Other Books by Stanley Weintraub

Victoria: An Intimate Biography
A Stillness Heard Round the World
The London Yankees
Four Rossettis: A Victorian Biography
Whistler: A Biography
Aubrey Beardsley: Imp of the Perverse
The Last Great Cause
Journey to Heartbreak
The War in the Wards
Private Shaw and Public Shaw

LONG DAY'S JOURNEY INTO WAR

LONG DAY'S

JOURNEY INTO WAR

December 7, 1941

STANLEY WEINTRAUB

T·T

TRUMAN TALLEY BOOKS
DUTTON
NEW YORK

TRUMAN TALLEY BOOKS · DUTTON

Published by the Penguin Group
Penguin Books USA Inc., 375 Hudson Street, New York, New York 10014, U.S.A.
Penguin Books Ltd, 27 Wrights Lane, London W8 5TZ, England
Penguin Books Australia Ltd, Ringwood, Victoria, Australia
Penguin Books Canada Ltd, 10 Alcorn Avenue, Toronto, Ontario, Canada M4V 3B2
Penguin Books (N.Z.) Ltd, 182–190 Wairau Road, Auckland 10, New Zealand

Penguin Books Ltd, Registered Offices: Harmondsworth, Middlesex, England

First published by Truman Talley Books · Dutton, an imprint of
New American Library, a division of Penguin Books USA Inc.
Distributed in Canada by McClelland & Stewart Inc.

LIBRARY OF CONGRESS CATALOGING IN PUBLICATION DATA:
Weintraub, Stanley, 1929–
Long day's journey into war : December 7, 1941 / Stanley
Weintraub.
p.   cm.
Includes bibliographical references and index.
ISBN 0-525-93344-1
1. Pearl Harbor (Hawaii), Attack on, 1941.   2. World War,
1939–1945.   I. Title.
D767.92.W45   1991
940.54′26—dc20   91-8352
CIP

Printed in the United States of America
Set in ITC Galliard with display in Palatino
Designed by Jack Meserole

For RODELLE,
My Wife and Collaborator

CONTENTS

Maps   x

THE DAY BEFORE: December 6, 1941   1

LONG DAY'S JOURNEY   17

THE DAY AFTER: December 8   627

CURTAIN CALL: Doomsday   651

Sources and Strategies   667

Acknowledgments   679

Index   683

THE RUSSIAN AND
MIDDLE EAST FRONTS
December 6, 1941

Germany and its Occupied Territories

Lake Onega

FINLAND
Lake Ladoga

U.S.S.R.

Tikhvin
Leningrad

ESTONIA

DENMARK

BALTIC SEA

LATVIA

Moscow

LITHUANIA

Smolensk

Konigsberg

Bryansk

Danzig   E. PRUSSIA

Minsk

Kursk

Berlin

Warsaw

Kharkov

GERMANY

POLAND

Kiev

BOHEMIA-
MORAVIA

Munich

SLOVAKIA

AUSTRIA   HUNGARY

ITALY

YUGOSLAVIA

BLACK SEA

ROMANIA

BULGARIA

ALBANIA

GREECE

TURKEY

Athens

MALTA

CRETE

CYPRUS

MEDITERRANEAN SEA

Tripoli   Benghazi   Tobruk   Bardia

El Gubi   Mersa   Alexandria
Matrûh

LIBYA   EGYPT   Cairo

Map by Virginia Norey

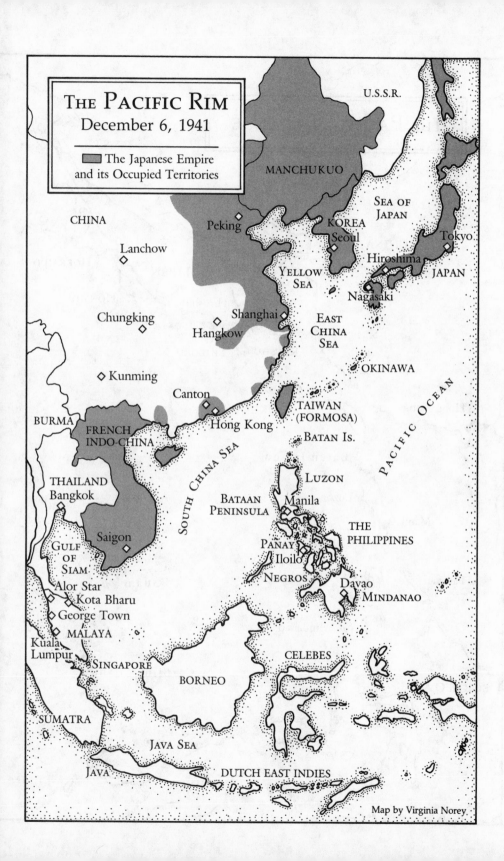

THE PACIFIC RIM
December 6, 1941

■ The Japanese Empire
and its Occupied Territories

U.S.S.R.

MANCHUKUO

SEA OF
JAPAN

CHINA

Peking

KOREA
Seoul

Tokyo

Lanchow

Hiroshima

YELLOW
SEA

JAPAN

Nagasaki

Chungking

Shanghai

Hangkow

EAST
CHINA
SEA

OKINAWA

Kunming

Canton

TAIWAN
(FORMOSA)

BURMA

FRENCH
INDO-CHINA

Hong Kong

Batan Is.

PACIFIC OCEAN

SOUTH CHINA SEA

LUZON

THAILAND
Bangkok

BATAAN
PENINSULA

Manila

Saigon

PANAY
Iloilo

THE
PHILIPPINES

GULF
OF
SIAM

NEGROS

Alor Star

Kota Bharu

Davao

MINDANAO

George Town

Kuala
Lumpur

MALAYA

SINGAPORE

CELEBES

BORNEO

SUMATRA

JAVA SEA

JAVA

DUTCH EAST INDIES

Map by Virginia Norey

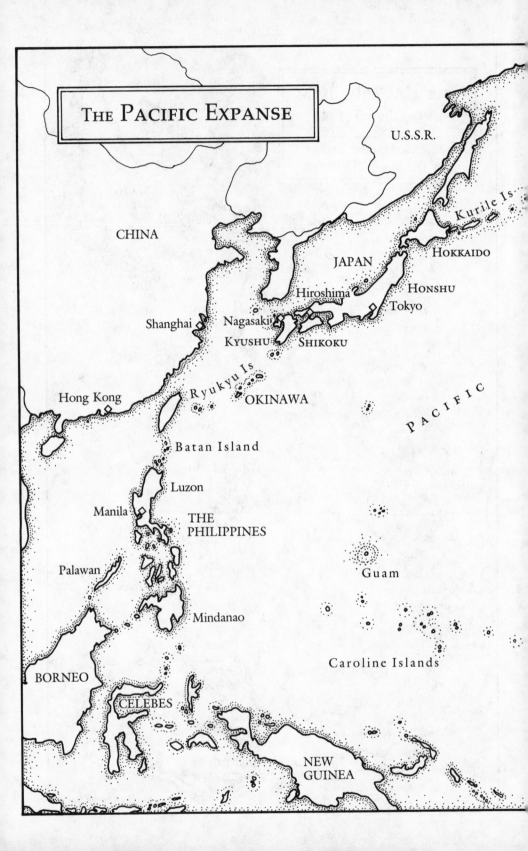

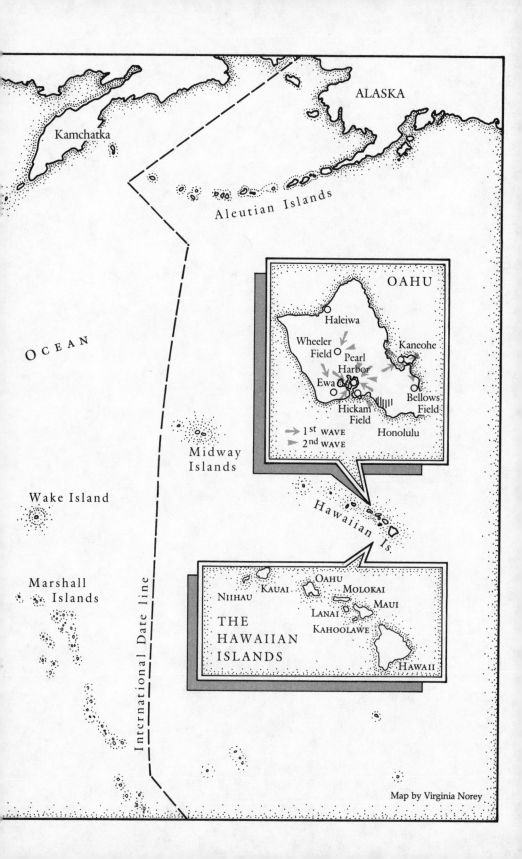

ALASKA

Kamchatka

Aleutian Islands

OCEAN

OAHU

Haleiwa

Wheeler
Field   Kaneohe

Pearl
Harbor

Ewa

Bellows
Field

Hickam
Field

Honolulu

→ 1ˢᵗ WAVE
▸ 2ⁿᵈ WAVE

Midway
Islands

Wake Island

Hawaiian Is.

Marshall
Islands

OAHU

KAUAI   MOLOKAI

NIIHAU   MAUI

LANAI

THE
HAWAIIAN
ISLANDS

KAHOOLAWE

HAWAII

International Date line

Map by Virginia Norey

THE DAY BEFORE

December 6, 1941

When all the oceans are as brothers.
Why must there be storm and strife in the world?

> —EMPEROR HIROHITO, quoting lines
> from a poem by his grandfather,
> Emperor Meiji, at the September 6,
> 1941, Imperial Conference on war
> planning

THE MOST CALAMITOUS December 7, reputedly, occurred in 2347 B.C. On that Sunday morning, so Archbishop of Armagh James Ussher calculated in 1597, Noah's Flood began. Less in dispute is a later December 7, also much associated with water, ships, mountains, and unheeded prophecies of catastrophe.

December 7, 1941, entered history west of the 180th meridian. The calendar day begins where the International Date Line straddles that artificial, often crooked band of turbulent ocean arching the earth from pole to pole just beyond Hawaii. Forty-eight hours are required to rotate a date worldwide. Over segments of three calendar days somewhere upon the face of the globe it was December 7, a swath of time that was simultaneously the flood tide of Axis power and the beginning of its ebb. Amidst an island-dotted expanse misnamed Pacific, what had begun half a world away in 1939 as a European war became the first truly global war.

When December 7 first arrived to the watery west of the Date Line, in the vicinity of Wake Island, it was 10:00 P.M. on the sixth in Tokyo, 1:00 P.M. that afternoon in London, only 8:00 A.M. in Washington, and a predawn 2:30 A.M. at Pearl Harbor. As the seventh limped to an end just west of Hawaii, it had long been December 8 elsewhere.

For Asians, the 8th was a date with its own ironies. On a long-past December 8, in the fifth century B.C., when the Morning Star had appeared in the eastern sky, Prince Siddartha, meditating beneath a bodhi tree, found his troubled mind suddenly as clear as the breaking day. He had, the legend relates, at last apprehended the path to Enlightenment. At thirty-five, he had become Buddha, teacher of asceticism and compassion, wisdom and tranquillity. His anniversary in 1941 promised to be very different.

The Japanese were assiduous searchers after good omens, but the linkage would go unnoticed. In a letter to the editor of the *Japan Times and Advertiser* on September 23, 1942, a reader noticed a different connection. "Can it be," he inquired, "a mere coincidence that . . . the figure 8 for the Japanese is an auspicious symbol, used in such words as *hakko ichiu*. . . . The War of Greater East Asia was declared on December 8th. These coincidences presage a final victory of the Japanese." The expression, meaning "all eight corners of the world under one roof" and used to signify universal brotherhood, came from ancient Chinese cosmography—the four directions and the four corners of the world. In Japanese it had first appeared in the eighth-century *Nihon shoki*, a myth-history, and had been revived as a euphemism for expansion into Asia as early as 1904; now it seemed a symbol revalidated.

The defeat of France had left its colony of Indochina ripe for an absorption that Japan had already begun. The Netherlands East Indies, rich with the oil to fuel Japanese industrial and war machines, and British Malaya and Borneo, rich with rubber and tin also scarce in the home islands, also looked like easy pickings. With the Nazi takeover of the Netherlands in May 1940, the Indies had become a colony without a homeland. And Britain had its hands full coping with the German blitzkrieg from the air and the threat of invasion across the Channel from a Nazified Europe. Russia, its major cities under siege or on the verge of falling to the Nazis before winter froze everyone and everything in place, seemed no threat.

Elsewhere the picture from the Japanese side also looked promising for a short war which the nearly helpless West would be eager to settle on terms that might rescue something. In North Africa, the British, evicted from Greece and Crete, their last footholds in Europe, were hanging on to Tobruk, lest they lose everything, including Suez and the lifeline to India. No ocean was safe from preying German U-boats, and Britain barely maintained a survival level of imports despite just-short-of-war American assistance. Even so, Australia, an underpopulated Commonwealth partner worried about Japanese ambitions, threatened to withdraw or withhold troops from Malaya and Egypt unless London did more to warn off Japan. Swallowing his misgivings, Winston Churchill ordered the new battleship *Prince of Wales*, the refurbished battle cruiser *Repulse*, and the aircraft carrier *Indomitable* to Singapore. Barely under way, the less than indomitable flattop went aground on a reef in the Caribbean, and had to put in for repairs. The largely symbolic capital ships went on without air cover.

As the last month of 1941 opened, Britain pressed for a commitment from the United States to intervene should British territory be attacked by Japan. Yet Franklin Roosevelt had been able to supply massive military assistance only by semantic evasions at home suggesting that America was not doing that at all. "Well, let me give you an illustration," FDR had told a news conference late in 1940 when he first proposed Lend-Lease for Britain. "Suppose my neighbor's house catches on fire, and I have a length of garden hose four or five hundred feet away. If he can take my garden hose and connect it up . . . , I may help him to put out his fire. Now what do I do? I don't say to him . . . , 'Neighbor, my garden hose cost me fifteen dollars. You have to pay me fifteen dollars for it. . . .' I want my hose back after the fire is over. . . . If it goes through the fire all right, intact, without any damage to it, he gives it back to me and thanks me very much for the use of it." The homily failed to hide that what he was proposing was to supply arms, even warships, to the British to fight Hitler.

The Lend-Lease debate in Congress became the last great divide between those favoring aid short of war even at the risk of war and the dwindling band of influential isolationists. Senator Robert Taft—"Mr. Republican" to his admirers, and the acknowledged leader of his party—had written to a political crony, "I feel very strongly that Hitler's defeat is not vital to us. Even the collapse of England is to be preferred to our participation for the rest of our lives in European wars." In the Senate he complained that lending weapons was "like lending chewing gum. You don't want it back."

On March 11, 1941, Lend-Lease, skillfully drafted to assure congressional majorities and titled with purposeful vagueness "A Bill to Further Promote the Defense of the United States and for Other

Purposes," passed. Stretched thin to supply weapons and equipment abroad before its industrial capacity had been mobilized, the nation could not meet the additional demands for its own two-ocean defense. As Roosevelt explained to Admiral Ernest J. King, he simply did not have enough butter to cover the bread.

Only four months before Pearl Harbor, Congress was more reluctant to renew the one-year conscription bill than it had been to draft young men for the army in 1940. Anticipating the demise of the unpopular law, conscripts chalked up barracks walls with the acronym "OHIO"—over the hill in October. At Princeton the "Veterans of Future Wars" suggested mockingly to the President that he appoint an Unknown Soldier of the next war at once, "so we can know who he is before he gets killed"; antiwar Vassar girls mischievously signed up in an "Association of Future Gold Star Mothers" and suggested a pilgrimage to Europe to select military cemetery locations for their unborn sons. Draft extension survived by one vote. The oceans separating America from war were wide, and to many the water seemed sufficient. Others felt that it was not the responsibility of a meddlesome Uncle Sam to pull other nations' chestnuts out of the fire. Yet as early as September 1940 the Japanese government had secretly begun the printing of "Occupation Currency"—military bank notes for Malaya, Burma, the Netherlands Indies, and the Philippines. The Philippines were "American," even to isolationists.

That wars in Europe and Asia were interrelated and would be more so was further assured when Hiroshi Oshima, the dapper general-diplomat who was Japanese ambassador in Berlin, reported to Tokyo in August 1941 a conversation in which Hitler affirmed that "in the event of a collision between Japan and the United States, Germany would at once open hostilities with the United States." Germany, in turn, demanded "a more active anti-British policy." Taking Singapore, Hitler and his naval chief, Erich Raeder, coaxed, would "frighten America out of the war." Oshima guaranteed that Singapore and Hong Kong would be seized before the British could somehow convey them to the U.S. under Lend-Lease. On delivery of the decrypt from British Intelligence, Churchill asked whether Roosevelt had seen it. He was assured that it had been sent to Washington.

The President had already frozen German and Italian assets in the U.S. By the time that Hitler had encouraged Oshima, Japanese assets had also been blocked; and on the same day in July, Roosevelt recalled

Douglas MacArthur, six years into his role as Field Marshal of the Philippine Army, into federal service with the three stars of a lieutenant general. The senior general with war experience, he had received his first star in Europe just before the Armistice in 1918. With his unready local army also summoned under the American flag, MacArthur began badgering Washington for more help. If the Japanese moved south for rubber and oil, he believed the Philippines would not be bypassed. (The islands, geographically, were an extension of the Dutch Indies.) But supply lines stretched across a thousand miles of Japanese-controlled Pacific mandates—a good reason for Washington to offer the Philippines more rhetoric than weapons.

As late as Friday December 5, 1941, a Cabinet discussion at the White House focused upon the exposed position of the Philippines, and participants turned to venerable Secretary of War Henry L. Stimson. "The Philippines are indefensible," he explained, "we have always known it. Every Army officer in the United States above the rank of lieutenant is familiar with the plan for the handling of the Philippines in case of war." What he was admitting, Labor Secretary Frances Perkins realized, was that defending the Philippines meant delaying the Japanese as long as possible, then writing the islands off.

The War Department had long assumed that Germany was its major concern, and with the Navy had sent officers to "observe" the Blitz and its consequences from the venue of the American embassy. The Army quietly rented nearby 18–20 Grosvenor Square, setting up a low-key military mission to prepare for inevitable war. Officers and enlisted men wore civilian clothes, used British ration cards, and, as inconspicuously as possible, planned American encampments in Northern Ireland, projected air offensives against Germany, and the release of British home troops for Middle East operations. As late as November 21, 1941, the mission discussed the European ramifications of a Japanese attack upon British and American territories in the Pacific. A report for the War Plans office on likely Army bases in Northern Ireland went to Washington on December 6.

Months earlier, the War Department had summoned a young colonel, Albert Wedemeyer, to coordinate planning a "Hitler first" strategy of engaging Germany on the continent of Europe before the Nazis could redeploy forces from Russia and wring defeatist concessions from the U.S. Three days before Pearl Harbor, on December 4, 1941, the document was somehow leaked to Colonel Robert McCormick's obsessively anti-British and isolationist *Chicago Tribune*. The banner headline "F.D.R.'S WAR PLANS" and the revelation of projections for a ten-million-man army confirmed to the conspiracy-minded that the President was plotting war while talking peace.

That Britain could not survive without America's direct involvement had long been obvious. American ships and planes were sharing anti-submarine missions with Britain and flying joint reconnaissance out of Gander in Newfoundland. Americans had occupied Iceland, relieving the British. American destroyers had been hit, and American sailors killed: anyone who could read a newspaper headline knew of the *Kearny*, and there was even a ballad on records and on radio about the torpedoed *Reuben James*. For the press, Roosevelt jauntily likened American patrols in the Atlantic to bands of scouts in the frontier West sent out ahead of the wagon trains to search for marauding Indians and to prevent an ambush.

While such moves enraged Hitler, he preferred limited and informal war to overt conflict. He ordered Joseph Goebbels's propaganda machine to assist, indirectly, all internal American anti-intervention groups, in particular the America First Committee. Goebbels had already praised that organization as "truly American and truly patriotic." Under its banner and those of supporting groups on its fringes, citizens ranging from self-styled patriots to racists, religious fanatics, pro-Germanists, isolationists, and paid German agents stoked the embers of pacifism.

Isolationism had drawn supporters from both Right and Left. Communists who compliantly became anti-interventionists when Stalin signed a non-aggression pact with Hitler in 1939 became enthusiasts for war against Germany only when the Soviet Union was invaded in mid-1941. Japan received little attention from the businessmen, politicians, pacifists, incendiaries, and ideologues in America First and kindred groups, from Keep America Out of War to the Silver Shirts. Bogged down in China, the Japanese had not been able to defeat Chiang Kaishek's poorly armed rabble. It was widely believed that the Japanese had weak eyes, and could not fly a straight course, let alone hit a target. Their weapons were shoddy and inefficient: look at the cheap toys they exported, famous for falling rapidly apart. Air hero and America Firster Charles Lindbergh thought that the U.S. could easily overwhelm the Japanese—but Hermann Göring's Luftwaffe was another matter. "No nation in Asia," he had assured an audience at

Yale without mentioning Japan, "has developed aviation sufficiently to be a serious menace to the United States."

America Firsters feared that Roosevelt was scheming to bring the U.S. into war on the British side through an Asian back door. Embargoes intended to thwart further Japanese encroachments in Southeast Asia were not only risky, they claimed, but bad for American business. In a newspaper advertisement, America First declared, "We have no real quarrel with Japan. We have no conceivable stake in Asia worth the terrific cost of a long-distance struggle with Japan." America need not be a "sentimental . . . knight-errant in Asia." Even a secret mid-1940 Government strategic study had concluded that "we must not become involved with Japan, that we must not concern ourselves beyond the 180th meridian. . . ."

.

In January 1941 Ambassador Joseph Grew in Tokyo had passed on to Washington information that a Japanese employee at the Peruvian embassy had overheard talk about the planning of a surprise attack on Pearl Harbor. Grew urged vigilance. The Japanese had a history of making surprise attacks, and the Navy had sets of "Orange" contingency plans for them, updated regularly between 1923 and 1940. (All were predicated upon a war initiated by Japan "without notice" following a period of "strained relations.") In 1932, as part of American war games in the Pacific, a mock carrier-force attack on Pearl Harbor was staged.

As early as 1925 a naval journalist, Hector Bywater, had published a novel, *The Great Pacific War*, in which the Japanese begin a surprise offensive in the Pacific by blowing up a ship in the Panama Canal. Bottling up the American navy in the Atlantic, the Japanese are then able to operate at will in Asia. In the novel—reprinted in 1932—the Japanese overrun Guam and the Philippines before losing command of the sea, relinquishing Manila and occupied China, and undergoing an air raid on Tokyo that leads to an uneasy armistice benefiting neither side.

Soon after, a novel appeared in Japan with a similar theme, *An Account of the Future War between Japan and the United States*. In Lieutenant Commander Kyosuke Fukunaga's fiction, Japan wins. Two Japanese admirals had written prefaces to the retired officer's prophecy, one of them confessing, "I cannot express any exhaustive comments on this work because of the relation which exists between the contents thereof and military secrets."

Fukunaga's war begins accidentally. A rash destroyer skipper, Eitaro Maki, sinks the USS *Houston* off the coast of China in 1936. Americans at home are irresolute. "Why should we risk our lives against unknown Japanese?" asks an isolationist-minded youth; yet the United States declares war. The Gatun Locks in the Panama Canal are blown up, trapping American naval reinforcements, and Japanese sabotage is suspected. Eventually the two fleets meet in the Pacific and Japan's superior air power decides the issue. Hawaii becomes a Japanese colony, and a statue of Maki is erected at Waikiki.

Arriving in Hawaii in the cargo of the *President Taft*, the novel was immediately seized by the Collector of Customs. The story was "not so good for local Japanese to read," an official decided. Copies were shipped to the War Department for study at the highest level. It was much—but quietly—read, possibly contributing to the pervasive and continuing concern about subversion and sabotage on Oahu. The date in 1933 when the novel arrived and was confiscated was December 7.

Japanese strategy was predicated upon a short war. When Admiral Isoroku Yamamoto had begun planning the Hawaiian strike on the chance that it would be authorized, and was asked what the chances were of victory against Britain and the United States, he said, "I can raise havoc with them for one year. After that I can guarantee nothing." In his view, Japan would be strongest at the beginning, then unable to make up its losses as American power regenerated. But severe early reverses might lead to war disillusionment in America, and a willingness to relinquish East Asia and the Pacific rim as the price of peace. But choices had to be made, and risks taken. Should the Siberian threat to Japan's rear be eliminated while Hitler kept Russia busy in Europe? Were the resources of Southeast Asia the first imperative, since armies fought on oil and rubber and metal?

Concerns about war were remarkably absent in Singapore, where Air Chief-Marshal Sir Robert Brooke-Popham, the British Commander-in-Chief, Far East, estimated the situation with placid confidence. "Taking into account (a) [Japan's] uncertainty," he forecast in September, "whether or not Germany is going to bring Russia to terms before the winter; (b) the time that would elapse before the Japanese could disengage from the north, even if Russia collapsed; (c) the bad weather in the South China Sea area between November and January inclusive, it is highly improbable [that] Japan can be contemplating war in the south for some months." He had time, he told the Advisory War Council in Melbourne soon afterward, to "perfect" his plans.

The decision for war had already been formally made, on September 6, at a conference managed by Emperor Hirohito's chief adviser, Marquis Koichi Kido. Prince Fumimaro Konoye was still prime minister. Everyone spoke unhopefully about Japan's minimum economic and political demands being met through negotiations in Washington. Further, the summer rice crop had been poor, emphasizing the island nation's needs for the produce of Burma and Thailand. Japan's war machine and industries depended on imported oil, and while its government called the American embargo, intended to reverse Japanese aggression in Asia, a provocation, it was openly evading restrictions through technicalities. Only Roosevelt's freezing of Japanese funds frustrated the eagerness of American producers to supply all the fuel Japan wanted. It was "ghastly," Treasury Secretary Henry Morgenthau had warned, to let Japan "pile up" all the oil needed to attack the U.S., but business was business.

The controlled Japanese press began describing the nation as "like a fish in a pond from which the water was being gradually drained away," with their only recourse the oil of the Indies. Their battleships, Admiral Osami Nagano warned, would soon become "mere scarecrows."

The Japanese dream of empire was perceived sweepingly as a question of survival. Abandoning China, its coastline still a patchwork of European enclaves and "concessions," was unthinkable; Southeast Asia was ripe for rescue, as it was the illegal property of outside colonial powers and within Japan's natural sphere of influence, its manifest destiny. Prince Konoye had resigned on October 16, permitting a War Cabinet dominated by the Army and led by General Hideki Tojo to take office. National aspirations, Tojo insisted to Konoye, were the biggest stakes a man could play, and one had to be a risk-taker. At some point, he explained metaphorically, one might find it necessary to jump, eyes closed, from the high veranda of the Kiyomuzu into the ravine below. Konoye reminded him that a prime minister of a nation of a hundred million, as Tojo had become, could not solve its problems by gambling with its fate.

Attacking the U.S. at all was risk enough, and few Japanese war planners coordinating the strikes across the Pacific were sanguine about taking on Pearl Harbor. Admiral Takijiro Onishi warned that America could not be "brought to its knees" by war and that avenues for compromise had to be left open. "For that reason, whether we land in the Philippines or anywhere else, we should avoid anything like the Hawaiian operation that would put America's back up too badly." But Onishi was overruled. A catastrophe might persuade war-reluctant Americans to "reconsider their Far Eastern policy."

"If negotiations succeed, fine," said Tojo, "but if not and we wait too long, it would be disastrous."

When imperial advisers vacillated in the Emperor's presence between recommending war or continued diplomacy, Hirohito, in his formal, high-pitched voice, remarked, "I am sorry the Supreme Command has nothing to say." From his pocket he withdrew a paper and began reading a poem written by his grandfather, Emperor Meiji:

> All the seas, in every quarter,
>   are as brothers to one another.
> Why, then, do the winds and waves of strife
>   rage so turbulently throughout the world?

The lines were less censure, or even recommendation, than the sort of cryptic message expected by ancient Greeks at the Oracle of Delphi. The lines reminded him, Hirohito explained, of his grandfather's love of peace. Yet they also spoke clearly of the inevitability of war.

While war was a gamble, the Japanese national psyche as cultivated throughout the 1930s would not allow humiliation. Tojo insisted that withdrawal from China "would not be in keeping with the dignity of the Army." And Admiral Nagano observed, in the Emperor's presence, that American intransigence could reverse Japan's destiny in Asia. He viewed the Empire as a patient who could be cured only through drastic surgery, without which "there was danger of a gradual decline."

One of Tojo's first, top-secret orders was to the Bank of Japan to ship all stored occupation currency to Army disbursing offices. By then Pearl Harbor planners had tentatively fixed upon Friday, November 21, as the attack date, something Konoye had not known. Sunday the 23rd had been an alternative. The early date was to have the fleet back to cover an invasion of Siberian Russia if Moscow fell. But Vice-Admiral Shigeru Fukudome, a key planner, feeling that the complex training had not been adequate, postponed "X-Day" to December.

When Admiral Heihachiro Togo destroyed the Czar's Far Eastern Fleet in Port Arthur in 1904, an unexpected strike that won the war before the Russians knew it had begun, Yamamoto had been aboard as a twenty-one-year-old ensign. To ensure complete surprise this time, Yamamoto wanted to have the U.S. not only lulled by negotiations but deceived by an unpredictable attack route. Instead of massing his fleet in the benign south of Japan he would assemble in the wintry islands of the Kuriles. And he would use an unorthodox northern arc traversed by no merchant shipping, a route tested late in October by sending the liner *Toyo Maru* to Honolulu.

Such surprises might have been foreseen by professionals alert to history, sensitive to leaks and to signal noise, and willing to take seriously evidence at odds with preconceptions. Stalin had eighty-four documented advance reports of the June 1941 Nazi attack, many with the exact date; the Western allies had incontrovertible warnings of the May 1940 invasion of France and the Low Countries, even to the routes; the American military had years, then months, then weeks, then days, then merely hours, of advance intimation of a Japanese strike, even to likely targets, yet ignored every opportunity to be ready. Japan's best weapon would be the wishful thinking that substituted more tolerable dreams for dark forebodings. Stalin had ordered messengers with the bad news shot; in the West they were merely ignored.

Two days before Tojo had assumed power, Lieutenant General Walter C. Short, U.S. Army commander in Hawaii, had responded to a query from Washington as to why he was planning to give his Air Corps enlisted personnel infantry training. Short reported "a surplus of 3,344 men with no assigned duties," and he wanted to give the men something to do. There was something wrong, Major General H. H. Arnold, Air Corps chief, thought, if airmen in Hawaii had nothing to do; but he reassigned neither them nor General Short.

On the mainland, many in the American military had little to do because they had yet to receive weapons with which to train. Even World War I equipment was scarce. Powerless constitutionally except to persuade, Roosevelt could warn the American people but could not undo decades of hostility to military appropriations, taxes, busybodies, foreigners of all sorts (although the U.S. was a nation of immigrants), people of skin hues other than something perceived as white, and customs that were different—and therefore "un-American." Intercourse with a less utopian culture seemed to many Americans a form of mis-cegenation. "I do not think it would be any use for me to make a personal appeal to Roosevelt at this juncture to enter the war," Church-ill wrote on November 9 to Jan Smuts in South Africa. ". . . We must not underrate his constitutional difficulties. He may take [warlike] action as Chief Executive, but only Congress can declare war. He went so far as to say to me, 'I may never declare war; I may make war. If I asked Congress to declare war they might argue about it for three months.' . . . Public opinion in the United States has advanced lately, but. . . ."

While American conscripts sometimes drilled with broomsticks—at Camp Funston, Kansas, on December 5, cavalry troops on maneu-vers used eggs for hand grenades—British and Commonwealth wives in Singapore and Hong Kong, ordered home for their safety, were either stubbornly returning or had never left. There would not be a war—at least not soon. And there was no telling how their husbands might stray if left to easy bachelordom in the permissive colonial milieu. The authorities fumed, but outgoing shipping was now hard to find. In North Africa, as the siege of Tobruk dragged on, the sandy harbor filled with sunken British bottoms and downed aircraft. In Russia, temperatures cold enough to congeal airplane oil and tank grease and snows high as a man's head had slowed German troops then almost within sight of the onion spires of Moscow. In a Japan chilled by autumn rain, the seventy-fourth liaison conference of the Cabinet and military chiefs had convened at 4:00 P.M. on November 29.

One Japanese code warning of war to its embassies abroad was to be "EAST WIND RAIN," while the go-ahead signal to the strike force moving toward Hawaii was "CLIMB MOUNT NIIKATA." Few in the meeting room in Tokyo knew the time of X-Day, the carefully guarded secret that had brought them together, or that it included a strike perilously close to the U.S. After some discussion, a participant ob-served, with the series of surprise attacks in mind, "I would like to see diplomacy carried out in such a way that we can win the war." Whether the speaker meant that diplomacy could gain Japanese objectives with-out war or that it would provide the screen for quick initial victories is unclear.

"We do have enough time," Navy Chief of Staff Nagano affirmed, but he offered no details. He knew that the Pearl Harbor force had already left Hitokappu Bay in the Kuriles, and he knew when it was due at its rendezvous point north of Oahu. There was, perhaps, a week of diplomacy left. Kept from the facts, the foreign minister, Shigenori Togo, appealed, "Tell me what the zero hour is. Otherwise I can't carry on diplomacy."

"Well, then, I'll tell you," said Nagano. And he bent low to whisper to Togo: "December 8." Then he noted more publicly to the conferees, "We have not [even] told our naval attaché [in Washington]." Someone remarked, "On this occasion the entire population will have to be like Kuranosuke Oishi"—a character in the celebrated story *The Forty-Seven Ronin*. Employing deceit about his identity, Oishi kept his intended victim off guard.

At the next liaison conference, on December 1, the Emperor was again present and listened carefully to the closing words of Privy Council chairman Baron Yoshimichi Hara. He did not doubt, said Hara, "that initial operations will result in victory for us. . . . This is indeed the greatest undertaking since the opening of our country in the nineteenth century. We cannot avoid a long-term war this time, but I believe that we must somehow work around this so as to bring about an early settlement. In order to accomplish this, we will need to start thinking now about how to end the war."

"His Majesty," the transcript of the conference notes, "nodded in agreement with the statements being made, and displayed no signs of uneasiness. He seemed to be in an excellent mood, and we were filled with awe."

LONG
DAY'S
JOURNEY

He that outlives this day and comes safe home,
Will stand a-tiptoe when this day is named.

—SHAKESPEARE, *Henry V*

WAKE ISLAND	TOKYO	MOSCOW	PEARL HARBOR
Midnight	10:00 P.M.	2:00 P.M.	2:30 A.M.
December 7	December 6	December 6	December 6

HOUR 1

TRANSMITTED at about 8:00 A.M., Washington time—already
10:00 P.M. in Tokyo—the message from Army G-2 (Intelligence) required little reading between the lines. The Japanese embassy
on Massachusetts Avenue "was reliably reported to have burned a code
book and ciphers last night." The information went to Army headquarters at Fort Shafter on Oahu, overlooking Pearl Harbor. But Pacific
Fleet headquarters at Pearl Harbor would not hear of it because the
Army and Navy in Hawaii seldom exchanged information unless specifically ordered to do so. The services on the islands took their turf
rivalries seriously.

The Navy was also preparing a warning about the imminence of
something. Eventually, Pearl Harbor would learn that forward installations were being instructed to do much the same thing as the Japanese
had done, and burning codes went beyond mere war games. At isolated,
Navy-run Wake Island, beyond the westernmost reach of the Hawaiian
chain and on the other side of the Date Line, it had just become
December 7. On Navy-administered Guam, adjacent to the Japanese-
occupied Carolines, it was an hour earlier. To Commander Lawrence
F. Safford at the Navy Department in Washington, both outposts
seemed in jeopardy.

Code destruction directives followed the usual bureaucratic channels. Safford's draft message went to a higher-up before going on to
Pearl Harbor for further transmission, and Rear Admiral Leigh Noyes
in Washington objected to the phrase "in view of the imminence of
war." Admirals were not paid to panic. Noyes was also certain that
the Japanese were bluffing.

"Well, Admiral," said Safford, too weary after his days and nights
reading decrypts to act deferential, "if all these [confidential] publications on Wake are captured, we will never be able to explain it."

Eliminating the offending phrase, Noyes ordered the watered-
down warning sent via Pearl Harbor, with an information copy to
Manila. Demonstrating further what he thought of Safford's sense of
peril, Noyes instructed that it be sent by "deferred priority." After all,
it was only 2:30 A.M. in Hawaii.

The message to Admiral Husband E. Kimmel would arrive twenty-
one hours later, just before midnight Pearl Harbor time. No one in
any command position would see it that Saturday night, or even on
Sunday. In Noyes's rewrite, the cable perversely permitted delay. "In
view of the international situation and the exposed position of our
outlying Pacific islands," it advised, "you may authorize destruction
. . . of secret and confidential documents now or under later conditions
of greater emergency."

Neither Navy nor Army headquarters in Washington directed their
Hawaii commands to exchange their Saturday warnings. Nevertheless,
the signs on Oahu that something was happening could hardly have
been overlooked. Japanese inquiries about the comings and goings of
warships in Pearl Harbor, the number and nature of planes on nearby
airfields, the weather over Hawaii, and the loyalty of local Japanese
had been intercepted for weeks. Such communications had become
more numerous. Washington and Honolulu were aware of them, just
as Washington and Manila knew about persistent Japanese overflights
of the Philippines.

•

Like his Japanese counterpart in Berlin, German Ambassador to
Tokyo Eugen Ott was a general, and a shrewd one. He had been
working well into the evening on what was normally a quiet Saturday.
Things were about to happen, he cabled Foreign Minister Ribbentrop
at ten. War in East Asia seemed probable, and soon, but not a war of

much use to Germany. America was questioning Japanese intentions toward Thailand, Malaya, and Burma, the likely new area of conflict rather than the front in Siberia so eagerly desired by Hitler to take the pressure off the Wehrmacht in Russia.

Although he had dangled the bait of Siberian territory for months, Ambassador Ott noted, the Japanese were skeptical "about favorable developments in the offensive against Moscow." Whatever the concerns of the United States, he felt, the Americans had no control over events on the Pacific rim of Asia. Nor, it was clear, did Eugen Ott.

Because of his close relations with the Imperial Navy, German Admiral Paul W. Wenneker, Ott's naval attaché, was better informed, but he did not always pass on everything he learned, except in coded cables to Berlin. Wenneker's role in monitoring German subs, surface raiders, and blockade runners which operated out of Osaka and Kobe offered him more military contacts than Ott had, and in a telegram which included the line "Ambassador unaware of the dispatch of this cable, but briefed about its content," Wenneker reported on the imminence of war. Imperial Navy Commander Shiba had told him that there would be war with Britain and the U.S. "by Christmas. . . . He cannot, possibly, tell me a precise date in consideration of the need for surprise."

Also at 10:00 P.M. in Tokyo—December 7 was two hours away—the Imperial General Staff, controlling events with precision, radioed *Kido Butai* ("mobile force"), approaching Hawaii in predawn although operating on Tokyo time, its latest intelligence from Honolulu. Despite radio silence, Admiral Nagumo's ships could receive signals, and the Japanese consulate in Honolulu had continued transmitting reports via Tokyo about the status of the Pacific Fleet at Pearl Harbor. The job of monitoring American warship movements had been easy. From the high ground around Pearl City anyone could look down and identify vessels. Assistant Consul "Tadashi Morimura" did exactly that each day, needing only a taxi. He also rented tourist aircraft, hired boats, even swam in the area. Any Hawaiian visitor could buy a packet of picture postcard views of the naval base, go on sightseeing flights from John Rodgers Field, take a tour bus with lei-swathed gawkers around Pearl Harbor, and purchase souvenir maps.

"Morimura," the indefatigable Japanese tourist, was actually Ensign Takeo Yoshikawa of Naval Intelligence. Playing his role of newly arrived junior diplomat with flamboyant zeal, he seemed too convivial

with local Japanese women and too fond of his sake to awaken sus-
picions from anyone shadowing him. He was never seen with a camera
or a notepad. Seldom did he share any of his data with Consul General
Nagao Kita, who preferred to know little about what his supposed
assistant was doing.

Kita himself transmitted messages to Tokyo from the bumbling
German spy Otto Kühn, who lived with his wife and daughter in a
house with a view of the sea, over the steep Pali hills in Kailua. In the
house, paid for in Japanese-supplied dollars, Kühn had concealed in a
suitcase a radio with a hundred-mile range, intended to contact Japanese submarines in the event war put the consulate out of business.
Kühn had even devised a bizarre scheme to signal subs about ships
moving in and out of Pearl Harbor by lights in his windows at night
and sheets on the clothesline by day. Kita would be sending a coded
message about sub signaling to Tokyo before December 6 was out—
a message not decrypted in Washington until December 10. The FBI
and U.S. Army Intelligence knew that Kita dabbled in spying, but they
respected his diplomatic immunity and considered him harmless.

Thirty-six minutes after Tokyo had received the coded radio message from "Morimura," it was being deciphered aboard the carrier
Akagi, now less than four hundred miles north-northeast of Oahu.

Arrived: *Oklahoma* and *Nevada* (having been out for eight days)
Departed: *Lexington* and five heavy cruisers
Ships in harbor as of 6:00 P.M., 5 December: 8 BB, 3 CL, 16 DD
In [dry] docks: 4 CL (*Honolulu* class), 5 DD

Everything about the Japanese operation was equally efficient. *Kido
Butai* was not only traversing an unfrequented portion of the North
Pacific with a reputation for stormy weather, but threading the gap
between the patrol paths of planes south from Dutch Harbor in the
Aleutians and north from Hawaii and Midway. The flagship *Akagi* was
receiving information about Pearl Harbor which was plotted on a grid
almost as if it had been transmitted on film.

Distributed before dawn because of the time differential with the
U.S. mainland—it was already eight in the morning in New York—
the *Honolulu Advertiser* displayed an ominous eight-column banner,
"AMERICA EXPECTED TO REJECT JAPAN'S REPLY ON INDO-CHINA."
Reports from the December 6 Tokyo newspapers were no less warlike.
The *Asahi Shimbun* of Tokyo had headlined, "U.S. USELESSLY

EXTENDING TALKS. HAS NO INTENTION OF COMPROMISE WITH JA-
PAN"; and even more foreboding, "FOUR NATIONS SIMULTANEOUSLY
START MILITARY PREPARATIONS." The four were Britain, the United
States, the Netherlands Indies—and Japan.

•

On board the converted troopship *Venice Maru*, which had embarked from Sakaide, on the northern tip of Shikoku, on the Inland
Sea, on November 22, the temperature below decks pushed past
82°F. Private Hisaeda Akiyoshi wondered where his unit was going.
A scare that morning had made him forget the stifling heat. "Because enemy ships crossed in front of us, our ship momentarily
stopped," he wrote in his diary. Several small American task forces
were in the central Pacific, one to ferry planes to Wake Island, another
to Midway, a third to Manila. None were really that close, although
something had been spotted that worried the flotilla commander, who
was heading for Guam. Akiyoshi, a draftee medic with a field hospital,
had been in uniform only since October. An hour before midnight,
there was nothing to do but wait. In the dark he could not pass the
time, as he did by day, filling in the many blanks in his diary with line
drawings.

•

Relman ("Pat") Morin, former Associated Press correspondent in
Tokyo, had not left the Japanese behind when he took up his window
on Indochina. In Saigon "the very air was electric" with tension. A
telegram from his home office came via the American consulate: "Washington says situation serious. Take all precautions."

He decided on a return to Bangkok, then found someone who
knew someone who could get him across the border from a town
where there were no Japanese security people. Monday would be the
day.

While he sat over a Saturday evening drink at a sidewalk table
outside his hotel, the Continental, two Japanese newspapermen he
knew walked by. He invited them over, but they seemed to Morin
"nervous, ill at ease." One of them asked, "Do you think there is going
to be war between Japan and America?"

"No," said Morin. The Japanese were unusually uncommunicative,
finishing their drinks in silence. Morin went into the hotel lobby to

telephone the local bus line to confirm a reservation. Then he had dinner with the American consul, Sidney Brown, and several of his British friends. They tuned in the BBC and heard military analyst Major Allan Murray expostulate, "If Japan would only stop this shilly-shallying and come to some decision." Brown had seven guests. "We all drank too much and laughed as loudly as we could. Nobody mentioned 'the situation.'"

•

After seeing *Sergeant York*, the Manila audience that had applauded Gary Cooper's almost single-handed defeat of the Germans in 1918 was leaving the theater. Captain Garry J. Anloff had an attractive Filipina woman on his arm but something else on his mind. He felt certain that war was going to break out that weekend and was grateful when they walked out under the bright lights "that nothing had happened while we were in there. It was the weekend."

He took his companion to dinner, always late in the Philippines, and, knowing that he had an early flight to catch next morning from Nichols Field, flagged a taxi—a new Willys rather than a vintage Ford—to take them home. He should be dropped off first at the apartment he always used, he told the Filipino driver, getting in after his companion and taking care that his white tropical suit didn't get smudged on the taxi doorframe. Then, Placida Lopez was to be driven home, he explained, and escorted to her door. "Yes, sir," said the driver; "that will be ninety centavos more to her house, sir."

"The cabbie knew who I am and whom I am with?" Anloff thought. "How unusual! I am in a white civvie suit, and he takes each of us without asking my address!!" He wondered if the Japanese had an intelligence network that included taxis. Routinely, Anloff, as Philippine Division assistant adjutant, had been taking classified papers to USAFFE (U.S. Armed Forces Far East) headquarters in Manila and carrying messages back to Fort Stotsenburg. His job had become one of breaking Major General Edward B. King's logjam of mail at Luzon North headquarters. Anloff would call the operations officer at adjacent Clark Field and have a car take him to an obsolete B-18. For his return north from Manila, the plane would still be at Nichols Field, its twin engines warming. At first he had wondered why he received a full crew for a milk-run, and why everyone was always so happy to see him. Later, he discovered that Clark Field had been on weekend alerts. No one without orders could leave the base. Anloff had made it possible for eight officers and enlisted men to enjoy weekends in the city.

He went to bed puzzled as to why Manila was still sleepily normal, and "wondering why we didn't get a war."

•

Operating in the snow and cold southwest of Moscow during the night that became the 6th, General Heinz Guderian had decided on his own initiative to withdraw the forward units of his XLIII Corps into defensive positions behind the River Don. Drifting snow and temperatures as low as − 37°F—or − 38°C—had immobilized most of his remaining armor. Even his own command tank, on the 4th, had been lost in an icy crevice. His troops lacked winter clothing, from boots to gloves to headgear. At every chance Guderian's soldiers stripped the frozen dead of both sides, defying discipline in search of warmth.

To the north, soldiers of the German 12th Infantry Division were wearing the summer clothes with which they had crossed the frontier in June. Division headquarters advised troops to wrap their bodies, under their uniforms, with newspapers. But there were no newspapers. Since freezing and thawing had deteriorated boots and gloves into inflexible lumps, Division command ordered men to "remove ruthlessly the civilian population's felt boots." The 18th Panzer Division instructed troops to use anything that could be wrapped protectively about the body, including "paper, tent sheets, . . . straw, hay," yet the division commander, comfortable in his command post, professed unhappiness with the improvisations his headquarters recommended. "The picture that one confronts . . . is far from gratifying at times," he deplored. "There are soldiers who both by their exterior as well as by their bearing can no longer be distinguished from Panje horses."*

The most sought-after prizes were *valenki*, the traditional Russian boots. Made of thick crushed black felt, they came up to the knees and kept feet warm and dry. The Germans took all they could find, from the living as well as the dead. That Guderian's troops looked more peasant than Prussian in *valenki* bothered few officers, however much it displeased Field Marshal Fedor von Bock, the austere commander-in-chief of Army Group Center.

* Panje horse: an East Prussian breed of small horse with a scruffy coat.

Admitting on the telephone to von Bock that his situation was so untenable that he had not been able to wait for permission to move back, Guderian paused for a response. "Where, actually," shouted von Bock angrily, "is your headquarters?" Von Bock had assumed that Guderian was too remote from the front to form a clear judgment. He was in the suburbs of Moscow.

At Krasnaia Polana, twenty miles to the north, troops could see the flashes of antiaircraft guns defending the Kremlin. Guenther von Kluge, commander of the Fourth Army, telephoned von Bock to report that the pressure on his forces was intolerable. He was reverting to a defensive posture, a euphemism for withdrawal. Then Maximilian Freiherr von Weichs telephoned from his Second Army command post that the Russians had broken into his ranks in several places; his line could no longer hold. He was ill, he pleaded, and needed relief. General Rudolf Schmidt was hastily reassigned to the Second Army sector. Georg-Hans Reinhardt, a panzer general, reported that his tanks had to withdraw from the Moscow-Volga Canal before they were trapped. Eric Hoepner's Fourth Panzer Army could not be contacted, but von Bock had already heard that Hoepner was shortening his lines.

No one was running away. It was too cold; the snow and ice were too formidable; and front-line troops were too tired and weak for real flight. Yet, when tank motors refused to run and gun recoil mechanisms failed to function, there was nothing left but to trudge out of range of Russian artillery fire, hoping not to become a casualty in the process. Little medical aid was possible; an incapacitating wound meant certain death.

Just below Tula, south of Moscow, Lieutenant Ludwig Freiherr von Heyl, with the 1st Advance Detachment 36, was close to the Russian capital. His artillery and machine gun transporters could not be steered in the cold; his radio truck moved, but the equipment could not transmit. He had received an order, "Maintain communication," but he could not. Somehow he secured a working half-track from another unit and moved a gun toward Arkhangel'skoye. The surviving men of Lieutenant Dreyer's platoon dug in there had "dealt brilliantly" with two enemy companies, he noted in his diary. "The 20 men are very proud. 70 Russians are lying between the village and the edge of the woods nearby, mostly killed with carbines." The heavy mortars were working but there were few "rewarding targets" in the frozen forestland.

"I make a few small probes . . . although my nose is freezing," he added. It was late afternoon; the sounds of gunfire were dying down. He was "dissatisfied" with his position "since I hear that it is supposed to look less good to the right," but a radio truck had caught up with them, bringing ammunition and field rations. It was so cold that farm buildings they torched—they were very likely unsafe as shelter—"absolutely refuse to burn."

Russian resistance, Hitler telephoned von Bock, was on the verge of collapse. Leningrad had been under siege for weeks, its population close to starvation. Moscow was within sight. There had to be a new attempt to take the city, with its unbombed blocks of potential winter quarters. The Kremlin, then, was to be demolished and the land leveled to symbolize the final overthrow of Bolshevism. In the optimism of August, Hitler had issued a similar directive for Leningrad, for which he refused to use anything but its pre-Bolshevik name. "The Führer has decided to have St. Petersburg," he had announced, "wiped off the face of the earth. The continued existence of this large city is of no interest." Hitler was not troubled about the population. Russians were *Untermenschen*, subhumans fit only for slave labor if they survived at all.

Few Germans on Russian soil were warmly housed. Snug in his own well-provisioned headquarters in East Prussia, Hitler conducted the war's strategy with his tame staff generals from the aptly named Wolf's Lair. Eight kilometers from Rastenburg, 450 miles northeast of Berlin and even farther from the Moscow front, Wolfschanze was hidden in a dark, gloomy pine forest, cloaked by a gray winter mist. Hitler's wooden hut concealed an underground bunker and was surrounded by barbed-wire entanglements, mine fields, sentry posts, and checkpoints. A hut nearby housed headquarters generals, a military library, and a briefing room. Spread farther out were barracks for guards, a radio station, a telephone exchange, a private railway line and station, and a small airfield.

Generaloberst Alfred Jodl called it "a cross between a cloister and a concentration camp"—but he had experienced neither. When Goebbels's Propaganda Ministry announced that the Führer was "in the field," it usually meant that after rising at noon he was in the pine forests of the Mauerwald, barking orders at his obedient wolfhound.

While complaining that he had sacrificed all pleasure by secluding himself at Wolfschanze to monitor the war, Hitler was clearly where he wanted to be. He had arrived on the Sunday the invasion of Russia began. The few people he trusted were received there; secretaries took down every word as he paced his office; communications specialists kept him in touch with the outside world; aides rushed him to the airfield for rare flying visits to advance command posts or to the railway station for an appearance in Berlin.

The only artwork he displayed was a painting of Frederick the Great in an ornate circular frame; it had accompanied him since 1934 and hung above the oak table at which he worked. Hitler's food was spartan; his clothes were a series of similar uniforms and trenchcoats. A singularly joyless existence by the standards of his staff—they could not even boast of victories because only the ultimate one counted—it was the unreal life that Hitler had chosen to live. One day, he predicted, the site would become "a historic monument, because here is where we founded a new world order."

Military matters absorbed him completely. His "I order," usually given only after long midday and late evening conferences, could not be questioned. Strategic decisions made from the warm underground bunker could be dehumanized. It did not snow on Wolfschanze maps, nor did the winter wind blow, or the temperature congeal fuel oil or freeze exposed flesh. One could not relinquish strategically vital positions; one could not abandon snowbound tanks and artillery; one could not surrender the Wehrmacht mystique of unyielding advance.

Yet by Saturday afternoon, even before darkness began to veil his moves, Guderian was already withdrawing, without orders. "Fortunately," General Günther von Blumentritt recalled after the war, "the Russians did not discover that [our forward elements] were moving back, so that we succeeded in extricating them and bringing them back to their original position in fairly good order. . . . The decision was just in time to avert the worst consequences of the counter-offensive that the Russians now unleashed."

As usual, the Führer was quick with statistics to substantiate his stubbornness. Although some figures were reasonably accurate and made his imaginative ones seem, in context, more persuasive, at Rastenburg he was not haranguing political lackeys or the docile bureaucracy, but career military men who could recognize military realities, whatever they were. German losses, Hitler told Generals von Brauchitsch and Halder, had been half a million. He would not admit the actual 800,000. The Russians, he boasted, had suffered a horrendous eight to ten million casualties; the crippled behemoth was about to topple. Russia had indeed lost five million or more men, over half to German prison camps, but endless manpower resources seemed to be at Stalin's summons.

Deluding himself that all the advantages lay with the Germans, Hitler pointed to his labor force from the satellite states, and to so-called volunteer divisions of Hungarians, Romanians, Italians, and Spaniards. Besides, there were additional makeshift ways to release more German manpower for the Eastern Front. Fighting units could be made of truck drivers without vehicles; of service troops who could be supplanted by civilian drafts; of factory workers who could be replaced by prisoners of war or foreign labor. Under no circumstances, Hitler vowed, would he comb troops out of western Europe or Norway.

Franz Halder wrote in his diary in desperation, Hitler "refuses to take any account of comparative figures of strengths."

On the Northern Front, Hitler viewed the endangered town of Tikhvin, south of Leningrad, as the fulcrum of the siege. "The enemy before Tikhvin has been reinforced," General Halder noted. "Very severe cold (38 degrees below freezing), numerous cases of death from cold," he added ominously. Reinforcements were lacking, and there had been some drop in strength from other causes than cold and casualties. Air units had been diverted to support Rommel in Libya, yet the Afrika Korps remained in trouble. "The situation no doubt is serious," Halder noted about North Africa. Armored operations had sustained "heavy losses, which cannot be replaced owing to shipping difficulties, while the British are bringing in reinforcements." Stalin would consider North Africa an irrelevant sideshow taking little pressure off his troops, but the evidence from Hitler's generals was different.

"Serious thinking about Tikhvin," Halder recorded. "Commanding generals take a grave view of the situation." But not Hitler, who brushed ominous projections aside. Weak and gaunt from a heart attack, Werner von Brauchitsch, on the edge of a nervous breakdown, resolved to relinquish his appointment and leave the army.

•

On the western edge of the South China Sea, in the gathering darkness, the Japanese minelayer *Tatsumiya Maru*, working alone, began laying 456 mines in British territorial waters between Tioman

Island and the Malay coast, just above Singapore. Then it slipped north toward Indochina, but not unobserved. En route from Cam Ranh Bay with a sister ship, the *Chosa Maru*, it was shadowed by British reconnaissance planes. To confuse them, the *Chosa Maru* turned back toward Indochina. When the *Tatsumiya Maru* resumed course it would be followed by planes and—so its skipper thought—submarines.

The Japanese had their own subs in the area—twelve of them in the waters east of Malaya. Off Kota Bharu the *I-56* was checking to see if the weather was "suitable for landing operations." Lying off Singapore the *I-122* monitored Royal Navy activity and the local weather. The *I-121* and the *I-122* were also to lay mines near the eastern entrance to Singapore; fear of disclosing their presence aborted the mission.

The mines were to protect the imminent Japanese landings on the Thai and Malay coast from British naval pursuit out of Singapore.* The invasion fleet, including nineteen transports, had weighed anchor on the 4th from Samah Bay on the occupied Chinese island of Hainan. By the time that the *Tatsumiya Maru* was laying its mines, the convoy was in the Gulf of Siam. The war in the Pacific had begun.

•

The tough, cocky Spanish "Blue Division" commanded by General Agustin Muñoz Grandes considered itself the elite of the Leningrad front. Even so, obscene gestures and Castilian curses were no match in the snow for fresh Russian troops fortified by vodka and willing to defend the Motherland with anything useful, from entrenching tools to icepicks. Once Nekrasovo had been lost Friday afternoon, the corps commander, General Friedrich-Wilhelm von Chappuis, wanted to withdraw. A new line northward from Novgorod might hold, but that would mean abandoning a bridgehead still held precariously by the Spaniards.

As Russian assaults were renewed with daylight on Saturday, Muñoz Grandes had met with the commander of his most exposed regiment, Colonel Jose Antonio Esparza. "What do you think of the situation?" Muñoz asked.

"I still think that we must pull back," Esparza confessed, "while

---

* Two casualties in the mine field were the Dutch submarines *O-16* and *K-XVII*, about a week later.

we have men that can walk out." The winter, and Russian replacements, had made a difference in the Spaniards, who were General Franco's gesture to erase the sting of refusal to enter the war against Britain and occupy Gibraltar. His country shattered by the civil war only recently won, Franco was unwilling to chance losing it all.

On their way to the front, rumor had it in Rome, the legionnaires paused in Warsaw, where they demanded women. Reluctantly, the Germans provided contraceptives and permission to visit local brothels. At Wolfschanze, Hitler was furious, withdrawing the authorization before many of the "french letters" could be used. Still in possession of their *cartes de visite*, the angry Spaniards, so admiring Italians said, inflated them and fixed them to the barrels of their rifles. Partisan spies watching the troop trains reported that the enemy was armed with a new weapon, possibly poison gas balloons.

Their situation was far different now. As early twilight materialized in mid-afternoon, Muñoz was arranging the evacuation of Esparza's men. Whatever the breach of authority, macho behavior was useless. In order to prevent any countermand from von Chappuis, Muñoz acted in secret. Heavy equipment, frozen in place, would be left behind. Their positions to the east of the river Volkhov, above Novgorod, were untenable; if Russians swept across the frozen river there would be no escape.

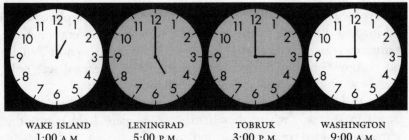

WAKE ISLAND	LENINGRAD	TOBRUK	WASHINGTON
1:00 A.M.	5:00 P.M.	3:00 P.M.	9:00 A.M.
December 7	December 6	December 6	December 6

HOUR 2

As December 7, 1941, began west of the Date Line, a convoy of eight American troop transports and freighters, carrying P-40 aircraft and crews for B-17 Flying Fortresses about to be flown from California via Hawaii and Midway, skirted Wake Island en route to the Philippines. Other convoys were bringing Marine F4F fighters to Wake and Midway. In Tokyo it was an hour before midnight on the 6th. From the *Nagato*, his flagship in Hiroshima Bay, Admiral Yamamoto waited for developments. He had already prepared a coded message to ships under his command announcing his assurances to the Emperor on the eve of hostilities. "I have the honor to tell Your Majesty that every man of the Combined Fleet will, with the Imperial order in his mind, do his utmost to accomplish the aim of waging war at any cost and justify Your Majesty's trust in them." Codes had changed on November 1 and again on December 1. American cryptanalysts had not yet caught up.

Radio silence aboard *Kido Butai*, the Hawaii strike force, had been enforced by rendering all sending apparatus temporarily inoperable. In fog, rain, and heavy seas, the lack of radio contact and the limitation to visual signals had left each ship's captain in agonizing tension. The chances of collision had been great. Refueling at sea was hazardous enough, and the possibility of encountering an unanticipated vessel sailing westward added to the sense of alarm.

Aware of the path of the Soviet freighter *Uritsky*, carrying Lend-Lease supplies from San Francisco to Vladivostok, the fleet kept away from it. Since the ship had to pass close to Japan as it neared port, the Russians had prudently informed Tokyo of its route. Anticipating other encounters, the Japanese Naval Ministry cabled their San Francisco consulate to radio "full reports" of any other ships leaving the Golden Gate. But no other vessel that could intersect with Nagumo's force had departed.

Kido Butai had now turned into a course due south, at twelve knots, heading for a point directly north of Oahu. In Washington, where it was only breakfast hour on the 6th, the Japanese envoys who had spent weeks in fruitless discussions with Cordell Hull saw their mission ending. A message sent to them from Tokyo that morning, in "Purple," a code that the Americans were breaking, pointed out that it was the Americans who had "invaded" Dutch colonial territory—Surinam, at the northern hump of South America—and that the Japanese had only occupied French Indochina "for joint defense." It seemed clear in Washington that the Japanese were preparing an elaborate rationale to justify the occupation of, at the least, the Netherlands East Indies. Of the two negotiators, special envoy Saburo Kurusu was the more pragmatic, having served his government in Germany. His colleague, Ambassador Kichisaburo Nomura, a former admiral with an American wife and long experience of the U.S., had given up weeks earlier. "I don't want to go on with this hypocrisy, deceiving other people," he appealed to the Foreign Ministry. "No, please do not think that I am trying to flee from the field of battle, but as a man of honor this is the only way that is left for me."

Instead, the ministry sent him Kurusu, who also had American connections, and who was preparing to meet an old diplomatic colleague, Ferdinand Mayer, at eleven that morning. Informal intermediaries might help. The United States would not budge regarding China or Southeast Asia, and Kurusu could see no compromise without both sides relinquishing something. Nomura, meanwhile, was alerted that a Japanese response to Hull was coming. The first of fourteen promised parts began transmission from Tokyo as December 7 was breaking west of the Date Line.

By three minutes after eight—not yet dawn on Bainbridge Island,

Washington, where Navy listening station "S" was copying it down—Part 1 was being teletyped to the Navy Department. It would take much of the day, and beyond, as the portions came sporadically, and out of numerical order. Yet it was sent in English, exactly as Tokyo wanted it delivered, which meant that no translation (beyond decoding) was required. Every paragraph was available to the Army, Navy, State Department, and White House before it was seen by Nomura and Kurusu. The Japanese embassy in Washington had to translate the English for study by its own personnel.

·

At 9:30 Stephen T. Early, Roosevelt's Press Secretary, held his morning press conference in the West Wing of the White House, but had nothing for the Sunday papers. He saw no need "for pads and pencils," as little had changed. The President, he said, had suggested that it was a good time for Christmas shopping. "I suppose," cracked a reporter, "he is . . . writing a declaration of war personally."

The President wasn't doing any writing at the moment, Early said. He was shaving. And he had "no appointments for today and none for tomorrow and I don't assume there will be [any]." But he did have appointments unconnected with the crisis. At eleven, Harold Smith, Director of the Budget, was to consult about the next year's estimates; then Attorney General Francis Biddle was to check with Roosevelt about language intended for a speech in Detroit on Sunday. Before either visitor arrived, the President was pushed in his wheelchair to the White House physician's office, where Rear Admiral Ross T. McIntyre worked on Roosevelt's lingering sinus infection. Few outsiders ever saw the President in a wheelchair. When guests were escorted in, his paralyzed legs were unseen behind his desk.

At the Navy Department on Constitution Avenue, Secretary Frank Knox, the Chicago publisher (and Republican vice-presidential candidate in 1936), was holding his daily briefing with his civilian and military chiefs. With his Army counterpart, patrician elder statesman and Hoover Cabinet member Henry L. Stimson, Knox represented Roosevelt's effort to build bipartisan unity in the military establishment. Earlier in the year, concerned about the implications of an effective British torpedo plane attack on the naval base of Taranto, located on the heel of the Italian boot, Knox had urged improvement of defenses on Oahu, writing to Stimson, "If war eventuates with Japan, it is . . . easily possible that hostilities would be initiated by a surprise attack upon the Fleet or the Naval Base at Pearl Harbor." Now, winding up the meeting, Knox asked, "Gentlemen, are they going to hit us?"

"No, Mr. Secretary," said Rear Admiral Richmond Kelly Turner, head of the Navy's War Plans Division. "They are going to hit the British. They are not ready for us yet."

•

On the Eastern Front a legacy of the Japanese decision to move south, rather than against Russia, appeared even before the first shots in the Pacific were fired. In his headquarters diary at Wolfschanze General Halder noted, "Identification of Siberian 65th Division, consisting of three regiments, one behind the other. . . . Our own troops physically overstrained. The situation is aggravated by the cold (30 to 35 degrees of frost [− C]). Only one out of five tanks was able to fire." As early as November 8, on the Moscow front, a captured officer from the Russian 61st Division identified himself as from a unit formerly in eastern Siberia. Stalin had learned from Baku-born spy Richard Sorge, ostensibly the *Frankfurter Zeitung*'s correspondent in Tokyo, that it would be safe to move troops from the Manchurian frontier. The Trans-Siberian Railway westward had overflowed with soldiers who had fought effectively for General Georgi Zhukov in 1939 in undeclared border battles with the Japanese. Now Zhukov's seasoned troops were fanning out in the western suburbs of Moscow.

Shrouded by snow and ice, encircled on land by Germans and Finns, Leningrad received its news of the outside world by radio. Its thin trickle of supplies arrived only after early darkness fell over "the ice road"—Lake Ladoga, to the north. Hitler was convinced that, once the lake thawed, the city would collapse. Despite its several million inhabitants, Leningrad was ghostly. Winter darkness lasted nearly all day. People trudged to work, empty stomachs protesting, through streets uncleared of snow, after surviving overnight in unheated and often windowless buildings. Garbage—fortunately frozen—lay uncollected. Except for what could be scavenged, bomb debris remained where it fell. Public transportation had virtually ceased. Water and sewage lines had mostly frozen and burst.

Holding the town of Tikhvin enabled the Germans to block the only paved supply route to Leningrad. The hazardous truck route over

Lake Ladoga was 190 miles. Until the ice thickened enough in winter, loads had to be light and speeds cautious. Sleighs drawn by the trucks spread the weight of the precarious shipments. There was a railhead, however, at Zaborie, a small station in difficult forest land one hundred miles east of Volkhov and sixty miles east of Tikhvin. When Tikhvin had fallen on November 9, the Leningrad War Council, in despair, ordered the building of a "motor road" of nearly two hundred miles, through virgin forest and along existing paths, in a wide circle from Zaborie to Novaya Ladoga. Encamped at stages along the route, working parties of soldiers, peasants, and factory hands employed makeshift tools when nothing else was at hand. By twilight on the 6th the road—a passage so narrow that trucks encountering each other had to pull aside into the deep snow—was declared completed.

The death rate from hunger, described on death certificates as "alimentary dystrophy," was nearly one thousand each day. Soldiers in front-line units received a pound of bread and four ounces of meat daily—estimated as 1,605 calories. Manual and technical workers in the city received only 1,087 calories, office workers a starvation 581 calories, less than the 684 calories for children. At least a thousand tons of food delivered daily were needed to maintain even that diet. While the Germans bombed and shelled the lake to make supply lines hazardous, traffic police stationed along the ice road laid temporary bridges across the gaps.

Although the forest road promised relief, famine was dehumanizing Leningrad. Cats, dogs and other household pets had long since gone into the stewpot. Children dug for leaves and plants and flower bulbs under the snow. Horse and cattle feed, bark, leather, carpenter's glue, and other organic substances were cooked. The bitter cold tortured wasted bodies; women ceased menstruating; everyone experienced weakness, swelling of the joints, the losing of control over one's body. The two basic sensations, a survivor remembered, were "the feeling of being cold" and "the feeling of hunger." One "gets up" with cold, "one walks with it, one goes to bed with it. . . . It penetrates the bones and sometimes it seems as if it enters the brain. One can't escape from it. It penetrates under all shirts, sweaters and jackets no matter how many one puts on." Hunger had "many shadings" of feeling—"from a dull, painful, sharp, unbearable one, which appears as soon as one has eaten one's ration . . . , to being tortured by fantasies."

Hospitals operated in temperatures that hovered at freezing; interior walls grew frost; water froze in pitchers. Hunger-caused diarrhea iced in filthy, unwashable sheets. Almost no medicine was available except sodium bromide, which was prescribed under various names. The medical staff, underfed and overworked, barely able to stand, operated in overcoats; patients lay in their beds fully clothed, under blankets and coats.

"Hungry people go mad," Lidiia Osipova observed in her diary after she was offered—and refused—a loaf of bread and half a pouch of tobacco for her wedding ring. She was not in encircled Leningrad, but in a German-occupied suburb where conditions were little better, as enemy troops supplied nothing, and desperate survivors turned to a black market where exotic valuables were bartered for any kind of food.

Her family was living on the proceeds from a ring sold to a German cook although Lidiia feared arrest "for corrupting the German army." Her head had spun "from the aroma of the sausage," but it was not offered. Instead, the cook "grabbed my knapsack and began to pour flour into it. . . . Then he asked if I wanted any sugar. Sugar! He thrust in a 2-kilo sack of sugar. I screwed up my courage and asked in a whisper for some bread. . . . Bread was now the thing we valued most because you could eat it at once and because it gave you the feeling of being full." She looked about. "He spotted a huge piece of meat, hacked off almost half of it and also stuffed it into my knapsack. I was afraid to breathe lest he come to his senses and the fairy tale come to an end."

A neighbor had stolen a Turkish rug from an abandoned flat and wanted help concealing it. The rug might be exchanged later for food. But Lidiia's frightened husband objected to hiding it. "I got furious at that stupid honesty and declared that as soon as we get rid of the occupation forces I'll divorce Nikolai. Now, really—such foolishness . . . when one is dying of hunger."

In Leningrad itself a woman gnawed by hunger resorted to the last precious object she had—the gold in her teeth. It would bring, she estimated to the dentist, two substantial loaves of bread. When, huddled in his overcoat, he had extracted the gold and filled in the gaps with something of less barter value, she asked his fee. "One loaf of bread," he said.

•

Edited and mimeographed in eight hundred copies on an Italian duplicator captured in the Libyan desert, the *Tobruk Truth* was the most dependable object of Italian origin in North Africa. Its motto, "Always Appears," had been in the left-hand corner of the pink sheets (or whatever other color was available) during all eight months of Tobruk's siege. Most of its news, even of Tobruk itself, came from BBC broadcasts. Isolated from British and Commonwealth forces to the east except by sea, Tobruk had been costly to both sides. It had pinned down General Erwin Rommel's panzers while creating, in its shallow harbor, a junkyard of downed aircraft and sunken lighters and relief ships. In return, the British, flying out of Malta and sneaking undersea out of Alexandria, had made resupply of the Afrika Korps by Italian ships crossing the Mediterranean all but impossible.

Generals Crüwell and Rommel could not agree on strategy. Ludwig Crüwell preferred waiting for the big advantage; Rommel would dispatch small groups of troops and tanks on local counterattacks to keep the British off balance and disorganize an enemy buildup. "He's winning a skirmish and losing the battle," Crüwell would mutter. "What does it matter anyway? Every battle won brings the Americans in that much sooner."

Aimed at relieving Tobruk, the British "Crusader" offensive launched on November 18 by General Sir Claude Auchinleck and his Eighth Army commander, Lieutenant General Alan Cunningham, had been predicated upon decrypts of German intelligence. Breaking the *Enigma* cipher brought knowledge of enemy fuel, food and ammunition shortages. North African temperatures in November and December were bearable—a major consideration when tanks often became boilers on treads.

"Inside our Crusader tank," Robin Maugham wrote about action near Bir Gubi, south of Tobruk, "the driver is hunched up . . . peering through a slit . . . in the steel wall which surrounds him. The slit is filled with a glass block four inches thick, and through it he can see dimly a narrow strip of sand." Levers to move the tank were between his legs, leaving him little room to move. An auxiliary turret blocked part of the glass, leaving him blind on his left side. Behind the driver crowded two crewmen and an officer.

"I stand in the center with my head half out the turret so that I can see. . . . If I crouch down . . . I can look through the commander's periscope but my vision is limited. . . . I must be careful where I put my hands because the two-pounder in front of me recoils to within six inches of my stomach. . . . The radio operator, crouched close to my right thigh, is loading the two-pounder for all he is worth. . . . He cannot see anything." The blast and rocking of the tank let them know when the enemy had found the range. Hardly able to see through the cordite fumes, the radio operator stoops to pluck more rounds to fire back. "The gunner's forehead is pressed tight against a padded bracket, placed so that his eye can look steadily through the telescope at the small circle of desert to which it is focused. . . . A tap on his right elbow tells him that the guns are loaded. He hears my fire orders . . . through his headphones."

"Two-pounder. . . . Six hundred. . . . Traverse right. . . . Steady. . . . On. . . . Fire! . . . Traverse left. Traverse left. Steady on. . . . Same target. Fire!"

"He's burning. He's burning. We got him."

"Traverse left. Quick. Traverse left. Steady on. . . ."

In the heat of each steel box, potentially a coffin, even over the grinding noise crews could hear the whining of incoming shells. They hoped for a towering cloud of sand and smoke that meant a miss.

On December 4 an Italian officer had arrived at Rommel's headquarters with a message that the *Panzergruppe* could not count on reinforcements or resupply before the end of the month, when the sea routes from Sicily could be protected by air cover. Rommel wanted to go ahead anyway with an attack at Bir Gubi. Counting upon support from often unreliable Italian mechanized units, especially the 20th Motorized Corps, commanded by General Gastone Gambarra. Instead, Gambarra, wearing two hats, one of them senior to Rommel, ordered Corps Commander Gambarra back. Meanwhile Crüwell radioed frantically and repeatedly, "Where is Gambarra?"—which soon became a rueful joke among the Germans about Italian timidity.

Despite the absence of the Italians, the Afrika Korps launched its counteroffensive on the morning of the 6th. By mid-afternoon the British 22nd Guards Brigade began falling back slowly while other units were organizing to outflank Rommel's weaker forces: he had no more than thirty serviceable tanks. Rommel's intelligence estimate, which the British had picked up, warned that if the German offensive failed to destroy "a substantial part of the enemy's force," a deep withdrawal would be inevitable, "breaking off the battle . . . in view of our own heavy losses in men and material." The Italians declared that their troops were exhausted and unfit for further action. Rommel went on, hoping to keep the momentum going into the next day.

Conferring on the Libyan situation with Mussolini in Rome, Marshal Ugo Cavallaro, his Chief of Staff, complained to the Duce that the Germans were blaming their plight on Italian ineffectiveness. In October, 30 percent of Italian supply ships crossing the Mediterranean had been sunk; in November, shipping losses had escalated to 80 percent—Cavallaro had raised the matter an hour earlier with Admiral Arturo Riccardi, Undersecretary at the Navy Ministry. Everyone, of course, Cavallaro assured Mussolini, had been performing valiantly, but they needed two more Italian divisions "*con urgenza*." Given their failure rate by sea, the troops might have to be moved by air. Mussolini suggested that Cavallaro talk to General Rino Fougier, Riccardi's counterpart at the Air Ministry.

At Acroma, on the western edge of the Tobruk perimeter, Michael Branch, a London stockbroker now an infantry captain with the 4th Indian Division, filled in polyglot fashion with Poles, Free French, and Australians, was supervising fire across a plateau when German Stukas began dive-bombing artillery positions behind them. When they returned, low, over the Indian positions, soldiers shouting *hawai-jahaz* ("airplane") placed their rifles between their thighs and fired happily, straight-up, without aiming. Two Stukas fell, hit by antiaircraft guns rather than the surprised Indians. Despite the craving for souvenirs no one chanced going forward.

•

A newly decrypted message should have been warning enough for American codebreakers on Saturday morning. By informing Germany of their unwillingness to fight Russia at the same time as they would be fighting the U.S., the Japanese were announcing a war against the United States. Foreign Minister Shigenori Togo's instructions to Ambassador Oshima in Berlin left nothing to the imagination except the day and place for the opening of the war. "We would like to avoid . . . an armed clash with Russia," Togo explained, "until strategic circumstances permit it; so make certain the German government understands this. . . . Explain to them at considerable length that insofar as American materials being shipped to Russia [are concerned], . . . if we start our war with the United States we will capture all American ships destined for Soviet Russia." But, he confided, "we cannot capture Soviet ships." Undecrypted, the message was filed away for the weekend.

GUAM	MANILA	MALAYA	WASHINGTON
1:00 A.M.	11:00 P.M.	9:40 P.M.	10:00 A.M.
December 7	December 6	December 6	December 6

HOUR 3

AT MALENGAS, on the southern coast of the big Philippine island of Mindanao, the Guam station ship *Gold Star*, in port to restock its lonely home base, had taken on a load of coal, fifteen hundred cases of San Miguel beer, thirty cases of Scotch whiskey, and one thousand tons of rice. At Cebu, its final port of call, where the *Gold Star* had sailed north to load one thousand tons of Philippine cement, its skipper, Commander J. W. Lademan, received new orders from Asiatic Fleet headquarters. Just getting up its steam for Guam, the vessel would have to skirt the Japanese-controlled island groups of the Carolines and the Marianas to return. The *Gold Star* was to make port in Manila.

Admiral Thomas C. Hart knew that a large Japanese force was heading south, somewhere. Uncoded Japanese radio traffic, most of it likely disinformation, was unusually heavy. To Captain George Johnstone McMillin, Navy governor of Guam, Hart sent a confirming message guaranteeing dry days ahead for the outpost:

DESPITE FACT THAT GOLD STAR READY TO SAIL STOP BECAUSE OF GENERAL SITUATION STOP INADVISABLE TO START NOW

Since MacArthur, as overall commander in the Philippines, had refused to permit flybys for crew recognition training, Hart had also issued orders for ships to fire on any aircraft making an approach. Earlier in the day, Captain A. H. Rooks, who commanded the cruiser *Houston*, anchored south of the Panay port of Iloilo, brought the message to Colonel Bradford Chynoweth, who had just arrived to command Philippine troops in the Negros and Panay region. "Ask your Air Corps people," he complained, "not to send planes over my ship at night without warning." Thirty-six unidentified aircraft had overflown the *Houston* at 0300. Rooks ordered his guns manned; he didn't want to fire upon friendly planes, but he didn't want to be "jumped on."

As Chynoweth had already discovered, the overflight had to have been unfriendly, but instructions were to fire only after being attacked. MacArthur was not about to be blamed for starting a war.

Chynoweth respected Japanese capabilities. As a boy of fifteen in 1904, son of an officer on Philippines duty, he had sailed into Manila Bay "past shattered remnants of the Russian fleet that had fled here after the battle of Tsushima." Aboard the *Coolidge*, on which he had just arrived, he didn't recall any officer who "didn't know things were about to bust open," but when he reported to USAFFE headquarters, no one "could care less." He was urged "to stay up in Manila and have a good time" instead of reporting immediately to his new duty station in the boondocks.* "That's what they were doing."

Career officers often downplayed the inadequacies of marginally trained Filipino troops about whom Dwight Eisenhower, when an aide to MacArthur, had seen "a minimum of performance from a maximum of promise." Since a positive assessment elicited additional support from Washington, MacArthur perceived a military potential in Philippine soldiery that was, to him, less fiction than prophecy. Nothing that MacArthur willed to see or to do could, in his own estimation, possibly go wrong.

Chynoweth knew nothing of the ramshackle army to which he was assigned, but he insisted on seeing MacArthur, who had "withdrawn into a magnificent inaccessibility." All questions vanished in the presence of the man. "The impact of his personality and his emotional

---

* *boondocks* (*bundocks*): Tagalog for mountain jungles in Luzon, brought home to the U.S. c.1902 by American troops as label for any remote rural area.

force . . . took me by surprise and left me at his feet." The experience buoyed Chynoweth until he arrived at the somnolent headquarters of the 61st Philippine Scouts Division, at Magallon on the island of Negros.

Many newly arrived colonels were without commands. "We were getting," Garry Anloff remembered, "loads of bird colonels who were a few years short of retirement and were surplus to the needs of every post in the U.S. Their seniority would have made them commanding officers of just about any unit to which they would have been assigned. The favorite solution was to 'attach' them to Headquarters, Philippine Department, and the colonels ended up answering the telephone, and getting in the way."

However ready for retirement himself, Tom Hart understood that he would command a desk a bit longer—that he would not be ending his career, as he once wished, swept off the quarterdeck by a fourteen-inch shell. On June 12 he had reached official retirement age but was being kept on until Washington found someone else to manage the Asiatic Fleet out of Manila. Younger officers manned quarterdecks. Hart wrote radiograms.

One message went to Captain Arthur G. Robinson, who flew his flag from the cruiser *Marblehead* and who commanded Destroyer Division 57. Robinson's firepower was largely concentrated on his flagship. Otherwise all he had were four 1918-vintage destroyers and the grimy *Black Hawk*, a destroyer tender just back from China duty, and labeled by sailors from the old four-stackers as "a tough ship . . . with the worst reputation in the Navy."

•

From Balikpapan, a Dutch oil port just above the equator on the east coast of Borneo, Captain Robinson's ships were ordered southward because of the undetermined whereabouts of the alleged Japanese invasion fleet. He solicited the Dutch port authorities, but they were reluctant to open the anti-submarine booms before daylight. Robinson had no choice but to lay over until morning.

Radioed orders seldom furnish details, but Robinson was aware that Japanese movements were considered potentially hostile and were being shadowed. He knew that the U.S. was using PBY "Catalinas" for reconnaissance, but nothing of what Roosevelt's critics would later call a "baiting feint" at the Japanese. On December 2, the President had ordered Hart "within two days if possible" to ready three small vessels, each to be commanded by an American officer, as a "defensive information patrol" into the China Sea and the Gulf of Siam. Hart had managed to prepare only two vessels, one of them his own "holiday flagship," the two-funneled *Isabel*. A second, the seventy-five-ton *Lanikai*, with sails and an ancient engine that could manage only six knots, was nearly ready to go.

Reporting to Cavite, on the south shore of Manila Bay, on his reassignment from China service, Lieutenant Kemp Tolley, Annapolis '29, found himself with a ship even less seaworthy than his flat-bottomed river gunboat *Oahu*. He recalled gratefully his sailing lessons at school. "Man her with a crew including Filipinos," he was ordered. "Have a gun mounted, load ammunition, food and water, and report here ready to go to sea." The navy yard commandant had been impressed that the original order came from the President. No paperwork would be involved. The *Lanakai*'s orders, like that of the *Isabel*, were: "Patrol off the entrance of Camranh Bay and report the direction taken by the Japanese fleet when it emerges." If the Japanese stopped him and wanted to know why Tolley was there, he was to claim that he was looking for the crew of a downed plane.

Although Hart was receiving British intelligence reports about convoys proceeding "perhaps [to] Bangkok, maybe Kra," he had more reliable sources of information. Ordering air reconnaissance on his own authority, he had personally briefed the Catalina crews. "Try to get confirmation and even full information, but try to do it without being seen, and don't bring on a war." The long-range PBYs, too slow to get in close, took advantage of cloud cover along the Indochina coast. Hart then radioed his information to Washington without saying how he got it. On December 2, he reported twenty Japanese transports and naval vessels in Cam Ranh Bay; on December 3, thirty. On December 4, they were gone, apparently sailing south. On December 5 the weather turned bad and there were no sightings. Then the weather lifted and the ships were spotted, apparently moving toward Malaya.

The news had come while British Vice-Admiral Sir Tom Phillips, having arrived to command naval forces in the Malayan region, was visiting Cavite on a courtesy call to Hart. Phillips knew almost nothing of the Southeast Asian situation except that it was ominous. Hart helped fill him in by having him meet the legendary MacArthur, who towered over the two tiny admirals. Phillips, at five foot two, was even smaller than the compact Hart. "Admiral Hart and I operate," MacArthur claimed, "in the closest cooperation. We are the oldest and dearest friends." In reality they detested each other, MacArthur envying Hart's four stars. "Small fleet, big admiral," he scoffed privately.

Not only was Hart's fleet small; so were his quarters in Manila compared to those occupied by MacArthur. A wag once called God "that quaint old subordinate of General Douglas MacArthur." His enormous penthouse suite atop the Manila Hotel, built and maintained for him as Field Marshal of the Philippines because he insisted that he was entitled to the equivalent of Malacañang Palace, was Olympian. He lived in state while, several floors below, Tom Hart had a modest bedroom. When Hart was in and available, he would put his hat in the window; those who understood the signal would know to come up and have a drink. Few saw MacArthur except as a distant Presence, strolling his quarter-mile of balconies, deep in thought and clenching a "Manila rope"—a black Filipino cigar. (The famous corncob pipe came later.)

Whether or not Tom Phillips understood the honor, he was filled in by MacArthur personally on how the general had prevailed upon Washington to exempt the Philippines from the "Orange" write-off, and how he expected to be up to adequate defensive strength by April 1942. MacArthur read promises as power, not long before putting on his bathrobe and slippers to trot down to Hart's room to show him a message about his getting additional B-17s.* "Now look at this, Tom. When you get something like this you can really call yourself something. You can pretend you've got power." And back he vanished into his penthouse.

For MacArthur the B-17s were more symbols than weapons. He had never taken aircraft seriously, and shared the bias of most Army brass about the efficacy of air power. Phillips understood the uses of air but also his own present limitations. He had only four destroyers to support the *Repulse* and *Prince of Wales*, and neither aircraft carriers nor adequate aircraft. Hart offered assurances that Destroyer Division 57, at Balikpapan, would be ordered immediately to move closer to

---

* MacArthur had been promised 240 fighter planes (107 had already arrived) and 165 modern heavy bombers (the first 35 B-17s had arrived).

Singapore. The ships would go first to Java "on pretext of rest and leave. Actually they will join your forces."

•

In rain squalls that concealed the moon, Lieutenant General Tomoyuki Yamashita's troopships, having left Hainan two days earlier, reached a position in the South China Sea due south of Cambodia Point (Pointe de Cau Mau) only ninety minutes before midnight, Thai time. To mislead British reconnaissance aircraft or submarines, the ships turned northwest into the Gulf of Siam as if heading for Bangkok.

The convoy already had its fill of scares about discovery. On the 5th the destroyer *Uranami* had encountered a foreign freighter, a Norwegian vessel innocently en route from Bangkok to Hong Kong. It was boarded and searched, and its radio smashed. Then it was ordered to head to the east, where it would pass no unfriendly ships until the Japanese force had made its landfall. The next afternoon a British Hudson bomber flying out of Kota Bharu appeared overhead, flying in and out of range of shipboard antiaircraft guns. Vice Admiral Jisaburo Ozawa had to decide whether to risk shooting it down, or risk his fleet. After an hour the plane was still maintaining pace. Belatedly— it was three in the afternoon—Ozawa signaled, "Large-type British aircraft in contact. Shoot down." At least, he may have thought, if the Hudson did not return, the British would have no reconnaissance photos.

Miscounting from his high altitude, and losing the convoy intermittently in the clouds, Australian Flight Lieutenant J. C. Ramshaw radioed just after noon that he had seen twenty-five transports with escorts, then ten with escorts. He was not sure whether it was the same group—but he had verified that a large hostile force had entered the South China Sea.

Darting in and out of cloud cover were three Lockheed Hudsons, all of which had evaded Japanese pursuit. From Kota Bharu, where Air Commodore R. H. S. Davis, commanding No. 1 Squadron, RAAF, was intercepting messages from the Hudsons, the information was forwarded by scrambler telephone to Singapore and then Manila, prompting Tom Phillips's return. "Admiral," asked his Cavite counterpart, Thomas Hart, "when did you say you were flying back to Singapore?"

"I'm taking off tomorrow morning."

"If you want to be there when the war starts," said Hart, "I suggest you take off right now."

The news also drew the *Repulse* back to Singapore. It had hardly arrived with the *Prince of Wales* when concerns were raised about its inadequate antiaircraft armament, and a move to Darwin ordered forthwith. The ship had only been en route to Australia for a few hours. Its initial docking in Singapore had not been announced, nor its return.

Assuming the worst, since the Hudson had not been shot down, Ozawa chanced breaking radio silence and sent a coded message to Combined Fleet headquarters in Japan. "It was," wrote Rear Admiral Matome Ugaki, Yamamoto's chief of staff, in his diary, "like living through a thousand autumns in a single day. What we are living through is a great drama for the human race, in which the fate of the nation and countless lives are at stake. But there is no anxiety. What will be, will be. This . . . is the will of the gods. And the country of the gods moves in accordance with that will."

In Singapore, Brooke-Popham delayed activating the Matador defensive scheme. He opted for more sea searches to confirm the destination of the convoy. Behind the vigorous facade, Brooke-Popham was a man of instant indecision. "Brookham," as he was known to airmen, was sixty-two and past his prime for a major command. For a desk post in a backwater, even an important one, he was what was available.

Lieutenant General Arthur Percival, the Army chief, nearly ten years younger, slight, red-faced, and dark-mustached, had also led more desks than soldiers. From Kuala Lumpur he commanded 89,000 troops, almost half of them Indian and inadequately trained. Nearly 20,000 were British and 15,200 were Australian. Few knew jungle warfare, least of all the local Malays, who had little interest in defending anything. These were Percival's polyglot pieces for the four-hundred-mile-long chessboard of Malaya, on whom Matador and much else depended.

Matador, Percival discovered on conferring with Phillips and Brooke-Popham, was not on. The watchword remained watchfulness. "There should be no undue alarm," Brooke-Popham judged, "because the Japanese expedition is directed at Thailand." Anyone with a map could see that lower Thailand was the vestibule to Malaya, but Brooke-Popham preferred, for the time being, to believe in the sanctity of political borders.

Percival's III Indian Corps, in the plans to execute Matador, had been on alert status since 3:15 P.M., when the corps commander, Lieutenant General Sir Lewis Heath, first learned of the Japanese armada. Breaking off his conference with Heath in Kuala Lumpur, Percival rushed to his car and raced south to Singapore only to be waved aside by the unhurried Brooke-Popham. Closer to the likely action, Heath felt even more frustrated. Because of his size, Heath was called "Piggy" privately by his men, but despite his bulk and a useless left arm crippled in the previous war, he had fought earlier in Africa. His military situation paralleled his physical disability. Each of Heath's two Indian divisions had only two of its three authorized brigades. But he had on his side, he was assured, the impenetrable jungle hinterland.

While Heath's inadequate and scattered army waited for orders, General Yamashita's troops at sea tried to sleep. Blacked out, they had little else to do, however crowded they were in the oppressive heat below decks. They hoped for better circumstances, especially better food, when living off the land. At sea, rations were bean soup, pickled radish, and buckets of boiled rice and barley. Officers and men, even stocky, rumpled Yamashita, shared alike, and he had selected the grimy and uncomfortable *Ryujo Maru* as 5th Division headquarters to make the point that he was living their lot.

In truth Yamashita's soldiers fared slightly better than the general. On Formosa, where they had trained and were exhorted by political officers that "Japan's fate is the fate of East Asia," they had bought sacks of dried eels which they baked aboard ship and sprinkled with salt. They were trained to be mobile; sneakers and shorts made them more maneuverable than if they were burdened with traditional combat gear. Besides, the Japanese economy could not have managed millions of tailored uniforms and sturdy Western-style service boots.

Soldiers carried pamphlets, largely written by Yamashita's balding, blinking-eyed Operations staff officer, Major Masanobu Tsuji, "designed to be read quickly, without strain," the preface explained, "in the cramped conditions of a transport vessel." Titled *Read This Alone— and the War Can Be Won*, it was a digest of political indoctrination, tips on jungle warfare and subsistence, and self-doctoring. South Asia was described as "a world of everlasting summer," a "treasure-house" in which a tiny minority of whites "tyrannized" the population. Troops were to "treat the natives with kindness—but do not expect too much of them. . . . Destroy the genuine enemy. . . . The British, the Amer-

icans, the French and the Dutch are mere armed robbers, while we
Japanese are brothers. At least, we are indubitably relatives. . . . But
countries of great natural blessings, where it is possible for men to live
in nakedness and to eat without working, breed large populations of
idlers. . . . These people have reached a point of almost complete
emasculation."

The soldiers they would face, the pamphlet explained, were largely
native although officered by whites; "consequently the sense of solidarity in each unit between officers and men is practically nil." Their
equipment was "outdated, and . . . the fact that the soldiers who operate
it are ill-trained and without enthusiasm renders it worse than useless.
Night attacks are what these people most dread."

Tropical enemies like malaria and syphilis, soldiers were warned,
loomed dangerously ahead. "To fall in a hail of bullets is to meet a
hero's death, but there is no glory in dying of disease or accident.
. . . Native women are almost all infected with venereal disease, and
. . . if you tamper with them you will also make the whole native
population your enemy." Since death, in any case, meant the possibility
that one's body would not be recovered, troops were enjoined to write
a will, "enclosing with it a lock of hair and a piece of fingernail," to
be sent back to a home base. Then "we shall not look back."

There were paragraphs on handling equipment ("Grow attached
to your weapons; care for them"), on conserving water ("Water is your
savior"), on behavior under fire ("the most vital thing of all is that you
should not panic"). Since soldiers would be arriving by sea, they were
reminded confidently that "when we reach the shore . . . the battle is
won. Our opponents are even weaker than the Chinese Army, and
their tanks and aircraft are a collection of rattling relics. Victory is
certain, and the only problem is to win in the cleverest way." And
victory was promised, for "if the rubber and tin of South Asia were
to be seized by Japan, it would create a situation far more intolerable
to America than even the present lack of steel and oil is to Japan." In
the process they would "set Asia free," and "change the course of world
history." It was a "holy crusade," and "the heroic dead [of past wars]
will be watching over us."

Inspired as well as reassured, Yamashita's divisions slept into the
morning of December 7.

•

At ten the President had been in the Oval Office for only fifteen minutes when his light schedule began unraveling. First, Associate Justice William O. Douglas, youngest member of the Supreme Court and an FDR favorite, came calling. Such things could still be done without an agenda. "It's always good to see you, Bill," said Roosevelt, who meant the compliment, as Douglas was a useful sounding board for ideas. The President had been considering his personal intervention with Emperor Hirohito, over the heads of the military. There seemed nothing else left but to wait for war to happen. Roosevelt had been revising a message, and intended to try out the new draft on Secretary Hull.

Accused of pushing a Japan eager for accommodation into a political and economic corner from which it could escape only through war, Roosevelt felt that he had pursued the only route that remained open to him. He did not know that Japan had been planning war since January nor that hostile fleets were even then closing in on several places where the American flag flew. What he did know was that Japan had been at war in Asia since 1931, had no intention of relinquishing its conquests, had every intention of expanding into Southeast Asia, and had a long record of barbarity in China as well as in Korea, which it had seized in 1910.

Though the Japanese regime might offer what it called a solution short of further war, it would be for a pause rather than a peace. Sooner or later, war with an expansionist Japan was likely. Although Roosevelt's generals and admirals preferred later to sooner, in order to prepare the nation better, even that arming was slow as long as isolationism remained influential.

The potent China Lobby in Congress and elsewhere was one of the more puzzling contradictions the President faced. Decades of American missionaries in China—their children often became politicians and opinion-makers—had led to a national sense of an American ethical stake; and years of American business investment led to pressure to keep ajar the "Open Door" to burgeoning Chinese markets. Yet many Americans who lobbied for the incompetent and corrupt regime of Chiang Kaishek as a counterweight to the Communists of Mao Zedong were otherwise largely isolationist, quite willing to leave Europe to Hitler or to Stalin.

Nor could Roosevelt escape domestic concerns. An early-morning memo came from Marvin McIntyre, his political liaison with Capitol

Hill: "Have a request from Congressman Lyndon Johnson who wants to see you next week." Young Johnson was persistent—and ambitious. Before the day was out FDR would learn that Johnson had also telephoned Edwin M. ("Pa") Watson at the White House. Watson handled presidential appointments, and passed a note to Roosevelt that Representative Johnson wanted to discuss a bill he was proposing which would merge two Depression-era agencies, the National Youth Administration and the Civilian Conservation Corps, into a single National Youth Administration. (Johnson had ambitions to head a NYA as a springboard to higher office.) "He hopes to go to Texas next Friday," Watson added, "and [he] would like very much to see the President before that time."

Running unsuccessfully for the Senate earlier in the year—he kept his seat in the House—Johnson had pledged to hawkish Texans who expected war, "If the day ever comes when my vote must be cast to send your boy to the trenches—that day Lyndon Johnson will . . . go with him." He vowed dramatically never to solicit a desk job; rather, he would be "in the front line . . . in the mud and blood with your boys, helping to do the fighting. . . . I shall never vote for war and then hide behind a Senate seat where bullets cannot reach me." What he did not say was that he had already obtained a commission as a lieutenant commander in the Naval Reserve, circumventing the mud and the trenches.*

In the Victorian clutter and gloom of the Executive Office Building adjacent to the White House, courtly Vannevar Bush chaired a morning meeting in his Office of Scientific Research and Development. The organization was one of the newest of the so-called alphabet soup of agencies established by executive order. In its first months of existence, it had been directed by the President to mobilize scientific resources for national defense. Former vice-president of MIT and chairman of the Carnegie Corporation, Bush was an applied mathematician and electrical engineer with major patents to his credit. Late in 1940 he

---

* A White House appointment for Monday would materialize. Roosevelt liked him. But the day was hectic and Johnson would get only a few minutes to announce that he was going on active service, and to say good-bye. Then he visited the office of Admiral Chester Nimitz and signed an application for active duty. Through Under Secretary of the Navy James V. Forrestal, Johnson arranged for himself an inspection tour of West Coast shipyards, then an assignment to an office in San Francisco for Navy liaison with New Zealand.

had reorganized the Uranium Commission to study all fission phenomena and to control publication of anything in the area of nuclear research that promised to have a military application.

German scientists had long been working at the frontiers of atomic physics. With war ongoing in Europe, émigré physicists were worried, and a Wall Street economist with access to the White House, Alexander Sachs, had brought to the President a letter signed by Albert Einstein urging support for research on a potential atomic bomb. "Alex," Roosevelt had said at the close of the interview, "what you're after is to see that the Nazis don't blow us up." Quietly, the President authorized an Advisory Committee on Uranium to investigate what might be done. An elderly physicist at the National Bureau of Standards, Lyman J. Briggs, became chairman to give the group a governmental base. Briggs had held federal posts since 1896.

The British had their own equivalent, code-named MAUD and headed by George P. Thomson of the Imperial Institute of Science and Technology. Since the fall of France they had been in desperate liaison with Briggs's group and had suggested, through Harold Urey, lately returned from London, that an isotope separation process was feasible. Urey's report went to Roosevelt through Bush, who told the group that Roosevelt had said that if atomic bombs can be made, make them first.

Gathered in Bush's small office with Briggs were Arthur Holly Compton, physicist and president of MIT; James Bryant Conant, a chemist, Bush's deputy, and president of Harvard; and Ernest O. Lawrence, the inventor of the cyclotron and director of the radiation laboratory at the University of California at Berkeley. Roosevelt, they realized, would find the money if they found ways to use it. All experiments with any practicality on the separation of uranium-235 were to be explored. "The possibility of obtaining atomic bombs for use in the present war," Conant interpreted the President's thinking, "was great enough to justify an all-out effort."

What Bush kept to himself was that, even at the risk of delaying the result, he did not intend to involve Einstein, the very begetter of the initiative. He had contacted Einstein through Frank Aydelotte, Director of the Institute for Advanced Study, then balked at furnishing the most brilliant scientist in the world with background data. Waiting until December 30, he explained to Aydelotte privately, "I am not at all sure that if I place Einstein in entire contact with this subject he would not discuss it in a way that it should not be discussed." (Army Intelligence and the FBI had reported that Einstein had supported pacifist organizations, an antifascist group, and even the Loyalist cause in Spain.) Even at its beginning, the bomb project was becoming entangled in security concerns that would eventually become as paranoid as they were ineffective.

Before ending the meeting, they agreed on ways to get things moving, and adjourned to lunch. But Lawrence was itching to get back to his experiments. He promised to meet with them again on the eighteenth and raced for a taxi to the airport. Soon, by the President's order, his flying would be over. All nuclear project chiefs would be forbidden to travel by air.

TOKYO	BERLIN	WASHINGTON	PEARL HARBOR
1:00 A.M.	TOBRUK	11:00 A.M.	5:30 A.M.
December 7	5:00 P.M.	December 6	December 6
	December 6		

HOUR 4

I N HIS OFFICE at the Japanese embassy in Washington, Saburo Kurusu had just sat down to confer with retired diplomat Ferdinand Mayer, an old acquaintance. During the initial pleasantries Kurusu kept turning his head watchfully, as if someone were listening in. Then, his voice rising just above a whisper, he confided, "Fred, we are in an awful mess." He had been delayed nearly two months, he explained, in arriving in the U.S. by an eye infection, lost time during which his government had sent no one to negotiate in his place. "This complicated the situation because time was running out, from the point of view of restraining the military element." All that the largely powerless civilian element in the government could do was to acquiesce in the further occupation of Indochina, as the "least harmful alternative." He rationalized the takeover as if Indochina were an unimportant toy for the Japanese Army to play with—in no way a menacing act to Britain or the U.S.

Cordell Hull, Kurusu complained, was "suspicious" of his motives, a good reason for Mayer, as a career diplomat, to vouch for his sincerity. He wanted both sides to give way a little, as that was the essence of accommodation, but each side was proving difficult. The State Department reflected the "national sentimentality" of Americans toward

China, which after all had been exploited by Europeans long before the Japanese had taken their turn. And Japanese "militarists," on the other hand, showed a "lack of humor" about leaving China. A "certain garrisoning" period would have to ensue to save face.

Personally, he did not believe that a German victory in Europe was in Japan's best interests, and he felt that most Japanese, irritated by the "arrogance" of Germans in Japan, agreed. But "hotheads" were gaining ascendancy, and he felt that he said as much as he could, "to the very extreme limits of a patriotic Japanese." President Roosevelt, he thought, might intervene usefully, as the State Department seemed to obstruct his efforts and those of the ambassador, Admiral Nomura. There was "extreme danger of war," even though it would be "suicide for Japan." The military could "upset the applecart . . . at any time."

To Mayer, Kurusu seemed to embody "extraordinary honesty and courage." He "begged" him to join Ferdinand Lammot Belin's dinner party at eight, to meet other influential people in the diplomatic community. Mayer had just come from an elaborate breakfast at Evermay, Belin's Georgetown estate, and he was returning there for dinner. Former Ambassador to Poland and a millionaire industrialist, Belin was a friend of one of Cordell Hull's assistants, James Dunn, and Dunn would be there. It was a chance for some personal intervention.

Without even checking with his colleague as to whether it would be an indiscretion, Kurusu agreed to come. Not only was he unaware of the President's initiative to Emperor Hirohito, still in preparation; he and Mayer had no idea that below, in the embassy cipher room, clerks were laboriously copying out paragraphs from the Foreign Ministry in Tokyo utterly at odds with what he thought was his mission.

•

At Wolfschanze, Adolf Hitler insisted to his generals that he could not be bothered with estimates of Russian strength: "Prisoner of war figures are conclusive proof of our superiority." (The Führer had, Halder noted, "the figures in his head.") Comparisons, Hitler scoffed, were "numerical notions only." His forces had lost, he figured, a few thousand per division. The Russians had lost "minimally ten times more than ours." They had lost, too, 78,000 guns, and their artillery was "at the zero point."

"Ours are no better," said Halder, thinking of the bitter weather, "because of immobility."

Each German division, Hitler continued, could hold a thirty-kilometer front; the Russians, despite their newly activated units, were incapable of such efficiency. Still, he insisted, it was important in the north to lose no ground and to link up with the Finns. "The enemy must not regain control of Leningrad as an industrial center, nor as a gate to the Baltic," he said, in a rare use of the Soviet name for the city. "Leningrad cannot hold out when it remains genuinely cut off." The Spaniards had to remain and help do that. Tikhvin had to be held.

"The Russians," Hitler insisted, "have not abandoned any place voluntarily; we cannot do so either." There should be "no thoughts of shortening the line." Then he hedged. If there were new positions prepared in which to withstand the winter weather, the principle of standing absolutely in place might be reconsidered. He was more optimistic about the south. The coal of the Donets basin and the oil of Baku beckoned. With "decent weather," Hitler suggested, fresh German divisions might be brought in from France to help if replaceable from other areas, but he could not spare troops from Yugoslavia because the Hungarians and Italians were not competent enough to cope with the guerrillas.

Halder was more concerned with shipments of "thick grease" to endangered positions to get frozen mechanized equipment moving. "Use airplanes," Hitler snapped.

•

"All day," a young Australian officer at Tobruk, Anthony Heckstall-Smith, remembered, "we could hear the gunfire like distant thunder, and at night the jagged edge of the escarpment was silhouetted against the brilliant gun-flashes and the red glows of fires." The British bombardment was taking a steady toll, including young 15th Panzer Division commander General Walther Neumann-Silkow, who had called for dive bomber support. Before the Stukas arrived, he was killed by a bursting shell. Although the Germans had no fresh equipment, troops, or supplies to bring up, at 8:30 A.M. General Crüwell had received an order from Rommel to stand fast until the arrival of Italian armor. Once before Rommel had admonished Crüwell, "We mustn't lose our nerve." This time, Rommel promised, there would be one final effort—the next morning.

With waning light, as forward movement petered out, Crüwell felt that he had forced a wedge into the center of the British line, but he had no way of reinforcing it or even of maintaining it. And help could not be expected from the Italians.

•

"The all highest," Captain Malcolm Kennedy noted in his diary before going on duty again at Bletchley Park, the British cryptanalysis center, "is all over himself at the moment for latest information and indications about Japan's intentions." Once reserved in Imperial Germany for the Kaiser, the expression was wry Bletchley parlance for Churchill, who "rings up at all hours of the day and night, except for the 4 hours in each 24 (2 to 6 P.M.) when he sleeps."

Bletchley Park in Buckinghamshire was a dark Victorian mansion much too ugly to be the focus of suspicion, but it housed under its gables and chimneys a small army of mathematicians, linguists, electrical engineers, crossword puzzle solvers, and experts in German, Italian, and Japanese. Once assistant military attaché in Tokyo, then a Reuters correspondent in Japan, Malcolm Kennedy headed the Japanese Section of the Code and Cipher School and had become convinced that the Japanese were about to move south against the British and Dutch. A month earlier he had written that "it should cause no great surprise." Churchill was not surprised that it seemed about to happen, but what he wanted to know was beyond Bletchley's arcane powers: the Japanese had given no hint whether they were going to land in Thailand or below the border in Malaya. All that was clear was that their force now at sea was simply too big to be a feint.

In London the leftist weekly *Cavalcade* was reporting erroneously that Japanese seapower was about to become even more formidable. "Hitler," it reported in its December 6 issue, out in time for Sunday readers of radical persuasion, "has dispatched his brand-new . . . battleship *Tirpitz* to Far East waters to join the Japanese fleet. With her are destroyers and U-boats. The idea is to get the United States into a cold sweat." The mightiest vessel in European waters was, in reality, holed up in Norway, in a fjord near Trondheim. Bletchley Park kept track of its whereabouts by reading German "Enigma" cipher reports. Because of its potential to harm North Atlantic convoys, the British would spend three years stubbornly trying, by air and sea, to disable *Tirpitz*.

The Japanese, *Cavalcade* added with equal authoritativeness, were watching the Russian front for the opportune moment to pounce.

"Most Tokyo observers believe that Japan will enter the war by attacking Borneo and Thailand when the Germans enter Moscow."

•

At the White House, Harold Smith was announced at 11:15 for his appointment to go over projected budget figures. He had hardly been seated with the President when a telephone call from Secretary Hull, on the new "scrambler" phone from the State Department, interrupted them. A "triple priority and most urgent" cable from American Ambassador John Winant had arrived from London at 10:40, "personal and secret to the Secretary and the President." The British Admiralty had reported Japanese convoys off Cambodia Point in the South China Sea, "sailing slowly westward toward Kra 14 hours distant." The Kra Isthmus was the neck of the Malay Peninsula at the Thai border. Fourteen hours was not much time to deal with events halfway around the world.

British and American military minds ignored the possibility that the Japanese Second Fleet might be moving with deliberate and misleading conspicuousness. Politicians, despite their experience with perfidy, gave no thought to that, and Roosevelt's response suggested that everyone had recognized what seemed to be the long-expected major new Japanese thrust.

The Director of the Budget could not help but overhear, and Roosevelt turned to him upon hanging up, remarking, "We might be at war with Japan [soon], although no one knows." Smith offered no response, and returned to the 1942 budget estimates, figures obviously now far too inadequate for what was likely to be required in the year ahead. As soon as he left the Oval Office he jotted the President's remark down on a scrap of paper and later transferred it to his diary.

•

Although noon in Washington was still a half-hour away, most of the desks in the Navy Department decrypting section were already vacant. Commander Safford and most others were taking Saturday afternoon off. Lieutenant Commander Alwin Kramer was away delivering several Japanese intercepts. In charge of the six translators was Chief Ships Clerk H. L. Bryant.

One of the six was Dorothy Edgers, a thirty-eight-year-old former teacher who had lived much of her life in Japan. All she saw in her incoming basket were "Magics" deemed to be in the non-urgent, deferred category, but she decided to scan them anyway rather than go home. One intercept, dated December 2, instructed the Japanese consulate in Honolulu to file ship-movement reports daily and asked about torpedo nets and air-defense balloons at Pearl Harbor. (Consul Nagao Kita had replied negatively about both.)

Another message capturing Mrs. Edgers's interest, recorded November 24 at the Army's Presidio listening station but still undeciphered, dealt with the pattern of U.S. fleet movements. A third, dated November 28, referred to the eight B-17s stationed on Midway and to the range of the island's antiaircraft guns. It appeared to have come from the Honolulu consulate. The longest—only three days old—was a telegram from Consul Kita to Tokyo, concerning details of transmitting fleet movement messages to sea—apparently to lurking Japanese submarines. All the intercepts suggested extreme and immediate interest in Pearl Harbor, and that the Japanese were up to something.

Dorothy Edgers took the December 3 message from Kita to Fred D. Woodrough, who was not only a colleague in the office, but her brother. Woodrough had secured the job as civilian linguist for her and recognized her fluency in Japanese. Together, they took the intercept to the Navy man in charge, Bryant, who agreed that it was "interesting." But, he added, looking up at the clock, since Mrs. Edgers would not be able to translate the entire intercept by twelve, it would "keep" until Monday. He was preparing to go home, as were the others. She had nothing special on for the afternoon, Dorothy Edgers said. She would stay and work on the Kita intercept until Kramer returned.

•

It was after midnight when Lieutenant Julien Goodman, ward surgeon in the station hospital at Fort McKinley, arrived with his medic friends at the officers' club. Over drinks they looked out over peaceful Manila Bay and put aside another boring day of dengue fever, parasitic infestations, and tuberculosis—the usual ailments of their constituency of Philippine Scouts. Nichols Field was three miles away, and quiet. The talk turned to Robert Montgomery's debonair performance in *Here Comes Mr. Jordan*. It was the last film that Goodman and the more fortunate of his friends would see for thirty-eight months.

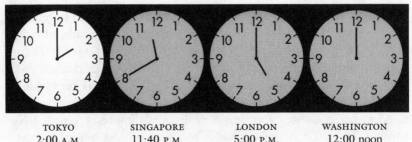

TOKYO	SINGAPORE	LONDON	WASHINGTON
2:00 A.M.	11:40 P.M.	5:00 P.M.	12:00 noon
December 7	December 6	December 6	December 6

HOUR 5

P UT IT in nicely drafted form," Foreign Minister Togo cabled Washington, "and make every preparation to present it to the Americans as soon as you receive instructions." A few minutes later came a cable postscript: the fourteen-part document would be so sensitive that an ordinary typist must not be used in preparing it. Nomura would have to find a junior official—on a Saturday afternoon—who could type in English. At the Office of Naval Intelligence, Lieutenant Commander Kramer, receiving teletypes from Bainbridge Island almost as fast as was the Japanese embassy, was listening in with deepening concern.

For transmittal in the other direction, Roosevelt had drafted a letter to Emperor Hirohito asking for his personal intervention as "a sacred duty to restore traditional amity and [to] prevent further death and destruction in the world." But he insisted on Japanese withdrawal from Indochina, since the peoples of the Philippines, the East Indies, Malaya, and Thailand "are asking themselves whether these forces of Japan are preparing . . . to make [an] attack in one or more of these many directions." It was time to let the message go. Roosevelt called for his secretary, Grace Tully.

·

General Sir Alan Brooke, Chief of the Imperial General Staff, was preparing to leave Whitehall at five when he learned from Singapore that sightings had been made of two Japanese convoys sailing westward toward Malaya. The report seemed to answer a question that had occurred to him two days earlier, when a group of foreign military attachés were presented to him. "I wonder," he had noted in his diary, seeing the gloomy appearance of the Japanese representatives, "whether we shall have them with us much longer." Since the movement reported was a naval one, the First Sea Lord, Admiral Sir Dudley Pound, took the initiative, calling a hurried meeting of chiefs of staff of the services. Sir Alexander Cadogan, Permanent Under Secretary of State for Foreign Affairs, represented Anthony Eden.

"We examined the situation carefully," Brooke wrote, "but from the position of the transports it was not possible to tell whether they were going to Bangkok, to the Kra Isthmus, or whether they were just cruising round as a bluff. P[rime] M[inister] called up from Chequers to have results of our meeting phoned through to him. Second message came in while we were there, but did not clear up situation in the least and it only said that convoy had been lost and could not be picked up again. Put off going home, dined at club, returned to War Office after dinner. Back to my flat expecting to be called out again."

·

"If you aren't at home," Margot Rosenthal had explained to her Berlin neighbor, Ruth Andreas-Friedrich, "they go away. Everything's all right if you aren't at home."

"But some time or other," Ruth noted in her diary, "you have to be at home. You can't be forever sleeping on strange sofas, aimlessly walking the streets, or sitting in stuffy movies. Once in a while you have to look after the flowers at home, the laundry. . . . Now and then everyone needs the feeling that one is not homeless." And even park benches were posted JUDEN VERBOTEN.

Ruth had expected a visit from Margot the night before. It was definite. She knew that it was dangerous for a Jew to visit an Aryan, but Margot was following the usual precautions. She "takes the [yellow] star off her jacket when she starts out in the evening. And before she goes back to her apartment in the morning, she slips into the nearest doorway, and sticks it back on her chest. Almost everyone does that, now that an unwritten law forbids Aryans to have any dealings with star bearers."

Margot chanced the stairs to her second-floor flat. After all, it was a Saturday evening; twilight was turning into deep darkness.

A policeman was waiting. Hauled off to the camp at Landshut, northwest of Munich, Mrs. Rosenthal was one of nine hundred in the evening's sweep, cargo for the night train south.

•

At noon in the old Cosmos Club on Lafayette Square, near the White House, Arthur Compton, Vannevar Bush, and James Bryant Conant sat down to lunch unworried about overheard talk in a public place. Cosmos habitués did not call attention to themselves. Conant lifted his "usual" glass of milk and took "a large swallow, only to discover it was buttermilk, which I detest. My sputtering and short outburst of profanity amused Van enormously but rather shocked Arthur." A few diners raised their eyes, but the scientists went on to discuss producing a new element, plutonium, to be separated from uranium in order to build an atomic bomb.

Compton was enthusiastic over the possibilities of plutonium, although element 94 was still largely theoretical. Glenn Seaborg, he explained, thought that it could be chemically extracted, making it a "worthy competitor" to alternatives requiring isotope separation. "Seaborg tells me that within six months from the time it is formed [by chain reaction] he can have it available for use in the bomb."

"Glenn Seaborg is a very competent young chemist," said Conant skeptically, "but he isn't that good."

Using natural uranium, as Enrico Fermi and Leo Szilard proposed to do, for "the construction of a self-sustaining chain reaction," Compton insisted, "would be a magnificent achievement" even if plutonium proved unusable for a bomb: "it would prove that the measurements and theoretical calculations were correct." He suggested beginning by setting up a secret project at Fermi's laboratory at the University of Chicago to construct a pile using natural uranium and graphite as a moderator. Bush proposed that General George C. Marshall be asked to furnish a high-ranking officer to oversee the bomb research programs as they multiplied across the country, and to furnish Army priority to get the work under way.

No one seemed to look up as they left.

•

Bringing in a light lunch with her stenographic pad, and lunches for the President and Harry Hopkins, Grace Tully sat down to business in the Oval Office. Time was running out for any peaceable solution. The Admiralty message on the Japanese convoy had reported its position as of 3:00 A.M. London time—8:00 A.M. Washington time—and had estimated fourteen hours to landfall. That time was now reduced to under ten hours. Hull and Roosevelt had talked the Saturday before of a last-minute direct appeal to Emperor Hirohito, and had even begun a message, then put it aside. Over lunch, the President tried some editing changes on Harry Hopkins, then ordered a final text sent to Cordell Hull for transmission via Ambassador Grew in Tokyo.

Slow troopships spread out over a wide area were difficult to miss even when slow reconnaissance planes over international waters kept wide of possible fire. But one had ventured close. A British Catalina flying boat—PBY to Americans—had located the convoy and was immediately shot down by Japanese aircraft flying cover from bases in Indochina. The crew had no time to send a distress signal. In Singapore the Catalina was reported late, and then missing. No one in London or in Washington heard anything about it.

At the Mayflower Hotel later in the afternoon, Miss Tully mentioned to the President, there would be a cocktail party hosted by columnist Richard Harkness. She had been invited. Could she go? Eager to downplay any sense of alarm in Washington, Roosevelt told her to enjoy herself.

•

Lieutenant Charles A. Fisher had begun a second tour of Singapore service early in December. Reporting for his first stint as night duty officer at Fort Canning—he would soon call Army headquarters "Confusion Castle"—Fisher arrived well before the day duty officer went off, and asked for instructions. The man he was relieving "was already straining at the leash to dash off for an evening in town." "It's all in the Standing Orders book here," he suggested. "Just read it through—it'll tell you all you need to know." Before he vanished he added, "If in doubt, ring Fortress."

On Fisher's second night as duty officer, the telephone rang just before midnight, and he took a message about the location of the Japanese ships in the South China Sea. He checked the Standing Orders book. On his earlier stint he had looked up "Fortress" in the telephone directory and found nothing, but now he knew there was a listing under "Singapore Fortress," where a breezy chap responded, "Yes, old boy. Get yourself another drink and leave it to me."

From Malayan Broadcasting, CBS newsman Cecil Brown cabled New York about "precautionary measures" in force. "All troops were called to their barracks and sailors recalled to their ships at five o'clock this afternoon. The mobilization of volunteers has been completed and there is widespread talk that there will be an emergency [declared] in Singapore over the weekend." Twenty Japanese businessmen scheduled to depart for Bangkok had been "yanked off with their baggage and their departure delayed," and most Japanese businesses—photography shops, barbers, dentists, and massage parlors—were closing, or being closed.

At a press conference earlier in the week, as Brown had arrived and received accreditation from the War Office, he had quoted Sir Robert Brooke-Popham's response to a question about how the RAF's Brewster Buffaloes—"Peanut Specials" to their pilots—could compare to Japanese aircraft. "They could give a very good account of themselves," "Brookham" offered reassuringly.

"Don't you think we need some of the machines that Britain has at home?" the Malayan Broadcasting reporter asked. Whatever the commander-in-chief's real feelings—he had asked for aircraft which were going instead to Russia and the Middle East—he responded, Brown thought, with scorn.

"Oh, no. If we need any of those super-Spitfires and hyper-Hurricanes we can get them out here quick enough." But Brown's first story had been killed, and the second emasculated into vagueness, with Sir Robert reduced in identity to "informed quarters." In another story, Brooke-Popham, described only as a "senior officer," explained confidently, "Malaya is the easiest country in the world to defend. There's one main road running roughly from north to south and a railway line. So long as we can hold these, the country stays ours." The beaches, he went on, were unimportant because there was impenetrable jungle between the coast and the main road. The Japanese military were unaware of any ultimate barrier. Japanese fishermen had long floated along the rivers or followed animal tracks into the interior.

Brown was incensed that a Japanese-owned paper, the *Singapore Herald*, was continuing to publish. "Peace can still be saved," its Saturday editorial claimed, and it suggested that Anglo-American "browbeating" of Japan—"the too-familiar Yankee big stick"—was less helpful than "calm reason and calm facts. . . . Japanese prestige and morale . . . are high enough to send a well-disciplined army and highly trained navy into action." To his diary that night, but not to CBS, Brown confided, "I don't know why the hell they don't bar the *Singapore Herald*."

Back in port since Saturday afternoon, their reassignment to Australia aborted, the crew of the *Repulse* grumbled about the denial of shore leave. Their presence remained a military secret, although no secret to anyone looking down on the naval base. Sailors lounged on deck in the evening heat as long as permitted, looking out on the beckoning lights of Singapore; then they went below glumly to closed portholes and blackout.

Not so for sailors from the *Prince of Wales*. Their presence was very public in the neon-lit evening, and until midnight curfew they filled the bars and dance halls, cinemas and restaurants. Grateful colonials bought them drinks, toasted their appearance in port, and offered them tickets for the services of dancing hostesses. It was definitely the way to fight a war.

TOKYO	MOSCOW	WASHINGTON	PEARL HARBOR
3:00 A.M.	9:00 P.M.	1:00 P.M.	7:30 A.M.
December 7	December 6	December 6	December 6

HOUR 6

S ATURDAY dawned rough and rainy for the crew and pilots on the aircraft carrier *Enterprise*. Retracing its route with Task Force 8 from Pearl Harbor to Wake Island, the ship had crossed the Date Line on November 30, losing December 1 in the process. By daybreak on December 2 the *Enterprise* had turned back slowly toward Oahu while waiting to retrieve the SBD bombers that had flown to Wake Island as navigational escort for the delivery of Major Paul Putnam's F4F Wildcats. The Grumman fighters of Marine Squadron 211 were to defend an atoll so small that the island airstrip occupied most of one coral-and-sand arm of wishbone-shaped Wake.

But for Battle Order No. 1, which Task Force commander Vice Admiral William F. Halsey had prodded the *Enterprise*'s captain, George D. Murray, to issue, everything would have seemed routine. Halsey intended to leave nothing to chance. "The *Enterprise* is now operating under war conditions," the message began. Any shipping sighted was to be sunk, any aircraft shot down.

Turning to Halsey once he read it, the operations officer, Commander William A. Buracker, asked incredulously, "Admiral, did you authorize this thing?"

"Yes," said Halsey, explaining that he was assured before he sailed that they would encounter no American or Allied shipping.

"Do you realize that this means war? . . . Goddammit, Admiral, you can't start a private war of your own! Who's going to take the responsibility?"

"I'll take it!" Halsey objected. "If anything gets in my way, we'll shoot first and argue afterward." To keep snooping subs or aircraft away he maintained rigid radio silence; and as TF 8 plowed ahead, Halsey's planes flew a three-hundred-mile patrol radius.

The hours of waiting during the turnaround phase of the voyage had not been without incident: Ensign John H. L. Vogt, flying reconnaissance for the *Enterprise* and its accompanying ships, had reported sighting a large unidentified fleet through the haze at the limit of his range. The fix seemed to validate Halsey's alert, but the fleet proved to be a visual trick of haze and sun and low clouds.

There were two December 5s when they re-crossed the Date Line, making the return leg seem longer than the outward one. The eastward voyage was stormy; the crew tired of battle stations and ready watches in the gloom. The convoy even slowed to make refueling from oilers easier for the lightweight destroyers rolling in the heavy seas. Hopes for an abbreviated weekend in Honolulu, with a Sunday morning docking at Pearl, were vanishing. All there was to look forward to was Gary Cooper in *Sergeant York*, showing at dark on the *Enterprise* hangar deck. Some griping was heard when the docking delay was announced. A movie about trench combat and World War I was no substitute for shore leave.

•

Before the evening meeting of Hitler and his staff at Wolfschanze, von Bock telephoned again to Halder. Some of his units had reported intercepting enemy radio conversations in English. "Had the Americans entered the war? Were there British or American troops or specialists at the front assisting the Soviets?" He directed forward units to report if any English-speaking soldiers were captured.

Very likely the Germans had overheard freakish transmissions. American P-40 Tomahawk fighters were being ferried to the Soviets as Lend-Lease equipment; possibly their American pilots had been communicating by radio, but they had not been permitted by Stalin to fly into Russia. Soviet crews had to take over at the point of entry—

usually the Iranian border, after a flight north from Basra. Even gift aircraft could not overfly Russia. "It is my opinion," the American military attaché reported from the temporary embassy in Kuibyshev, "that the greater the Soviet successes, the lesser the probability [of cooperation]."

The cynicism of Stalin's restrictions on aid from Britain and the United States may have been matched by the Western powers' own rationale for assisting an unfriendly and suspicious police state, but on the donor side the motives were plainly put. Churchill had joked when Russia was attacked, "I have only one purpose, the destruction of Hitler. . . . If Hitler invaded Hell I would at least make a favorable reference to the Devil in the House of Commons." His comments were on the record, while only three months before the Nazi invasion the Soviet Foreign Office had secretly informed its diplomats, "We have no intention of endangering the German-Russian [non-aggression] treaty, which is necessary to fulfill our most urgent aim, namely, the destruction of the British Empire."

Reports to von Bock from his own reconnaissance planes—a few were aloft—were of increasing concentrations of Soviet forces west of Moscow. He had given his commanders in the field, he confided to Halder, freedom of decision so that they could conduct operations according to their best judgment. That his generals had taken the option before he had given it went unsaid. Halder understood that he had heard the code words for withdrawal.

Writing for *Red Star*, the army's newspaper, Konstantin Simonov reported that at Gremiacheye he saw "a hastily dug German graveyard. Several hundred birch crosses topped by helmets had iron or wooden plates with inscriptions in black paint. . . . When [the Germans] began to retreat they had no time to put up additional crosses. Twisted corpses littered the roadside."

Simonov's account was a litany of horrors. "Frost-bitten, starving women with babies at their breasts [who] had spent the last two nights in the fields, emerged after hiding in haystacks and snowdrifts." Withdrawing troops who had tried to burn peasant stocks of potatoes, now prisoners in a reoccupied house, "light a lamp, undress, sit naked on a table, and squeeze their lice." Fourteen Red soldiers who had been locked in a cellar are found "burned alive." In a charred house, of which only one room remained, sits "a five-year-old girl with a serious, old woman's face and hollow cheeks and eyes." Simonov had no need to invent what he saw. Similar scenes recurred from north to south over hundreds of miles of frozen front.

Near Tula, a Guderian salient nearly surrounded for weeks, the Russians forced a wider opening, but the Grossdeutschland Regiment, an elite motorized infantry formed from the Guards Regiment of Berlin with young volunteers from all over Germany, hung on with heavy losses. Almost cut off by the counterattack was General I. V. Boldin and his divisions. Zhukov, growing more confident, telephoned him asking why he had not reached Laptevo. This was the third time he had been encircled, Zhukov reminded Boldin sarcastically. Wasn't he overdoing it a bit?

.

Joseph C. Harsch of the *Christian Science Monitor* had just arrived on the Matson Line's gleaming white, double-funneled *Lurline*. Having a nose for news—he had been in Berlin, and on returning had covered the Army's maneuvers in Louisiana—Harsch was in Admiral Kimmel's office overlooking crowded Pearl Harbor at five minutes to eight for one of the Pacific Fleet commander's rare interviews. Several of Kimmel's staff hovered about, including his public relations officer, Lieutenant Commander Waldo Drake.

Finding his time taken up by questions about wartime Germany, Harsch began to protest that he was being interviewed. "Admiral," he interrupted, "it's my turn now to ask a question."

"All right, go ahead," said Kimmel.

"I know nothing about the situation out here in the Pacific theater. I'll ask the obvious question. Is there going to be a war out here?"

"No."

"Would you please explain why you seem so confident that there won't be a war?"

During Harsch's voyage to Hawaii, Kimmel observed, he may have missed some of the news. "Moscow is not going to fall this winter. That means that the Russians will still be in the war in the spring. That means that the Japanese cannot attack us in the Pacific without running the risk of a two-front war. The Japanese are too smart to run that risk."

Waldo Drake rephrased the admiral's words a little more pungently: "I don't think they'd be such damned fools."

While not language suitable for the *Monitor*, Drake's version, like the admiral's own, emphasized an optimism not backed up by the morning papers and their headlines, nor by Kimmel's early morning Intelligence briefing, concluded just before Harsch arrived.

Rising to indicate that the interview was over, Kimmel suggested that Drake show Harsch "around Wheeler Field and the Army areas over the hill." Later in the day the off-the-record conversation would be followed by an off-the-record look at bombers and big guns.

SINGAPORE	WASHINGTON	SEATTLE	PEARL HARBOR
1:40 A.M.	2:00 P.M.	11:00 A.M.	8:30 A.M.
December 7	December 6	December 6	December 6

HOUR 7

TROUBLESHOOTING for his boss, Air Corps chief "Hap" Arnold, Lieutenant Colonel Ira Eaker had been ordered to fly from Washington to the Republic Aviation factory on Long Island. A test pilot who preferred big bombers, Eaker had been in the cockpits of nearly every type of aerial hardware manufactured in the U.S. since the end of the biplane era. The first model of the P-47 Thunderbolt—a big, overpowering pursuit plane—had been rolled out, and Arnold wanted Eaker to compare it to the new British Typhoon fighter he had test-flown in England.*

Arnold was leaving in the other direction. He wanted to see a flight of B-17s off from California to Hawaii, on the first leg of a journey to reinforce American bomber squadrons based in the Philippines.

Eaker took the prototype P-47 up for about two hours. "I did two or three [simulated] missions, made a number of landings, took it up to maximum altitude and tried out its manueverability." Then he decided to remain overnight and return to Washington the next morning

* Every American warplane to fly in World War II had been designed before December 1941—including the B-29.

71

with his wife, whom he had brought along, in time to take his mother-in-law to Sunday brunch.

•

At dusk the day before, the two-man Vildebeeste torpedo bombers at Seletar airbase, north of Singapore city, had been ordered north to beef up British air strength already at the Kota Bharu field. It was well into the weekend, which meant, Richard Allanson remembered wryly, that it was a surprising "compliment" on the part of the station commander in "turning up and in fact standing at the salute as we taxied into position for a formation take-off." About halfway to "KB" the squadron plowed into "a huge group of violent electrical storms." Six planes turned back, one pilot claiming engine trouble. For the others, flying into the dark clouds, it was about forty-five minutes before there was a break in the blackness through which they could see fires on the ground and assure themselves that they were still over land.

Primitive and slow, the Vildebeestes were far from watertight. Raindrops, "very large and very close together," found their way into Allanson's airspeed indicator, "which went haywire, swinging from one end of the clock to the other." He radioed the squadron commander for permission to make Kota Bharu on his own. It meant "stirring the pudding," or moving the control column gently from side to side to maintain lateral control and keep from stalling. Thanks to the ground crew's flare path he found the Kota Bharu strip, lowered his nose, and landed in the darkness.

Settled in, so they thought, 36 Squadron's pilots were awakened in the early hours of Sunday morning to move to a field about fifty miles south, "Runcie's Airstrip." Runcie—"either a Norwegian or a Swede—was also known as 'Mad Runcie' for in his dedicated zeal to get the airstrip into useable condition, he had offered a bribe to every coolie on the job out of his own pocket if it could be finished by a certain deadline date."

Going out to his Vildebeeste in the half-darkness, Allanson saw the plane appear to move, and was horrified to discover that masses of yellow Kerengga ants were "marching to and fro" on the wings. "But in those circumstances," he remembered, "one could not cry off for such a reason, so I settled myself in the cockpit and hoped for the best. Fortunately, Kerengga ants evidently did not like flying." Without being nipped, he managed to take off, and his reduced semi-squadron settled in again, next to the makeshift airstrip that Mad Runcie had hacked out of the jungle.

•

With antiwar feeling high in the summer of 1941, Congress had passed a law that all draftees over twenty-eight years of age would be released, but by the time it went into effect Private Tom Hardwick's ammunition company was on maneuvers in the pea patches of North Carolina. On return to Fort Jackson, South Carolina, Hardwick and other elderly soldiers were processed for release, and a warm sun shone as the "over-twenty-eight men" stood in formation as a separate squad on the parade ground they had grown to detest. The commanding officer explained that their release was technically only a transfer to enlisted reserve status. If an emergency arose, they would be called back. Then he strode down the line as they stood at attention, to shake the hand of each man. "As he was the ultimate martinet," Hardwick remembered, "I ignored his outstretched hand." Nothing could be done, he thought, to punish petty insubordination: Hardwick was now a civilian, although he would have to get back to New York to retrieve his civilian clothes.

There were no trains north on Saturday afternoon. Hardwick lifted his duffle bag to his shoulder and began hitchhiking toward Wilmington, Delaware, where he could get a ferry to New Jersey. If all went well, he might be there by Sunday afternoon.

•

With a model of a flag-draped petition before him, in its right-hand corner a wreath enclosing the words "Peace On Earth, Good Will Towards Men," Otto A. Case, the Washington State Chairman of the America First Committee, dictated a letter to retired General Robert E. Wood at the national office in Chicago. The board chairman of Sears, Roebuck was as militant as anyone in his anti-interventionism, Anglophobia, and anti-Rooseveltism. R. Douglas Stuart, Jr., ran the Committee from Wood's business base of Chicago, home also for such Firster stalwarts as Colonel Robert R. McCormick, publisher of the Anglophobic *Chicago Tribune*.

Full of good intentions, the document read, "WE THE UN-DERSIGNED, Citizens of the United States and residents of the State of Washington, do not believe that American boys should be sent to fight in foreign wars; hence we hereby respectfully but urgently petition you, our President, and our Members of Congress, to keep OUR NATION at peace and to do everything possible to help lead the world back to 'Peace On Earth, Good Will Towards Men.' "

Case urged that every state prepare a similar plea. "Of course, if the interventionists plunge us into war with Japan before we begin the circulation of petitions, that will be different and we would, then, certainly be guided by your further advice."

He mailed it on leaving his office in Seattle late that morning, affixing an air mail stamp so that the America First office in Chicago might receive it on Monday the 8th.

•

At Pearl Harbor a clerk in Fourteenth Naval District Intelligence typed out the bland daily summary for distribution. Radio activity of Japanese origin, it began, remained "very heavy with a great deal of old traffic being transmitted. Messages as far back as 1 December were seen in the traffic. This is not believed [to be] an attempt to maintain a [deceptively] high traffic level but is the result of confusion in traffic routing with uncertainty of delivery." Most signals intercepted, so the report went on colorlessly, seemed to emanate from Tokyo (three separate wave lengths), the Formosan port of Takao, Saipan in the Marianas, and Ominato, an obscure naval base in far northern Honshu. "Practically all of Tokyo's messages carry prefixes of high authority."

There was implicit concern in the lack of signals from the Second and Third fleets, which were transmitting only through Takao and Tokyo. As for Admiral Yamamoto, unmentioned by name, "The Commander in Chief Combined Fleet originated several [undecrypted] messages to the Carriers, Fourth Fleet and the Major Commanders."

Briefing Admiral Kimmel hardly an hour earlier, Commander Edwin T. Layton, Pacific Fleet Intelligence Officer and the clerk's boss, had expressed certainty that something was up. Interpreting the curious radio traffic in the context of other data, he assumed a big operation. At the least, an invasion of Thailand or Malaya was imminent. Further, the absence of direct transmissions from Japanese carriers "suggested that one or more [carrier] divisions were tied up in the southward advance."

Dubiously, Kimmel had sent Layton out to get an opinion from Vice Admiral William Pye, the battle force commander, and Layton took a harbor gig from his office at the submarine base to the *California*. It was already a "glorious" morning as he pulled up alongside the flagship of the battle force, "moored in majestic isolation off Ford Island at the head of Battleship Row." On the quarterdeck were Pye and his acting chief of staff, Captain Harold C. Train. Layton filled them in on the news from Gulf of Siam, and on the unusual radio traffic his staff had identified.

Pye scoffed, Layton recalled, at the idea of an attack on the British, and Train backed him up. The Japanese, they suggested, were positioning themselves to interdict the Burma Road lifeline to China, very likely through Thailand.

Disagreeing politely—they outranked him—Layton saw Japan's objective as "farther south, probably the oil of the . . . Indies. They might not leave our forces in the Philippines unengaged on their flank. . . . They would take us out on the way down, and we would be at war."

"Oh, no," said Pye. "The Japanese won't attack us. We're too strong and powerful." He turned to Train. "Harold, do you agree?"

"Emphatically," said Train.

Pye handed the briefing sheet back to Layton. "Please thank Admiral Kimmel for this information," he said.

Taking the harbor launch back to Kimmel, Layton reported his own estimate, now upscaled, and Pye's dismissal. "I want you to repeat that again," said Kimmel.

TOKYO	MOSCOW	WASHINGTON	PEARL HARBOR
5:00 A.M.	11:00 P.M.	3:00 P.M.	9:30 A.M.
December 7	December 6	December 6	December 6

HOUR 8

T HROUGHOUT the daylight hours, Marshal Zhukov's counter-attacks had broadened. He had reoccupied Kalinin, to the north of Moscow, and was using skis and sleighs to move artillery within range of deeper German positions. The frozen Moscow River was crossed; Staritsa was retaken.

Eighty-five miles south of Moscow, Tula had long blocked the capital's encirclement. Tula's inhabitants had once rushed to the western approaches with bottles of gasoline ("Molotov cocktails") to throw at approaching tanks, setting some afire. Less crude weapons were now available. Russian soldiers deploying the new "Stalin organ," multiple tubes on a truck that launched rockets at close range, attacked those enemy tanks which still moved.

While German generals were apt to telephone Hitler whenever anything went wrong, General Zhukov was reluctant to call Stalin, who, after initial hysteria and confusion, was running the Moscow front from the Kremlin with grim confidence. Like Hitler, Stalin oversaw every move on his maps and picked up the telephone whatever the hour, a few days earlier admonishing Zhukov, "Do you know that they've occupied Dedovsk?"

"No, Comrade Stalin," said Zhukov, puzzled, "I didn't know that."

The town was only ten miles from Moscow. In German hands it would have been the catastrophic breakthrough for which Hitler had been pressing.

"A commander should know what's going on at the front!" Stalin snapped. He ordered Zhukov to proceed to Dedovsk and organize an immediate counterattack, and Zhukov had argued that it was unwise to leave headquarters at such a time.

"Never mind," Stalin said stubbornly. "We'll get along somehow."

Zhukov hung up and contacted General Konstantin Rokossovsky of the Sixteenth Army. Rokossovsky knew nothing about Dedovsk either; there had to be some mistake. There was fighting around Dedovo—a different place, unthreatening to Moscow.

"I decided to call Headquarters and explain the misunderstanding. But it was like trying to drive a nail into a stone. Stalin was in a towering rage and demanded that I go immediately to . . . do everything necessary to see that this miserable village was recovered from the enemy." But when Zhukov had left for the Dedovo area, unnecessarily, Stalin rang the command post three times, asking, "Where is Zhukov? Why has he gone away?" Stalin had found another threat that needed attention. Settling the new matter, finally, by telephone, he concluded, "Well, and what about Dedovsk?"

Zhukov replied that he had sent a rifle company supported by two tanks to oust the Germans from Dedovo. Stalin was satisfied, and Zhukov was again reminded that every village was somehow being watched from the Kremlin. During the First Secretary's lifetime and for some years after, war histories would preface almost every account of a victory, no matter how minor, with the ritualistic "*s initsiativy Stalina*"—"thanks to Stalin's initiative."

•

Lieutenant Commander Kramer returned to the Cryptographic Section in Washington at three, just as Dorothy Edgers was translating the last sentence of the Kita intercept. "If the above signals and wireless messages cannot be made from Oahu, then on Maui Island, 6 miles to the northward of Kula Sanatorium." She pressed it on Kramer before he had a chance to sit down, and she watched with astonishment as he not only failed to share her excitement, but reacted with irritation that she had stayed late to bother with a "deferred" intercept. Instead of seeing it as more evidence of an obsessive Japanese interest in Pearl

Harbor, he scrutinized its prose style. "This needs a lot of work, Mrs. Edgers," he concluded, finally. "Why don't you run along now? We'll finish the editing sometime next week."

"But, Commander," she protested, "don't you think this intercept ought to be distributed right away?"

"You just go home, Mrs. Edgers," Kramer insisted. "We'll get back to this piece on Monday." He had worked too many hours and seen too many Japanese intercepts. Some of the forty-nine Tokyo-Honolulu messages picked up between November 15 and December 6 were routine; many others pointed to Pearl Harbor. None was an open revelation of intent, but at a time when war seemed imminent they had surfaced in numbers that had overwhelmed the staff. Safford had gone home; Kramer was too tired. The decrypting searchlight of "Magic" would not be directed upon them until they were of only historical value.

•

In mid-afternoon, the Japanese embassy staff began returning from a luncheon at Washington's posh Mayflower Hotel in honor of Hidenari Terasaki, the embassy's Second Secretary. He was being transferred to Rio de Janeiro. Others had been ordered to Mexico and Argentina, a depletion of personnel which suggested an approaching break in diplomatic relations. Although by 11:58 the first thirteen parts of the Foreign Ministry's message to the American government had been received at the embassy, only the earliest paragraphs had been worked on. No hint of tension had emerged amid the sake toasts and artificial hilarity.

Among those returning to the embassy—it was a Saturday and most staff simply went home—were the correspondents for the *Osaka Mainichi* and the Domei Agency. Someone suggested going out for a round of golf while the light lasted, but Mazuo Kato, the Domei man, thought it was too cold. Instead, the newsmen began a table-tennis game in the basement while Katsuzo Okamura, an embassy official with time on his hands, watched. As the ball clicked back and forth, they discussed the whereabouts of the *Tatuta Maru*, on which many expected to sail home. It should be nearing Honolulu, Kato estimated. When the others appeared skeptical he insisted, "Of course it is coming."

"I doubt it," said Okamura.

"Why do you doubt it?"

"It just looks that way."

"How about a bet?" Kato offered.

"All right," said Okamura. "I'll bet you a dollar she never gets here." They shook hands on it, American style.

Upstairs in the ambassadorial suite, NBC Blue Network commentator H. R. Baukhage was conducting an interview with Saburo Kurusu "just to have some filler material for my Monday broadcast." Although Kurusu was politely oblique, and Baukhage realized that he had gotten nothing for his pains, such an outcome was nothing new for a reporter. He left through the main corridor, where hurrying employees were straining under loaded wastebaskets and cartons.

"Aren't you rather busy for Saturday afternoon?" he asked.

"Yes, very busy, so very busy," one admitted.

•

When, the day before, Australian External Affairs Minister H. V. Evatt had transmitted a message to his envoy in Washington, Richard G. Casey, asking him to keep a close watch on the war situation, there still appeared to be some maneuvering time. Everything, he cabled, "seems to turn on whether Japanese reply to Roosevelt . . . can reasonably lead to negotiations or whether it should be rejected out of hand." The State Department, Casey now cabled back to Canberra at 3:37, was trying to have it both ways, emphasizing to Roosevelt "the constitutional difficulty" of assuring a military response to further Japanese military adventures, while the Secretary of State himself was "trying to get the United States army and navy to show naval and air activity in the Gulf of Siam in order to hearten Thailand." But, Casey added, "The President has to watch that his activities, prior to the Far Eastern situation reaching a breaking point, do not enable his opponents here to say that 'the United States is acting in advance as if already an ally of Britain' [—] which would increase his political difficulties."

There was nothing further, he confessed, that either he or the British ambassador could do.

•

At 9:57 P.M. Berlin time—three minutes before the ten o'clock news—Karl-Heinz Reintgen switched on his microphone at Belgrade military radio and said, as he did every evening, "And now just for you, for everyone here and there—'Lili Marlene.' " And he lowered the needle of the station phonograph onto the record—its actual title "Song of a Sentry"—which Propaganda Minister Joseph Goebbels had once banned as harmful to morale. *"Vor der Kaserne, vor dem grossen Tor . . . ,"* Lale Anderson sang plaintively. "Underneath the lantern, by the barrack gate, Darling I remember the way you used to wait. . . ."

At night the Belgrade signal reached into North Africa, and the west as far as England. Reintgen had already been told by General Fritz Bayerlein of the Afrika Korps that in the seven months since Belgrade had begun broadcasting "Lili Marlene," everyone on both sides ceased firing at 2:50 to listen in. Major General Rudolf Schmundt, Hitler's aide-de-camp, had called the Führer's attention to the song, and Hitler listened for it too. "Schmundt," he concluded, "this hit will not only enrapture the German soldier, it will probably outlive us all." Churchill thought so too, remarking that "Lili Marlene" might be the only thing to survive the Nazis.

Reintgen would play the poignant, march-time lament more than a thousand times before fleeing the Balkans.

TOKYO	BERLIN	WASHINGTON	PEARL HARBOR
6:00 A.M.	10:00 P.M.	4:00 P.M.	10:30 A.M.
December 7	December 6	December 6	December 6

HOUR 9

IN BERLIN, Foreign Office State Secretary Ernst von Weiszäcker, a career diplomat in high standing as drafter of the Munich pact that dismembered Czechoslovakia in 1938, sat down to his diary after a long Saturday at work. He had just learned of the General Staff decision to forgo further offensive action in Russia: "The Caucasus war is being dropped until the summer of 1942." The Russian front was not "a pleasant outlook," but perhaps the bleak situation was "as overestimated as the Russians were underrated at the beginning."

He was certain that war was about to erupt in the Pacific. For nearly a week the Japanese had been insisting that a clash with the U.S. "could hardly be avoided," since the Japanese Navy was pressing for it. Berlin had been asked for assurances that no peace would be concluded with Britain or the U.S. separately from Tokyo, and that Germany consider itself at war with the U.S. if war occurred between Japan and the U.S.

"I think we cannot say no," he noted; but he thought that reciprocity was required, as Germany could be at war with the U.S. before Japan began any adventure in the Pacific. In any case he saw little advantage for Germany in Japan's involvement. Dino Alfieri, the Italian ambassador, had even confided his fears that it would prolong the war.

"Militarily," Weiszäcker concluded his diary page with less than his usual caution, "advantages and drawbacks may balance each other. . . . Were I more optimistic for our cause than I am, then I would rather be opposed to Japanese participation."

·

Once cable 5918 arrived from Ambassador Winant in London at 3:05, with more details about the Gulf of Siam convoy, activity at the White House—most of it off the record—increased as the afternoon lengthened. Regarding war in the Malaysian area as imminent, Netherlands military authorities were putting into effect their own Rainbow Plan A-2. By prior arrangement it involved British and Commonwealth forces, and it included sending Dutch planes to Singapore. Both governments hoped to draw in the United States.

"British feel pressed for time," Winant reported, "in relation to guaranteeing support [for] Thailand, fearing Japan might force them to invite invasion on pretext [of] protection before British have opportunity to guarantee support but wanting to carry out President's wishes in message transmitted . . . to Halifax."

The tall, lean Lord Halifax, once a leader in the Cliveden group eager for an accommodation with Hitler, had undergone a conversion after the failure at Munich in 1938. The British ambassador understood the President's political problems—there were many Americans unwilling to believe that a deal with Japan, at someone else's cost, could not be struck. Thailand, he and Roosevelt realized, was only the gateway to Malaya, Burma, and the Indies, not a stopping place. Also, he knew that the Philippines could not survive a thrust south. General Marshall and Admiral Stark, the American service chiefs, had already urged the President—on November 27—to warn the Japanese that a move into Thailand "may lead to war" with the U.S.

Churchill had urged Roosevelt to go even further. Through Winant he confided that while recognizing the "constitutional difficulties"—an oversimplification of the President's domestic problems, as Churchill knew—he hoped that at the appropriate moment, "which may be very near," Roosevelt would warn Japan "that any further . . . aggression would compel you to place the gravest issues before Congress or words to that effect."

The message prepared for Emperor Hirohito was essentially that response, but everyone involved now sensed not only that it was too late, but that it would not have altered events even had it been sent weeks earlier. With Winant's cable in hand, Roosevelt sent urgently for Halifax.

•

Alger Hiss, an aide to East Asia political relations chief Stanley Hornbeck, had already left the State Department for the day. "With no thought of impending catastrophe," he remembered, "those of us who were responsible for our Far Eastern policy had not stayed late in our offices. . . . I got home with no sense of crisis." All of Cordell Hull's underlings had dismissed Japanese entry into the South China Sea as "likely to be merely a feint and the fleet would probably turn north into the Gulf of Siam. Since French Indochina had already been overrun by the Japanese . . . , [that] would mean no new aggression and would therefore be of no consequence to us." Hiss had "no foreboding of any . . . change in the unpromising negotiations Secretary Hull was patiently carrying on."

Daylight was fading when Halifax and the President met in the Oval Office. Both knew that Britain needed every effort short of a declaration of war. A cable from Captain John M. Creighton, the American naval attaché in Singapore, to Admiral Hart in Manila, transmitted two hours earlier, indicated how far down the levels of command that understanding had reached. Brooke-Popham had told him, Creighton reported, that London had received "assurance of American armed support" if British, Dutch, or Thai territory were violated. Although isolationists later claimed that the American offer had no constitutional legitimacy yet committed the U.S. to go to war, Halifax knew that even without Congress, Roosevelt could do in the Pacific what he had already done in the Atlantic.

Having received no direct confirmation about obligations beyond the Philippines, Hart cabled Washington, "Learn from Singapore we have assured British [our] armed support under three or four eventualities." He liked Tom Phillips, but the British, Hart worried, were still willing "to disperse forces, guard everything and be so thin that nothing is really guarded. . . . We were quite frank, laid our cards down and wore no gloves."

Committing his ships on the basis of a message from a naval attaché and making war plans with a friendly admiral who was not a legal ally was not Hart's usual operating method, but he had already seen enough of Roosevelt's style to realize that some things could not be written down. "In ordinary times," he told his diary for December 7 about the way he was being informed of his commitments, "such treatment as that would force me to ask for my immediate relief. . . . Guess there is a war just around the corner, but I think I'll go to a movie."

Briefed by Halifax after his White House meeting, Richard Casey rushed cable 1096 to Canberra, appending a text of Roosevelt's entreaty to Emperor Hirohito. "President said that if he received no answer . . . by Monday evening December 8th Washington time he would publish text of his message that evening and that on Tuesday afternoon or evening he would give 'warning' to Japanese government." This would be followed by "warnings or equivalent" from "British and others." Roosevelt, Casey closed, still felt that Japanese movements might only be intended to improve their bargaining position short of war, while Hull had no illusions: "British Ambassador tells me that the President does not believe that the Japanese will make an aggressive move as soon as the Secretary of State does." But that may have been something that Roosevelt had to say in order to justify a dramatic gesture to Hirohito.

•

At 4:00 A.M.—4:20 the previous afternoon in Washington—Sir Shenton Thomas was awakened at Government House, Singapore. An urgent cable had arrived from the Colonial Office. Word in London was that the Japanese convoy in the Gulf of Siam had disappeared. Where was it? What was it up to?

Since he was already up, Sir Shenton went to the early service at St. Andrew's Cathedral.

•

It was nearly eleven at Pearl Harbor, where a meeting that Admiral Kimmel had convened would delay everyone's lunch. He had shared Edwin Layton's fears that the Japanese would strike at the Philippines, and wondered what precautionary measures might be useful thousands of miles of ocean away, as they were. Should the battle force go to sea, to somehow stand by? Around the table with Kimmel and Layton were Captain William ("Poco") Smith, Fleet chief of staff; Captain Charles E. McMorris, war plans officer; and Captain Walter DeLany, operations officer.

The more they talked, the more reasons emerged to remain where they were. With no carriers available for air cover, their battleships would be vulnerable at sea. And where would they go? Steaming about uselessly would drain oil reserves on Oahu. Sending large numbers of ships out on a weekend would also raise unnecessary alarm. Long-range operations against Japanese bases in the Marshalls and Carolines, to protect Hawaii and to take pressure off the Philippines, required a state of war, and preparations for which the Navy was unready.

They decided to do nothing.

TOKYO	MALAYA	LONDON	WASHINGTON
7:00 A.M.	4:40 A.M.	10:00 P.M.	5:00 P.M.
December 7	December 7	December 6	December 6

HOUR 10

K ATHLEEN HARRIMAN'S twenty-fourth birthday was on the seventh, and she and her father were invited to Chequers for the weekend to celebrate. Ambassador Winant was to join them on Sunday. Prematurely, Churchill instructed the kitchen staff to have a birthday cake at Saturday dinner. When it was carried in, a day too early, the Prime Minister offered an elaborate toast and presented Kathleen with a signed copy of his 1899 (and second) book, *The River War*, inscribed with his "best wishes." Only one other youngish member of the opposite sex was at the table, Pamela Churchill, Randolph's wife,* who with Randolph away at war spent much time with her parents-in-law. Churchill's inappropriate birthday present, apparently pulled off a shelf at the last moment, when he needed a gift, reflected the very different preoccupations of the men at Chequers.

Realizing that the Foreign Secretary and his deputy, with the Russian ambassador, were about to embark for the Invergordon naval base in Scotland on the first leg of a dangerous sea journey through the Arctic Sea to Murmansk and Moscow—and that it was a bad time for Anthony Eden and Alexander Cadogan to be away—Averell Harriman

---

* Later, Mrs. Averell Harriman.

had already cabled Harry Hopkins in Washington to reinforce Cadogan's last warnings:

> The President should be informed of Churchill's belief that in the event of aggression by the Japanese it would be the policy of the British to postpone taking any action—even though this delay might involve some military sacrifice—until the President has taken such action as, under the circumstances, he considers best. Then Churchill will act "not within the hour but within the minute." I am seeing him again tomorrow. Let me know if there is anything special you want me to ask.

In London, Cadogan contacted Winant again, and also told the Dutch government-in-exile "to get ready." But, he noted hastily in his diary (which he was not taking to Russia, as the ship might be torpedoed and sunk), all plans might be in the "melting pot"—and one sees the racist component in the slur—"if the monkeys are going for [the] Kra Isthmus."

Cadogan went home to dinner and to pack. "So far," he noted finally, "10:30 p.m., quiet. This Diary (if we start tomorrow) will be continued on scraps of paper."

•

The Office of Civil Defense in Washington, D.C., was a disorder of disparate older organizations and new volunteer groups, headed by the feisty and garrulous mayor of New York, Fiorello La Guardia. Like several other Roosevelt appointees, he was a likable but inefficient amateur. He worked part-time at the post and filled his staff with other well-intentioned amateurs, most of them mayors. The OCD offices at DuPont Circle were an amiable confusion, into which Eleanor Roosevelt had intruded. Organizing a Volunteer Participation Division, she enlisted, among others, another New Yorker, Judge Justine Polier, whose specialty was family welfare, and Paul Kellogg, who edited a social work journal. All afternoon Mrs. Roosevelt had conferred in her study with Judge Polier and Kellogg on community organization, using as a model what England had already learned, however difficult that would be to apply to a vaster country, one which, besides, did not take the possibility of attack seriously.

As her guests arose to leave she took them in to see the President, who had been working through the day and seeing a stream of advisers. "Well, Justine," said Roosevelt, reaching out his hand to the daughter of Rabbi Stephen S. Wise, "this son of man has just sent his final message to the Son of God." It was, he explained, the final card he could play to keep the peace, a personal appeal to someone who had only moral authority, but it was enough if the Emperor of Japan chose to employ it. Startled by their moment in the Oval Office, they said their good-byes and left.

•

At 11:40 A.M. Hawaiian time the *Akagi* began signaling a message to the other ships in the strike force which it had kept in readiness for the occasion. With a fine sense of drama, Admiral Yamamoto had paraphrased the battle order of his hero, Admiral Heihachiro Togo, to be read to all hands. Under continuing radio silence, the *Akagi* had waited only for authorization to release the text already in every captain's hands as Combined Fleet Operational Order No. 13. The appropriate signal flag went up, and on each ship all hands were read the exhortation, "The moment has arrived. The rise or fall of our Empire is at stake! Every man is expected to do his utmost!" On the *Akagi* itself, to shouts of *"Banzai!"* repeated on other ships, the historic flag hoisted by Togo in 1905 prior to the Battle of Tsushima, when the Russian fleet was annihilated, was raised once more.

•

On board one of the capital ships in *Kido Butai* ("Force Z" to copy Togo's code name of 1904), the Third Battleship Division's diarist could not contain himself to the usual laconic prose of naval logs. "Nothing more contents us, as sailors," he wrote, "than to look at the same signal hoisted up when we are about to meet the enemy's Pacific Fleet on the Pacific Ocean. There is none [aboard] who does not make up his mind to accomplish the great deed comparable to those accomplished by his ancestors, thereby making the Empire everlasting."

In the vicinity of Pearl Harbor, "Tadashi Morimura"—Ensign Takeo Yoshikawa—was making another survey of conditions around the base, for a final report to Tokyo. The Navy Ministry was concerned about antiaircraft preparations, especially barrage balloons. They could get in the way of dive bombers. Although Consul Kita's telephones were being tapped by the FBI, no agency had placed a watch on the Japanese consulate in Honolulu, and, as usual, no one tailed "Morimura" about as he played tourist.

TOKYO	LONDON	WASHINGTON	PEARL HARBOR
8:00 A.M.	11:00 P.M.	6:00 P.M.	12:30 P.M.
December 7	December 6	December 6	December 6

HOUR 11

I FEEL I should now . . . address you," Roosevelt's message to Hirohito explained, "because of the deep and far-reaching emergency which appears to be in formation." There was no need to explain what that was. "I address myself to Your Majesty at this moment," it concluded, "in the fervent hope that Your Majesty may, as I am doing, give thought . . . to ways of dispelling the dark clouds. I am confident that both of us, for the sake of the peoples not only of our great countries but for the sake of humanity in neighboring territories, have a sacred duty to restore traditional amity and prevent further death and destruction in the world." Proofreading Grace Tully's typescript— she had been summoned back from her party—the President added a note to Hull: "Shoot this to Grew. I think it can go in gray code— saves time—I don't mind if it gets picked up. FDR."

The best hope would have been that the message escape confidentiality. On November 29 the Japanese Censorship Office had secretly ordered that all incoming and outgoing cables except those sent by the government be delayed in delivery by five hours. On December 6 the order was amended to five hours one day, ten the next. Sunday was the first full day for operation of the system. Lieutenant Colonel Morio Tomura had telephoned Tateki Shirao, a censor official at the

Ministry of Communications, to begin with a ten-hour lag. In Tokyo it was already close to nine on the morning of the seventh.

•

A taxi brought Aloha-shirted "Tadashi Morimura" back to the Japanese consulate in Honolulu from his latest reconnoitering of Pearl Harbor, and since it was a crucial moment, he and Nagao Kita ceased their usual pretense of being unaware of each other's real duties and reviewed "Morimura's" draft message to Tokyo. Keeping the Imperial Navy spy's cover intact, the report was signed by the consul general.

Few indications of alertness could be seen; the base appeared as quiet as on any other Saturday. "At the present time there are no signs of barrage balloon equipment. . . . It is difficult to imagine that they actually have any." Still, "Morimura" explained, while the American forces could be expected to "control the air over the water and land runways of the airports in the vicinity of Pearl Harbor, Hickham, Ford and Ewa, . . . I imagine that in all probability there is considerable opportunity left to take advantage of a surprise attack against these places." In response to another question from Tokyo he added that there seemed to be no torpedo nets protecting the battleships lying off Ford Island. Then he added a postscript: "It appears that no air reconnaissance is being conducted by the fleet air arm."

Since the elaborate "Purple" code had been destroyed on order from the homeland, Kita encrypted the information in the low-priority PA-K2, a system with complicated spelling tables and transpositions. It would be decoded in Washington on December 8.

•

Ambassador John Winant did not reach Anthony Eden's London house at 17 Fitzhardinge Street until nearly midnight. He had driven there from the embassy in Grosvenor Square in an embassy car, intending to go on in the morning to Churchill's official country residence at Chequers. The American car was thin protection against German bombs or spent British AA shells: when driven to and from Downing Street by Churchill's people he was usually in a vaultlike steel-reinforced Humber Snipe limousine. "Gilbert" Winant—the British familiarly used his middle name—was comfortable with the youngish Eden, who was forty-four to Churchill's sixty-seven, and not the Great Man to the shy ambassador. Churchill had the knack of saying riveting things that left Winant in awe; Eden was straightforward. The week before, Winant had steered a party of isolationist congressmen to Chequers for lunch with the Prime Minister, and the American visitors had made it clear that they expected Britain to be invaded and to fall. "What will happen if the Germans gain a foothold in this country and you are overrun?" one asked.

"With dying hands," Churchill shot back, "we shall pass the torch to you."

Two weeks earlier he had said publicly, at the Mansion House of the Lord Mayor in London, "Should the United States become involved in war with Japan, the British declaration will follow within the hour." It was Winant's vain task to keep Churchill from such grand gestures, which only frightened the isolationist Right into believing, correctly, that the P.M. was trying to edge America into war by one means or another. Ever the diplomat, Eden chose his public words with caution, but he and Winant understood each other.

The Foreign Minister was busy packing. "He found me some supper and we stayed up until the early hours of the morning discussing his mission to Moscow. We both had great faith in the Russians as fighting allies and equal belief in their ultimate desire for a peaceful world."

BANGKOK	LENINGRAD	TOBRUK	WASHINGTON
7:00 A.M.	3:00 A.M.	1:00 A.M.	7:00 P.M.
December 7	December 7	December 7	December 6

Hour 12

S OUTH OF LENINGRAD, under cover of darkness, Muñoz Grandes dispatched his deputy, Colonel Miguel Rodrigo Martinez, with deliberately unwritten orders to Esparza to accomplish a withdrawal as early as possible once darkness came again. The retreat was to be orderly, with casualties kept to a minimum. If possible, it was to be done without either the Russians or von Chappuis discovering what was happening. In forward positions, several of Muñoz's protégés were already dead, their frozen bodies unretrievable. Another, Dionisio Ridruejo, was in the grip of a nervous breakdown to which he would owe his life, as it meant evacuation to a hospital in Riga.

Standing guard by his frozen and useless antitank gun, which he had fondly named *Yola*, Juan Eugenio Blanco was partly sheltered from the wind by the shattered walls of an abandoned monastery. At $-25°C$ ($-12°F$) it was still rather mild; his posting was nearly over, and his greatcoat did not keep him warm. From a nearby bunker he heard voices, even laughter, and cautiously peered in, wondering whether he could warm his feet. The men inside had a working stove.

A half hour later—it was now past four, and the sky was getting faintly light—his relief, Mariano Ferrer, had not yet come. Ignoring earlier inhibitions about abandoning his post, Blanco strode into the onetime monastery building where Ferrer lay sleeping and shook him awake. "Consider yourself relieved and go to bed," Ferrer mumbled.

Blanco forced himself back onto the courtyard until Ferrer appeared, then took his place inside. He warmed his hands and feet, opened a can of sardines, quickly chewed down the contents, and dozed off just as the drone of Russian aircraft could be heard. Few left their beds for the frigid safety of the bomb shelter. Blanco closed his eyes again, then heard an explosion followed by screams that jolted him awake. There was a hole in the ceiling. In the row of camp beds opposite, a sleeping soldier had been killed instantly; an unexploded bomb could be heard, ticking. Blanco rolled out of bed and flattened on the floor; too terrified to run, he began muttering a Paternoster but had not gone beyond "Our Father, who art" when the bomb detonated.

Coming to, unknown minutes later, he could see the clearing night sky through the mist of dust and fallen roof timber. Uncontrollably shouting with joy at his survival, he climbed out from beneath the rubble to see nine others also emerging. Thirty were dead.

·

To ease the pressure on Tobruk, the British organized an assault on Bir el Azazi, to begin at 8:30 P.M. At 9:00 the infantry had still not arrived. When supporting machine guns and artillery opened at 9:30, according to plan, the infantrymen, only now moving up, had to hustle out of the way. Since the tank commander and his armor had failed to materialize, according to the 70th Division log, the bombardment was rescheduled for 10:30.

On the other side of the line, puzzled Germans guessed some clever ruse was in the making. At 10:40 the British brigades were told that the tanks still could not be found; at 11:45, leaderless, the tanks arrived, although at the wrong gap, and the zero hour for Operation Snowwhite was reset for 2:00 A.M.

At 1:40 a brigade officer reported that the tank commander had turned up but had not yet relocated his tanks. Z-hour was delayed to 3:30. As night faded, gunners and infantrymen dozed at their duty stations.

·

Monitoring reports on the movement of the Japanese convoy in the Gulf of Siam, Captain William Smedberg, an aide to "Betty" Stark, worked at the Navy Department into the evening. The fleet appeared on a direct path to the Kra Isthmus, and the major operation that everyone was expecting. When its direction seemed unchanged, and no other Japanese movements could be traced, Smedberg and his associates decided to call it a day. He remembered Secretary Hull's conversation with Stark a few days earlier, about the inevitable failure of an accommodation with the Japanese: "Admiral, I'm afraid the fat's in the fire. It's up to you military fellows now."

The admiral, however, had gone off duty. From the standpoint of the stage, Washington was a wasteland, and Stark's choices of live theater were few. There was Shakespeare's Trojan War dark comedy, *Troilus and Cressida*, at the Wardman Park. The Gayety, at 9th and E, offered "Glorified Burlesque" with Rosita Royce doing her "daring dance of the doves." And at the old National Theatre on Pennsylvania Avenue was a revival of Sigmund Romberg's operetta in the Viennese manner, *The Student Prince*. The 1924 musicalization of *Alt Heidelberg* celebrated a bygone Germany of harmless principalities and charmingly medieval universities, un-Hitlerite and unthreatening.

Already out in early editions were Washington's Sunday papers. Buried deep inside the *Washington Post* was Mark Sullivan's weekly column titled "We Face a World War." In aid to Britain and hostility toward Germany he saw "little left of the Neutrality Act." As for the other side of the globe, "At the moment this is written we are very close to war with Japan."

On the way out the door at the Navy Department at 7:30 Captain Charles Wellborn summed up the long day succinctly to Smedberg as they walked out into Constitution Avenue, now dark and nearly empty of traffic. "Well, the British are sure going to catch it tomorrow at Singapore."

•

Maverick actor-director Orson Welles, his stock high after *Citizen Kane*, was downing a drink in the lobby of the Blackstone Hotel in Chicago with his traveling companion, Pare Lorentz. Signed up for RKO, Lorentz was working on an ambitious documentary which he called alternately *Ecce Homo* and *Name, Age and Occupation*, about the condition of the industrial worker in America. He had shot tens of thousands of feet of film in Detroit and with Welles had gone to New York to find new faces to put under contract for the movie. They had chosen two, and taken the train back to Los Angeles, but with the wait to change trains in Chicago long, they had detoured to a familiar oasis.

Recognizing them was William Benton, a publicist and entrepreneur who had become vice-president at the University of Chicago. Benton, later a senator from Connecticut, had founded the lucrative Benton and Bowles advertising agency, which had offered its services to America First. The slick publicity firms under retainer to a number of big corporations with isolationist executives, including Quaker Oats, Hormel, and Sears, Roebuck, had been steered to America First, among them the influential J. Walter Thompson agency and Benton's own. (Chester Bowles was already working for Quaker Oats heir R. Douglas Stuart, Jr., from New York.) "Don't forget it," was Benton's familiar boast. "The smart money is on our side." Ordering more drinks, he assured Welles and Lorentz that they failed to understand "the real feelings of the country." The heartland of America was behind Charles Lindbergh, and solidly isolationist. "Roosevelt will never get us into war, no matter how hard he tries."

Feeling uncomfortable, Welles announced that they had to leave to catch their train.

·

Off Hvalfjordur, Iceland, thirty-one miles north of the overgrown village of Reykjavik, the capital, Lieutenant Paul R. Schratz, Annapolis '39, scaled the familiar six ladders from his cabin on the cruiser *Wichita* to "sky forward." His antiaircraft watch, with half of the five-inch, 38-caliber AA guns manned despite the impossible flying conditions, was 0000 to 0400 on the seventh, and he was at his post seventy-five feet above the sea a few minutes before midnight.

Below, behind the stout submarine nets closing the entrance to Hvalfjordur, another British-American convoy was huddling for the hazardous final five hundred miles southeast to Scotland. The dark and the pelting rain and sleet made the scores of ships in the fjord just below the Arctic Circle, all of them blacked out, invisible.

The *"Witch"* had been operating off Iceland, on the edge of the war, for five dreary months. When the Germans occupied Denmark in May 1940, Iceland's thousand-year-old link with the home country had been severed. The King of Denmark had also been Iceland's sovereign. Now Iceland, on Britain's western flank, was independent of Copenhagen, with an elected regent. Britain had sent ships and troops to keep the Germans out.

American anti-sub patrols ranged as far east in the Atlantic as twenty-five degrees longitude, midway between Africa and Brazil; in the north a presidential order in July had bent the imaginary line to include all of Iceland. Troops and aircraft were dispatched, and the British, stretched thin worldwide, were happy to redeploy much of their own small forces.

While protecting convoys as far as Iceland, the U.S. on occasion was venturing even further, once just short of Londonderry, to goad the Germans into provocative acts. When Hans Thomsen, the German chargé in Washington, protested, isolationists forced a temporary retrenchment, although the convoy protection quietly resumed. Secretary Stimson wanted to push the U.S. closer to the inevitable war with Germany, which had to happen before Britain was past saving. A major incident, he confided to his diary, was like "trying to make the Confederates fire the first shot. Well, that is what apparently the President is trying to do here."

U.S. forces in Iceland were operating under orders that the approach of any Axis forces to within fifty miles would be "conclusive evidence of hostile intent." Still, German planes from occupied Norway reconnoitered unmolested. There were few all-weather roads for supplying the thirty-nine lonely observation posts, which could warn but do little else.

Occasionally U-boat commanders hit, or narrowly missed, an American warship or war-cargo ship. Flying out of Gander, B-17s and B-24s of the Newfoundland Base Command had been operating under war conditions and making routine sweeps over the North Atlantic, now and then bagging a U-boat or at least intimidating one out of range. Roosevelt had told the nation by radio, "When you see a rattlesnake poised, you don't wait until it has struck before you crush it." That was, U-boat chief Admiral Karl Dönitz complained, "completely contrary to every tenet of international law, [and] was of the utmost military, material and moral benefit to Britain." But the Germans were restrained by headquarters in Kiel from direct challenges that might draw the U.S. in even deeper. Hitler was not ready.

Aboard the *Wichita*, 650 feet long and displacing 16,700 tons,

Paul Schratz, the gunnery control officer, could see nothing but his instruments, and think of little but his wife, far along in her first pregnancy. The low conversation of the changing watch crews was inaudible over the rain, "wind-driven needles of [which] found every crevice," he remembered, "in my salt-stained parka, stiff and crinkly from long exposure to sea and wind." The subdued throb of the ship's eight engines, sometimes a consolation, failed him. Iceland at midnight-to-four was miserable, lonesome duty, and he "succumbed to immediate personal misery."

TOKYO	WASHINGTON	SAN FRANCISCO	PEARL HARBOR
10:00 A.M.	8:00 P.M.	5:00 P.M.	2:30 P.M.
December 7	December 6	December 6	December 6

Hour 13

A T 8:00 P.M. the State Department dispatched a brief cable to Tokyo alerting Grew that an important communication to him was being encoded and that it contained the text of a message from the President to Hirohito. Grew was to deliver it personally to the Emperor at the "earliest possible moment." It was initialed for Hull by his assistant Stanley Hornbeck, suggesting that Hull had now left after a long day and the prospect of a longer one on Sunday. A further hour would elapse before the message to Hirohito was fully encoded and left Washington.

A copy went also to Ambassador Clarence Gauss in Chungking, with a message also initialed by Hornbeck instructing Gauss to ask Chiang Kaishek not to make difficulties for the U.S. Roosevelt knew well that it was in Chiang's interest to abort any accommodation with Japan: peace in China could pull his shaky coalition of warlords apart and foreclose the external support that kept him in power. Inform Chiang, the cable went, that the message has already gone to Hirohito, and represented "very nearly the last diplomatic move that this government can make toward causing Japan to desist from its present course; . . . and that it is very much hoped that Chiang Kaishek will not make or allow to be spread in Chinese Government circles adverse comment."

·

At 2:15 a British brigade commander in the Libyan desert, impatient with the delay in moving against Bir el Azazi decided that to open at 3:30 would be too late, yet to start earlier, while the tanks were still five thousand yards away—about three difficult miles—was impracticable. He called the attack off, and instead sent out a patrol to check conditions at Outpost Queen (formerly Bondi). Rommel's men were still alert. The patrol was flushed from Queen with the loss of nine men. The night's action was over.

·

There were thirty-two invited for dinner at the White House, nothing extraordinary for a Saturday evening. Having done all he could do until the receipt of more news, Roosevelt sat over drinks in his study with his Dutchess County neighbor and friend Vincent Astor, who had offered his yacht to the Navy for coastal patrol duty. The President joked about Astor's wanting to "unload" it on the government to save on its upkeep. Then Roosevelt's valet helped him dress for dinner and seated him before the guests arrived at eight. He preferred to make as few wheelchair entrances as possible.

British Vice-Admiral Sir Wilfred French and his wife were the principal guests. Others ranged from Breckinridge Long, Assistant Secretary of State, whose wife sat at the President's right, to his son and daughter-in-law, Captain and Mrs. James Roosevelt. An old Albany friend at the dinner, Bertie (Mrs. Charles) Hamlin, thought that the President "looked very worn . . . and after the meat course he was excused and wheeled away." Whether cares of state, or the violin recital by Arthur LeBlanc to follow, had propelled him off, no one knew. But Roosevelt had slipped back into his second-floor study, and in the light of a green-shaded lamp he toyed with his stamp collection and chatted with Harry Hopkins, who had come out of the hospital a few days before and looked thin and haggard.

Since Hopkins knew that he was the President's favorite sounding board, and had been missed, he abandoned any hopes of retiring early. Roosevelt wanted to talk about political problems arising from the *Chicago Tribune*'s exposure of the "Victory Plan." With that spun out, he aired hopes to escape from the Washington winter and fish in the Key West sunshine if all went well. It seemed clear to Hopkins as he listened that the President was marking time, waiting for news. The next day, he may have thought, everything would get straightened out as they would know whether the Japanese were continuing negotiations, or whether they were moving as expected against Thailand. Anticipating the answers, Roosevelt had called a meeting of all top advisers in the White House for three in the afternoon.

At former ambassador Belin's Georgetown mansion, where Ferdinand Mayer and Saburo Kurusu were dining, guests had barely been seated when Kurusu received a telephone call from the Japanese embassy that the President had dispatched a personal plea to Emperor Hirohito. It was, he told the others on returning to the table, "a very clever move" that would cause "many headaches in Tokyo." Table talk had been about the Germans, who would be, Kurusu said, untrustworthy allies, and if it came to that, would attempt to make Japan the Italy of the Pacific.

.

At Hamilton Field, near Sacramento, thirteen B-17s, comprising the 38th and 88th Reconnaissance squadrons, and their flight crews were inspected by General Arnold and hurried off while there was still twilight for takeoffs. Most of the crews were inexperienced. None had ever been on such a long flight—and Oahu was only the first leg on the route to Mindanao. If all went according to plan, Hawaii landfall would occur at about breakfast time. Their ground crews were already on the high seas, with ammunition, weapons and other supplies as part of a support effort for the Philippines.

To save on weight and to economize on fuel, the B-17s were not yet fitted up to fight. The newest models had a tail-gunner blister and a more formidable tail assembly than the earlier models, but no guns projected: they were still wrapped in protective Cosmoline, to be installed at the final destination.

The worrisome news from the Gulf of Siam had speeded up departure. Despite newspaper headlines and briefings, the airmen, according to Arnold, "could not be told all the various factors in the case except that we wanted them to leave as quickly as possible." Telephoning General Marshall earlier, Arnold observed that the B-17 crews "don't realize how serious this thing is."

"Well," said Marshall casually, "they're your people. You start them out."

Arnold did. He told the crews that they would "probably run into trouble somewhere along the line . . . and might have a fight on your hands." The men thought that he meant the mandated islands near Guam.

"If we might face a war situation on our trip," Major Truman H. Landon asked, "why don't we have the bomb sights and machine guns for our aircraft aboard, instead of having them shipped by surface vessel?" Arnold agreed, and some gear in packing boxes was loaded aboard for installation later, perhaps in Hawaii. But they carried no ammunition, since weight had to be conserved for fuel on the 2,400-mile first hop, the longest leg of the journey. As it was, Arnold thought, the skeleton crew of pilot, copilot, navigator, engineer, and radioman left no one to man a gun if one had to be fired.

Conferring separately with the Hamilton Field headquarters staff, Arnold warned that war was close. He ordered that their own planes be dispersed. The West Coast could be vulnerable and he disapproved of planes "being huddled together."

It was after five before the big bombers roared off for the fourteen-hour flight to Oahu.

•

The Saturday afternoon Honolulu *Star-Bulletin* headlined stories about war preparations in Singapore and a possible new peace plan from Japan. The picture on page one displayed a sentry on Oahu beside an American flag. The caption: "Army on the Alert." (The current *Collier's* magazine, which had not yet reached newsstands in Hawaii, featured an article by Walter Davenport, "Impregnable Pearl Harbor.")

•

In San Francisco a seaman first class in Intelligence, Robert D. Ogg, although assigned to bug suspected agents in the area, had discovered earlier what appeared to be Japanese communications on new frequencies.* Signal traffic picked up by American listening posts

* Identified only as "Seaman Z" in John Toland's *Infamy*, a 1982 polemic that accused Roosevelt of conspiring to drive Japan into war, Ogg denied the implications which Toland had attributed to him.

seemed heavy as December 6 wound down in the West. Suggestions as to where to look had come to Ogg's boss, Lieutenant Ellsworth A. Hosmer, from two commercial telegraph agencies. To Ogg, the proposed fixes seemed suspect, although they emanated from somewhere across the Pacific. Weather conditions played tricks with frequencies. The air all week had been filled with Japanese signals, authentic and false. The Japanese were masking fleet movements by a massive and shrewd effort at dummy radio traffic, some of it created by veteran carrier radiomen deliberately kept home so that their recognizable "fists" would be traced to ports on the Inland Sea.

It was clear that something was up, or that the Japanese wanted to leave that impression. Stations as far north as Dutch Harbor in the Aleutians were picking up signals on unfamiliar frequencies, and in codes that changed on December 1 after changing on November 1. Signals from phony sources as well as from such real ones as fishing fleets and diplomatic traffic overwhelmed American intelligence, which was simply unable to process all of them.

Among the messages extracted from "Purple" was one, on the last day of November, in which the Foreign Ministry in Tokyo had urged Ambassador Oshima in Berlin to "say very secretly" to the Germans "that war may suddenly break out between the Anglo-Saxon nations and Japan through some clash of arms and that the . . . breaking out may come quicker than anyone dreams." Since a war warning had gone to Manila and Honolulu only three days earlier, Kimmel and Short were not made privy to the new decrypt.

Kimmel had been wondering about the whereabouts of the Japanese carriers. On December 2 his intelligence officer, Lieutenant Commander Edwin Layton, had guessed, "I think they are in home waters, but I don't know where they are. The rest of these units, I feel pretty confident of their location."

"Do you mean to say," Kimmel asked, half jokingly, "that they could be rounding Diamond Head and you wouldn't know it?"

No one in the Western camp was expressing any concern that the Gulf of Siam strike force *seemed not to have a single carrier.* Ogg, who did not know that, had guessed as late as the 6th that his unidentified signals came from some fuzzy area "east of the International Date Line"—but Japanese naval discipline was absolute, and commanding officers on the ships of the strike force had not only removed transmitting tubes from radios, but locked the hand keys afterward. Even the radios on carrier aircraft stored on deck and below were inoperable until manned for flight. *Kido Butai* could receive but not send.

When Ogg went off duty on Saturday afternoon he knew no more than when he had reported for duty at the beginning of the week.

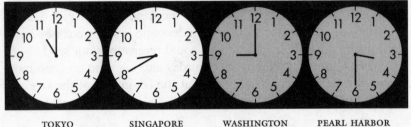

TOKYO	SINGAPORE	WASHINGTON	PEARL HARBOR
11:00 A.M.	8:40 A.M.	9:00 P.M.	3:30 P.M.
December 7	December 7	December 6	December 6

HOUR 14

THE SUNDAY EDITION of the *Malaya Tribune* appeared in Singapore with a large black headline, "27 JAPANESE TRANSPORTS SIGHTED OFF CAMBODIA POINT." It was not a scoop—press services all had the story. Elsewhere in the paper was the government warning that it was a bad time to travel and urging people away from home to return. Jimmy Glover, for fifteen years the *Tribune*'s editor and managing director, wondered "how long the peace and serenity which I had come to regard as my right in Malaya would last." Glover was on the balcony of his house in Holland Park, then outside the city, when his telephone rang. It was a very angry Brooke-Popham, protesting Glover's "pessimistic view of the Far East situation." "Brookham" had been in Hong Kong the previous December long enough to visit the New Territories and peer at the Japanese across the border in occupied China. "I had a good close-up, across the barbed wire," he informed General Hastings Ismay in London, "of various sub-human specimens dressed in dirty grey uniforms, which I was informed were Japanese soldiers. If these represent the average of the Japanese army, the problems of their food and accommodation would be simple, but I cannot believe they would form an intelligent fighting force."

The chiefs of staff in Whitehall apparently agreed, cautioning Brooke-Popham that the Japanese "should not be over-estimated," and two months later "Brookham" himself had reported that one of his battalion commanders, reviewing troops in Malaya, had deplored, "Don't you think they are worthy of some better enemy than the Japanese?"

"I do hope, Sir," another officer lamented to Brooke-Popham, "we are not getting too strong in Malaya, because if so the Japanese may never attempt a landing."

Outshouted now, Jimmy Glover had to listen to similar expressions of confidence from the Far East commander-in-chief. "I consider it most improper," Brooke-Popham expostulated in his Sunday-violated voice, "to print such alarmist views at a time like the present. The position isn't half so bad as the *Tribune* makes out."

"That's not fair," said Glover unapologetically. "The news was released by Reuters and passed by the censor. To me the presence of the Japanese transports off Cambodia Point means war."

Getting nowhere, Brooke-Popham put down his phone, releasing Glover for his Sunday morning ritual of drinks at the Seaview Hotel, on the coastal road to the east. There, while the orchestra played, expatriates sat in the shade of the pillared terrace and sang songs. When the breakfasters left, the tables were cleared for Sunday curry tiffin.

Reading the morning paper at his bungalow, Brigadier Ivan Simson, Chief Engineer of the Malaya Command but in the Far East only four months, looked at the headline story and quickly put it down. A few days earlier, inspecting up-country installations, he had discovered that no one knew much about coping with enemy tanks. There was no need to know. Tanks were useless in Malaya. The British themselves had none. An Australian battalion commander held that "in the jungle, anti-tank guns hindered mobility and were an encumbrance."

At Fort Canning, Simson knew, there were thousands of official War Office publications on tank defense, neatly bundled and undistributed because tanks were not considered practical in jungle country. He thought that the possibility for tank use existed. There were long, empty beaches; there were improved roads; and there were wide, neat paths through the rubber plantations.

Securing General Percival's permission, Simson had drafted a non-technical condensation. It had just come off the press, and, deciding that Sunday was a good day to begin planning its distribution, he drove to his office at Fort Canning.

.

Not for nothing are the Siamese among history's perennial survivors. When, on Sunday morning, it became clear that no matter where else the Japanese landed, they were first going to subdue Thailand, Ambassador Crosby in Bangkok telegraphed frantically to Brooke-Popham in Singapore. The Thai Minister for Foreign Affairs had insisted in the strongest terms that his nation would resist any preemptive occupation. There could be no British crossing of the frontier until and unless Japan struck first. A violation of Siamese neutrality would almost certainly, the minister had explained for his government, result in immediate occupation by Japan.

"For God's sake," Crosby pleaded, "do not allow British forces to occupy one inch of Thai territory unless and until Japan has struck the first blow at Thailand."

After the fall of France, Thailand had claimed Laos and Cambodia. The French in Indochina fought off the Thais, forcing them to accept, with relief, a cynical Japanese offer of mediation. The peace signed in Tokyo awarded areas west of the Mekong River to Thailand, whose premier gushed that his country would "forever remember the friendly efforts" of Japan, in whom it had "placed implicit confidence." Having occupied the rest of Indochina the following July, Japan became Thailand's neighbor. Now the debt was being called in.

The British needed at least twenty-four hours to set Operation Matador in motion if the Japanese were to be forestalled, but the Thais preferred Japanese occupation to becoming a battlefield. The ornate temples would lose none of their gingerbread.

At a cocktail party in Bangkok on Friday, December 5, Foreign Minister Direk had asked British military attaché Captain Andrew Gilchrist, "Could Thailand rely on Britain?"

Although almost alone, with her war production stretched to the limit, said Gilchrist, Britain always won the last battle. And there was, he reminded, the formidable Far East Fleet.

"It's a question of *confidence*," the minister insisted. "If you leave us out on our own, exposed like this, you just can't expect us to behave like Greece and die to the last man." But, he added, keeping his balancing act going, "We shall resist."

Whom they would resist remained a military riddle for the British. Yet there was no question but that even with the prospect of resistance, it would be better to be on Thai beaches before the Japanese took them than to dawdle and then face a land-based enemy with airfields that threatened Malaya. While the problem still seemed more a political one, Churchill had sent a trusted crony, Alfred Duff Cooper, with promise of Cabinet rank as Resident Minister for Far Eastern Affairs. Duff Cooper pushed for troops and planes to be diverted from Libya. "There seems to me no defence at all," his wife Diana had written to a friend in England a few days before, "but I expect I'm wrong. Today a little fleet arrived to help." She had seen the *Prince of Wales* and the *Repulse*, and she was right. There was no defense, and the fleet was indeed little. At first, Duff Cooper thought that the sparkling capital ships "conferred a sense of complete security," but he evaded any responsibility for Matador.

In Washington, meanwhile, M. R. Seni Pramoj, the Thai minister, had been sending message after message requesting instructions on political alternatives. "I even suggested," he recalled nearly a half-century later, "that in case of an invasion [by the Japanese], a Free Thai movement be organized which I would serve in Washington." There was no reply.

•

For Japanese embassy personnel in Washington it was unfortunate that the fourteen-part message was not only arriving piecemeal but was encoded *in English*. Besides, the entire staff of the cable section had gone to Secretary Terasaki's farewell party, and it was 9:30 in the evening before the interrupted decrypting of cable 902 was continued. Much sake had been consumed, and few of the thin complement that had returned to the embassy had been in condition for serious work. While some awaited the promised fourteenth part, held back for maximum secrecy, they passed the time by hacking apart what was left of the machine which coded messages back to Tokyo. It had been rendered useless on order from Japan only the day before, although two days before that the instructions as received specified "immediate and complete" demolition. There was little else to do, but the cable personnel had been told to remain, and they waited.

Not until midnight could the staff turn into Japanese the first thirteen parts of the fourteen-part message received earlier in the day.

Commander Safford's men had decoded it before nine o'clock. Lieutenant Commander Kramer ordered copies made for the regular Navy recipients of "Magic" messages as well as for the White House. Meanwhile, he telephoned everyone whom he could reach on his distribution list, mostly Navy brass, to explain that he was delivering something that should be examined at once. He was not always able to leave a message—it was a Saturday night—and he could not leave documents of that secrecy in a mailbox or on a doorstep. Then Kramer telephoned his wife, Mary, to fetch him at the Navy Department and chauffeur him about.

Abandoning her wrapping of Christmas presents, she drove Kramer about, first to the Executive Office Building adjacent to the White House. It was 9:30 when they delivered a locked pouch to Lieutenant Lester Schultz, who took it to the President's study on the second floor. FDR was clipping stamps—"for the children at [the hospital in] Warm Springs," he told Schultz. Hopkins was pacing back and forth in conversation with Roosevelt, but stopped while Schultz removed the typewritten pages from the pouch and handed them to the President. Both Hopkins and Schultz stood by quietly while Roosevelt read the entire packet. Then he passed it to Hopkins, who read the sheets and returned them to the President. Turning to Hopkins he said, Schultz recalled, "This means war."

There was still a crucial paragraph unreceived, but while Schultz waited for instructions, Roosevelt and Hopkins discussed the imminence of war and where it might happen. Since it would be "at the convenience of the Japanese," Hopkins observed, "it was too bad that we could not strike the first blow, and prevent any sort of surprise."

"No, we can't do that," said the President. "We are a democracy and a peaceful people. We have a good record." He reached for the telephone to contact Stark, and learned from his switchboard that the admiral had gone to see *The Student Prince*. Paging Stark might "cause public alarm," Roosevelt told Schultz, returning the documents. The White House would find the admiral "within perhaps another half an hour."

Kramer dropped off other pouches, including one to Frank Knox at the Wardman Park Hotel. Knox excused himself to study the documents while Mrs. Knox entertained John O. Keith, a business associate from Knox's former paper, the *Chicago Daily News*, and his wife. Alarmed at what he inferred, Knox telephoned Stimson and Hull to set up a morning meeting at ten. By that time, Knox thought, the complete message would be in hand. He had already absented himself earlier, to telephone Hull, Stimson, and then Stimson again, between 8:30 and 8:47, routing the calls through the White House switchboard. Discovering this time that Colonel Rufus S. Bratton, delivering "Magic" documents to the Army's list, had left Hull's copy with the night duty officer at the Department of State, Knox furnished Hull by telephone at home with all he would know until the next morning. It was, Bratton had explained to the night man, "a highly important message" for Mr. Hull. With care, it was taken to his office and put on his desk.

•

With a flight of B-17s due from the mainland, Lieutenant Colonel Clay Hoppough, telephoning for the Air Corps' commanding general, Frederick L. Martin, contacted radio station KGMB in Honolulu. Martin wanted KGMB, which usually signed off at midnight after its *Night Owl* program, to broadcast through the night, linking with its regular sign-on time in the morning. Flying Fortress navigators could home in on the Honolulu signal.

Lieutenant Colonel George W. Bicknell of Army Intelligence was dismayed by the makeshift system. It exposed information about incoming flights. Hoppough promised "to take that up later" with Martin. For the present there was no other way to keep inexperienced pilots from missing the islands.

Bicknell was sure that he had done enough work from home on a Saturday afternoon, but just before four the phone at his Aiea Heights residence rang again. It was Robert Shivers, who ran the FBI office in Honolulu. "You better come right down here, George," Shivers said. "I want you to see something which I think is a matter of great importance."

Shivers and Bicknell often shared information. Bicknell drove down palm-fringed Kamehameha Avenue into the city center, and parked at Merchant and Bishop streets, close to the Dillingham Building. He found Shivers very excited. "This thing," he said, showing Bicknell a wiretap transcript, "looks very significant to me. I think something is going to happen."

The wife of a local Japanese dentist on the FBI "suspicious" list, Mrs. Motokazu Mori, identified herself as a correspondent for the

Tokyo *Yomiuri Shimbun*. Her home telephone and her husband's office line had been tapped for weeks; calls to the newspaper were especially monitored. The evening before, she had telephoned Tokyo, conducting with someone at the newspaper office a lengthy, expensive conversation which had taken most of Saturday for the FBI to transcribe and translate. Once he scanned it, Shivers was struck by the utter triviality of the two-hundred-dollar long-distance call. It had to mean more than its surface, as military references were tucked into its banalities. The questions came from Japan, the answers from Mrs. Mori:

> I received your telegram and was able to grasp the essential points. I would like to have your impressions on the conditions you are observing at present. Are airplanes flying daily?
>
> Yes, lots of them fly around.
>
> Are they large planes?
>
> Yes, they are quite big.
>
> Are they flying from morning till night?
>
> Well, not to that extent, but last week they were quite active in the air.
>
> What about night time?
>
> There seem to be precautionary measures taken.
>
> What about searchlights?
>
> Well, not much to talk about.
>
> Do they put searchlights on when planes fly about at night?
>
> No. . . .
>
> What is the climate there now?
>
> These last few days have been very cold with occasional rainfall, a phenomenon very rare in Hawaii. Today, the wind is blowing very strongly, a very unusual climate.
>
> Is that so? . . .
>
> Do you know anything about the United States fleet?
>
> No, I don't know anything about the fleet. Since we try to avoid talking about such matters, we do not know much about the fleet. At any rate, the fleet here seems small. . . . It seems that the fleet has left here.
>
> Is that so? What kind of flowers are in bloom in Hawaii at present?
>
> Presently, the flowers in bloom are fewest out of the whole year. However, the hibiscus and the poinsettia are in bloom now. . . .

The conversation seemed very strange to Shivers. Among the items discussed was the stopover of Ambassador Kurusu, which had been weeks earlier, and no longer news. The question about the fleet in harbor was clearly answered erroneously. Anyone on the hilltops above

Pearl could see the battleships clustered about Ford Island, but the question may have concealed interest in whether any carriers were in port. Further, the query about searchlights was so open as to suggest that the Japanese might have wanted any furtive tappers to think in terms of attacks only after dark.

Then Mrs. Mori went on to a clutter of trivia that suggested it meant more, explaining, according to the FBI summary,

> that the Japanese sake brewed in Honolulu is called "Takara-Masamune," that a person named Takagishi was the technical expert in charge of the brewing; that said Takagishi is a son-in-law of Grand Chamberlain Hyak-utake, being married to the latter's daughter; and that said Takagishi returned recently to Japan. . . . [The Tokyo party] adds that Japanese here and the Americans also drink sake. He informs that Japanese chrysanthe-mums are in full bloom here, and that there are no herring-roe for this year's New Year celebration.

After that came statistical questions about the Japanese population in Hawaii—something that the *Yomiuri Shimbun* staff must have known, but which furnished numbers of possible significance. Like the talk of flowers, it may have concealed a code. And finally—inexplica-bly—the Tokyo man signed off, after Mrs. Mori's apologies, "I'm sorry I couldn't be of much use," with "Oh, no, that was fine. Best regards to your wife." But Mrs. Mori *was* the wife. A slip, or a code?

From the Dillingham Building, Bicknell telephoned his G-2 su-perior, Lieutenant Colonel Kendall Fielder, and told him that he had a matter "of great importance" to take up with General Short "right away."

"Couldn't it wait?" Fielder urged. The general was going out for dinner. What about tomorrow morning?

"It *cannot* wait," Bicknell protested. When he sounded genuinely alarmed, Fielder offered to call back. He had only to inquire next door. He and Walter Short lived in adjacent houses at Fort Shafter, and their wives were good friends. In fact, both couples were going out to dinner together.

"If you can, get out to Shafter in ten minutes," said Fielder, tele-phoning back.

HOUR 15

M AZUO KATO left the Japanese embassy wondering whether Katsuzo Okamura's habitual pessimism or some more intimate knowledge had accounted for his acceptance of the bet over the *Tatuta Maru*. At a Chinese restaurant near Union Station he had dinner with Ichitaro Takata, the *Osaka Mainichi* correspondent with whom he had played table tennis at the embassy, and Clark Kawakami and his wife. It was Kato's second farewell meal that day. Kawakami, the second man for the Domei Agency, was an American citizen but his wife was not; she was planning to return on the *Tatuta Maru*.

Walking back from the restaurant, Kato and Takata could finally confide in each other about the possibility of war and internment.

"What will you do in prison?" Takata asked.

"I may write a book. What will you do?"

"I can play *Go*," he said. "I'll teach you."

A difficult board game comparable to chess, *Go* requires special apparatus, including 181 specially fashioned black stones and 180 white ones. "Where would you get the stones?" Kato asked.

"We'll probably have ample time, and we can make them one way or another. We can make a board," he suggested, warming to the idea, "and gather ordinary stones, if necessary."

"You are an American citizen," Kato said, turning to Kawakami; "*you* won't be interned."

Kawakami laughed. "I'll send you plenty of whiskey."

Returning to his office alone, Kato ran into an International News Service reporter who asked whether he knew that the President had just sent a message to Emperor Hirohito appealing for peace. Kato scoffed, but made a hurried check of his teletype and found that although a message had been sent, its text had not been released. He sent a dispatch about it to Tokyo, in case the news had not yet reached Japan some other way.

.

At the Georgetown home of F. Lammot Belin, a note was brought in to Saburo Kurusu, who was still lingering on after dinner. Discussion of Japanese-American relations with Belin and his guests had been affable but was leading nowhere. It was vital, they agreed, for Roosevelt to get through personally to the Emperor. Kurusu glanced at the note. The embassy, it read, expected him back without delay. His chauffeur was waiting.

.

Assuming that the Hudson which had spotted the Japanese convoy in the Gulf of Siam had radioed its position to Malaya, Admiral Ozawa prepared for attacks by air and sea after dawn on the 7th and ordered watches from 3:00 A.M. In heavy rain and zero visibility they saw nothing. Neither did a British Catalina flying boat sent up before dawn; but a second one, dispatched later in the morning, was located by Lieutenant Ogata, flying a Zero float plane, at 9:50. Ogata estimated that the Catalina would encounter the convoy, then sixty miles away, in less than half an hour. His *geta-baki*—Japanese for "planes with clogs on"—had only one 7.7mm gun to the Catalina's three machine guns, but he had surprise on his side. Slipping underneath the slow Catalina, he fired into its belly.

In Singapore no one knew of the first actual shots in the war. (When no distress call came long after the Catalina was due back, it was presumed lost to bad weather.) Minutes later the Japanese force reached "Point G" in the South China Sea, the area fixed for splitting into smaller units for its seven landfalls. One target was so small that only a single transport was designated for it. Even at that, Yamashita felt that he had too many men and kept one division back. He knew that he would be outnumbered, but the Kra Isthmus was narrow, and he did not want his troops getting in each other's way or creating problems of supply.

The major landing would be at Kota Bharu, just below the Thai border. A British airfield was nearby. It had been left to Ozawa to determine whether Kota Bharu should be attacked at the same time as the other landing sites, or whether that should wait until the British had committed their forces in the area—perhaps elsewhere, like Singora (Songkhla) in Thailand. Assuming that a delay could furnish opportunity for British warships to move north, Ozawa signaled to Yamashita from the *Chokai*, "Execute landings as planned. Simultaneous landing at Kota Bharu."

The Japanese intended to keep Thai resistance minimal. The day before, an officer from Saigon had visited Colonel Hiroshi Tamura, the Japanese military attaché in Bangkok, to plan the presentation of an ultimatum to ensure peaceable passage. They agreed that a smoke signal from the embassy early on the morning of the 8th would confirm to a low-flying plane that the demands had been met. A dinner-and-dance party for the foreign colony at the Oriental Hotel that evening suggested that public tension remained low.

While Bangkok newspapers played down war fears, Ozawa's fleet rendezvoused in the stormy Gulf of Siam with a smaller convoy carrying the 143rd Regiment from Saigon, combining nineteen transports with seven more. British planners were correct in assessing the December weather as inappropriate for an invasion attempt, but that was why the Japanese convoy was there. Subdividing into smaller strike forces, seven groups headed for locations in lower Thailand and upper Malaya.

At 9° 25′ north, 102° 20′ east, the separated groups were on their own momentum. The plan was to coordinate all strikes across the Pacific in order to maximize the possibility of surprise. Yet despite the cleverness of Japanese strategy, it was impossible to evoke simultaneous sunrises across seven thousand miles of the earth's surface and eight time zones. Farthest apart were Malaya and Hawaii. The Malaya force was to strike just after midnight, *Kido Butai* soon after sunrise.

For the ultimatum to work before landfall, and before separate incursions the following dawn from Indochina, Premier Phibun would have to confirm its acceptance for Thailand. If he refused, resident Japanese would be at risk; and to prepare for that possibility, Colonel Tamura collected representatives of the Japanese community at his office in Bangkok on Sunday morning to discuss sweeping up all civilians by twilight to house them, for their own safety, in the compound of a local Japanese school.

As they gathered, Pananon Vanit, a Thai cabinet minister and expected collaborator, burst into Tamura's office with the news that Premier Phibun had disappeared. Phibun, he claimed, had been angered by a report that a Thai official had been arrested by a Japanese officer somewhere at the Thai-Indochina border. An officer of the Imperial Guards Division, about to cross the frontier, assumed that the man was spying. Neither could communicate in the other's language; the Japanese officer, frustrated, kicked and slapped the Thai, then let him go. When the released official told Bangkok of the affair, Phibun acted highly agitated and declared that he would investigate for himself.

The motive to rush from the capital seemed flimsy. Why would the country's chief official—almost a dictator—vanish at such a precarious moment? Had he seized upon the incident in order to lie low? Vanit did not know.

·

To the flourish of bagpipes and a brass band, seven hundred members of the Royal Scots and 1st Middlesex battalions marched before midday to St. John's Anglican Cathedral in the park just above the Royal Navy docks in Hong Kong. Although Sunday Church Parade was the norm, the situation was anything but normal, for everyone now expected the Japanese to strike. The question was where, and whether by sea or by land. Major Cecil Robert Templer,* 8th Coast Artillery Regiment, had been scheduled to play the hymns and had been practicing them on the piano when he received orders to report for duty. Someone else would fill in.

Major General Christopher M. Maltby, wiry and bowlegged, redfaced and trimly mustached, with sandy hair turning gray, marched

---

* Later a major general and anti-insurgency chief in postwar Malaya.

with his men in a rolling gait. Then, in the church, to stress the importance of the occasion, he read himself from the Book of Matthew. Soldiers sang the hymn, "Praise My Soul, the King of Heaven."

As the service continued, an officer entered and strode down the aisle to Maltby's front pew. A Punjabi border patrol in the New Territories had been watching Japanese troop movements across from the village of Fanling. Intelligence already knew that the 38th Division had been augmented by heavy artillery from Canton and that the force was commanded by a six-year veteran of China campaigns, Lieutenant General Takashi Sakai. The alignment appeared to be no exercise. It was time to activate everyone. Alarmed, Maltby left the service, then sent inside for senior officers.

Inside St. John's the puzzled minister preached to a congregation that continued, disconcertingly, to dwindle.

.

A cable from Washington had arrived in Tokyo just before noon on Sunday requesting Ambassador Grew to stand by for an urgent message. It was not delivered. Roosevelt's personal entreaty to the Emperor arrived a few minutes later—ten in the evening the previous day in Washington. It was also withheld.

Grew waited impatiently. Although the embassy had been cut off, without his knowledge, from Washington, he had learned about the message anyway. The Associated Press had an arrangement with Domei, and through Domei's domestic service, Max Hill had received a cable from New York on Sunday morning, "Roosevelt appeals to Emperor for peace in Pacific."

Hill had already written a confidential memo to his AP home office warning that there would be war by mid-January; on talking with Grew, he had found the ambassador even more pessimistic. Three weeks earlier, Grew told him, he had sent a message to Washington warning that war was imminent and would probably come with dramatic suddenness. Hill telephoned to Grew. "I have received a cable from New York," he began, "that President Roosevelt has appealed to the Emperor for peace in the Pacific. Will you receive the message or does it go directly to the Palace?"

Since it was Grew's first hint of the message, he knew that something was seriously wrong. "There's nothing I can say," he answered guardedly. "Absolutely nothing I can say at this time. Thank you for calling." Grew dropped the receiver back on its cradle. He was worried. The cable had to come through him.

Otto Tolischus, Berlin correspondent of the *New York Times* until he was ejected for reporting that won him a Pulitzer Prize, had been reassigned to Tokyo, where he lived in a house adjacent to the American embassy grounds. Ignoring the good weather—an unusually sunny, mild December day—he sat at his typewriter over an article on Ambassador Grew for the *New York Times Magazine*. Tolischus could read no Japanese, and what spoken Japanese he possessed came from his living in Tokyo. He was dependent on the English-language press. The *Japan Times & Advertiser*, subject to unacknowledged force-feeding and censorship, offered little hope for many more days of peace. Under its major headline, "Easier Atmosphere in Talks Reported by Japanese Press," it reported that deliberately circulated "wild rumors about immediate Japanese action" had "frightened Roosevelt administration leaders" into more conciliatory terms for Nomura and Kurusu. Yet it added that the Japanese negotiators were "firm as a rock" in negotiating nothing away.

There was nothing in the Sunday edition to engender anything but gloom. A parallel story headlined a speech by Lieutenant General Tei-ichi Suzuki, President of the Cabinet Planning Board (many top officials were now military men), on the East Asia Co-Prosperity Sphere. The "Manchurian Incident" and the "China Affair," Suzuki argued, were the beginnings of "permanent peace in East Asia," a pre-George Orwell exercise in Orwellian language. Equally ominous were stories from the West: "German Artillery Shelling Moscow in Furious Battle," and "Rommel's Soldiers Recapture Gambut." A story inside dealt with military confusion and political rivalries in Manila that were being blamed for "lack of defensive preparations" in the Philippines. An American congressman from Michigan was claiming that the U.S. had to "save [President] Quezon from his own crowd." A story buried farther inside foreshadowed trouble even closer at hand. The Japanese Foreign Office had announced the transfer of Katsuo Okazaki, Consul-General in Hong Kong, to the post of Counselor at the Embassy to the puppet Chinese regime at Nanking. That Okazaki was not being replaced was the key element in the announcement.

There were other warning signs. Vichy France "declared that all reports on the dispatch of strong Japanese troop contingents to Indochina and all allegations about Franco-Japanese tension are pure inventions." And a Japanese scholar was quoted as saying in an article in *Hochi*, "We want to tell the United States to take her dirty feet out of the [East Asian] flower garden into which they have intruded. We wish that she will leave the garden quietly. Where can be found such a gentlemanly country as Japan? Both Great Britain and the United States should look closely at Japan's peaceful attitude." And Bunsho Takemura went on to identify the countries in the garden, including "Indochina producing iron, Thailand producing rice, Malaya producing tin, India producing cotton, the Netherlands East Indies producing oil and rubber, and New Caledonia producing chrome and nickel." The geographical sweep of implied Japanese ambitions was breathtaking. "Japan desires to live in a wide and happy atmosphere," Takemura concluded, and *wide* seemed meant literally.

A visitor interrupted Tolischus's typing. Ruth Kelley, a clerk at the American embassy, was interested in tips about magazines and newspapers which might buy a piece on Japan. Diplomatic activity was at a "standstill." She had little to do; time was hanging heavy. Tolischus promised to think about it, and Miss Kelley left for a Sunday afternoon party at Max Hill's.

Tolischus went back to his Grew article. He wanted to finish a draft that he could offer to Grew for his reaction. It turned out as he typed to be more about the times than about the ambassador. The "long-predicted war," he wrote, "between the white and yellow races in general, and war between Japan and the United States in particular, has become an imminent possibility. And whether it shall become a grim reality is now the great issue being decided in Tokyo and Washington." It sounded a bit strong to him as he read it over but he let it stand. Grew could modify it if he thought it extreme.

•

Saturday evening, December 6, was fixed in 1941 for American armed services pre-Christmas Officers' Club parties around the world. "The Japanese must have known this," Charles W. Utter, then a lieutenant in the Canal Zone, thought later. One of the first three jungle officers trained in Panama, he thought it was curious that two of the three—all reservists—came from un-tropical New England. At his club in the Zone, Utter found the happy atmosphere right for announcing his engagement to a girl in Chicago. The news raised the level of alcoholic enthusiasm even further, "and I was asked to join the Fort

Commander's and Regimental Commander's table, where their wives directed their husbands to assign us quarters as soon as possible—and to do it now!"

Unfinished drinks in hand, as well as a seltzer siphon bottle, the general, the colonel, and the lieutenant paraded to Headquarters, where married officers' quarters were assigned. "A little scrap followed as the two wives argued where my bride-to-be would stay while I was out in the jungles and before we were married. The Colonel's wife flipped her fingers through her drink in the direction of the General's formal white uniform—and hit her mark. The General replied with a squirt of the seltzer bottle at the Colonel's lady." Utter made haste to disappear from the scene, and, as unobtrusively as possible, he joined the bachelor officers at the bar.

HONG KONG
12:00 noon
December 7

MOSCOW
7:00 A.M.
December 7

WASHINGTON
11:00 P.M.
December 6

PEARL HARBOR
5:30 P.M.
December 6

Hour 16

A T NOON the last of twenty-six merchant ships ordered out of Hong Kong harbor to safer waters cleared the bay, most of them en route to Singapore. Eight others, given more time to make ready, had twelve additional hours, after which the Gap Rock Lighthouse thirty miles to the southwest would be dismantled.

After a brief stay in barracks on the Kowloon side, at Shamshuipo Camp,* the two Canadian battalions that had arrived on November 16 on the *Awatea* from Vancouver were in the process of moving to defense positions on the island. Some of the Canadians had been in uniform less than sixteen weeks, three of those at sea and three since at Shamshuipo, and could do little more than march.

"The minute I got off the boat," Private Wilf Lynch recalled, ". . . I realized that if the Japanese attacked, they'd wipe us out. 'We've got no air force, no navy, no place to go,' I told my pals. 'The Japs can back us up to the sea and even the best goddamned swimmer in the Grenadiers couldn't make it all the way home to Canada.' My pals laughed. 'We won't have to worry, Wilf. It's them that will be running away.' "

* Afterward a Japanese-run prison, and then a refugee center.

The Canadians spilled out of the Star ferries from Kowloon. Keeping most of them on the mainland appeared useless. The only seemingly defensible perimeter, familiarly known as the Gin Drinkers Line, ran close to Kowloon where the peninsula narrowed, from Junk Bay over Smugglers Ridge to Gin Drinkers Bay. Although much of the island's water was piped from the mainland, the system of protective pillboxes and earthworks, partially constructed in 1936, had been abandoned as futile. To guard Hong Kong from the sea, fixed naval guns pointed out from the harbor, particularly from Stonecutter's Island—"Upside Down Island" to the Chinese. Aircraft defending Hong Kong were more appropriate in a museum than on an airstrip. The four Vickers Vildebeeste torpedo bombers and three Supermarine Walrus amphibians could have fit into a small exhibition hall. None had guns—or torpedoes.

Planners in London once estimated that if Hong Kong could hold for 120 days it could be relieved. No one now seriously credited that, but until late on Saturday, December 6, when Maltby had issued a "warning of impending war," even he had believed that the Japanese buildup along the New Territories was for psychological reasons. Major General A. E. Grasett, the former military commander in Hong Kong—he had been transferred out in September—had glowingly called the colony "an impregnable fortress." Sir Geoffrey Northcote, the governor, agreed, but he had left, too.

The battalions from Winnipeg had arrived at Holt's Wharf without vehicles or heavy weapons. Why the Canadians had been sent to Hong Kong at all had puzzled their officers. Bureaucratic bungling kept their motorized equipment from being loaded in Vancouver, and they crossed the Pacific with 12,000 empty cubic feet of vehicle storage. An American freighter, the *Don José*, had followed on November 4 with all 212 unshipped vehicles, proceeding without lights via Honolulu and the Torres Strait (between New Guinea and Australia) on a route to Manila, then to Hong Kong. Avoiding Japanese-patrolled waters doubled the sailing time. At eight and a half knots, maintaining radio silence, the *Don Jose* was well north of New Guinea and in Philippine waters.

Churchill's view early in the year had been—so he had told General Sir Hastings Ismay—"There is not the slightest chance of holding Hong Kong or relieving it. It is most unwise to increase the loss we shall suffer there. Instead of augmenting the garrison it ought to be reduced to a symbolic scale. . . . Japan will think long before declaring war on the British Empire, and whether there are two or six battalions at Hong Kong will make no difference to her choice." Even so, the Dominions Office in London thought that a show of strength might make Japan hesitate, and Canada was asked to contribute. J. L. Ralston, Minister of National Defence in Ottawa, agreed that "it was Canada's turn to help. . . . Australia had been doing a great deal in Libya and elsewhere; the New Zealanders had been in Crete; and the South Africans in Abyssinia."

·

At 7:00 A.M. on Sunday morning in the western suburbs of Moscow the temperature dipped to Fahrenheit −20° (−29°C). As a result of poor, and poorly cooked, food, and the need to warm the body with schnapps of any description, intestinal disorders raged among the German troops. It was death to squat in the open, not because of Russian snipers, but because in the extreme cold performing one's natural functions could result in what military doctors called "a congelation of the anus." Soldiers breakfasted on horse and cattle feed found in captured barns, as even axes rebounded harmlessly off frozen horseflesh—the only meat available. One soldier, so a report went, "was drawing his ration of boiling soup at the field kitchen [and] could not find his spoon. It took him 30 seconds to find it, but by then the soup was lukewarm. He began to eat it as quickly as he could, without losing a moment's time, but the soup was already cold, and soon it would be [frozen] solid."

"When will they at last pull us out of the line . . . ?" a young recruit wrote, with difficulty, in his diary. "What is all this for? . . . When will we ever get back home? . . . With an empty belly almost everyone is suffering from dysentery. We feel weak and miserable as dogs. And add to this the terrible cold. The frostbite in my feet is growing ever larger and infected with abscesses every day. . . . And there are the Bolsheviks! . . . We cannot halt them."

The temperature was no different on the Russian side of the line. Marshal Zhukov would later insist, with obvious exasperation, "Bourgeois historians and former Nazi generals have tried to convince the public that the million picked German troops were beaten at Moscow not by the iron steadfastness, courage, and heroism of Soviet soldiers, but by mud, cold and deep snow. The authors of these apologetics

seem to forget that Soviet forces had to operate under the same conditions." Zhukov was correct about the thermometer and the heroism,
yet Russians were fighting for the soil they stood upon, in a climate
they knew, supported by short supply lines and dressed in winter garb.
Further, the Russians had only to hold out in order to win, while the
Germans had to win in order to hold out.

.

Armed with the FBI tap, Bicknell rushed to his car and bucked the
crowds returning from the University of Hawaii-Willamette football
game. Hawaii had won, 20–6. Fans were exuberant. Instrumentalists
from some of the fourteen bands at the stadium were snarling Honolulu
streets. Nevertheless, Bicknell kept close to the ten minutes he had
promised, arriving at 5:40. With Fielder reading over Short's shoulder,
both scanned the Mori exchange with more anxiety about being late
for dinner—it was a half-hour drive to Schofield Barracks—than about
the telephone transcript's implications.

The conversation could be quite innocent, Short concluded weakly,
but it was "a very good picture of the situation in Hawaii."

He hadn't yet had time, Bicknell confessed, to analyze it for "anything hidden," but he thought it appeared "very significant and an
indication of something in the wind." He assumed that Short could
add it to other discomforting clues, like the burning of codes at the
Japanese consulate.*

Fielder downplayed the conversation. It appeared "silly from our
Western mind's point of view"—only an exchange of legitimate information "that would sell a paper."

Bicknell, Short agreed, impatiently getting into his car, was "a little
too intelligence conscious." Anyway, "no one of us could figure out
what it possibly meant." The general and his aide went off to dinner;
frustrated, Bicknell drove home through the emptying streets.

.

The popular cartoonist of "Terry and the Pirates" was on a transcontinental, multi-stop plane heading east from Los Angeles for Sunday
arrival in Washington. Milton Caniff's relationship with the authorities

---

* Both Fielder and Bicknell would later testify that Short had been told about the
consulate code burnings; Short denied such knowledge.

was mixed. Some thought he was exposing military secrets; some thought he was exposing too much of the Dragon Lady's cleavage. Isolationist papers had objected that his villains in China were labeled as Japanese and ostentatiously flew the meatball flag. Caniff withdrew the flag and the name, kept the uniforms, and called the Japanese "invaders." His four hundred newspapers stayed with him, even the *Chicago Tribune* and the *New York Daily News*.

Assistant Secretary of War Robert Patterson had called him in "and said these invaders are obviously Japanese," which would not cost Milton Caniff "any Japanese circulation," but the U.S. was engaged in sensitive diplomacy and "maybe we should soft-pedal this political stuff."

"Sir, I disagree with you," said Caniff, and he "could see the others in the office sinking through the floor." One didn't argue with Secretary Stimson's right-hand man.

"Son," said Patterson, without taking his feet off his desk, ". . . we're gonna do it my way."

"Yes, sir," said Caniff insincerely, never expecting to hear from the Assistant Secretary again, but the Chemical Warfare office telephoned as the weekend was beginning. The War Department was concerned about public ignorance of air-raid precautions. Could Caniff "get together a poster on what to do in case of an air raid?"

Now he was flying out on the first plane he could get. People in Washington, he thought, "expected something."

•

At about 11:30, General Sherman Miles, Chief of Army Intelligence, returned home. He had been at a dinner party in Arlington, across the Potomac from Washington, at the home of Captain Theodore S. ("Ping") Wilkinson, the Navy Intelligence head, when the Kramers had delivered the thirteen-part decrypt. Miles found a message to telephone Colonel Bratton, and realized that Bratton had tried to deliver a set of the documents to him. He had already discussed the papers privately with Wilkinson in Arlington, where they had concluded that although a break in negotiations was certain, that had no immediate "military significance." The President and several of his Cabinet had interpreted the decrypt more dramatically. Still, Miles expected that the fourteenth part would be in soon after midnight.

They would understand the message better then. There was plenty of time to distribute the complete text early on Sunday.

Bratton was relieved. He was not sure that Hull had received his copy; a receipt evidenced its delivery only to State. And he had made no attempt to go to Fort Myer, where the chief of staff lived, as he knew that the Marshalls "were leading a rather monastic life." They would both have the full message in the morning.

Unless the *Washington Times-Herald* was wrong, and reported an event from which George Marshall had begged off, the general had been less than monastic Saturday evening, attending a dinner of veterans of his college ROTC unit. The reunion, at the University Club on 16th Street, NW, only a short walk from the White House, had slipped his mind years later when it seemed to him that he had stayed home with his wife, who was recovering from two rib fractures. He had been ill, too, although putting in his usual long days. To his stepdaughter, Molly Winn, he had written earlier in the day of his wearying flood of crises, but he had not mentioned Japan. Everything, he explained vaguely, was "so unsettled." He was "taking a rather heavy political beating" from isolationists who were fighting the "large appropriation bills" for military expenditures, and had "just about enough steam to do this job."

He could have delegated more authority, but he hadn't, yet he was unable to examine all the paper that flowed in. That General Short's response to Marshall's "war warning" had misinterpreted Washington's intent escaped everyone. A "Number One Alert" was not a state of full readiness but a sabotage watch. Stark, writing unhelpfully for the Navy Department—and without informing Marshall or Roosevelt what he had done—had watered the warning down by predicting possible Japanese targets while omitting Hawaii. Stark had even instructed Admiral Kimmel in Pearl Harbor to show the message to Short.

Paging Marshall—if the President considered that possibility as he had with "Betty" Stark—would have resulted in the same sense of alarm which the White House had feared in the admiral's case. Although Marshall could not have left the War Department for the day in ignorance of the "pilot" message from Tokyo about the Foreign Ministry memorandum, it appeared then to be State Department business. Stark, whom Roosevelt knew longer and better, could consult with Marshall and his people if he thought it urgent to do so. War in the Gulf of Siam, if it came to that, did not involve the United States Army.

The Starks returned from *The Student Prince* at 11:30, much later than Roosevelt expected. They had guests with them, Captain and Mrs. Harold D. Krick, and had gone for a post-theater snack. The Chief of Naval Operations lived in a Victorian mansion (now the official residence of the Vice-President) with long open porches and a conical tower at one corner, on the grounds of the Naval Observatory. When an aide reported a call from the White House, the admiral excused himself to climb to his second-floor study under the tower, where he had a direct line to the President. Descending after a few minutes, Stark observed that while "relations with Japan were in a critical state," he saw no reason for immediate action on his part. However anxious the Washington establishment, few lights would burn late.

•

In the port of Osaka at the same time, which was 1:30 in the afternoon on the 7th, Admiral Wenneker, the German naval attaché, managed, after four hours of negotiations with Japanese officials, to get aboard the freighter *Rio Grande*, which had slipped through the British blockade from Bordeaux. At sea for seventy-three days, it had traveled 19,303 nautical miles, losing one man swept overboard but encountering no aircraft and only five ships, each of which it evaded. It had anchored off Osaka the afternoon before, its 7,272 tons of cargo "completely in disorder," Wenneker observed, from the heavy seas.

The *Rio Grande*'s mission was to carry a cargo of rubber back to Germany to eke out the synthetic equivalent on which the Nazi war effort was dependent, but first it had to off-load in Osaka and then in Yokohama. Less than happy about each *Blockadebrecher*, the Japanese had to accept unwanted machinery, while new military weaponry they could appropriate and put into production arrived only rarely and grudgingly. And each ship had to be refueled with scarce oil. The Axis powers had agreed on a division of Asia at the 70th parallel of longitude, east of Iran, but the oil of Iraq and Iran, the Caucasus and Borneo, remained to be seized.

Representing the Navy Ministry, Captain Hasama explained via an interpreter, Commander Sato, the complicated Japanese customs technicalities, and the German representatives, including the ship's master, Captain von Allwörden, were invited "in friendly fashion" to dinner ashore, even though Hasama "was extremely busy (as a result of the outbreak of war)." Very likely Wenneker could see war preparations all about the sprawling harbor, but he asked no questions and assumed that it was the reason why the *Rio Grande*'s crew of forty-eight, including ten marine AA gunners, all desperate for dry land, would have to gaze at it from the dock. Christmas appeared about to arrive early. "Crew informed in an address about a ban on going ashore," Wenneker noted, "and the necessity for this emphasized. This understood, even though there was disappointment at first."

HONG KONG	SINGAPORE	MOSCOW	LONDON
1:00 A.M.	12:00 noon	8:00 A.M.	5:00 A.M.
December 7	December 7	December 7	December 7

HOUR 17

AFTER the Government House meeting of the Hong Kong Defence Council, General Maltby's aide, Captain Iain MacGregor, had his hands full. The head of a large bank, protesting that the alert was bad for business and a waste of time, wanted to see the general. "The Chairman paced the room, all the time telling me the whole thing was bloody nonsense, and that only two days before he had received a coded cable from one of his Managers [in China] who had been dining the previous evening with the C-in-C of the Japanese Kwangtung Army. The C-in-C had assured the Manager that under no circumstances would the Japanese ever attack their old ally, Great Britain. 'Good God, Iain,' said the banker, 'you're a civilian, really, a Far East merchant. You know how these Army fellows flap. You know our intelligence is far better than theirs. What the hell does Maltby think he's doing, calling up and deploying the Volunteers, taking more than half my staff away? Doesn't he realise it will cause a panic among the Chinese and a run on the bank tomorrow, with only a skeleton staff to deal with it? The whole damn thing is ridiculous.' "

MacGregor was "glad indeed" when the general returned at one. Maltby would not rescind the call-up. Orders were going out across the colony because the Japanese were indeed coming. Hong Kong banks would have to make do with fewer staff. He was sorry about it.

·

It was just past Bangkok noon when a pilot radioed to the *Ryujo Maru* in the Bay of Siam, "We have brought down an enemy patrol plane." Although the morning skies had cleared enough for reconnaissance aircraft from northern Malaya to search for the Japanese convoy, also darting among the cumulonimbus clouds were covering Zeros. The squadron of Lieutenant Colonel Tatsuo Kato operated from Phiquok Island, just off the coast of Cambodia. Quan Phu Quoc—as it is currently called—had been turned into an air base, the closest available to the Kra Isthmus.

Anxiety gripped the convoy. Had the enemy plane opportunity to radio a fix? Had there been, as some of Kato's pilots thought, a second plane that had escaped into a whirling cloud? "The discovery of the convoy sailing to the northwest," Lieutenant Colonel Tsuji, on the *Ryujo Maru*, thought, "we could bear with patience, but from two o'clock in the afternoon our change of course must be concealed even from the gods."

The weather worsened. Fog reappeared, and low clouds cut visibility across the bay. Tsuji considered his prayers answered.

·

Mrs. E. Innes-Kerr and a friend had driven to the Singapore camp at which their Volunteers husbands were based, and found the area nearly deserted. There had been a sudden scare, a bored sentry told them, and everyone had gone off at an hour's notice to battle stations. He had no idea how far that meant.

The Innes-Kerrs knew there were reasons to be anxious: she worked as a secretary at Malayan Broadcasting. Reality had come only the day before as they were watching a matinée of Bernard Shaw's *Major Barbara*. A half-hour into the film a notice flashed on the screen, "ALL BRITISH TROOPS TO REPORT BACK TO BARRACKS IMMEDIATELY." There had been "a great rustling" in the audience and nearly everyone had departed. The experience was repeated all over the island. Squadron Leader Donald B. Pearson, in charge of training at the Kluang air base, had gone to play rugby football for the RAF team against the Army squad and found a notice posted at the entrance to the Singapore

Cricket Club, "The match between Army and RAF is cancelled. All Service personnel are to report to their units immediately." Instead of footballing he found himself converting training aircraft into makeshift dive bombers and mounting two Vickers guns on each. That had been the day before.

When, on Sunday morning, "Tam" Innes-Kerr telephoned that he was stationed at a machine gun post between the Seaview Hotel and the Swimming Club, the women packed some supplies for their husbands in the Innes-Kerr auto and tooled down the East Coast Road.* "Tam" was the senior sergeant in command; the men, Mrs. Innes-Kerr recalled, "were stationed in the garden of one of the lovely big houses along the coast, and they were putting up barbed wire all through the garden. It was a scene of such peace and beauty that, even with men in uniform, and the pillboxes, and the barbed wire going up, it was quite impossible to visualise that it could ever be touched by war." The preparation fit the rigid strategic pattern of Singapore defense. No enemy—not even snakes—could reach the island through the impenetrable Malayan jungle, or across the Johore Strait, much like a castle's moat. Only a frontal assault from the sea could be expected, and for that the military authorities had prepared a welcome of coast artillery—fixed naval cannon.

The ritual Sunday morning singalong down the road at the Seaview Hotel came to a close at noon when the bandleader signaled the final number, and dozens of gin drinkers burst into

> There'll always be an England,
> And England will be free,
> If England means as much to you,
> As England means to me.

It was not so much what England itself meant: for many that was a very distant memory. It was what England contributed to the good life in the polyglot city of three-quarters of a million, where even a private who had enlisted to escape a life of pinched penury could live what seemed a princely existence. Sent from England with the 18th Division to reinforce Singapore, John Mutimer recalled "months of

---

* A broad Marine Parade and even broader East Coast Parkway, as well as massive buildings, now separate the East Coast Road from the coast, a result of gargantuan postwar landfill operations that have enlarged Singapore and moved the seafront outward.

sheer luxury and joy." At the end of each barracks sat an Indian servant. "At the call of 'Boy,' the Indian would come running to your room, an old boy of about 90, I imagine, and say 'Yes, sahib.' Shades of the Imperial past. He swept the hut, cleaned boots, and in the sergeant's room looked after . . . one's laundry, which was simply dumped on the floor, and returned the next day immaculately washed, starched, and ironed, until the creases on the short shirt sleeves, and on our shorts, were like a knife edge."

The camp barber would complete each haircut with a massage that left the scalp tingling; and, D. G. Cotton, a private in an antiaircraft unit, remembered, "men could be shaved in bed each morning by [electric] torchlight before reveille; a small boy wielding a lather brush preceding the barber who lifted the mosquito net, and resting a[nother] torch on the chest of the occupant, used a straight razor with great speed and dexterity." After a while, Mutimer was sure, "you became so used to it you didn't want to wake up, so soft was his touch. . . . Somehow I felt as though all my life I was destined to live in a place like Singapore. . . . I loved the teeming city. . . . The armies of ants on the march, the birds, the trees and bushes, the fireflies at night, and the noise of the insects, the smell, the people, the food and the clothes, all were a part of me, a wonderful world which I embraced with all my heart."

For expatriate civilians, Singapore offered an even more opulent contrast to English realities. The Malays, Indians, and Chinese were all gentle adult children born to serve the servants of the Empire. Colonial shibboleths that demanded collars and ties at the office, or over drinks at the posh Raffles Hotel, were crosses eagerly to be borne in upholding the Victorian-era traditions that kept the island an exotic and sweaty appendage to England. Everything important was cheap —gin, cigarettes, strawberries, jewels, native mistresses, the cricket club, ball gowns, rickshaw wallahs, taxis. The wartime price—it was necessary to be reminded that there was a war on somewhere—was the presence of soldiers showing no traces of anxiety; occasional aircraft displaying the RAF symbol overhead; warships gliding in and out of port; campaigns to enlist volunteer nurses, auxiliary firemen and air-raid wardens; and practice alerts with brownouts of building illumi-nation. The good things would all last, the denizens of Singapore were certain, as long as there was an England.

In the veins of the master race in white-skinned Burma and Malaya,

Rhodesia or Kenya, ran British blood. The atmosphere was only slightly different in the Dutch Indies, where racial attitudes were more relaxed. Hadn't they been there for three hundred years? And hadn't the wharves and refineries and plantations created wealth that had trickled down? Yet the Japanese did not expect the native beneficiaries of such largesse to do battle with them when they came in guise of liberators. After all, Malayans and Burmese could not be expected to know how brutally the Japanese had colonized Korea, or what freedom in a puppet state was like in Manchuria. Some ethnic minorities might even be induced to sign up for a Japanese-organized army to liberate the home country into someone else's satellite—and some Indians eventually did that in Malaya.

·

An *Oberleutnant* from Vienna, Wilhelm Prüller at twenty-five was a product of the Hitler-Jugend active in Austria even before the Anschluss. His *Schutzenregiment* 10 was a motorized battalion belonging to the Fourth Light Division, on the southern flank of Army Group Central, below Moscow. As protection from the cold, his men had let their beards grow since moving eastward from Kursk. Icicles, elongated by every painful breath, hung from them. Contrary to regulations, Prüller's men wore white rags around their helmets and torsos as camouflage in the snow and for extra insulation. It was no longer a war, he told his diary, "but a fight for billets."

Early in December, his platoon of thirty-nine men had one room in a Russian hut in which to sleep, standing up. The wounded died. "Yesterday," he wrote on the 7th, "we had 32 degrees below zero [C]," which was − 26°F. "It will get worse. We are not advancing any more, however. . . . The villages lying in front of us are burned down now, so that the Russians can't use them against us. Behind us on the hills, bunkers will be constructed as a winter defense line. Probably we shall move back from here, too, and burn down all these villages behind us."

The peasants they had evicted and driven away, Prüller concluded, were not to be "envied"—but all "softer emotions" had to be "sacrificed for tactical necessity." The Russians, he was told, were doing the same. "I only don't understand what is to happen to us. Are we, in an armoured division, supposed to sit in a bunker? . . . With my inborn optimism, [I] still believe that we shall get [back] to Germany sometime." His division had been promised Christmas leaves, which would get two men in each company home for the holidays. Yet there was no transport to make it good, and every able-bodied soldier was needed as the Russians pressed their counteroffensive.*

Among the Western nations urgent cables were flying about in such numbers that confusion was inevitable. Although Lord Cranborne, Secretary of State for Dominion Affairs, had been up all Saturday night fielding messages as soon as they were decrypted, he still did not know whether Roosevelt's warning to Emperor Hirohito had left Washington. At 5:06 A.M. on Sunday he sent circular message M438 to all Dominion prime ministers with the draft (M439) of what was to be a follow-up message to Tokyo—"that if Japan attempts to establish her influence in Thailand by force . . . she will do [so] at her own peril and His Majesty's Government will at once take all appropriate measures. Should hostilities unfortunately result, the responsibility will rest with Japan."

The exercise was akin to stopping a bullet already fired.

---

* Prüller would survive to return to Austria, becoming proprietor of a shop in Vienna which offered local souvenirs and Catholic *Devotionalien*. Gaunt and alcoholic after the war, he wore his SS ring unashamedly.

HOUR 18

S INCE the telephone call from Otto Tolischus just after noon, Ambassador Grew in Tokyo had kept his shortwave radio turned to KGEI in San Francisco, listening for news of the President's message to Hirohito. Nothing of the sort had turned up as a cablegram to him. Finally the evening news—it was ten the previous night in California— went on, and Grew learned what he already knew—that Roosevelt "had sent or was sending a message to the Emperor." Nothing of its substance, or how it was being sent, emerged. Grew remained baffled, never suspecting that the Japanese military was keeping it from him, and from the Emperor. To withhold it from the Emperor was a deed too enormous to conceive.

•

When in Manila, Sir Tom Phillips had revealed his desperate short- age of destroyers in Singapore. Could he expect, in the event of war, any assistance from the Americans? "Yes," said Admiral Hart, "pro- vided you order those two old destroyers you have tied up out of indefensible Hong Kong, and recall them to Singapore." They were 1918 vintage, useful largely as escort vessels. On one, HMS *Scout*, Christopher Briggs was a lieutenant and executive officer, a transfer from the merchant marine. Although his wife, Alice, and their daughter, Patricia, had been evacuated unwillingly to Manila, en route to Australia, Alice had managed to get back. In order to stay she got a job with a firm in the Hong Kong and Shanghai Bank Building.

On Sunday afternoon the Briggses went for a walk in the hills behind Kowloon, unconcerned by the Volunteer Force trainees they saw. (Volunteers, many of them Hong Kong and Shanghai Bank employees, were out most Sundays.) Returning to their flat in Argyle Street, Kowloon, for dinner, they discussed retrieving Patricia from the Philippines, and mother and daughter returning to England. Briggs was not sure that he would see either of them again very soon. Though his ship was undergoing bottom-painting and boiler-cleaning at Taikoo Dockyard, all leaves over Sunday night had been canceled, and he had to return to the *Scout* by evening, to sleep on board. They arranged to meet on the Hong Kong side for lunch the next day, if possible, before the ship cleared the drydock.

·

In the first daylight of Sunday, Munich was nearly empty of vehicles, a time for prisoner-of-war crews from the Westende *Lager*, in overalls and boots, to be sent in to clean the streets. John Tonkin, of the 151st Anti-Aircraft Battery, had been taken prisoner in Crete. Shipped to Stalag VIIA in Moosburg, he was trucked about for street-cleaning duty, then moved to Westende, which was closer to the city. In the beginning his companions were often elderly Jews, clad, despite the early morning frost, in thin cotton clothes emblazoned with a yellow, six-pointed star. Domestic dustpans and brushes in hand, they were compelled to sweep the streets on their knees.

Alongside, British PWs suffered at first from "nausea," but, Tonkin remembered grimly, they had to "absorb the environment." The Jews were, "poor devils," disappearing into a huge work camp called Dachau, a "dreadful place" just to the northwest where "harrowing scenes" occurred at the adjacent railway terminus. The camp seemed to be filling up, but few Jews came out anymore. Almost all the street details were now PW labor.

·

It was after 1:00 A.M. in Washington when Assistant Secretary of State Adolph Berle went to bed. After taking his daughters to *The*

Student Prince matinée, he had returned to the State Department to work on a message to Congress that Hull was drafting for the President if nothing came of the appeal to Emperor Hirohito. With the message to the Emperor en route, Berle was working on the follow-up when Colonel Bratton's packet arrived. Berle took it from the Secretary's desk to glance at it, noting in his diary that the thirteen parts of the Foreign Ministry memorandum were enough that he didn't need the rest of it. The reply was "not only a flat turn down, but a coarse and gratuitous and insulting message as well."

The accompanying cable on how and when the completed text was to be presented to Hull seemed ominous to Berle. It meant war—somewhere. When the U.S. would be involved seemed still a puzzle, and with a piece of it missing, he "turned in . . . feeling very uneasy. The waltzes of 'The Student Prince' seemed like a dirge of something that may have existed once, but certainly had very little relation to anything one knew today."

•

Although the *Nevada* was supposed to remain at sea off Oahu through the weekend, so junior officers aboard had expected, it was already back and moored as usual at Ford Island. Unidentified submarine contacts were blamed. It seemed prudent for the big battleship to be in port. Ensign Charles J. Merdinger, for whom the *Nevada* was a first assignment after graduation from the Naval Academy in June, was assigned to the plotting room, but there was no reason for him to stay aboard: his duty was the next day. He went ashore into Honolulu for the evening, bought an artificial Christmas tree for his cabin, listened to entreaties from his friends to stay in town for the night, and decided to return. Hotels were high living. Ensigns made only $1500 a year.

•

Just east of the Date Line lay isolated Midway Island, an atoll used as a refueling stop for transpacific aircraft. The carrier *Lexington* was steaming northwest from Pearl Harbor to ferry planes to reinforce Midway, only half as far from Oahu as was the even less defensible Wake Island. Protecting the carrier was Task Force 12, three heavy cruisers and five destroyers, with Rear Admiral John H. Newton flying his commander's flag from the *Chicago*. There were no docking facilities for large vessels at Midway. The planes were to fly the final 400 miles to the atoll.

Takeoff from the *Lexington* was scheduled for 11:00 Hawaii time on the morning of the seventh. The fleet had cleared port early on the fifth, zigzagging at seventeen knots with scout planes overhead by day and radar sweeps after dark. Had its course taken TF 12 more north than northwest, the *Lexington*'s aircraft might have encountered evidence of *Kido Butai*, now moving due south toward Oahu. At first, nothing seemed unusual—a routine job—but Captain Frederick C. Sherman of the carrier became eager to return when his escort ships began picking up on sonar the churning of what seemed to be a tailing sub.

To shake the shadow, the task force zigzagged at more frequent intervals, and in the darkness and the empty ocean, sonar technicians listened tensely. The signal was persistent. No American undersea craft were to be in the area.

The skipper of the *I-74*, one of nineteen crack subs from three Japanese squadrons on blockade and interception missions around Hawaii—there were eight more subs on special assignments—had been tracking the *Lexington* for hours. Frustratingly, there was no way he could radio to Admiral Nagumo's strike force that the carrier was not tied up at Pearl Harbor, but he could send it to the bottom himself when the time was ripe. Orders to all subs were to hold off torpedoing any targets before 8:00 A.M. Hawaii time. However tempting the kill, nothing was to alarm the Americans too soon.

TOKYO	MANILA	SAIGON	CALIFORNIA
4:00 P.M.	3:00 P.M.	2:00 P.M.	11:00 P.M.
December 7	December 7	December 7	December 6

HOUR 19

T O FOSTER the illusion of unwarlike activity, especially for lurking spies and Western journalists, Chief Cabinet Secretary Naoki Hoshino and several of his aides made a Sunday afternoon appearance on a Tokyo tennis court. To a knowledgeable foreign agent their presence would have seemed so unusual as to excite suspicion. To participate in the charade, Marquis Kido, the mustached, balding, bespectacled confidant of the Emperor, had already played a game of croquet, which he had lost.

To further the illusion of an average Sunday, Prime Minister—and War Minister—Tojo, almost always garbed as a general, left his family quarters at four, wearing a Western tweed jacket and riding breeches, and carrying a riding crop. If he were seen on horseback in the park, it would have appeared, he imagined, unwarlike in the extreme. Tojo's Military Affairs Secretary, Colonel Susumu Nishiura, was appalled at the exposure. Ultra-militarists might try assassination to remove Tojo for a more radical leader. After listening to Nishiura's objections, the Prime Minister settled for a lower-profile automobile ride with his wife and daughters.

Suggestions of normality appeared everywhere in the military and governmental establishment, including Kido's attendance at an afternoon funeral, and a banquet given by the Emperor at 6:15. But Kido's diary also notes, later, "9:30. Secretary Hoshino came [to the Palace]. Discussed the war against America and England."

.

Restless, telling himself that by the next afternoon, having made his bus trip to the border, he would be safely in Thailand, Relman Morin walked the Saigon sidewalks. He had tried to read, "but the print was meaningless." Encountering a French friend "connected with the airlines," he learned that the Japanese had seized the last commercial airport, just outside the city. "The French had refused for months to hand it over. . . . Now [the Japs] had taken it by force. There had been no fighting because the French had nothing to fight with. They had simply locked the gates, and the Japanese had broken them open."

Two weeks earlier he would have tried some scheme to get the story past the censors. Clearly there was some imminent anticipated use for the airfield. "The only thing that was important now was sheer physical danger. . . . I found myself looking at my watch and making the effort to realize that a war might be coming. War was something you read about in school." He went back to his hotel and chain-smoked.

.

Back in the Philippines only three days after China duty on the Yangtze, Lieutenant Alfred Littlefield Smith, a Navy doctor on the river gunboat *Luzon*, was eager for home. His orders to the States were awaiting signature, but he was still on duty on the *Luzon*, although it was Sunday and his friends in port were ashore. Two of Smith's buddies were getting in a round of golf at the Cavite course; after the eighteenth hole they turned into the clubhouse for a drink. At a conspicuous table was Admiral Hart, alone. Assuming the freedom of his medical insignia, Commander Harris sat down and asked about his own release for home.

"Your orders are on my desk," the admiral said, raising a hand well above the table surface, "with a stack that high. If everything is all right tomorrow at 10 o'clock, come by and I'll have them signed."

Harris reported the good news to Smith.

.

At 9:00 P.M. Assistant Consul "Tadashi Morimura" cabled his final report to Tokyo for the Pearl Harbor grid.

The following ships were observed at anchor on the 6th: 9 battleships, 3 light cruisers, 3 submarine tenders, 17 destroyers. In addition there were 4 light cruisers and 2 destroyers lying at docks. It appears that no air reconnaissance is being conducted by the fleet air arm.

"So it was," he recalled, "that as I sat at my desk in the darkened consulate building in Honolulu late in the evening . . . , I knew that the message I was working on might well be the last which the Japanese attack-force commander would receive. . . . After giving the message to the waiting code clerk . . . I strolled about the consulate grounds. . . . The bright haze in the distance indicated that the lights were on at the Pearl Harbor naval base, and I could hear no patrolling aircraft aloft. It was a quiet Saturday night and all seemed normal, so I finally turned in."

Five hundred miles to the north, *Kido Butai* had reached the meridian of Oahu. In conference on the *Akagi*, Chief of Staff Kusaka observed that the ships in port at last count would very likely leave on Tuesday.

"It is most regrettable," Commander Minoru Genda, the Operations Officer, observed, "that no carriers are in."

Lieutenant Commander Kanijiro Ono, the Intelligence Officer, explained that the *Enterprise*'s task force had left on the twenty-ninth, and only the two battleships that had escorted it were back. Since the *Lexington* had returned from a previous exercise on the twenty-ninth and left again on the sixth—Ono referred to Tokyo time—a pattern seemed suggested. He expected the *Enterprise*'s return "today," one carrier replacing the other. Ono also wondered where two other flattops, the *Yorktown* and the *Hornet*, were, as he counted them as "belonging to the Pacific Fleet." A rare Japanese intelligence lapse, the shift of the *Hornet* to anti-sub work in the Atlantic had not been picked up; the *Yorktown* was expected back imminently from the West Coast. "They must be out here," Ono insisted.

"If that happens," said Genda, referring to the return of the carriers, "I don't care if all eight of the battleships are away." (He understood that the ninth battleship referred to in Yoshikawa's report was the obsolete *Utah*, now reduced to target ship, with a deck of concrete and planks.)

Commander Tamotsu Oishi, the senior staff officer, disagreed. "As an airman," he told Genda, "you naturally place much importance on carriers. Of course, it would be good if we could get three of them, but I think it would be better if we got all eight of the battleships."

The last word went to Rear Admiral Kusaka. He saw only a slight chance that any carriers would be in port, yet little chance, too, that any battleships would leave on a weekend. "We can't do anything about carriers that aren't there. I think we should attack Pearl Harbor tomorrow."

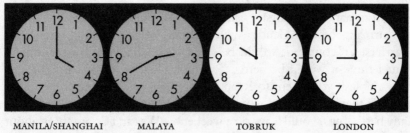

MANILA/SHANGHAI	MALAYA	TOBRUK	LONDON
4:00 P.M.	2:40 P.M.	10:00 A.M.	9:00 A.M.
December 7	December 7	December 7	December 7

HOUR 20

S HANGHAI was largely under Japanese occupation, yet free. There was the French Concession, and independent of it the International Settlement, with its famous Bund fronting the Whangpoo River. Surrounding both was the Chinese Municipality of Greater Shanghai, dominated by Japanese military overlords. Battalions of foreign troops, supplied from the river and abroad by gunboats and larger vessels flying foreign flags, symbolized the colonial regimes and their extraterritoriality. Although French power had faded with Vichy, two gunboats, the *Wake*, flying the Stars and Stripes, and the *Peterel*, with the Union Jack, survived from a once-colorful naval presence. When commissioned in 1927, someone's error had given the *Peterel* an extra *e* stubbornly maintained thereafter as a matter of pride. The locally built *Wake* was too shallow-draft to be oceangoing. Few crew remained; it housed only radio equipment for the American consulate. The *Peterel* displaced only a few hundred tons and was equally unseaworthy. The breech blocks of her two three-inch cannon had already been sent to Hong Kong. Two Lewis machine guns were her entire firepower.

On the afternoon of December 7, *Peterel* was moored off the French

Bund; *Wake* was tied up to the British naval buoy downstream. Some sailors from both ships were on the town. Two rugby football matches were enlivening Sunday afternoon at the Shanghai Club. The Royal Navy eleven, mostly off-duty personnel from the *Peterel*, played the Way Foong team of Hong Kong and Shanghai Bank employees, quickly taking a lead it never relinquished. On the adjoining pitch the Japanese Rugby Club was playing the Shanghai Rugby Club, with the winners of both matches to play the following Sunday for the Tse Ling Cup.

Finishing first, with a 7-0 victory, the Royal Navy team, without waiting to find out who their opponents would be, hurried into the club's dining room for supper after a quick change of uniform. Since their service launch returned from the Bund dock to the *Peterel* at 11:30, the sailors wanted to crowd in a movie and a round of the dance halls, politely called "cabarets." Only the duty telegraphist—Liddington—the engine-room rating, and the duty quartermaster had to be sober after midnight.

One man per party was permitted all-night leave. Although it was Jack Honywill's turn, he elected not to take it—girls were expensive. Undeterred, Seaman Cumming volunteered himself for a longer haunt of the cabarets. No one worried about the token Japanese force, the old, three-funnel cruiser *Idzumo*, a destroyer, and a gunboat. They were part of the riverfront scene.

With his family back in England, British businessman Arch Carey had moved in with his boyhood friend of earlier days in Shanghai, Jack Bowker. For the afternoon, Bowker and Carey were at a favorite spot off the road to Tsinpu. Some suburban parks were lush gardens, tenderly cultivated for absentee owners by Chinese caretakers, but the Japanese had forbidden visits after dark. To make sure they were not in violation, Bowker and Carey hurried back to their car as the sun was going down and began the drive back.

At the junction of the Tsinpu and Hungjao roads they noticed a white line drawn in lime across the road. It had not been there earlier, but they gave it no further thought. The next day they realized that the Japanese had marked off all exits from Shanghai.

•

Late on Sunday afternoon in Manila, Hart heard from his *Isabel*. It had been buzzed by Japanese planes while still far from Indochinese waters. At 4:30 P.M. he radioed Washington in the same message that he announced the departure of the *Lanikai*, "ISABEL RETURNING WAS SPOTTED AND IDENTIFIED WELL OFF COAST HENCE POTENTIAL UTILITY OF HER MISSION PROBLEMATICAL. HAVE NOT YET FOUND THIRD VESSEL." Since the Japanese seemed uninterested in sinking the *Isabel*, Hart wondered whether they were trying to avoid a provocation.

By 4:45 the *Lanikai*, its armament a newly installed Spanish-American War three-pounder, had moved fifteen miles from Cavite to an anchorage near Corregidor, at the mouth of the bay. Ships were permitted to transit the mine field channel at the entrance to Manila Bay only by daylight. Not enough of that was left for the pitifully slow *Lanikai* to make it to open sea. The mine field was something of a joke, as the barnacle-clogged mines were largely inoperable. Still, orders were orders—and a mine might, if nudged, actually go off. Tolley's crew settled down to a supper "at sea," having been away from port all of three-and-a-half hours since hoisting sails and being towed clear by a tug. The reconnaissance into Indochinese waters would wait for dawn. In the gathering dusk they could see the lights of Corregidor popping on.

•

Churchill was up early at Chequers to draft a message to Bangkok. "There is a possibility," he warned Luang Phibun Songkhram, the Thai prime minister, "of imminent Japanese invasion of your country. If you are attacked, defend yourself. The preservation of the full independence and sovereignty of Thailand is a British interest, and we shall regard an attack on you as an attack on ourselves."

Almost simultaneously, the Japanese ambassador, Teiji Tsubogami, was assuring Japanese respect for the "independence, honor and sovereignty" of Thailand, but at a price that would empty the words of meaning. Whichever side the Thais invited in to protect it from the other, Thailand would be creating the conditions for counterresponse. Phibun would have to place his bets.

•

From Singapore the "1st degree of readiness" order ("Raffles") was sent north at 3:15 P.M. by the Green Line scrambler telephone. It meant that the off-again, on-again Matador operation was almost on. In torrential rain, troops of the 11th Indian Division prepared to move forward to the border, and across. The strategy was simple—seize Singora before the Japanese plucked it and occupy the narrow "Ledge" position at the neck of the peninsula, a high point from which to fire at invaders attempting to move into Malaya. On paper it looked simple, but to forestall the Japanese, operations had to be activated quickly.

While troops patiently stood to in the rain, Matador remained more submerged by politics than by weather. What if the Japanese fleet was a feint, to lure the British into Thailand as Ambassador Crosby in Bangkok feared? Would that commit the Thais to the Japanese side, after which the Japanese could occupy the country? Wet and frustrated, the 11th Indians waited while the generals and the politicians dithered Sunday away.

.

As the Malaya force's segments moved closer to landfall—now 120 miles north of Kota Bharu—the lead destroyer, *Uranami*, spotted an unexpected ship, and all hands braced for trouble. It was another Norwegian freighter. Sailors boarded it, forced the crew into lifeboats, and scuttled it. Even if not on a British intelligence mission, it had time to radio its distress. Little surprise seemed left.

With dusk approaching, the last fighters from the Kato Squadron hovered protectively over the convoy. Unwilling to risk other pilots without risking himself, Lieutenant Colonel Kato had ordered only senior officers on the final mission of the day, exchanging ceremonial cups of water with them and designating a major left behind as successor if that became necessary. Younger flyers protested being left behind. "Fools!" Kato snapped. "If we do not return, then indeed you will follow later. At least only wait until then."

In darkness and fog the Zeros wandered back separately. Unable to find the airstrip, several planes ran out of fuel and crashed into the bay. Kato managed to locate Phiquok Island and escaped with his life.

Moving to the southwest, the heavy cruiser *Chokai*, flagship for the operation, blinked a signal during a break in the rain: "The main business now is to proceed to Kota Bharu to cover the landing of the Takumi Detachment. Pray for the success of the disembarkation. Vice-Adm. [Jisaburo] Ozawa."

.

At 9:30 on Sunday morning, Rommel arrived at Crüwell's command post, just out of sight of the Libyan coast. "If the enemy was not beaten today," he put the matter as if he had not already ordered a disengagement after dark, "we would have to abandon the Tobruk front and go back to the Gazala position." Preliminary measures, he told Crüwell, had been taken the previous night. Gazala was on the Via Balbia, the coastal road west of Tobruk. Heavy artillery had been withdrawn, and the understrength Italian divisions had also been moved back. "The Sollum front," Rommel added, referring to a southern anchor, "would also have to be abandoned."

With forty tanks still serviceable, Afrika Korps was "to hold out today and keep the enemy off, and to counter-attack if the enemy pressed too hard. During the night it was to withdraw 30–35 km northwest." Crüwell, then, was to cover the retreat of the 90th Light Division as well as the Ariete, Pavia, Trieste, Brescia, and Trento divisions. The Italians, who had fought ineffectively, if at all, were to be rescued by a German rearguard.

•

At ten, Minoru Genda awoke from a Sunday evening nap in the noisy Operations Room of the *Akagi* due north of Oahu, and went on deck. Planes were being checked for the last time; mechanics gunned the engines, and in the darkness, flames darted from exhaust pipes. Genda walked to the ladder leading to the bridge and climbed up for a better view, the sea breeze across the flight deck flushing any last drowsiness from him. He felt cleansed of uncertainties about the Pearl Harbor mission—"as bright and clean as a stainless mirror." Regrets about not flying with Mitsuo Fuchida and the others vanished in the exhilaration of getting the operation going. Although only a commander, he had organized it. Once the planes took off, all decisions were his until the planes were again down.

On deck observing the tuning-up had been Commander Fuchida, the first-wave leader, also a mere commander among admirals. There was nothing left for him to do but to get some sleep. In the wardroom he advised the pilots still up to get some rest. Peeling off his own flying suit he made ready for bed, feeling, "I had set up the whole machinery of attack, and it was ready to go. There was no use worrying now." But he laid out for the flight—as did Lieutenant Shigeharu Murata, who would lead the dive bombers—red underwear and a red shirt to wear under his uniform. If they were wounded, they reasoned, the sight of their blood would not demoralize brother officers. Then, while other fliers, just in case, were writing farewell letters home, he slept soundly.

MALAYA	LENINGRAD	LONDON	PEARL HARBOR
3:40 P.M.	12:00 noon	10:00 A.M.	10:30 P.M.
December 7	December 7	December 7	December 6

Hour 21

WITH some of Rodrigo's forces below Leningrad surrounded, General Muñoz Grandes appealed to von Chappuis for permission to withdraw. The regiment's most forward troops, Muñoz warned, soon "would be dead, sacrificed to bombs, shells, tanks and crushing enemy infantry attacks." He would lose half his division, and perhaps even Novgorod, his southern pivot. He conjured up a picture of diminishing effectives that was worse than the precarious actual situation. With orders to remain in place, Chappuis sent Muñoz back. Still, he would order Rodrigo to begin the retreat at nine in the evening, and to keep it disciplined he told Esparza that any measure necessary, including summary execution, could be employed.

In preparation, troops began prying crosses out of the frozen graveyard that they had expected would be in their rear rather than abandoned to the enemy. A wry Eastern Front joke was that a wooden cross was easier to get than an iron cross.

Army Group North desperately needed winter quarters. In an order dated December 7, the 12th Infantry Division was ordered to evacuate within nine days all civilians along a six-mile-deep stretch parallel to the front. The dispossessed could take some food and goods, but their houses were either to be used for troops or burned to the ground. (A few weeks later II Corps admitted that civilians had been evicted "with entirely inadequate food supplies.") The homeless were to be prodded in the direction of the Russians; no one was to be concerned with what became of them.

The 18th Panzer Division ordered the arrest of any civilians of military age; these were to be sent to the rear for forced labor. The rest of the population was to be driven ruthlessly eastward, their livestock not needed by German troops destroyed and houses torched. A later order stipulating a "desert zone" recommended poisoning all abandoned wells with dead cattle.

Some villagers hid in the forests; a few of the very elderly were abandoned, the Germans assuming that, isolated and alone, they would not survive. At least once the price was high. Early one evening the Germans came to the village of Kurekino near the town of Velikiye-Luki, to the south of Lake Il'men, and became players in a snowy equivalent to Mikhail Ivanovitch Glinka's opera *Susinin*.

In the opera, Ivan Susinin is a peasant who volunteers to guide a group of foreign invaders through the marshland and leads them instead to their death. At Kurekino a German ski detachment was looking for a shortcut. Matvei Kuzmin, an eighty-six-year-old farmer, offered himself as guide. He had been too old to be of use to anyone and had been left behind. All through the night, so Vasili Rybakov wrote, "the old peasant led the enemy detachment in deep snow and through forests and ravines. Meanwhile his grandson Vasili found a Soviet unit and warned it of the danger. At daybreak Matvei Kuzmin led the German detachment into the open, where the Soviet troops had already laid an ambush. When the Hitlerites realized that the peasant had lead them into a trap, they killed him, but they met with severe retribution."

Below Klin, north of Moscow, *Assistenzarzt* Dr. Heinrich Haape had just learned that his leave was postponed. He had been authorized a Christmas trip to Duisburg, to celebrate his engagement to Martha Arazym, a young opera singer,* but conditions had changed drastically in only a few days. Earlier in the week the 6th (Bielefeld) Division of Westphalian Grenadiers, of Army Group Center, had expected to begin the final trek to Moscow. The front in their sector had congealed into a frozen stillness. Most of Haape's cases were men whose only winter garment was a woolen *Kopfschutzer*—"head protector." Frostbitten ears

---

* He would eventually marry her at long-distance, by proxy.

were rare, but the rest of the body was vulnerable to the cold. The farthest he had got from his own unit, in the falling snow that deadened the sound of their Mercedes, was to the 106th Division, astride the main road from Klin to Moscow, where he had gone with Oberleutnant Graf von Kageneck.

An occasional Wehrmacht signboard in code left them confident that they were in safe territory; riding in the tracks of two heavy trucks made driving easy. Huge propaganda signboards with the usual slogans and pictures of Stalin and Lenin remained, but most of the wooden buildings were flattened. For a while it seemed that they could drive, unhampered, right to Red Square. At a regimental command post they encountered two officers wearing precious heavy leather coats. Observing the Bielefeld divisional crest on the car, out of place in the zone, one of the officers, his rank concealed under the coat, asked, "Well, where are you off to?"

"To Moscow," Kageneck had said.

"That's where we're going, too," said the taller of the pair. "Perhaps you'd better wait for us."

Haape wondered where they were, explaining that they had "got off our track."

"Quite simple," said the plump officer, pointing with a leather glove. "A little to the left of us are the Russians, and directly ahead of us—over there—is the train station for Moscow. If the tram hadn't been put out of commission by the carelessness of our soldiers you could have had a free ride into Moscow. It's only ten miles away. But if I were you I wouldn't try to follow the tram lines in your car."

They exchanged information. Haape bragged of only one serious case of frostbite; the officers of the 106th admitted to 25 percent casualties from the cold, and no winter clothing for the ranks. Their men, though, were "behaving magnificently. They're thinking of one thing—taking Moscow . . . and having warm winter quarters. To them . . . the fall of Moscow means the end of the war."

"One more jump and we shall be there," the tall officer said. ". . . Surely we can't be denied it now."

Close by was the abandoned trolley station, beyond which the telegraph poles pointed toward Moscow. "Let's walk across and have a look," Kageneck urged. "Then we can tell [Major] Neuhoff that we were only a tram ride from Moscow."

The wooden benches in the waiting room were empty. Rummaging in a wooden bin, Haape pulled out a fistful of tickets marked, in Cyrillic, MOSKVA. Finding no other souvenirs, they left for their car, trudging through a curtain of snow to the west. "It must fall," Kageneck mused, thinking of the destination on the tickets, "yet I wonder . . ."

They had returned on the night of the 5th—St. Nicholas's Eve— and Haape was to set off on his leave on the 8th. In the commandeered building that was the officers' mess, Haape and Kageneck laid out bottles of cognac secured from a Luftwaffe unit—Kageneck's brother was a Luftwaffe ace, with seventy aircraft kills claimed. A fire blazed in the open hearth. Outside, *Leutnant* Stolze, just back from the hospital, warned, it was −35°C (−31°F). "Even the Wehrmacht report [for the day] no longer talks about the encirclement of Moscow."

"On the thermometer," Haape confirmed, "you can read how the attack on Moscow is going."

"Exactly."

It hadn't seemed so to Haape in the tram station, but on the morning of the 7th, with the leave cancellation in his hands, he knew it was true.

•

In Berlin, Joseph Goebbels's ministerial conference went on as usual on Sunday morning. At the Reich Ministry for Propaganda, he had gathered his deputies for radio, film, the press, army and party propagandists, and upper administrators without portfolio, to listen to a predictable monologue and a dispensing of decrees. The minutes for the 7th note that the minister dressed down his aides—who had been scrupulously following his orders—for withholding "all unpleasant news." Germans had become "over-sensitive about any possible temporary reverses."

The public, said Goebbels, never embarrassed by contradictions, always knew more than emerged from official bulletins, and could take what he called "unpalatable truths." (One he could not bring himself to mention was his press directive of November 18, declaring that the Wehrmacht in the East had already been supplied with winter clothing.) It was all right to note, he explained, that "the overall situation"— he meant Russia—ruled out sending Christmas presents to troops, or Christmas leaves. There were transportation constraints that "are expected to last, not just a few days, but some length of time."

Churchill, not normally singled out for Nazi praise, "did the right thing," Goebbels observed, when he promised the British "blood, toil, tears, and sweat." Nevertheless, the Reichsminister reminded his functionaries, "justified optimism about the outcome of the war" had to prevail.

The major propaganda problem, in his view, was "how the resistance of the Russian troops and the Russian population should be explained." His solution was to emphasize that Russians were more used to hardship than Germans, just as in the earlier phase of the war the Germans were tougher than the French. More "inner superiority" was now required of Germans. It was not a directive he would have anticipated a few days earlier.

As usual he asked whether there were any questions, but it was only a formula to end the session. There were never what Goebbels himself described as "awkward discussions."

•

Early on Sunday morning, Churchill's military chiefs gathered in the War Room below Whitehall. The question remained whether a waiting game would give too many initial advantages to Japan. Did they have the capacity to interdict the Gulf of Siam strike force well out to sea? The troop transports would be most vulnerable in any case once anchored offshore. The chiefs—Dudley Pound, Charles Portal, and Alan Brooke—minuted to Churchill their consensus not to fire the first shot if it would be represented by isolationists in America "as a deliberate attempt on our part to drag them into a British war." Yet—it seemed a contradiction—they also wanted assurances of "U.S. armed support."

From Chequers, Churchill telephoned that he and the President had agreed that if the invasion force seemed about to invade Thailand, Britain "should obviously attack Japanese transports," but not move ground troops in unless a landing had taken place. This upgraded the promise of "armed support" effective only for Malaya. Roosevelt was to make the pledge publicly on December 10, a date he may have chosen because whatever was going to happen in the Gulf of Siam would have happened by then anyway. Still, Churchill would telegraph to General Auchinleck in Egypt later in the day, "This is an immense relief as I had long dreaded being at war with Japan without or before the United States. Now I think it is right." If the U.S. came to Britain's aid and were attacked by the Japanese, all would be well—except that the Japanese would have landed. The Prime Minister was willing to pay that price. Even the temporary loss of Malaya was a cheap investment if it would make America a full ally.

•

As Saturday darkness fell, some routine work went on at Pearl Harbor; a few ships went in and out on patrol and work in the dry docks continued under lights. Eight battleships were moored snugly in pairs off Ford Island; most of their crews were ashore on passes. At Army airfields, planes were clustered equally snugly, to guard against possible sabotage. At the Bloch Center near the main Pearl Harbor gate a "Battle of Bands" attracted crewmen from the fleet, especially from the *Arizona, Argonne, Detroit, Pennsylvania*, and *Tennessee*, whose bandsmen were performing. The Center was new, an enlisted men's mecca for beer, boxing competitions, pool-shooting, jukeboxes, and visiting entertainers. For men who remained near their bases, service clubs at Hickam, Kaneohe, Schofield, Wheeler, DeRussy, and Ruger were jumping with music and the noise of slot machines and clinking glasses. Near the harbor under neon lights, the bars of Pearl City overflowed with sailors drinking the night away.

For Ed Sheehan, a Pearl Harbor ironworker who had come from Malden, Massachusetts, the year before looking for a job, Saturday evening meant work. In Dry Dock One, the destroyer *Downes* was being refitted. Neatly cut rectangular openings in her hull awaited new plates, and Sheehan had been given the swing shift to speed up the repairs. On the dry dock floor with the *Downes* was the *Cassin*, the next assignment; and behind them soared the bulk of the battleship *Pennsylvania*.

When Sheehan returned from supper, lights were glowing in the huge concrete chamber; cranes lowered plates to be hung on the *Downes*. "We fought [the plates] into place with crowbars and sledge-hammer blows. Welders made blinding contact, and bright streams of molten metal cascaded down to bounce off the dry dock floor. The intense blue-white light sent great shadows dancing on the dock's walls." When the heat and haze became oppressive, Sheehan slipped inside the *Downes* to cadge some coffee. (Crewmen remained aboard ships in dry dock: whatever housekeeping functions could be maintained were carried on.)

A chief bosun's mate was on duty; Sheehan joined him to share "a thick brew." Since Christmas cards had a long haul to the States, the sailor was keeping busy addressing a batch—"with troubled pauses" because "he was writing the same goddam thing on the goddam cards" and was searching for something new to say. (Sheehan taught him to spell *Mele Kalikimaka*—"Merry Christmas" in Hawaiian.) When the fumes from the heated galvanized iron seeped into their compartment, they took the coffee mugs topside for fresher air, and the chief exchanged merry obscenities with a friend on the nearly dark *Cassin*.

They could also see workmen sandblasting the crusted bottom of the *Pennsylvania*. Its spade-shaped bow loomed over their heads. Beyond the dry dock the lights of the cruiser *Helena* glistened at Ten-Ten Dock. "Off Ford Island we could see twinklings from the *Avocet*, *Neosho* and *California*, and beyond, the beady lights of other battleships. The destroyer *Shaw* and tug *Sotoyomo* presented only a small scattering of lights in the floating drydock. The chief said the whole fleet was in, except he hadn't seen any carriers lately. It was a lovely night, . . . air turning cool as time moved toward midnight. We went back below."

HONG KONG	MALAYA	MOSCOW	GERMANY
6:00 P.M.	4:40 P.M.	1:00 P.M.	11:00 A.M.
December 7	December 7	December 7	December 7

HOUR 22

BY NIGHTFALL, General Maltby had his Mainland Brigade of Royal Scots, Punjabis, and Rajputs in their positions along the Hong Kong frontier, with Brigadier Cedric Wallis, who had long worked with Indian troops, commanding the Gin Drinkers Line below. Canadian Brigadier John K. Lawson was in charge of the island forces, British and Canadian infantrymen on the beaches and the slopes. Lawson knew he had insufficient troops and had persuaded Maltby to cable the War Office to ask that Canada furnish a third infantry battalion, as well as engineers and an ambulance unit. Only the day before, in London, the Dominions Office had been asked for more men.

Artilleryman Bob Yates of the Royal Scots had no illusions about reinforcements, or their value if they were there. "I personally knew we couldn't win. We were told there would be no Dunkirk. No relief. I wrote to my sister that I'd be dead or a POW by Christmas. We had two old destroyers. Old airplanes. The gun I was on was manufactured in 1902. Our rifles were First World War types—Enfields. I was twenty-four, stupid, prepared to die there, to fight to the last man."

At Fanling Golf Course, four miles below the frontier, G. A. ("Andy") Leiper, who worked for the Hong Kong branch of the Chartered Bank of India, and his friend Frank Harrison, were walking toward the tenth tee, followed by Chinese caddies. Leiper wondered aloud what might be going on "over there" to the north. Whatever it was, it had kept players they had expected to encounter off the course. Almost everyone who golfed there was a member of the Volunteer Defence Corps; many had been called to duty that weekend. Caddies who normally thronged the clubhouse shop waiting for jobs were absent. "Caddies think more better stay at home today," the caddie-master confided.

At the tenth tee they turned back. "Finishee. *Faan hui*," Leiper said. With relief the caddies shouldered the bags and trudged off.

For a Sunday the clubhouse was deserted. A few men were eating a cold lunch; others were hunched over drinks at the bar. Leiper asked whether there had been "any developments" in the two hours they had been out. "Nothing official," said a man at the table. "There's a hell of a lot going on amongst our own military, and the Armoured Car Company of the Volunteers is supposed to be near Shatin.* Also plenty of the usual rumours that the Japanese are massing in the villages just over the border. Altogether we think it's a good idea to push off home."

Leiper and Harrison were having lunch and a drink when a waiter ("boy") called Leiper to the telephone. Mobilization was on. Volunteers would get preference for ferry crossings. The word was to be passed quietly.

At 2:30 David Bosanquet left the eighteenth green and headed for the clubhouse bar. "I remember thinking how good a couple of gins would be . . . and wondering why there was so much activity outside. . . . Many people were leaving hurriedly. . . ." On the door was a large notice which read: "ALL VOLUNTEERS MOBILIZED. REPORT TO HEAD-QUARTERS BY 16.30 HOURS." He had little sleep the night before, and was decidedly unready for duty.

The night before had been active enough. Bosanquet had played rugger for a club team against the Army. It was a Saturday off from Jardine Matheson, where he had worked his way up to £400 a year, on which one could live in many-servant splendor in Hong Kong. But at a dinner dance at the Gunner Officers' Mess at Lyemun, at mid-Peak, he had been handed an urgent message to get business documents aboard the *Yu Sang*, which was to sail in two hours. Taking his girl-

* Southeast of Fanling, north of Kowloon Tong.

friend, he raced for his office keys, and then for the papers lodged in the firm's safe. Arthur Piercy of the Shanghai office was taking them to India via Manila.

There were mad dashes in Bosanquet's Ford, a ferry ride to Kowloon, a dash to the *Yu Sang*'s wharf, drinks on board with Piercy, and an improvised ride back. Bosanquet's girlfriend was brought home, still in high heels and long dress, hobbling up to the Peak in the first light of dawn.*

At 9:00 A.M., after a few hours of Sunday morning sleep, Bosanquet had teed off at Fanling. At 6:30 P.M. Sergeant David Bosanquet, 5th AA Battery, Hong Kong Volunteer Defence Corps, would report for duty, two hours late.

Above Fanling, a VDC group huddled on Sunday afternoon maneuvers, instructed by Middlesexer Captain Mickey Mann. Showing them how to sight indirectly, Mann held a rifle and mirror and gazed into it across the emptiness toward the frontier, suddenly seeing something that caused him to exclaim, Arthur Gomez remembered, "My God! The situation is serious!" They did not press for an explanation. At sunset the volunteers were trucked back to Kowloon, dirty and tired. Eager for a bath, Leo Landau found a notice tacked to his door summoning him to duty. He went "straight out to our gun," a shore battery on Cape D'Aguilar.

Ten minutes after Leiper had been warned to leave quickly and quietly, the clubhouse was empty and a queue of cars was snaking its way southward to Jordan Road and the car ferry in Kowloon. The dock area resembled an overturned anthill. A large board nailed to two uprights announced, in white block letters, "VOLUNTEERS, NURSING AND OTHER SERVICES. THIS WAY."

A professor at the University of Hong Kong, Robert K. M. Simpson had played Fanling earlier and left on his own, frustrated by messages recalling his partners to their units, "literally from the first tee." A reserve officer himself, he "knew that such alarms and excursions need not mean anything serious. Yet on the way back to the ferry his party "met a good deal of military traffic, troops and lorries, moving

---

* The *Yu Sang* would be sunk by Japanese bombs in Manila harbor, with the documents still aboard. Arthur Piercy waited out the war in prison camp, suffering what Bosanquet described as "dreadful privations."

forward towards the frontier through the dusk." Just as he entered his house, the phone rang—a message from Headquarters asking "whether I'd be free on Monday to take part in a 'morning exercise.' "

He had to oversee his half-yearly examinations, he explained. He could "come along after nine if really necessary." On the other end of the line the officer said that he might ring again in the morning.

A constable had redirected Leiper and Harrison into the Volunteers priority queue. They bumped their way to the loading stage, boarded, and on the Hong Kong side checked in at VDC headquarters near the Star Ferry docks. There Leiper learned that his company was mobilizing at 10:00 A.M. on Monday, also that his bank had asked for an exemption for him, as head of the Cash Department. A run was anticipated when they opened in the morning.

Once home with his wife, Helen, he began to pack valuables away and discuss what else had to be done. Helen had been permitted to remain in Hong Kong as an auxiliary nurse. Neither might be home for days at a time, if ever. Their three Chinese servants would almost certainly disappear. Helen burst into tears.

They called on a friend who was veterinarian at the Jockey Club and asked him to "put down" their two dogs.

·

At 5:00 P.M. on December 7, the trading firm of Echigoya and Co., Ltd., at 131 Middle Road, Singapore, shut its doors. On October 25 the British administration had begun curtailing the operations of Japanese businesses, and Kurahachi Fukuda and his associates had no option but to return to Japan. Closing "until further notice" was set for December 9, and an announcement appeared in the *Straits Times* and the *Singapore Nippo* on December 5. On Monday they would sail for Japan via Bangkok.

Throughout Sunday they moved their merchandise from the ground-floor shop to the third floor. "All the day along," Fukuda wrote in his diary, "keeping all the stocks in good condition and have asked Mr. J. C. Cobbett to inspect the firm before the closing." Cobbett certified "the condition of our firm," and at 5:30, at a meeting of stockholders, Cobbett was appointed alternate director with C. V. Miles. The entire group adjourned to a jolly dinner at the Southern Restaurant, all still good friends.

•

Flying in to confer with General Guderian east of Orel was Lieutenant General Lothar Freiherr von Richthofen, commander of the only air force on the Russian front left to Army Group Center. Most of Air Fleet 2, commanded by Field Marshal Albert Kesselring, had been transferred to North Africa, to support the hard-pressed Afrika Korps. "We had a long conversation together and discovered that we agree on the general situation," Guderian confided to his wife, who would understand what he had written between the lines. "I also talked to General [Rudolf] Schmidt, who is in the same position as myself and who commands the army on my right. He too shares my views."

Whether the Führer also did they had yet to discover, but they assumed the worst. General von Brauchitsch used the daily conference at Wolfschanze to tell Hitler that he contemplated retiring for reasons of health. Others were now suggesting at least limited withdrawals, but when Keitel claimed that he needed to rest and rehabilitate the army before offensive operations could be resumed in better weather, Hitler called him a moron. Jodl intervened to prevent Keitel from saying something intemperate. "I was the one who always had to suffer and make good the consequences," Keitel complained, "of each . . . crisis of confidence. Gradually I was becoming fed up with being the target of everyone's obloquy, as though I was to blame every time Hitler found that the face of this or that general did not fit any more." Afterward, Jodl talked Keitel out of a threat to commit suicide that seemed lacking in seriousness anyway.

By afternoon, von Leeb had telephoned to Hitler several times about his difficulties. "Very tight situation at Tikhvin," Halder noted. Von Leeb's Army Group North "thinks it cannot hold the town and is preparing to return to a defensive position. . . . In the Ladoga sector, enemy reinforcements have apparently been arriving from across the [frozen] lake. Violent attacks at Leningrad."

Persuaded that there were no practical alternatives to evacuating Tikhvin, Hitler ordered the salient "eliminated." The previous day Halder had reported "serious thinking about Tikhvin," but no solution. Now Hitler had solved the problem on his own, approving small-scale adjustments which would not lead to a wholesale deterioration of the German position. The Führer, Halder noted, was leaving local commanders "freedom of decision." Von Bock was "given a free hand" after his telephoned pleas from Army Group Center about the Moscow situation. In the north, "von Leeb must not withdraw further than artillery range from Tikhvin," to keep the relinquished area useless to the Soviets.

"The occurrences of the day," Halder mourned, "have again been heartbreaking and humiliating. Headquarters is now no more than a messenger boy, if that much. The Führer, over the head of Supreme Headquarters, gets in direct touch with the commanders of Army Groups. But worst of all, the Supreme Command"—his careful allusion to Hitler alone—"does not realize the condition our troops are in and indulges in paltry patchwork where only big decisions could help."

Although Halder wanted Hitler to concede to a withdrawal from precarious positions around Moscow just as he had grudgingly permitted a fallback below Leningrad, Hitler found new reasons to hesitate. After all, the head of military rail transport had reported that although the railroad situation had been "aggravated . . . due to technical failures from frost," there was "no cause for anxiety." Halder was anxious anyway.

•

Vera Inber, a poet and wife of a prominent Moscow physician, had come with her husband, Ilya Davidovich Strashun, to work in the north just before Leningrad had been cut off. In midafternoon twilight the dwindling electricity was just enough to illuminate the white-columned Philharmonic Hall for its Sunday concert, an element of strained normality in the ghostly city. The matinée had been canceled the previous Sunday "in view of a strong artillery bombardment." Her husband had a few hours off from duty at Erisman Hospital, where the frozen dead were piled up "like cordwood," and for whom there was no wood for coffins. She had seen "a corpse on a small sleigh. . . . It was wrapped in a white shroud, and the knees were clearly discernible; the sheet was bound tightly round. . . . The shape of a human form was clear enough, but one couldn't tell whether it was of a man or a woman. It had become merely a body belonging to earth."

The concert hall was "increasingly somber and hellishly cold. The chandeliers burn only a quarter of their power. Some members of the orchestra wear quilted jackets and some wear half-length sheepskin coats. As violinists need to keep their hands and arms free, and the cellists even more so, they wear . . . quilted coats. The double basses can wear sheepskin coats, as their movements are directed downward." For the Tchaikovsky *Overture 1812* and the Beethoven *Fifth Symphony* the drummer "has the best of it. He warms himself by striking blows on his drums." Most difficult for the dwindling orchestra—it was the radio ensemble, as the Symphony had been evacuated to Novosibirsk— were the demands upon the wind instrumentalists. In near-starvation, as Radio Leningrad broadcaster Olga Bergholtz realized, they "had nothing to strain their diaphragms against." Determinedly in tailcoat, Karl Eliasberg, the conductor, Vera Inber noticed, "was badly shaven. Probably he lacked the means to heat up water or had no light to see by."

•

At the prisoner-of-war camp at Elbersdorf, near Kassel, Ian Campbell, once a battalion commander and a future general, went to Sunday morning prayers. "One could not help wondering a bit at the nature of things," he wrote in his diary, "when sitting in church looking through the windows and observing the very religious local inhabitants, with the men wearing tall black top hats, walking to their local church. Both parties praying that their side would win the war." His group had no "canary"—no smuggled radio—and looked forward to leaving church at lunch hour to watch for friends imprisoned "in the castle above us" who signaled "the canary's news" by Morse code while their guards were having lunch. At a window they would raise and lower a towel ("shorts and longs") to relay what the BBC had to say. The next occasion would be a busy one for the towel.

•

Anthony Eden left at ten o'clock for his meeting point with the mission to Russia. At the door to say good-bye was John Winant, who had spent the night at the Edens' but with only a few hours' sleep. Eden urged him to go back to bed. "I told him no," Winant wrote; ". . . I wanted to go to Chequers to see the Prime Minister. . . . I thought the Japanese were on the road to war. Whom, when, and where they were going to attack I said I did not know; but . . . I thought it would be soon, and wanted to be with Churchill."

Eden expressed his own concern about going away at a moment when his country "was in for trouble," but he was expected in Moscow. Winant left soon after. Chequers was a hundred miles away.

•

Everything had gone according to schedule at the Foreign Ministry in Tokyo, with the fourteenth part of the *saigo no tsukoku*—the final notification—sent out, for safety, on two circuits, at five in the evening via Mackay Radio (MKY), and at six via RCA. Then at 6:28, and at 6:30, an additional message went out, again via two circuits, to instruct Nomura and Kurusu on the exact delivery time to Secretary Hull. But within the hour two mistakes were found. A line had been omitted in the delivery note, and a key word in the third paragraph had been mistranslated into English. Correcting cables on both circuits followed, and lights in the Foreign Ministry finally went out. It was 5:20 A.M. in Washington.

•

Through a break in the clouds a Hudson bomber located the largest element of the Japanese force closing in on Kota Bharu. The Hudson slipped away, then returned, and at 5:25 P.M. the busy *Uranami* opened fire, driving the plane away from any closer contact with the transports. An alert again went to Singapore, followed by another, thirty-five minutes later, from a second Australian Hudson, reporting small convoys now sixty-five miles offshore and heading south. More than an hour would pass before the telephoned messages reached Brooke-Popham.

Returning just before dark to the Operations Room at the Kota Bharu airbase, RAAF Flight Lieutenant John Lockwood declared cockily, "I am the first to be fired at in this war!" Flying Officer Donald Dowie, the observer in the second Hudson, described the armada as in the form of a T, with naval vessels forward and the transports behind. "Very impressive," he recalled, ". . . like a giant scorpion in the water."

A Japanese account glorified the voyage in Hollywood fashion; Ryuichi Yokoyama wrote, "The escorts of our warships in formation on both flanks kicking up surging waves, and our airplanes circling above, with the Rising Sun glistening on their wings, presented a very spectacular panorama of the great overseas operation." The description may have fit better weather as they set out. As they approached the

Kra coast, thick clouds and heavy rain forced the Hudsons shadowing the ships to fly at two hundred feet above the water for the final fifty miles.

•

At the naval base in Singapore, Admiral Sir Geoffrey Layton and Lady Layton were entertaining the Thomases for Sunday tea. General Percival had just reported to Sir Shenton (so the governor noted in his diary) "that one Japanese ship has fired on a reconnaissance aircraft of ours." That hardly seemed sufficient reason to deprive Daisy Thomas and himself of the fluid that bonded the Empire. From the base the *Prince of Wales* and *Repulse* were an imposing sight against the unbroken blue sky.

MANILA	PARIS	WASHINGTON	PEARL HARBOR
HONG KONG	BERLIN	NEW YORK	12:30 A.M.
7:00 P.M.	BELGRADE	6:00 A.M.	December 7
December 7	12:00 noon	December 7	
	December 7		

HOUR 23

O UT OF ST. LOUIS via Shanghai, Emily Hahn was a thirty-five-year-old free-lance writer who had taught geology at Hunter College and worked for the Red Cross in the Belgian Congo. In Hong Kong she was writing a life of the famous Soong sisters. One was Madame Chiang Kaishek; another was married to the multimillionaire banker H. H. Kung. The third was the widow of Sun Yatsen. As an American, "Mickey" Hahn had escaped the edict that had sent most British women packing. "Go to Australia?" she quoted them as objecting. "Do you know how difficult it is to get maids in Australia, or cooks? Who's going to help me with Baby? Why do I have to go if those Eurasian women can stay? Why must I go and leave my husband free to play around with Chinese tarts? What about my house? Why, this is my home!! If I were living in England would you make me go away, just because there's danger of an invasion from the Germans? And who says we are in danger here anyway? Didn't you say you could manage those silly little Japs?"

And the husbands complained, Miss Hahn went on, "Who's going to pay the expenses of double households for me? Can you guarantee that my wife will behave herself? There's a law . . ."

Some women had remained by signing on as "essential war workers," usually as nurses to be called up in an emergency that most saw as remote. Others merely evaded regulations by pulling strings, or by leaving, then slipping back. Emily Hahn had a special problem. She had just given birth to Major Charles Boxer's child. And he was married to someone else, to a lady who had been evacuated unwillingly to safer Singapore.

A Sandhurst product and East Asia expert who knew Portuguese, Chinese, and Japanese, Boxer was on the Army Intelligence Staff. Intending to stay with him, Emily signed up for "essential service" through the good offices of her friend Hilda Selwyn-Clarke. Hilda's husband, known on the Peak as "Septic Clarke," was chief of medical services for the island. Emily arranged that she and the baby, Carola, would move in with the Selwyn-Clarkes if war came. "Red Hilda" was a socialist unbothered about such bourgeois niceties as a marriage license. "The minute it strikes," Hilda had assured Charles Boxer, "I'll come down and pick her up with the baby."

On Sunday evening Charles and Emily had friends in for cocktails at Charles's flat halfway up the Peak—for propriety Boxer kept his separate domicile. Two evenings earlier, over drinks, he told Maya Rodeivitch, a photographer, and Colin MacDonald of *The Times*, he had been at a dinner party across the frontier at Shumchun, given, so Emily described it, "by his old friend the [Japanese] general, out on the border of the New Territories." Boxer had practiced his Japanese, and nothing seemed unusual—obviously the reason for the invitation to a member of Maltby's intelligence staff.

Another guest was buxom, ebullient Australian journalist Dorothy Gordon Jenner, a former silent film actress who wrote as "Andrea" and, thanks to a successful face-lift, did not look her fifty winters. Emily Hahn recalled that the party "went on to a buffet supper, but none of us was really merry. Charles's uniform, and the fact that he sat at the radio most of the evening, had a dampening effect upon our spirits." Even more dampening, according to Dorothy Jenner, was that when the vanilla soufflé came round for second helpings, and she refused, contending that she'd eaten enough, Boxer advised, "You'd better take some more. You never know when you will next be offered vanilla soufflé." And so she did, remembering the words often in Stanley Camp, where her ample figure shrank over three and a half years to eighty pounds.

•

On the evening of November 27, Major Joe R. Sherr of Radio Intelligence at Fort McKinley had been informed of suspected Japanese overflights of the Philippines. He was directed to look for unusual Japanese radio traffic; then a week later he was asked to examine what he was decoding for short messages from Tokyo ending—usually—with the English word "STOP." No explanation had come from Washington, only that such transcripts be radioed urgently to the U.S.

At about sunset on Sunday Tokyo began sending such signals and Sherr's code room intercepted "twenty-five or thirty" similar messages going to diplomatic offices worldwide. Lieutenant Howard W. Brown took the first message to Fort Santiago for transmission to Washington. While he was away, Sherr translated the full text. It was only, Brown remembered, "that a couple of Jap officials had been shifted to other positions STOP." It seemed unimportant.

At the officers' club at the Army's Sternberg Hospital in Manila, dietician Ruby F. Motley sat over drinks with a colonel who was "down in the dumps."

"It's here, practically," he said. "Jap planes were flying over today." He meant the early hours of the morning, in darkness. Miss Motley professed surprise that it was "so close."

•

Although Yugoslavia had been dismembered into satellites and fiefdoms, subservience to the occupiers existed largely in official accounts. A civil war in the resistance split Right from Left, each side publishing newspapers, maintaining a command structure complete to uniforms and insignia, and receiving assistance from abroad. Josip Broz "Tito" had needed all the support he could get from Moscow to keep his men active. In the mountains of southern Serbia and Montenegro, the first snow and sleet of winter had fallen on December 4. Three days earlier, poorly trained and equipped Montenegrins had attacked Plevlja, held by Italians, penetrating to the town square before being driven out. They had lost three hundred dead and twice as many wounded, bringing charges from Draza Mihailovic's allegedly counterrevolutionary Chetniks of imprudence, especially after Tito released

German prisoners only to find that his own men held captive by the Germans were shot.

Hanging on into the weekend, Tito began a series of meetings in partisan headquarters in Drenovo, a village where a cook and a cow were kept to supply him with something better than mere rations. Communist equality had its limits. Before noon, survivors of the Plevlja fiasco were gathered by Milovan Djilas, Tito's aide, to offer the Montenegrins the option of going home. All refused, the session ending abruptly, Vladimir Dedijer wrote in his diary, when Italian occupation troops, who usually avoided the hinterland, came to try to "rescue" a truck seized the day before. Chasing the Italians off delayed the start of Tito's "Central Committee" meeting, which he was planning to chair himself, but it gave the partisans their resistance accomplishment of the week.

·

When his personal train, code-named *Asia*, stopped at a station in the Rhineland just after noon, Reichsmarschall Hermann Göring telephoned to Hitler at Wolfschanze. Göring had noted in his diary for the 6th "visits to art dealers and shopping" in Amsterdam, where, in a bemedaled and tentlike white uniform jacket, he toured collections with his agent, Alois Miedl, a Munich merchant who kept an office in occupied Holland for such purposes.

Asia included lounge cars with plush upholstery and lush tapestries; a bedroom carriage with outsized bath for the outsized Göring; a barber shop, darkroom, theater, and even a mobile hospital. It had flat cars mounted with AA guns and others loaded with an assortment of the Reichsmarschall's vehicles, in case he wanted to take to the road—a Citroën, a six-wheeled Mercedes and a sportier one, and five American autos. Most important were the two freight cars which held the Luftwaffe chief's latest purchases, bought with cash on a Reichsbank order he approved personally. After all, he contemplated bequeathing his collection to the German people, an unwritten intention which made his blissful hours appropriating art at bargain prices, usually from confiscated Jewish collections, appear to him as crucial as if he were attending to the nation's crises in the East.

Before that, Göring had been in France, largely because his wife's couturier was there, and at Cartier's; yet he had also called upon Vichy officials, and at 26 Fighter Wing he inspected the "hot" new Focke-Wulf 190. Only after admiring his acquisitions back home at Carinhall would Göring visit Wolfschanze. Hitler understood his old comrade's priorities.

•

The Jews of "unoccupied" France were a little better off, for the moment, than those in the swath of the country, from Flanders to the Pyrenees, under German military authority. Sustaining the fiction of an almost-free nation with administrative unity across all of France, the Vichy government, under German pressure, used the anti-Semite Xavier Vallat, ironically its General Commissioner for Jewish Affairs, to negotiate a structure under which French Jews would handle their own concerns. Despite a few exceptions, Jews were gradually being deprived of the opportunity to do anything but menial work. They had already been barred from government posts and were not permitted to teach or to practice law, medicine, dentistry, or architecture. They could not be university students. In December came laws forbidding them to be midwives or pharmacists; next they would be kept from the stage. Vallat claimed that he was a surgeon, not a butcher, and was only cutting the canker of Judaism from the French soul.

Vallat was actually as anti-German as he was anti-Jewish. Early in 1942 the Germans would force the fifty-year-old former deputy, a one-legged, one-eyed veteran of the 1914–1918 war, out of his job, labeling him a *Judenschutzkommissar*—Commissioner for the Protection of the Jews. Still, in the first week of the second December under Nazi rule, Vallat was carefully following instructions from occupied Paris on how to render the Jewish population, freed from legal disabilities since Napoleon, more and more helpless. Few cared. Marshal Henri Philippe Petain received protests in silence. The Catholic church was in vocal support of applying Nazi racial edicts to France. As a bishop in Toulouse put it in a letter to heads of religious orders in his region, "The common good of the nation comes before that of the Jews." And a Jesuit publication, *Construire*, called the *Statut des Juifs* "a measure of moral purification."

The new law, promulgated November 29, had become effective December 2. The Union Générale des Israélites de France (UGIF) was to be an umbrella for Jewish communal, charitable, and religious organizations. It meant folding in the CCOJA—the Commission Central d'Oeuvres Juives d'Assistance, which dealt primarily with immigrant and refugee Jews. Having fled oppression earlier, they were now no better off than they had been.

Drafted with crafty ambiguity, the new law permitted Vichy to do, or veto, anything, and when the UGIF and CCOJA leaderships met on December 7 to merge into a new board, its members resisted Vallat's terms. William Oualid was instructed to draft the risky note to Commissioner Vallat stating their position. On the same day Vallat convened the Association des Rabbins Français, which was obstructive for unexpected reasons. Placing a religious ban on cooperation proved more Nazi than Vichy in effect, for refusing to do Vichy's bidding ended any way to protect, under an organizational cover, stateless refugee Jews. Many were already in concentration camps and would next be in Auschwitz. And it was French, rather than Jewish, chauvinism on the part of the rabbis that did all of them in, for the mandate most resisted was the blurring of legal distinctions between French and foreign Jews.

Vichy's diluted anti-Semitism identified a Jew as a person with three or more Jewish grandparents; the Nazi rule required only two. The rabbis were interested in French Jews; and Oualid's message to Vallat, who could only have laughed at its innocence, suggested that Franco-Jewish organizations should be given the leading role in Jewish affairs, and that the presidency of the UGIF go to a sitting president of an existing French organization. Such hierarchical minutiae were of no moment to Nazis and their collaborators, interested in meek acquiescence until efficient machinery was in place to remove all Jews. Fewer would be deported to death camps from the Vichy side of the demarcation line than the other, and fewer French Jews than stateless pawns, but that was only because the Germans would run out of time before they ran out of Jews.

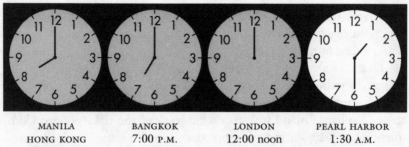

MANILA	BANGKOK	LONDON	PEARL HARBOR
HONG KONG	7:00 P.M.	12:00 noon	1:30 A.M.
8:00 P.M.	December 7	December 7	December 7
December 7			

Hour 24

S OME MYSTERIES of the 7th, turntable of the war, may always remain so, buried with their dead. Among them is the conversation Sunday evening, at a French restaurant on Dewey (now Roxas) Boulevard in Manila, between veteran foreign correspondent Karl von Wiegand of the Hearst newspapers and Rear Admiral William Glassford, former commander of the Yangtze Patrol. Its barely seaworthy ships, including his own flagship, the gunboat *Mindanao*, had abandoned China for safer havens. Glassford was again under the wing of Admiral Hart, and awaiting new assignment.

Von Wiegand had turned up on the last boat from Shanghai with his cosmopolitan assistant and companion, Lady Drummond-Hay, an attractive widow of forty-six. An old Asia hand with good German and Japanese connections, he was welcome everywhere and privy to information often planted with him to test advance reaction. Even Roosevelt had used him.

In Shanghai on October 17, von Wiegand claimed later, he ran into Glassford, whom he knew familiarly as Bill and classified as a "drawing room admiral" and favorite of the ladies in the International Concession. Von Wiegand had some inside information he couldn't print, he told Glassford. It is possible—yet improbable—that he had

been leaked information from Tokyo. There would be a mission to
Washington headed by Saburo Kurusu. If he failed to find an accommodation with Secretary Hull and President Roosevelt by November
26, American time, "War in the Pacific will begin any hour after midnight December 6."

In 1957, the foxy reporter, eighty-three years old and nearly blind
as a result of injuries received in an air raid on Manila soon after the
war began, also remembered the admiral's hinting to him that on Hart's
retirement Glassford might become the new commander of the Asiatic
fleet. Since there were only a few hours left to the 7th, von Wiegand
recalled to Glassford their conversation in Shanghai and ordered a
bottle of champagne "to drink to victory." Recognizing Japanese
strength and American weakness, he added when the cork popped,
"Let's drink to victory[,] but you have been given a suicide assignment.
You and our allies are so outnumbered you haven't a ghost of a chance."

Glassford remained so moody during the meal that Grace
Drummond-Hay whispered, "Karl, don't you think another bottle
would help to lift his spirits?" Von Wiegand nodded to a waiter, and
another bottle arrived.

"I wonder," said the admiral on parting, "if your information will
be correct."

.

When Francis Braun returned to the Arlington Hotel in Kowloon,
his abode for several years, the streets were already dark. In the lobby
someone was waiting—a policeman, with an arrest warrant.

"What on earth for?"

"Your country, Hungary, has declared war on Great Britain. You
are now an enemy alien and you are to be interned." Finland, Romania,
and Hungary had been allies of a sort to Germany and had sent troops
into Russia. Hitler had pressured them to acknowledge a state of war,
also, with Britain.

A mild-mannered employee of a printing company, with few interests other than the journal he published in Esperanto, Braun was
no danger to Hong Kong. He made his dinner, the policeman watching, packed a few essentials as well as his passport, and was escorted
to Stanley Prison.

Booking him, the prison clerk wondered, "Did you not know that
war was coming? Why didn't you leave?"

"Where to?" asked Braun. "This is my home."

His passport was exchanged for a registration card reading "F-13 European"—his block and cell number. The only internee whom he found he knew was Maurizio Sasso, the Italian former maître d' of the Hong Kong Hotel.

•

At 7:30 P.M. Bangkok time, Ambassador Teiji Tsubogami was announced at the Foreign Minister's residence. Forewarned, Chaiyanam Direk was waiting with the Thai police head, Detcharat Adun. With the utmost politeness, Tsubogami explained that Japan was about to declare war on Great Britain and the United States. Thailand was not an enemy, but Japan was "obliged by necessity" to request passage from Cambodia through Thai territory, by road and rail, to the Burmese and Malayan borders. Troopships were already offshore.

Its clocks set twenty minutes earlier than Thai time, Malaya was itself little more than five hours from invasion; Hawaii, across the Date Line where it was now after one, was six hours from attack. The government of Thailand—it had been Siam until June 1939, when the name had been abandoned as of foreign origin—was being advised not to contest an invasion.

Direk explained that although the Japanese government desired an immediate response, he could not give it. He had to consult with the Cabinet and the Regent. Besides, the premier, Field Marshal Phibun, was out of town. And Phibun had issued instructions that any infringements of Thai sovereignty from whatever side were to be resisted to the last man. They bowed to each other, and the ambassador departed, certain that the secret he had shared would not leap the borders of Thailand. Direk would later even deny that he had spoken to Tsubogami.

Phibun had already acquired a picture of Japanese plans from Colonel Tamura. Tamura's colleague, the consul general, Wannito Asada, had returned on December 1 from a quick trip to Japan with a secret document informing the embassy of the decision to make war on an unspecified "X-day." He had heard it was to be either the 5th or the 8th, only a few days away. It was up to Ambassador Tsubogami and his aides to secure Thai cooperation and end the temporizing by which the Thais had kept a precarious equilibrium between the British and the Japanese.

After some informal hints from Tamura, Phibun found himself trapped into condoning what seemed to him like a partial invasion, although that in reality was like being partly pregnant. "Should Japan start a war against Britain, it would . . . have to capture Singapore. To do this there is no other way but for you to pass through southern Thailand, so I have been thinking of averting my eyes from what happens south of Prachuab Kirikhan.* But I want you to avoid sending forces through the central plains because this would have its impact on Thailand's honor and dignity. Should you have to invade Burma, you will need to pass through central Thailand. However I would like you to postpone this until I have been able to get [the nation] prepared for it. To try to pass through by forcing us will certainly disgrace me before the people of Thailand."

After a second meeting with Phibun on the 4th, Tamura had reported to Tokyo that Thailand would cooperate if the central plains were respected. Meanwhile, still trying to have it both ways, Phibun had appealed to the British ambassador, Josiah Crosby. A Japanese invasion was imminent, yet might be headed off if London declared that an attack on Thailand meant war with Britain. A veteran of thirty years in Asia, the stout, amiable Crosby took seriously Phibun's desire not to let Thailand become the Poland of Asia. "I do believe," Crosby had told *Collier's* correspondent Frank Gervasi, "that we have sold the Thais the idea that they are to commit hara-kiri on behalf of the British Empire." Now he was no longer so smug. Phibun had disappeared from Bangkok, almost certainly to cover his preference for letting events happen without his having to take obvious sides. But the Japanese "proposal"—as Ambassador Tsubogami described it—was an ultimatum that expired at 2:30 A.M. local time on Monday.

Adun hurried to Suan Kulap Palace to have a message sent to Phibun on the border, imploring him to return quickly. Then Adun called an emergency cabinet meeting for eleven in the morning.

•

* A coastal town about a quarter of the distance toward the Malay border down the narrow Kra Isthmus shared by Burma, Thailand, and Malaya.

Early Sunday morning Churchill had sent to Roosevelt a draft of a message to the Japanese government, to follow up the White House appeal to Emperor Hirohito. A forwarding note asked for "any comments which the President may have." The "declaration" stressed that Britain had "no designs against Thailand" but that any attempt by Japan to impair Thailand's independence "would affect the security of Burma and Malaya and His Majesty's Government could not be indifferent to it. . . . Should hostilities unfortunately result the responsibility will rest with Japan."

At noon Ambassador Winant arrived by embassy auto at Chequers. He had last been at the Prime Minister's country house on the Sunday in June when news came that Hitler had invaded Russia.

Greeting him outside, Churchill asked, referring to Malaya, "Do you think the Japanese are going to attack?"

"Yes," said Winant.

Churchill paced back and forth in the driveway. "If they attack you," he added, "we will declare war. If they attack us, you declare war."

"I'm sorry, Mr. Prime Minister," Winant reminded, "but I can't guarantee this. Only Congress can declare war."

"Well," Churchill said, a riposte having evaded him, "let's go in and have lunch."

After lunch Churchill compensated as usual for his interrupted nights with an afternoon nap while Winant went for a walk in the placid country lanes.

TOKYO	MANILA	PARIS	PEARL HARBOR
10:00 P.M.	9:00 P.M.	2:00 P.M.	2:30 A.M.
December 7	December 7	December 7	December 7

HOUR 25

WAITING UNEASILY into the night for any scrap of news about the Roosevelt appeal to Hirohito, Ambassador Grew had kept his shortwave radio tuned to KGEI in San Francisco. Through static and wavering sound he picked up renewed confirmation that the President had indeed sent an urgent message to the Emperor. Yet only when the Japanese military decided that it was too late for the cable to be of any use was the triple-priority message from Cordell Hull delivered to the embassy, informing Grew that a telegram would follow which he was to deliver to the Emperor at the earliest possible moment. At 10:30 P.M. Roosevelt's message, ten hours delayed, finally arrived at the embassy. From its markings and stampings, Grew knew that it had been held up all day. Anger was useless. He asked his assistant, Counselor Eugene Dooman, to telephone the Foreign Minister.

To Togo's private secretary, Mr. Tomoda, Dooman explained the circumstances and asked that Togo meet with Grew. The time depended upon the decrypting of a telegram just received from Washington. The minister, Tomoda said, trying to spare his chief awkwardness, wished to retire as soon as possible. Perhaps Mr. Grew could call the following morning, a business day.

The ambassador would not think of disturbing Togo at such a late hour, and on a Sunday, Dooman apologized, had the matter not been one of such extreme urgency. Togo knew the date scheduled for hostilities to open. Little more than an hour remained before that calendar day began. He had protested ineffectively against giving the enemy no advance notice. Now the message from Washington could have no effect upon movements that were irreversible. He permitted Tomoda to make the appointment, but only if Grew could arrive before midnight.

In the American embassy, code clerks worked frantically, although the Japanese could have given them their own translation with the message.

•

On Sunday afternoon in Berlin, State Secretary von Weiszäcker gave his annual talk to German air attachés in Europe, a sparse audience of two dozen men, he noted, because there were fewer neutrals. He had no need to add that the numbers reflected fewer free nations. "I reminded the gentlemen," he wrote, "that in December 1940 I had to say as the view of the leading authorities in the Reich that the war was won, that it was only a matter of bringing England to admit its defeat." He thought that a concession from Churchill could still end the war, despite the new Russian situation, the possibility of which he admitted having "negated" at the previous December's meeting. Now he knew that they were in for a long war with Russia. "I tried to be as honest as possible. Yet that had its limits."

"Almost nothing useful comes to mind anymore," he admitted in his diary, "that my office could contribute to the war. We are still longer and more on the path of violence." And he recalled the "Berlin Congress" held the week before to bring the foreign ministers of Nazi satellite countries into the planning for reconstituting Europe. One delegate, the Bulgarian Foreign Minister, Ivan Popov, had told von Weiszäcker "openly" that such plans had to wait "until one knows the outcome of the war." The other diplomats, he noted ruefully, "were swindlers or swimmers too much for such an admission."

•

Colonel Bonner Fellers, American military observer in Egypt, had the run of Royal Air Force headquarters and was puzzling over a

```
67    434.02.02.10  06/28/93 11.02 1460
B.DALTON BOOKSELLER        PRESCOTT, AZ

  0517098792
                                  7.99
                 SUBTOTAL         7.99
                 SALES TAX        0.48
                 TOTAL            8.47
                 CASH             9.00


---------------THANK YOU---------------
```

prediction just offered. Air Chief Marshal Sir Arthur Tedder had greeted him with, "Bonner, you will be in the war in twenty-four hours. We have had a secret signal [that] Japan will strike the U.S. in twenty-four hours." When Fellers recalled the episode in 1967, it was without corroboration. But, he added, when he observed that it would not be in Japan's interest to gain a powerful enemy, Tedder declared that it was in Britain's interest, and he was happy about it.

Fellers thought of cabling to Washington, but assumed that the War Department had the same information. If he committed anything to paper, the Germans and Italians knew it. In September, Italian "black bag" operatives had quietly broken into the American embassy in Rome and photographed its code books. With the U.S. diplomatic code in the Mediterranean cracked,* Axis agents had been eavesdropping on Colonel Fellers, who was sending his information to Washington— and, it seemed, Berlin. In North Africa, as long as the colonel had the confidence of the British high command, Rommel received packets of military plans and directives which he described as "little fellers."

The British were just as successful in reading Italian plans, courtesy of their having solved "Ultra." From Bletchley, English analysts were identifying almost every ship sailing from Italian ports, and the mission of every Italian submarine. The foreknowledge did not prevent some embarrassing sinkings of British ships, but it had made it difficult to supply Rommel.

•

Marshal Cavallaro, meanwhile, was on another afternoon visit to Benito Mussolini's ballroom-sized office. No reinforcements had been moving by sea to Libya, but the German military attaché in Rome, General Hans von Rintelen, had promised fifty Junker transports which could fly from Brindisi (in the heel of the Italian boot) to Bardia. "I see the *Duce*," Cavallaro wrote in his diary. "I tell him that if we do not send

---

* Anti-Nazi lawyer-diplomat Helmuth von Moltke wrote to Lionel Curtis in England, in a letter never received because the Swedish intermediary feared it would endanger the sender, "We get highly confidential stuff from practically every British and much worse still every American legation or embassy. Probably your people repay us the compliment in tapping the stuff inside our own legations. . . ." The letter, dated March 23, 1943, did not compromise von Moltke but he was arrested later, anyway, and executed.

two divisions we will lose North Africa and if we lose Africa we lose the war. *Duce* agrees. Promises to telegraph the Führer right away."

The loss of more German planes from the Eastern Front would aggravate the already desperate supply situation in Russia.

•

Captain Ernst Jünger, forty-five, fourteen-times-wounded veteran of the 1915 trenches and author of the 1920s Western Front bestseller *In Stahlgewittern* ("Storm of Steel"), was spending his Sunday afternoon in Paris at his job of co-opting French intellectuals. It was almost too easy a task. The Deutsche Institut occupied the former Polish Embassy, an eighteenth-century mansion on the Rue Saint-Dominique. The name suggested cultural interchange; its mission was to enlist collaborators, which required little effort among rightist writers—some newly converted—who welcomed the Nazi supermen. Parisian fascists had changed little since the perjured trials of Captain Alfred Dreyfus two generations earlier.

Frenchmen on tight rations ate and drank enthusiastically at the Institute's soirees and signed up with the Propagandastaffel; unashamedly self-interested publishers, theater people, academics, and churchmen had few qualms about contributing a spurious respectability to the Occupation. More a pragmatist than a Hitlerite, Jünger appreciated the sleazy French Nazis far less than he did the fine French wines, especially champagne. He had already laid by a stock of Chambertin 1904 in case of reassignment.

Eager for Jünger's ear was Louis-Ferdinand Destouches, a physician who wrote novels as "Céline." His literary fame—at thirty-eight in 1932 he had published the influential *Voyage au bout de la nuit* ("Journey to the End of the Night")—made him a prize propaganda catch. Jünger despised him. "Tall, bony, strong," he described Céline, "yet lively in discussion or rather in his monologue. He speaks with the inwardly turned look of maniacs that shines as if from caves."

Céline's newest book, *Les Beaux Draps* ("A Fine Mess"), was a tract advocating the killing of anyone with "a single Jew among his grandparents." Too vicious even for the Vichy sector of France, it was banned there. "I have death always beside me," he boasted, and he pointed beside his chair, as if, Jünger thought, Death was a small puppy at his feet. Céline was astonished, he declared, even amazed, "that we soldiers do not shoot, hang, exterminate the Jews, . . . that somebody who has bayonets at his disposal does not make unlimited use of them." The Nazis could hardly have been accused of excessive kindness to French Jews, had long persecuted them economically and physically, and had seized thousands for deportation to an unknown fate in the East. To add to their misery a curfew was to go in effect the next day, at 6:00 P.M.; a hundred hostages were executed in reprisal for attacks on German soldiers; and a fine of a billion marks was imposed upon the Jewish community in France.

For Céline it was not enough. "If the Bolsheviks were in Paris, they would show you and teach you how one combs through the inhabitants quarter by quarter and house by house. If *I* had the bayonets, I would know what I would have to do."

"It was instructive," Jünger observed in his diary, "for me to hear him rage in that manner for two hours because the monstrous strength of nihilism shone through. Such people hear only *one* melody, yet this one uncommonly intensely." Céline was like "an iron machine" that could not be stopped until broken, perhaps like a specimen from the stone age. "When such men speak of science, of biology, for instance, . . . it becomes a mere means of killing others. Their happiness does not lie in having an idea. . . . They abandon themselves to the delight of killing."*

•

A special fast train left London at 1:00 P.M. to take Eden, Cadogan, Ambassador Ivan Maisky, and their party to Scotland to board a destroyer which would ferry them to Scapa Flow. In the Orkneys, to the stormy north, they were to be transferred to a powerful cruiser speedy enough at twenty-seven knots to evade a U-boat. Few at the Soviet embassy knew of the journey, but to shake off any possible informants, Maisky set off for a midday walk through nearby Kensington Gardens. It was a mild afternoon, but he had his warmest clothes on his back, including a yellow wool imitation fur coat. Weaving through Sunday strollers he ducked into the Queensway Underground station in his attention-getting garb and took a train to Euston Station, where the

---

* Two weeks after the Allied landings in Normandy in 1944, Céline fled into Germany. "Curious to see," Jünger observed, still enjoying his Parisian champagne, "how people capable of demanding the heads of millions of people in cold blood worry about their dirty little lives. The two facts must be connected." (Jünger hung on until Paris was evacuated, on August 14, 1944.)

delegation's unmarked express was waiting at a siding. He said good-bye to his wife and joined Anthony Eden in a carriage where the Air Ministry had thoughtfully delivered, in his size, a pair of pilot's fur-lined boots.

•

By eight o'clock on Sunday morning, Japanese embassy officials in Washington had located the disconsolate and sleepy Katsuzo Okamura and set him to work. He was familiar with an English-language type-writer and had diplomatic rank. By orders from Tokyo, low-clearance clerical staff could not be entrusted with what would become thirteen double-spaced typewritten pages for delivery to Cordell Hull. Con-ditions at the embassy were in disarray. The iron gate had been left unlocked overnight; milk bottles and the Sunday papers were on the doorstep and telegrams were stuffed in the mail slot. The few employees about had used a back entrance, and the Massachusetts Avenue frontage had an abandoned look. The farewells and departures and code-room chaos during the night of waiting had exacted its toll.

A messy two-fingered typist, Okamura was a secretary only in em-bassy administrative title. As he pecked away, an official higher-up proofread. Several pages had to be typed over again, and as Okamura labored over them a cable labeled "EXTREMELY URGENT" arrived by commercial telegraph, Tokyo assuming that the embassy may have already destroyed its receiving capacities. It was the final section of the long memorandum but not the final message, as minutes later cable 907, marked "EXTREMELY URGENT, VERY IMPORTANT," instructed No-mura and Kurusu to hand the fourteen-part response to Hull at one o'clock that afternoon, hardly a normal time to expect the Secretary of State to be in his office. Nomura had not yet seen it: it had not been deciphered. But Okamura was beginning to feel that he had won his bet about the *Tatuta Maru*.

Across the Potomac at Fort Myer, General Marshall arose to take his usual Sunday morning horseback ride—at a "pretty lively gait," he recalled—around the experimental farms now the site of the Pentagon. He was relieved to be alone and away from telephones and telegrams. It was a crisp, quiet morning.

•

In the spacious lobby of the Manila Hotel, officers in dress attire and fashionably gowned women—most of them Filipina since civilian

Americans had largely been evacuated—streamed in for one or another of the posh parties and dances of the evening. Gold-braided top brass gossiped under pillars and palms. At 9:45, Admiral Thomas C. Hart and his chief of staff, Rear Admiral William ("Speck") Purnell, returned to the hotel from nine holes at the Manila Golf Club at Caloocan, and an unscheduled several hours afterward at their offices in the Marsman Building. Hart had not been able to keep his mind on his game; they had left the fairways to follow up the latest bulletins. Hart ascended to his room while Purnell remained in the lobby chatting with new arrivals.

Hurrying in was Major General Lewis H. Brereton, MacArthur's nervous aviation chief, to whom Purnell passed along his freshest news. "In confidence"—so Brereton claimed in his diary—Purnell reported that Hart had received a warning of imminent war from Washington. Although Hart had not told him so, he believed that Hart and MacArthur were about to confer with High Commissioner Francis Sayre and even President Manuel Quezon. It was only a question "of days or perhaps hours," Purnell predicted, until the shooting began. (That the leadership should have been in conference was obvious, but MacArthur disliked Hart, distrusted Sayre, and was distant from his admirer, Quezon, who was weekending away.) All commanders, Purnell thought, would be briefed in the morning, when the new working week started.

The warning—if not an invention after the fact—failed to surprise Brereton. He had guessed that the Japanese might attack on the previous weekend, on the day of the annual Army-Navy football game. Officers in faraway places gathered at their Army or Navy clubs to listen to teletyped or radioed reports of the game's progress—a period of minimal alertness. With no attack the previous Sunday—Saturday in the U.S.—Brereton had pushed his war estimate forward, requesting permission from MacArthur to conduct photo reconnaissance over bases in Formosa (Taiwan) from which any assault on the Philippines might be expected. "In view of War Department instructions to avoid any overt act," MacArthur replied, denying the request, he was limiting flights to two-thirds the distance between northern Luzon and the coast of Formosa. MacArthur's actual orders from the War Department were less cautious than his interpretation. Negotiations with the Japanese, they confided, were, to all practical purposes,

TERMINATED. . . . HOSTILE ACTION POSSIBLE AT ANY MOMENT. . . . THE
UNITED STATES DESIRES THAT JAPAN COMMIT THE FIRST OVERT ACT.
THIS POLICY SHOULD NOT, REPEAT NOT, BE CONSTRUED AS RESTRICTING
YOU TO A COURSE OF ACTION THAT MIGHT JEOPARDIZE YOUR DEFENSE.

Even as he turned Brereton down, MacArthur knew that Iba Field
radar had picked up blips identified as "forces of strange aircraft estimated at 9 to 27 bombers," traced from Formosa to as close as twenty
miles off the Lingayen Gulf, an expected invasion point on northwestern Luzon. "Presumably," Brereton had written after four occasions of such flights, from just before dawn of the 30th through the
3rd, "they were making trial navigation flights to familiarize themselves
with the air route. Homing radio instruments could easily have been
tuned in on the Manila radio. . . . On the return flight to Formosa
these formations undoubtedly used their own Takao radio station."

At MacArthur's insistence, Brereton ordered sixteen—nearly half—
of his B-17s transferred to Del Monte Air Base on Mindanao, to the
south, but "in the event of hostilities" they were to return to Clark
Field, near Manila. On the 6th he cabled Washington that his planes
were "dispersed and each under guard" and that defenses were manned.
He had gone to Clark himself to check on the state of readiness.

Also in the Manila Hotel, Brereton saw MacArthur's lean, smartly
dressed chief of staff, Major General Richard K. Sutherland. They
shared Purnell's concerns. There might be war at any time. Brereton
telephoned his office. All fields and commands, he ordered, were to
go on "combat alert" as of daylight Monday morning. As for Sunday
night, however, the partying continued, the biggest of the bashes the
Twenty-Seventh Bombardment Group's party for Brereton himself. (It
goes unmentioned in his published diary.) Airmen and officers alike
were among the twelve hundred guests, the arrangements committee
having promised "the best [striptease] entertainment this side of
Minsky's."

Among the attendees were the seventeen Flying Fortress crews still
stationed at Clark Field, over which high-flying unidentified planes
had been traced that afternoon. In the penthouse upstairs, MacArthur,
no partygoer, kept his own counsel.

As the cream of the Air Corps danced and drank into the night,
eighty-five Japanese troop transports guarded by nearly as many warships were ferrying 43,000 soldiers of Lieutenant General Masaharu
Homma's 14th Army south in the darkness toward Luzon.

•

At 3:20 A.M. Honolulu time, cable 864, sent via RCA from the Foreign Office in Tokyo to Consul General Kita, was received in Hawaii and duly sent on in the waning darkness by bicycle messenger. It was in the simple OITE code. If the Americans intercepted it almost simultaneously it would have made no difference in the backlog of undecrypted messages picked off Japanese radio. The new cable, last that Kita would receive, read, "Relations strained between Japan and the United States and Britain." He understood that it meant imminent war, but despite all the work that Kita and his staff had done to enlighten Tokyo about American defenses on Oahu, he had been told nothing.

In Washington, where it was not quite nine on Sunday morning, few people would have fixed on Oahu as a target. The Naval Intelligence chief, Captain Wilkinson, had seen decrypts of numerous requests to Kita for Pearl Harbor data and assumed that when Tokyo posted on a grid nearly daily the positions of every American ship in port, and plotted the whereabouts of others at sea, Kita's superiors were interested in how quickly the Pacific Fleet could sortie from Oahu to interdict a Japanese move into Malaya or the Indies.

Arriving in his Navy Department office, Alwin Kramer found the decrypt of part fourteen of the Japanese message to Hull and went through its unhopeful language about the chances of promoting peace in the Pacific "through cooperation of the American Government" having now "finally been lost." In the last line came regrets "that in view of the attitude of the American Government" Japan had concluded "that it is impossible to reach an agreement through further negotiations."

Another message relating to the fourteen parts and intercepted by Navy Station "S" at Bainbridge Island four hours earlier was still being processed, but rather than wait for it, Kramer began preparing packets of what was ready for delivery to his distribution list. His superior, Commander Arthur McCollum, left to update Wilkinson. Shortly, all of them were in Stark's office. The language of the fourteenth part was stronger, they all agreed; it was "a confirmation," Stark ventured, that Japan was "likely to attack at any time in any direction." It appeared to end a diplomatic minuet, but no clear military significance emerged.

TOYKO
11:00 P.M.
December 7

TAIWAN
PHILIPPINES
10:00 P.M.
December 7

MOSCOW
LENINGRAD
5:00 P.M.
December 7

TOBRUK
3:00 P.M.
December 7

Hour 26

FREIHERR VON HEYL climbed out of his new bunker at five. Taking advantage of the fading early evening light, the Russians had begun attacking the village of Besborodowo, moving quietly across a frozen lake. Several clerks from a German administrative company lay dead. The command post at Mokschino was threatened; von Heyl moved toward it with his troops, finding a pioneer (work) platoon already pushed into combat to help, and even four antiaircraft guns pressed into ground service. One gun, and the house next to it, were burning. Nearby a pioneer sergeant had been killed. "His group is running around confusedly with a defective machine gun. With the radio truck I drive to the location of another anti-aircraft gun, see the Russians crawling down the hill on the left and fire at them properly. Furthermore, I send the pioneers back to their positions."

As the Russians broke into the northeastern edge of the village, two platoons of reinforcements arrived to help von Heyl, reoccupying what was left of Mokschino. The Moscow front was holding, shakily.

In his warm headquarters trailer, Field Marshal von Bock was setting down his explanation of why things had gone so wrong. First, the early onset of autumn mud (*Herbst-Schlammzeit*), which bogged down the advance even before the snows did. Second, the failure of the railway system to handle the huge volume of army needs before the beginning of winter. Third, he admitted, the gross underestimate of Russian resistance and of their personnel and materiel reserves. The Russians, he thought, better understood the problems of distance and supply, and had moved in fresh divisions and firepower from Siberia, the Caucasus, and the Iranian border. It was a war of numbers, of vast reaches of territory and vast accumulations of soldiers and equipment, and an error (*ein Irrtum*) to think of quick or easy success against such Russian advantages.

·

"I remember," Captain Michael Branch wrote, "we passed through an abandoned Eyetie position too hastily to spend time on looting the usual tins of tomato sauce, etc. It was an amazing sight, a bare black hillside with thousands of love-letters blowing everywhere in the strong wind. I just had time to scoop up one of those splendid Carabinieri hats with cock-comb feathers on it. . . . Not long afterwards we came to an unexpected escarpment about 100 feet high and apparently miles long, . . . and massive boulders the size of a room. We just had to get down it . . . but it was a hair-raising business finding a way where the guns and trucks would not overturn."

Among the papers picked up in the desert by the Australians was a laconic Italian diary abandoned by a soldier apparently from Milan, filled with primitive drawings. Almost every day's entry was "All's well that ends well"—including December 7, which began with *"Un grande bombardemento."*

The *Tobruk Truth* for the 7th featured the remarriage of the King of the Belgians, and Britain's declarations of war on Finland, Hungary, and Romania. Since most troops were too busy for leisure reading, the remote irrelevancies were exactly right.

·

Arriving at the Munitions Building on Independence Avenue at nine, Colonel Bratton mulled over the fourteenth part of the Tokyo memorandum with some of Marshall's aides. It was "one of the formalities," they agreed, on the road to war. "There was no military significance to its presence in Washington as long as the Japanese ambassador kept the note locked up in his safe."

When the activating cable, "Will the Ambassador please submit to the United States Government (if possible to the Secretary of State) our reply to the United States at 1:00 p.m. on the 7th, your time," was decoded, the long message suddenly took on ominous implications. The timing—a specified hour early on a Sunday afternoon—was unprecedented. Bratton was convinced that some American location in the Pacific was being targeted for attack, only a few hours away. In near panic, he went in search of superiors with authority to send a warning to someone, somewhere. But it was Sunday morning.

Calling Marshall's quarters at Fort Myer, Bratton found that the general was still out riding. He urged Marshall's orderly to find him and ask him "to go to the nearest telephone, that it is vitally important that I communicate with him at the earliest practicable moment." Then Bratton telephoned Miles. Sherman Miles had no command authority, but Marshall would want to consult with him. Leonard Gerow was next on Bratton's list.

Examining the "one o'clock" instruction from Tokyo, Kramer mentally converted it into Manila time and Honolulu time—and into Tokyo time as well, because the Japanese navy used that clock exclusively. He wondered "how this . . . tied up with the movement of the big Japanese convoy down the coast of French Indochina; in other words, to get an idea of whether it was evening or midnight or early in the morning around Kota Bharu." The calculations brought him to predawn, dawn, and early morning at all likely targets. Seeing "an extreme likelihood of war" even though the message appeared unwarlike, he sealed all the new intercepts in folders and began dropping them off, encountering McCollum leaving Stark's office. It was another chance to stress the time relationships, and he made his point to his chief, who then went back to talk to Stark.

Unaware of all the fuss since he had not seen any part of the long decrypt, Marshall was cantering home on his bay gelding, King Story, with Fleet, his Dalmatian, at his heels.

•

Early risers in the East found an ominous lead story in the hefty Sunday papers. Stuffed with Christmas advertising, the *New York Times* was of near-record bulk. The chief news item was headlined, "ROOSEVELT APPEALS TO HIROHITO AFTER NEW THREAT IN INDO-CHINA," but page-one readers could take confidence in another major story, "Navy is Superior to Any, Says Knox." The Secretary's annual report was out, and registered pride in the defense buildup. Readers of the *Washington Post* were reminded that kickoff for the football game at Griffith Stadium was 2:00 P.M. and that the new Soviet ambassador, Maxim Litvinov, was arriving at National Airport at 9:40 A.M. Knox's report and the President's message received page-one treatment.

In the *Times* the face of war appeared in advertisements for Lillian Hellman's anti-Nazi melodrama, *Watch on the Rhine*, but otherwise Broadway advertised, at prices from $1.10 to $2.75 (55¢ seats at matinees), a feast of escapist theater. Noel Coward's *Blithe Spirit*, Gertrude Lawrence in *Lady in the Dark*, Danny Kaye in Cole Porter's *Let's Face it*, Ethel Merman in *Panama Hattie*, Boris Karloff in *Arsenic and Old Lace*, Ethel Barrymore in *The Corn Is Green*. *My Sister Eileen* was selling out and *Hellzapoppin* was nearing its 1,400th performance. In the movie houses older wars turned up (at 50¢ for the cheap seats) in *Sergeant York* and *The Chocolate Soldier* (with Nelson Eddy and Rise Stevens). Humphrey Bogart brooded in *The Maltese Falcon*; Greta Garbo pouted in *Mata Hari*; Carmen Miranda fractured the English language in *Weekend in Havana*; Vincent Price scowled in *Angel Street*; Jack Oakie ran for comic touchdowns in *Rise and Shine*.

The hit novel for Christmas giving was Edna Ferber's *Saratoga Trunk*, at a hefty $2.50, the price of a two-record set of the *1812 Overture*, with Artur Rodzinski and the Cleveland Orchestra. Gift crates of oranges and grapefruit from Florida were $2.79 at Bloomingdale's. Hattie Carnegie's dresses began at $15.00 while pricey Rogers Peet had men's suits and topcoats from $38.00. Henri Bendel offered silk stockings at $1.25 a pair ($1.65 in the current "wonder fabric," nylon). And Abraham and Straus featured in a page of Christmas toy offerings, at $1.98, a remote-control bomber that attacked a battleship. "Running along on a suspended wire, the all-metal dive bomber sweeps over a battleship target and electrically releases the bomb when you press a button. A fascinating game. It takes skill and you can play it by the hour."

•

In a memo to his staff on October 14, 1941, Admiral Kimmel warned as he had done before that a Japanese surprise attack on Hawaii was possible and that an advance clue might be the discovery of a lurking enemy submarine. Even a single sub "may indicate the presence of a considerable surface force probably composed of fast ships accompanied by a carrier." Under such conditions it would be necessary, "as quickly as the situation and daylight conditions warrant . . . to pursue or meet enemy ships that might be located by air search or other means."

At 3:42 Sunday morning the destroyer *Ward* and the minesweepers *Condor* and *Crossbill* patrolled off the entrance to Pearl Harbor. In the lifting darkness about two miles south of the entrance buoys the *Condor*'s officer of the deck, Ensign R. C. McCloy, noticed a suspicious wake. It appeared to be a periscope, and in an area where American subs were forbidden to operate submerged. The two vessels were on a collision course; the mystery shape turned sharply to port and the *Condor* swerved to starboard, blinkering the *Ward*, "Sighted submerged submarine on westerly course, speed 9 knots."

The *Ward*'s skipper was Lieutenant William W. Outerbridge, on his first patrol during his first command. He had inched up only from one stripe to two in his fourteen years out of Annapolis. The prewar navy was slow, but Outerbridge was not. Sounding general quarters, he slowed to ten knots and prowled the area by sonar. By 4:35, having located nothing, he sent his men back to their bunks and did not report the incident to Harbor Control. Nor did the *Condor*. The Navy radio station at Bishop's Point had monitored the conversation, but it was between two of its own ships and neither had requested that any message be relayed. No early warning was triggered; the Japanese sub survived.

•

Puffing on a briar pipe and talking with Counselor Dooman, Ambassador Grew paced nervously in his walnut-paneled library. Messengers from the embassy, down a wooded two-acre hill from the ambassador's residence, dashed up the steep stone steps to bring snatches of the decrypted message to Grew. He wondered about trying to get a taxi to the Foreign Ministry, as no embassy automobile was in the compound. As he and Dooman wondered whether taxis might suffer the same fate as embassy cables, Second Secretary Merrell Benninghoff churned up the gravel driveway in his Ford coupé.

"I guess," he said later, "I just had a hunch I ought to take a look around."

By 11:45 a complete document was ready, and Grew climbed into the Ford beside Benninghoff, his long legs squeezed up against the dashboard. The streets were dark and deserted. They reached Foreign Minister Togo's official residence by 11:50. Grew was hurried up the crimson-carpeted staircase to a second-floor reception room to be greeted by the Minister's principal secretary, Toshikazu Kasé, who doubled as interpreter. Neither Grew, who had served in Tokyo for nine years, nor Togo, who had been in the Washington embassy for nearly four years, in the 1920s, needed an interpreter. For the Foreign Minister, however, the buffer furnished time to formulate a response. It was after midnight when Togo, in full diplomatic dress, entered. Kasé motioned them to two blue-plush overstuffed chairs.

Grew knew that he had no time for niceties. "I have here," he explained, displaying the paper in his hand, "a personal message from President Roosevelt to His Imperial Majesty. It is a message of such momentous importance that I respectfully request the opportunity to deliver it in person to His Majesty at the earliest possible moment."

Grew was not surprised when Togo—peering at his watch—claimed that an audience would be "most difficult" to accomplish at the unusual hour. "And of course such an audience would have to be arranged through the Imperial Household Ministry. I cannot possibly say when it would be granted."

Grew would not be put off. He urged the immediacy of the message, and, putting on his glasses, he read it in full to Togo, who waited after each paragraph for Kasé's unnecessary translation. There were no American concessions in it. Rather, Roosevelt wanted immediate assurances of withdrawal from Indochina—"every Japanese soldier or sailor." Neutralization of that area, he assured Japan, would create conditions for peace, while a continuation of Japanese encroachments was "unthinkable." The message was a request for an Imperial order to restrain military forces already in motion. There was even an implicit threat in it. "None of the peoples whom I have spoken of," the President said, ". . . can sit either indefinitely or permanently upon a keg of dynamite."

"I shall give the President's message the most thorough study," said Togo in accepting his copy. Grew could read nothing on Togo's face.

"Does that indicate some doubt," Grew inquired, "as to whether you will request an audience for me?"

Delivery of the message would serve no American purpose, Togo knew, but there was a Japanese advantage. The prospect of an Imperial interview would keep the Americans from any ultimate alert. It implied that there was still time, and Togo assumed that this misinformation would be relayed to Washington, where it was still early on Sunday morning.

Promising to intervene with the Imperial Household, Togo shook Grew's hand and ushered him out into the chilly Tokyo night.

At 12:40 he telephoned Marquis Kido to ask how to handle the situation. Kido suggested a call to Tojo, and another to the Minister of Imperial Affairs. Roosevelt's message could change nothing already set in motion, but Kido was concerned about its "diplomatic effects."

•

With *Kido Butai* making its final run toward Oahu, the Eleventh Air Fleet on Taiwan was preparing for its strikes in the Philippines. All personnel at the Takao (Kao-hsiung) and Tainan (T'ain-nan) air bases had been restricted to quarters earlier and told of their targets. Few but the Operations staff knew the entire picture. Lieutenant Commander Koichi Shimada remembered his misgivings on discovering how closely timed and integrated were operations planned to unfold on schedule over a quarter of the earth's circumference. "On seeing the outline . . . I had been struck by its resemblance to a railroad timetable and [I] wondered if a war could really be fought in this manner, so completely at the will of one side."

Before the 194 aircraft assigned to bomb airfields on Luzon could take off, the naval high command in Japan had to approve the routes and target times. A special courier had flown to Tokyo to avoid a radio intercept. As a result, Shimada was flabbergasted when a radiogram arrived at Takao with a warning that "to assure the success of the Hawaii attack, it is imperative that the Eleventh Air Force in Taiwan take every precaution to guard against the enemy's learning of our military movements before that attack takes place." The initial segment of the message had been even more disconcerting: "Imperial General Headquarters is quite confident of success in jamming the enemy's radio frequencies so that any warning dispatched to the Philippines as a result of the Carrier Strike Force's attack on Hawaii will not get through."

Kido Butai was just moving into position. The radiogram, Shimada thought, was unforgivably stupid. "Here was the highest headquarters instructing us to take precautions when, by sending out a message filled with such ultra-secret information, it was itself guilty of a breach of security!"

Fortunately for Tokyo, no one was listening—or at least no one heard. Yet surprise was not enough. Since aircraft would have to fly most of the route from Formosa in darkness, it was urgent to know what weather conditions would be encountered over Luzon. To obtain data, a scout plane was launched at 8:30 and a second was to lift off at 10:30.

"The weather that we encountered," Shimada wrote, "while not ideal, was not so bad that the attack would have to be postponed. I gave my opinion, in brief radio reports, that our planes could take off on schedule. Use of the radio was kept to a minimum so as not to alert the enemy; nevertheless, there were clear indications that either my plane or the earlier one had been detected."

At 11:15 the radio monitoring center at Takao overheard warnings being sent to Iba and Clark fields. At the same time the Air Corps listening station at Iba began jamming the frequencies the weather planes were using. When that happened, the two aircraft disappeared into the night and took a roundabout return route in case they were followed. The morning adventure, Shimada worried, could no longer catch the enemy unaware.

TOKYO
Midnight
December 8

HONG KONG
SHANGHAI
PHILIPPINES
11:00 P.M.
December 7

MALAYA
9:40 P.M.
December 7

PEARL HARBOR
4:30 A.M.
December 7

HOUR 27

A
T 0000 hours, Tokyo time, on December 8—one second after midnight—the master of the *Tatuta Maru*, en route to San Francisco via Honolulu with thirty-seven Americans and other evacuees from Japan, and scheduled to pick up Japanese nationals eager to return home, opened, as he had been instructed on leaving Yokohama December 2, a sealed box. His well-publicized sailing dates included a call at the Mexican port of Manzanillo on December 19, and at Balboa in the Canal Zone on December 27. When the ship had cleared home waters its voyage seemed to infer peace in the Pacific at least through mid-January, but the box from the Navy Ministry contained orders to reverse course immediately to Yokohama at top speed and in radio silence. The box also included twenty pistols—in case irate passengers, discovering the elaborate hoax, tried to take over.

•

On Sunday evening Arch Carey enlivened his new bachelor existence in Shanghai by dining with friends, then going to the movies. In the next seat he discovered the British Consul General, Sir Anthony George, an old friend from Hankow days. It was obvious to Carey that there was nothing to worry about, or the chief British presence in the area would not have been there. Shanghai's preferential status had survived the earlier world war, and the Japanese legally were partners in the International Settlement.

John B. Powell, who had also sent his family away, felt more troubled. Editor of the *China Weekly Review*, he had just put out the December 6 issue and expected to be in his office on Monday morning to plan the issue to be dated the 13th. Chinese postal clerks who ran what amounted to a dual postal service, working for the Japanese censors on one hand and eluding them with mail destined for Free China with the other, had already smuggled the latest *Review* out of Shanghai. The city somehow worked to everyone's advantage.

Powell also ran a radio station owned by Press Wireless, the only communications link not under Japanese control. He wanted to keep it going, and to keep his loyal Chinese on the payroll, even the coolie who slept in the office and eased mail past unsuspicious sentries.

In the Hongkew area, the mostly Japanese eastern neck of the Settlement, all Jews were being resettled in a ghetto. (The Bureau of Stateless Refugees would distribute passes to leave it daily.) The Bund Garden, near the Beth Aaron Synagogue, across the bridge, was a popular destination, but few risked any kind of border violation. Just getting to the refugee community had been difficult enough. From 1938 through 1941 nearly seventeen thousand Jewish refugees from central and eastern Europe had arrived via neutral countries and were being cared for by the American Joint Distribution Committee. There were also about fifteen hundred "non-Aryan Christian" refugees, technically Jews according to Hitler's Nuremberg Laws, facing an uncertain present and even bleaker future.

To the Chinese, the ultra-orthodox Jews in their unusual black garb and their beards and earlocks, little changed since seventeenth-century Poland, were "little Indians"—somehow akin to the turbaned and bearded Sikh police employed by the British. To the Japanese, anti-Semitism barely existed except through the shrill German propaganda literature shipped to the East and Nazi diplomatic exhortations to its Axis ally. In December 1940 Japan's then Foreign Minister, Yosuke Matsuoka, had told a Jewish businessman from Manchuria, "I have concluded a treaty with Hitler, but I never promised him to be an anti-Semite." To the Japanese Navy's resident expert on Jewish affairs in Shanghai, Captain Koreshige Inuzuka, Jews were to be exploited. In a 1939 report he had written that Jews were like a globe fish—a *fugu.* "When you eat it, it is delicious; but if you do not know how to fry it, it may kill you." In Shanghai, expertly combining tolerance and intimidation, he would fry his fish well.

Laura Margolis had worked in Cuba with refugees from Hitler. Latin America was a limbo in which arrivals waited for immigration into a United States unwilling to shelter many of them. China was very different. "I came out [to Shanghai]," she recalled, "very naive with low-heeled shoes and work clothes." Then she discovered that nothing could be accomplished for refugees with the ruling elite except through the social nexus. "I quickly had to buy a long dress. . . . Everybody was partying. It was that kind of city. I didn't like it. It was a colonial atmosphere. Nothing can ever touch them; nothing can ever happen to them. The Chinese were not people, really. The war was going on across the bridge, and it didn't affect [the foreign residents]. . . . So there was nothing to do but play the game. You had to. I did this, plus meeting Inuzuka at these parties. They would invite the important Japanese people."

•

Scattered light rain was falling in Kowloon when Harold Bateson, the bespectacled Australian night clerk at the posh Peninsula Hotel, telephoned a nearby radio repair shop. Two Japanese sisters on the cleaning staff who lived with their uncle's family behind the shop had not shown up for their shift. When the uncle answered, Bateson asked if both girls were ill. "Yes, sick," said the uncle, unconvincingly. "Won't come work for long time." And he hung up. Although the hotel was still cleaning up in the aftermath of the "Tin Hat Ball," Bateson would have to do without the young women. Held the evening before, the benefit was to raise £160,000 for a bomber squadron promised by "the people of Hong Kong" to defend Britain. Hong Kong itself had no modern military aircraft, but that seemed to bother no one.

A Swiss businessman stopped at the desk for his key and chatted. He had been walking past the Matsubara Hotel, a gathering place for local and visiting Japanese, and wanted to share his puzzlement. Through the window the lobby looked deserted; even the desk clerk was missing. He asked whether the hotel had closed. Bateson wondered whether the two episodes were related. The *Shirogane Maru* had left Hong Kong for occupied Canton the day before with a boatload of homeward-bound passengers, including all the colony's Japanese barbers. Other Japanese, the same day, had sailed across the bay to the Portuguese colony of Macao.

Sergeant Major E. C. Ford and his mates on Mount Davis were having pints and sandwiches all around until 11:30, griping about the constant alerts and alarms. He had been awakened by his houseboy—on a Sunday—at 11:30 A.M. to take a telephone message to report at 7:20 P.M. instead of the next morning. His Sunday had been ruined. They talked about the Japanese threat and decided that it was nonsense. "Give 'em stew," said another sergeant.

•

Notre Dame Academy in Midsayap on Mindanao was run by the Missionary Oblates of Mary Immaculate, a small order that reached out to the Philippines from Boston. Even in Mindanao, where war seemed remote, the teenage boys had decided to form a military unit which they called Knights of Our Lady. The Knights had planned a military Mass on December 8, the Feast of the Immaculate Conception. Knowing nothing about marching or drilling, they came to pug-nosed, jug-eared Father Edward Charles Gordon. He applied to the constabulary for help and found that Captain Macario Guballa, although the only Protestant in the town, was willing to train the boys into parade readiness. His sister was a Carmelite nun.

At Sunday Mass, Father Gordon had announced an afternoon practice, and Captain Guballa drilled the boys into the darkness. Then the group had to prepare for the Monday morning fiesta. "One boy came along with a sack on his back," Father Gordon wrote in the gold-edged pages of his diary. "Coming from it were all kinds of squeals. It was a young pig that would soon be butchered. Another came up with a sack tied to the back of his bicycle. It was another pig."

The Knights had collected enough money over a two months' campaign for five small pigs. "You should see these kids kill pigs," the priest wrote with some awe. "They just tie their snouts . . . and then stick them in the Adam's apple with a small knife. Then they collect the blood in a basin to make a delicious sauce (delicious for them but not for me). They then pour scalding water on the 'porker' and scrape the hair off it. Well, about eleven o'clock I told them to go home and go to bed. I went back to the *convento*. A few minutes later one boy came over and wanted to borrow the keys to the school. He asked if they could sleep there for the night."

"Why don't you go home?"

"We live very far, Father."

Gordon gave them a key "and about twenty piled into the room. I heard them singing and talking for about twenty minutes—and then all was silent."

•

Returning to Fort Myer at 10:15, Marshall let Bratton's many messages wait until he had a quick shower. By 10:25 he was on the phone to Bratton, who would only say over an insecure line that he had "a most important message" that the general "must see at once." He would bring it over.

"No, don't bother to do that," said Marshall. "I'm coming down to my office. You can give it to me then."

The urgency in Bratton's voice got Marshall moving. First, he ordered his War Department car over to Virginia for him. Then, feeling that it would not arrive soon enough, he instructed his orderly, Sergeant Semanko, to get "the roadster" out—a flashy red car belonging to Marshall's stepson, Clifton Brown. Semanko had never done such a thing before, but in Brown's roadster the two roared away through the quiet Arlington National Cemetery toward the Memorial Bridge over the Potomac.

Reaching the bridge approaches, they saw the general's khaki-painted official sedan racing in the other direction. Both vehicles jammed their brakes. Marshall transferred to the Army vehicle and Semanko took the roadster back. The chauffeur accelerated through the empty streets, past the Lincoln Memorial and on to the War Department. Ten minutes had been saved.

•

It was after nine in the evening before Brooke-Popham and Percival got together in Singapore to discuss how to cope with the Japanese. There was no longer sufficient lead time, Percival concluded, to move Indian troops of the 11th Division across the border to oppose a landing at Singora. Without Thai opposition, they might arrive by two in the morning; the Japanese would land by midnight. It might be best, the generals rationalized, to defend Malaya from positions more favorable to them. Taking their views to Phillips at the Naval Base—Phillips had just returned from Manila—they secured his agreement that Matador was now unworkable. Since Josiah Crosby had been making a fuss from Bangkok that Matador was impolitic, they now had another reason not to execute it.

Their joint cable to London was a model of blindness and passivity. They had decided against Matador—and almost anything else—because, they explained,

1. Conditions for reconnaissance were very bad and there can be no real certainty that ships seen were an expedition.
2. If expedition is in fact aimed at Singora region it can reach there before we can arrive. Matador is designed only to forestall a Japanese expedition.
3. If conclusion[s] drawn from reconnaissance prove incorrect we should incur all the disadvantages of breaking Thai neutrality.
4. Japanese movements are consistent with a deliberate attempt to induce us to violate Thai neutrality.

Only if the Japanese land south of the Thai border, *in Malaya*, they concluded to London, "is it to be assumed that we are at war with Japan." Further, Brooke-Popham postscripted, "C-in-C Eastern Fleet concurs."

Paralyzed by indecision, the Singapore command wanted desperately to believe that the Japanese strike force was only bait to commit the British to a mistake. Whether or not Brooke-Popham knew of the attacks on the two Allied ships, he knew that his own aircraft had been fired on; and he knew that the Japanese "expedition" he was still unwilling to label as hostile or even real was very large indeed, and up to no good.

To keep watch on Japanese intentions, Brooke-Popham ordered, in lieu of action, a dawn air reconnaissance of the Singora area on Monday. Near the Thai border, rain-drenched Indian troops of the 11th were still standing to, unaware that they, and Matador, had been abandoned.

•

The train from Singapore via Kuala Lumpur arrived on schedule at the Kota Bharu station at 10:30. Debarking as if everything were normal was Flight Lieutenant Peter J. Gibbes. There was even a man from RAAF Transport to meet him. Several days earlier he had delivered the first Australian-manufactured Beaufort bomber to Singapore, and he was joining No. 1 Squadron to fly Lockheed Hudsons as a replacement pilot. He had hundreds of hours on multiengined aircraft with Australian National Airways, and had qualified at home on Hudsons as well.

Arriving at his post, he was plunged into darkness. Kota Bharu was not yet on alert status but the air base was; its fliers had been shadowing what appeared to be a Japanese invasion fleet for two days. On the train he had learned nothing, but as his driver crawled along the base without lights, Gibbes was filled in.

With headquarters dark, Gibbes was delivered directly to his officers' mess and told to report for duty in the morning. It was all very strange. Total blackout conditions prevailed, and he had little idea of his surroundings. He unpacked his kit, undressed, and went to bed.

.

It took about ten minutes for the gate in the antisubmarine nets across the mouth of Pearl Harbor to swing open. At 5:08 the minesweeper *Crossbill*, which had been working with the *Condor*, passed in, its routine tasks done. Normally *Crossbill* would have been accompanied by its sister ship. *Condor* and *Ward* had been delayed by combing for the elusive sub, neither making a new sighting. At 5:32 the *Condor* slipped behind the net, two minutes later receiving a message from the *Ward*, "We will continue search."

Since the tug *Keosanqua* was due to go out at 6:15, the gate tenders did not bother to close the protective net. It would remain open until 8:46, making it easy for minisubs hovering in the area to slip in. The Japanese planned for such neglect. On November 18 five "large-type" subs of the "I" class had left Kure in southern Honshu, each carrying a secret weapon identified only as "Target A" concealed in a large tube clamped to the deck. These were two-man midget submarines, eighty-one feet long and resembling a torpedo with a conning tower. Each carried two torpedoes and could run about nine hours at low speed—sufficient to return to the mother ship if possible—but none of the ten crewmen expected to be alive at the end of the day.

Self-sacrifice appealed to Japanese concepts of ultimate courage and dedication to the Emperor and led inevitably to the kamikaze pilots of 1944–1945. (No carrier pilot about to take off for Hawaii had a parachute.) The competition for minisub crews was so intense that even Lieutenant Naoji Iwase, whose idea the venture was, had to compete. (He skippered the sub clamped to the mother-ship *I-22*.) Each crewman had left clippings of his hair and nails, neatly wrapped with a letter of farewell to his parents, in a stamped envelope at Kure. The subs were to slip into the harbor and torpedo the largest target available. Each sailor had a pistol and a samurai sword to kill himself if in danger of capture, and explosives to destroy the vessel.

Ensign Kazuo Sakamaki and Chief Warrant Officer Kiyoshi Inagaki had the least expectations of survival. Although tests aboard revealed that their gyroscope was defective, they refused to be left behind. Clambering into their minisub from the deck of the surfaced and swaying *I-24*, they clutched bottles of wine and lunch in their left hands, their right hands free for gripping the catwalk. "On to Pearl Harbor!" they shouted over the slapping waves to their skipper, Lieutenant Commander Hiroshi Hanabusa.

Clasping his lunch and his bottle on the deck of the *I-20*, from which the lights of Oahu could be seen, Ensign Akira Hiroo, at twenty-two the youngest of the ten, observed happily, "We must look like high school boys going on a picnic. . . . The ice cream sold at Honolulu is especially fine. I will bring you some when I come back."

The last to be cut loose was Sakamaki. Since his minisub threatened to surface and had to be navigated by magnetic compass alone, the periscope wake seen by the crew of the *Condor* could not have been his. The sub hovering near the net had been too elusive. But the waters around Oahu were alive with Japanese submarines—twenty-seven of them, as well as three with *Kido Butai* and the five midget subs. Any ships flushed out of the harbor by the air raid appeared to have little chance. Admiral Yamamoto had thought of everything.

"At the moment of my release," Sakamaki wrote later, "my submarine nearly toppled over into the water. . . . My aide and I crawled back and forth inside the submarine, removing the lead ballast and filling the tanks with water to correct the trim of the craft. . . . After ten minutes I lifted the ship slightly to see through the periscope where we were going. . . . To my horror the ship was moving in the wrong direction!" The sub had gone ninety degrees off course, and Sakamaki had to manage manually and by sight when necessary, which put him at greater risk. "My hands were wet with cold sweat. I changed direction three or four times."

By guesswork and his periscope, he inched to the harbor entrance and awaited an opportunity to sneak in. "Have no fear," he assured Inagaki, his crewman. "Now that we have come this far . . . we will somehow break through. . . . We will loose our torpedoes at an enemy battleship. If necessary, let us dash into one of them. That's our mission. In a few hours our fate will be decided. So cheer up."

TOKYO	MALAYA	BERLIN	PEARL HARBOR
1:00 A.M.	10:40 P.M.	5:00 P.M.	5:30 A.M.
December 8	December 7	December 7	December 7

HOUR 28

B Y 11:00 A.M. in Washington, decrypted cable 907 had been
handed to Ambassador Nomura, who only then discovered that
he had to deliver the long message still being typed in English to the
Secretary of State in two hours. He had not even read the whole text.
The first thirteen parts had been typed so poorly that Katsuzo Okamura
began a cleaner version while waiting for part fourteen. This time he
worked from the dictation of a junior interpreter. Errors multiplied;
near-panic occurred when code clerks transcribed two further cables
ordering corrections in the text, one resulting in a single page to be
retyped, the other requiring two pages.

At the State Department, Secretaries Hull, Stimson, and Knox were
conferring. Stimson's minutes note, "Hull is very certain that the Japs
are planning some deviltry and we are all wondering where the blow
will strike." They agreed that it was vital for "the main people who
are interested in the Far East" to stay together and respond in common
to Japan. "The British will have to fight if they attack the Kra Peninsula.
We three all thought that we must fight if the British fought." Hull
proposed a draft to be presented to the President. The Japanese thrust
southward, he began, "inevitably means . . . control of islands, con-

tinents, and seas from the Indies back near Hawaii." It was part of an Axis strategy "to conquer and destroy, with Hitler moving across half the world and the Government of Japan . . . moving across the other half . . . and collaborating or cooperating whenever to their individual or their mutual advantage."

Knox noted points to make to Roosevelt, the first being, "We are tied up inextricably with the British in the present world situation." The loss of Singapore and Malaya would jeopardize the entire British war effort and cost the Dutch their Indies. If that happened, "We are almost certain to be next, being then practically Japanese-surrounded."

"I think," he proposed, "that the Japanese should be told that any movement in a direction that threatens the United States will be met with force. The President will want to reserve to himself how to define this." Then Knox ticked off territories he had in mind, from British to Portuguese. None of the secretaries suggested listing any area over which the American flag flew as in immediate danger. The Japanese, they guessed, would seize vulnerable colonies of occupied or weak colonial powers, but not be so foolhardy as to push the U.S. into war.

With such advice prepared for the President's three o'clock meeting at the White House, they adjourned. Stimson had a long ride home to lunch. Knox said that he was returning to the Navy Department. Hull remained in his office to await Nomura and Kurusu.

•

At 5:30 A.M., the two *Kido Butai* cruisers which had catapult capability, *Tone* and *Chikuma*, each lofted into the murky morning light a Zero-type* reconnaissance floatplane. Two hundred twenty miles to the south, Private Joseph L. Lockard and Private George E. Elliott had been manning the mobile radar unit at the Opana station for ninety routine minutes. Opana, near Kahuku Point on the northernmost wedge of Oahu, consisted of a few tents and two equipment-laden trucks. To save money, manpower, and wear and tear, the equipment was only used part-time. Convenient for practice, the hours had been 6:00 to 11:30 each morning. In response to the war warning from Washington, General Short on November 28 had moved the operating schedule up, estimating 4:00 A.M. to 7:00 A.M. as "the most dangerous

---

* "Zero" came from the year of Mitsubishi's introduction of the fast, maneuverable plane—1940, the 2600th year of traditional Japanese history.

hours" for a carrier-based attack. No other change in alert conditions followed.

The maximum effective reach of the oscilloscope was about 130 miles. Usually about twenty-five "targets" were plotted in the early hours, but not on Sunday. Plotters at Fort Shafter—weekdays—moved arrows about on a large map, based on information phoned in from the new radar stations or transmitted by coast watchers. It was not always clear what the blips on a radar screen represented, or how to tell friend from foe.

The *Tone*'s scout was to overfly Lahaina Roads on Maui, to the southeast, which submarine *I-72* had advised the day before was empty of ships; Admiral Nagumo was still looking for the missing *Enterprise* and *Lexington*. The *Chikuma*'s plane was to radio a last-minute report on conditions at Pearl Harbor, carefully keeping about five miles off target. As they gained altitude above the strike force, Genda observed, there was some apprehension aboard nearby ships that enemy planes had been sighted, "but in a minute they proved to be ours, and the slight commotion was settled."

•

At the Peninsula Hotel in Kowloon the dance band was playing "The Best Things in Life Are Free" when it was interrupted by a man waving a megaphone from a balcony above the dance floor. "Any men connected with any ships in the harbor," he shouted, "report aboard for duty." Then he added, in the sudden silence, "At once!"

Men hurriedly said their good-byes, some tugging their ladies through the lobby to the queue of waiting rickshaws.

On the island, at the Hong Kong Hotel, several large parties had packed the ballrooms; then an announcement activating volunteers sobered up most revelers, and the hotel emptied. In the Jockey Club bar, even gimlets were abandoned. An army officers' party enlivened by British nurses broke up as rumors spread, but at another the Commissioner of Police, John Pennefather-Evans, vowed that no Japanese was going to break up *his* party. Alone soon after, he caught the last ferry from Kowloon.

•

Sunday had been a busy day for Captain Desmond Brennan's B Company of twenty-five ambulances, hundreds of miles north of the

Australian 8th Division's main forces. From Ipoh they had crawled up
the narrow, winding road to the border, above Sungei Pattani. Above
was a sliver of Thailand and the panhandle of Burma, which shared
the peninsula above Malaya. A Punjabi battalion was in place to protect
the west coast road.

Most of Dr. Brennan's soldiers were from Tasmania, and used to
relative isolation; getting used to Indian troops—"Dogras"—was another matter. They carried their meat supply on the hoof, decapitating
goats with a cleaver after what Brennan called "much ritual," which
concluded with rejection of the carcass if the head had not been severed
with one blow. "Whilst this was on, word arrived that the truck bringing *our* rations had slipped off the road and down the hillside, and was
balancing dangerously over a sheer drop of several hundred feet. 'Tassie'
Watt, our lieutenant, organized a food rescue and took a group to the
vehicle. Linking arms, they were able to get our lightest man onto the
truck and empty quite a lot of the food before the truck tilted over
and plunged down the cliff. The soldier, one 'Judy' Garland, was firmly
clasped by 'Tassie' himself."

At the camp, Brennan had lunched with the battalion officers, "and
I remember a Lt. Col. Collins warning us about our perception of the
Japanese. We all thought they were little short-sighted men with buck
teeth, whose rifles were old scrap iron and whose bullets wouldn't fire.
He said to forget it. They were dogged soldiers with good leaders and
dangerous weapons. We all agreed war was imminent, but at least a
week off."

It was bedtime; Brennan was assigned an Indian soldier as servant.
"This embarrassed me, as the idea of someone waiting on me was all
wrong. To make matters worse, this dark gentleman took his job
seriously and since he knew no English and we couldn't communicate,
I began to worry lest he should interpret my refusal as racial discrimination. He wanted to take my shoes and socks off and so I agreed to
that at most, but when he commenced to massage my feet, I thought
perhaps this servant idea wasn't bad at all. That evening he lay across
the door of my hut, after tucking in the mosquito net securely and
assuring me with gestures that his large knife was able to be drawn
readily to protect me."

On Sunday the Volunteers in Penang, just off the northwestern
Malayan coast, remained at their pillboxes and drilled as they had every
day since they had been mobilized the previous Monday—"perhaps,"

Charles Simon thought, "because we were much nearer to the impending battle area and Singapore was thought to be an impenetrable fortress."

Holiday bungalows for colonials were clustered a cool half-mile above sea level, remote from the bustling, largely Chinese, population of the Crown Colony. In more serene times, Sir Shenton Thomas reached his Governor's residence by funicular railway. Below, in George Town, the second city of the Federation, Simon had to beg two hours' leave one evening to go to his office in Beach Street, where he was manager of the Remington Rand branch office, in order to telephone his director in Singapore. With tin and rubber the chief products of the region, and both coveted by the Japanese war machine, George Town had been blacked out nights through the week. "We had regular stand-to and stand-down watches, and we really did take the whole thing much more seriously than our comrades in Singapore." But Sunday was "a day like any other day, and nothing untoward happened."

•

Sembawang Aerodrome was in north-central Singapore, relatively remote from the city. (Few places could be more than twenty-five miles away from someplace else.) Duty pilot was W. R. Halliday of 453 Squadron. It was a twenty-four-hour stint, and he had been on the job since 8:30 A.M., when he received a call from the operations room. No aerodrome lights were to be visible because Japanese aircraft were expected shortly. He did not ask how the information was acquired. News of the Japanese fleet in the Gulf of Siam had been public all day.

Sembawang was not a lively spot late on a Sunday night. Most personnel were in bed. "I tried to get a message to the pilots that the war was going to start but I could not leave my job and the phones in quarters were not answered. I also tried to get one of the aerodrome guards to take a message but they were Sikh troops and could not understand me. So I waited for the start of the war by myself."

•

As Detcharat Adun, deputy premier in Bangkok, awaited members of the Cabinet for the emergency session he had called, a message from absent Premier Luang Phibun arrived, answering Adun's urgent plea that the premier return. He would be back, Phibun assured, by dawn.

To the Cabinet, Adun explained that he had dispatched an airplane to fetch the premier, but Phibun refused to fly, sending an excuse with the pilot that he would come by car. A babble of voices calculated that he could not get back any sooner than eight in the morning, by which time events would have taken their course. Phibun may have been timid about flying at night, or worried about Japanese planes. More likely, he foresaw rewards for a passive Thailand in Japanese territorial gifts. Accusations of guilt from Britain could be explained by a surprise attack in his absence.

The debate was brief. Ministers agreed that they would have to permit the Japanese to pass through, but without Phibun they would not commit themselves to a vote. Ignoring the 2:30 A.M. deadline, they agreed to meet again in the morning.

•

At seven in the evening, von Chappuis finally telephoned Muñoz with permission for his division to retire across the Volkhov. He had already issued orders, he told Muñoz, that Tikhvin, once to be held at all cost, was to be evacuated the next day. Muñoz did not reveal that the withdrawal was already in progress, the Spaniards torching Russian villages as they pulled back. To appear in compliance, Muñoz issued order 73 at 10:14, with the instructions he had received for falling back. The last truck across the Volkhov carried the birchwood crosses removed from the Spanish cemetery.

The Spaniards were not ideologues depopulating the country of its *Untermenschen*, but no one worried about the villagers driven off into the frigid night with nothing but what they could carry. It was war.

•

When Tito convened a Central Committee meeting in a small, inconspicuous, overcrowded house in Drenovo, it was already dark. The pretentious Moscow-borrowed title identified the circle of Tito's closest subordinates. They gathered, Milovan Djilas wrote, "in the corner of a room, around a little table which one could reach only by stepping over the bodies of sleeping soldiers. It was stifling and dark, except for a gas lamp." The "armed struggle against the occupation," Edward Kardelj held forth with ideological unreality, "had developed into a class war between the workers and the bourgeoisie." His Communists had put up little resistance until the Germans attacked Russia ten weeks after the invasion of Yugoslavia, but he scoffed at Britain's "passivity toward Hitler" and deplored the "tensions between the West and the U.S.S.R."

Workers and peasants, Kardelj pontificated, had to ally against the occupation "because we thereby affirmed ourselves as a patriotic force [and] . . . because this was part of a worldwide class struggle led by the Soviet Union." Tito suggested organizing scattered Serbian units into a brigade, "not [to] be tied to any specific territory but [to] fight wherever needed." He would resign as party secretary, Tito offered, because of the succession of recent defeats, but he would continue to lead the army. "The party should not shoulder the responsibility for all failures."

Djilas barely had time to protest, "But that doesn't make sense," when others also raised their voices to reject Tito's "self-abnegation," for the unsentimental reason that Moscow would interpret the act as disintegration within the party. Tito was pleased. He would stay. They talked instead of reorganizing the Serbians. When the others left, Tito remained. (A few days later the Italians surprised his forces at Drenovo. His security guard fled without firing a shot. Tito ran under fire into the woods. The Italians looted the house and shot the only inhabitant, the daughter-in-law of the owner of the cottage.)

•

In the portion of Poland the Nazis were Germanizing as Wartheland, slightly east of the midpoint between Poznan and Lodz, was the town of Chelmno—famous in Jewish folklore as Chelm, the place where the most gullible and incurably optimistic of all Jews dwelt. Simple innocence was the hallmark of Chelm. In one tale a Chelm farmer was startled by news that the long-awaited Messiah was coming; indeed, he was at that moment only a few hours from Chelm. The farmer wrung his hands. "I have only recently built this house, and have invested the rest of my kopecks in cattle; besides, I have only just finished sowing our crops!"

"Don't worry," his wife soothed. "Think of all the troubles our people have survived—slavery in Egypt, the wickedness of Haman, the Inquisition in Spain, the pogroms of the Czar. All of these the good Lord has helped us to overcome; and with a little help from Him, we will overcome the Messiah too!"

There was no Messiah of any sort on Sunday, December 7. In the early darkness, seven hundred Jews loaded into trucks sealed with improvised canvas tops were moved into a compound on the edge of Chelmno closed off by a thick spruce forest and high wooden fence. They had been shipped from the town of Kolo, informed only that they were en route to a railway station and work in the "East." Since there was no prisoner grapevine to prepare them for disbelief, they clutched at the hope that they were on their way to "resettlement."

Michael Podklebnik, who somehow survived, recalled that, unsuspectingly, he escorted into one truck "my own father, my mother, [my] sister with five children, my brother and his wife and three children. I volunteered to go with them but was not allowed." He also watched as a man he knew only as Goldberg, owner of a confiscated sawmill, "approached the Germans with a request to be appointed manager of a Jewish camp in the East. His application was accepted and he was promised the . . . position."

The Barlogi station was nowhere in sight, but no one inside would know it. The Nazis of SS Captain Herbert Lange's Sonderkommando identified the area as Precinct 77. The Poles called it, because of a villa on the grounds, "the Palace" or "the Mansion." German assumptions were that the extermination process would be quick, quiet, and above all, secret. Within fifteen minutes after exhaust fumes were redirected into the cargo compartment of a van, the trapped captives, so tightly packed that they could only stand, would be asphyxiated. When the prisoners ceased writhing—the SS men were to wait for the vehicles to cease shaking—it would be time, according to plan, for the grisly task of stripping clothing, removing rings from limp fingers—cutting off a joint or two if necessary—prying gold teeth loose. Then the corpses were to be dumped into pits prepared by other prisoners.

So, at Chelmno, the Holocaust went into its first phase. However barbaric, the method would prove insufficiently massive. Soon there would be other abbatoirs, devised with manic efficiency and constructed about permanent gas chambers. To keep the systematic murders cloaked by euphemisms, as their scope and the numbers of people needed to operate them made them less than secret, they were labeled as Special Treatment (*Sonderbehandlung*) Centers, of which Auschwitz (Oswiecim), Treblinka, and Majdenek were among the most infamous. In the Warsaw ghetto Emanuel Ringelblum would write in his diary that "the world was deaf and dumb to our unparalleled tragedy." In December 1941 so were many of the future victims.

A conference in Berlin at 56–58 Am Grossen Wannsee had been planned for December 9 to organize more systematic methods of effecting a Final Solution. Rolf-Heinz Höppner, Sturmbannführer of Posen, had written to his "*Lieber Kamerad* [Adolf] Eichmann" that his "expedient means . . . do sound somewhat fantastic but, in my opinion, they are entirely feasible." Göring had first (on July 31, 1941) signed an order confirming Reinhard Heydrich's authority to "solve the Jewish problem as rapidly and conveniently as possible by emigration or evacuation." Heydrich was to make "all necessary preparations in an organizational, logistical, and material context for an overall unraveling of the Jewish problem within Germany's sphere of influence in Europe." Abetted by Heinrich Himmler, Heydrich would find extermination a more satisfactory "logistical" process.

With the news from the Pacific complicating priorities, and the massive problems arising from the stalling of the Russian offensive, the Wannsee conference would be postponed to January 20. There was, however, no cancellation of the killing, as the German chief forester (*Forstmeister*) of the county recalled. "I was traveling from Chelmno to Kolo accompanied by the *Landrat und Kreisleiter* [district head] Becht. As we were driving through the forest, Becht said, pointing in the direction of Precinct 77, 'Your trees will be growing better soon.' When I looked inquiringly at him, he replied that Jews make good fertilizer. I wanted more information but Becht was very mysterious and changed the subject."

In the Lodz ghetto, crowded with hundreds of thousands of "resettled" Jews, some of whom had assimilated unnoticeably—so they thought—into the German populations of their towns, the captives were separated. The children, the elderly, the ill were going to Chelmno; those classified as fit for slave labor remained for the factories constructed nearby to exploit them—until the captives broke down from hunger and maltreatment and enriched the soil of the Ladorudz Forest.

•

At ten minutes after midnight, Gunner's Mate First Class J. Daniel Mullin, on the 0–4 watch, stood by as four young officers returned to the destroyer *Ford* in a motor whaleboat. An old salt—Mullin had joined the Navy in 1936—he knew well what to expect at the close of a Manila weekend. "As usual, Mr. Smith had his camera slung from his shoulder, and in turning to descend the ladder to his cabin, gave more attention to its safety than to his own feet." As they proceeded below, Mullin "wondered what Mr. Cross had done with the tennis racket and golf clubs which were . . . in his luggage when he reported aboard in Jolo. . . . The ship's employment allowed little time to develop those skills, . . . the tennis courts and greens so needed not existing in the[se] places. . . ." It was a quiet watch.

．

While Merrell Benninghoff drove Ambassador Grew back to the Tokyo embassy compound, Foreign Minister Togo was on the telephone to Prime Minister Tojo. Tojo slept in a dwelling on the well-guarded grounds of his official residence. The formal building housed offices and meeting rooms. Only Tojo's wife and two youngest daughters lived with him. Since he was War Minister in his own Cabinet, he also had title to that ministerial residence, three blocks away, where his elder unmarried children lived.

That Tojo was asleep reflected either his self-discipline or his confidence. Although he had been prime minister for only seven weeks and had troops and ships and planes deploying over seven thousand miles, he had left word that he was only to be informed when circumstances warranted. News from Malaya was imminent, and after that, Hawaii. Togo's concern about how to react to Roosevelt's intervention seemed a triviality. It would soon be two o'clock—midnight at Kota Bharu and dawn at Pearl Harbor.

Tojo had suggested that they discuss the President's message, and Togo offered to bring it. The Prime Minister donned his round, thin-rimmed glasses, dressed in his high-collared general's uniform, and walked through the quiet gardens to the lobby of the official residence.

Togo, now in a business suit, handed a Japanese translation of the message to the Prime Minister, who asked whether there were any concessions in it.

"None," said Togo.

"There is nothing that can be done," Tojo observed. It was too late even for conciliatory words to make a difference.

Ambassador Grew, said Togo, wanted to present the message in person. Although that was impossible, he had telephoned Marquis Kido, who thought it was proper to acquaint the Emperor with it.

Tojo had no objection, but wanted a reply prepared in advance for the Emperor, as would be the case with any other matter of state. Without benefit of secretaries, they sat down in Tojo's office and composed one. Then, bowing a good-bye to the Foreign Minister, Tojo remarked about the good fortune of the lateness of the telegram.

Togo hurried out to return to his residence. He could not go to the Palace, whatever the time of day or night, without formal attire.

From the Palace, Minister of Imperial Affairs Matsudaira telephoned Koichi Kido that the audience with Togo was on.

•

At 11:25 Malaya time (11:45 in Bangkok) ships without lights had been reported off Kota Bharu. At 11:55 Bangkok time the Japanese force off Singora dropped anchor. Under cloudy skies and a moon just past full yet fuzzy in intermittent rain, observers on the troopships could see lights on shore at both locations. At what seemed exactly midnight the lights at Kota Bharu went out. The 7th had become the 8th.

At Kota Bharu the Japanese assumed that they had been spotted; at Singora a light appeared onshore, flashing on and off regularly, half-hidden as the ships pitched in heavy swells. Someone shouted, "It is a lighthouse. The Singora lighthouse!" Despite nine-foot seas, landing barges were launched; men climbed down rope ladders from the lurching transports. Peacetime maneuvers in such heavy weather would have been canceled; now the Japanese had to take their chances. It took about an hour to off-load men and heavy equipment; then a red light from the gunwale of the *Ryujo Maru*, General Yamashita's flagship, signaled a go-ahead.

As landing craft crashed together at the water's edge, seasick soldiers held weapons over their heads. Last to wade through the surf was the headquarters staff. It was already two o'clock, Thai time. The streetlights of Singora looked close. What was known informally as the Dream Plan, a bloodless takeover, seemed attainable.

•

Neither Bratton nor Miles had taken any initiatives to alert overseas commanders, nor had anyone else. It was a matter of perception of service responsibility—Marshall was Chief of Staff; decisions were his. The Army in Hawaii had fought the Navy for years for primary responsibility for the defense of the islands, and had prevailed. In Oahu, Short was well aware of that, but neither Marshall nor anyone else in Washington knew that Short's only concern for Sunday morning was a golf date with Kimmel.

When Bratton and Miles arrived in Marshall's office at about 11:25 they found him painstakingly reading through the entire fourteen-part message. Neither interrupted: he was a four-star general. Finally Marshall looked up over his glasses. Did they have any views on the significance of the one o'clock Sunday delivery instructions?

They might be timed, Bratton ventured, to coincide with a morning attack somewhere. It was already past five in Hawaii, and after midnight in Manila. Persuaded, Marshall scrawled an updated warning to commands in the Pacific:

> Japanese are presenting at one pm eastern standard time today what amounts to an ultimatum also they are under orders to destroy their code machine immediately. Just what significance the hour set may have we do not know but be on alert accordingly.
>
> Marshall

Calling Stark, he asked whether Navy counterparts should be notified. The CNO's first reaction was that previous alerts were enough; as soon as he hung up he telephoned back and asked that "Inform naval authorities of this communication" be added to the text. Stark also offered Navy radio facilities, but Marshall preferred familiar channels, and handed the message to Bratton.

·

Domei correspondent Mazuo Kato awoke late in his Sixteenth Street Washington apartment. Since it was Sunday, he breakfasted American-style on pancakes with butter and maple syrup. Then he wrote two brief news stories, one—based on the Sunday papers—about the President's appeal to the Emperor and the chances of peace, the other on Colonel Kenkichi Shinjo. The assistant military attaché at the embassy had died of pneumonia a few days earlier and was to be buried that afternoon. Kato planned to attend the funeral. He was checking his typing when the Western Union messenger he had telephoned picked up the dispatches for Tokyo.

Embassy Second Secretary Hidenari Terasaki, whose long farewell had consumed the previous afternoon for the diplomatic staff, had also arisen late. His daughter Mariko read the Sunday comics, while over coffee the Terasakis discussed whether to drive into Virginia for southern fried chicken. Gwen Terasaki was a Tennesseean, and her mother was visiting. It was a last chance to use the new Buick convertible, purchased before the sudden reassignment orders. One of Terasaki's tasks had been to co-opt American pacifists, and he had enlisted potential peace brokers, from businessmen to Roman Catholic priests with Asian ties, to intercede with the White House. That strategy was now exhausted.

Secretary Hull had just completed his discussions with Stimson and Knox when Ambassador Nomura telephoned to secure his appointment at one. Nomura had finally read the text of the note he was to deliver—long after American authorities in Washington had chewed over it. While the military chiefs were less anxious than the Cabinet Secretaries, Hull had been expecting the call with foreboding.

In an office down the corridor from Nomura's, Secretary Okamura was still retyping a clean copy. The code room had not yet sent him part fourteen of the message.

•

As Colonel Bratton was leaving for the Signals Center to send Marshall's message, General Gerow shouted after him, "Tell them to give first priority to the Philippines if there is a question of priority." Army Intelligence head Sherman Miles acknowledged that the Sunday afternoon appointment was "very unusual," but he saw only diplomatic intimidation in it. With Marshall, Gerow and his War Plans Division associate for Pacific Affairs, Colonel Charles W. Bundy, agreed that hostile action against some American installation was possible at one o'clock Washington time, but that Thailand remained the likely target, and the safest one for the Japanese. Overseas commands could make the best local judgment, Miles suggested. Get a warning to them "and let them translate it into their own time."

Hearing "some commotion in the code room," the imperturbable Lieutenant Colonel Edward F. French, who ran the Signals Center, left his desk to see what was going on. Excited, Colonel Bratton was waving a scrap of notepaper. "The Chief," he said, "wants this sent at once by the fastest safe means."

French took the paper, looked it over, and handed it to an assistant. "Well," said French, "will you help me get this into readable script? Neither I nor my clerk here can read General Marshall's handwriting." In his haste, Marshall had scrawled something that resembled a doctor's prescription.

Bratton retrieved the memo and dictated it. Then he left to report to Marshall. Glancing at his watch he saw that it was 11:58. Marshall immediately sent him back. "Find out how long it is going to take."

French took the question and did some figuring in his head. It would take, he told Bratton, about thirty or forty minutes to reach all the persons addressed. Bratton relayed the estimate. Everyone would have the alert by one o'clock Eastern time.

•

Still 215 miles west of Oahu, the *Enterprise* was eight hours from port at Pearl. Scouting Six in eighteen Dauntless SBDs was airborne at 6:15 A.M. to search ahead of the fleet on routine sub patrol and to precede it to Ford Island. The lucky crewmen would salvage something of Sunday, all of which would be lost by the men on the carrier.

In Lieutenant Commander Howard L. ("Brigham") Young's plane was Lieutenant Commander Bromfield B. Nichol of Admiral Halsey's staff, with a report on the Wake delivery. With radio silence still maintained, landing early was also a way of getting the message back that TF 8 would be entering the harbor late—near dusk on Monday afternoon, Halsey estimated. Originally he had hoped to make port by Saturday evening; heavy seas had slowed them, then one of the escorting destroyers, USS *Dunlap*, began experiencing engine trouble, and the convoy had slowed even more to accommodate the *Dunlap*'s reduced power.

After a cup of coffee on deck while he watched the takeoffs, Halsey went below to shave and shower. He would have a leisurely breakfast with his assistant, Lieutenant H. Douglas Moulton. Everything appeared routine.

•

The six Japanese carriers off Oahu were turning slowly into the wind, their bows dipping fifteen degrees and taking powerful slaps from the sea. "The weather was very disheartening," Commander Mitsuo Fuchida, who would guide the attack, told listeners on Tokyo radio nearly a month later. "The sun was not up yet and dense, heavy clouds hung over us and over the waters of the Pacific about one thousand to two thousand meters over our heads. The sea was rough and we could hear the waves splashing against the sides of the ship with a thunderous noise. Under normal circumstances no plane would be permitted to take off in this sort of weather."

In the near-darkness, carrier pilots in the first wave assembled for breakfast; *sekihan*, a special dish for ceremonial occasions, consisting of rice boiled with small red beans, replaced the routine salted fish with rice and barley. On their way to their planes, wearing *hachimaki* headbands reading *Hissho*—"certain victory"—they picked up food for the flight: traditional rice balls and emergency rations of chocolate. While Fuchida briefed his *Akagi* group, other squadron leaders did the same, making sure that men knew the latest ship berthings in Pearl Harbor, wind and cloud conditions, and rendezvous points. On the *Hiryu*, Commander Takahisa Amagai went to each plane and removed the slips of paper he had inserted into the radio transmitters to prevent even an accidental break in radio silence.

As Fuchida prepared to climb into his plane, a senior deck officer handed him a white *hachimaki*. "This is from *Akagi*'s crew," he said. "We would like you to carry this to Pearl Harbor on our behalf." The seamen with their names inked on the scarf would be represented on the raid by proxy. Fuchida bowed his thanks and wound the *hachimaki* around his helmet.

On flight decks, green lamps were waved in a circle to signal each takeoff. Pilots gunned engines and timed their runs before the ships, lurching in heavy seas, took a downward pitch which might have plunged planes into the sea. The next was already moving before the plane ahead was in the air. In fifteen minutes, all 182 fighters and bombers were up, following the signal lights of the lead plane. It was 6:15 Hawaii time and they were 230 miles due north of Oahu. Above the thick cumulus cover, Fuchida tuned in Honolulu. "Partly cloudy, with clouds mostly over the mountains," the KGMB announcer advised between musical numbers. "Visibility good. Wind north, ten knots." Fuchida corrected his course by five degrees.

TOKYO	SINGAPORE	WASHINGTON	PEARL HARBOR
2:00 A.M.	MALAYA	12:00 noon	6:30 A.M.
December 8	11:40 P.M.	December 7	December 7
	December 7		

HOUR 29

WHEN Finance Minister Okinori Kaya himself telephoned Hisatsune Sakomizu at 2:00 A.M. and asked him to hurry over to Kaya's official residence, an old house across the street from the Diet Building, Sakomizu was surprised. He no longer worked for Kaya. As Kaya's private secretary the young economist had undertaken confidential missions at all hours, but he had been promoted to the Planning Board five weeks before. Although he was the son-in-law of Admiral Keisuke Okada, prime minister in 1935–1936 and considered unreliable by the militarists, Sakomizu's future appeared unimpeded.

Kaya let his protégé in on the secret. War was about to begin; it might have already begun in waters off Hawaii and Malaya. The Finance Minister was concerned that when investors and brokers learned of war with America, the bottom would drop out of the Tokyo stock market. He wanted to ward off financial chaos as well as to suggest that the war was a popular one. Sakomizu was authorized to do whatever was necessary, including using government funds discreetly to prop up the market.

Having spent nearly two years in New York for the Finance Ministry, Sakomizu had no illusions about overpowering the United States, or even bringing it to the negotiating table. Still, he promised to work on the stock market. Then he returned home and tried to sleep.

•

As December 7 lengthened into late afternoon, Rommel remained in a precarious political and strategic situation. He was short in aircraft and armor, and had lost three generals. Johann von Ravenstein of the 21st Panzer Division had inadvertently driven into a New Zealand position the week before and was a guest of the British; Max Süm-mermann of the 90th Light Division and Walther von Neumann-Silkow of the 15th Panzers had been lost to enemy fire. In addition, his Afrika Korps deputy, Ludwig Crüwell, was jaundiced and ill.

Italian generals and Italian promises were poor substitutes. Rommel's patience with Roman pomposity had grown short. Although Libya was Italian, he liked to think that his orders came from Hitler. Nevertheless, his superiors, from Mussolini down, all men he despised, were in Rome. And the general to whom Rommel was technically subordinate in the field was the mustached, autocratic Ettore Bastico, a personal friend of the *Duce*.

Shocked by the death of Neumann-Silkow—a revelation of enemy firepower—Bastico sent for Rommel, who responded that he was too busy to leave his post, newly established in a ravine near Gazala. In a huff, Bastico drove to Rommel's headquarters.

The interview was as hostile as if they were on different sides in the war. As it dragged out past sunset, events were going badly near Tobruk to the east. According to the Italian record, Rommel kept the difficult Bastico waiting for fifteen minutes, then let him into the head-quarters trailer and "very excitedly and in an uncontrolled and impet-uous manner" blamed the defeat they were facing on the uncooperative and inefficient Italians.

Outraged, Bastico interrupted, but Rommel, "very heatedly, and acting like an overbearing and uncouth boor, yelled that he had strug-gled for victory for three weeks and had now decided to withdraw his divisions to Tripoli—and to have himself interned in [Vichy French] Tunisia." Hoping to hold Benghazi for a resupply effort, Bastico—he reported—tried to get in some words of his own, but Rommel snapped, "We haven't won the battle, so now there's nothing to do but retreat!"

Although Rommel had no such intentions, some falling back was essential. Even so, he wrote to his wife, Lucie, after Bastico stormed out, "I'm feeling okay and hope my lucky star won't leave me."

He needed his lucky star more than ever. At 6:00 P.M. the mobile column of the 2nd South African Division, sent out earlier to mop up between Tobruk and Gambut, returned with fifty prisoners and information that the Germans were withdrawing. One prisoner was especially well received. According to the 70th Division report, " 'Bardia Bill,' the heavy gun which had so constantly shelled the harbor in the past month and had become a by-word among the garrison, was discovered intact together with the German master-gunner who had refused to leave his gun."

•

For French laborers in the Nazi-occupied zone of France, the work-day that ended on December 7 also concluded one of their few successful attempts to hurt the German war effort. Immigrants, many of them Jews, toiled in factories supplying the Wehrmacht. They worked in order to live, but their labor was helping the Germans enslave them. Illegal organizations, many of them Communist, looked for safe ways to disrupt the war in Russia, and in September, as the winter loomed, targeted the manufacture of gloves destined for the Eastern Front. Production dropped as workers, claiming illness, turned up four days a week rather than six. By the time the covert strike was called off on December 7, 160,000 pairs of gloves had been lost in missed production; but to play safe the slowdown shifted to another branch of the knitting industry, winter underwear. Production would fall by 375,000 garments. The underground Solidarity movement on December 6 had issued leaflets urging workers not to "willingly work" for the Germans; "whenever forced to do so, sabotage production, work slowly, all means are to be used to counter the needs of the Fascists!" The news of the Eastern Front that could be read between the lines of censored Paris newspapers suggested that hope still existed, and that resistance helped.

•

The *Antares*, a Navy supply ship with lighter in tow, was a familiar sight along the southern Oahu coastline. As the sun was coming up at 6:30, casting a sheen on the water, the skipper, Commander Lawrence C. Grannis, noticed something partially submerged nearby. It looked like a submarine and had a conning tower, but it was experi-

encing "depth control trouble and . . . trying to go down." He passed
on the sighting data to the *Ward*, still on watch outside the harbor.

Observing the same dark object, Ensign William Tanner, on a
routine PBY patrol, guessed that an American sub was in distress, and
at 6:33 dropped two smoke pots to mark the location. The *Ward*'s
helmsman called Outerbridge, certain that whatever it was, it was
unfriendly and was maneuvering to follow the *Antares* into Pearl Harbor. Outerbridge ordered general quarters at 6:40; for the second time
his men left their bunks. This time, ordering his four-inch guns to fire
from fifty yards, he headed for the sub. The number three gun struck
the intruder at the waterline, separating the conning tower and periscope from the sub; it heeled over and began to sink. To make sure,
Outerbridge ordered depth charges released, and an oil slick rose with
the surge. Above the *Ward*, the PBY dropped its own charges.

At 6:45 Outerbridge ordered a cease-fire. Six minutes later he
radioed what he had done to 14th Naval District Headquarters, and
at 6:53 a confirmation: "We have attacked fired upon and dropped
depth charges upon submarine operating in defensive sea area." He
did not want headquarters to think he had mistakenly put away a whale.

•

Ignoring General Gerow's priorities, Colonel French in the Army
Signals Center fired off the first of Marshall's war warnings from Washington to the Caribbean Defense Command in the Canal Zone. It was
12:00 noon. The message to Manila went off at 12:06, and to the
Presidio in San Francisco, for Pacific Coast operations, at 12:11. Since
10:30, atmospheric conditions made sending anything to Hawaii
chancy. French even had his doubts about the West Coast—although,
curiously, not about the Philippines. He assumed that the Navy would
be having the same problems; in any case his instructions were to reach
Fort Shafter, not Pearl Harbor. Army authorities could notify the Navy
on Oahu.

With a direct teletype to Western Union in Washington, French
used the commercial services. Western Union would wire to San Francisco, and RCA Radio from there to Hawaii. Arranging that took a
little longer, but the message was clocked out at 12:17. It was 6:47
A.M. in Honolulu.

No one thought of resorting to the scrambler telephone, a rather
new device of uncertain security. A teletype message could be en-

crypted. Revealing accidentally on the telephone that the Japanese code had been broken seemed too great a risk.*

If Lieutenant Outerbridge was certain that he had sunk an intruder, Lieutenant Commander Harold Kaminsky was convinced that the incident meant more than that. Receiving the message as the watch officer at Harbor Control, he was even more alone than it seemed, as his Hawaiian telephone operator was "perfectly useless and had not been instructed." A World War I retread, Kaminsky had been on duty since four the previous afternoon, with no relief. According to the book, in an emergency he was to contact the Naval District chief of staff and the commandant's aide. Kaminsky had read the newspapers, and had no doubt that the U.S. was "in it."

He tried reaching a list of designated officials. Failing to find any of them, he dialed their assistants and the assistants of their assistants. On his own initiative he ordered the destroyer *Monaghan* into the defensive sea area and finally located Admiral Claude C. Bloch's chief of staff, Captain John B. Earle. Although Kaminsky's voice registered intense excitement, Earle shrugged the matter off. It seemed to him "another of those false reports." Reluctantly, he agreed to reach Bloch. It was 7:12.

Wasting precious minutes on the telephone mulling over the reliability of the report, Bloch instructed Earle to check whether the incident was "bona fide," and then to await developments. One of the people Kaminsky had reached was likely to notify Admiral Kimmel anyway. Earle decided to shave and dress while waiting for more news.

•

When the fourteenth part of the Japanese note was delivered to the flustered Okamura and his fumbling helper it was already 12:30 in Washington. They had not yet reached part thirteen of the retyping. Ambassador Nomura had been inquiring persistently about their progress. Now he felt that he had to telephone the State Department to apologize that the message he was to deliver was not yet ready, and that he might be delayed. Hull agreed to be available whenever they arrived. That it was lunch hour, and Sunday, had not occurred to the

---

* Colonel (later General) Walter C. Phillips, then General Short's chief of staff, afterward was furious about the failure to use the scrambler. "With these remarkable instruments," he wrote, "conversations are absolutely secret." His naval counterpart in Hawaii, Admiral Bloch, disagreed.

envoys, but Hull—who had already read the message he was to receive—waited anyway.

In the foyer of the embassy, Nomura and Kurusu stood in their morning clothes, coats on their arms, while outside their official car idled. They knew less than Hull did about events, and no one in Tokyo had informed them what had already begun across the Pacific in Malaya. Nor had a counterpart in London been instructed to hand over a message to somehow legitimize the war with Britain before the first blows were struck.

In the White House, the President received his first official visitor of the day at 12:30, Dr. Hu Shih, the scholarly Chinese ambassador. Roosevelt wanted to acquaint Ambassador Hu with the appeal to Emperor Hirohito, and read aloud selected passages, stopping here and there to point out a telling phrase that might be useful when made public. He was ready to release the letter on Tuesday, he assured Hu, and if the Emperor did not step in and use his moral authority, there would be no way to avert a Pacific war. "Something nasty" would happen there soon—possibly even involving the Philippines. And he mentioned the very suspicious appointment that Kurusu and Nomura had made with Hull. That meeting was going on, he observed, at the very moment that he and Hu were parting.

·

The five mobile radar stations on Oahu were to close their practice hours at 7:00. Four of the five shut down promptly. At Opana, Private Elliott asked his operator, Private Lockard, to stay on longer for more plotting instruction. From 6:45 to 7:00 they had tracked a lone blip close in, and had duly reported it to Fort Shafter, where it was yawned off. It was one of the float planes reconnoitering ahead of Fuchida's first wave.

Elliott was at the screen at 7:02 when he observed "something completely out of the ordinary." Taking over, Lockard plotted the flight they had picked up. It was at the edge of their reach—137 miles and nearly due north, then 132 miles, then . . .

Lockard telephoned Shafter; the operator could find no one on duty. A few minutes later, someone called back. It was the watch officer, Lieutenant Kermit A. Tyler, a fighter pilot in the 78th Pursuit Squadron. The early morning hours, especially on Sunday, were dreary; he was looking forward to going off duty at eight. Because a bomber-pilot friend had told him that KGMB played music through the night when mainland flights were expected, to help them home in on Hawaii, he had flipped on his car radio en route to duty just before four, to cut through the quiet. Sure enough, there had been music.

The blips he was seeing, Lockard told Tyler, suggested "an unusually large flight—in fact, the largest I have ever seen on the equipment." The phenomenon was now less than 130 miles away, three degrees east of north.

Tyler sounded relieved. The B-17s from California were on course. "Well," he assured the Opana crew, "don't worry about it." In the paradise that was Oahu, everyone—or nearly everyone—lived in a haze of immunity from attack. By then it was 7:15 and the blips had closed to 88 miles. Lockard wanted to shut down but Elliott, insisting, "It is a fine problem," wanted to stay at the dials. He was posting a new and shorter distance every three minutes. By 7:30 he posted 45 miles.

•

To maintain surprise on all fronts, the Kra Isthmus landfalls were planned for midnight Malayan time, which was dawn in Hawaii. The Kra coast would see the beginning of the Pacific war, but given the inefficiency of military communications, or at least the inefficiency of the command structure, the British would keep Japan's surprise attack—no real surprise in any case—secure.*

Malayan beaches were wired, mined, and peppered with pillboxes. Units of the Indian 9th Division were up and down the many miles of threatened coast, with a field artillery regiment and the Indian Mountain Artillery. At Pattani, just above the border, other Japanese transports anchored, but troops would remain aboard until dawn, and even then would encounter Thai resistance. At Kota Bharu the Japanese directed naval fire on the 9th's #13 and #14 pillboxes. Giving away their location resulted in five Australian Hudsons and five Vildebeeste torpedo planes taking off from a flooded runway to find the Japanese. The first pass of the Hudsons was frustrated by fire from the ships;

* News of the landings quickly reached Singapore, where Brooke-Popham conferred hastily with Air Marshal Pulford and General Percival and ordered air attacks on troops and shipping; but it would take more than three hours before the information reached London. It was also unknown in Washington—and in Pearl Harbor, where it might have quickened predawn alertness.

weather conditions proved too much for the Vildebeestes, which turned back.

Into a stubborn east wind the Japanese lowered landing barges for the first wave of the 5,300 men aboard the three transports. Gingerly, soldiers climbed down on ropes and nets. In the heavy swells several of the twenty launches capsized, and men in flotation vests clung desperately to handholds to keep from being washed out on the strong tides. (Orders were to return the vests with the launches once they landed, for the next wave.) Less to hit fortifications than to frighten the Indian soldiers manning them into fleeing inland, cruisers and destroyers threw shells at the beach in the darkness; but gunners seemed to have a good idea of pillbox locations. It was not only the catch that had long lured Japanese fishermen there.

"The enemy," Colonel Tsuji reported, "reacted violently with such heavy fire that our men lying on the beach, half in and half out of the water, could not raise their heads." The commander of the landing force, Colonel Yoshio Nasu, knew that his men would have problems with the terrain. The beach was only an approach to dry land, as the area was cut up into shallow islands formed by the mouth of the Kelantan River. To get to the mainland meant fording the sandy flats while under fire. The Japanese might have picked an easier landfall, but the water was navigable near the shore, and close inland was their objective, the RAF base that might become their staging area for raids deep down the peninsula.

Colonel Nasu climbed down from the pitching *Ayatosan Maru* into a crowded barge lowered into the sea on the side of the ship away from shore fire. He beached it amid a debris of capsized landing craft, waterlogged supplies and equipment, and bodies—his first losses. About two hundred men—two boatloads—were exposed on the sandbar. Wading toward the mainland, they encountered barbed wire. "See if you can cut that wire," Nasu ordered. A captain crept toward it and a buried land mine scattered sand in all directions. The wire parted and the Japanese crawled forward.

In Singapore at 1:15 A.M., Sir Shenton Thomas was awakened by a call from an agitated General Percival. At nearby Fort Canning, Percival was receiving reports that the Japanese had begun landing in the darkness at Kota Bharu.

"Well," said the governor, "I suppose you'll shove the little men off!" Then he picked up his green scrambler telephone and ordered the police to begin the long-planned roundup of all Japanese adult males in Singapore. On the long peninsula any such attempt was bound to be ineffectual. Japanese farmers and small businessmen, many pretending to be Chinese, had long infiltrated the eleven separately administered Malay states. As fishermen they knew the coast; as photographers they had snapped anything of possible significance; as merchants and importers they had supplied the British Army and knew its strength from its needs.

Sir Shenton had sounded no less confident than he had on Saturday morning, when he had strolled into the office of Mrs. Mollie Reilly, his civilian cipher officer. Having worked for him since March 1939, she thought she knew all his pomposities, but on that morning only thirty-six hours earlier he had seated himself on the edge of her desk and said solemnly, "Well, Mrs. Reilly, I have bad news for you. We are at war!"

She put down her pencil. "Well, we've been expecting it for a long time now," she said. "Let's be thankful it didn't happen a year ago when we had that scare."

He looked at her over the top of his glasses and laughed, "Oh! But you didn't ask me with whom we are at war?"

"But of course you mean Japan."

"Ha!" he chuckled again. "I thought I would catch you. No, we are at war with Finland." British declarations of war on several Nazi satellites, including unhappy Finland, had been formalized that weekend.

As he walked back to his own office still pleased with his joke, Mrs. Reilly called after him, "Oh! I thought you were going to prepare me to expect a Jap bomb on my head any moment."

Thomas turned toward her. "What did you say? Japanese bombs in Singapore? You can take it from me there will never be a Japanese bomb dropped in Singapore. There will never be a Japanese set foot in Malaya."

After telephoning some of his staff to stand by Thomas ordered coffee and began dressing. Then, on the balcony of Government House, with its view of the city and harbor, and the hills silhouetted beyond in the brilliant moonlight, Sir Shenton and Lady Thomas, in the muggy air, sipped the earliest morning coffee of his seven-year stay. He would remain up, he told his wife as the coffee service was taken away; she could return to bed. Kota Bharu was 400 miles away, and there was nothing more to do until daylight.

•

Alerted for the Foreign Minister's limousine, Imperial Palace guards in Tokyo were waiting when Togo wheeled through the outer gardens to the Sakashita gate in the high east wall. Up a ramp to the left was the Emperor's residence, a large wooden structure in Japanese style, in which the waiting room for government officials was incongruously Western. In his morning coat, Togo paused until Marquis Kido arrived. Together they walked to the palace library, where the Emperor, anticipating the first war bulletins, had remained awake by his high-powered shortwave radio. Kido went in alone. Hirohito's study echoed with electrical poppings and static, through which could be detected occasional unintelligible words. Kido bided his time. The Emperor took several telephone calls, then fiddled with the radio dials until he picked up a transmission from the assault force off Malaya.

No warrior, Hirohito was less prepossessing than his title, even in military uniform. Small and slight, he wore rimless glasses, and at thirty-nine he looked too unimposing for his august honorary rank. Looking up, he saw Kido. Foreign Minister Togo, the Marquis announced, was waiting in an anteroom with a message from President Roosevelt. Kido had not read the message, but he explained that it was a belated and thoroughly inadequate plea for peace. The issue was moot. War already existed in Malaya; it was nearly three o'clock Tokyo time, and if all went according to plan, war with America would occur within the half hour.

The Emperor instructed Kido to escort Togo in.

•

Lieutenant Commander Kaminsky was keeping busy. In between his dialing skeptical Navy brass, the *Ward* managed to get a message to him at 7:20. Outerbridge had intercepted a suspicious small boat in the defensive zone. "We are escorting this sampan into Honolulu. Please inform Coast Guard to send cutter [to] relieve us of sampan." The sampan's crew had improvised a white surrender flag, which struck Outerbridge as odd. Kaminsky continued telephoning.

En route to the Coast Guard station, the *Ward* encountered what looked like another undersea object three hundred yards away. Outerbridge ordered five depth charges released. Deckhands thought they saw an oil bubble rise to the surface and burst, but the water was seething with the explosions.

In his minisub, Ensign Sakamaki "heard an enormous noise and felt the ship shaking." He hit his head against something and was knocked out—his "first contact with war." Quickly regaining consciousness, he saw "white smoke" in the sub and turned away from the harbor so that he could check for damage. He noticed none, and Chief Warrant Officer Inagaki, his crewman, was unhurt; Sakamaki felt the blast and pressure of additional depth charges, and the sub rocked. He knew from having surfaced earlier that there were old four-stacker destroyers above him. "I did not want to waste my torpedoes on those destroyers. . . . The depth charges fell near us but not as close as the last time. I had to speed up again and turn the ship."

No one at 14th Naval District headquarters thought of telephoning their Army counterparts about the *Ward*'s encounter, nor had the Navy learned anything about Lockard's radar blips.

Readiness was scarce on Sunday morning. The 300-mile air patrols from Oahu maintained by Admiral James O. Richardson until December 5, 1940, had not been continued by his successor, Admiral Kimmel, because the pilots protested seven-day-a-week duty, and Patrol Wing headquarters complained that air reconnaissance was wearing out its sixty PBYs. Three-quarters of the 780 AA guns on ships in the harbor were unmanned altogether, and only four of the Army's 31 AA batteries were in position—without ammunition, which had to be returned to depots after practice, as it was allegedly "apt to disintegrate or get rusty." Most ammo was stored remote from the guns, often locked up by someone with a key who was nowhere nearby. Especially on weekends.

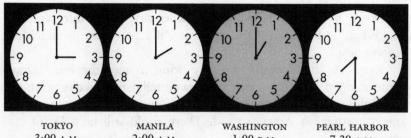

TOKYO	MANILA	WASHINGTON	PEARL HARBOR
3:00 A.M.	2:00 A.M.	1:00 P.M.	7:30 A.M.
December 8	December 8	December 7	December 7

Hour 30

O N a CBS broadcasting assignment, burly Bill (William J.) Dunn was having trouble getting out of Burma to continue to Bangkok. Although only 360 air miles from Rangoon, it was inaccessible by commercial plane. He would have to change ships in Singapore. While he worked that out, the Strand Hotel offered luxury he owed himself after seedy Chialing House in spartan Chungking, the government guest quarters for foreign visitors and diplomats. The only inconvenience in Rangoon was the nightly practice blackout.

Sunday dinner with Lieutenant General D. K. McLeod, two colonels, and the general's aide was running past midnight, but the broad, screened veranda in McLeod's quarters, fanned by lazy ceiling punkahs, was comfortable, and the postprandial coffee and liqueurs added to the Somerset Maugham atmosphere. The general came to the point briskly over his cognac. "Mr. Dunn, is it possible for your country to get into this war—as it has to before long—on a unified basis, without dissension among your people?"

Every conversation with British, Dutch, and Chinese military people, sooner or later, came to that question. "Sir," said Dunn, "I've got to admit I can't answer that. As you know, a large and sincere portion of our population believes that we should let Europeans fight their own wars, in Europe or Asia, and opposes any type of intervention."

"What," asked one of the colonels, "if Japan were to attack the Philippines?"

"Such an attack would certainly bring us into the war," Dunn acknowledged, "but not necessarily as a united nation. We've promised the Philippines their early independence, and a lot of Americans no longer consider it American soil. There could still be a lot of dissension."

McLeod left no doubt that Britain would soon be hard-pressed in the Pacific and needed all the help it could get. He also doubted the loyalty of the Burmese and expected them to switch sides if invaded. As they arose for good-byes, they agreed only that matters were likely to get worse. On that bleak note Dunn returned to his comfortable room at the Strand.

•

From Cairo, Australian war correspondent Kenneth Slessor filed a dispatch home, having just flown back after "a brief visit to an Australian warship"—it was the HMAS *Hobart*—"which has been bombarding enemy positions off the Mediterranean coast. I was in the ship's wardroom when its radio announced the sinking of the *Sydney*. There was a brief silence in which only the announcer's voice could be heard and the piping of a bosun's whistle from the quarterdeck above. Officers rose from their chairs and stood round the radio listening intently to the laconic details. . . . The *Sydney* was not discussed that night. Hardly a man on the ship had not lost a personal friend amongst her crew, but work went on as usual."

The mustached, forty-year-old Slessor, looking in his uniform and cap more like a senior officer than a onetime poet and editor from New South Wales, was as much cheerleader as reporter, writing about how well Australia's forces played their roles and creating emotional linkages with home. The Libyan shore off Tobruk, he wrote, was flat and dreary, with a low dark flange that was the escarpment. "It reminds you of the West Australian coast," he quoted a bearded young lieutenant as saying. But the continuing shock of the *Sydney* was palpable, and Slessor knew what it meant at home.

The heavy cruiser had been the pride of the fleet. On November 30, a German raider, the *Kormoran*, had crept close, off the coast of Western Australia, disguised as a Dutch freighter. The *Sydney* went down like a stone, with all hands. Only a few survivors from the *Kormoran*, soon after encountered and sunk, could tell what had happened. After giving a good account of itself in the Mediterranean, the Australian cruiser had been lost in home waters. The nation that weekend was stunned and bereaved, and Prime Minister John Curtin was already beginning a citizens' fund for the construction of a new *Sydney*. The campaign was national therapy.

•

At the RCA cable office in Honolulu, Tadao Fuchikami, a bicycle deliveryman who had reported for work at 7:30, began assembling the telegrams for his route, which included the Kahili district. Just tucked into the pigeonhole at 7:33 was George Marshall's urgent warning to General Short at Fort Shafter, advising of a deadline in Washington, now three minutes past. There were no priority markings on the message. Fuchikami put it into his bag for routine delivery.

Also at 7:30, Mitsuo Fuchida began looking for landfall—specifically, Kahuku Point on the north shore of Oahu. A few minutes later a long, uneven coastline rippled beneath. His aircraft began to deploy, most curving to the west and south over the Oahu coastline, some cutting sharply east to surprise the patrol base at Kaneohe, to the southeast of Kahuku. To avoid confusion and to split up pursuit craft which might rise to head them off, the dive bombers, torpedo bombers, and horizontal bombers each took separate counterclockwise arcs toward Pearl Harbor and Hickam Field. The fighters followed the dive bombers, which were to hit Wheeler Field in central Oahu before proceeding on. Fuchida's order for attack was to be one shot out his canopy from his signal pistol. A second shot would mean that surprise had been lost. The torpedo planes swooped almost to sea level; dive bombers rose to 12,000 feet; level bombers slipped down just beneath the clouds. The island slumbered below.

•

"The enemy fleet is not in Lahaina anchorage." At 7:38 the message came in from the *Tone*'s floatplane over Maui. It was the first break in *Kido Butai*'s radio silence, but the only one listening was Admiral Kusaka aboard the *Akagi*. No one was tracking the small radar blip produced: Opana was intent upon the massive signal closing in from the north. Immediately after the *Tone* plane's report came another, from the *Chikuma*'s scout over Oahu: "Cloud ceiling over the enemy fleet, 1700 meters. Its density, scale 7. 0308." The time registered Tokyo reckoning. The fleet was in harbor—by the pilot's count ten battleships, ten light cruisers, one heavy cruiser, and other vessels. By the time he had signed off, at 7:39, Elliott had traced the flight to twenty miles north; but the truck from their barracks at Kawailoa, ten miles away, had come to fetch him and Lockard. Taking the station log with them, they shut off their equipment, pleased at their "very good reading."

•

Although Admiral Kimmel finally heard of the *Ward*'s encounter with a submarine at 7:40, he was unwilling to believe that the Japanese were about. Lieutenant Commander Logan Ramsey, operations officer of Patrol Wing Two, who had learned of the reported sinking at 7:30 from the PBY report (it claimed the same sub as did the *Ward*) asked "if the message had been properly authenticated." It was possible, he felt, that it was "a mistake, a drill message of some variety that had gotten out by accident." Yet he knew the rules that such messages were required to begin with the word "Drill."

The instinctive response in the command structure for verification—born of skepticism that the real thing could happen where they were—resulted in inaction almost everywhere. Ramsey refused to accept the reports as "definite information of an enemy attack." Instead, "for no reason that I know of, [I] drew up a search plan for our aircraft under the conditions prevailing that day. . . . Meanwhile I was waiting for an authentification of the message." He donned slacks and an aloha shirt and drove the short distance from his quarters to the Ford Island operations center for the 14th Naval District.

Kimmel had arisen at seven for his every-other-Sunday golf game with General Short. More visible than most others, he symbolized command inertia, the paralysis of will that had immobilized brass hats despite all the danger signals over two weeks and in particular that weekend. Despite his eight o'clock golf date, when the call came forty minutes after he had awakened about the very real sinking of a very real submarine intruder, he had neither shaved, dressed, nor breakfasted. "I'll be right down," he told Commander Murphy, his staff duty officer. But Kimmel had seen "so many reports, false reports of submarines in the outlying area, I thought, well, I would wait for verification." That the attack had occurred only a mile and three-quarters from the entrance to Pearl Harbor had rung no bells in his brain. Besides, all the headlines emphasized masses of Japanese ships thousands of miles distant in the Gulf of Siam. Even the information that the Honolulu consulate had been burning papers had failed to stir him. "Such reports had been made to me three or four times in the course of the year. The first time . . . I was considerably concerned."

Earlier in the year Kimmel's Japanese-speaking fleet intelligence officer, Lieutenant Commander Layton, had given Kimmel a translation of parts of a new book, *Shall America and Japan Fight?*—which speculated on the possibility, *after* a declaration of war, "of a Japanese raiding squadron, centered around a couple of *Akagi*-class carriers . . . , making a raid on Pearl Harbor." Kimmel wanted to know whether the author could be writing "from any official or semiofficial point of view," and Layton had pointed to the Japanese "mania for secrecy." Would the Japanese take such a gamble, Kimmel wondered, and Layton's answer was that it was possible "if they thought they could get away with it." Sending for his war plans chief, Captain Charles H. McMorris, Kimmel had raised the question again, and McMorris was skeptical—"too many risks involved for the Japanese to involve themselves in this kind of operation."

"So with that," Layton reflected later, "we sort of put the book out of our minds and went about our business."

•

For a Sunday morning, Hickam Field was extraordinarily active. Twenty-four men were in a hangar preparing to wheel out obsolescent B-18s for an 8:00 training run. There was also a modern B-24 that needed work, and mechanics had reported to Hangar 15 for that. Besides, Major Landon's flight of B-17s was due in from California, and at 7:45, worried about their whereabouts, Lieutenant Colonel James A. Mollinson called the control tower from his quarters to check on them. A navigation error had added to their flight time. One of the crew on Lieutenant Karl Barthelmes's plane had accidentally thrown a switch that sent the B-17 off course. By the time Barthelmes recovered and turned due south, his fuel indicator showed empty; he was flying on the below-zero reserve. Yet at least one of the incoming planes had been heard in Oahu through the static. They were close.

At Hickam, Colonel William E. Farthing had been waiting anxiously in the tower since six. Below, clustered together for ground security, was most of the Hawaiian Air Force bomber strength—twenty older B-17s, twelve A-20 light bombers, and thirty-two useless B-18s. On General Short's orders, all were being protected against sabotage by a guard force armed with pistols. One hundred miles out, Landon's planes were homing in on KGMB's syrupy Hawaiian music, for which the overtime bill was being paid for by the Army.

Also homing in on the signal, five minutes closer to Oahu in time, and on a bearing only 3° to the west of the B-17s, were Fuchida's 183 planes. At 7:48 one group broke through the clouds near Kaneohe, fanning out over the PBYs of Patrol Wing One. Of Commander Harold M. Martin's thirty-six PBYs, four were moored in the bay; three were away on patrol and four were in a hangar; the rest were on ramps. By the time Martin had run from his quarters to the administration building, the first plane on the water had begun to burn. Struck by bullets and by flying debris, service crews being ferried to the planes in the bay splashed feebly and went under. Men who had leaped from bed in their skivvies had nothing with which to defend themselves; the only arms available were a few dozen Springfield rifles, a few old Lewis guns, and several Browning BARs, all locked away in the armory.

Martin's duty officer telephoned nearby Bellows Field to warn personnel there as well as to ask for assistance; his call was considered— until the Japanese appeared overhead—a bad joke. Seeing the red sun on the wings, a local contractor, Sam Aweau, had already telephoned Bellows, then Hickam, with neither duty operator taking him seriously. The Pearl Harbor operator scoffed, "Boy, you sure must have had a big time last night!" By then, dive bombers were making short work of Martin's planes as well as his only fire truck, and a petty officer who had run out to turn over the propeller of Martin's lone utility plane was riddled by a Zero.

The most immediately available weapons were the .50-caliber machine guns mounted in the parked PBYs; sailors ran to man them, firing away until the planes were in flames. Twenty-seven Catalinas were destroyed, some with crews still aboard; only the planes in the air on patrol were undamaged.

Lieutenant Commander Shigeru Itaya's Zeros swept along the shore to Ewa, where they strafed the Marine air base, destroying 33 of the 49 planes on the ground and disabling the rest. Installations along Kaneohe Bay were a shambles. Shooting off the lock of the "ready storage" ammunition shed, Ordnanceman Alfred D. Perucci, with Aviation Chief Ordnanceman John W. Finn, dragged out a machine gun. While Perucci handed out small arms, Finn mounted his BAR, using a garbage can lid as a pitiful shield. Wounded several times, he gritted his teeth and kept firing. (Finn would get a Medal of Honor.) Nearby, marines blazed away with anything they could load. Cannon fire from the Japanese planes blew holes in the quarter-inch steel doors of the ammunition lockers, also hitting a car in which five pilots were racing to their aircraft. The car burst into flames. A sailor ran to the base's lone gasoline truck, which one bullet could have turned into a torch—and hurtled to cover.

"As I got back to the armory . . . ," Seaman Doyle A. Bell remembered, "everything became quiet—no planes, no gunfire; just the smoke, the fire, the dead, and a terrible, lingering confusion. I was eighteen and I had never imagined that I would see war, or that this would be what it was like."

•

When Fuchida's fighters approaching Pearl Harbor did not seem to respond to his signal pistol at 7:41 he fired again a minute later. The dive-bomber squadron took the second shot as a "Surprise Lost" warning, under which circumstance it was to attack first. The fifty-three planes divided, heading for nearby Wheeler and Hickam fields. With surprise complete, it would make no difference. From his horizontal bomber squadron, Fuchida radioed the code to launch attacks— "*To, to, to, to. . . .*"—at 7:49, and the first bombs fell at 7:53, about seven minutes ahead of plan.

At the Navy Ministry in Tokyo, Fuchida's radio frequency was being monitored, and his "*to—to*" was picked up in the message room. Puzzled, the code officer called Operations. The signal wasn't in his code book. Commander Miyo understood. As a squadron leader on the *Kaga* he had coined the order. "They're doing fine," he said. "It means *charge.*"

In the harbor were 96 warships, most with no schedule except to hoist colors at eight and to hold Sunday divine services on deck soon after. Fuchida radioed to Admiral Kusaka the signal for successful surprise: *"Tora—tora—tora."** On the *Akagi*, Kusaka turned to Nagumo and shook hands.

Anchored off the island of Hashirajima, in the Inland Sea near Hiroshima, was the battleship *Nagato*, flagship of Admiral Yamamoto. 7:49 in Hawaii was 3:19 on the morning of the 8th in Japan. The message room on the *Nagato* had been tuned to *Kido Butai* and to Fuchida's aircraft radio since 2:00, waiting for a break in the radio silence and the first news of the attack. Yamamoto was prepared to order his home fleet out, if necessary, to steam to the aid of the strike force.

From the code officer crackled the message, "We have succeeded in surprise attack." He had picked up Fuchida's *"Tora—tora—tora."* The staff officers around the admiral shook hands and watched Yamamoto for signs of emotion. When his steward could not conceal his own excitement, he brought out sake to celebrate, and even *surume*— dried squid. A succession of toasts broke the tension, the noisy celebration continuing until additional radio reports turned them again into listeners.

•

Leader of the 4th *Shotai* of fighter escorts from the *Kaga* was another Yamamoto, stocky, mustached Flight Petty Officer Akira Yamamoto, who quickly scored what was credited as the first "aerial victory" of the war. An unarmed civilian sightseeing plane was cruising the Oahu shoreline. In the morning sunlight the bubbling surf seemed to splash silently against the beachfront rocks below. A single burst of gunfire brought the tourists down, and Yamamoto flew on to strafe aircraft parked wing-to-wing at Hickam Field.

•

At 3:10 Tokyo time, when Fuchida was one minute from Pearl Harbor, Foreign Minister Togo bowed his way into the Emperor's library. Marquis Kido discreetly exited. Bowing deeply again, Togo asked whether he might read to the Emperor a personal message addressed to him by President Roosevelt. Hirohito nodded. And as both stood, he listened to the appeal he had no power to heed. The actual

---

* In Japanese, *tora* means "tiger." The code was suggested by the saying, "A tiger goes out two thousand miles and returns without fail."

response had already been made in Malaya and was about to be made even more dramatically in Hawaii.

Brandishing another paper, Togo observed that he and the Prime Minister had prepared a response for the Emperor, and assuming the further permission of His Majesty, he would read it. He began with a paragraph about Indochina, to which the thirteen-part note was declared the Emperor's reply through his government. Then he concluded, "Establishment of peace in the Pacific and consequently in the world has been the cherished desire of His Majesty for the realization of which He has hitherto made the Government continue its earnest endeavors. His Majesty trusts that the President is fully aware of this fact."

Hirohito listened impassively to the rhetoric of rejection, and when Togo had concluded, the Emperor nodded his approval. "That will do well," he added. In most matters, Kido was the Emperor's ventriloquist, but Tojo and Togo had saved the Marquis the trouble. Shut out from affairs now, Kido had not even been offered Roosevelt's cablegram.

"Thank you for your graciousness, Your Majesty," Togo said. He bowed again from the waist and waited until the Emperor left the reception room before he made his own exit, escorted by a chamberlain through quiet, red-carpeted corridors. Kido had already gone. When Togo reached his residence at the Foreign Ministry compound it was just in time to receive a call from Navy Minister Shimada that Japanese aircraft were attacking Pearl Harbor. First strike reports were highly favorable. Surprise had been achieved.

Kido's diary noted, only, "3:30. Came home."

•

The *Helena*'s engine-room clock lapsed into paralysis at 7:57. Lieutenant Tsuyoshi Nagai's torpedomen from the *Soryu* had hurtled toward the western shore of Ford Island, with Nagai himself looking past the island to the *Pennsylvania*, in dry dock. Normally it berthed at Ten-Ten Dock. When Nagai realized that the drydock protected the battleship from torpedoes, he turned to Ten-Ten Dock and loosed a torpedo at the two ships there. The old, shallow-draft minelayer *Oglala* escaped as the missile skimmed under its hull, hitting the *Helena*, alongside, amidships. Three explosions rocked the cruiser, while the ancient seams of the minelayer were ruptured by the force of the blast.

The noise echoed into Admiral Kimmel's quarters as he listened on the phone to Commander Vincent R. Murphy's verification of the *Ward*'s sub sighting report. Murphy had not yet finished when a yeoman, Harry Rorman, burst into his office, shouting, "There's a message from the signal tower saying the Japs are attacking Pearl Harbor and this is no drill!"

Dropping the *Ward* business, Murphy relayed the report. Kimmel banged down the phone and ran outside, buttoning up his uniform as he went. He was just in time—his home had a splendid view of Battleship Row—to see the *Arizona* "lift out of the water, then sink back down—way down." His heart sank with it, and so he knew, too, his naval career.

Ordered to telephone senior officers, Rorman began with his boss, Captain Willard A. Kitts III, the Fleet gunnery officer. The Japanese were bombing Pearl Harbor, Rorman announced to a very sleepy Kitts, and he was to report to duty immediately.

"Rorman, you're drunk," said Kitts.

"I am not drunk and am I to tell the Admiral that Captain Kitts will not come in?"

"I will come in immediately," said Kitts, "and when I get there I will put you in the brig for insubordination."

Rorman called other brass. All but one remarked about the bad joke on a Sunday morning, or asked whether it was "another drill." Lieutenant Commander Layton merely said "thank you" and rushed over. For days he had been wondering where the Japanese carriers were. Now he knew.

In his high-flying horizontal bomber, Fuchida had more to do than release bombs. He was to monitor the mission and photograph the results. As he left his lead position, another plane taking his place, he set his bulky camera, mounted on a swivel, so that it could take pictures over the side of the opened cockpit. He also had a peephole in the floor of the fuselage.

Puffs of smoke all about him showed that American return fire, at first scattered and inaccurate, was increasing. As his pilots concentrated on the big capital ships, the AA crews on the cruisers and destroyers were becoming active. A plane on Fuchida's wing dropped its bombs prematurely, and Fuchida ignored the flak bursts to move in close and reprimand the pilot in a way that suggested the subsonic slowness and primitive communications that made the attack in some ways as medieval as a cavalry charge. As Fuchida neared he shook his fist in anger; then, noticing that the plane was trailing gasoline, he chalked on a small blackboard—all Japanese aircraft carried them—"What happened?"

The pilot scrawled on his own blackboard, "Fuselage hit."

Fuchida messaged him to return immediately to his carrier, but the pilot scribbled some shorthand for "Fuel tank destroyed. Will follow you." But having failed with his bombs, he peeled off and began to dive directly toward a battleship, to become his own bomb. Another AA shell caught the crippled plane. It exploded, twisting down in fragments.

A shell splinter pinged into Fuchida's plane, ripping a hole in the fuselage and severing all but one strand of the rudder cable. Still, his pilot moved into position over Battleship Row, where Fuchida could see a tremendous explosion. A column of fire and smudge rose high over a capital ship, which "cracked right in the middle. Oil gushed out of the hull of the ship and covered the water with a thick, dark curtain." It settled into the mud of the harbor. Through his binoculars, Fuchida recognized the crow's nest superstructure as "of the *Arizona* type."

Turning to his peephole, he watched his own plane release its four bombs toward the *Maryland*, then bank away as its remaining rudder cable screeched. "They grew smaller and smaller until they looked like poppy seeds and finally disappeared just as [two] tiny white flashes appeared on and near the ship." The other two bombs—near misses—left widening rings in the water. "Two hits!" Fuchida shouted. Elated, he ordered his forty-eight bombers to return to their carriers on completing their passes. His own Mitsubishi circled Oahu airfields to assess damage inshore.

From the lanai of his home in the easeful Army officers' area above the harbor, Lieutenant Colonel Bicknell watched in anger. His wife heard mumbling about "poinsettias" and "hibiscus"—Bicknell was remembering the Mori telephone call which had failed to interest General Short. Now it seemed more than ever like a code—perhaps for types of ships in harbor.

Lieutenant Heita Matsumura's *Hiryu* torpedo group had deployed simultaneously with the *Soryu* force, Matsumura himself coming in so low over southern Oahu that, with his cockpit canopy open, he could not only see the sugarcane bend to the force of his passage but also feel "the warm air of an unending summer land." One of his planes ejected a torpedo toward the target ship *Utah*, which Matsumura realized was a wasted shot. With its timber-lined deck, the old battleship, now only a bombing target, appeared to the inexperienced Lieutenant Timostsu Nakijima like an aircraft carrier.

By 8:00 A.M. the hits by bomb and torpedo already reported by radioed shouts of *"Atarimashita!"*—"It struck!"—were wreathing smiles on the faces of Nagumo, Kusaka, and Genda aboard the *Akagi*. Shouted radio reports in clear—there was no time for code—from American ships and installations confirmed even more strikes than the efficient Japanese could verify from their aircraft. Eight o'clock was also time aboard ship for morning colors. Crews were lining up in neat rows to raise flags, and bandsmen were preparing to play "The Star-Spangled Banner." In some cases the ceremonies continued until strafing planes scattered the participants. They could not hear the aircraft over the boom of the brass bands.

·

At two minutes before eight, from Ford Island, a terse signal was relayed to the Mare Island Naval Station in San Francisco Bay and picked up in shock by installations half a world away: "AIR RAID PEARL HARBOR. THIS IS NO DRILL."

Rear Admiral Patrick N. L. Bellinger, Pacific Air Arm commander, had wanted no mistake about the reality of the event, and in his haste had failed to identify the attackers, although no one who heard the message had any doubts about the enemy. Chief Radioman Frank A. Ackerson in Naval Communications in Washington fielded the relay and passed it on to Rear Admiral Leigh Noyes, who the morning before had stricken "imminence of war" from Commander Safford's warning to Pacific commands. In the corridor outside Frank Knox's office, Noyes encountered the Secretary, his aide, John H. Dillon, and Rear Admiral Richmond Kelly Turner. "My God, this can't be true!" said Knox. "This must mean the Philippines!"

"Betty" Stark was just coming up the corridor to meet Knox for a late lunch. He glanced at the scrap of paper. "No, sir," Stark insisted. "This is Pearl!"

At General Marshall's offices—it was now 1:30 P.M. on the East Coast—a Navy enlisted man rushed in and handed Colonel John R. Deane a penciled note, "Pearl Harbor attacked. This is no drill." Deane telephoned Marshall at lunch. It had been an awkward time for the general, who seemed never to be at the right place at the right time. As Marshall asked Deane "to contact Hawaii if possible and verify the message," confirming accounts began pouring in. Everywhere in War and Navy the reaction was much the same stunned surprise as that of Rufus Bratton, who threw up his hands and cried, "Oh, my God!"

J. Edgar Hoover had his own lines of communication. His Honolulu chief, Robert L. Shivers, found him in New York via FBI headquarters in Washington. "I know Japanese airplanes when I see them," said Shivers. "You can hear the bombs yourself! Listen!" He held the telephone mouthpiece out his office window so that Hoover could hear the explosions.

As general counsel of the Immigration and Naturalization Service, Edward Ennis was working in the annex to the block-square offices of the Department of Justice at Tenth Street, working on contingency plans regarding aliens in event of war. Suddenly there was a call from the Immigration Office in Honolulu. A Japanese attack was in progress. He telephoned Attorney General Francis Biddle in Detroit; then he called other Department of Justice bigwigs, and finally those assistant attorneys general who were available.

Ennis had worked with Assistant Secretary of War John J. McCloy on what to do in such an event. There were over a million Americans of Axis nationality, most of them merely people who had neglected the formalities of naturalization. The 117,000 residents of Japanese descent on the West Coast, many of them citizens, were considered suspect whether or not they had citizenship papers and even if they were of American birth. Ennis drafted Emergency Proclamation 2525 for the President's signature. It authorized the FBI to interrogate and detain suspected Japanese sympathizers and to conduct searches for "contraband"—anything from radios and cameras to literature in Japanese. The aim was less to catch anyone or anything than to allay public panic. Even before it was signed, its authority for "summary apprehension" of Japanese aliens "deemed dangerous to the public peace or safety" was flashed to FBI offices in the West.

McCloy had been reading "Magic" intercepts, having come in only for a few hours in the afternoon. "Don't kid me," he admonished an aide who had come running in with the news. "Perhaps they're attacking someplace farther west, like Singapore, but they wouldn't dare attack Pearl Harbor." He took with him to Knox's office Brigadier General Ulysses Grant III, who was in charge of guarding Washington, and Sherman Miles. "Here's the whole goddam Union Army," Knox joked—the only thing he would find funny all day. Miles was the grandnephew of General William Tecumseh Sherman.

Acting to protect key installations against security breaches or sabotage, McCloy sent Marines to the White House, and ringed the Capitol and other government offices with bewildered troops. Military units around the country were authorized to protect dams, docks, factories, and other vital installations. The fixation with sabotage dated back to World War I and several incidents attributed to German tampering, notably the "Black Tom" blast of 1916, when explosives-laden railway cars on a New Jersey siding blew up. Fear of Japanese subversion had underlying racist aspects, intensifying the problem. It was difficult for provincial Americans not to believe that clandestine sympathies with Tojo existed on the part of Americans who spoke his language at home and possessed his skin hue.

•

Just after two in the morning, Philippines time, a radar technician in Colonel Harold H. George's Interceptor Command detected a blip between Formosa and Luzon. When three radar revolutions confirmed that the object was moving south, the operator telephoned George's office.

Radarmen had been picking up blips for more than a week, usually in the hours just before daylight, and George had commented to Brereton, "It's my guess that they're getting their range data established—possibly a rendezvous point from Formosa." After a Wednesday overflight near daybreak George added, "They've got all they need now. The next time they won't play. They'll come in without knocking." But there had been more blips and even sightings of formations rather than lone aircraft, from twenty to fifty miles offshore. A Saturday sighting had prompted Brereton to call a staff meeting at which he declared that war was imminent—a prophecy which MacArthur contradicted in an off-the-record press conference. He agreed that war was coming, but in 1942, perhaps by April.

This time George ordered P-40s from Iba Field up toward the targets, and the radar operator watched tracks converge and cross. When the pilots reported sighting nothing, George ordered a second attempt. Again there was nothing—radar had sensed location and direction, but could not estimate altitude. Whatever had been there had apparently flown thousands of feet above the P-40s.

To the east at Fort Stotsenburg, the men of the 192nd Tank Battalion had been living well. National Guardsmen from Harrodsburg, Kentucky, blighted coal-mining country, they were surprised at the catcalls from troops on the docks when, on November 20, they arrived in the Philippines. "Sucker! Sucker!!" came the cry from soldiers who expected the newcomers to replace them. "We thought, boy, they was really foolish," Private Cecil Vandiver remembered; "we thought it looked like a paradise to us." At Stotsenburg they seemed to be on "extended maneuvers." Officers told them "we were supposed to show the Filipinos how to operate our tanks and everything and then we'd go back home. . . . It seemed like we were in for a pretty easy time. A little Filipino boy, for a few pennies, would make up your bed and shine your shoes. We really thought we had it made."

Among the draftees in the 192nd were some with ham radio experience. Almost immediately they converted several government-issue radios to operate on the amateur band and spent hours of their nights— since the time difference was thirteen hours—sending messages home. At 2:30 A.M., working the ham nets and picking up Honolulu, they learned, before MacArthur did, that they were at war. At the communication tent in their tank park, they began picking up garbled messages about the Japanese and bombing and Pearl Harbor. "They were scattered," remembered Lieutenant William Gentry, who had been elevated from National Guard sergeant, "and the first reports were not too accurate except that we knew there was a tremendous amount going on there." Yet Oahu seemed too far away to matter. "Well," the reaction was, "the war has started."

•

The dawn patrol of Ford Island's Patwing 2—three PBYs—was making its search of all fleet operating areas for suspicious objects while four other PBYs engaged in communications exercises with submarines. In addition, five PBYs had lifted off from Midway Island to scout a sector of ocean, and two had gone in search of the *Lexington*, to escort its Marine planes. First Class Petty Officer Maury Meister remembered that it had been Navy Day—October 27—when his squadron of PBYs made its mass flight from San Diego to Oahu to reinforce the wing. Air time was a grueling 24 hours 15 minutes. In the final descent to splashdown Meister recalled hearing someone comment on the aircraft intercom, "We'll probably be at war with Japan in six weeks."

The days that followed were filled with routine navigation exercises, working with fleet units for radar identification and target practice. Then came regularly scheduled antisub patrols, carrying depth charges and surface explosives, as there were reports of Japanese tankers heading eastward low in the water and returning westward riding high—a phenomenon suggesting the refueling of submarines at sea. Anything that looked like a sub that was not in a known position for American submarines was to be hit. "We were told to drop the depth charges, then find out who it was."

Sunday December 7 was the forty-second day since departure from the West Coast. The dawn patrol had taken off at 3:30, alerted to look for targets on or near the surface, and Meister's PBY had flown its assigned vector, crossing and crisscrossing until sunup. It was to proceed to the Hawaiian island of Molokai, where an American sub would be standing by to practice visual communications.

About five miles offshore they saw their contact. The First Radioman was at a signal gun to communicate with the sub while the Second Radioman manned the radio. From his post he began shouting excitedly, "Are we using some special code for radio today? I just received this message and I can't decode it!" He showed Meister the strip "WAR WITH JAPAN COMMENCED WITH AIR RAID ON PEARL."

"These typed letters looked at least six feet tall, and when I showed the message to the First Radioman, he signaled it to the sub. There was no answer; the sub made a crash dive and that was the last we saw of it."

Suddenly war was a reality. The enemy might be in the vicinity. Petty Officer Meister, from a broken, nonchurchgoing family, suddenly found himself "praying to a God I did not know, 'Dear God, please make it possible for me to go through this war and may it be possible for me to never have to kill one of my fellow men.'" The intensity of his feelings surprised him. Momentarily he was distant from the crew members around him. Then he heard the Second Radioman calling known units in their area and drawing no responses. Finally he raised Pearl Harbor and asked, "Is this a drill?"

"NO, NO," came the answer, "AND GET THE HELL OFF THE AIR."

"Here we are," Meister thought, "about a thousand feet above the Pacific Ocean, about fifty miles from our base at Ford Island; our country is at war with Japan, and we have nowhere to go." They circled around the spot where they had last seen the friendly sub, keeping quiet Molokai in sight.

•

At 8:04, KGMB in Honolulu interrupted its morning program of Sunday music with a summons to all military personnel to report immediately for duty. The call kept being repeated; soon it was also on KMU. (No reason was given until 8:40.)

In an elegant Victorian mansion on six lushly landscaped acres at 2661 Nuuanu Avenue, Una and H. Alexander Walker awoke to the noise of what seemed like distant gunnery practice. Chief executive officer of American Factors, a sprawling mercantile conglomerate that included posh Liberty House, the politically conservative Walker was outraged. "Here they go again," he spluttered to Una, "wasting the taxpayers' money on a Sunday morning. This fellow Roosevelt even spoils my sleep."*

Walker's wife reminded him that a display of bad temper was not a way to begin their twenty-first wedding anniversary. Fifty guests were coming for a celebratory dinner at six, the top local brass from Admiral Kimmel on down. A band was engaged, and Honolulu's best caterers. It would be a big day.

They did not turn on their bedside radio.

•

Archie Pence, a sailor on the *Oklahoma*, remembered his ship as being "never less on the alert" than the morning of the 7th. The *"Okie"* was due for an inspection by Admiral Kimmel and was as tidy as it was unready for action. "I was told that our antiaircraft guns had no

---

* According to a Domei (Japanese) dispatch from Germany, quoting the *Berlin Borsen Zeitung*, the NBC radio station in Honolulu interrupted its Sunday morning broadcast with "two flash reports that Japanese planes were approaching Hawaii. The islanders, however, took the announcements as a Sunday morning joke and remained in bed. Suddenly a heavy drone of airplanes and a terrific downpour of bombs greeted these late-Sabbath risers."

firing pins and I recall that our ammo ready boxes had no ammunition in them. This was so the guns and ready boxes would be clean for inspection."

Crews on ships in Pearl Harbor heard bells and alarms which seemed reminders to go to church. Ignoring all signals, many dozed in their bunks. A torpedo took out the *Oklahoma*'s electricity—a real message—and three more laid open the ship's port side. Boatswain Adolph M. Bothne heard the order on the ship's public address system, "Man your battle stations! This is no shit!" He found the antiaircraft ammunition storage boxes locked, as were the fire and rescue chests. He went for a hammer and chisel as the *Oklahoma* began to list so heavily to port that he had to walk uphill. Sliding into the oily water, Archie Pence floundered about until he located lines from the nearby *Maryland* and was pulled up to the deck.

While musicians on the *Nevada* finished morning colors and packed away their instruments before going to gun stations, seamen on other ships smashed magazine locks to get at ammunition. On the cruiser *Phoenix*, inspected the day before by dust-obsessed—and white-gloved—Rear Admiral H. Fairfax Leary, the awnings over the AA guns had to be pulled down as well. The destroyer *Blue* and the repair ship *Vestal* were firing vigorously by 8:05—just as the *Vestal* was taking two bomb hits. The *California* absorbed its first torpedo at 8:05, and more followed. Also scheduled for inspection on Monday, the battleship had been made ready early, to keep Sunday free. Covers had been removed from six of the manholes opening into her double bottom, and a dozen more loosened. Water surged through them.

In a searing flash at 8:08, which Fuchida saw from his plane, an armor-piercing bomb detonated in the forward magazine of the *Arizona*. The ship crumpled and sank with a thousand men trapped below, including Rear Admiral Isaac Campbell Kidd and the *Arizona*'s skipper, Captain Franklin Van Valkenburgh. Debris from the *Arizona* engulfed the *Vestal*—chunks of the ship and its equipment, even, Ensign B. C. Besser remembered, "legs, arms and heads of men—all sorts of bodies." On the *West Virginia*, Captain Mervyn Bennion was mortally wounded, almost at the same moment, by a bomb fragment that punctured his stomach. Flooded by torpedo hits, the listing *Nevada* tried to get up steam and move away from the burning oil pouring out of the *Arizona*. Realizing it, Japanese pilots saw a chance to block the channel with the hulk of the *Nevada*. They went after the crippled ship again.

In the plotting room of the *Nevada*, Ensign Charles Merdinger received a call to send half his men topside to man the 5-inch AA guns. Five decks below the main deck, they were already below the surface of the water outside the ship. No one was safer above, where crewmen had already been strafed and killed, but the big guns directed from below were useless against aircraft. "This was a real Hobson's choice," he felt, "because . . . those men who were singled out to go topside thought they were going to their deaths. And the ones who were staying thought . . . we might get trapped down there." No sailor hesitated. The most junior officer aboard, but for his roommate, Merdinger gave his orders to men all older than he was, and they replied, "Aye, aye, Sir," and went. On his telephone he heard that the nearby *Oklahoma* had turned bottom-up.

Near Wheeler Field, 27th Infantry Lieutenant (later Lieutenant General) Harry Kinnard bent to pick up a fallen, still warm, spent cartridge case and realized, in shock, "it was not our caliber at all." Watching from his office window at Pearl with Commander Maurice E. Curts, Admiral Kimmel was struck on the chest by a spent bullet. A dirty splotch materialized on his white uniform jacket. Retrieving the bullet he murmured to Curts, "It would have been merciful had it killed me."

Since the harbor was not visible from Fort Shafter, all that General Short could see were puffs of smoke in the sky. As Colonel Phillips ran over to tell Short that the island was indeed being bombed and strafed, Colonel Bicknell arrived in the peaceful, palm-ringed circle of headquarters buildings from his Aiea Heights home and Short asked, "What's going on out there?"

"I'm not sure, General," Bicknell confessed, "but I just saw two battleships sunk."

"That's ridiculous," Short snapped, turning his back.

•

Chatting with Ambassador Hu Shih, Roosevelt was in unpresidential garb—flannel slacks and an old gray pullover sweater that James Roosevelt had worn until his father had admired it. Afterward, lunch was delivered to his study on a tray, and he ate and chatted with

Hopkins, awaiting calls from Stimson and Knox about their meeting with Hull. He had excused himself from Mrs. Roosevelt's luncheon to be available.

Eleanor Roosevelt was entertaining thirty guests in the Blue Room. A diverse group, it included family, friends, government functionaries, even an officer in the Army Medical Corps. "Mrs. Roosevelt's secretary," said one guest who had expected the President at least to appear, "is cleaning up the edges of her social list."

Franklin, Mrs. Roosevelt apologized to the luncheon group, was "so sorry" he could not join them, but the press of business was responsible. "The news from Japan was very bad."

Official Washington was busy with luncheons. In Olney, Maryland, nearby, where Secretary of the Interior Harold Ickes maintained a working farm, his table included his own produce: he kept chickens and pigs, and had even gotten into trouble over his use of Interior Department vehicles to deliver eggs to Washington groceries. Ickes was entertaining—among others—Supreme Court Justice Hugo Black, Texas Senator Tom Connally, and Donald Nelson, the former Sears, Roebuck executive whom Roosevelt had appointed war production chief with the unwarlike title of Chairman, Supply, Priorities and Allocations Board. Ickes had never met Nelson before, but was betting that he would be a power in Washington. Connally had "a fund of funny stories he tells well," Ickes noted in his diary, but their minds were elsewhere. "We knew that the situation with respect to Japan was critical, as everyone knew it who had been reading the newspapers. Naturally, we talked of the possibility of war."

At the home of Assistant Secretary of State Long, the former ambassador to Italy and staunch political conservative had been writing in his diary before his luncheon guests arrived—the Turkish ambassador, Mehmet Münir Ertegün; Brigadier General Clifford L. Corbin; businessman and bureaucrat Will Clayton; and Orme Wilson, State Department liaison with the War and Navy departments—all with their wives. "The Japanese problem," Long observed, "is practically at a crisis. . . . Here, Nomura and Kurusu kill time."

Knox was on the line to the White House at 1:47, seventeen long minutes after receiving the news from Hawaii, insisting on being put through to the President, who had just finished his lunch. "Mr. President," he said quietly, "it looks as if the Japanese have attacked Pearl Harbor."

"No!" said Roosevelt in disbelief.

Knox quickly hung up to make more calls. "It was just the kind of unexpected thing the Japanese would do," Roosevelt said, turning to Hopkins. "At the time they were discussing peace in the Pacific they were plotting to overthrow it. If the report is true, it would take matters entirely out of my hands."

Few further Sunday appointments would be kept. Speaker of the House Sam Rayburn had arranged, through "Pa" Watson, for FDR to see Gerald Mann, the liberal-minded Texas attorney general. With Lyndon Johnson he was one of the losers in the June 28 special election which propelled spurious hillbilly Governor W. Lee ("Pappy") O'Daniel, a folksy former flour salesman and radio personality—and outspoken isolationist—into the Senate to fill out a vacancy. Roosevelt had supported Johnson; now, with the full term to be fought for in 1942, Rayburn hoped to test the New Dealing Mann on the President, but Pearl Harbor had intervened.

•

At the Japanese Embassy it was 1:50 when Secretary Okamura, now with a translator named Kemuishi at a second typewriter to correct typographical errors, finished the document from Tokyo. The appointment had been delayed again until 1:45, but Hull still waited. They dashed for their car.

Roosevelt knew he had to reach Hull, but first he asked his switchboard to ring Press Secretary Stephen T. Early. Still in his bathrobe, Early was in his second-floor study reading the Sunday papers. "You'd better tell the press right away," said the President, offering only the bare facts he had, and knowing that Early would check further. "Have *you* any news?"

"None," said Early, "to compare with what you have just given me, sir."

•

On the *Enterprise*, Halsey was on his second cup of coffee when the telephone rang. Lieutenant Moulton answered. "Admiral," he said, turning to Halsey, "the staff duty officer says he has a message that there's an air raid on Pearl!"

"My God!" said Halsey, thinking of his planes flying in unexpectedly and due at 8:15—it was then 8:12—"they're shooting at my own boys! Tell Kimmel!"

Frantic at the thought that trigger-happy AA gunners had failed to recognize their own aircraft, he was ready to break his radio silence. But just then his communications officer, Lieutenant Commander Leonard J. Dow, handed him a message: "AIR RAID ON PEARL HARBOR X THIS IS NO DRILL."

All hands on all ships in TF 8 were being informed on loudspeakers when a second message arrived: "ALERT X JAPANESE PLANES ATTACK-ING PEARL AND AIR FIELDS ON OAHU." Neither report solved the mystery of the *Enterprise*'s own planes.

·

Colonel Farthing's view from the Hickam control tower included Pearl Harbor. Watching for incoming B-17s he first saw what he took to be Navy aircraft, "coming around to the Navy base at the east of the island, and we heard a bunch of airplanes . . . coming from about 10,000 feet. . . . They dived down on Pearl Harbor. I saw a black object leave the first and hit with an explosion. The first plane turned its wings up and I could see the Rising Sun. . . . That airplane im-mediately came to Hickam Field."

Running down the tower stairs, Farthing hit the dirt just as a wave of planes strafed the runways. Methodically, the high-level bombers and dive bombers remained in formation and, with perfect timing, dropped their explosives after the Zeros pulled away from strafing runs.

Into the melee droned the B-17s, fourteen hours out from Cali-fornia. "Jesus Christ, the Japanese are really coming in now!" exclaimed Chief Petty Officer Harry Rafsky on Ford Island. American AA gunners opened up. "Here comes the Air Force out to greet us," Truman Landon had thought when he first saw the Zeros over his B-17. "Damn it, those are Japs!" someone shouted on the intercom. But the B-17s had sacrificed ammunition for fuel, and for balance the armor plate in the rear was shifted forward. They could only attempt evasive action. Trying to escape the Zeros as well as AA fire from his own side, Landon throttled his own B-17E into a handy cloud.

Major Richard Carmichael and Lieutenant Harold Chaffin brought their planes down on the too-short, 1,200-foot runway at Haleiwa. Captain Raymond T. Swenson was landing at Hickam while a Zero pilot, Lieutenant Masanobu Ibusuki, was radioing the *Akagi* that he had shot down "a flying B-17." He had landed a shot amid Swenson's stock of magnesium flares, and the B-17's tail was blazing as it touched down. As the tail assembly fell off, the plane skidded to a stop on its nose. The crew ducked to safety—all but Lieutenant William R. Schick, who was strafed as he ran down the runway.

The Flying Fortresses scattered across Oahu. Lieutenant Frank Bostrom gave up on Hickam when ships in Pearl Harbor began firing at him. He found a cloud, then tried Hickam again. This time Zeros pounced on him, disabling two of his engines, and he bumped down on the Kahuku Golf Course. Evading friendly fire, other Fortresses sneaked into Hickam. Landon radioed the tower to say that he had enough fuel for Hilo, on the big island of Hawaii, but was also talked down into chaotic and burning Hickam. As he banked to land, Captain Gordon Blake in the tower warned, "You have three Japs on your tail and the antiaircraft fire is erratic!" Somehow Landon got in. Touching down at Hickam, Lieutenant Charles Bergdoll thought he was in the most realistic drill he had ever experienced, until he saw the debris of a B-24—newest bomber in the Air Corps arsenal and the only one in Hawaii—burning beside the runway. It was no smoke-pot exercise.

Lieutenant Robert Richards's bullet-riddled B-17, with three of the crew wounded, limped toward Bellows Field with enemy planes on his tail. A few miles further were the thousand-foot Koolau cliffs overlooking the sea—and he was running out of gas. Crash-landing, downwind, on the too-short runway, he skidded into the grass. The B-17 affair had taken all of ten minutes. By 8:20 all were down, somehow. Of the twelve that had flown the route, four were wrecked.

A UP bulletin from Honolulu reported, "A group of four-motored bombers bearing the rising sun insignia of the Nipponese Air Force . . . [was] met by a terrific barrage of anti-aircraft fire," and another two hours later observed that the Japanese raiders had included "four-motored Flying Fortresses." No such planes could have lifted off from carriers, and in any case the Japanese had no such bombers. But the cost in misidentification of American planes over Oahu would bring with it a lesson. No more would the American star insignia on aircraft include a red disk. Panic and poor training may have been more responsible than a misread meatball, but the red circle would disappear from American planes.

On his way to breakfast, Major General Frederick Martin heard noise and poked his head out the door. His men were not supposed to be so busy on Sunday morning. Red balls on aircraft wings, fixed landing gear, and pillars of smoke from the harbor and from Hickam Field told him more than he cared to know. Rushing to his telephone—despite his being Air Corps chief in Hawaii no one had yet informed him—he ordered a slightly less surprised Brigadier General Howard C. Davidson, commanding the Fourteenth Pursuit Wing at Wheeler Field, "Get your pursuit ships in the air just as fast as you can!"

Davidson explained that his unit was under attack and that they were "struggling" to get some planes in the air. Because the war warning had been downgraded in Hawaii into a sabotage alert, most of his aircraft, including 75 newly delivered P-40s, some of them already gutted and burning, couldn't fly. Not only were they parked in a clot; they were empty of fuel and ammunition. "Concentrating" the planes had been Martin's idea; "dispersal" might have "alarmed the populace."

Jumping into his car, Martin rushed to headquarters. Dive bombers and Zeros were scoring hits as he arrived, and Army AA shells were dropping erratically. As Martin turned to rush upstairs to his office, Lieutenant Colonel James A. Mollinson, his deputy, warned him to remain on ground level: "If you stay here, at least you'll have two ceilings between you and the enemy."

Although Martin said later that his aim, other than repelling the attack, was "to get the carrier," Air Corps Lieutenant Denver Gray, then at Hickam, reported Martin as hesitating to attempt a bomber mission to find the fleet: "I can't order them up. We are not at war." In any case he had few bombers left that were operational, and could not have sent any up while Zeros were swooping in to strafe easy targets which the dive bombers had overlooked. And Martin had no idea where the Japanese carriers were because no one had paid any attention to the Opana radar tracking.

Captain Brooke E. Allen rushed to save his own parked B-17. In a bathrobe when the shooting began, he had pulled on flying gear and hurried to Hickam. Orders be damned, he thought; if he could get airborne, he might locate an enemy carrier. As he got to the runway he saw a direct hit on a repair hangar, then others on a supply building and a mess hall. Bombs were falling everywhere, and hitting something every time—a beer hall, the firehouse, the base chapel, the guardhouse. Liberated prisoners rushed to help a sergeant mount a machine gun for antiaircraft fire. Allen improvised a crew, loaded several bombs, and tried to start his engines. Number one would not turn over, although the other three started; Allen taxied across the field trying to get going, counting his blessings when the dive bombers moved on.

Then the dive bombers returned with Zeros, and Allen and his crew scrambled out and hid behind a bulldozer. When one man panicked and ran, a burst from a Zero separated his head from his body; others shot out a wheel and an engine from the B-17. Leaving the cover of the bulldozer to search for a flyable B-17, Allen watched a private whom he knew only as an orderly room clerk climb into the nose of a B-18 and blaze away with a machine gun. The bomber had been on fire when the soldier had taken over the nose gun; he was still firing as flames enveloped the plane.

Lieutenant Ken Taylor awoke groggily in the officers' quarters at Wheeler Field. He and Lieutenant George Welch had been out nearly all night, on the town, carousing at hotels in Waikiki and moving on after closing to the officers' club at Hickam. They belonged at Haleiwa on the north shore, on temporary assignment with their 47th Pursuit Squadron, but in their condition the beds at Wheeler had seemed more inviting than the tents of Haleiwa. When a second shock wave rattled the windows, Taylor reached for his pants, tuxedo trousers with a shiny black stripe. He had been in formal uniform until sacking in.

In the hallway he found George Welch. Looking outside, they saw gray planes with red disks. Bullets were kicking up everywhere. Taylor dashed in and called Haleiwa to get their planes ready. His car was outside and unhit. How to evade the strafing became a matter of acutely exact timing. "Let's wait until we hear the plane's engine, then run," Welch suggested.

They dashed for the car and made Haleiwa, on an empty road, in ten minutes. Crews had the props of their P-40s turning over. Jumping in, they took off into the empty sky and headed back to Wheeler.

Lieutenant Colonel William C. Farnum ducked into Air Force Headquarters at Hickam as a spent Navy AA shell buried itself in the driveway much too close to him. He heard General Martin on the telephone talking painfully to Washington. His responses offered no comfort except perhaps to the Japanese, who were getting information from radio messages and telephone calls made hastily in the clear: "I don't know. . . . I don't know how many. . . . No, we don't know where they came from. . . ." When the President summarily relieved

General Short and Admiral Kimmel, he would also relieve General Martin.

.

Flying in from the *Enterprise*, "Brigham" Young was five minutes behind schedule in reaching Pearl Harbor. Passing close to the Marine airfield at Ewa, he saw planes circling, and puffs of antiaircraft bursts. First he wondered about practice on Sunday morning; then he became concerned about passage through flak. Violations of drill regulations seemed enormous.

One of the circling planes peeled off and turned toward Young's SBD Dauntless. From the rear seat Lieutenant Commander Nichol watched what looked like a stream of burning cigarette butts flash past. Some struck the plane's wing, and pieces of aluminum skin shredded away. Then Nichol saw the red ball of the Rising Sun. Young's wingman in the other leading SBD dived for the Ford Island runway; as Young slowed to follow he saw a sailor on the field point a machine gun at him, and then a pilot run toward the gunner, warning him off, rock in hand. "What the hell goes on here?" exclaimed Young as he climbed out of his plane.

Ten minutes later Lieutenant Commander Halstead Hopping brought in the remnants of Scouting Six, peeling off toward Luke Field on Ford Island. Not all his SBDs had made it. On the *Enterprise*, startled radiomen had heard the voice of Ensign Manuel Gonzales break silence on their frequency with "Do not attack me. This is six baker three, an American plane!" Then, to his rear gunner, "We're on fire. Bail out!" Contact was broken. Bomber and crew disappeared without trace.

Lieutenant F. A. Patriarca had swung north toward Kauai on his patrol leg; as he turned toward Oahu he encountered the first Japanese wave. Realizing that they were unfriendly, he turned out to sea, radioing the *Enterprise*, "White 16—Pearl Harbor under attack. Do not acknowledge." There was no chance that Halsey's ships, under radio silence, would respond. But none of the fixed-landing-gear planes followed Patriarca to Kauai, where, his tank near empty, he crash-landed in a field.

Ensign Vogt, who thought he had seen an enemy fleet off Wake, had not spotted the actual attack force, which was farther to the north and east. But planes from the fleet he had somehow sensed turned up in his path as he came over Oahu. On the ground at Ewa, Marines watched his Dauntless mix up with a pair of Zeros, pouring tracer bullets into one of them. When a Zero lost speed and pulled up, Vogt had no chance to turn aside. Both planes disintegrated, spraying flaming wreckage over Ewa and the cane fields nearby.

Two other SBDs from Scouting Six came in together at 1,500 feet. Both Lieutenant Clarence E. Dickinson and Ensign J. R. McCarthy saw smoke rising from the island while they were still miles out and assumed that it came from the clearing of cane stubble until they recognized antiaircraft fire from the harbor. Emerging from the smoke of burning ships, Japanese fighters swarmed around them; the slow dive bombers could not get away. Bullets riddled Dickinson's plane; his gunner, Roger Miller, managed to down a Zero before dying. Dickinson bailed out.

McCarthy also parachuted, the spinning tail of the SBD's fuselage brushing him and breaking his leg; his gunner, unable to get loose, died in the wreckage. Landing unscathed, Dickinson ran past Ewa Field toward flaming Ford Island and was knocked flat when the destroyer *Shaw* exploded as he approached. Picking himself up, he hitchhiked a ride to Pearl. Flaming from Zero tracers, another SBD from the *Enterprise* glided without power toward Hickam Field, hitting the water just short of the runway. Ensign E. T. Deacon managed to get loose and inflate his rubber raft; lifting his wounded gunner aboard, he paddled ashore.

Aboard the *Enterprise*, still more than a day out, the disaster unraveled in fragments of radio intercepts. Only the frantic message from Gonzales's plane had suggested a connection. Six of the *Enterprise*'s planes had gone down.

TOKYO	MANILA	WASHINGTON	PEARL HARBOR
HIROSHIMA	3:00 A.M.	NEW YORK	8:30 A.M.
4:00 A.M.	December 8	2:00 P.M.	December 7
December 8		December 7	

HOUR 31

ELATED OFFICERS dashed in and out of the *Nagato*'s wardroom to listen to the latest messages read from the map table. Reports from the Hawaiian task force were overwhelmingly good. Ship anchorages in Pearl Harbor had been plotted so precisely that with few exceptions the reports from fliers were accurate; at the map table Lieutenant Commander Yasuji Watanabe confidently shouted out the names of ships and the condition in which the first wave thought they had left them:

"Battleship *Pennsylvania*, direct hit!"

"Battleship *West Virginia*, sunk!"

"Cruiser *Helena*, heavy damage!"

"Battleship *Oklahoma*, capsized!"

Radio messages had become more and more of a jumble in the thirty-five minutes since aircraft over Hawaii had begun sending reports to ships at sea. Many were being picked up by communications units at Hashirajima, tuned to the fleet's wavelength. Even American radio messages flooded in, creating a problem in sorting out competing signals. A reluctant smile creased the face of Admiral Yamamoto, standing silently at one end of the map table with his chief of staff, Rear

Admiral Matome Ugaki, next to him. Nothing seemed to be going wrong.

Even to Yamamoto, the list of American ships apparently put out of action, and estimates of planes destroyed, grew astonishing. When Lieutenant Commander Watanabe took the list he had been compiling to the end of the table and handed it quietly to the Admiral, Yamamoto glanced at it and said, cautiously, assuming overlapping claims, "Actually, it will be only half as good as you estimate." Then, while radio signals continued to crackle over the amplifier in the wardroom, he turned to Commander Shigeru Fugi, his political officer. The Japanese government's final declaration to the United States, Yamamoto observed, had been planned for delivery before the attack on Pearl Harbor had begun. He wanted the timing confirmed.

"I believe the note was delivered as scheduled," Fuji offered.

"Nevertheless," Yamamoto insisted, "I want you to check it."

Concerned that the rules of war had been bent by a failure to deliver some suggestion of a war note to Washington in time, Yamamoto set down a poem to register his feelings:

> What does the world think?
> I do not care,
> Nor for my life;
> For I am the sword
> Of my Emperor.

General Tojo was awakened soon after four o'clock by his secretary for naval affairs, Captain Empei Kanaoka. The attack, he said, was succeeding. Sitting up in bed, Tojo asked whether the Emperor had been informed. Not yet, said Kanaoka, who promised to take care of it. Tojo turned out the light and went back to sleep.

.

The telephone rang in Admiral Hart's Manila Hotel bedroom just before three o'clock. He recognized the voice of Lieutenant Colonel William T. Clement, Marine duty officer at the Marsman Building naval headquarters just three-hundred yards down the road: "Admiral, put some cold water on your face. I'm coming over with a message."

By the time that Hart had toweled his face, there was a knock on his door. He opened it, then sat on his bed to look at the paper in Clement's hand: "AIR RAID ON PEARL HARBOR. THIS IS NO DRILL."

Clement explained that the duty radioman had identified the "fist"—the sending technique—of the operator at Pearl Harbor and was positive that the intercept was authentic.

Sitting on the edge of his bed, Hart seized a scrap of notepaper and drafted a dispatch: "Asiatic Fleet. Priority. Japan started hostilities. Govern yourseles accordingly." In his haste he omitted the *v*. He telephoned his chief of staff, Admiral Purnell, dressed, ate a hasty breakfast, and left for his office. Although Purnell rushed the news to General Sutherland in the walled city across from the hotel, the Signal Corps had picked up the same message, and Signals chief Spencer B. Akin, a brigadier general, had already been to the sleeping quarters in the Army command offices. "Pat! Pat! Wake up!" he whispered to Colonel Hugh ("Pat") Casey, chief of engineers. "The Japanese have just bombed Pearl Harbor."

Sutherland and Brigadier General Richard J. Marshall, Jr., his deputy chief of staff, sat up in their beds. Sutherland reached for his telephone and the private line to MacArthur's penthouse. "Pearl Harbor! Pearl Harbor!" MacArthur repeated. "It should be our strongest point!"

Sutherland put down the phone, then lifted it again to call MacArthur's air chief, Lewis Brereton. Lieutenant Colonel Charles Caldwell answered but the ringing had already awakened Brereton. "General, Pearl Harbor's been bombed," said Caldwell. "Sutherland is on the phone and wants to talk to you."

Hastily dressing, Brereton shouted to aides to notify all units and have them ready for action. It was still dark, and he expected attacks any time after daylight. Many of his men had barely made it to bed. It had been a long and not always sober ride home after the balls and parties at the Manila Hotel.

A note on Harry Hopkins's memorandum pad written between two and three in the afternoon Washington time reads, cryptically, "MacArthur ordered 'execute.'" With the War Department's radio message number 736 to him explicitly invoking Rainbow 5 went assurances of "every possible assistance and support within our power." Hours elapsed before MacArthur executed anything.

In his penthouse the bedside phone rang again. This time it was Brigadier General Gerow in Washington. It was 3:40 in Manila. Aircraft and installations at Pearl Harbor had suffered "considerable damage," he confirmed. The raid was still in progress, and, Gerow warned,

"I wouldn't be surprised if you get an attack there in the near future."
Later, MacArthur would recall that as his first news of the war. Stunned
and confused in the predawn darkness, he asked his wife, Jean, to bring
his Bible to him.

While shocked members of MacArthur's staff were gathering in
Intramuros, he sat on the edge of his bed, turning the pages of his
Bible. (It was his practice to read from the Scriptures for ten minutes
every morning.) Finally he dressed and crossed palm-lined Dewey
Boulevard to his office.

Also at 3:40 the telephone in Lieutenant Colonel William C. Braly's
Harbor Defense Command Post on Corregidor jangled. It was Captain
Bob Brown, aide to Major General George F. Moore, the commanding
general of Harbor Defenses. "Rudie Fabian," he reported—Fabian was
a lieutenant at the Naval Intercept Station—"just phoned me two
messages he picked up"—and he repeated what Hart had learned. All
the harbor batteries in Manila Bay were alerted—there were about four
thousand officers and men on the islands in the Bay. Mine fields had
been laid during the summer, but no one knew that many of the
mines were so defective that no provocation could explode them. The
Navy's antiaircraft guns were three-inch weapons built to interdict low-
flying early 1930s biplanes; the coast artillery was of World War I
vintage. The huge mortars hidden in Corregidor's hollows which
gave the island its reputation of impregnability were embossed, if one
looked closely, with an identity of manufacturer and date which made
one feel less sanguine about the fortress-island's chances: Bethlehem
Steel, 1898.

Awakening his coastal battery, Lieutenant John M. Wright, later
a general, assembled his men in the darkness and told them the news
from Hawaii. "Go [back] to bed," he said, dismissing them; "get a
good night's sleep, and I'll get you up before daybreak so you can get
in a hole, and get ready for an air raid." There was no comfort in his
remarks, and few slept.

At 3:45 Hart followed up his war message with a second one. As
received by the sub *Sturgeon* it read, "Submarines and aircraft will wage
unrestricted warfare." Hart had few planes useful for combat, but he
had twenty-eight subs and was an old submariner himself. If anything
could ward off slow troop transports, it would be his subs. Four,
however, would not survive the devastating and nearly unopposed air
raid on Cavite on the tenth, which also cost all but 150 of the torpedoes

in storage onshore. With few exceptions, American subs, slipping among fat targets from merchantmen to a carrier, would fire wide of the mark, even against targets at anchor. Some "fish" exploded prematurely or failed to penetrate. The exploders on the diminishing and irreplaceable stock of precious torpedoes were defective.

.

Settling in his bed at the Kota Bharu air base, Peter Gibbes heard "what sounded like shells exploding in the distance. I noticed half-dressed officers and airmen rushing past my room and shouting at each other. I yelled out 'Shut up, you bastards and let a fellow get some sleep!' "

"You'd better get off your ass," someone shouted back. "The war has started; the Japs have landed!!"

"Bewildered, scared and confused," Gibbes confessed, "I found myself some two hours later in a Hudson with 3 perfect strangers as my crew, in darkness, setting off to bomb the invasion fleet. Not too sure where the coast was, or how far, I followed the flashes of gunfire and exploding bombs and dropped my bomb load." It was his only sortie of the night.

Ashore at Singora, Japanese troops waited for Major Yoshihiko Ōsone. Ostensibly a clerk in the small Singora consulate, he was planted there to deliver the town. When Ōsone failed to appear, Major Masanobu Tsuji seized a Thai pulling an empty rickshaw, and through an interpreter ordered him to the consulate. A dog growled as Tsuji pounded on the gate, and a corpulent, pajama-clad man, rubbing his eyes with sleep, came to the door. "Ah! The Japanese Army!" said Consul Katsuno. Behind him, sleepily, appeared Major Ōsone. They had not received the secret embarkation plan to be sent via the Saigon embassy, Ōsone claimed. Yet he had, and he had been given before taking up his assignment in Singora a letter of instructions on deciphering telegrams, including the one giving the date and time of the landing. In his anxiety he had burned the instructions too soon and had not known that an innocuous message had concealed his orders to co-opt the Thai police and army units in his district. In particular the Japanese wanted to keep the bridge over the Perak River from being blown up by the Thais. Tsuji had even brought the payoff money to quiet the Thai police. In a white linen suit, the consul led Tsuji, his orderly, and an interpreter to his car, and they drove off to the police station, the orderly carrying, in a large silk *furoshiki* square, 100,000 ticals in Thai currency.

At the station gate shots rang out; a headlight on the consulate car shattered. Several more shots followed; the four emptied out of the car, abandoning the *furoshiki* and taking cover in a drainage ditch. Over and over again the frightened interpreter shouted, "Don't shoot! It is the Japanese Army. Ally with us and attack the British."

The consul's muddy white linen suit attracted further fire, as did the car. Recklessly, Tsuji's orderly crawled back to the car and retrieved the money, and the four retreated toward their beachhead until they found a battalion moving up. Tsuji clasped hands with Major Kobayshi, who had been in military school with him. "Somehow or other," suggested Kobayshi, "we ought to come to terms and not fight the Thai Army; don't you think so?"

Tsuji agreed, but by then Thai machine gunners on high ground above the beach were spraying the landing site, where soldiers took cover under, and behind, coconut trees. The first light of dawn was emerging. Tsuji went to General Yamashita for instructions. This was not the way the Dream Plan was supposed to have worked.

•

The coordinator of the American Hour on Rome Radio, beamed by shortwave to the U.S. and other parts of the world, was George ("Giorgio") Nelson Page, a Virginian who had renounced his citizenship and become an Italian. Other English and American expatriates, admirers of Mussolini, contributed to the English Hour and the American equivalent. Weekly, Ezra Pound would take the train south from Rapallo to record his ten-minute contribution, sometimes also to write propaganda slogans for Page, and to collect his 350 lire per presentation, about 17 dollars.

On December 7 Pound remained to hear his broadcast about how cozy life was under Fascism and how venial were the Western democracies as misled by crypto-Jews Churchill and Roosevelt. The night before, Pound had run into an American journalist who confided that concerns about Japan were unfounded "and that the Japs would never etc. etc." Huddled in his shabby double-breasted tweed overcoat, Pound hurried back to his hotel, the Albergo d'Italia, grateful for the reassurance.

Since his early days in London, when he learned about Asian literature from Ernest Fenollosa, Pound had been devoted to Japanese writing and art. War with Japan would only complicate his already difficult life. He had even explored, unbeknownst to Fascist friends, the possibility of taking his family back to the U.S. on the Pan Am Clipper from Rome. But, he told his sixteen-year-old daughter, Mary, the bureaucrats at the American consulate "had been very nasty." Whether it was cause or effect, Pound had made "undignified remarks" about the U.S. to George Wadsworth, the Chargé d'Affaires at the Consulate General, and on leaving the office he arrogantly offered, Wadsworth reported, "the Fascist salute."

By the time Pound's broadcast aired, just after seven, the Japanese were at war with Britain and the U.S., but no one in Italy knew it, and the gaunt, cranky self-exile was introduced as if the world had not changed. "The Italian Radio," his announcer began, "acting in accordance with the Fascist policy of intellectual freedom and free expression of opinion by those qualified to hold it, [and] owing to the tradition of Italian hospitality, has offered Dr. Ezra Pound"—he had an M.A. from the University of Pennsylvania—"the use of the microphone twice a week. It is understood that he will not be asked to say anything whatsoever that goes against his conscience or anything incompatible with his duties as a citizen of the United States of America. And now Professor Ezra Pound, the well-known American poet and economist."

"They say," Pound began, "an Englishman's head is made of wood and the American's head made of watermelon. Easier to get something into the American head but nigh impossible to make it stick there for ten minutes." He wondered "what good I am doing," but he had in mind "some things you folks on both sides of the wretched ocean will have to learn, war or no war, sooner or later." While Pound didn't "cotton to the idea of my country bein' an octopus," he hoped for an American takeover of Canada. That was all right because the British Empire was only a "syphilitic organization" run by Jews. The U.S. could be next, he warned; it was already being run by "ex-European Jews" who would make "another peace worse than Versailles." Pound put his trust in noninterventionists like "Brother Hoover," the former President. "I do not want my compatriots . . . to get slaughtered to keep up the opium and other British Jew rackets in Singapore and Shanghai. This is not my idea of American Patriotism."

America's job, he insisted, was to stay out. "I repeat; the rot and

stink of England are from inside and have been from the time of
Cromwell and no number of rabbis and bank clerks in Wall Street and
Washington can do one damn thing for England save to let her alone."
Roosevelt, he warned, was "in the hands of the Jews" and only "a
Fascist solution" would save the country.

Next week, Pound volunteered, he would expand on that subject.
"Good evening. Ezra Pound speaking."

The war news astonished and confused Pound. It was evening;
there was no way to return home to Rapallo, to get his bearings among
the rustling olive trees. He thought he remembered rushing home at
noon on "Arbour Day, Pearl Arbour Day," but that noon was eight
hours past. The United Press bureau chief in Rome, Reynolds Packard,
recalled Pound unexpectedly coming to his house that evening to talk
about the inevitability of war between the U.S. and Italy. He intended
to stay, Pound confided, realizing that he would be a pariah at home.

"I told him," Packard remembered, "that he would be a traitor if
he did so, and now was the time for him to pipe down about the
alleged glories of Fascism."

"But I believe in Fascism," Pound insisted, offering the Fascist
salute in emphasis, "and I want to define it. . . . I tell you I want to
save the American people."

There was no way, Reynolds found, "to reason with him." Pound
pulled his long overcoat around him and left.

•

Secretary Stimson was having lunch at Woodley, his estate overlooking Rock Creek Park, when the telephone rang. In a "rather excited" voice the President asked, "Have you heard the news?"

"Well," Stimson said, "I have heard [of] the telegrams which have
come in about the Japanese advances in the Gulf of Siam."

"Oh, no, I don't mean that. They have attacked Hawaii. They are
now bombing Hawaii."

Stimson recovered from the shock with some confidence and hope.
Since the Japanese had attacked America's strongest base, it was possible that the alerted forces there might score a tactical defensive success.
As he would say when he found that they had failed, "It is not the
duty of the outpost commander to speculate or rely on the possibilities
of the enemy attacking at some other outpost instead of his own. It
is his duty to meet him at his post at any time and to make the best

possible fight that can be made against him with the weapons with which he has been supplied."

In his diary for the day he wrote, "My first feeling was of relief that the indecision was over and that a crisis had come in a way which would unite all our people. This continued to be my dominant feeling in spite of news of catastrophes which quickly developed. For I feel that this country united has practically nothing to fear, while the apathy and divisions stirred up by unpatriotic men have been hitherto very discouraging."

At 2:05 the President reached Hull. An hour late, Nomura and Kurusu had just arrived at State. Hull was to say nothing about Pearl Harbor—only "to receive their reply formally and coolly and bow them out."

In the company of Hull's assistant, Joseph W. Ballantine, Nomura and Kurusu—clearly distressed—were ushered in. The Secretary did not invite them to sit down. Offering Hull a typescript, Nomura explained, "I was instructed to hand you this reply at 1:00 P.M. We were late, because it took longer than expected to translate the cable of the memorandum."

Hull made a pretense of scanning the message—he had read it hours earlier. "Why one o'clock?" he wanted to know.

"I don't know the reason," said Nomura, "but I was so instructed."

Leafing through more pages of the typescript, Hull asked whether it was being shown on the instructions of the Japanese government. "That is so," said Nomura, with Kurusu standing silently next to him.

His usual courtly Tennessee courtesy overwhelmed by anger, Hull exploded that in his fifty years of public service he had "never seen a document that was more crowded with infamous falsehoods and distortions on a scale so huge that I never imagined until today that any Government on this planet was capable of uttering them."

When Nomura looked as if he were about to protest, Hull raised a hand for silence, then signaled for them to go. Nomura's memoirs mention shaking hands silently with Hull before leaving. (Hull recorded accepting no such gesture.) Heads bowed, they emerged into a corridor crowded with reporters. "Scoundrels!" Hull muttered after them. "Pissants!" (Hopkins's notes read, "Hull delivered message from Japs 2:20. Hull indignant.")

None of the newsmen trailing the envoys out into the feeble December sunlight knew any more than did Nomura or Kurusu. "I had not even dreamed of the attack on Hawaii," Nomura wrote afterward, "for my concern and attention had been concentrated on the Southwest Pacific."

At the embassy, where the curious were already gathering at the gates, military attaché Major General Saburo Isoda—an old friend of Rufus Bratton, from his Japanese assignment—greeted Nomura with tears in his eyes and the news they had only learned from the radio. It was regrettable, he said, that "things should have come to such a pass. But, alas, this is fate."

"I can even now," Nomura wrote five years later, "recall how deeply moved I was at seeing his tears consoling me. I did not know at that time whether the Secretary of State already knew of the surprise attack."

•

Ed Sheehan had worked late at Pearl and was hard to awaken. His apartment mate, Al Sharkay, shook him into consciousness. When Sheehan saw Sharkay's face, he knew he had better get up. Stumbling into their living room, where a radio blared, he heard Webley Edwards, the familiar "Hawaii Calls" announcer, repeating, "Pearl Harbor is under attack. This is no drill. This is the real McCoy. . . . Those are real planes up there with red spots on them. Please believe me!" They rushed outdoors and looked toward the harbor. Columns of black smoke were rising. "Specks darted about in the sky, looking like gnats from our distance."

While Sharkay was suggesting that they ought to "get out there," Edwards appealed to all Pearl Harbor workers to report for duty. In minutes they were on their way. Driving east on Kapiolani Boulevard and across downtown Honolulu, it seemed to Sheehan and Sharkay like any other Sunday. Solitary walkers alongside the silent office buildings appeared unaware that their world had changed. Sharkay drove faster. As they neared Hickam and the harbor they could hear the booming of bombs and see oily black smoke rising above the treetops.

At the main gate to Pearl there was a chaos of cars. They parked illegally at the side of the road and walked. At the entrance "half-dressed Marines, waving rifles with fixed bayonets," were passing people through. Separated from Sharkay, Sheehan hopped on an open truck ferrying other arrivals. "A whistling sound came from the direction of the submarine base and a plane flew over, low, less than a hundred feet above our heads. We could see the red suns on its wings and the head of the goggled pilot. Marines lifted their rifles and fired wildly. The plane's guns clattered briefly, digging up pieces of road and clods of dirt."

As New York surgeon Dr. John J. Moorhead was being driven to his Sunday morning lecture at Honolulu's Mabel L. Smyth Auditorium—he was to speak at nine on "Burns"—his driver clicked on the car radio and picked up a bulletin at 8:40 that Pearl Harbor was under attack. Moorhead—an Army doctor in 1917–1918—had lectured on Friday on "The Treatment of Wounds." Of the three hundred in his audience, most had been service medical officers, interested in hearing someone with real battle experience.

As if Pearl Harbor had no connection with Honolulu, Moorhead went on to his lecture date; the streets he drove through appeared convincingly at peace. But the lecture hall was nearly empty, and shells suddenly began falling outside—spent and erratic Army AA fire. A local doctor rushed in breathlessly with an appeal for extra surgeons at the Army's Tripler General Hospital, and the hall emptied. Moorhead's own improvised surgical team worked the rest of the day and into the night with little relief.

All the hospitals on the island were quickly more than full; one of them, the hospital ship *Solace*, was tied up across the harbor from Battleship Row. Its big red cross was visible to the Japanese pilots, who had explicit instructions to avoid dropping bombs on Honolulu or other civilian sectors and to stay clear of hospitals, including hospital ships. (The stray shells that landed in the city were American.) On the *Solace*, Radioman Glenn Lane awoke from a morphine shot and thought he had been taken prisoner. His attendant was a Filipino. Filipinos, Chinese, Japanese, and other Asians were in jeopardy throughout the day and into the night as panicky Americans assumed that anyone not a pale-skinned *haole* was the enemy. (Negroes, as they were called, were a special category—always in service rather than fighting units. Yet one, burly Mess Attendant 2nd Class Doris Miller on the *West Virginia*, manned a machine gun although untrained to use it.)

As Major Leonard D. Heaton and Major Lawrence Ball, both M.D.'s, were waiting for their car and driver to take them to Dr. Moorhead's surgery lecture in Honolulu, the first-wave dive bombers screamed down, machine guns chattering. Investigating the noise, Mrs. Heaton had come to the door. Heaton pushed her down behind a palm tree and hit the ground himself. (Later he added one of the spent bullets to his decorations case. Years after, when he was Army Surgeon General, he visited his former house and paid his respects to the palm tree.)

The Schofield Barracks Hospital was little more than a mile from the Wheeler Field fighter base. Heaton and Ball rushed to duty, remembering their hospital C.O.'s warning of a few weeks before to have one's life insurance and emergency packing instructions in order, to discuss with one's wife "where she will go with the family in the United States," and to do so without causing alarm. "Because, gentlemen, we are in a very dangerous period and anything can happen from Japan."

Colonel Austin J. Canning had taken his own warning so seriously that when Heaton arrived to prepare for surgery he was told that Canning was nowhere to be found. As senior officer, Heaton found himself temporary C.O. Fortunately, he had laid in, for an emergency, stocks of saline and glucose fluids, and the new sulphanilamide powder. No one had any experience of triage—determining which patients were too far gone for high-priority help—but Heaton designated Captain Robert Hardaway as his triage officer, asking him also to operate when he could.

Heaton and Hardaway discharged anyone taking up a bed for a minor ailment, ordering released soldiers to get back to their units. With casualties pouring in, they ignored the usual bureaucratic paper for outgoing or incoming patients. "I knew we needed all the manpower available. We thought the Japs were coming right in on an invasion. . . . That created a little bit of trouble when Colonel Canning returned, a couple of days later, because he bitterly resented the fact that I hadn't completed the paperwork on these patients. . . . I told him we just didn't have time for that kind of business. I never inquired where he was or what happened to him." Heaton had been a specialist in abdominal surgery. After Pearl Harbor he also knew a lot about amputations.

Schofield's corridors were full of casualties, but nothing like Tripler, which took the bulk of wounded from Hickam and the overflow from Pearl. At Tripler, where Phyllis Walen, wife of an Army sergeant at Fort Shafter, had just had her baby delivered, the thump of what seemed practice with smoke bombs seemed reassuring. It was time for infants to be brought for morning feedings, and she listened for the squeals over the outside noises. "Suddenly a young Filipino nurse rushed in, crying and yelling—'Oh, my God! The Japanese are bombing Pearl Harbor! We'll all be killed!' She collapsed in tears. All of the women in the ward, including myself, were in a state of shock. We never did get to see our babies that morning."

She remembered a rush of stretchers by her door, and new mothers set to work making gauze pads and bandages, while from the corridor they could hear a Catholic chaplain giving the last rites to some of the arrivals. Amid the hubbub Mrs. Walen wondered whether her newborn son "would ever get to meet his grandparents, aunts and uncles."

.

Ed Sheehan jumped off a truck at the shipfitter's shop at Pearl, across the road from the docks. Men were running about the decks of moored ships, some loading and firing antiaircraft guns. Above the roof of the machine shop he saw clouds of smoke, but the building hid his view of the outer harbor. "Get under cover, you dumb bastard!" a Marine yelled. Sheehan dashed inside. Out of habit he went to punch the time clock, and his boss, Dave Melville, shouted, "Never mind that, Eddie, for Christ's sake. Go over to Ten-Ten Dock and do what you can to help."

Slipping around crouched Marines at the door, Sheehan took a shortcut through the machine shop, passing men who stood by their lathes nearly paralyzed by what they saw from the windows facing Ford Island. "It was like looking into Hell on a sunshiny day. Each of the great battleships . . . was in agony. Only the cage-like top sections of the masts on the *West Virginia* and *Tennessee* were visible through the roiling filth. The *California* looked half-sunk, listing on one side in snapping fires. The *Arizona* . . . tilted at a crazy angle amid oily clouds rising like thick black cauliflowers." Having absorbed seven torpedoes, the *Oklahoma* had rolled over and exhibited only its long whalelike underside, on which desperate sailors clustered, risking a slide into the oily water. Stubbornly, the ship's executive officer "walked the hull" to stay topside. Small boats ducked in and out of the flaming wreckage in the harbor, picking up flailing, oil-slicked men. Internal explosions vomited fragments of ships and gear and crew.

Aboard the cruiser *Helena*, men were shouting and waving at people on the pier, and Sheehan found himself in a queue passing AA shells aboard. He felt relief in doing something. When the ammunition gave out and the group broke up, he felt suddenly useless and ran on, thinking, "There must be something I can do. Or perhaps someone will tell me what to do."

Berthed close to a dockside crane, the heavy cruiser *New Orleans* was a difficult target for dive bombers. Pulling up to clear the gantry, pilots had to release bombs prematurely or hold their fire. After cutting away an awning to get a better shooting angle at the planes, seamen were hacking with fire axes at locked ammunition boxes when all electric power vanished. To prevent the *New Orleans* from becoming a sitting duck, the duty officer had called for cutting the ship loose, and an eager sailor had chopped at the cable to the dock, severing the "hot" line to shore. Lacking steam to start the cruiser's own generators, gunners had to feed AA shells by hand.

With Sunday morning church services above deck abruptly canceled, Presbyterian chaplain Howell Forgy descended below deck to offer encouragement in his own fashion. "Praise the Lord and pass the ammunition!" he exhorted. Someone remembered, and later told a newspaperman, prompting one of the more memorable songs of the war.*

One foreign vessel, the Dutch merchantman *Jaegersfontein*, was unexpectedly contributing to the defense of Pearl Harbor. Just before eight it had been lying outside for a harbor pilot and approval to enter. Captain Walter Bahr, the pilot, had left the dock in his launch seeing puffs of smoke in the distance; the noise and smoke had increased as he closed in on the freighter, inbound from the West Coast. Seizing a chance to block the channel with her, dive bombers turned toward the freighter, but the Dutch had been at war for nearly two years and knew how to defend themselves. While Bahr guided the *Jaegersfontein* in at its sluggish top speed, the Dutch crew, canvas stripped from their AA pom-poms, blazed away.

From the old supply ship *Vega*, nearby, Fireman Tony Gellepis watched the *Jaegersfontein* "making her entry into the harbor and firing away as if beset by the Devil." Only one bomb dropped harmlessly near her, about five hundred yards away on Sand Island. Once in port, the crew queued up at Queen's Hospital in Honolulu to give blood,

---

* The cover of the sheet music for Frank Loesser's song—the words of which had nothing to do with Pearl Harbor—showed soldiers in 1917-vintage helmets, on a beach at the edge of a tropical rain forest, loading huge shells into a coast-artillery piece to fire at a Japanese Zero.

along with hundreds of donors who ranged from brawny Hawaiian laborers to prostitutes of every hue.

•

At 2:20, as Eleanor Roosevelt's luncheon guests were leaving, a White House usher whispered to Captain Frank E. Beatty, Frank Knox's aide, that the Navy Secretary was on the phone. "They said it was urgent."

Returning to ask his wife to drive him to the Navy Department, Beatty paused to tell Mrs. Roosevelt and, one of the guests, "Bertie" Hamlin, remembered, the others "stood around in stupefied knots—there was nothing to say. . . . The guests seemed to melt away—nobody bothered to say goodbye to anyone." Mrs. Roosevelt recalled hearing more bulletins from the usher, and "the information was so stunning that there was complete quiet."

Upstairs, the President had been on the telephone since Frank Knox's call. "I wanted to tell you," he explained to Hu Shih, whom he had just seen at the White House, "that the Japanese have bombed Pearl Harbor and Manila"—at first there were reports about a simultaneous attack on Manila, which may have been a garbled reference to Malaya. "It is terrible, simply terrible. Since you were the last person I talked to before this happened, I thought I ought to call you and tell you about it."

From home, Steve Early was telephoning the three American wire services—Associated Press, United Press, and International News Service. His wife had jotted down a brief bulletin—"not more than ten key words," he had instructed. It was 2:22 P.M. "This is Steve Early," the Press Secretary began. "I am calling from home. I have a statement here which the President has asked me to read." The bulletin was slightly more than ten words: "The Japs have attacked Pearl Harbor, all military activities on Oahu Island." He was going to the White House, he closed, and "I will tell you more later."

At 2:28, Stark called to update the President on Pearl Harbor. He reported considerable damage to the fleet, and many casualties. The attack was continuing. Roosevelt told him to execute—in the words of Hopkins's notes—"the agreed orders to the Army and Navy in event of an outbreak of hostilities in the Pacific."

Before Early could get out of his house—it was 2:36—he called the White House three-way press hookup again to advise—erroneously, it turned out—that there had been an air attack on Manila. There were reporters at the White House before he got there. Unruffled, Ruth Jane Rumelt, his secretary, asked them to wait and offered no news as their numbers grew.

Eleanor Roosevelt had begun a letter to her daughter Anna Boettiger in Seattle before lunch, finishing with news of the family. There was one mishap to report. Anna's brother Franklin, Jr., was a naval officer aboard a destroyer on convoy duty. At night in the Caribbean there had been a collision, and his ship had to put into Puerto Rico for repairs. "He is o.k. & was not the officer who had the watch. Pa 'forgot' to tell me till today when I heard rumors from other sources & asked." When lunch broke up she completed her letter. "The news of war has just come & I've put in a call for you & Johnny [Boettiger] as you may want to send the children East. I've just talked to the mayor [Fiorello La Guardia] & all plans will change from now on." (In Manhattan, La Guardia called a press conference, broadcast over WNYC, imaginatively identifying "Nazi thugs and gangsters" as "the masterminds" of the Pearl Harbor attack. East Coast residents, he warned, should have no false sense of security.)

In Seattle, John Boettiger was pulling the editorial from the next edition of the *Post-Intelligencer* and preparing a replacement, under the heading "War Comes to the U.S." After the predictable "die has been cast" opening he worried about the attractive target presented by the industrialized Pacific Northwest. "It is not altogether impossible that a Jap aircraft carrier could slip through close enough to our coast to conduct a foray upon our airplane and shipbuilding plants."

•

Oahu was so mountainous that some residents saw no sunsets and others no sunrises. There were areas so sheltered through the attack that war came only by telephone or radio. Reporting from London and Berlin, Joseph C. Harsch had experienced his share of air raids, but in Honolulu he awakened thinking only of an early Sunday swim. Seeing the puffs in the sky from Waikiki, he invited his wife to see what a practice air-raid exercise looked like. Others on the beach, enjoying the morning sun, knew nothing until neighboring bathers flipped on their portable radios. Admiral Milo Draemel had driven to a golf course unaware of anything his destroyers had been doing that morning. Intercepting him as he checked in, Mrs. Draemel gave him the news on the telephone. Rushing back, he took a launch to his flagship, the *Detroit*, off fiery Ford Island.

Surreal episodes proliferated. An officer foursome playing the Schofield Barracks golf course had knocked a ball into a sand trap. Going after the ball, they encountered an infantryman firing away with his rifle at airplanes above them. In the distance at the shoreline, smoke was boiling up from ships in the harbor. "Get out of here and play your war games somewhere else!" snapped one of the golfers.

Amidst the attack the usual troupe of Hawaiian girls in native— or what passed for native—costumes appeared at the Pan-American Airways dock for the customary alohas and presentations of leis to departing *Clipper* passengers. There was no *Clipper*, and they were told that their services seemed not to be needed. Disappointed, they left.

•

At about 8:50 A.M. General Short's new alert reached Schofield Barracks. It warned that the enemy was making an attempt to occupy Oahu. Reports of parachutists were coming from everywhere on the island, all of them erroneous but for sightings of Americans who had abandoned disabled planes. No Japanese bailed out. One pilot climbed from a plane that had crashed in Middle Loch, but resisted rescue, which would have meant becoming a prisoner. The boat crew from the destroyer *Montgomery* finally shot him. "Parachutists," the UP wired, "appeared off Harbor Point, five miles from the center of Honolulu. It was assumed that they were suicide squadrons of saboteurs." Short feared a landing in force, an impossibility since the Japanese had no ground troops aboard *Kido Butai*.

On the stricken *Nevada* a radioman picked up news that the Japanese were landing at Diamond Head; on the *Tennessee*, word was that Waianae Beach had been stormed; the seaplane tender *Swan* heard that Waikiki had been taken. At the Navy Yard civilian workers learned that the entire north shore of Oahu had been lost, and other reports at Pearl Harbor had Schofield Barracks captured. Rumors had the island ringed by armed Japanese sampans, and eight enemy battleships were imaginatively observed seventy miles offshore, moving in close to bombard Oahu.

Worried that the attack was the softening-up preliminary to invasion, units scrambled for weapons. At Schofield, Lieutenant (later Lieutenant Colonel) David T. Coiner found that his supply sergeant was requiring, amid the strafing, a written hand receipt on issuing small-arms ammunition. Coiner "gently admonished the sergeant to discontinue the paperwork." Marine Lieutenant Paul Becker, manning a post between the harbor and Hickam, rushed a detachment to the Laululei ammunition dump for resupply. Lacking properly processed orders, they were refused. Laululei was twenty-five miles away from the war. "My men finally took it at gunpoint," Becker remembered. "In effect, we had to steal our own ammunition."

A company clerk in the 27th Infantry Regiment at Schofield Barracks, Private James Jones had wanted to be a fighting man, but only pounded a typewriter. Sunday, at least, was special because of the bonus of a half-pint of milk at breakfast. Milk was a luxury in Hawaii, an expensive import. Real eggs were also special for Sunday, and Jones was gobbling two fried eggs with his pancakes when he heard the rumble of explosions from Wheeler Field two miles away. Carrying his half-pint protectively, he rushed out of the mess hall with other curious G.I.'s. Approaching low was a Zero, its guns rattling down the company street. "As he came abreast of us, [the pilot] gave us a typically toothy grin and waved, and I shall never forget his face behind the goggles. A white scarf streamed out behind his neck and he wore a white ribbon around his helmet . . . with a red spot in the center of his forehead."

In Jones's novel vividly evoking the day, *From Here to Eternity* (1951), little more than the names are changed. In the novel a young red-haired soldier lies sprawled on the asphalt, a victim of the Zero's guns, and another soldier, bending down to inspect the body, concludes, "Them's real bullets that guy was usin." Strafing the guardhouse where Jones usually slept, Japanese planes also killed his buddies still in their beds, including, he wrote to his father, "three of the best friends I've had since I've been in the army."

Fiction or fact, many expected a landing, and as shudders from explosions at Wheeler Field shook their barracks, Jones's sergeant announced, "The CQ will unlock the rifle racks and every man get his rifle and hang onto it. *But stay inside.* . . . This ain't no maneuvers. You go running around outside you'll get your ass shot off. . . . You want to be heroes, you'll get plenty chances later. . . . You'll probably have Japs right in your laps by time we get down to beach positions." Orders were to disperse along the Oahu shoreline, on an invasion watch.

The first carrier wave had spent its force. At Fort Kamehameha, a harbor installation, Sergeant (later Lieutenant Colonel) Ronald D. Moton watched enemy planes bank overhead and return to the docks and airfields. There were few targets at Kam. In an open field he and a supply sergeant were firing .30-caliber rifle ammunition helplessly at the dive bombers. A third soldier joined them—until a captain, the local motor pool officer, drove up and ordered them to stop: "You'll make the Japs mad and they'll start shooting back at us!" It was an order. They stopped. As they put their obsolete Springfields down, a private ran by to ask where the camp ambulance was. A Zero had crashed into a building and killed four men "watching the show." The plane had been "flying itself" with a dead pilot at the stick.

"Well, I went over to see what I could do, but they were dead—just torn to pieces. I went up to the aircraft and pulled the canopy open. The pilot's face had gone forward and smashed onto the top of the control stick." Moton had seen the red ball on the wings but wanted to assure himself that the occupant was "a goddamned Jap." He "picked his head up by the top of his helmet and pulled his head back and all I could see that wasn't smashed was his slant eyes."

A truck turned up from a Marine unit on the beach and asked the way to an Army ammunition depot. "We fired up all our ammo down there," one Marine explained. "Do you have any that we could use?"

"Back up your truck over at that building," the ordnance officer pointed, "and take anything you can use."

Later the post commander chewed him out. "I thought Marines were part of the United States forces," the captain shot back. "I'd give those people anything they could use."

There were many attempts on Oahu to down Zeros and dive bombers with hand-held weapons, the most cumbersome of them the Browning Automatic Rifle. James Jones put one of the successful efforts into vivid fiction, in which a noncom, timing his BAR fire for sufficient lead, sprays a plane's nose, then the cockpit, then the tail assembly. "The plane shivered like a man trying to get out from under a cold shower and the pilot jumped in his seat twice like a man tied to a hot stove." Soldiers saw the pilot "throw up his arms helplessly in a useless try to ward it off, to stop it pouring on him. There was a prolonged cheer. A hundred yards beyond . . . the little Zero began to fall off on one wing and slid down a long hill of air into one of the goalposts of the 19th Infantry football field. It crashed into flames. A vast happy college-cheer yell went up . . . as if our side had made a touchdown against Notre Dame."

·

Commanded by Lieutenant Commander Shigekazu Shimazaki, the second wave of 171 planes reached Kahuku Point at 8:40 and deployed widely over Oahu, keeping clear of the black smoke and away from energetic antiaircraft fire. Leading the torpedo bombers, Lieutenant Commander Takashige Egusa chose runs at ships sending up the heaviest volleys, assuming that these—in Fuchida's words—"had suffered least from the first attack." Cruisers and destroyers were targeted as well as damaged battleships.

Return fire was fierce from Pearl Harbor, but the airfields had lost much of the potential to strike back. The leader of the 3rd Covering Squadron of nine Zeros, Lieutenant Fusata Iida, an old hand of twenty-seven with experience in China, was shot up when his planes encountered the few P-40s and nearly useless P-36s that were airborne. Several outgunned Americans went down, but Iida leaked gasoline. Realizing as he headed north near Kaneohe that he would not make it back to the *Soryu*, he determined to take something with him. Closing his cockpit canopy, he began to descend in what Lieutenant Iyozo Fujita assumed was a strafing run. "I immediately began a wingover to follow his plane down," Fujita reported. "I realized abruptly, however, that Lieutenant Iida was flying in a . . . manner quite different from his usual tactics. I watched his plane as it dove in its vertical, inverted position until it exploded on the ground between the airfield hangars." From the wreckage the Marines retrieved a Japanese flag and Iida's *hachimaki*.

Most Air Corps planes that had managed to get into the air had come from Haleiwa. Many of the several dozen sitting on the grass strip—ancient P-26s and stubby P-36s—weren't worth strafing. The primitive field was not on the list of Japanese targets, leaving the sky clear for Taylor and Welch to get their P-40s up, and over to smoking Wheeler Field, which the dive bombers and Zeros had left for fresh targets. Pursuing, they found the Japanese at Ewa, methodically destroying parked Marine Wildcat fighters. To Taylor the disciplined formations were "like a traffic pattern" into which he and Welch intruded, firing everything they had.

Running out of ammunition—few planes had been ready to fight—

they raced to Wheeler, staying clear of burning aircraft and keeping their engines running as the planes were rearmed. Crews were shouting instructions when the second wave appeared, strafing the men on the ground. Taylor and Welch gunned their P-40s over the grass, Taylor just clearing an ammunition dolly. A few more planes from Haleiwa joined them, and, Taylor recalled, "things got kind of jumbled" as the Americans mixed into the Japanese formations.

Welch and Taylor claimed seven Japanese planes, but Taylor had to be pulled from his P-40 to patch a shot-up arm. Very likely the only pilot ever to go into combat in tuxedo trousers, he had made a mess of them.

Despite the racket around Pearl Harbor and the airfields, the Japanese, avoiding civilian targets, had not awakened many on Oahu to what was going on. American gunners firing excitedly in every direction altered that; and to the unbelieving at their radios in Honolulu, Webley Edwards on KGMB began repeating with each new and uninformative bulletin, "This is the real McCoy."

•

At 5:30 A.M., as Australia's Monday morning papers were being delivered, with news of Roosevelt's message to Hirohito and Japanese movements at sea, an aide to the prime minister awakened John Curtin in Melbourne to tell him about Malaya and Pearl Harbor. The *Sydney Morning Herald*'s editorial was titled "Twilight of Peace in the Pacific." Curtin dressed and began drafting a message to be broadcast countrywide.

On his way home for a long Christmas holiday, the prime minister had expected the long railway trip to Western Australia to be punctuated by appearances at every stop, fund-raising for a new cruiser *Sydney*. Worried about the Japanese, Curtin had hung on at Melbourne, holding conferences in his dingy sitting room in the Victoria Palace Hotel, the aspidistras and potted palms in the suite veiled in a fog of tobacco smoke.

Before leaving Canberra, he had been bidden a dramatic farewell by a Japanese diplomat seemingly going home only on leave. It had left Curtin uneasy, and the prime minister discovered extensive but quiet departures of Japanese diplomats and businessmen. He shared his concern in a cable to President Roosevelt. "Something *was* going to happen," he told a friend on arriving in Perth.

•

On the *Lanikai*, rocking in the swells at the edge of the Manila Bay mine field, the ancient radio beeped at 3:30. It could receive but not transmit. In the darkness the radioman found his sleeping skipper, Kemp Tolley, and nudged him awake. The message was "Orange war plan in effect. Return to Cavite." (Despite MacArthur, the Navy thought "Orange.") "There was no point in waking the crew before dawn," Tolley remembered thinking. "I went topside to collect my thoughts in the cool night air. The lights that had twinkled in profusion last evening on Corregidor had gone out."

On the old four-stack *John D. Ford*, anchored off Cavite, Radioman William J. McMahon burst out of his shack at 3:30, yelling to the empty quarterdeck, "Pearl Harbor is being bombed. *No drill!*" The duty messenger, R. W. Williamson, went to the captain's and the executive officer's cabins with the news while McMahon, hearing another call sign, rushed back. It was a message, in the clear, to all ships, Asiatic Fleet. While tearing off the tape, he saw Commander P. H. Talbot in the doorway, in his bathrobe. Talbot ran Destroyer Division 59. McMahon handed him the tape: "From CinCAF to all ships— Attacking aircraft at Pearl Harbor identified as Japanese—Act accordingly."

By then the *Ford*'s captain, Lieutenant Commander J. E. Cooper, was at the threshold. The two officers withdrew to his cabin, clutching their bathrobes closed, the teletyped message still in Talbot's free hand.

Nearby on the destroyer *Parrott*, Bill Slagle, assigned the slow watch because he had not yet completed his basic radio course, had picked up the message. Disbelieving, he sent for a repeat and asked whether it was correct. "Hell, yes" came the answer. "Get your damned clumsy fingers off the air!" Slagle decided that it was time to wake his commanding officer, Lieutenant Commander Edward N. Parker. Parker asked to have the message read; then he changed his mind and reached for the paper. "Sound General Quarters," he ordered. "No, I'll do it. Get back to the radio room." And he bounded out of bed.

On the *Ford*, the 4:00 relief watch began gathering early, coffee mugs in hand. Light switches were checked. A "Darken Ship" order seemed certain. To Ken Tillman, his replacement, Dan Mullin, mused, "Who would dream that Pearl Harbor would get it first?" Thinking of the likely size of the strike force, Kelly Bowen, just off the bridge, added, "What the hell do you think they'd have done to two little World War I-built destroyers?"

·

Using the United Press bulletin, the Mutual Broadcasting System was first by a fraction of a minute in getting the news on radio, prompting a telephone call to its New York switchboard by an irate New Jersey listener who had been panicked by Orson Welles's "War of the Worlds" in 1938. "Ha! You got me on that Martian stunt. I had a hunch you'd try it again."

Mazuo Kato had already left his apartment, walking in the direction of the funeral chapel where services were being held for Colonel Shinjo but hoping to hail a taxi. One appeared quickly, and its radio was on as Kato opened the door and climbed in. Manila had been bombed, the report went. Damage and casualties were heavy. Kato missed hearing about Hawaii.

"God damn Japan," said the cabbie, not looking back. "We'll lick hell out of those bastards now."

Kato asked him to keep the radio on, and gave the address in precise English. When they arrived at the chapel, he paid his fare and did not wait for change. The services had already begun. Sitting up front were two American Army officers detailed to the obsequies. Kato squeezed in between a Japanese Army officer from the Embassy and Yuichi Kobayshi, correspondent for the Tokyo daily *Yomiuri*.

"Did you hear that Manila was bombed?" Kato whispered to the Army man, who shook his head, puzzled. Kato turned to the *Yomiuri* reporter. "There's no use staying here," he whispered to Kobayshi. "Let's go." They waited for the close of a prayer and tiptoed out, guessing now why Nomura and Kurusu, who had been expected, were not present.

A taxi dropped them at the Japanese embassy. The driver did not have his radio turned on. A growing crowd of Americans huddled curiously in quiet Massachusetts Avenue. The embassy gate and chancellery door were locked, but Kato rang for admission and slipped in unmolested.

"Who did the bombing?" he asked the first person he saw. "The Army or the Navy?" He was assuming that a belligerent young officer had acted without authority, perhaps in another Panay incident—or as in a novel.

"They both did" came the reply, apprehending his meaning. "As a matter of fact, Japan did."

From the embassy teletype and radio, Kato and Kobayshi learned about Pearl Harbor. Staff gathered round the radio, talking under it in hushed tones. "The atmosphere," Kato noted, "was more like that of the funeral from which I had just come than that of an embassy . . . on the first day of a war. Someone remarked soberly that 'Colonel Shinjo died at the right time.'"

•

At 2:31 (Eastern Time), music lovers whose radios were already tuned to CBS for the 3:00 New York Philharmonic concert heard John Daly break in to say, "The Japanese have attacked Pearl Harbor, Hawaii, by air, President Roosevelt had just announced. The attack was also made on naval and military activities on the principal island of Oahu." In his excitement the last word became "O-ha-u."

With no further bulletins, commentators on the networks substituted speculations about the Far East—until a second news flash from the White House mistakenly reported an attack on Manila. CBS in New York attempted contacts with KGMB in Hawaii ("Go ahead, Honolulu . . .") and with a station in Manila, each time with no success, and filled in instead at 2:46 with military analyst George Fielding Eliot.

The Japanese, Eliot guessed, were attempting "to delay and impede American operations in the Far East" and were attacking from aircraft carriers, "a very desperate measure" because of American patrol planes and long-range bombers guarding Hawaii. "The question is how much delay they have purchased with the carriers they have risked." They were "likely to suffer severely as soon as they can be located."

A telephone call to KGMB, abruptly cut off, confirmed that enemy planes—estimated at fifty to one hundred—were still overhead, and that steady antiaircraft fire could be heard. When contact was finally made with Fred Wilkins in Manila, who had not heard of either attack, and suddenly faded out, listeners as well as radio personnel in New York were certain that Wilkins was wrong. The Wrigley Chewing Gum program of piano music resumed.

On the twenty-ninth (editorial) floor of the Time-Life Building in Rockefeller Center, Theodore H. White, recently back from an Asian trip with his boss, Henry Luce, was writing a story for *Time* about the inevitability of war with Japan, "no matter what the Japanese were saying in Washington." The phone rang. James Aldridge, who would quit journalism later to write novels, lifted it, then let the receiver drop. "Jeezus Christ!" he yelled. "The Japs are bombing Pearl Harbor; it's on the radio."

Rushing to a news ticker, they read the first flash. When no details followed, they went back to their office and looked out the window at the streets crowded with people and automobiles. Throngs were reconnoitering Christmas decorations and shop window displays. Above them, unaware of the extent of the catastrophe, White and Aldridge were "gleeful." It was "the right war, a good war, and it had to be fought and won." They scrawled sheet after sheet of typing paper with "We are at war with Japan" and "The Japanese are bombing America," folded them into paper airplanes, and sailed messages into the distant streets below.

Henry Luce wanted America in the war. His ailing father had been a missionary in China; "Harry" had been born in Tengchow in 1898. Only the U.S. could save the country. The guests invited for lunch at Luce's Greenwich, Connecticut, estate included peripatetic journalist Vincent Sheean, Ambassador to Russia Laurance Steinhardt, philosopher Lin Yutang, popular historian Mark Sullivan: twenty-two in all. The Luces had made it a rule that meals were not to be interrupted by telephone calls, but one seemed so crucial to the butler that he brought the message in on a tray. FDR did not like Clare Boothe Luce, whom he classified as an intellectual glamour girl and privately called "Clearly Loose," but he would have approved of her reaction. Glancing at the message over her dessert, she tapped a glass with her spoon for attention. "All isolationists and appeasers, please listen," she began. "The Japanese have bombed Pearl Harbor."

Guests gasped, then, etiquette forgotten, ran for radios and telephones. Only Dr. Lin remained, impassively finishing his dessert. "You see," he explained to Mrs. Luce, "this is all so very expected."

Henry Luce's public enemies were the isolationist publishers Robert McCormick in Chicago, and the Pattersons—Cissy in Washington and Joe in New York. Before abandoning his guests and rushing to Manhattan, Luce ordered roses sent to Cissy Patterson with a note: "Hiyi: How do you like everything now?" He was at Rockefeller Center in under an hour, supervising the remaking of the seven lead pages of *Time*, then about to go to press. At the *New York Daily News*, Joe Patterson's staff rewrote his early Monday editorial, appealing for defensive warfare only and arguing against adventuring too far from home.

Across Sixth Avenue from the Time-Life Building, in Radio City Music Hall,* cathedral of the cinema, the film unreeling was *Suspicion*, with Cary Grant and Joan Fontaine, and between screenings a platoon of Rockettes kicked their heels with military precision. But the center of attention, usually only a curiosity in the vast Art Deco lobby, was a news ticker, spilling out a spaghetti of repetitive war bulletins from Washington. Unbelieving, moviegoers gaped as the tape unwound, then most disappeared into the oblivion of the silver screen. Others rushed home.

In Cleveland, Ohio, eighty delegates to a conference of the Institute of Pacific Relations—congressmen, journalists, industrialists, academics—opened their final session after lunch at a swank country club. No speeches had been permitted; the aim had been "back and forth discussion" about the course that the United States should pursue in the Far East. Two participants were Tokyo correspondents invited back for their expertise, Hugh Byas and James R. Young. Just as the afternoon segment was beginning, the war news came, and reporter Clayton Fritchey estimated "dead silence for two minutes."

Breaking the stillness, the chairman finally turned toward an isolationist congressman, asking what response he thought America would give. "Our answer," he said, to noisy cheers and applause, "is probably being given by the American fleet right now."

The attack, one delegate volunteered, seemed an insane move, but he had a curious explanation which he claimed came from the State Department. Japanese warlords had concluded that they could not win in China, but to admit that and withdraw would cost them the government. "A defeat by the U.S. and Britain combined would cause no loss of face. Therefore the best solution was a short war with the Allies and quick surrender."

•

Taking the long southern route to Hawaii and San Francisco, the *President Coolidge* had sailed from Manila on December 1 with the

---

* In October 1989 the Mitsubishi name, associated in December 1941 with the Zero fighter and the bombers that blasted Pearl Harbor, was linked to Rockefeller Center when the Mitsubishi Estate Group purchased control of the Rockefeller Trust properties, including Radio City Music Hall, for just under a billion dollars.

cruiser *Louisville*, the lumbering transport *Scott*, and two destroyers. On the *Coolidge* were service dependents evicted from the Philippines by Admiral Hart, an order which had earned him the sobriquet "Hard-hearted Hart." Also aboard were military people transferred to other stations, including Colonel Ivan D. Yeaton, who had been attaché in Russia. In Singapore before he flew on to Manila, a veteran diplomat warned Yeaton that the American cutoff of oil to Japan, however morally appropriate, would lead sooner rather than later to war.

As they neared the International Date Line to the east, Yeaton remembered that he would be repeating Sunday, December 7. Coming on deck soon after sunrise to a beautiful morning, he saw to his surprise land on both sides of the ship. "Seeing a ship's officer I inquired as to our location. . . . 'We are passing through the Torres Straits,' he answered. The *Scott* had been cutting our speed badly. A short time later news came over the loudspeaker that Pearl Harbor was under attack. At that moment we were off Rennell's Island, about 100 miles south of Guadalcanal."

●

Still sleepless, Sir Tom Phillips was at the naval base in Singapore at 2:15 A.M. when a signal arrived from the Admiralty in London. It transmitted a telegram from Lord Halifax, sent from Washington about nine hours earlier, that the U.S. would regard Japanese invasions of Thailand, Malaya, or the Dutch Indies as hostile acts against the United States itself. Japanese vessels steering west or southwest across the Gulf of Siam were to be attacked, "since they were either going for Thailand or Malaya." Kota Bharu had been under attack for two hours, and Phillips was now being given permission to head off the ships that had already begun off-loading their troops.

The Admiral called an urgent staff conference in his war room. The subject was not how to put Humpty Dumpty together again, but what to do about Force Z—his capital ships. Lieutenant Commander J. W. McClelland, Base Signals Officer, took informal minutes. Phillips began by suggesting that the Japanese would not employ battleships or aircraft carriers in the area as long as the U.S. fleet remained powerful. (He knew nothing of what was happening in Hawaii.) He worried, rather, about submarines, because torpedo planes and dive bombers had to be launched from carriers if their targets were far from land. To work near the shore he needed the fighter escort left aground at Jamaica. If his ships were only to be used to advantage later, he had better retire westward.

Although he had already determined privately to take the offensive, he wanted to be told that by his superiors. Sir Shenton Thomas, up from Government House, arose to do just that. If the capital ships were only a bluff, he challenged, the Japanese would call it. Exploiting the *Prince of Wales* and *Repulse* might alter the circumstances. He "made disparaging remarks about Japanese efficiency. He did not expect a [serious] sea-borne landing of large ground forces during the northeast monsoon, and still hoped that [only] the occupation of Thailand was the Japanese objective." Brooke-Popham offered what McClelland described as "his usual cliché": "Once he is in a fight, the only way to get a Jap out of it is to kill him!"

Air Vice-Marshal Pulford emphasized the limitations of his aircraft, especially in covering ships out of sight of land. Sir Shenton wanted the big ships protected from the air, or not used. Then, contradicting himself, he challenged Phillips, "Do you know, Admiral, I am beginning to believe that *if* the Japanese intend to attack"—he remained in a dream-world that the Kota Bharu affair might yet be a feint—"your intervention is the only thing that can prevent the invasion succeeding."

A sudden convert to reality, Thomas predicted "a regular pot-mess and no mistake," and as if punctuating his warning, an air raid alert sounded. "Red" indicated imminent attack. "Those in the War Room," McClelland minuted, "lay down on the floor under the conference table. When the 'All Clear' sounded"—it was a false alarm—"the meeting broke up in a hurry."

•

From 8:50 to 9:10, the *Nevada* struggled down the harbor past the capsized *Oklahoma* and the blazing *Arizona*, drawing planes away from undamaged ships. A torpedo at 8:03 had torn a gap 45 feet long and 30 feet high, flooding many of the forward compartments. Fifty men aboard had already been killed; the bow section was nearly destroyed. Dive bombers had obliterated most of the ship's superstructure. Its skipper was ashore in Honolulu for the weekend and Lieutenant Commander Francis J. Thomas, two grades too junior to handle a battleship, guided the *Nevada*, listing to port and moving under partial steam, through Egusa's swarming second wave, grounding it into the mud off Hospital Point. In the acrid smoke, Thomas was not sure where he was except that the *Nevada* was on an even keel. For the moment that was good enough. Five minutes later a launch with the ship's captain, F. W. Scanland, pulled alongside.

A radio message to VP-24 PBYs on patrol south of Oahu ordered them to return to Barber's Point—the southwest corner of Oahu— and fly "the wide part of a wedge," then return to base. They were to search for the Japanese fleet. Flying toward Diamond Head from the thin rectangle of Molokai, the island just southeast of Oahu, they could see spreading columns of oily black smoke rising from the vicinity of Pearl Harbor. Familiar ships had taken unfamiliar shapes. The *Arizona* was afire and settling in the water; the *California* was deep in the harbor mud; the *Utah* had buckled; the *Oklahoma* was belly-up; the *Nevada* was beached near Ewa. Planes were burning at the naval air station; hangars appeared "blown to pieces."

As Maury Meister set his compass, his crew saw Egusa's wave approaching. "Big yellow-orange images of the rising sun glared at us from the bodies of the planes and the wings; they passed us by without as much as a look in our direction as they had much larger targets in their sights." Escaping, the search craft flew to the south as instructed, never realizing that the arc of intersection with the enemy aircraft suggested that the carrier force was to the north. Knowing what an easy target the lumbering PBYs were, crews "searched diligently for our targets, hoping we would find them and at the same time praying that we wouldn't."

•

When Ensign Sakamaki poked his periscope above the surface again, risking the wrath of four-stack destroyers, he turned toward Pearl Harbor, intending to make a run inside. Columns of black smoke rose from burning ships. "I was hot throughout my body. I breathed faster and my heart was beating at a terrific speed." Clutching his periscope he shouted to his crewmate, "They've done it! Look at it!"

Heading toward the harbor with new enthusiasm, Sakamaki jarred a coral reef. Reversing power, he managed, on the fourth attempt, to work loose, but the crash had wrecked a torpedo and tube; compressed air and gas from his battery were leaking, and the air was becoming foul. On a second try at the harbor mouth, he hit another reef. This time reverse power failed to budge the sub, but ships in the harbor were too busy to notice.

As the two crewmen crawled back and forth shifting lead ballast from front to rear, cringing at shocks from the leaking battery, a destroyer began firing, but the sub floated loose before the four-stacker found the range. Sakamaki plunged as deep as he could, hoping that the sub would hold together, and again inspected the interior. His remaining torpedo tube appeared useless. "What are we going to do, sir?" Inagaki asked.

"The only thing we can do now is to plunge right into the *Pennsylvania*," Sakamaki declared, reeling from exhaustion and not realizing that the battleship was in dry dock. Once more he began inching the crippled sub toward Oahu. He knew it was daylight, but he had lost any sense of time.

·

William Hayter, Lord Halifax's First Secretary, had just returned to the British embassy from the White House, where he had delivered the latest Admiralty messages. Halifax was on his way out; after lunch he was going riding. Hayter said that he and his wife would take advantage of the mild Sunday to drive into the country and take a walk. But just as they were about to leave, the ambassador returned. The President had telephoned to say that the Japanese were bombing Pearl Harbor. "I asked Lord Halifax if he were sure he'd got it right. . . . This seemed to me an improbable story; we had always thought they were much more likely to go for Hong Kong and Singapore, leaving the American possessions alone."

"The Pwesident"—Halifax always pronounced it that way—"*said* Pearl Harbor." And Halifax placidly wondered what they should do about it.

Hayter suggested telephoning London, getting through to a "rather somnolent" Foreign Office Resident Clerk. Although Hayter considered his news "interesting" and asked that it be conveyed to the Prime Minister, the Sunday duty official seemed unacquainted with the significance or the location of the event. "What was that place? Could you spell it?"

"The sensation created in Washington," Hayter judged, "was of course rather stronger." The embassy switchboard was jammed with misinformation that was an index to the "disorder and confusion. . . . At first it seemed to take the shape of panic. The whole Pacific fleet, we were told, had been sunk, the Atlantic fleet couldn't get through the Panama Canal, and there was nothing to prevent the Japanese [from] landing on the West Coast wherever and whenever they liked (and presumably marching on Washington)."

His Australian counterpart, Alan Watt, "could not understand . . . why Japan did not attack only British territory in the first instance, to test whether Roosevelt could have persuaded an isolationist Congress to declare war in such circumstances. . . . To force a largely isolationist America into a war from which it might conceivably have abstained seemed to me a gambler's throw." With Watt, several of the legation staff discussed the new situation with "tremendous relief that, whatever trials lay ahead, the resources of the United States would now definitely be thrown into the balance. . . . Hitler had attacked the Soviet Union; Japanese military leaders had attacked the United States. Whom the gods wish to destroy they first make mad."

•

Before noon—it was just after nine at Pearl Harbor—Ernest O. Lawrence was in the Radiation Laboratory at Berkeley with Frank Oppenheimer, Robert's younger brother. They were optimistic about extracting experimental quantities of U-235 through Lawrence's calutron, which he predicted would hold the key to the core of a bomb. Robert Oppenheimer and his wife, Kitty, were still at home with the San Francisco Sunday papers, their radio turned on to the first war news, about which no one else in the laboratory was yet aware. "I decided that I had had about enough of the Spanish cause," he remembered, "and that there were other and more pressing crises in the world."

Foremost now was nuclear fission. Physicists were suddenly turning up at the Radiation Laboratory without concerns about unpaid overtime. "I remember that Sunday," said Paul Aebersold, who had arrived nearly ten years earlier as a graduate student transfer from Stanford. "We worked all through the day, and that night we ran the first uranium-235 samples on the calutron. They took the form of faint green smudges on the collection box." Lawrence was—prematurely— elated. "When I saw the first micrograms of uranium-235," Aebersold recalled, "I couldn't envisage, as he could, the miles of electromagnetic separation plants that waited in the future."

Several hours after the production run, keeping his own reaction to the war news to himself, Lawrence left the laboratory for a walk in the gathering darkness. The surrounding fence was casually guarded by campus police. Alone, he would circle the fence all night long.

•

Ed Sheehan saw a launch approaching from one of the stricken battleships and ran to the dock to haul in its lines. They were slithery with oil, but he hung on and tied the boat up. Most aboard were in shock or worse, and the coxswain urged haste. Slick with oil, the wounded were hard to hold. "Two or three were quite still. A few others made weak movements or clutching motions. . . . I knew that one was dead. He was utterly limp, and his head rolled from side to side against my chest. And I could tell from the eyes of the sailor helping me that he, too, knew his shipmate was gone. We put the boy down gently among the wounded lying by the side of the road."

Soon the launch was heading back for more. "The coxswain looked small, his legs apart on the stern as he held the tiller under his arm." Sheehan found a bucket and some water, and brought it to the row of men lying between the crane tracks and the machine shop. By the time he returned, someone had covered the faces of the dead with caps or bits of clothing.

He turned and saw the destroyer *Shaw* hit in the floating dry dock. A huge fireball rose. Twisted scraps of metal soared thousands of feet into the air, each trailing streamers of smoke. A quarter of a mile away, Sheehan picked up "a curl of steel, ripped clean and shiny, handball sized." He thought of keeping it as a souvenir, then threw it into the harbor. Approaching Ten-Ten Dry Dock he saw smoke rising amidships from the *Pennsylvania*. Immune to torpedoes, it was hurt less badly than the other battleships. The *Downes* was nearly broken in two at the bridge; the *Cassin* alongside had been ripped apart and had fallen against the *Downes*. "Looking down into the dry dock brought another shock. Someone had ordered it flooded for safety and the three ships sat in a rising pool of thick black oil. . . . It was a loathsome mess." On the *Pennsylvania*, crewmen dashed about with hoses, soaking locations from which steam hissed in clouds.

While Japanese planes searched for fresh targets, gangs of sailors and civilians at dockside were working to clear debris and fight fires. In a varnished straw safari helmet from Singapore, giving orders in fractured English, was Tai Sing Loo, officially the Navy yard photographer. While AA gunners fired from the *Pennsylvania*, the stubby, energetic Loo tried to protect the new hoses he had brought round. "I were little worry," he remembered, "because I have no nails and lumber to nail between the two planks . . . while the heavy traffic going by with emergency cases to the Naval Hospital without crushing the hoses." He found Captain Charles D. Swain, who telephoned for Loo, and "within few minutes four men marching down with nails and lumber. . . . Suddenly the roaring Anti Air Craft Guns in action, I call my men to dodging for safety, after the Enemy Planes disappear we all returns to our duty." Since his carpenters had fled, Loo commandeered "two of our local boys passing by." Then he directed traffic.

Sheehan recalled thinking, "He is the yard photographer and suddenly he is giving us orders." But Loo had metamorphosed from local character. "He had taken charge and his instructions made sense. We obeyed without question, . . . clearing tracks for the cranes, hauling hoses, moving debris, and servicing trucks. Crewmen carried blanket-covered bodies off the *Pennsylvania*. Others stared down at the tangled . . . *Cassin* and *Downes*. Time did not move."

•

At 9:21, Task Forces 3, 8, and 12, all in the vicinity of the Hawaiian Islands, received messages to rendezvous. Each closed, "FURTHER IN-STRUCTIONS WHEN ENEMY IS LOCATED." The *Enterprise* also intercepted a series of fantastic bulletins that suggested either panic or catastrophe. "Two enemy carriers thirty miles bearing 085 from Barber's Point." "Enemy landing party heading for ammunition depot." "Japanese paratroops and gliders heading for Kaneohe." "Eight enemy transports rounding Barber's Point."

"So many false reports being received from unknown sources concerning presence of enemy ships, carriers, transports, and submarines," Halsey jotted impatiently in his diary, "that it is very difficult to glean the true from the false."

Whatever was actually happening, it was war, as an intercept urging medical officers in the Pearl area to rush all available anaesthetics to the naval hospital confirmed. Halsey ordered the "PREPARE FOR BATTLE" signal flags hoisted to the yardarm and four fighters to go aloft on continuous search. The alarming messages continued to flood in.

•

At Barking Sands Airfield on Kauai, the ten airmen and eighteen engineers and the two hundred mixed-race soldiers of the 299th Infantry of the Hawaii National Guard were each issued a World War I rifle and 20 rounds of ammunition to repel the expected enemy hordes. To further drive off the Japanese, the 299th set up three machine gun positions along the beach with all of 550 rounds for the ancient guns, and a World War I 75-mm howitzer with only enough ammunition to be symbolic. A little later someone got the idea that the engineers' dynamite could be used to turn the old trucks they had into road missiles. As Private A. J. Winser described it, they were to volunteer themselves as "suicide drivers," to ram any Japanese airplane that attempted a landing. Fortunately the first plane—two weeks later—was American, a bullet-riddled cargo plane from Hickam, patched up after the raid to bring them their first supplies in a month. For days they had been living on "rice, crumbs of bread, jelly and a little coffee."

.

Having spent the night moored at Wake Island, the Pan American Airways *Philippines Clipper* took on passengers soon after sunrise Monday morning. It taxied out into the quiet green lagoon at 5:40, taking off uneventfully at 5:55. Travelers going on to Guam, 1,300 miles west, and then to Manila, were relieved to be airborne. Lonely, wishbone-shaped Wake, 450 miles from the nearest land, was actually three scraps of sandbar and coral reef with a surface of 2,600 acres—the size of a large farm. There was no high ground and no place to hide. A directive from the President in 1939 had placed Wake, with Guam and Midway, under Navy jurisdiction so that funds could be diverted for their defense. Wake was host to 1,200 civilian construction workers—many of them Chamorros from Guam—building runways, revetments, and other installations. The excess population complicated life on an atoll with no fresh water except what could be distilled from the sea.

After reveille at six the Marine contingent was finishing breakfast, and its commandant, gaunt, balding Major James Devereux, was shaving in his tent. Since B-17s had begun island-hopping across the Pacific to the Philippines, an Army radio van set up near the airstrip was active around the clock. Wake was taking seriously a warning received at Pacific bases two weeks earlier: "INTERNATIONAL SITUATION INDICATES YOU SHOULD BE ON THE ALERT." Signal Corps Captain Henry

S. Wilson was standing by when his operator, after the *Clipper* disappeared into the dawn sky, intercepted an uncoded transmission from Hickam Field: Oahu was under attack.

Wilson ran to Devereux's tent. Within minutes a coded message followed that the Japanese were bombing Pearl Harbor. Walter Bayler, an Army captain scheduled to proceed to Midway Island to set up air-ground radio communications on the order of the Wake system under construction, saw Devereux with the decoded radiogram. "Of course it may be just another false alarm," said Devereux, "so I have requested verification. If it comes through, I'll let everyone know immediately."

Frantic bulletins in the clear were verification enough. On his second try, Devereux located the base chief, Commander Winfield Scott Cunningham, who telephoned the radio shack to recall the *Clipper*, only ten minutes out, before it ran into a swarm of oncoming Japanese aircraft. Devereux had his bugler sound "Call to Arms," and Marines swarmed over the atoll. Atop the watchtower that was the highest point on Wake—otherwise only twenty-one feet above sea level at the topmost dune—signalmen waited for the return of the Pan Am flying boat and the first signs of the enemy.

HONG KONG	SINGAPORE	WASHINGTON	PEARL HARBOR
MANILA	MALAYA	NEW YORK	9:30 A.M.
4:00 A.M.	2:40 A.M.	3:00 P.M.	December 7
December 8	December 8	December 7	

HOUR 32

FOLLOWING a tour of Japanese duty, Associated Press correspondent Clark Lee had expected to rest at home in Hawaii, but he was still in the Philippines. Of the newsmen who gathered, glass in hand, in the Manila Hotel lobby to gossip, all but one, C. C. Chapman of Mackay Radio, who had lived in Japan longer than any of the others, had felt that war was imminent. Lee had bet "Chappie" the cost of a radiogram to Honolulu that war would break out within a week. Borrowing Chapman's pencil, he confidently wrote out the message to be sent to his wife: "TAKE CARE OF YOURSELF OKAY HERE." She received it before the last Japanese plane had left Pearl Harbor, the last civilian message received before censorship began.

Lee got the news himself from Ray Cronin at the Manila AP office, who telephoned, "The Japs have blasted hell out of Pearl Harbor!" Sleepily, Lee could not comprehend the message, and Cronin shouted it again. It was very likely close to four o'clock, but Lee remembered it as two—which would have been before the attack began. He scrambled out of bed, pulled on slacks and sandals, and hailed a taxi to the *Manila Bulletin* building. There were always taxis hovering around the Manila Hotel.

By then Manila radio had the news, and nervous antiaircraft gunners were firing into the empty black sky. Awakened by the explosions, Jorge Vargas groped for his telephone. Private secretary to President Quezon and unofficial assistant president, Vargas called Philippine Army headquarters. War had broken out, he was told. Pearl Harbor had been attacked. American wire services had picked up the news from radio intercepts. Vargas tried MacArthur's headquarters and got the same report. He knew he had to reach the president, but to disturb him even for such news as that bothered Vargas. Quezon was in Baguio, in the hills to the east of Lingayen Gulf, more than a hundred miles to the north. It was the summer capital, where officials went to escape the worst of the Manila heat. Quezon had gone to his private bungalow there near the Government Mansion to recuperate from a flare-up of the chronic tuberculosis which had been dogging him for twenty years. Vargas dialed Baguio anyway.

•

Just before 4:00 A.M. Shanghai time Commander Stephen Polk-inghorn of the gunboat *Peterel* was awakened by a telephone call from the British consulate just off the Whangpoo River. Pearl Harbor had been bombed. He could expect trouble by daybreak. Polkinghorn, a sixty-three-year-old reserve officer and former pilot on the Tientsin River, ordered "Action Stations" piped, and prepared to scuttle his gunboat. Tugging on an overcoat and a wool cap, he went out on deck in the chill predawn air.

He was not surprised when a Japanese launch drew alongside in the darkness and an armed party climbed aboard. Presenting a written order to surrender the *Peterel* was Commander Inaho Otani, officially naval attaché at Shanghai, but actually chief of staff of the *Idzumo*. Stalling for time, Polkinghorn read the paper over very slowly, then fibbed that the commanding officer was ashore and would have to be telephoned for instructions. Otani insisted that the senior officer aboard was responsible for his ship.

"Yes," Polkinghorn conceded.

"Then," said Otani, "make a ready answer on your own judgment."

He would, said Polkinghorn, if his officers and crew could remain on board.

"Such a matter makes no sense at this moment," Otani argued. "Say *yes* or *no* right away! Resistance is useless and you should answer *yes* for the peace of Shanghai. You must surrender your ship."

"Come into the wardroom and discuss the situation."

"No, we must have an immediate reply."

"Definitely, *no*. Get off my ship!"

He understood, Otani said, and, remembering the naval niceties, put out his hand to be shaken before withdrawing to his steam launch. Polkinghorn turned his back. Standing watch, armed with a pistol, A. E. ("Jim") Mariner, who had been listening to the proceedings with awe, retreated further into the shadows. Below, Otani's launch cleared the *Peterel*, then sent up two red flares. In an instant Japanese warships in the harbor opened up, and the undeterred Polkinghorn returned the fire with his two ineffective Lewis guns.

Sound asleep on Shanghai booze, Jack Honywill was awakened by a "terrific explosion" and discovered his small cabin, facing portside toward the French Concession, brightly lit. Searchlights from Japanese ships had found his porthole, as had some shell fragments. Looking at his wristwatch to check the time he found his hand covered with blood. Shells were striking the *Peterel* as he swung out of bed to reach for his shoes; a piece of shrapnel pierced his calf. Still in his pajamas, he ran to the aft ladder and climbed to the deck, where Stoker Usher, already wounded, had reached for a lifejacket. "You better get a life belt," shouted "Jack Dusty" Hayne, but Honywill, bleeding from two flesh wounds, was rushing to the starboard gangway to destroy radio gear.

The *Peterel* was being hit continuously; Honywill could hear Polkinghorn shouting, "Bring the motor-boat round the starboard side." There was another shattering burst in the vicinity of the potbellied stove on the mess deck; Honywill realized that his right leg was now broken at the knee. Ignoring the pain, he stumbled, then crawled, toward the guardrail, aware of someone lying face downward as he groped for the ladder. Of the living, only Polkinghorn seemed aboard now; Honywill heard an "Abandon ship!" order repeated several times above the din. It was 4:45.

Flopping into the water, Honywill struck out toward the drifting motor launch, already crowded with survivors. He saw Jim Mariner standing up in the boat, trying to remove his greatcoat—if waterlogged it could drag him under—while tracer bullets flew past. In the glare of the searchlights and the burning *Peterel*, Honywill realized that the Whangpoo current was drawing him away from the launch. Exhausted, he was "swallowing a lot of this extremely filthy river." The *Peterel* was plunging nose-first when a life belt from the deck drifted by. He struggled to wrench it under his body as Seaman A. B. Holman, bleeding from a head wound, swam by, and a small sampan came alongside both. It looked like rescue.

As they hung limply to the gunwale, the Chinese boatman demanded one of their dripping watches. Holman offered his. With the extortion paid, they were hauled in and deposited onshore in the French Concession, where police took them by rickshaw to L'Hôpitale Sainte-Marie in the rue Père Robert. Stoker Dunbar was already there, unconscious and dying. Nursing sisters, assisted by a seventeen-year-old English volunteer, Evelyn Gander, whom the sailors gratefully called "Girlie," cleaned off the blood and grime and dressed their wounds. The women knew that sooner or later the *Kempeitai* would claim the sailors; meanwhile there was a chance they would survive.*

Ashore even earlier, in a hotel on the Bund, was the captain of the USS *Wake*, unaware at first that his deck officer had surrendered to a boarding party. The *Wake*'s unscathed crew joined the remnants of the *Peterel*'s in the camp at Woosung. The Japanese press would trumpet the capture of the helpless American sardine tin as one of the day's victories.

At the Cathay Hotel, on the Bund, where the Joint Distribution Committee's representatives, Laura Margolis and her new assistant—Manuel Siegel had arrived December 1—lived, the pair had front-row views of the war. "The whole harbor seemed aflame," she recalled. "Japanese troops had come over the bridge from Hongkew and . . . occupied our hotel. . . . The first thing we did when we saw all the flames was that we tore up all our papers and flushed them down the toilet because we knew we were imprisoned. . . . There were broadcasts—'All enemy nationals stay put; don't move.' And so we did not.

---

* Dunbar died the following night. Holman was seized by the Japanese. Honywill, given a few more days, made friends with "Girlie" Gander, daughter of a British customs official, but lost contact when he was taken to a prison camp. Repatriated in 1942, Evelyn Gander returned to England, married a Yankee soldier, and moved to America. Eventually the marriage broke up and she returned to England. Years later, knowing that Honywill had come from a Welsh village with the unforgettable name of Cwmfel-lnfach, she wrote to him, "Dear Jack, Forty years ago you told me I could reach you at this address." They were married the next May; seven months later Honywill died of a heart ailment.

We watched what was going on from the lobby . . . and saw the Japanese guards with their bayonets standing there. We couldn't go out; we were stuck."

From the tenth floor of the Palace Hotel, also on the Bund, J. G. Ballard (young "Jim" in his re-creation of the scene in *Empire of the Sun*) watched the *Peterel* go under after his parents vainly tried to keep him from the window. His father, an English businessman in Shanghai, had taken his wife and son to a hotel for safety because of war anxieties; now the war had come too close and he wanted to take them back home. The Ballards, already dressed in the early morning light, seized suitcases, and Jim, and encountered other guests—suitcases in hands—surrounding the silent lifts, pounding on the metal grilles, shouting down the empty shafts.

In the lobby, Chinese kitchen staff, guests who had taken the staircases, and White Russian clerks "crouched behind the leather furniture and potted palms, but Jim's father strode past them to the revolving doors." Crowds of Chinese filled the Bund "between the stationary trams and parked cars, old amahs hobbling in black trousers, coolies pushing empty rickshaws, beggars and sampan boys, uniformed waiters from the hotels."

The panic, if it existed at all, was short-lived. The Japanese were not, at least yet, interested in interning frightened European civilians. It was more important to move troops over the Soochow Creek bridge and into occupation of essential services. To fifteen-year-old Michael Blumenthal,* a refugee child on an expired German "J" passport walking to his Fifth Form class at the Jewish School on Seymour Road, it was "an unaccustomed, unwelcome and frightening sight" to find the deserted U. S. Marine barracks—the Marines had left for the Philippines in October—already occupied by the Japanese, "with their sentries posted in front."

•

Takeoff for Luzon was set for four o'clock. At two in the morning an orderly had gone through the pilots' barracks at Tainan, on the southwest coast of Taiwan, waking Saburo Sakai's group of NCO naval

---

* W. Michael Blumenthal became Secretary of the Treasury in the Jimmy Carter administration.

airmen. Flight Petty Officer Sakai and the others quietly slipped into their flying gear and went outside to check the weather. Skies were clear, with stars stretching from horizon to horizon.

The "Nell" medium bombers and Zero fighters of the 21st Air Flotilla (Eleventh Air Fleet) were fueled and ready. For weeks Sakai's squadron of Zeros had practiced flying at reduced propeller revolutions—just short of stalling—and at an optimum 12,000 foot altitude, to conserve fuel and stretch their endurance aloft from six to ten hours. The distance due south to Clark Field, 90 miles above Manila, was over 450 miles, and they knew that they could cruise the distance and back, yet have fighting time over the Philippines, on their 182-gallon capacity.

In the near darkness the crunch of boots on gravel was the only evidence of preparations. No engine had yet been started when thepilots grouped about Captain Masahisa Saito, the flotilla commander, for briefing. Reports from reconnaissance planes were that the weather over the target areas was satisfactory. At the Takao airbase, headquarters for the Eleventh Air Fleet, the pilots of the 23rd Air Flotilla—54 "Betty" bombers and 50 Zeros—were being briefed to hit Nichols Field, in the Manila suburbs. At each base, orderlies brought crews breakfast as they sat cross-legged on the tarmac beside their planes. The attacks were planned for 6:15 A.M., just before dawn.

It was about three when a mist began to close. By four, ground visibility at Takao and Tainan had dimmed to five yards. From the control towers, loudspeakers crackled that takeoff was delayed. Pilots looked at their watches and cursed the fog. They had missed their chance of catching the Americans asleep.

It seemed only a few minutes later when the loudspeakers lost in the fog again called for attention and announced that "this morning a Japanese task force has succeeded in carrying out a devastating surprise attack against the American forces in the Hawaiian Islands." Flight crews were shocked; their own friends on the mission had long kept the secret. At Tainan a roar arose in the near-darkness. Breaking discipline, pilots danced and slapped each other on the back. Then the realization dawned that not only might the Americans be waiting for them on Luzon; long-range bombers, which the Americans had, could hit their aircraft on the ground the moment the fog lifted. Gun installations were manned, and men on the field strained for the sounds of enemy planes.

•

In the Hotel Continental in Saigon, it had taken hours for Relman Morin to fall asleep. There had been no point in trying to file stories for the AP that would not pass the censor and would only call attention to himself. He had gone to bed early in the breathless heat and lay in the darkness listening to the inanities of the radio. Then he clicked it off and moved a chair onto his tiny balcony and watched nothing happen in the vacant square. The cathedral bells chimed one, then two o'clock. He went back to bed, dimly hearing in the rue Le Grand de la Liraye "the whine of a siren that died away in a low snarl. Then another and another."

It seemed to him that he had been asleep only a few minutes when he felt someone tugging at his shoulder. It was exactly three o'clock. "For a moment I was all mixed up. I thought I was back in Singapore. . . . Then I saw the face of a French friend." While Morin stared in confusion his friend said, "The war has started. The Japanese have bombed Pearl Harbor."

Morin began to laugh, uncontrollably, the tension having broken. Pulling a cigarette from a pack on the night table, he scratched a match, his hand quivering more than the flame. Although he felt "scared to death," the act of taking the cigarette settled him.

"All the British and Americans have been arrested," his friend said. "I didn't know whether you'd be here yet."

"But this country is supposed to be neutral."

"I don't understand why they haven't come for you."

"I heard sirens," said Morin. "So that's what it was."

"It was all arranged. They went to every house at the same time. . . . Everything is closed. The trains and buses have been stopped. Everything."

"I had a seat on a bus going beyond Hue this morning."

"It won't go. You can't get away."

They went to the window and Morin wondered why there was no excitement to see. "There hasn't been any excitement," said the Frenchman. "It was all done quickly." They sat until daylight, when reality interposed. Morin had only seven piastres and no place to go. His friend gave him some money. Banks would be closed. Morin urged him to leave. "If they find you here—"

There was a rap on the door. The Frenchman froze against the wall, his eyes bright with fear. Before either could move, the door opened. It was a hotel clerk with a telegram from AP colleague Clark Lee in Manila: "UNABLE TO REACH YOU BY TELEPHONE STOP SUGGEST YOU PLACE CALL."

Morin's friend shook his head. There were no phone circuits open. "Now I must go," he said. They shook hands and he slipped out.

•

Previously known as Samara, Kuibyshev, on the frozen-solid upper Volga on the edge of the Urals, had been named for the author of the first Five Year Plan. When C. L. Sulzberger of the *New York Times* had tried to cable his home office in October that correspondents as well as most others in Moscow not needed for its defense were being evacuated eastward, he tried evading the censorship by filing that he was keeping an appointment with John O'Hara.* The shabby city, swollen with excess population as informal temporary capital, was a funnel for the snowy blasts of Asia, which rattled its most prominent symbol, an enormous cloth banner decorating a former church and extolling the blessings of atheism.

With Stalin having stuck it out in Moscow, Kuibyshev's most visible citizen was the thirty-five-year-old Dmitri Shostakovitch, who had been flown out of Leningrad in October with his family. He was too valuable a symbol to be abandoned and had left his native city reluctantly. On Leningrad Radio on September 17 he had noted scoring the second movement of his new symphony, his seventh. In a two-room apartment dominated by a piano provided by the Kuibyshev music school, he was finishing the last movement. Labeling it the "Leningrad Symphony" for propaganda purposes, he worked at it late into each night. The Party authorities "were less strict . . . and didn't care if the music was too gloomy. . . . All the misery was put down to the war." Most of his symphonies, he confided later, were "tombstones."

Subsisting on bread, beer, and soup bought at the Foreigners' Shop,

---

* O'Hara's fatalistic 1934 best-seller referred to the ancient and different city of Samarra (seventy miles from Baghdad), to which, in legend, a young man flees, unaware that he has an appointment there with Death.

correspondents who lodged at Kuibyshev's misnamed Grand Hotel warmed themselves with hard-to-get whiskey from the West. "They were sure," Soviet newsman Ilya Ehrenburg party-lined, "that in a month or two Hitler would conquer the whole of Russia, and sometimes comforted themselves and us with the thought that the struggle would continue in Egypt or India. When the news came of the Japanese attack on Pearl Harbor, the Americans in the Grand Hotel came to blows with the Japanese journalists."

Little of it was true, Sulzberger remembered: "We were all pro-Red Army, and our relations with the Japanese were quite affable." The news had come late at night. Sulzberger had already retired to his room, but the ever-courteous Tokyo newsman for the *Asahi Shimbun*, Masaharu Hatanaka, who lived on the same floor, came to his door bowing and smiling with a "So sorry, we sank your fleet this morning. Supposing we are at war."

Sulzberger was skeptical, but he pulled on his clothes and struggled through hip-high snow to the schoolhouse that was the temporary American embassy. Still up, the assistant military attaché, Mike Michela, confirmed Hatanaka's news if not his damage estimate.

·

"Berlin," United Press reported from Germany, "was electrified tonight at the news of the Japanese attacks. The story, datelined New York, was carried by the official news agency DNB a few minutes before 10:30." No one in Germany was more electrified than the Führer. At Wolfschanze, after the usual late dinner, Hitler had gathered assorted minions willing to listen to him soliloquize into the small hours—adoring secretaries, his personal physician, desk officers, and his diplomatic adviser with the rank of ambassador, Walther Hewel. Having shared imprisonment at Landsberg in 1923, the loyal Hewel had a special relationship with the Führer.

Hitler had been indulging in reflections about how the emergency collection of warm winter clothing among the civilian population, for the troops on the Eastern Front, had been going. Everyone understood that it had not been in his plans to be frozen in Russian snows in December, but such observations were out of place. Toward midnight Hitler's press officer, Heinz Lorenz, burst in with a bulletin. An American radio broadcast picked up in Germany had mentioned a surprise Japanese attack on the U.S. fleet in Hawaii. Japan had joined the war.

Hitler leaped to his feet. Slapping his thighs in delight he shouted, "The turning point!" Then he rushed out of the room to find Keitel and Jodl. To Hewel, following him, he predicted, "Now it is impossible for us to lose the war: we now have an ally who has never been vanquished in three thousand years, and another ally"—he was recalling a remark about the Italians which Talleyrand had attributed to Napoleon—"who has constantly been vanquished but has always ended up on the right side."

It was the only time in the war, Keitel recalled, that Hitler "came bursting in" excitedly with news, violating the austere hierarchy he had created at his headquarters. "I gained the impression that the Führer felt that the war between Japan and America had suddenly relieved him of a nightmare burden; it certainly brought us some relief from the consequences of America's undeclared state of war with us."

In his war diary General Halder penned into a corner of the first page of his daily entry, "Japan opens hostilities against U.S." It was not that matter-of-fact. The abstemious Hitler called for champagne and invited headquarters officers to an impromptu celebration. According to General Warlimont, Hitler himself "*hat an einem Glase genippt.*" Nothing like that had happened before at glum, gray Wolfschanze.

As a symbol of his enthusiasm, Hitler would award Ambassador Oshima the Grand Cross of the Distinguished Order of the German Eagle in gold. The sneak attack on Pearl Harbor appealed to Hitler. "You certainly gave the right declaration of war!" he told Oshima at the investiture on the fourteenth. "This method is the only proper one . . . , [to] strike as hard as possible, indeed, and not waste time declaring war." He compared Japan's sincere desire for peace to Germany's and praised Japan for its "patience of a saint toward this lout, Roosevelt."

The news was a great relief, Hitler went on as Ribbentrop listened. A neutral but openly hostile America made the submarine campaign impossible. "How can a commander know when he should fire his torpedoes and when he shouldn't? The American vessels were sailing in convoy with their lights out, and they also supplied the British with 50 destroyers of a type that they themselves owned 80 of. One cannot imagine that a U-boat commander should read through a whole book before he fires a torpedo in order to discover if the ship is a British or an American one! U-boat commanders have been put under an intolerable psychological strain, for . . . as a result of a single mistaken torpedo being launched . . . his country could be drawn into a new war."

Roosevelt, he insisted, "must be smashed. It has been the major accomplishment of the Japanese that they have destroyed the myth of American superiority from the start." As a soldier in the last war, he learned not to overrate American fighting qualities. "Then, German troops were tired and worn out and the American troops were fresh and well-fed. In spite of that, where German and American forces clashed, the Americans just folded up and needed weeks before they could be put back in the front line. How can we expect troops to fight to the uttermost when they have the dollar as their God?"

Now, Hitler felt, "All the Jewish concepts like the 'Western Hemisphere,' the '300-Mile Zone,' and the like have become things of the past." The Japanese had already presented the Kriegsmarine with seventy torpedoes of the type used at Pearl Harbor, and construction drawings, and he would see to their manufacture and deployment. "If the British ports and shipyards were wrecked, Britain would be helpless." But there were other priorities too. He would "turn his whole attention to North Africa" until the winter was over and he could complete "the destruction of Russia."

•

Conveyed in modern luxury across France, Belgium, and Holland, then through Germany, Göring was back in Berlin. His special train was being off-loaded of new plunder, all legally paid for in appropriated Reichsmarks. The shopping had been rewarding, but the conference with doddering, whitebearded Marshal Pétain, the excuse for the jaunt, left much to be desired. To air ace Adolf Galland, who had been along for ceremonial visits to Luftwaffe bases, Göring had remarked at St. Florentin-Vergigny, a small town north of Paris, that his meeting with the collaborationist Vichy chiefs was likely to take about twenty minutes, just long enough to issue instructions.

Göring emerged three hours later with his feathers ruffled. Both Marshal Pétain and Admiral Jean Louis Darlan, for whom the aged Marshal was largely a façade, used German problems in Russia and North Africa to press for concessions. Darlan was next going to Turin to talk to Count Galeazzo Ciano, Mussolini's son-in-law and Foreign Minister. Petain had behaved as though France had won the war, Göring warned the *Duce*. The old man had tried to hand Göring a

document setting out Vichy France's conditions for further collabo-
ration, and when the Reichsmarschall refused to accept it, tucked it
calmly into his breast pocket.

Göring was particularly frustrated by lack of access to French North
Africa, still securely in Vichy hands. The Germans were looking for
safer ways to resupply the Italians and their own Afrika Korps in Libya
than the routes being interdicted by British planes and submarines.
"Dark news from Libya," Ciano noted in his diary. "Our forces are
no longer such as to attempt a long resistance; they must break contact
with the enemy, and break it decisively"—the Foreign Minister's euphemism for the withdrawal that Rommel had already begun. ". . .
Mussolini is calm; in fact, he talks about the possibility of a counter-
attack. . . . It all depends on cession of the port of Bizerte by the
French." But Tunisia would face a Gaullist rebellion, Darlan had
warned Göring; besides, it might open French Africa to attacks by the
British and provide an excuse for American intervention.

"During the evening," Ciano added, "[Field Marshal Hans Georg
von] Mackensen comes to tell me in the name of Ribbentrop that I
must start no such negotiations with the French. This is the will of
Hitler, communicated to Mussolini. . . . Hitler is right: Tunisia is de
Gaullist 101 per cent. . . . This morning the Duce was very much
irritated by the paucity of [Italian] losses in eastern Africa. Those who
fell at Gondar number sixty-seven; the prisoners ten thousand. One
doesn't have to think very long to see what those figures mean."

•

With Harry Hopkins at his side, the President convened a meeting
in his Oval Office at three o'clock. Secretaries Hull, Stimson, and Knox
were there, Hull having had just left Kurusu and Nomura. Admiral
Stark and General Marshall offered information from Hawaii, Stark
doing most of the talking. He had just been on the phone to Pearl
Harbor, listening to Rear Admiral Bloch, commandant of the 14th
Naval District. Despite the scrambler Bloch had been vague in his
damage estimates, and Stark, exasperated, asked sharply, "Claude, how
about it?"

"It's pretty bad. I don't know how secure this telephone is."

"Go ahead and tell me," said Stark. And Bloch did, with Captain
John McCrea, afterward naval aide to the President, listening in. "If

any unauthorized person has heard the remarks I have just made to the Chief of Naval Operations," Bloch concluded, with deep concern, "I beg of you not to repeat them in any way. I call on your patriotic duty as an American citizen." The worry was real, and suggested why Marshall, earlier, had not wanted to warn General Short yet again, or to do it by telephone.

Interrupted by telephone calls, which Roosevelt took personally, the conferees learned bit by bit about further damage to the fleet. It was, Hopkins felt, "not too tense an atmosphere because I think that all of us believed that in the last analysis the enemy was Hitler and that he could never be defeated without force of arms; that sooner or later we were bound to be in the war and that Japan was giving us an opportunity." It would be "a long, hard struggle."

Roosevelt had long anticipated war with Germany and hoped that a policy of bluff and stall would keep the Japanese from anything more than nibbling gains. At his shipboard meeting with Churchill in August, he had confided (Lieutenant General Henry Pownall of the Imperial General Staff had noted it down) his hopes of being drawn into war with Hitler. The President, Pownall noted, "was *all* for coming into the war, and as soon as possible . . . but he said he would never *declare* war; he wishes to provoke it. He wants to create an incident that brings war about, being no doubt sure that he will then be fully supported by the people."

Everyone around Roosevelt registered genuine surprise at the audacity of the Pearl Harbor attack. Press censorship and executive orders to carry out internal dispositions were suddenly needed. Go ahead and execute the orders, said Roosevelt; he would sign them later. With Marshall he discussed troop and aircraft movements. With Hull he declared the need to keep the South American republics "not only informed but . . . in line with us." He would submit a "precise message" to Congress to ask for a declaration of war, and Hull urged that the President use the occasion for a "strong statement" on Japanese-American relations.

Hopkins suggested two emergency meetings at the White House, with the Cabinet and with congressmen. The first was set for 8:30 and the second to follow, with a small list of invitees rather than all senior leaders and committee chairmen. Hamilton Fish of New York was ranking Republican on the Foreign Affairs Committee of the House of Representatives, and the President would not have the stubborn isolationist in the White House.

.

On maneuvers at Fort Bragg, North Carolina, Paul W. Tibbets, Jr., a former medical student whose infatuation with airplanes had diverted him into the Air Corps, had been flying war-games missions. After interdicting trucks with TANK painted on the sides, and troops with sticks and logs simulating nonexistent rifles and mortars, he was returning to Fort Benning, Georgia, in his A-20. "It was a reasonably sunny day, and I had tuned my radio to a station in Savannah and was following the needle home. Every weekend pilot will understand this method of navigation. . . . I was able to find some music instead of the sermons that were on many stations that Sunday. Suddenly the music in my earphones ceased and a voice broke in. A mile over the red clay earth of Georgia, I learned that the Japanese had bombed Pearl Harbor."

When Tibbets landed, he saw "people . . . out of the buildings and all over the field. You would have thought that they expected a Japanese attack on Savannah that day."

That this seemed even remotely possible was a product of the geographical innocence of most Americans. In New York, in Woody Allen's film *Radio Days*, Sally White, a night club cigarette girl, asks, "*Who* is Pearl Harbor?" And in a seedy little café on the Virginia coast, where prep school student William Styron and three friends were drinking illegal beer "so crudely brewed that gobbets of yeast floated in it like snowflakes" and gnawing late-afternoon hamburgers, the waitress came to their table and announced the perplexing radio news. "I'll never forget her homely face, which was like a slab of pale pine with two small holes bored in it, nor her voice, which had all the sad languor of the upper Pamunkey River. 'The Japanese,' she said, 'they done bombed Pearl Harbor. God help us, it's so close. Imagine them gettin' all the way to South Carolina.' That woman's geography was only a little less informed than our own." It was not much different from the reality of the singing Andrews Sisters in Cincinnati, where Maxine Andrews walked out in front of the theater expecting to see the usual crowds standing in line to get tickets. Only there were no crowds or lines. Puzzled, she walked in through the untended stage door and found the doorman and the stagehands sitting round a radio and talking about Pearl Harbor. "Where is Pearl Harbor?" she asked.

Exhausted after taking a prototype P-47 Thunderbolt on a test run the previous day, Lieutenant Colonel Ira Eaker was worried "about all this [high-]altitude flying I had been doing." Back home after taking his visiting mother-in-law out to Sunday brunch, he crawled into bed for a nap, and it seemed to him that he had hardly dozed off when he saw his wife standing nearby. When he looked up she said, "The Japs have attacked Pearl Harbor!"

"You'll have to think of a better story than that to get me out of bed," he said sleepily. She turned up the volume on the radio and Eaker could hear an observer in Honolulu describe the attack, still going on.

Reaching for the telephone, he called General Arnold's office. Colonel Carl Spaatz answered. He and his wife had been remodeling an old house they had just acquired in Alexandria, across the river in Virginia, when his office telephoned, and Ruth Spaatz had rushed him across the Potomac to the Munitions Building. "I think I'll catch a civil airliner tonight," Eaker suggested, "and get back to the West Coast and join my old 20th Pursuit Group."

"I think you are headed in the right direction," said Spaatz.

•

At Fort Davis, near the Panama Canal, the morning began as an ordinary Sunday, which was fortunate for officers who had partied strenuously the night before. It was a free day except for the Anti-Tank Company and Lieutenant Utter's Jungle Platoon. At three they were to go on guard duty on the Atlantic side of the "ditch." It would be a peacetime spit-and-polish formation and inspection, with a lucky G.I. plucked from the ranks to be a general's orderly for twenty-four hours and then to have a three-day pass. Since he would be officer-of-the-day for twenty-four hours, Utter was catching up on his daily paperwork before Guard Mount when his First Sergeant arrived and said, "Compliments of the General, Sir, and he wants you down at his office immediately." Utter recalled the disaster at the officers' club and was sure that he was in trouble. "Tell the General for me," he said, "that I am going on guard duty shortly." The sergeant returned with "The General knows that, Sir, and says to get your ass down there pronto!"

Expecting to find the general in Sunday attire—usually golf shorts—Utter was astounded to see him instead in full battle dress, with tin hat and .45 in his holster. They were at war with Japan, he announced. Pearl Harbor had been bombed. A patrol out of Rio Hato on the Pacific side of the canal had reported unidentified aircraft—and an enemy carrier was thought to be lurking to the south, near the Galapagos Islands.

Utter wondered how to get the news to his father, who published, in Westerly, Rhode Island, the only Sunday afternoon daily newspaper either of them knew of in the United States, but he could not get through. It proved unnecessary. The pressmen at *The Sun* knew all about it. They gutted the front page and ran "JAPANESE BOMB HAWAII AND THE PHILIPPINES" in twenty-four-point type. Although the news had been released by the White House at 2:22 P.M., they had only two brass mats available to print the numeral 2. Altering history by one minute *The Sun* rushed out its paper with the President's announcement set at 2:23 P.M.

On the Caribbean side of the Panama Canal Zone, Lieutenant (later Lieutenant General) Arthur S. Collins of the 14th Infantry had accepted an invitation to Sunday dinner at the home of a canal engineer. It was an opportunity to get away from military messes and alerts that proved false alarms. Sabotage of the canal was a constant worry, as was the possibility of air attack from the sea, and Navy patrols were flying long missions outward from both ends of the waterway, reaching to the limits of their fuel.

Both Army and Navy personnel had been taken off alert at noon, and on the Pacific side, Lieutenant Andrew J. Goodpaster (later a general and military aide to President Eisenhower) and his wife decided to play "a little round of golf" on Fort Clayton's nine-hole course. In khaki work clothes, on the edge of the steamy jungle which was never far away from anything in the Zone, and close to the 25th Bombardment Squadron's base at France Field, Lieutenant G. Robert Fox, a chemistry major just out of the University of Michigan (later a lieutenant colonel and afterward a professor), gathered palm fronds to decorate the officers' club for Sunday evening festivities, planning to change into dress whites afterward.

There were a lot of personnel in the Zone garrison—over 30,000—yet inadequate aircraft for reconnaissance, only enough ammunition for one minute of fire per gun for the new 37mm antiaircraft guns, no barrage balloons, no planes equipped for night pursuit, only two radar units with few trained to operate them, and eight long-range bombers and twelve light bombers that were not obsolete. The new P-39 fighters, engineered to fire a 37mm cannon, were flying without their still undelivered guns. The most obvious signs of war were the German and Italian ships interned in Cristobal harbor, a matter being handled by consuls as a problem of international law, with crews living aboard ship while the question was adjudicated.

As the Goodpasters putted near a barracks area, a onetime West Point classmate also with the 11th Engineers shouted from his doorway, "Come to the radio; the Japs are bombing Pearl Harbor!"

"Oh, hell," Goodpaster shouted back. "We've been through the Orson Welles thing. Forget it!"

"No, no, no! This is real. You come and listen."

It was no invasion-from-Mars fiction, and the golf game was over. So was Collins's dinner. At Fox's quarters, he was nearly into his whites—pulling up his trousers—when the telephone rang. Suddenly he was officer-of-the-day, effective immediately, and ordered to draw a .45 pistol from Armament. His unit was placed on round-the-clock security.

Goodpaster quickly learned that he was to arrange for the immediate construction of a cantonment to hold all the local Japanese who were being rounded up—250 was the first estimate of likely internees. Collins and his friend Tommy Callan rushed back to frantic messages "that the Japanese fleet was coming to hit the Canal, and maybe try to make a landing. At any rate, orders came out immediately that everyone was frozen wherever they were." Collins had just shipped home most of his goods and had been living out of a footlocker while waiting for transportation to Fort Leonard Wood, Missouri, to join the newly mechanized 6th Division. He had already spent two sultry, oppressive years in the Zone. Now he was little better off than the Germans and Italians on their ships. He wasn't going anywhere either.

·

The final football game of the season for the Washington Redskins and the Philadelphia Eagles went on in ancient Griffith Stadium before a sell-out crowd. The green-painted steel-and-wood grandstands were rickety, but Redskins fans were loyal and uncomplaining. Sparked by Tommy Thompson and Jack Banta, the Eagles scored first, but the

Redskins would go ahead in the second half on three touchdown passes by Sammy Baugh to win, 20–14.

The second half was under way when sportswriter Shirley Povich of the *Washington Post* saw AP writer Pat O'Brien receive a teletyped message in the press box, "Keep game [account] short. Unimportant." (UP teletyped all bureaus, "PLS HOLD SKEDS TO BONE; OFFER ONLY HOTTEST; DON'T BREAK EXCEPT FOR CERTAIN HOT BULLETINS.") Puzzled, O'Brien teletyped an angry objection and received an immediate reply, "Japs just kicked off. War now."

Povich's story the next morning would be headlined, "War's Outbreak is Deep Secret to 27,702 Redskin Game Fans." It was not information to keep quiet about, and the rustle of war bulletins trickled out of the press area and down the seats, becoming more garbled with each exchange. International News Service reporter Eric Friedheim and his boss, Washington bureau chief William K. Hutchinson, were sitting separately. When the writers in the press box got the news, "Hutch" tracked Friedheim down and sent him to the White House, remaining himself to see the rest of the game. Another reporter in the grandstand got the news from his wife, who heard it on the radio, then telegraphed, under his name, "DELIVER TO SECTION P, TOP ROW, SEAT 27, OPPOSITE 25-YARD LINE, EAST SIDE, GRIFFITH STADIUM. WAR WITH JAPAN! GET TO OFFICE!"

Military notables as well as lesser ranks in uniform, ranging down even lower than Ensign John Fitzgerald Kennedy, were at the stadium. Between plays, loudspeaker appeals blared for various generals and admirals to report to duty immediately. The Resident Commissioner of the Philippines was asked to return to his office. Newspaper circulation managers and delivery boys were asked to show up at their jobs without delay. Yet the Griffith management refused to air the Pearl Harbor news on the public address system, explaining, "We don't want to contribute to any hysteria." Besides, George Preston Marshall, owner of the Redskins, pointed out, "non-sport news" was never broadcast at the stadium.

In the Polo Grounds before 50,051 fans, the New York football Giants were hosting the Brooklyn Dodgers. Again the audience was told nothing, although Colonel "Wild Bill" Donovan, head of what was not yet called the OSS, was repeatedly summoned by loudspeaker to telephone Operator 10 in Washington, a link to the White House. Leaning over toward Frank Morris, a draftee on furlough, a retired

Navy man commented, "History could be in the making, you know." But the old salt stayed in his seat and kept his eyes on the gridiron.

As Brooklyn crossed the New York 45-yard line, radio listeners understood. "Japanese bombs," an unfamiliar voice broke in, "have fallen on Hawaii and the Philippine Islands. Keep tuned to this station for further details." With the score 21–0 and Pug Manders scoring all three touchdowns for the Dodgers, the tension had evaporated from the game but not from the crowd. The ominous buzzing grew with each loudspeaker entreaty to other VIP types to go to a box-office telephone. A stiff, cold wind drove others from their seats, including the *New York Times*'s Harrison Salisbury, who left with his wife for a restorative drink at the flat of a friend. They turned on the radio to the game as the announcer cut in with "additional details of the Japanese bombing of Pearl Harbor."

"Those poor little Japanese bastards," said Salisbury. "The suicide boys have got them in the soup. They are finished. They are through. They haven't a chance." Then he put his coat back on and hurried to his office.

The 34th Bomb Group at Westover Field in Holyoke, Massachusetts, had two new B-17s and three obsolete B-18s. It took most mornings, including Sundays, to fit inexperienced crews into the Flying Fortresses for training, and Major Curtis LeMay decided to knock off for the afternoon and have a few hours with his three-year-old daughter. The car radio went on when he turned the ignition key, and he listened to the Giants-Dodgers game until it was interrupted by war bulletins kept from fans in the stands. He felt "some sense of relief" that the waiting was over. Accelerating home, he broke the news to his wife, then returned to the base, which was already in confusion.

With twenty-three seconds remaining, the Giants scored a touchdown and avoided the embarrassment of a shutout. As the crowd that had remained until the last play began to leave, the public address system announced that all military men were to report to duty immediately.

·

Chain-smoking Donald Downes worked for three masters. He had kept his position with the Free World Association in New York as cover when he became a spy for British intelligence, and he was permitted to pass on any relevant information to an appropriate American agency. His job had included penetrating anti-interventionist organizations to discover whether they were involved overtly with German agents or were only Nazi dupes. Downes was spending his Sunday afternoon preparing a report for Colonel Donovan.

Focusing on German consulates and the German embassy, he had looked for persons who might have been conduits for Nazi funds. Senator Burton K. Wheeler of Montana and Senator Gerald P. Nye of North Dakota, Charles A. Lindbergh, and James D. Mooney, head of General Motors overseas operations, as well as Kingman Brewster, Jr., the student leader of the America First movement at Downes's alma mater, Yale, were among his suspects. The FBI had already learned that the wife of a former German embassy officer was working with Mrs. Wheeler in America First. "Magic" intercepts had connected Second Secretary Terasaki of the Japanese embassy with American anti-interventionists, including lesser-fry Firsters. Downes had hoped to establish clear links with Nazis. Instead he had established only that they shared some views, although a few members remote from the leadership did have Axis contacts. Only the Boston and Cleveland groups had traceable connections to Nazi money. The known recipients of German funds, he typed out, were rather minor figures—a Republican county chairman in Ohio, an Amherst College instructor, and similar nobodies.

.

The first part of the program had been short—the First Symphony of Shostakovitch. Scheduled to play the Brahms Piano Concerto in B-flat with Artur Rodzinski and the New York Philharmonic on a national radio hookup, Artur Rubinstein was just about to mount the steps to the Carnegie Hall stage when he heard "an outcry of horror from several stagehands and from Rodzinski himself, who arrived gesticulating dramatically." Rubinstein was "thunderstruck," but the concert had to continue. Still, Rodzinski felt he had to inform the audience, which had already begun seething as the news drifted in from the foyers and cloakrooms.

"You must first play 'The Star Spangled Banner,' " Rodzinski advised Rubinstein as he proceeded to the piano. With them came Warren Sweeney, the CBS announcer for the broadcast, who confirmed from the stage what had been murmured through the aisles. Raising his baton, Rodzinski repeated the National Anthem, which by custom had begun the program, this time with Rubinstein at the piano. The audience stood at stiff attention, order returning with the first bars. Everyone sang lustily, then settled down to the Brahms concerto, which, Rubinstein recalled, "we played with special fervor." But when it was over, the audience raced for the doors, and the orchestra, conductor, and soloist scurried backstage to find a radio.

In the Bair household on Cornell Avenue in Swarthmore, Pennsylvania, after-church dinner was followed as usual by the New York Philharmonic concert, piped into their parlor on the faithful Atwater Kent console. Mrs. Elizabeth Posey from next door had telephoned earlier to ask whether her father, Clarence Dykstra, might visit to listen, and he had come over with her. Dykstra was on leave from the presidency of the University of Wisconsin on appointment as chairman of the Selective Service Board. The weekend with his daughter's family was a rare retreat from the harried and unpopular job of drafting men for a year's military service.

Ceremoniously turned on to the Philharmonic, the radio broadcast instead what appeared to be a repeat of an earlier bulletin about a Japanese attack on Pearl Harbor. Dykstra rushed for the kitchen telephone and called the White House switchboard. The Bair family overheard talk of mobilization and how quickly Dykstra could get on a train to Washington. John Bair's father, a sergeant in 1918, wondered aloud if he were too old to get back in the Marines.

On a train from Washington, bound for New York, where he planned to consult with key physicists about atomic bomb research, Arthur Holly Compton made room for a boarding passenger at Wilmington, Delaware. He was bursting with news. Compton would no longer need to be persuasive.

•

At his isolated home on Martha's Vineyard, Lindbergh turned on his radio for the latest news. He had moved to the island retreat in August for more privacy, a posture at odds with his increasing speech-making for America First. Lindbergh was working on his next exhortation, scheduled for Boston, where he would urge that Americans keep out of England's war.

"I did not think it would come quite so soon," he wrote in his journal. "But Pearl Harbor! How did the Japs get close enough, and where is our Navy? Or is it just"—he lapsed into wishful thinking—

"a hit-and-run raid of a few planes, exaggerated by radio commentators into a major attack?" Any attack, he thought, would be costly to the Japanese in carriers and planes, "unless our Navy is asleep—or in the Atlantic. The question in my mind is, how much of it has been sent to the Atlantic to aid Britain?" If it could be proved that Roosevelt had left Hawaii defenseless in order to protect English shipping, America First might have a case.*

Lindbergh's wife, Anne, was listening to the radio in her car as she drove to Woods Hole, Massachusetts, later in the day recalling the moment in her diary. "It is the knell of the old world. . . . If C. speaks again they'll put him in prison, I think, immediately. . . . I listen all afternoon to the . . . Philharmonic, a beautiful concerto of Brahms. But it is interrupted every ten minutes with bulletins about the war. This is what life is going to be from now on. . . ."

The big America First effort that afternoon was in Pittsburgh, at the Soldiers' and Sailors' Memorial Hall three miles from downtown. Senator Nye was to address a capacity crowd, fifteen hundred of the faithful, at three. The speaker's platform, set against a backdrop of Lincoln's Gettysburg Address in huge black letters on a buff background, was empty as the clock struck the hour. A *Pittsburgh Post Gazette* reporter, Robert Hagy, had slipped into the little backstage room in which the red-nosed, gravel-voiced senator had been closeted with Firsters on the program, and shoved the pasted-up teletype of the Pearl Harbor flash at Nye. Irene Castle McLaughlin, the still-trim, remarried widow of the dancer killed in the Great War, and local Firster John B. Gordon bent over Nye to share the dispatch.

"It sounds pretty fishy to me," Nye rasped. "Can't we have some details? Is it sabotage or is it open attack? I'm amazed that the President should announce an attack without giving details."

When it was clear to Hagy that the senator preferred to disbelieve, he asked what effect war with Japan might have. Would America First disband?

"If Congress were to declare war, I'm sure that every America

---

* Like many other isolationists and conspiracy theorists, Lindbergh would never cease believing that Roosevelt was not only "determined" to drag an unwilling America into the war, but ready "to stoop to almost any means"—including provoking the Pearl Harbor debacle—to accomplish that. So he wrote in 1957 to Admiral Robert A. Theobald, who had defended Husband E. Kimmel in various military and congressional proceedings, and in an anti-FDR book, *The Final Secret of Pearl Harbor*.

Firster would be cooperative and support his government in the winning of the war in every possible way," said Nye, "but I should not
expect them to disband even if Congress declared war." Then he and
the others pushed through the curtain and paraded onto the platform
to loud applause.

Leading off, Vernon Castle's widow denounced Roosevelt as a
warmonger and dabbed at her eyes when recalling her husband's death
in the trenches. Then a state senator, Charlie Sipes, attacked Roosevelt
for making "everything Russian appealing to the U.S." To roaring
approval from the crowd under the draped red, white, and blue bunting
he went on, "In fact, the chief warmonger in the U.S., to my way of
thinking, is the President of the U.S.!" People in the audience shook
"Defend America First" signs.

From an aisle seat well to the back of the hall a stocky white-haired
man stood up as the cheers echoed, and tried to make himself heard.
Although in civilian clothes, he was Colonel Enrique Urrutia, Jr., chief
of the Pittsburgh Organized Reserve, and a thirty-one-year veteran.
"Can this meeting be called"—he meant "held"—"after what has happened in the last few hours?" he shouted. "Do you know," he challenged Sipes, "that Japan has attacked Manila, that Japan has attacked
Hawaii?"

Firster loyalists were used to hecklers. There were shouts of "Warmonger!" and "Throw him out!" Several large men converged upon
him, and policemen from a detail of ten assigned to the hall to keep
order escorted Urrutia out through a cacophony of shrieked insults.

"I came to listen," he told Hagy in the lobby, purple with rage. "I
thought this was a patriots' meeting, but this is a traitors' meeting."

From the platform, Sipes was telling the audience, "Don't be too
hard on this poor bombastic man. He's only a mouthpiece for FDR."
Finishing his speech, he introduced several local Firsters before Nye's
turn came.

"Whose war is this?" Nye began, referring to occupied Europe.

"Roosevelt's," chorused the Firsters.

"My friends," said Nye, "are betting twenty to one that if we don't
stop in our tracks now, we'll be in before Great Britain gets in." It
was the usual isolationist routine of claiming that Britain was keeping
its casualties down while encouraging further American involvement.
Nye had long felt that only the English and the Jews were behind the
anti-Hitler rhetoric, and Lindbergh had publicly agreed with him. One

of the authors of the first Neutrality Act, forbidding Americans to sell or ship weapons to belligerent countries, Nye opposed every defense measure in Congress and any proposal of any kind made by Roosevelt. Now each crack at the President raised howls of laughter, still rising and falling when Hagy was tapped by an usher and told that he was wanted on the telephone.

As he listened, he copied out the message with his pencil in block printing: "The Japanese Imperial Government at Tokyo today . . . announced a state of war with the U.S. and Great Britain." Hagy walked up to the platform and put the scrap of paper on the rostrum before Nye, who glanced at it and went on with his prepared speech.

                                    •

Hard by General Marshall's office in a corridor crowded with messengers running back and forth, a new brigadier general promoted from lieutenant colonel only months before (skipping colonel) was "phoning and doing different things because there was a great clamor to get troops to the west coast." And Mark Wayne Clark thought to himself "how lucky we are that we just had maneuvers. We'd moved a corps. Two or three months before that you would say, 'How do you move a corps?' " Now he ordered two Army corps headquarters companies to California overnight, so they could prepare to receive the rest of their units, and he remembered how, on maneuvers in Louisiana, "we had used Standard Oil (Esso) road maps because the Army had nothing better." He wondered what the quality—and quantity—was of the maps they had of Far East areas that were likely war zones. Clark, Dwight Eisenhower, Walter Bedell Smith, and others jumped up quickly under Marshall represented his solution to the Army's age-old problem, which he had once described as "a collection of old officers at the head of every division who had ceased mental development years before."

Under an exchange program with Japan, Captain Maxwell D. Taylor (soon a general) had trained with a Japanese artillery regiment only a few years before. In shops near the training camps he bought Japanese military manuals and brought them home. They were the only Japanese military guides the Army now had.

Returning from the Carolina maneuvers in a long, dusty convoy of "six-by-six" trucks, Lieutenant George M. Trostle of the 110th Infantry Regiment was puzzled by what he saw. Heading south three weeks earlier the clattering queue of trucks and support vehicles had woven through towns and villages seemingly devoid of population. No one had paid the slightest attention to them. Now they were greeted by cheers from clusters of flag-waving townspeople. Above the din and clatter of the convoy they could hear enthusiastic shouts as well, but could not make out the words. Only when they bivouacked for the night would they learn from portable radios pulled out of duffle bags, Trostle remembered, "that the United States was at war and I was in it."

In dry dock at the Norfolk Naval Shipyard in Virginia was the elderly battleship *New York*, having a propeller shaft replaced and undergoing other refitting. As was the yard rule, all hazardous material had been removed, including ammunition. But when the war news broke, the *New York*'s captain ordered that all antiaircraft batteries were to be fully manned, even though no AA ammunition could be brought on board for the guns. "How were we supposed to shoot?" wondered William Gregg, Assistant Communications Officer. "What German or Japanese plane could reach Norfolk?"

The next step was to discover the battleship's classified instructions in event of war. Gregg and a colleague went to the naval base to find out. On the way they stopped to alert his immediate superior officer. "He had already heard the news, but . . . was on his way to play golf, and felt that nothing was to be gained by his immediate return to the ship." Gregg's companion was "deeply incensed" by the lack of devotion to duty, but at the naval base they "found the admirals and other top brass wandering about as if in a trance. It was Sunday, and the classified material was protected in the vaults by bank-type time locks. It was impossible to open the vaults before 0800 Monday."

Cramming electricity and underwater demolition after having acquired his irrelevant degree in journalism, Ensign Glenn Addington was agonizing over the unfamiliar material at his kitchen table. Newly married, he and his wife, Lucy, had a tiny apartment near the Naval Mine Warfare School in Yorktown, Virginia.

Lucy stopped stirring her oatmeal-cookie batter when the scratchy table radio began transmitting recall-to-base orders. Addington had not been commissioned long enough for the bright gold braid on his cap device to tarnish, and he had stubbornly refused to try the surreptitious salt water dip method of achieving what his wife called "the honorable green corrosion" of the experienced seaman. He had chosen the Navy because the Army suggested mud and mire and trenches. The radio seemed to confirm a waterborne war.

Addington telephoned his base. He was to report in the morning for reassignment, and Lucy wondered about the laundry frozen on the line, and what from it she would have to iron in a hurry. She thought of their wedding-gift china still unpacked in barrels, and realized that the Navy would transfer everything—somewhere.

Addington would ship out on sub patrol in the Caribbean. Four years later the Navy delivered their china; six months after that "a Navy truck with armed enlisted men delivered a mysterious crate—our ironing board."

At Fort Benning, Georgia, a group of officer candidates were five days from commissions as second lieutenants. Jack A. Marshall watched a veteran sergeant in the class go to pieces in the squadroom. He had come to OCS from Schofield Barracks. "I should have been there," he cried. "Those are my men getting killed, my men. . . . I don't even know who is left. I should be there!" He wept—a sight no one had ever seen before—and banged brawny fists on a table. General Omar Bradley, the school commandant, called an emergency assembly, and in his quiet, scholarly manner reported the details that were known and added that General Marshall had told him by telephone from Washington that OCS was not to be interrupted.

The event of the afternoon at Camp Wheeler, Georgia, was the last lunch chow line for about seventy-five draftee privates who would complete their year of active duty the next day. Their packed duffle bags were piled in one end of Private Fred Warrick's barracks, ready to go. The screams of rage when someone ran out of the barracks to report the war news were not, in choice of vocabulary, identifiably patriotic. "They knew," Warrick was certain, "that their time had been unilaterally extended."

At the Marine Corps base in Quantico there was concern that the Germans "had submarines ready to sail up the Potomac," and that the ocean was not enough protection. R. H. Patterson, a seventeen-year-old private, was assigned Fire Watch on the roof of his barracks, "custodian of two buckets of water and two buckets of sand to smother the incendiary bombs. He also was issued a five-round clip of ammo for his 1903 Springfield rifle, "to repel paratroops or saboteurs." Only war in the Pacific had come, but the Marines in Virginia were ready. Patterson "dreamed of warplanes overhead."

Similar scenes were enacted at other military bases thousands of miles from Oahu, where green troops who had never heard of Pearl Harbor were being rushed to dubious duty with equipment that had already been obsolete in 1917. At Virginia Beach, the movie suddenly stopped and young Lieutenant Henry A. Miley (later a general) and his wife Peggy discovered that the country was at war. Miley read on the screen that his 57th Coastal Artillery was to return to duty immediately. At headquarters his colonel "shocked us young fellows who wanted to live forever by saying that he had called Washington and volunteered his regiment to go overseas immediately." They had no bolts for their last-war machine guns, but before they boarded the SS *President Johnson*, converted to a troopship, everyone was issued a pith helmet.

Watching a movie in Amarillo, Texas, Tom Cartwright, at seventeen a junior-college freshman, was puzzled when the screen went blank, the lights came on, and the theater manager stepped forward to announce that the country was at war with Japan. Newsboys rushed through the aisles with local extras, "which had very large headlines and a brief account." Insulated from the real world, he brought a paper home, asking his uncle, with whom he lived, if the situation were as serious as all that. His uncle explained. When Tom's eighteenth birthday came around, he joined the Air Corps.

.

Their field exercise ended, the Royal Canadian Artillery officer class hauled their antiquated Great War-vintage eighteen-pounder guns back across the snowy prairie to Camp Shilo in western Manitoba. Pretending to load, fire, and correct sightings of pretended targets until someone was satisfied about the imaginary effectiveness of their fusillade was exhilarating in the bright chill of early winter. Now in the officers' mess there was hot buttered rum for thawing out. Paying no attention to a radio dispensing popular Christmas music, they talked of the big show to come in Europe until someone near the radio shouted, "Hey, shut up for a minute. There seems to be an important news item coming over."

Donald Greene remembered being "properly sobered" and that the men "said the obvious things about how this would make a big difference." Someone remembered a remark attributed to George VI, whose commission they held, about the fall of France: "Now we won't have to be bothered anymore by bloody allies." Now they had one again, although the outspokenness of the America First segment of their neighbors to the south—Manitoba was not far removed from Wheeler's Montana and Nye's North Dakota—suggested that America was a reluctant ally. "Well," said a voice in the background, "the Yanks had it coming to them."

•

The white armada of Japanese-manned and -owned tuna and sardine boats from San Pedro and Long Beach went out in the warm late-morning sun, with the sky a sharp blue. From the Terminal Island wharf, Jeanne Wakatsuki and her mother waved good-bye to Papa's boat, *The Nereid*, and waited for the last bright specks to disappear. They seemed to be floating, suspended, at the horizon's limit. Then they began growing larger again.

"They're coming back," Mrs. Wakatsuki said, puzzled.

"Why would they be coming back?" asked Chizu, wife of a crewman.

They guessed engine trouble, a storm coming, an injury, an illness. No one had ever seen the eager fleet turn on its tail. As they watched and waited, a cannery worker came running toward the wharf shouting that he had heard on the radio—as had, certainly, the fishermen returning—that the Japanese had bombed Pearl Harbor.

"Mama yelled at him," Jeanne remembered, " 'What is Pearl Harbor?' But he was running along the docks, like Paul Revere, bringing the news, and didn't have time to explain."

That night, Papa Wakatsuki would burn the flag he had brought with him from Hiroshima thirty-five years before. "It was such a beautiful piece of material," Jeanne thought. "I couldn't believe he was doing that."

Before long, at the Terminal Island ferry landing, two busy Army Intelligence men, with local policemen to help, were searching every car for "alien Japs." Bewildered detainees were lodged in a makeshift chicken-wire compound. Wakatsuki and the others had scurried home before the patrol had been ordered out, but for all of them it would only be a matter of time.

George Kondo in Berkeley was working with a friend in his garden, entertained by a portable radio. Despite a college degree, he was working weekdays in a laundry, having lost his job in an import-export house when tension with Japan escalated. Most of the laundry employees had degrees. The music stopped, and bulletins began popping about Pearl Harbor.

"Holy cats!" was all he could say.

"Don't worry," said his friend. "Nothing can happen to you."

A year later, he was able to leave a relocation camp at Topaz, Utah, when he and his wife accepted jobs as domestics in Chicago.

In Los Angeles, Frank Chuman, twenty-four, had just returned with his sister from church and sat down to lunch when the radio blared the bad news. The family ate almost silently; then his father left the table and went to the locked drawer in the cupboard where he kept two ceremonial swords he had brought to America in 1906. Chuman's father had promised the larger of the two, with an ornamental ceramic scabbard, to Frank as eldest son; but now he took both swords into the backyard. Frank followed.

"My father proceeded to separate the component parts of the sword. He removed the steel handguard and left the bare, naked steel sword blade itself. He did that with both swords while I watched him. Then he thrust the naked blades of both of the swords deep into the ground . . . as deep as they would go and covered them so that they couldn't be seen from the surface. Then he threw away the scabbards." The act not only reflected concern at being found with an apparent weapon; it was a symbolic rejection.

Wilson Makabe was working with his family at the "back end" of their hundred-acre fruit farm in Placer County, California, about a hundred miles west of Reno. His eldest sister came out with the war news. "It was hard for us to believe. But shortly after that, while we were eating [lunch], a car pulled up and people got out and identified themselves as being from the F.B.I." Although apparently never in the house before, they "knew just where to go to look for things." An agent pulled out papers that went back thirty years, and ordered Shinzo Makabe to go with them. "My father never had a chance to pack his clothing, or his suitcase, or anything." He went off in an FBI vehicle and was not seen again until the family was reunited in a camp at Tule Lake.

In San Francisco, Shirow Uyeno, the editor of a bilingual Japanese paper, the *New World Sun*, had just put his paper to bed with a front-page story about the President's appeal to Emperor Hirohito when a telephone call came from a staff member who had turned on his radio at home. "Don't joke!" said Uyeno. More calls came in. Uyeno stopped his press and replated for an extra based on what he was hearing on his own radio. One story he translated contended that Japanese paratroops were dropping into Honolulu, a fantasy that fed anti-Japanese hysteria.

A reporter telephoned the Japanese acting consul in Portland, Yutaka Oka, who refused to believe the news. "It is just a wild rumor. I have had no word at all. I have just heard what is on the radio; I don't believe it. . . ." (A happy Chinese consul in New Orleans, on the other hand, told reporters, "As far as Japan is concerned, their goose is overheated.") Soon, Oka was burning papers in the consulate stove, and smoke seeped into the eighth-floor corridors of the Board of Trade Building. At the sprawling Oregon Shipbuilding Company along the Willamette River, Mrs. Henry Kaiser was christening the freighter *Thomas Jefferson*, and workers and guests were cheering the vessel down the launching skids.

In North Platte, Nebraska, Mike Masaoka arrived to speak to local descendants of the three hundred Issei (Japan-born Americans) who used to ice the refrigerator cars on transcontinental freight trains. As Nisei went, he was a celebrity, having written and published the patriotic "Japanese-American Creed" read to the Senate by Elbert D. Thomas of Utah the previous May. But the North Platte police were waiting at the station to throw him into jail. "We are at war with Japan," they explained.

It would take three days before he could reach Senator Thomas, and leave his cell, but the freedom was temporary. Soon Masaoka, his widowed mother, and his five brothers were shipped to an internment camp.*

The panic on the West Coast began at the top, even before General Marshall's message to Lieutenant General John DeWitt at noon, Pacific time, ordering his Fourth Army command to operate under Defense Category B, which meant that his area, commanding the Pacific coast from the Presidio in San Francisco, "might be subjected to minor attacks." DeWitt was paranoid about the Japanese population on the coast. Troops from Fort Ord were ordered to stand guard every fifty yards along the beach to shoot at anything resembling an enemy sub-

---

* Five of the brothers, including Mike, later joined the Nisei 442d Regimental Combat Team. One was killed in action, the others wounded.

marine. Every Japanese vegetable farmer near the coast, and every Japanese fisherman, was treasonous until proven otherwise.

The hysteria DeWitt generated was at its greatest in the San Francisco area and southward along the coast. In Carmel that warm December morning, Major General and Mrs. Joseph W. Stilwell were holding open house for new junior officers from Fort Ord. Stilwell's house looked out over the Pacific, and guests in civilian clothes (they were off the post) chattered over the sound of the crashing surf. They did, at least, until a neighbor rushed to Mrs. Stilwell to tell her the radio news. Everyone searched for a radio, and guests listened, stunned. The party dissolved.

Stilwell began receiving wild messages. Fourth Army reported a "Jap fleet 20 miles south, 10 miles out [of Monterey]." He ordered his chief of staff of III Corps, Colonel Thomas Hearn,* "to start reconnaissance." Periscopes allegedly were sighted; San Francisco was expecting—or at least General DeWitt was expecting—an air raid.

A draftee who looked on Regular Army men as "Cossacks," Ray Wax was on the beach with other G.I.'s on leave when someone with a radio said that Pearl Harbor had been attacked. "We all got up in our swimming trunks and headed back to camp." Back at camp—Fort Ord—they were shipped out to protect the coast. "What we really did was terrorize the Japanese up around San Francisco. . . . I remember two bandoliers around me with a hundred rounds of ammunition and an M-1 rifle, riding in the back of a truck making Japanese farmers observe six o'clock curfew. So help me God, we were told to shoot anything that moved."

At Camp San Luis Obispo, Private (later Major) John P. Smith of the federalized California National Guard found himself pressed into dubious defense of the Pacific coastline. None of the enlisted men had ever heard of Pearl Harbor. Overnight his mates of Japanese ancestry "disappeared without explanation." Admired for their soldiering abilities, they had, nevertheless, been quietly taken into custody.

•

The *Lurline* was still keeping Hawaii time. The gleaming white ship had left Honolulu just after noon on the fifth, jammed with vacationers returning to the mainland and Hawaii residents anticipating

---

* Later major general, chief of staff of China-Burma-India theater.

Christmas in the U.S. There had been the usual aloha farewells—streamers and leis and Hawaiian music; but there had also been a bonus. As they drew out of the harbor, *New York Herald Tribune* reporter Joseph Newman remembered, military aircraft "staged an elaborate demonstration, diving at our vessel and sweeping past with breathtaking speed at excitingly close distances." It was a Friday; there was a lot of activity around Pearl Harbor.

At ten on Sunday morning the steward knocked on Newman's cabin door. He had some interesting news. "The Japs just bombed Pearl Harbor." Unbelieving, Newman checked with the purser. The *Herald Tribune*'s man in Honolulu had missed the biggest story of his life.

Seamen began blacking out the windows and portholes, and worried passengers became even more concerned when the captain called them together to announce formally what had happened. The news, embellished at every telling, had "swept through the ship like a terrifying blaze at sea." He pointed out that there was some danger of attack, especially by Japanese submarines, and ominously instructed everyone "either to sleep in his life preserver or keep it handy." He hoped, he concluded, to bring the *Lurline* into San Francisco safely.

The captain told no one that his radioman had picked up an SOS from the *Cynthia Olsen*, perhaps a hundred miles from the *Lurline*'s position. Commander Minoru Yokota in the *I-26* had been stalking the small freighter through the night, waiting for the hour of the attack on Hawaii. When the time was right the *I-26* surfaced and fired over the bow of the freighter to warn it to stop. When it kept moving, Yokota ordered a torpedo fired. It missed, but the *Cynthia Olsen* stopped, and the crew began lowering their two lifeboats. When the last seaman clambered aboard and the boats pulled away from the doomed freighter, the *I-26* began hammering at it with a 15cm gun; then, frustrated that the *Cynthia Olsen* was taking so long to sink, Yokota sent a torpedo into it. The ship rolled onto its right side. But it had taken Yokota so long to dispatch the little wooden freighter that the *Lurline* was out of danger.

Few G.I.'s were up for Sunday breakfast in the less-than-rigid routine of what was still a peacetime sailing out of San Francisco. There had been no cheering crowds or speeches at dockside the day before when another Matson line ship, the *Matsonia*, set sail west to Manila via Honolulu. The departure had seemed solemn, yet there had been no secrecy as soldiers spilled out of their troop trains and marched to the gangplanks. Despite the tiers of new bunks in the bow, meals were served in the resplendent main dining room, using the *Matsonia*'s dinnerware and silver service. After field training at Camp Shelby, Mississippi, and Camp Beauregard, Louisiana, Corporal Robert Kidd of the 101st Signal Battalion, New York National Guard, had found amenities on the partly converted cruise ship not what he had expected when he joined the Army. The *Matsonia* was a day out when sleeping soldiers were awakened by unpleasant rumors sweeping the ship. Finally the voice of the ship's captain boomed over the loudspeakers, "This is it, we are in the midst of a war."

The ship seemed to continue on its course, sailing alone; then "we made a big circle and turned back to San Francisco."

•

In Manila Bay at 4:10 A.M. the *Ford*'s Executive Officer, Lieutenant N. E. Smith, ordered Bos'n Mate Tillman to pipe "All hands" and inform them of the news, and to add that the ship would be darkened at 4:30 but that breakfast would be served as usual. They would be getting up steam and soon cutting loose.

On the gunboat *Luzon*, Lieutenant Alfred Littlefield Smith heard a tapping on his door. He was tired of medical emergencies. His orders home were awaiting Admiral Hart's pen. As Smith turned in the darkness to flip the switch on his lamp, the voice on the other side of the door identified himself as the pharmacist's mate. "Doctor," he warned, "don't turn on the light and don't light a cigarette. We're at war with Japan."

"And there I was," Smith remembered ruefully. Bad luck. But nearly four years later he was the only one of the *Luzon*'s officers—although nearly blind and weak from prison camp malnutrition—to make it home.

The crews of Motor Torpedo Boat Squadron 3 were asleep at Cavite when telephones began ringing. Ensign Anthony B. Akers was sure the reports about Pearl Harbor were a joke. "It's a hell of a time to declare war," he mumbled. His senior officer, Lieutenant John D. Bulkeley, was ordered to the Commandantia, a venerable building where Rear Admiral F. W. Rockwell was already scanning the predawn sky. "They ought to be here any minute," he predicted. Bulkeley's six seventy-foot-long plywood speedboats were easily incinerated targets.

Rockwell ordered him to rouse his men—twelve to a boat—and to move to war stations at Mariveles Harbor on Bataan, opposite Corregidor.

His own boat, Lieutenant Robert B. Kelly claimed, was ready to go. He was so certain that war was coming that he had gone to the Army and Navy Club in Manila the day before and bought a large steak and assorted trimmings to put aboard, guessing that it might be his last feast for a long time. While one PT-boat patrolled the bay, the other skippers took turns loading standard supplies—corned beef, canned potatoes, canned fruit and vegetables, soon-rare coffee—before moving to Mariveles. They tied up a hundred yards apart to avoid being wiped out together.

•

At latitude 23°46′N, longitude 170°56′W, about 420 miles southeast of Midway, the carrier *Lexington* was moving into position to release Marine Scout Bomber Squadron 231, Grumman Wildcat fighters for the island garrison at Midway. With morning they had ceased picking up signals from the sub thought to be tracking them. The *I-74* had lost contact toward dawn, but Task Force 12 still felt exposed. The carrier, destroyers and cruisers *Astoria, Portland*, and *Chicago* were still on alert when, at 9:42 A.M. Hawaii time, Admiral Kimmel radioed and ordered Newton back before he could deliver his planes. Already shelled by Japanese destroyers racing by from bases in the Carolines, Midway would have been the best base from which to search for the returning *Kido Butai*, but the reinforcement flight was aborted.

Task Force 12 (with the *Lexington*) was to rendezvous with Halsey's TF 8 (and the *Enterprise*) at latitude 22°N, longitude 162°W, about 120 miles west of Kauai. Also at sea was Vice Admiral Wilson Brown, who had left the same day with the smaller Task Force 3 to conduct a simulated bombardment and landing exercise. His flag flew from the cruiser *Indianapolis*, which was escorting five newly converted destroyer-minesweepers. Isolated Johnston Island, 700 miles southwest of Oahu, had just been practice-shelled by Brown's ships when Kimmel's signal, "Air Raid Pearl Harbor," came through. TF 3 was ordered to close with the *Lexington* at its best speed.

Kimmel's messages altered routes everywhere in the Pacific. South of Oahu, and spared the ignominy of being tethered targets in port, were the heavy cruiser *Minneapolis* and several light cruisers and destroyers. These also were ordered to close with Halsey, making a combined force, including everything the Navy had but battleships, that would have multiplied the catastrophe at Pearl Harbor had they not been on missions at sea.

Long past Hawaii, and diverted from its Philippine destination, now too risky, was another cluster of ships. The heavy cruiser *Pensacola* was passing through the lonely Phoenix Islands, far to the south of Johnston Island, escorting Navy and Army transports bound for Manila with thousands of soldiers, aviators, and naval personnel, and P-40s as well. The convoy was radioed to proceed well to the south of the Carolines, via Fiji, and to off-load in Australia. It was early evidence that the Philippines could not be reinforced and were effectively to be written off.

One of the seven ships in the *Pensacola* convoy, the 3,300-ton *Coast Farmer*, carried 150 tons of letters and Christmas parcels for U.S. military personnel and their families in the Philippines. The Christmas mail would spend the rest of the war in Australia, under a warehouse tent in Brisbane.

Kimmel also ordered Halsey's force to intercept an enemy whose position was unknown. The Opana radar, which had been reactivated at nine, had tracked the second Japanese flight as returning northward, but the Army failed to inform the Navy. The cruiser *Minneapolis* picked up a report that two enemy carriers were about ten miles off Pearl Harbor, an unlikely location—and the exact position, then, of the cruiser. The captain of the *Minneapolis* ordered a message sent to CINC-PAC, "No carriers in sight." His flustered radioman sent, instead, "Two carriers in sight." The planes that rushed to check out the sighting recognized "*Minnie*" and veered away.

In the confusion the operator of a direction finder on Oahu picked up a transmission from a Japanese carrier at 358°—or almost exactly due north—and misinterpreted it as 178° or nearly due south, because the instrument recorded simultaneously reciprocal bearings. The misreading then seemed to make sense when one of Halsey's SBD scouts identified Rear Admiral Draemel's cruisers and destroyers south of Pearl Harbor (TF 1) as an enemy force, and Halsey ordered his torpedo bombers after them. Turning south also, the *Lexington*'s task force found nothing until a patrol plane reported an enemy carrier with a flight deck "camouflaged to look like a heavy cruiser," and a destroyer "with the rising sun painted on her bows."

The rising sun turned out to be the red-lead showing beneath the chipped paint on the bows of the destroyer *Porter*, accompanying the cruiser *Portland*—and not a single contact was made with any element of *Kido Butai*.

At Kaneohe Naval Air Station, the dive bombers in the second wave had little left to hit, but dropped 500-pound bombs on their first runs, then 132-pound bombs from under each wing on the second run. When the planes withdrew at 9:50, sailors were sure they would be back, perhaps with a landing force. Charges were set to blow up the remaining fuel if necessary. Then, tension drained, exhaustion followed. "We slept anywhere we could," Doyle Bell recalled. "I collapsed on some cloth gunnery targets." They were of no further use anyway. Henceforth there would be real targets.

That there were seventeen dead and sixty-seven wounded made Commander Martin's next task easier. With the unfounded report that parachute troops were landing and observed to be wearing dungarees, Martin decided to have all his surviving men wear khaki-dyed whites. Although the supply officer had his hands full, he had only half his complement to outfit.

That a hangar continued to burn into the night was also less of a problem than it might have been in normal times. Martin had no planes.

·

On December 7, Captain Arthur G. Robinson's log on the cruiser *Marblehead*, anchored at Tarakan on the northeast coast of Dutch Borneo, noted only the sighting of a drifting mine to the starboard. The Dutch authorities retrieved it. Events became more complicated a few hours after midnight. At 3:15 the ship's radio picked up Hart's laconic war orders. Robinson logged, "We're off at daylight. To hell with my cold."

The *Marblehead* could leave no sooner because the Dutch cautiously kept the antisubmarine booms at the harbor mouth closed during darkness. Robinson ordered a general alarm sounded to call all hands to battle stations. Then he dressed hurriedly and went to the bridge, pausing, he remembered, to pray to be granted the strength and courage expected of him. On the cruiser's intercom he broadcast Hart's war message. The supreme moment toward which they had been readying themselves had come, Robinson told his crew, and he was confident that they could meet their responsibilities. He sent an aide ashore to inform the Dutch and to arrange for passage through the mined harbor; then he called for coffee and toast.

No one went back to sleep. The messages received—and intercepted—made that certain. There was shock that Pearl Harbor rather than Manila had been hit, and disbelief at the devastation. Hart's messages included one to his vessels in the Indies to proceed at best speed to the Java port of Surabaja, where the *Marblehead* would rejoin Destroyer Division 57. There were still two hours of darkness to wait out.

·

"I have just a little additional information to give you," Steve Early told reporters milling about the White House, "besides what I have already flashed to your offices. So far as is known now, the attacks on Hawaii and Manila were made wholly without warning—when both nations were at peace—and were delivered within an hour or so of the time the Japanese Ambassador and Special Envoy Kurusu had gone to the State Department and handed to the Secretary of State the Japanese reply to the Secretary's memorandum of November 26. . . . The President directed the Army and Navy to execute all previously prepared orders looking to the defense of the U.S. The President is now with the Secretary of War and the Secretary of the Navy and steps are being taken to advise congressional leaders."

Reporters rushed to telephones; late arrivals demanded fill-ins; then at 3:23 P.M. Ruth Jane Rumelt came to the pressroom and read from her notebook, "So far as present information goes, and so far as we know at the moment, the attacks are still in progress. We don't know, in other words, that the Japanese have bombed and left."

In a minute or two she popped back in and offered another bulletin: "The President has just received a dispatch from the War Department reporting the torpedoing of an Army transport, thirteen hundred miles west of San Francisco. Fortunately, the transport was carrying a cargo of lumber rather than personnel." Reporters rushed again to the phones.

·

By 4:30 A.M. MacArthur was at his headquarters in Intramuros, the "House on the Wall," officially No. 1 Calle Victoria. He was just in time for a radiogram from General Marshall that had also gone to commanders in Hawaii:

> Japanese are presenting at 1:00 P.M., Eastern Standard Time today, what amounts to an ultimatum. Also they are under orders to destroy their code machine immediately. Just what significance the hour set may have we do not know but be on alert accordingly. Inform naval authorities of this communication.

It was the message that should have arrived more than three hours earlier.

A minute later the United Press Manila Bureau was wiring New York, in contradiction to reports out of Washington, "MANILA WAS QUIET THIS MORNING AT 4:31 A.M."

At 4:35 the phone in Major General Jonathan Wainwright's house at Fort Stotsenburg rang. It was in the room next to his bedroom, and he stumbled toward it in the darkness, "sensing it was bad news." On the line from Manila was Colonel Pete Irwin, MacArthur's assistant chief of staff for operations. Admiral Hart, he reported, had heard from Pearl Harbor that Japan had "initiated hostilities." Hanging up, he began to dress with one hand while trying to telephone his aide, Captain John R. Pugh, with the other.

"Johnny!"

"Hello? Yes, General."

"The cat has jumped."

At 4:50 Irwin telephoned again. "The battleship line at Pearl Harbor," he reported, "and our big Hickam Field air base have been heavily bombed." More calls came, each bringing "progressively worse information." Authorities in Manila had little idea what was happening except that wherever it was, it was not the Philippines.

•

Night came early and remained late in Iceland. Colonel (later General) Theodore W. Parker stood on the pier at Reykjavik with visiting General Chesley Bonesteel, waiting for the return of a small ship carrying the American minister and his party. The general wanted to meet the official American representative before he continued on.

Parker and Bonesteel were pacing the quay in the cold when the captain of the British station ship, a floating dormitory for naval staff, saw the pair. "The weather was lousy. So he sent an aide down to invite us to come up on the bridge." They could see the harbor and watch for the minister's arrival, and be more comfortable. "So General Bonesteel accepted this nice invitation," Parker recalled, "and we went up. . . . They weren't using their best captains to run station ships. They had their best captains out at sea, fighting the war." The British skipper had already heard about Pearl Harbor, which meant that the U.S. was in the war on his side. "He had obviously been celebrating with the bottle and he had a hell of a job concealing his great joy that Pearl Harbor had happened."

Sitting down to dinner in Hvalfjordur to the north, officers aboard the *Wichita* prepared to celebrate the news of the afternoon that Paul Schratz had been reassigned to submarine school in New London, Connecticut, effective January 2. Groggy after only three hours' sleep following midwatch, Schratz had sacrificed his nap to searching for a way back across the wintry North Atlantic, but the wardroom news stirred him awake. Ship's radio had picked off signals about Pearl Harbor, and after the first excitement, gloom fell as "Witch" officers chanced guesses about the fate of the fleet, and their friends. Straining for further terse bulletins, they learned little more, but the reality of the losses would become obvious when they produced a way back to the mainland. There were two battleships on the Iceland watch. Both were to be transferred at maximum speed to the Pacific. Schratz did not need to be told why, but he would have a berth home on the *Idaho*.

•

At thirty-three, CBS London correspondent Edward R. Murrow, or at least his disembodied voice, deepening in resonance from chain-smoking four packs a day, was famous. By radio he had brought the Blitz into millions of American homes, and when he confessed about the British, "They want us in this war," he had proved equal to the massed militants of America First.

Usually he reported only the facts, which spoke for themselves over the background of bombs and air-raid sirens and city noises of day-to-day London. Murrow seldom dealt in personalities, but once, walking with a friend in the Kent countryside, he had passed a house that sheltered young evacuees from the devastated city, and referred to the Firsters' chief ornament, Charles Lindbergh. The country house had been the home of the Lindbergh family on fleeing the U.S., and a voracious press, after the kidnapping and murder of their son. From England the intrepid aviator, idolized after his solo flight to Paris in 1927 as no man before or since, had visited Nazi Germany. Receiving a decoration from Hermann Göring and a tour of factories and airfields, Lindbergh reciprocated with admiration for Hitler's New Order, returning convinced that war in Europe was not America's business and that, in any case, the Luftwaffe was invincible. He had preached both premises at large public meetings arranged by America First.

Passing the country house in Kent now crammed with evacuee children's beds, Murrow pointed, with unconcealed bitterness, to "the house which gave refuge to Charles Lindbergh—now giving refuge to children who had to leave London because of the bombing by Lindbergh's friends."

CBS had called Murrow home on leave to be lionized, and the network had arranged a testimonial dinner in New York on December 2. A weekend in Washington followed, complete to a Sunday afternoon of golf with several of Roosevelt's New Deal stalwarts and dinner that evening at the White House. FDR himself had sent a message to the banquet, but it was poet Archibald MacLeish who spoke the memorable words, on a national hookup, about how Murrow's broadcasts had altered the way people thought about what radio could do. "You burned the city of London in our houses and we felt the flames. . . . You laid the dead of London at our doors and we knew that the dead were our dead. . . . You have destroyed . . . the superstition that whatever is done beyond three thousand miles of water is not really done at all."

On the fourth hole, a CBS messenger came running down the Burning Tree fairway to alert Murrow to a bulletin. The Japanese had attacked Pearl Harbor. Murrow asked whose report it was. Although CBS had been as quick as any competitor in airing the flash from the White House, for some reason the messenger answered "Reuters."

"Pay no attention," Murrow dismissed, and his foursome went on to play the next hole, putting their clubs away only when the news began sweeping the course. Janet Murrow assumed that their dinner invitation was off, but telephoned to Eleanor Roosevelt to make sure.

"We still have to eat," said Mrs. Roosevelt. "We still want you to come."

·

With fires forward still out of control, the beached *Nevada*'s stern began to swing out toward the Pearl Harbor channel. There was concern that if the ship sank it might block the only way in and out of port. Harbor tugs came alongside and began pushing the stern toward the beach. The ship broke loose, drifting toward the western side of the channel. Then its undamaged engines began turning over at two-thirds reverse speed, and by 10:45 the *Nevada* was regrounded on the western side, listing to starboard. Five more hours would be needed before the fires were sufficiently out that work could begin to remove the dead.

Burning slowly—as it does under atmospheric pressures and temperatures—fuel oil from ruptured tanks enveloped the broken hulk of the *Arizona*. When Lieutenant Commander Samuel Fuqua, the senior surviving officer aboard the *Arizona*, abandoned ship with the rest of his men at 10:02, there were few able to leave with him. Only 39 aboard the *Arizona* survived; 1,102 bodies remained below. A motor launch from the overwhelmed *Solace* took the wounded. Seaman Second Class Oree C. Weller and Lieutenant Jim Dick Miller were picked up from the black water by another launch. The luckiest of the crew—about 250—were already ashore on weekend liberty, granted only to officers and the top two grades of enlisted men—first class petty officers and chief petty officers. (For the rest of the seamen, there had been little reason to weekend ashore anyway: the bars and brothels were too expensive for men paid thirty dollars a month.)

Climbing down from the mainmast, Weller noted the paint-seared but undamaged stack. Returning to Pearl Harbor years later and recalling the legend of "a bomb down the smokestack," he checked and found that the interior stack gratings, installed to prevent anything or anyone from falling through to the fire rooms, were still intact. Little else on the *Arizona* was in such good shape.

At the *West Virginia* the launch picked up more oil-soaked men from the water, then off-loaded the unwounded at the submarine dock. Weller was wearing nothing but skivvy shorts, shirt, and a black film of fuel oil. "An enlisted man from the Sub Base," Weller remembered, "took off his shirt and wiped my eyes and mouth. Then he took me to his barracks and gave me a pair of dungarees to wear."

•

By 7:35 A.M., positions on *Wake* were manned. Turned about by its captain, John H. Hamilton, the *Philippines Clipper* dumped 3,000 pounds of fuel to make the maximum landing weight of 48,000 pounds, and splashed down on the lagoon. Passengers hurriedly disembarked and were returned to the Pan Am Hotel to await developments.

Major Paul A. Putnam, commander of aviation on the atoll, had just arrived on the 4th with a squadron of twelve Grumman F4F fighters, ferried to within flying range on the carrier *Enterprise*. Looking younger than his thirty-eight years, Putnam was full of ideas. The *Clipper* could not take passengers anywhere. Why not conduct a long-range search toward Japanese territory to the south—with fighter escort—early that afternoon to see whether an invasion force was en route? Although a civilian, Hamilton agreed; while Marines were being fitted with World War I helmets, six five-inch shore batteries were camouflaged at Peacock Point, and sixty antiaircraft guns were manned, everyone listened for the first sounds of the enemy. "The harder we listened," Walter Bayler later wrote, "the more surf we heard. . . . We realized that a plane would have to be almost overhead before we could expect to hear the drone of its engines."

•

The pitch and roll of the Japanese carriers forced some planes returning from Oahu to stack up aloft until they could hazard a landing. Some came down hard and buckled landing gear, wings, or tail sections. Some landed badly shot up. (To speed up recovery of both waves, the worst cases were pushed overboard.) Climbing out, pilots and crews gathered on the flight decks near blackboards that had been marked with a Pearl Harbor grid so that they could identify hits and overlapping claims. Other planes overhead scouted for American subs, patrol planes from Hawaii, and aircraft from the unlocated carriers, a particular and nagging concern to Nagumo. Homeward-bound pilots, to conceal the position of their own carriers, which had moved to within 190 miles of Oahu to recover planes short on fuel, were faking a turn southward. Still, Nagumo and Kusaka thought, the enemy had to realize the direction from which the attackers had come.

Pilots offered to go on a search operation to locate the elusive U.S. carriers. Some talked of a third strike, and bombers from the first wave were moved below to be refitted. Commander Naohiro Sata of the *Kaga* debriefed his first-wave crews, who were "enthusiastic and joyous" over the success of the shallow-water torpedoes and the efficiency of armor-piercing bombs dropped by high-flying horizontal bombers. Lieutenant Commander Itaya claimed that his forty-three Zero fighters had encountered only four pursuit planes and had destroyed all of them. Control of the sky had been achieved easily. Chief Flight Petty Officer Juzo Mori, flying a torpedo bomber, had hit, it appeared, the *Nevada*, and reported happily, "I didn't expect to survive this attack, since I and the other pilots anticipated heavy enemy resistance. If I were going to die, I thought, I wanted to know that I had torpedoed at least an American battleship." All the crews reported fierce, if belated, AA fire, and expected the second wave to undergo heavier weather.

At 10:47 the first-wave recovery was declared completed. Only a few planes were missing and presumed lost.

.

Four tracking stations in Malaya were operating in the early hours of the 8th when one of them, Number 243, picked up approaching aircraft seventy-five miles north and on a line for Singapore. Other stations began plotting the blips, and the information was relayed to the Filter Room at the Kallang Airbase, east of Singapore city. A large table displayed an outline map of the Singapore area, superimposed on a grid where each square represented distances in kilometers. Plotters wore headphones to take calls from outstations, and moved position counters. A teller passed the information on to Fighter Operations. All active stations were soon tracking what they described as 12+ aircraft. It was 3:20 A.M. "I labelled the plot of these incoming aircraft, seventeen of them as it transpired," Flight Lieutenant Harry Grumbar, the filter officer on duty recalled, "as 'X' (unidentified) because I knew we were not at war and so had not yet got an official enemy."

The planes were twin-engined "Nells" of Rear Admiral Sadaichi Matsunaga's 22nd Air Flotilla. The Genzan and Mihoro air groups had flown from Indochinese bases into increasingly bad weather. Strong winds lashing sheets of rain against the bombers drove them lower and lower, until they were hugging the sea; finally the Genzan Group, unable to maintain formation, gave up and turned back. By the time RAF stations picked up the planes, the Mihoro Group, which had been flying precariously almost at wave-top level, had found better weather and regained altitude.

Grumbar had been a broker in his family firm, with a seat on the

London Stock Exchange. He knew how to plot a complex situation, but once he issued tracking data, his responsibility ended and the matter moved to someone else's jurisdiction. Nevertheless, he left the Filter Room for the adjacent Operations Control office to offer his opinion that there was "not a shadow of a doubt" that a raid was imminent, whether or not they were at war.

When he returned, the approaching aircraft were fixed at thirty miles off the southeast tip of Johore Strait, turning west. With his direct line to Air Raid Precautions headquarters in Singapore, he put a call through.

•

Just across the road from St. John's Cathedral, the "Battle Box," 102 steps in thirteen flights below street level, was the underground complex adjacent to Murray Barracks,* the Defence Headquarters for Hong Kong. There, before dawn, Major Charles Boxer, as intelligence officer on duty, monitored the Japanese radio while the man he had relieved, Major "Monkey" Giles, dozed on a camp bed. At 4:45 Radio Tokyo was droning into Boxer's earphones when a second announcer broke into the broadcast, announcing that the Imperial Army and Navy had attacked British and American forces in the Pacific. Boxer ripped off his headset and shook Giles.

"Wake up, Monkey!" he shouted. "The war's started. You don't want to miss it, do you?" Then he telephoned Maltby's aide, Lieutenant Iain MacGregor, who awakened the general and alerted forward companies near the still-quiet frontier to begin demolition of anything from which they were going to fall back which might be of use to the enemy, particularly road and railway bridges into occupied China.

Fifteen minutes later, Naval Headquarters just below the Battle Box received news from Singapore. The Japanese were landing on the Malayan coast. It was still nearly two hours to sunrise, hours of optimum potential for an attack. The entire Hong Kong garrison was ordered to stand to arms.

---

* The Murray Barracks area is now in part the site of the tallest building in East Asia, the I. M. Pei-designed Bank of China. Much of the area in which the Volunteers assembled, the Army organized, and the Navy operated, is now a forest of steel-and-glass offices and hotels, such as the Hong Kong Hilton, across the street from what is left of the Murray Barracks. The venerable Peak Tram still runs from the street crossing above. Barely visible, St. John's Cathedral remains, just above the Hilton.

Henry Ching, acting editor of the *Hong Kong Telegraph* while Stewart Gray was away in Australia—he had sailed the day before—was asleep at his home in Village Road, Happy Valley, when the telephone rang at five. On the line, excited, was Bill O'Neill of Reuters. "Sorry to wake you up, old chap, but I thought you'd like to know. The bloody balloon's gone up. The Japs have attacked Pearl Harbour and the Philippines. Britain and America have declared war. Hell of a show. They'll be here for breakfast." (The United Press, Reuters's American competition, had bulletins to its Hong Kong offices held up for hours by British censors, "a gesture that we had met with on two or three previous occasions," its local manager recalled.)

•

Trying to create a script that would please M-G-M, Anita Loos (*Gentlemen Prefer Blondes*) had suggested Joan Crawford as Madame Chiang Kaishek. Via Hunt Stromberg, M-G-M proposed instead a remake of *Tell It to the Marines*. Miss Loos, who had been in the silents—she was fifty-three but looked fifteen years younger—retorted that it had been charming, but failed to relate to the American situation. "Play around with it," Stromberg urged; "maybe you'll come up with something to prove us wrong."

A comedy about the 1918 war was not what she wanted to update. Returning to Beverly Hills after a dinner party the night before, she had thought of an angle that might work, and had sat up all night writing. She was still trying out ideas when her maid interrupted to tell her that a man on the radio was talking about a catastrophe in Hawaii.

It seemed only minutes later when Preston Sturges and Ray Goetz arrived, breathless with news about Pearl Harbor, and bringing with them three young Marines they had met on the way, one with a bride of less than three days. Anita thought tearfully of how they would be reporting back in only hours to risk their lives, and instructed the maid to uncork the champagne she had been hoarding to celebrate her impending divorce from actor John Emerson. Soon Aldous and Maria Huxley and others arrived. The atmosphere, assisted by alcohol, took on a brighter aspect. "Everyone," Anita wrote in her diary when the house again quieted, "feels relieved, almost exhilarated, that America is forced into the war."

•

When the surviving Kota Bharu landing craft, under fire and in heavy seas, had returned to their home transports, it was already 3:30 A.M. In the darkness, British aircraft from northern fields were flying hazardous low-level bombing and strafing runs over the convoy. Gunner Bob Thomson, crewman in Captain John Lockwood's RAAF Hudson of No. 1 Squadron, was certain that he fired "the first angry shot for Australia" against Japan in going after the lurching troopships. Commander Hashimoto held back the next wave despite Army concerns that the infantry ashore had to be reinforced. Letting only a further 396 men off the *Awagisan Maru*, he ordered the ship to withdraw farther offshore.

Coming over only in twos and threes—there were not very many of them to spare—the Hudsons and even the obsolete Vildebeestes were deadly. "Our transports," Tsuji wrote, basing his account on an eyewitness, "soon became enveloped in flame and smoke from the bursting bombs and from shells fired by the shore batteries. The *Awagisan Maru* after ten direct hits caught fire; later the *Ayatosan Maru* did likewise after six hits." Unmentioned was the third transport, the *Sakura Maru*, which was also badly damaged. The light cruiser *Sendai* and other ships escaped serious damage only by retiring out of range. "The officers and men of the antiaircraft detachment," Tsuji continued, "although scorched by the flames, finally shot down seven enemy planes."

One of the downed Hudsons was J. C. Ramshaw's plane; he had shadowed the convoy for two days, and it had finally claimed him. He was on his second sortie with a load of four 250-pound bombs that he deposited on the *Awagisan Maru*. It took a day of settling in the water to sink. Ramshaw's observer had been Donald Dowie, victim now to one of the segments of the "scorpion in the water" he had earlier seen sailing unopposed. Orders from Brooke-Popham had been not to engage the Japanese, as perhaps they were heading somewhere else—"a bit of a joke," Dowie thought afterward. Luckier than Ramshaw, he spent ten hours in the water with the broken neck and fractured vertebrae he carried with him to a Japanese prison camp.

"As the fire burst through the decks of the ships, the soldiers still on board, holding their rifles," Tsuji wrote, "jumped over the side. Kept afloat by the[ir] lifejackets, . . . some managed with difficulty to get into boats while others swam toward the shore."

The 8th Brigade of the 9th Indian Division kept up a steady fire in the lightening night as the Takumi Detachment came within point-blank range. Japanese soldiers on the beach "instinctively dug with their hands into the sand and hid their heads in the hollows. . . . They burrowed until their shoulders, and eventually their whole bodies, were under cover." They were so close to the enemy that some could raise themselves just enough to lob hand grenades toward the pillbox loopholes.

Much depended on the barbed wire as the 8th Brigade had twenty-two miles of coast and ten miles of frontier to defend. The pillboxes were set at intervals of a thousand yards—just enough, planners thought, for fire to cover the area. But it took only one inoperative pillbox to open a stretch of beach. "Moving over corpses [of their own dead]," according to Tsuji, "the wire-cutters kept at their work. Behind them followed a few men, piling up the sand ahead of them with their steel helmets and creeping forward like moles. The enemy soldiers . . . fought desperately. Suddenly one of our men covered a loophole with his body and a group of the moles sprang to their feet in a spurt of sand and rushed into the enemy's fortified position. Hand grenades flew and bayonets flashed, and amid the sound of warcries and calls of distress, in a cloud of black smoke the enemy's front line was captured."

Of the two hundred men who had landed with Colonel Nasu, 120 were still on their feet. Two pillboxes had been silenced—Numbers 13 and 14; 15 at the Badang side of the beachhead and Number 12 at the Sabak end would take hours longer. The Kelantan River was the second line of defense. Men still wearing lifejackets plunged in and crossed, attacking Indian defenders at bayonet point.

One of the most costly actions in the Malayan campaign, the seizure of the Kota Bharu beachhead cost the Japanese an admitted 320 dead and 538 wounded, much foundered equipment, and three ships. It disproved, there at the least, the condescending language in the training manual read on shipboard about the fighting qualities of British colonial troops. And it proved that Kota Bharu had been appropriately named. In Malay, *kota* meant "fort."

•

The service chiefs had sat in Whitehall in almost continuous session through the day, waiting for the blow to fall. The Cabinet War Rooms, deep underground below Downing Street where Horse Guards Road intersected with King Charles Street, ran under the eastern edge of St. James's Park. The chiefs of staff used Room 67, situated near the Map Room (65), as an emergency conference room. A large relief map of Malaya hung on the wall. (For greater detail they resorted to the *Times Map of the Far East.*) The difficult terrain and the long coastal gap between Singora in Thailand and Kota Bharu in Malaysia seemed inhospitable to seaborne invasion. Every possible Japanese objective had been analyzed again and again, using up irretrievable hours. Uppermost in the discussions was how to ensure that whatever the circumstances of the seemingly inevitable hostilities, the United States would be brought in. When the news came—of far-flung attacks on British territories, and on Hawaii—Brooke noted in his diary with mock ruefulness, "All our work of the last forty-eight hours wasted; the Japs themselves have now ensured that the U.S.A. are in the war!"

No one would be going home for a while, but it would be more a matter of waiting and listening. Orders covering every imaginable alternative had gone to field commanders long before. Someone had to notify the Prime Minister, they suddenly realized—before he learned the news on the radio.

•

East of "the Rock"—Gibraltar—Lieutenant Commander Gordon W. Stead, a Canadian on loan to the Royal Navy, was patrolling the sub-infested sea in the *I-26*. Wooden, and all of 128 feet long, it bobbed like a cork when destroyers sliced by, but the Mediterranean itself was calm as Stead surveyed the waters toward Malta. From the wheelhouse, the ship's radio blared a warning of an incoming signal, and Stead rushed from the bridge to take it down. It began, he thought, with "the widest possible address":

To: All Concerned Home and Abroad From: Admiralty
Commence hostilities against Japan repeat Japan at once.

"Back in the bridge, bemused by the peremptory tone of the signal, I looked around. No Japs in sight, nor, so far as I could guess, were there any within 10,000 miles." Soon after, he turned on the BBC and learned the meaning of the message.

Hour 33

ROBERT TROUT, CBS's temporary replacement in London for Ed Murrow, had the news first. The network leased a transatlantic telephone line for ten minutes for its nightly reports from England, and Trout was waiting, earphones on, for his cue to speak. Studio voices from New York that he recognized were filtering through. He heard John Daly, then Major Eliot, then a clatter of teletype. Someone across the Atlantic was supposed to lead in, "And now we bring you Robert Trout in London. Come in, Bob Trout." Instead he heard, faintly, "Of course it means war . . . but why Pearl Harbor?" Suddenly his prepared script was useless.

John MacVane, NBC Blue Network correspondent in London, walked into his office as the BBC news reader at nine o'clock itemized the lead stories. "I was sure that Pearl Harbor was in the Philippines . . . and when Florence Peart said she had heard the announcer say Hawaii, I could not believe it. While we were getting out the atlas, the BBC . . . gave us the full story. We were stunned. Most of the correspondents I talked with that night believed that we would shortly be in the war against Hitler as well." From his perch off Nazified Europe, MacVane realized that Britain and its cause could not win

337

without the U.S., and he felt "that eventually the United States *would* be forced by its self interest to enter the war." But he was appalled by "the reports of the isolationist speeches at home, the Lindberghs, the fanatic right-wing isolationist congressmen and senators, men living in a political dreamworld, combined with the reaction of so many Americans that their hearts were with Britain in its most gallant hour, but of course, America couldn't really do anything but stand on the sidelines and cheer. . . . Suddenly, at a stroke, Japan had wiped away the indecision."

In a BBC temporary studio at the Bedford Corn Exchange, the story of Alexander Nevsky's defiance of the Teutonic invaders, dramatized earlier by Sergei Eisenstein in his famous film, was about to go on the air. The version by poet Louis MacNeice featured a large cast, chorus, and orchestra, and Serge Prokofiev's cinema score. Poised for the green "ON" light once the evening news was over, the conductor put down his baton. A note handed him declared an indefinite delay for more bulletins. Elsewhere in London, the news came as a surprise to M.P. Harold Nicolson ("I do not believe it") and to American-born M.P. Henry ("Chips") Channon ("I was flabbergasted"). Reporter Mary Welsh (Hemingway) was telephoned by London friends offering commiseration, one adding, "Too bad for you but I'm feeling a slight sadistic pleasure that the war has caught up with our people who rushed over to your country."

•

Pleading indisposition, Clementine Churchill did not come down for Sunday dinner, which left only Pamela Churchill and Kathleen Harriman at Chequers to represent the opposite sex. "The Prime Minister seemed tired and depressed," Averell Harriman recalled. "He didn't have much to say throughout dinner and was immersed in his thoughts, with his head in his hands part of the time." Just before nine, when Winant and Harriman were alone with him at the table, General Hastings ("Pug") Ismay and his naval aide, Commander C. R. ("Tommy") Thompson, joined them. Churchill's butler-valet, Frank Sawyers, carried in a small fifteen-dollar portable radio that Harry Hopkins had given Churchill for the evening ritual of the BBC nine o'clock news.

Fumbling about to switch it on—it required lifting the lid—

Churchill missed part of the first item; in his cool, authoritative voice, Alvar Liddell was already into his opening summary of the "headlines."

"We heard him say something," Thompson recalled, "about air attacks on the Hawaiian Islands. Before it had dawned on us what this meant he was already talking about a tank battle south of Tobruk, but the P.M. sat bolt upright in his chair and asked, 'Didn't he say there has been an attack on American bases?' . . . By now the summary was dealing with a new German thrust toward Moscow and daylight raids by the R.A.F. We were still staring at one another and wondering whether we had been imagining it when Liddell began again."

Blandly, Liddell repeated the first item. "The news has just been given that Japanese aircraft have raided Pearl Harbour, the American naval base in Hawaii. The announcement of the attack was made in a brief statement by President Roosevelt. Naval and military targets on the principal Hawaiian island of Oahu have also been attacked. No further details are available."

"The Japanese have raided Pearl Harbor!" Harriman repeated in astonishment.

"No," Thompson argued unbelievingly. "He said Pearl River."

Returning from the kitchen, Sawyers confirmed Pearl Harbor. "It's quite true. We heard it ourselves outside."

Churchill rose from his chair. "We will declare war on Japan," he said. Malaya had been under attack for more than three hours, but he had not yet been informed.

Looking at the gift radio, Ismay thought—so he remembered—"Anyhow, Harry [Hopkins] will be pleased that we are all in it together."*

Churchill turned to Winant. "Does that mean war?" he asked. "Will the United States [now] declare war?"

"You can't declare war," Winant said, "on a mere radio report. Let me call the President. The Germans know what's going on, so it doesn't matter even if they do listen in."

At the door, excited, was John Martin, Churchill's principal private secretary. The Admiralty was on the phone. After the service chiefs offered more news, Winant put through a call to the White House,

---

* After midnight, the Prime Minister, with Harriman, dispatched a joint cable to Harry Hopkins: "Thinking of you much at this historic moment.—Winston, Averell."

and in two or three minutes he had the President. Churchill listened on an extension. "I've got someone with me who wants to speak with you," said Winant.

"Who's that?"

"You'll find out when he speaks."

"Mr. President," Churchill began, "what's this about Japan?"

"It's quite true," Roosevelt said. "They have attacked us at Pearl Harbor. We are all in the same boat now." He added that he would go to Congress the next morning for a declaration of war, and Churchill assured him that although Parliament was not scheduled to meet until Tuesday, he would summon them to formalize the situation with Japan, and follow the President "within the hour."

Winant asked whether any warships had been sunk. Roosevelt replied that there was no precise count of casualties yet, but losses were heavy. There were even reports that enemy warships "had been sighted between Hawaii and San Francisco."

"This certainly simplifies things," said Churchill. "God be with you."

William Hayter's message to the Foreign Office from Washington had still not been relayed to Churchill, but Whitehall telephoned again with further information. "Soon after the first excitement," Martin recalled, "I was able to obtain . . . from the Admiralty news of the Japanese attack on Malaya." It was already four o'clock in the morning in Malaya; the news had taken nearly four hours to reach London. Admiral Layton as commander-in-chief of the China Station had signaled, "Report from Kota Bharu. An attempt is being made to land from 3 or 5 transports. One landing craft already approaching mouth of river." Although the word *Japan* did not appear, Churchill ordered that His Majesty's ambassador in Tokyo be instructed to inform the Imperial Japanese Government that a state of war existed "between our two countries." (The message was withheld from Sir Robert Craigie by the Japanese.)

"The inevitable had finally arrived," Harriman remembered thinking. "We all knew the grim future that it held, but at least there was a future now. We . . . had realized that the British could not win the war alone. On the Russian front there was still a question whether the Red Army would hold out. At last we could see a prospect of winning."

"I do not pretend to have measured accurately the martial might of Japan," Churchill wrote, "but at this very moment I knew the United

States was in the war, up to the neck and in to the death. So we had won after all!" Later he would claim that "being saturated and satiated with emotion and sensation, I went to bed and slept the sleep of the saved and thankful." In fact, he would stay up with Winant until five in the morning.

.

In the War Ministry press room in Tokyo the atmosphere was electric. Alerted to be there at the unusual hour of six in the morning, Japanese newsmen hastened there even earlier, to pick up whatever scraps they could. Knots of smiling officers moved in and out with messages, but the journalists were left to their own speculations.

At the rostrum was Major Masahiko Takeshita. He had spent more than two hours in the code room, reading *Kido Butai* messages beginning with the first—"Very, very big success." With Navy personnel he had prepared the initial communiqué, which he now stepped aside to let a naval officer read, an honor agreed upon because the Navy had struck the first blows. "Today, before dawn, the Imperial Army and Navy entered into a state of war with American and British forces in the western Pacific."

From the prime minister's offices in the official residence, a Cabinet meeting was called for seven; all members had been notified by telephone. Most military business was already out of the way—the automatic unwinding of long-prepared plans. The Cabinet needed to approve civil edicts to put the country more fully on a war footing, and the Imperial Rescript to be issued in the name of the Emperor, legitimizing the war and exhorting the Japanese people to effort and sacrifice. Although Japan had been fighting in China intermittently since 1931 and continuously since 1937, the nation had not been legally at war. China remained an "incident."

Shuichi Inada, a senior member of the Cabinet's secretariat, had written the Imperial Rescript in late November once *Kido Butai* had embarked, and Cabinet Secretary Hoshino had revised the draft. That the Cabinet would adopt it and the Emperor approve it were formalities. Hirohito had no choice, and the Cabinet would appreciate the formal court language. Inada's only instructions had been to keep it short: the entire text had to appear in all Japanese newspapers to give the war its proper historical and cultural context. He had limited it to six hundred words, beginning with "We, by grace of heaven, Emperor of Japan, seated on the Throne of a line unbroken for ages eternal, enjoin upon ye, Our loyal and brave subjects . . ." and ending with the "confident expectation" that "the sources of evil will be speedily eradicated and an enduring peace immutably established in East Asia raising and enhancing thereby the glory of the Imperial Way within and outside our homeland."

The final line, under the places for the Imperial Sign and Seal, dated the rescript "The 8th Day of the 12th Month of the 16th Year of Shōwa," a curious combination of West and East. The Japanese Empire, traditionally older than Christian or even Imperial Rome, used the Gregorian calendar as well as the Japanese dating of imperial reigns. *Shōwa* ("Bright Peace") designated the reign of Hirohito, who had become Emperor in 1926.

Tojo quickly scanned the document handed to him by Hoshino, and nodded his approval.

·

From the bridge of the destroyer *Amatsukaze*, Commander Tameichi Hara watched twenty light bombers and fighters take off from the carrier *Ryujo*, fifty miles off the coast of Mindanao and about one hundred miles from Davao. It was just daybreak. His task force had seen no enemy ships or planes in the two days during which they had approached the Philippines from Palau, westernmost of the Caroline group under Japanese mandate. Certain that Washington talks would work, Hara had spent two days and nights on the bridge expecting with every message a countermanding of the operation. The deadline for turning the fleet about had been midnight, and when that passed with no signal, he dozed in his chair, weary with the strain. At 3:30 a blinding rain squall awakened him, and he realized that Lieutenant Toshio Koyama, his navigator, had matters under control. "How stupid to be napping on such an important day!" he remembered thinking. "I cursed myself and phoned the radio room for any new messages. There were none."

The launching of the planes at 5:00 cut through his drowsiness with a "rousing and inspiring effect." As the planes lifted out of sight, four destroyers broke from the ring around the carrier and steamed for Davao Bay, to intercept any ships leaving their anchorages for safety in open water. Hara's *Amatsukaze* remained with the eight other escort ships to await the return of the *Ryujo*'s planes. To confuse possible

American submarines, they steamed alternately east and west on either side of the carrier. It would be a long time until the Japanese discovered that the Asian fleet, whatever the heroics of American undersea crews, was equipped with torpedoes armed with defective fuses.

•

The persistent ringing of his bedside phone finally got through to Manuel Quezon in Baguio. The ailing President realized that only Jorge Vargas would be calling him at that number and hour. "Yes, Jorge?" he began, with some annoyance in his voice.

"Mr. President," said Vargas, trying to sound calm, "the Japanese have bombed Pearl Harbor. Also Clark Field. War has been declared." Clark Field was a guess. Vargas thought he had heard antiaircraft fire from that direction.

"Jorge, you're crazy!" Quezon shouted into his phone. "War might be declared but the Japanese would never dare attack Hawaii. Are you joking? Where did you get this nonsense?"

Vargas had kept his radio on, and as he began telling Quezon that MacArthur's office had confirmed the report, a broadcaster began, in great excitement, to read a news update: "Pearl Harbor attacked . . . American battleships sunk . . . heavy casualties . . . !" Vargas held the telephone mouthpiece close to his radio.

"Tell General MacArthur," Quezon instructed Vargas, "that I am going down [to Manila] this morning." Remembering that he would need his senior aide, Colonel Manuel Nieto, who could carry him, if necessary, in his burly arms, he added, "And tell Nieto to come here right away." The colonel was nearby, but Vargas duly made the long-distance call. Then he summoned a driver to take him to Intramuros. While he waited for his car, Vargas gulped down a hurried breakfast.

•

At a high table in his Manila waterfront office, Admiral Hart stood reading bulletins. "If anyone spoke," Lieutenant John Horton remembered, "it was in a low voice, because of the admiral's being there. . . . A plain language message, torn from a radioman's typewriter, was posted on a board on the bulkhead. . . . Officers came in from the dark, wondering why they had been summoned, and someone would nod toward the message. They would read it and then read it again, turning away without exclaiming as they would have if the admiral had not been nearby." The tacked-up strip was the first Pearl Harbor report, ending, "THIS IS NO DRILL."

•

General Brereton's published diary (1946) has all the earmarks, in its December 1941 segments, of being improved after the fact—after he had been kicked upstairs in 1942 to command Allied air forces in the backwater of India. In the diary he reported to MacArthur's headquarters in Intramuros at five, where he had to cool his heels. Even then he was kept from MacArthur. "After General Sutherland had given me all available information I requested permission to carry out offensive action immediately after daylight. I told Sutherland I wished to mount all available B-17s at Clark Field for missions previously assigned and to prepare the B-17s at Del Monte [in Mindanao] for movement, refueling and bomb loading at Clark Field for operations against the enemy on Formosa. General Sutherland agreed with my plans and said to go ahead with preparations; in the meantime he would obtain General MacArthur's authority for the daylight attacks."

When Brereton left No. 1 Calle Victoria, he had what he described as instructions "to prepare our heavy bombers for action but not to undertake any offensive action until ordered." In actuality he had little authorization but to keep the engines warm. Later, Sutherland would claim that he reminded Brereton that "there were 20 [air]fields in Formosa" and that the general "had no notion of what he would attack, and he would almost certainly lose his planes." Sutherland may have been angry, too, that Brereton had any B-17s in Luzon, as he had ordered all of them flown to Mindanao, where they would be of little use, but out of harm's way, and "the order was not executed."

Returning to his own headquarters at Nielson Field, just southeast of Manila, Brereton informed his staff about the failure of his plea to unleash the B-17s, and "everyone was puzzled over why we couldn't bomb Formosa since the Japs had committed the first overt act at Pearl Harbor." Sutherland, who had some flying experience and regularly interfered, as he would all through the war, with Air Corps strategy, knew that there were contingency plans to interdict bases on Formosa. Even the Japanese were aware of them. At eight o'clock they would intercept an American message which they misinterpreted as meaning that a raid was scheduled to take place in two hours. At 10:10 a patrol plane mistakenly reported B-17s approaching, and the apprehensive

Japanese ground crews began distributing gas masks. The 27th Bombardment Group at Clark Field did have sketchy plans, lacking bomb-target maps and bomb-release lines for particular speeds and altitudes. Yet even without optimum guidelines, Captain Alison Ind, a B-17 pilot, recalled, "we had something complete enough to make this bombing mission a very far cry from [a] blind stab."

No one could have been unaware of aircraft and antiaircraft batteries on Formosa, but the B-17's long-distance and high-altitude capabilities were ideal for offensive missions without short-range fighter-plane protection. Its defensive power lay only in its ability to keep an attack from materializing. On the ground it was useless.

At 5:30 Major John Mamerow of the Adjutant General's Office, Philippine Department, was awakened at Fort McKinley and told that war had begun and he was to report to Air Corps headquarters at Nielson Field. ("I thought it was nuts.") A car came to pick him up and soon after he arrived at Nielson, General Brereton "arrived from MacArthur's headquarters and gave us as much of the story . . . as he knew. . . . We were told to stand by for orders. General Brereton also told us he had requested permission to bomb Formosa and that we were to begin to draw up that plan. I was told by the General's chief of staff [Colonel Francis M. Brady] to sit on the telephone and keep the war diary. The next thing I knew we got a call from General Sutherland . . . saying the Formosa plan had been disapproved, but to make sure our aircraft were secure."

At Nielson Field, Brereton explained the situation to Lieutenant Colonel Eugene L. Eubank, who had flown down from Clark Field. Enemy transports were almost certainly massing in Formosa's Takao Harbor, if they had not already steamed south. B-17s could hit them if not hit first. Brereton decided it would not be contrary to orders to prepare three planes for a reconnaissance. Brereton's diary entry referred to "missions previously assigned"—suggesting that no further reconnaissance was necessary. Sutherland admitted to an interviewer in 1945 that "there was some plan to bomb Formosa, but Brereton said that he had to have photos first. That there was no sense in going up there to bomb without knowing what they were going after."

Brereton and Eubank knew more than Sutherland rationalized, and had worked on plans to bomb bases in Formosa. Captain Garry Anloff, who was close to Clark Field and its operations, had gone along on a cautious "recon flight to Formosa" and "from five miles away . . .

personally saw over 100 twin-engined bombers on each of two fields."
Brereton's people knew that there were only a few major airbases there,
and in Anloff's terms "had the initial requirement for their B-17s, to
go after the two or three big airports." Eubank got one B-17 in his
19th Bombardment Group ready. John Carpenter (later a lieutenant
general), his Intelligence Officer, who had already scouted Formosa,
was put on standby, with fuel loaded and cameras aboard.

While Manila had been cloaked in predawn darkness, and Brereton
had failed to see the ultimate authority to approve his strike, MacArthur
had been more active as Philippine proconsul, laying out for Jorge
Vargas what had to be done in Quezon's name. One directive placed
the Philippine Constabulary and the volunteer guards component of
the Civilian Emergency Administration under USAFFE control. Sabotage had to be guarded against, and Japanese nationals rounded up.
Vargas promised to issue additional emergency orders as Quezon's
proxy.

Warnings remained in effect not to shoot at overflying planes unless—in Anloff's words—"that aircraft had dropped an object and that
object had hit the ground and exploded." The Philippines, by this
reasoning, as an almost-independent nation which MacArthur served
as Field Marshal of its army, might somehow be spared. To attack
Japanese bases or aircraft was to commit an overt act of war on behalf
of the Philippines, drawing Quezon's country into the conflict before
its time. Later MacArthur defended his inaction. His orders, he said,
"were explicit not to initiate hostilities against the Japanese." Yet those
orders predated Pearl Harbor. And if he had not known for hours that
the war was on, radiogram 736 from the War Department received at
5:30 officially informed him of it and authorized him to carry out
responsibilities assigned in Rainbow 5. Still, the heavy bombers sat on
Clark Field.

•

British troops disembarking at Cape Town had spent dreary weeks
at sea. In order to sail in American-flag vessels under American protection, they had to be ferried across the rough North Atlantic to Nova
Scotia. In Halifax harbor they were transferred to American transports
convoyed by American cruisers and destroyers for the long voyage
around Africa to India or Singapore. The shorter Mediterranean route

was impassable, a gauntlet of Axis subs and planes, even for the technically neutral United States.

With too many ships for Cape Town piers to handle, some transports were still at sea, awaiting entrance until their turns came. A delirium of freedom ashore for each shipload followed while the convoy refueled and reprovisioned. Some troops heard the news of the widening of the war while at sea. Teenage lieutenant Ian Watt, later to write, as a Stanford professor, about Joseph Conrad in the Malay waters which Watt had yet to traverse, learned about Pearl Harbor on descending the gangplank of the *Wakefield*, once a smart transatlantic liner. Radios had just broadcast the news. "It seemed wonderful to me; in the long run it guaranteed an Allied victory."

Onshore also were the *Wakefield*'s crew, mostly American Coast Guard volunteers who had expected to remain close to home. Reluctant to be involved in England's war effort while supposedly at peace, so Watt thought, the American sailors now found themselves in it altogether. Rushed off to a dance for the officers of the Suffolk Regiment (18th Division) at the Kelvingrove, a posh country club, young Watt found himself dancing with "a lovely girl called, I remember, Bubbles Du Plessis," when the music stopped and a man at a microphone announced that Prime Minister Jan Smuts, newly annointed a field marshal, would speak briefly. The wizened, seventyish Smuts materialized on the emptying dance floor and announced wryly to the guests that "whatever we might think of the temporary successes of the Japanese we should all be deeply grateful to them; they have scored a major and strategic success—for the Allies. The sudden, and dastardly attack on the United States has brought about a miracle; it has forced the Americans, after wavering already much too long, to commit themselves to the battle against Hitler." Then the dance went on, but everyone was much too excited to care. And there were lots of free drinks, to toast the turnaround of the war. For Watt and others the euphoria was premature. Captured in Malaya, he would toil to build the bridge on the River Kwai.

•

George Kennan remembered his homeward progress as he left the American embassy in Berlin, where he was administrative officer. Winter evenings were always grim. Blackout rules were severe and fuel restrictions left one feeling always cold. Being out at night meant "groping in pitch blackness from column to column of the Brandenburg Gate, feeling my way by hand . . . to the bus stop; the waiting for the dim blue lights of the bus to come sweeping out of the obscurity; then the long journey out five and a half miles [in] . . . the dim, hushed interior of the bus, lightened only by sweeps of the conductor's flashlight; the wonder how the driver ever found his way over the vast expanse of unmarked, often snow-covered asphalt." Then, when the bus stopped to let Kennan off somewhere on the wide and endless street there was "the eerie walk home . . . , again with much groping and feeling for curbstones; the subdued voices of other pedestrians heard but not seen; and finally the confrontation with the facade of what appeared, from outside its blackout curtains, to be a dark and deserted home."

There was always, on entering, a "tinge of surprise" that behind the bleak walls "was light, at least a minimal measure of warmth, at times (when she was not taking the children somewhere) a wife, and a coziness all the more pronounced for the vast darkness and uncertainty of the war that lay outside." Day by day at his office he followed on a large wall map "the advance of Hitler's army across the great regions of forest and swamp to the west of Moscow, comparing it at every turn with the similar advance of Napoleon's army in the year 1812." As the penetration of Russia proceeded, American relations with Germany had deteriorated. Kennan sensed that the break was near; but it did not come as he expected. Switching on his shortwave radio to pick up the "faint signals" of American news broadcasts, he learned about Pearl Harbor.

Kennan went to his telephone and roused Leland Morris, the chargé d'affaires at the embassy. Berliners went to bed early in the cold and dark. Kennan then called as many other officials as he could find. They all found their way back to the embassy "to consider our course now that the end [in Berlin] seemed near. Our country was at war with Japan; and it was clear that this situation might at any moment develop into war with Germany." He knew they had little time left even in the constrained freedom in which they lived and worked. Codes might be seized, and sensitive documents; communications might be cut off at any moment; they might be taken into custody without warning. They closed the metal blinds on the ground floor and explored the uncertainties.

Having picked up the BBC nine o'clock news about Pearl Harbor, the German Foreign Broadcast Monitoring Service twisted dials for a confirming second report before awakening Joachim von Ribbentrop. Listening impatiently, the Foreign Minister shouted into his bedside telephone that it was "probably a propaganda trick of the enemy's for which my Press Section has fallen." Then he asked that further inquiries be made and the results reported to him in the morning. But the phone rang again: it was Ambassador Oshima, with the same news. He wanted to meet immediately with Ribbentrop rather than discuss the new state of affairs on the telephone.

By the time Oshima arrived, Ribbentrop had new confirmation from the Foreign Office. Although he "had not yet secured Hitler's sanction," Oshima cabled Tokyo, "the immediate participation in the war was a matter of course." The secret agreement would have to come out, perhaps as soon as the next day, Ribbentrop promised. And, Oshima reported, Ribbentrop "rang up Ciano then and there and notified him of the foregoing."

His counterpart in Berlin, so Count Galeazzo Ciano noted in his diary, "is joyful over the Japanese attack on the United States." Ribbentrop "is so happy, in fact, that I can't but congratulate him, even though I am not so sure about the advantage. One thing is certain: America will now enter the conflict, and the conflict itself will be long enough to permit her to put into action all her potential strength."

Equally cynical about the news was Ernst Jünger, in Paris. Finishing his diary page for the night, he noted the Japanese raid. Then he added, "Maybe the year 1942 will become the one in which more people than ever before cross over to Hades at the same time."

Just back from France, and new intimacy with Göring that revealed a decadence he had not imagined, air ace Adolph Galland found his misgivings compounded by the news from Japan. With Werner Mölders dead in a crash near Breslau, Galland was only in his first weeks as commanding general of the Luftwaffe's Fighter Arm, but he had seen enough from the inside to realize that "the curve of the graph [of] . . . German victories had passed its peak and would descend from now on." The Japanese success would be an aberration, but the curve would now begin "moving toward its final end with almost mathematical precision at a constantly steepening angle."

•

In Hildburghausen, between Meiningen and Coburg, the only sign of war was the infantry battalion in training; there had been a garrison there for a hundred years, but now soldiers did not remain very long. Snow had not yet fallen, but townspeople were preparing for Christmas. Santa Claus Day, traditionally December 6, was just over, with fewer gifts for children available than in past years. Blame was placed on the godless Bolsheviks, who had stubbornly refused to accept the New Order in Europe that had barely touched out-of-the-way Hildburghausen.

Memories of the last war and the old order were still acute, and the venerable Kaiserhalle was crowded when a local military authority, former *Oberleutnant* Franken, one of the last officers with German troops in South-West Africa in November 1918, began an evening talk about the lost colonies. Like Franken, most Germans considered the surrender of German Africa one of the injustices of Versailles. Hitler had exploited the issue.

The onetime *Oberleutnant's* exercise in imperial nostalgia was lengthening into the evening when a message was handed to him at the lectern. (Someone in Hildburghausen had been listening to the BBC.) Franken glanced at the note, then read it to the audience. Japanese aircraft had attacked Hawaii and destroyed most of the American battle fleet. The announcement, Dietrich Zapf remembered, "was followed by frenetic applause and hurrahs. People jumped up yelling as if the Berlin-Rome-Tokyo triangle had just won the war." There was no way the major could go on, but people were too excited to go home. They "pushed aside all ideas that the war could be lost"—a feeling Zapf sensed underlying the wry popular joke, "Children, let's enjoy the war; the peace will be horrible."

Another grim joke that had arisen with winter on the Eastern Front had been the question, "Can Germany lose the war?" "Unfortunately not," was the answer. "Now that we've got it, we'll never get rid of it."

Standing in small groups in front of the emptying Kaiserhalle, townspeople discussed what might now happen. Dietrich Zapf lit a cigarette in the darkness and in the glare of the match his teacher, Dr. Guenther, recognized him, rushed over, and boxed his right ear. It was shameless public behavior for a youth.

Two years later both Dietrich and his teacher were drafted.

•

Robert Murphy had been counselor at the American embassy in Paris when it fell to the Germans in June 1940. He had been reassigned to Algiers by Roosevelt to maintain contacts with French Africa. Between the lines had been the understanding that anything Murphy could do to bring the French colonial empire into the war against the Nazis, or at least to deny it to the Nazis, would be useful. Vichy's chief representative in Algeria until then—he had been summoned home—had been General Maxime Weygand, who had signed the armistice with Germany. That seemed a bad start for the Rooseveltian strategy, but in a year in Africa, Murphy had become intimate with Weygand and had the support of Admiral William Leahy, the ambassador in Vichy.

"I was dining in Algiers," Murphy wrote, "at the home of my French friend Count de Rose when the radio announced the Japanese bombings in Hawaii. Everyone turned to me as the only American present. I certainly underestimated both the power of the Japanese and their willingness to take risks, for I told the dinner guests that I could hardly believe the Japanese would be so reckless." Then Murphy added, frankly, that "it would solve the principal problem which weighed on President Roosevelt: How would the United States enter the war? . . . I could only feel relief that the chips were down at last, and Americans no longer need pretend to be neutral."

It was an hour later in Cairo. Quentin Reynolds, with two other reporters back briefly from the front, had been dining well at luxurious Shepheard's Hotel, which still had champagne, when Douglas Williams walked in. Officially the Ministry of Information representative, he was the censor of their dispatches. For the well-fixed, soldier or civilian, even the surface intrigue and gossip in Cairo were little changed. Social life was almost unruffled by what was happening in the Libyan desert. Polo afternoons at the Gezira Sporting Club occupied more officers in Cairo than did the war, and roulette at the Mohammed Ali took up evenings after gourmet, unrationed dinners at oases like the Turf Club. Women of every hue—and equivalent males—offered themselves, at a price, for Nilotic nights that often ended only with the dawn summons by the muezzin from the minaret of the Ibn Tulun. Nothing of the sort reached newspapers at home.

"Any news tonight?" Reynolds asked.

"Only that Japanese thing," Williams said casually.

"Oh, those Japs," said Reynolds. "They talk and talk and never do anything."

Williams stared at him in disbelief. "Haven't you heard? They bombed the hell out of Pearl Harbor, and whether you three great reporters know it or not, your country is now at war."

The reporters leaped from their table to the teletype ticker in the lobby. "What date is this, anyhow?" Reynolds asked Ken Downs.

"December 7."

"I guess that's a date to remember."

They went up to Reynolds's room to figure out what to do. "All three of us wanted to get home. . . . It didn't seem right to be in Cairo with America at war. . . . We were pretty excited, especially in view of the fact that all three of us had been yelling, 'We'll be next' for two years. But none of us had expected that it would be the Japs who'd go to work on us."

•

Returned from Tom Phillips's emergency meeting at the naval base just before 4:00 A.M., Sir Shenton Thomas was pacing the flower beds under the veranda at Government House. There was a bright moon, and sleep was out of the question.

A servant emerged to summon him to the telephone. It was Air Vice-Marshal C. W. H. Pulford, RAF chief, whom he had seen only an hour before at Phillips's headquarters. "Hostile aircraft," Pulford warned, had been tracked on a course for Singapore. Should the city be alerted?

Under no conditions, Thomas insisted, should the air-raid sirens be sounded. They would only "alarm the civilian population." Orders were orders, and Pulford relayed the prohibition to Wing Commander Cave in the Filter Room at Kallang.

Sir Shenton had hardly returned to the veranda when Pulford telephoned again. Aircraft were definitely headed for Singapore. All right, Thomas conceded, the sirens could be activated. In his diary he wrote that he "had just time to phone Rodgers of Harbour Board and Jeans"—the Air Raid Precautions chief—but all he had actually done was to order Wing Commander T. C. Carter to communicate with the appropriate civilian authorities. Ruefully, Cave recalled, either "the arrangement for sounding them went astray or the responsible city official could not be found."

At Kallang, Flight Lieutenant Grumbar had acted on his own to alert Air Raid Precautions on his direct line, "but I was told that they were powerless to sound the air raid sirens because their Chief Warden was at the late night cinema (some . . . had all-night viewing), and only he had the keys that controlled the Alarm switch. I also tried to get the city lights extinguished as a first priority, but with equal lack of success." Bureaucracy marched to a different drummer.

•

A *New Yorker* editor turned down the volume of his radio after another repeat of the shocking news from Honolulu and searched his magazine rack for the November 22 issue. Thumbing through to page 32 he found what he was looking for—a small advertisement headed "*Achtung Warning Alerte.*" Below was the instruction, "See advertisement Page 86. Monarch Publishing Co. New York." The remainder of the space was occupied by a drawing of two dice, one black and the other white. On the first was a double cross and the number 12; on the other the number seven appears moving into the top position.

He riffled through the rest of the magazine, finding many additional pages with the same small advertisement referring to page 86, on which he found a full-column enjoining the reader, "We hope you'll never have to spend a long winter's night in an air-raid shelter, but we were just thinking . . . it's only common sense to be prepared. If you're not too busy between now and Christmas, why not sit down and plan a list of the things you'll want to have on hand. . . . Canned goods, of course, and candles, Sterno, bottled water, sugar, coffee, or tea, brandy and plenty of cigarettes, sweaters and blankets, books or magazines, vitamin capsules . . . and though, it's not time, really, to be thinking of what's fashionable, we bet that most of your friends will remember to include those intriguing dice and chips which make Chicago's favourite game THE DEADLY DOUBLE $2.50 at leading Sports Goods and Department Stores Everywhere."

Above the message, in a drawing, a group played dice in a shelter while searchlights above swept the sky in a pattern suggesting—at least in twenty-twenty hindsight—the rays of the Rising Sun on the flag of the Japanese navy. Below, a two-headed traditional Prussian eagle appeared, with a shield in the center marked with a double cross. The elaborately enigmatic puzzle of a game advertisement suggested a double cross on the seventh day of the twelfth month, involving Germany and possibly Japan—and war. At least in the light of events it looked like more than a coincidence.

All that the magazine's advertising office personnel could recall when the affair was checked out was that a man who paid in cash and did not leave his name had brought in the text of the advertisement with the plates to be used. By the time the FBI was called, the company, which curiously listed no address or telephone number in its advertising—it received mail only during 1941, and at 500 Fifth Avenue—was out of business.

J. Edgar Hoover's office scoffed at the idea that someone had tried to warn the nation through what appeared to be a board-game advertisement, or that it alerted Axis agents to lie low after a certain date. The FBI dismissed the matter.

•

"Baukhage talking." The gravelly opening was as familiar to American radio audiences as the lead-in of a Lowell Thomas or H. V. Kaltenborn, or even of Gabriel Heatter's suddenly inappropriate preface, "There's good news tonight." At 4:09 and 50 seconds, H. R. Baukhage cut into NBC Blue Network programming from the White House pressroom. He had served with Steve Early in Paris in 1918 on the Army newspaper *Stars and Stripes*, and, given the emergency, asked to have a mike installed.

Word got out quickly; the White House was already a war zone. Bill Lawrence of the *New York Times*'s Washington bureau, listening to the Redskins game, headed for the White House in his car as soon as the flash was broadcast. Eric Sevareid of CBS was sitting in his living room talking to Phil Potter, a college classmate who was then a news editor at the *Baltimore Sun*, when a neighbor tapped on his window and shouted, "Turn on your radio!" Chalmers M. Roberts of the *Washington Times Herald* was reading the Sunday comics at his house in Georgetown when the flash broke into his day. He rushed to the office in time to hear publisher Cissie Patterson, who considered FDR the Enemy, challenge her staff, "Do you suppose *he* arranged that?"

UP White House man Merriman Smith had been shaving belatedly when his wife pounded on the bathroom door and asked, "You know what the radio just said?"

"No, what?"

TOP: Emperor Hirohito receiving his army's obeisance. *(National Archives.)*

Japanese newsreel photo of pilots being briefed on a carrier before taking off for Oahu. *(Capt. Roger Pineau, USNR, Ret.)*

BELOW: A Mitsubishi ("Val") dive bomber being sent off by its carrier crew toward Pearl Harbor. *(Capt. Roger Pineau, USNR, Ret.)*

RIGHT: The airfield (foreground) on Ford Island, with flames and waterspouts in the background rising from bombed battleships. *(Naval Historical Center)*

A Zero strafes parked American bombers, Hickam Field. *(National Archives.)*

BELOW: Buildings afire at Hickam Field below a shell-tattered Stars and Stripes. *(Smithsonian Institution photo 3A 41720.)*

TOP: Planes afire on the ground at Ford Island naval air station. *(National Archives.)*

BELOW: Hasty mass burial of American military dead on Oahu, Sunday afternoon, December 7, 1941. *(National Archives.)*

TOP: The destroyer *Shaw*, hit in the floating dry dock at Pearl Harbor, explodes. *(National Archives.)*

BELOW: Battleship Row aflame, Pearl Harbor. *(National Archives.)*

TOP: The superstructure of the *Arizona* crumples and settles into the mud of Battleship Row. *(National Archives.)*

BELOW: Pearl Harbor still ablaze as night begins to fall on the evening of December 7, 1941. *(National Archives.)*

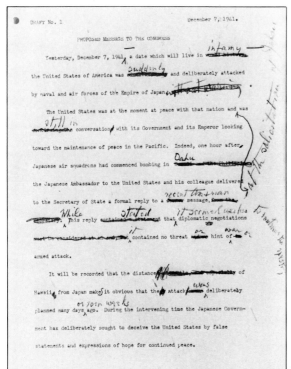

LEFT: President Franklin D. Roosevelt's "date which will live in infamy" war message to Congress, draft revised in F.D.R.'s hand. *(Franklin D. Roosevelt Library, Hyde Park, N.Y.)*

BELOW: Navy men in the Atlantic listening on ship's radio to the President's war message to Congress, December 8, 1941. *(National Archives.)*

President Roosevelt
signing the war resolu-
tion against Japan,
December 8, 1941.
(National Archives.)

Prime Minister Winston
Churchill arriving at
Downing Street on
Monday morning,
December 8, 1941,
with a copy of *The
Star* headlining
"JAPS ATTACK. . . ."
*(Hulton Picture
Company.)*

LEFT: General George C. Marshall on an early morning canter with his dog, Fleet, at his heels. Fort Meyer, Virginia, 1941. *(Marshall Research Foundation.)*

BELOW: The "war warning" to the Philippines command, November 27, 1941. *(National Archives.)*

BELOW: The *Lanikai* in all its armed might, Manila Bay, December 1941. *(Rear Admiral Kemp Tolley, USN, Ret.)*

TOP: General Douglas MacArthur with President Manuel Quezon of the Philippines. *(National Archives.)*

BELOW: Clark Field on Luzon as photographed by Zero pilot Saburo Sakai. Puffs are bomb explosions and anti-aircraft fire. *(Colonel Edward M. Jacquet, Ret.)*

LEFT: A British soldier taken prisoner in Malaya. From captured film. (*Imperial War Museum FE 277.*)

BELOW: Japanese troops moving through the Malayan jungle, December 1941. From captured film. (*National Archives.*)

TOP: General Sir Robert Brooke-Popham with reporters in Singapore. In the white tropical suit is CBS reporter Cecil Brown. *(Imperial War Museum FE 429.)*

RIGHT: The *Prince of Wales* in Johore Strait, Singapore. *(Imperial War Museum FE 483.)*

BELOW: The *Prince of Wales* and the *Repulse* on fire off Malaya, as seen from a Japanese plane in captured film. An unscathed British destroyer is in the foreground, deliberately left by the Japanese to rescue survivors. *(National Archives.)*

LEFT: General Erwin Rommel of the Afrika Korps in the Libyan desert, December 1941. *(Imperial War Museum HU 5625 [LRGD].)*

BELOW: British soldiers preparing an edition of the *Tobruk Truth* on a captured Italian mimeograph. *(Imperial War Museum E 4866.)*

A British armored column in the outskirts of Tobruk, December 1941. *(Imperial War Museum E 6969.)*

TOP: Jews being pressed aboard Nazi trains "west" for alleged "resettlement" late in 1941. From captured German film. *(National Archives.)*

BELOW: Straw boots being manufactured for foot soldiers on the Russian front by slave labor in a Polish ghetto. From captured German film. *(National Archives.)*

TOP: Adolf Hitler with *Luftwaffe* General Hans Jeschonnek in the snow-covered woods at *Wolfschanze*. From captured German film by Hitler's photographer Heinrich Hoffmann. *(National Archives.)*

LEFT: Spanish "Blue Division" troops trying to right a vehicle in the Russian snows. *(From G. B. Kleinfeld & Lewis A. Tambs,* Hitler's Spanish Legion.*)*

RIGHT: German graves on the Russian front near Orel, December 1941. From captured film. *(National Archives.)*

TOP: Leningrad, December 1941. A woman pulls a sheet-wrapped corpse through the snow on a child's sled. *(Vera Inber.)*

BELOW: Dusk on the "Road of Life" across frozen Lake Ladoga, near Leningrad, December 1941. *(Sovphoto.)*

Some of the early atomic bomb scientists. Left to right: Ernest O. Lawrence, Arthur H. Compton, Vannevar Bush, James B. Conant, Karl T. Compton. *(From R. G. Hewlett & O. E. Anderson, The New World, Penn State Press, 1962.)*

LEFT: The Hiroshima A-Bomb exploding, August 6, 1945. Taken from the accompanying Air Force B-29. *(Smithsonian Institution 3A 03381.)*

"It said the Japanese bombed Hawaii."

Racing to the White House from Arlington in his car, he paused long enough to hail a motorcycle policeman and explain. "How about an escort?" Smith entreated.

"Why, those little bastards," said the policeman, comprehension dawning, and jamming down the starter lever on his cycle. "What entrance do you want?"

Washington bureau chief of the *New York Sun*, Glen C. H. Perry had been visiting, with his wife and three-year-old son, Christopher, in Virginia on Sunday afternoon. As a friend in Alexandria opened the door he asked Perry what was new in the war. "What war?" said Perry.

Inside, they crowded around the radio and listened to instant Far East experts ponder the situation. One isolationist pundit, Upton Close, suggested that the attacks in Hawaii "might well be German submarines trying to provoke us into war, and that the Japanese government would probably disavow the attack even if its own navy was responsible." A few minutes later came news of Japan's official declaration of war.

•

Just after four the air-raid siren at Sembawang Aerodrome went off. Groggy airmen of the Australian 453 Squadron stumbled to their parked aircraft and readied them for takeoff. While engines warmed, an order to abort arrived. No one took off. Air Command feared that in the confusion of antiaircraft fire, searchlights, and enemy planes, inexperienced gunners might hit their own night fighters. Frustrated pilots watched their own searchlights pick out twenty-seven twin-engined bombers, and, as they crossed the island, Duty Officer Halliday saw what appeared to be "every gun on the island, rifles, machine-guns plus anti-aircraft guns," fire. It was "a beautiful sight," but there were no hits. Since Sembawang was slightly elevated, with a vantage north into Johore Strait, Halliday was able to see the superstructure of the *Prince of Wales* at the naval base, "lit up, all right, as bright as day. . . . So the war was on."

Flight Lieutenant T. A. Vigors, a young Irishman already a veteran of the Battle of Britain, and in temporary command of the squadron, was eager for action, as were two Australians, R. D. Vanderfield and B. A. Grace, who had flown missions over England and in the Middle East. For the three, Vigors sought permission from headquarters to intercept, and intimated that they might take off "anyway." If he did, he was warned, he would be placed on charge for disobedience. Dismayed, they watched the bombers traverse the island at high altitude, unaffected by the fire from below.

•

As his train rushed north into Scotland, Ambassador Maisky mused about how British-Soviet negotiations might affect the course of the war, and indeed what the course of the war in Russia actually was. He remembered his conversation just before the Prime Minister had repaired to Chequers. Maisky had remarked in passing that he would be glad to see Moscow again. Looking at him sideways through a blue cloud of cigar smoke, Churchill asked, "Are you sure that the meeting will take place in Moscow?"

The import of the question was obvious. There was concern in Britain that the Russians would not be able to hold the capital. Although Stalin himself had stayed behind in Moscow, "Why otherwise had Moscow been evacuated [by officialdom]? Why had Kuibyshev become the new seat of government?" Maisky had wondered himself, but said the patriotic thing. "What a question! Of course the negotiations will take place in Moscow." In a conciliatory tone, but stumbling over the pronunciation of Kuibyshev, Churchill had wished for complete success "wherever the negotiations take place."

At teatime on the special train, all of the official party gathered in Eden's carriage, paying little attention to the crowds at stations they hurtled through without stopping. Later, in the darkness, the crowds began to look excited and very different from the ordinary. Becoming concerned, Eden ordered a short halt at the next station, where a porter on the platform reported that the stationmaster had heard that Japan had attacked the U.S. "Very agitated," Eden asked Maisky what he thought of the news. It was to be expected, said Maisky. "Now the war in essence has engulfed the whole world: but the relationship of forces between the two camps has clearly changed to our advantage."

"What do you think? Should I now go on with the journey to Moscow? Perhaps it would be better to return to London?"

"Not on any account," Maisky objected. "On the contrary, your journey to Moscow has now become even more necessary."

The train rumbled on through the night.

•

Charles De Gaulle's chief of staff, Colonel Philippe Billotte, brought the news to the leader of the Free French at his house in Hampstead far removed from the subterranean war rooms in Whitehall. "Well," said the general, in his usual pontifical tone, "this war is over. Of course, there are more operations, battles and struggles ahead; but in fact the war is over, as its outcome is no longer in doubt. In this industrial war, nothing can resist the power of American industry." But he added a concern, since the U.S. still recognized the Vichy government. "From now on, the British will do nothing without Roosevelt's agreement." Vichy still controlled French colonies in the Caribbean, and the tiny islands of St. Pierre and Miquelon, in the Atlantic off the Canadian coast. De Gaulle could not understand why colonies in America's back-yard which supported Nazi spies and could radio to and refuel sub-marines were not considered a threat. That Roosevelt did not want to furnish a pretext for the Germans to overrun the rest of France was an absurdity to de Gaulle. Vichy was in any case manipulated by Nazi surrogates, and he saw no difference.

"Now the war is definitely won!" he stressed, nevertheless, to Cap-tain Passy, his Intelligence chief since the beginnings of the Free French movement. "And after that," De Gaulle prophesied, "will come two phases. The first will be the rescue of Germany by the Allies; as for the second, I fear that will be a war between the Russians and the Americans." He already had entrusted Admiral Émile Muselier with the mission of seizing St. Pierre and Miquelon, whatever Roosevelt's likely objections. De Gaulle saw even less reason now to shelve the idea.

•

It was 4:00 A.M. Singapore time when Flight Sergeant C. H. Lock-wood heard the sound of aircraft. The RAF at Seletar Air Base was expecting a Dutch squadron from Java, and Lockwood had been su-pervising the conversion of the canteen into temporary quarters for the Netherlands East Indies crews. He had to wake the airmen who were to prepare the flare path, and by the time he had assembled them, bombs were falling into the flying boat area. It was not the Dutch. Airmen took cover wherever they could, Lockwood diving under a truck parked at the Guard House.

Then he remembered that there was a Malay prisoner trapped inside. "I went and unlocked him. He had been sleeping naked, and took off into the rubber estate behind the airfield. The last I saw of him was spurts of dust from his feet as he took off down the road." Bombs continued falling; the canteen was hit before the planes continued south toward the city.

In the Guard Room the telephone rang. It was Lockwood's fiancée, a nurse at the Tyersall Park hospital. "What was all that noise?" Pat asked. Lockwood said that he couldn't discuss it on the phone. "I can guess," she said. "What shall we do about our wedding?" The romance had been frowned upon higher up, as Pat ranked as a captain, but the wedding had been scheduled in any case for the 10th. He'd be off duty at 6:00 A.M., Lockwood said. He'd see what he could do to move the date up.

Just after four, Cecil Brown's telephone had rung at the Raffles Hotel, and he stumbled out of bed to grope for the receiver. It was Major C. R. Fisher, an officer with Services Public Relations, in the Union Building. "Will you come to press headquarters right away? We have an announcement to make." As Brown put the phone down he heard a heavy boom, then three more in quick succession. "It can be only one thing," he realized. "I know a bomb when I hear one."

While scrambling into his clothes he looked for his portable typewriter. At the hotel entrance a rickshaw coolie was wide-eyed with wonder and interrupted sleep. "What is, master? What is, master?"

"Bombs!" Brown shouted. "To hell with them. Take me to the Union Building."

"I no go there—not go." The explosions had come from that direction.

"Like hell you're not going. I'll give you two dollars." (The fare was usually thirty Singapore cents.)*

"All light—go."

There were few vehicles to be seen on Beach Road (now inland), and every light in Singapore and in the harbor seemed on. People were gathering where bombs had fallen. At Union Building the rickshaw wallah grunted to a stop and accepted Brown's two dollars.

An Englishwoman who lived above her dress shop near Raffles

---

* A Singapore dollar was then worth sixty cents American; eight Singapore dollars equaled a British pound.

Place, blasted out of her bed by a bomb, telephoned the police. "There's a raid on!" she screamed.

It must be a practice, said the duty officer.

"If it is," she charged, "they're overdoing it. Robinson's has just been hit!" The smartest emporium in the Far East, Robinson's was the Harrods of Singapore.

Robert Payne's father was construction manager at the Singapore naval base, beneficiary of £63,000,000 of new port facilities, which the gray, indestructible-looking *Prince of Wales* and *Repulse* had been guarding from their anchorages. Later a biographer, Payne had spent the 1930s wandering from one university to another, working in a shipyard, reporting the war in Spain. In Singapore he was shipyard armaments officer. "I never could have imagined," he wrote thirty years later, "that a naval base would be so like paradise. . . . Flame trees grew in the base; the air was scented with frangipani blossoms; king cobras streaked through the high grass. Malay princes worked side by side with Chinese coolies in the machine shops." He lived near the blue Straits of Johore, which separated the island from Malaya, and worked amid "the immense drydocks, the humming of machinery, the turbaned Sikhs standing guard, the big guns facing out to sea."

The big warships opened fire, "but the silver planes flew serenely overhead, out of range of the guns. I was duty officer that night, and . . . as soon as I heard of the presence of the Japanese planes, was to see that all the lights in the base went out. I gave the order over the telephone, and suddenly the whole base was plunged into darkness except for the floating dock moored in the straits, blazing with lights like a Christmas tree." Frantically, he telephoned the dock, but got no answer. It was Sunday night. At last Payne reached the head of the base's night crew and hurled curses at him. "I know all about that," he told Payne, "but I can't find the bloody switch."

In a palm-fringed barracks at Changi, near the eastern edge of the island, Private John Boulter, an underage gunner who had just reached seventeen, was trying to drop off to sleep. He was still not used to the heat at 2° above the Equator. Hearing the drone of aircraft, he got up. Other men followed him outside. No night exercises were on, they assured each other. "The engine noises faded away; we were just about to go in when flashes lit the sky and a deep rumbling noise began. 'Bombs,' I said."

"Not likely," a barracks mate scoffed. "The Jerries couldn't get here. The Japs haven't declared war."

The rumbling continued; they could see over the glow of Singapore the distant flashes of antiaircraft guns. But the older men were "fed up with clever talk," and they "beat a retreat to bed."

In a schoolhouse in Geylang, closer to the city, a Singapore Volunteer Corps company, alerted that there was a war on to the north, tried out their newly dug slit trenches. Amateurs, they did not know that they should be in bed. One of them, Private David Marshall, who worked in the law offices of Allen & Gledhill, had been accepted in the Volunteers only reluctantly, because he was "neither a European, nor a Chinese, nor Eurasian"; rather, he was a Jew whose family had lived in Asia for generations.* Finally he was placed "with the odds and sods, East Europeans and some English volunteers." From their trenches he saw "beautiful birds in the night sky, . . . lit up by our searchlights. They dropped anti-personnel bombs, some of which exploded in our car park, distributing a vast number of very small circular phosphorescent felt rings aflame, difficult to extinguish. I went round, trying to stamp them out with my military boots."

Sounds of gunfire awakened Sir Shenton Thomas's code officer, Mollie Reilly. She sat up in bed to listen; then she went to the window and saw three planes caught harmlessly in antiaircraft searchlights. Awakening her husband, she pulled him out to the veranda to see. By then there were five planes visible. "There had been no air raid warning—Singapore streets were all lit up as usual."

Atop the observation tower of the old Ocean Building, Charlie Gan was on duty as a clerk with Volunteers. It was "a very nice place to sleep. Oh, the breeze blowing in and out. I was sleeping and my chapee woke me up, 'The Japanese have landed!' And I cursed him for that. . . . I was very tired working round the whole day. . . . I just cursed that fellow, 'What the hell are you doing? The Japanese? Go to hell. Let them land anywhere. I want my sleep.'" And so Gan slept through the report from Kota Bharu, only to be awakened again by "the first experience of bomb. And that time the Japanese were using a very small bomb. . . . And yet the whole building was rocking and shaking."

* His service to Singapore escalated from private in 1941 (and Japanese prisoner thereafter) to ambassador to France in the 1980s.

This time someone yelled, in Malay, "Charlie, wake up! The Japanese planes are here!" He heard and felt the bombs fall, then he saw one hit the Chartered Bank. Two others straddled Johnston's Pier, and the water spouted up. While Gan watched with awe, the guard on the dock remained impassively on duty. "He had the guts to stick around. . . . Every one of us ran for our lives except this poor fellow. He was on duty."

Lee Kijo Lin's family in Kapong was awakened by the wail of sirens which went off only as the bombers were leaving. His father, a warden, had not known of any practice alert. With the radio having ceased broadcasting, as usual, at midnight, and the street lights on, nothing out of the ordinary seemed to be happening, but Mr. Lin had heard ominous radio bulletins about Japanese ships as well as confident ones about the invulnerability of Singapore. He decided to telephone his friend Chua Chin Liat, the district warden for Kapong.

Liat wasn't sure; it might have been a training exercise he hadn't known about. Lin decided to call some British friends.

In the western countryside, Edwin Thumboo, although only eight and in a house without radio or telephone, knew that the air raid was real, for he could see flames leaping from the oil refinery and storage tank area at the distant shoreline. The family had arisen to watch, realizing that the war had begun. Since they knew that Singapore was impregnable and that the Japanese would surely lose, they worried aloud only about Edwin's step-grandmother. His grandfather's second wife, she had returned as a widow the year before to her birthplace in Nagasaki.

At Lee Kijo Lin's house the telephone rang. It was Liat, now very excited. There had been a raid, with damage and with casualties going to the hospitals. It was war. Suddenly the sense of unpreparedness came home to Lin's father, usually not given to anticolonialist sentiments. "What's the difference?" he shrugged to his son. "A change of masters now!"

In Woodlands Camp, on the road linking the island by causeway with Johore, John Mutimer turned over in bed, wondering "what silly buggers were practicing at that time of night." He heard the bombers, then dozed off again, dreaming that he was back in England in the Blitz. "Next minute I was out of bed and standing outside, listening to the bombs screaming, whistling and crashing to the ground. . . . I couldn't believe it. We weren't at war in the Far East; the Germans couldn't get that far. . . . They couldn't bomb us [anyway], there was no blackout. Then the truth dawned." He would never be shaved at dawn, before awakening, again.

A White Russian émigré, Constantine Constantinovich Petrovsky had joined the British Army in Hong Kong as a physician. His Field Ambulance Company in Singapore had been used to war rumors and restrictions to camp—"a silly game." Now he assumed he was dreaming. "There were rumbling noises going on, like engine noises from planes. And I woke up. . . . The aircraft were high in the moonlit sky, and beautiful. Then came his first sounds of war, first the antiaircraft fire: "pomp-pomp." Then "bang, bang, buzz, buzz . . . bap, bap, bap, bap, bap, bap . . . zzzzzzzing, brooomh, crrrrumb, crrrrumb." Singapore was "full of lights. . . . And only when the raids stopped were lights [put] out. Only then [the city] woke up, you see, to put the lights out." His unit "tried to ring up" to see if they could be of any use, and "found that the casualties [were] in the city, mainly in [the] Chinese area." Soon the radio went back on the air and they discovered that they were not alone in having been taken by surprise.

While the noise outside Changi Prison suggested that what he had been imprisoned for had actually happened, consular official Mamoru Shinozaki was pulled from his cell and taken before a sleepy Colonel Lily, the superintendent. His status had changed, said Lily. Shinozaki was now a prisoner of war.

In the guise of consular aide, he had escorted a plain-clothed businessman, actually Colonel T. Tanikawa, Imperial Army planning chief, about Malaya and Singapore, an exploration that had convinced Tanikawa—later a general—that Singapore had to be taken from Johore, to the north. Shadowed while passing data to Lieutenant Colonel Tsuji for General Yamashita, Shinozaki had been arrested and sentenced to three years' hard labor for assisting Japanese officers to obtain "information which might be useful to a foreign power." Given nothing to write with, he passed his free hours composing Chinese poems, scratching them on his cell floor, then committing them to memory. In his iron-barred cubicle that "reminded me of a bird cage. . . . I could see the sky. . . . As the anti-aircraft guns fired, a screen of grey dots could be seen against the blue."*

* In February, on the surrender of Singapore, renamed by the Japanese *Syonan*, he joined the Military Administration.

•

Still exhausted in the aftermath of maneuvers, the chief of staff at Headquarters, Third Army, in San Antonio, had tucked in an early lunch and was going to nap the afternoon away. The new brigadier general, his star recognizing brilliant mock warfare in Louisiana, had left instructions not to wake him under any circumstances. When he saw his aide hovering over him anyway, Dwight Eisenhower understood. He had expected war somewhere, but he hadn't known where. Five days later a call came from Washington. Marshall wanted him "to hop a plane and get up here right away."

At the War Department after his White House meeting, Secretary Stimson joined the Army service chiefs and Assistant Secretary McCloy in preparing emergency orders. The President, Stimson observed, was drafting a declaration of war against Japan. He wondered whether the United States "should declare war on Germany at the same time." The others liked the idea.

Rushing back to his office from his own luncheon party, Assistant Secretary of State Breckinridge Long ordered all communications with Japan stopped, the provisions of the Trading with the Enemy Act made operative, Japanese diplomatic offices protected, ships at sea informed. The wealthy, patrician bureaucrat was mad as hell. Viscerally racist, he had no desire to see the United States at war with Germany, which was saving the world from Jewish and Communist contamination, and he had used his influence in the State Department to keep refugees— "who could never become moderately decent American citizens"—out. But war with the Japanese was different, and Long was angry only that his government had not been ready. He was, he would write in his diary, "sick at heart. I am so damned mad at the Navy for being asleep at the switch in Honolulu. It is the worst day in American history. They spent their lives in preparation for a supreme moment— and then were asleep when it came."

The reaction of another assistant secretary, Adolph Berle, was that "if there is anyone I would not like to be [at this moment], it is Chief of Naval Intelligence." Yet almost anyone who had been exposed to evidence which in hindsight pointed to Pearl Harbor had downplayed or ignored it. It was too distant from Japan to risk a fleet, too strongly defended, too well patrolled, too shallow for torpedoes. References to Pearl Harbor by spies or agents were red herrings, to mask the real targets.

Staff admirals were stunned by the reports of ship after ship settling into the mud of Pearl Harbor—all but brawny Rear Admiral Ben Moreell, chief of the Bureau of Yards and Docks, who walked into the gloomy exchange late. "Well, gentlemen," he said in his usual confident manner, "I've lined up every heavy contractor in the United States ready to go to Pearl Harbor to start raising those ships." And he meant it. Some ships would be operational in weeks; only three would never sail again.

Trying to weather his wife's discontent with politics and with Washington, Adlai E. Stevenson, an aide to Frank Knox, had taken Ellen and the boys on a family picnic. Winter dusk had come by the time they returned to R Street. Stevenson had hardly opened the door when the maid showed him a stack of messages by the phone. It must be, he told Ellen, the Kearny Shipyard business again; it would wait until he washed up. While he was showering the phone rang again; it was a newspaperman acquaintance who wanted a statement. "About what?" Stevenson asked.

The voice on the other end evidenced irritation, then surprise, that the Secretary of the Navy's right-hand man did not know that the Japanese had been bombing American installations in the Pacific. He rattled off a list, some of the places rumored rather than real targets. Stevenson hung up with an apology and rushed to his office, adjacent to Secretary Knox's, remaining there through the evening and most of the night as place names the newsman had ticked off rolled by in earnest.

Secretary Ickes's guests were gone before he received word of the war, but he saw no reason to rush back to the Department of the Interior. He was feeling old and tired. He took a walk, and was lying down afterward when the summons to a meeting at the White House came. Donald Nelson was tuning in the New York Philharmonic on his car radio as he drove home from Ickes's farm when he heard an excited voice say, "In ten minutes H. V. Kaltenborn is going to give you more information on the bombing of Pearl Harbor."

Captain Dean Rusk, John Kennedy's Secretary of State in the 1960s, had been at his desk in the old Munitions Building on the Mall since six in the morning, trying to make sense of the flood of intelligence reports. When a punch-card sorter located him, he was a company commander in the 30th Infantry Regiment, 3rd Division, called up as a reservist from law school in Berkeley. Rusk's branch of intelligence

(G-2) was British Asia, which, when he arrived late in October, was a filing cabinet drawer with a tourist handbook on India (marked "Confidential"), a military attaché's report on the Indian Army dated 1925, and clippings from the *New York Times*. His immediate superior was Colonel James Compton, who had given him a free hand to assemble a staff. By December it included a green new second lieutenant, Robert Goheen, a future president of Princeton.

The lack of intelligence had amazed Rusk, who began to collect information on Southeast Asia wherever he could—from former missionaries, scholars, merchant seamen, and the like. When word came that the principal instrument of American strategic planning—the Pacific Fleet—had largely been sunk at its moorings, he realized that the Japanese section of G-2 shared some blame. Colonel Compton showed Rusk a memorandum, only a few days old, listing possible Japanese targets. Pearl Harbor was not on it. "I thought I'd better show you this memorandum," Compton said, "because you are never going to see it again. All copies are being gathered up and destroyed."

•

Mazuo Kato left the Japanese embassy after about an hour. Nomura and Kurusu had returned from the State Department in shock, speechless after Hull's outburst and unaware of the events that had overtaken all of them. "I thought there was something very funny"—meaning *strange*—"there," Nomura said about Hull's agitation, "but I didn't get it." They had known only that the message prepared in such a frenzy was a rupture in negotiations, no more. An "East wind; rain" signal fully breaking relations—yet not in itself a declaration of war either—had been listened for in a nightly vigil by embassy staff since the instructions regarding it had been received thirteen days before, but Okamura told Kato that the anticipated code had never been picked up.

When Kato slipped out of a side door that opened on an alleyway leading to Massachusetts Avenue, it was getting dark and the air was chill. In front of the embassy the throng of protesters was getting larger. Obscenities were shouted against the invisible occupants. As Kato reached the street the crowd parted quietly; then someone told him, "You're the last son of a bitch we're going to let out."

Kato thought it prudent not to try to hail a cab there, and hurried along Massachusetts Avenue; but one man detached himself from the crowd and followed behind him, shouting at the cabbie who slowed for Kato, "Don't let him in. He's a Jap." Kato walked further, worried that it was dangerous to be alone in the gathering dusk. Soon a cab stopped, and he had to make a quick decision about where to go. At his apartment there might be police waiting to pick him up. He asked, instead, to be driven to the home of a woman friend at the State Department who lived nearby with her parents. He owed her $150, which he had borrowed because his expected Domei remittance had not arrived. The day before, Secretary Hull had personally intervened to enable him to draw dollars from a Washington bank, and Kato could now repay the loan. In any case, he might not need dollars much longer.

At his friend's home he listened to the flurry of news on the radio. He knew there was no chance of sending further messages to Japan. When he was invited to stay for dinner, he gratefully accepted.

•

The flash on NHK—Nippon Hoso Kyokai (Japan Broadcasting Corporation)—had been read by announcer Morio Tateno at 6:30, his excitement evident in the repetition. "We now present to you urgent news. The Army and Navy Divisions of Imperial General Headquarters jointly announced at six o'clock this morning, December 8, that the Imperial Army and Navy forces have begun hostilities against American and British forces in the Pacific at dawn today."

The news blared from street loudspeakers in towns and cities throughout the islands as people began going to work. Men and women in the streets instinctively had been clapping their hands to the infectious rhythm of the "Warships March" when the music had ceased abruptly. Once the bulletin ended—there were still no details—thousands of listeners in Tokyo began drifting toward the gates of the Imperial Palace to bow in prayer for victory. Others clustered about loudspeakers, wherever they were, bowing silently. Preceding the news were the first bars of the Beethoven Fifth Symphony, the dot-dot-dot-dash anticipation of the Morse code for *V*, popularized, people did not realize, by their new enemy Winston Churchill the year before as symbol for victory.

Although in charge of planning for the Personnel Bureau of the Navy Ministry, Commander Atsushi Oi had been bypassed in the planning for the first strikes. He had even been sent on a week-long trip with a naval aide-de-camp to the Emperor to check on the quality of physical examinations for new recruits in southeastern Japan. Men in poor shape were turning up in uniform. Although he had been puzzled when Vice-Admiral Tomoshige Samejima failed to appear on the railway platform and Captain Jisaburo Sato, the junior aide, materialized instead, Sato explained that the admiral suddenly found that he had to remain in Tokyo. On the morning of the eighth they were back at Ueno Station, where they parted, and Oi was soon at his house in the Setagaya district. He turned on the radio to catch up with the news and went to wash his face just as the music changed abruptly. "A very familiar song with us Navy men called 'Gunkan-machi' ["Warships March"] was heard, followed by a stern-voiced announcement."

Oi had not yet reached for the faucet. "I shuddered," he remembered, "and felt as if icy cold water was streaming down my back from neck to waist." Washing his face and hands hastily he rushed upstairs to a window from which he could see the snowcapped cone of Mount Fuji. Almost every day since his appointment in October he had argued with zealous Navy Ministry staff who were "strongly insisting on war." More than most military men, he knew the limits of Japan's resources and understood their long-range chances. "The sky was very, very clear and the always beautiful view of Mt. Fuji was more beautiful than ever. I clasped my hands before the splendid sight and tried to compose my shocked heart." The radio music, no less martial, had now switched to "Batto-tai"—"The Drawn Sword Brigade."

•

At the Manila Hotel, Karl von Wiegand heard a pounding on his bedroom door. He looked at his alarm clock. It was five, and still dark. Lady Drummond-Hay had the room with the telephone. "The Admiral is on the telephone," she shouted. "He says it's urgent."

Von Wiegand ran to her room. "What's up, Admiral?" he asked.

"The war is on. Your information was correct." Glassford told him about Pearl Harbor, adding that casualties "are very heavy." He was going off to his ship, he said. "God love you." And he left for a plane bound south to his new assignment—the American cruisers and destroyers scattered over a thousand miles of the Dutch Indies. His flagship would be the cruiser *Houston*, then at Iloilo.

Later, Glassford denied it all; von Wiegand stuck to his story.

•

His voice trembling, seventy-two-year-old Joseph E. Poindexter, Governor of Hawaii by presidential appointment, went on the air from his office via a KGU microphone to read a proclamation of emergency. It was less than necessary, since getting the chaos under control required martial law, which would make General Short military governor. Poindexter had more reason to be shaken than most residents. A misdirected AA shell had landed in his driveway, and another had burst near him as he had driven to his office. He assumed that every wild AA shell sent up by jumpy gunners meant another enemy attack.

As he was closing, a telephone message was handed to the governor. Short wanted him off the air: another attack was expected, and the Army wanted to shut down Honolulu's radio stations to prevent the Japanese from homing in on the broadcasts.

Poindexter wept. "We are going off the air for the first time. We have been under attack and the sign of the Rising Sun has been plainly visible on the underside of the planes." Blotting out Oahu's radio signals was a good idea, but eight hours too late. Still, the governor's aides, panicking that another raid was imminent, hustled him down the stairs as soon as he completed his peroration, pushed him into his car, and drove him away.

Bewildered, Poindexter thought he had said something wrong on the air and was being rushed off to house arrest.

At 11:42 both KGU and KGMB dutifully went silent, compounding the misery of families who wanted to know what was actually happening, and how their sons, husbands, and fathers were faring from Kahuku Point to Ford Island. Even more than before, Honolulu became an incubator for exotic rumors.

•

It took only thirty minutes for Flight Petty Officer First Class Shigenori Nishikaichi to fly the 124 miles from Kaneohe Bay on Oahu to the tiny island of Niihau. The Zero he had been following in Iida's squadron trailed white smoke, then disappeared. Both were going to fail their rendezvous with the *Soryu*. His gas tank punctured by a bullet, he was running out of fuel.

From the air Niihau resembled a crouching seal. At the base of the seal's spine Nishikaichi saw a cluster of frame houses—the village of Puuwai. To await a rescue sub, he wanted to ditch near the coast. Picking what looked like pasture land, he pulled on his control stick.

His wheels snagged on a wire fence. The plane pitched forward on its nose. His harness broke and the impact knocked him unconscious.

Owned by the Robinson family, which operated the eighteen-mile-long island as a sheep and cattle ranch and restricted residence to its 136 Polynesians, Niihau had, by design, no modern conveniences, not even a radio or a telephone. Kauai, from which the once-a-week supply boat came, was eighteen miles away.

Hawila (Howard) Kaleohano saw the plane from his front yard. When it sputtered and came down, Kaleohano, who could lift a sheep like a feather pillow, ran over and yanked up the cockpit canopy. Startled, Nishikaichi reached for his Nambu pistol—much like a Luger. Kaleohano slammed the pilot's head against the instrument panel, lifted him out of the plane, and dumped him on the ground. Waving the gun, which he had no idea how to use, Kaleohano motioned Nishikaichi toward the house.

Understanding that he had captured a Japanese enemy, Kaleohano sent for the head beekeeper, Ishimatsu Shintani, and Yoshio Harada and his wife, Irene, who kept house for John Rennie, the elderly Scot who ran the Robinson homestead two miles off. In her kitchen, Mabel Kaleohano gave Nishikaichi Sunday pancakes, and the puzzled pilot offered Japanese money in return. Shrugging it off with a laugh, Howard Kaleohano returned to examining the papers he had taken from the pilot's flight jacket—drawings of bases, ships, and aircraft, and what Kaleohano did not recognize as a rendezvous map. "Give paper back!" Nishikaichi demanded. Kaleohano shook his head negatively. He had seen the bullet holes in the plane, even stuck his fingers into them, and understood what must have happened.

Shintani arrived. He was a quiet man of nearly sixty who lived with a Hawaiian wife. He spoke briefly in Japanese with the pilot, gasped at what he learned, and left abruptly. Puzzled, Kaleohano and the curious villagers who had gathered in his kitchen learned little more from the Haradas.

"What happened to you?" Yoshio Harada asked Nishikaichi. Harada was a Nisei of thirty-seven.

"Can any of these people understand Japanese?"

"No, that's why they sent for me."

"Don't you know that Japan has attacked Pearl Harbor?"

The only radio on the island was locked in Robinson's house and Harada had the only key. He decided not to translate that exchange.

GUAM	TOKYO	SHANGHAI	PEARL HARBOR
8:00 A.M.	7:00 A.M.	HONG KONG	11:30 A.M.
December 8	December 8	MANILA	December 7
		6:00 A.M.	
		December 8	

Hour 34

O N a clear day," Edward Wayne Settles remembered, "you could look from the island of Guam and see the island of Saipan, which belonged to Japan. We'd go out on patrols at night and we'd see lights flashing all over; it was the Japanese fleet out there. They were taking pictures and seeing how strong we were." Neither strong nor big, Guam had been voted nothing by Congress for defense. On the edge of the Marianas, war booty for Japan after the German surrender in 1918, the thirty-mile-long by seven-mile-wide island was defended by a one-stack former Yangtze River minesweeper, the *Penguin*, and two patrol boats that each carried a crew of five.

Guam had no military airfield. The Navy, however, had quietly slipped funds to Pan American Airways to develop a chain of flying-boat landing sites across the Pacific, including Guam, with the idea that each would have military potential when needed. Since the island was the property of the Navy, its governor, known as "King" by the 23,000 Guamanians, was a naval captain, G. J. McMillin. Six weeks earlier, all American women and children, including McMillin's wife, son, and daughter, had been evacuated. Except for servants, he had the block-long seventeenth-century Spanish governor's palace at Agaña all to himself.

At 8:00 A.M. the *Penguin*, its twenty-four hours of circling Guam completed, tied up at its buoy in Apra harbor. Eddie Howard and the rest of the boiler room crew shut off steam to the engines. Howard had gone from brass instruments—he played the trumpet—to brass fittings. A twenty-one-year-old from Indiana who had joined the Navy as a bandsman, he climbed up to the main deck with his firecrew for disembarking. A station boat from the Piti Navy Yard came alongside, and a sailor ran up the gangway to deliver a note to their skipper. J. W. Haviland III, his crew thought, was old for a lieutenant, but short of war, promotions came slowly. An aging skipper seemed appropriate for an ancient ship.

Glancing at the note, Haviland turned and shouted, "Get underway immediately!" Howard ran for the boiler room, the General Quarters alarm sounding as he went. While the crew began working to get steam pressure up again, the engine room chief took a call from above on the voice tube, returning to warn his men that they were already drifting out toward the harbor reefs. "We're loose from the buoy," Howard yelled. "To hell with warm-up time. Cut those boilers in at full power NOW!"

The *Penguin* picked up speed as it began to roll in the rough water at the mouth of the harbor. From below the crew could hear the full complement of the *Penguin*'s guns firing—two three-inch antiaircraft deck guns and two .50-caliber machine guns. The ship shuddered; insulation broke loose from the overhead pipes onto the heads of the boiler crew.

Farther out, Howard remembered, "I heard a bomb. Whooom! It went off and the ship shook a bit, and there were holes in the bulkhead. . . . One of my men had blood running down his head, and he was going to get out of there, and I wouldn't let him." When the *Penguin* slowed, Eddie decided to go above to see what was happening. A mess hall door led to the main deck. He opened it into a burst of flame and a tremendous noise. Slamming the door, he plunged down the ladder as a second and then a third bomb exploded. The *Penguin* lay dead in the water.

The six boiler crewmen waited. Howard buzzed the voice tube to the engine room. "We hollered . . . and there's no one out there." Several crewmen took wrenches and banged on the bulkhead door. Still there was no response. "They're all dead out there, I guess," said Howard.

"What are we going to do?" asked one sailor.

"We're going to stay right here."

Soon a hatch opened above them and someone shouted down into the noise, "Everybody out down there!" The crew imagined a Japanese voice.

"Well," said Howard, resigned, "we've been boarded. We might as well go up." It was his own executive officer. The "Abandon Ship" order had gone to everyone but the boilermen.

A year older than Howard, and almost a neighbor in that he came from a farming village in Illinois, Edward Settles had joined the Navy after working for thirty dollars a month in the Civilian Conservation Corps, a Roosevelt program to furnish useful environmental jobs for the unemployed. It was winding down in 1940, and, deciding that the Army meant mud and the Navy clean sheets, Settles evaded the draft by enlisting to get "a ship under me." It was the *Penguin*, and while Howard had rushed below, Settles saw the Japanese planes coming and dashed to a .50-caliber machine gun. "One plane dove on the ship and got so close that I could see the bandana on the pilot's head. . . . I ran 250 rounds of ammunition . . . between the prop and the cockpit of this plane and he began to smoke. He went down before he got the ship."

Without time to fire short bursts, he had let the gun get too hot, and reloaded gingerly with his back propping up the gun. "Anyway, a first class boatswain's mate named Obby Bryan was standing out in front of me, and this damned gun fired a round." Brandishing his .45, Bryan shouted, "Settles, you son-of-a-bitch, you tried to kill me!"

"Honest to God, chief, I didn't do it!" Settles pleaded, and, as if in corroboration, the overheated gun fired another round, saving his life—although a run by "Betty" bombers riddled the ship and nearly did away with both of them. "You could read a paper through the side of it," he remembered. Only in "shorts with the ass ripped out of them," he jumped overboard and began swimming toward the harbor, close to a carpenter's mate notoriously tight with his money who struggled in a lifejacket and pair of shorts from which a thick wallet bulged. "But the sucker couldn't swim . . . [and] then his billfold came out of his shorts." Instinctively he went under after his sinking wallet, and Settles had to clutch at his hair to keep him from washing farther out to sea with his money.

Haviland, the skipper, had remained aboard until the last, his left arm "shot to pieces, nothing but bone and shreds of skin left." When he could see that everyone still alive was off, he threw a mop over the side, jumped overboard, cradled his mangled arm around the mop handle, and swam the two miles to shore with his good arm.

Exhausted, the sodden survivors who made it to the beach watched the *Penguin* slowly sink, stern first. Wearing makeshift bandages torn from their scanty clothes, they trudged toward the nearly deserted town of Agaña. On the way they met someone who told them about Pearl Harbor.

By 8:27 the planes that had riddled the *Penguin* were glide-bombing Marine harbor installations. It was nearly three hours since the war news had arrived, at 5:45, from Manila, and shore patrol squads had gone out to arrest all Japanese nationals. The garrison of 385 Marines and naval personnel and 308 local Guamanians was little more than a moral force. With no defense appropriation for Guam, Roosevelt had juggled funds to begin an airfield on the Orote Peninsula, but that had only gone as far as the arrival of an advance echelon of workmen. There, the Marines dug in and waited.

.

Stubbing out another of his sixty daily cigarettes, Hideki Tojo began his first wartime Cabinet meeting just after the NHK news aired. Military aides had filled him in on war bulletins. The Cabinet room was dominated by a large round table at which ministers sat, with assistants at seats behind them. Tojo stood. "As you must all know," he began, "we are now at war. Our Army reports success at Kota Bharu in Malaya, and also in Thailand. But the operation about which you may want to hear is the Navy's attack against Hawaii. Admiral Shimada will tell us about that."

The Navy Minister, Shigetaro Shimada, arose at his seat. "The Navy's attack against Hawaii has no doubt been a great surprise to all of you," he said. "I am sure you understand it was necessary to maintain absolute secrecy. A very large task force, including six carriers, took part in the mission. Radio reports indicate great success. Pilots above Pearl Harbor say they have sunk several American battleships and have accomplished other good results. This is wonderful to hear, but I want to point out that it seems to us in the Navy Department that the damage to the enemy must have been overestimated. When we heard the report, we felt it was necessary to discount it to a certain extent.

Even so, the news is great. The attack on the American fleet, which was the main purpose of our Hawaiian operation, has been accomplished."

Shimada's caution impressed the Cabinet. Aerial photography would prove his strike force's claims. Meanwhile he could take pride in a mission that cost none of his surface vessels.

Next on the agenda was the Imperial Rescript. Copies had been furnished to each minister. Tojo asked for objections to its language. There were none. It was only 7:20, but the general had no desire to prolong the session. Normal business could be conducted at a less pressing time. He had to meet with the Privy Council and with the Emperor. "At last the war has begun," he concluded. "There is no other way but to fight. We must announce this to the people." What he meant was a broadcast message of his own. Radio had already brought the fact of war to every Japanese awake.

Already apprised of events, Marquis Kido left at 7:15 for his Palace office, eschewing his chauffeured car. He had managed three hours' sleep. "As I walked up the slope of Akasakamitsuke to Miyakezaka, I saw the sun freshly rising above the distant buildings. Our country is really going into a great war today with two mighty nations, America and England. . . . Anxious about the result, I closed my eyes and prayed toward the sun."

Again in the Palace only four hours after he had last left it, he met with Tojo and the military chiefs prior to the Privy Council session, scheduled for eight. "On hearing of the great success of the attack," he noted in his diary, "I deeply appreciated the divine help."

Ambassador Grew had been awakened just before seven by a telephone call from Toshikazu Kasé, the Foreign Minister's secretary. Grew was to come to Togo's office as soon as possible. Kasé regretted the urgency—he had been trying to reach the embassy since 5:00 A.M. but had not been able to get through. Knowing that his cables had been held back, Grew suspected that the military had also blocked telephone lines. While dressing, he heard from servants that NHK Radio had confirmed that war had begun.

At his home nearby, Grew's deputy, Eugene Dooman, was awakened by his houseman, Kyobashi, who drew his bath and laid out his clothes. It was not quite seven, Dooman's usual waking time, but Kyobashi reported that Max Hill of the Associated Press was on the telephone. Dooman shouted a hello into the phone several times, hearing only "background noises." Finally, Hill's housekeeper answered, apologizing that Dooman's caller had been "obliged to leave."

Suspecting an arrest, Dooman telephoned Merrell Benninghoff and asked Benninghoff to take his Ford over to check. Then Dooman dressed, and he was still breakfasting when Benninghoff returned. "Well, it's here," he said matter-of-factly. "Japan attacked Pearl Harbor this morning."

"Kyobashi, did you know this?" Dooman asked.

"Yes," he acknowledged. "I heard this on the 6:30 broadcast."

Dooman called Grew, who was already gone. Soon after, Dooman's car arrived, on schedule. Oyama, his driver, had heard the news, but took the streetcar to the embassy garage anyway and came to the house. "Oyama," Dooman asked, "what do you think of this?"

"It's terrible. Our government must be crazy." Oyama had a job to lose.

Max Hill had been awakened by his housekeeper, Katsu. "Domei," she announced. She was used to early morning calls.

"Switch it up here," Hill said, waiting for a voice at the other end.

"This is Domei, the English Translation Department. We have sent the following telegram to [AP in] New York for you: 'Imperial Headquarters announced at six a.m. that a state of war exists between the Anglo-American powers and Japan in the far Pacific."

"Jesus!"

"Do you understand?" asked the Domei man.

"Read it again!" was all Hill could think to say. The Domei caller obliged. Hill decided to check with the cable desk. "Something very bad has happened," he was told, cautiously. Domei had also heard that Pearl Harbor was being bombed; perhaps Mr. Hill wanted to come to the office.

"I'll never make it," said Hill.

"Why?" asked the voice from Domei. Then, becoming cautious, "Are there—er—people waiting outside?" Both were thinking of the same thing, but could not say it.

"Not yet, but it's a cinch they will be damn soon."

Hill put down the phone and went to tell his associate, Joe Dynan. Dynan's bed was rumpled and empty. Suddenly Hill remembered that Joe had gone to an early Mass. Monday the 8th was the Feast of the Immaculate Conception. Hill decided that he would risk a run to Domei. Bob Bellaire of the United Press lived next door, with Max

Stewart of the Canadian Legation. Stewart had a car. They might make it to the Dentsu Building before the police were at the door. Hill pulled on his shoes, fumbling ineffectively in the cold with his shoelaces. Laces flying, he ran for the next house.

Entering through the kitchen he began shouting, "War's been declared!" Both bedroom doors flew open.

"Quit your bloody fooling!" said Stewart, rubbing his broad hairy chest to get warm. Looking at Bellaire he realized that Hill was in earnest. "The bloody bastards," he said. "The bloody—"

"Let's get moving," Hill broke in. "The embassy's our best bet, if we can get inside. We can file from there, maybe, or at least keep in touch with Domei. . . . I'll be back in ten minutes."

He asked Katsu to telephone Dooman while he packed a suitcase. "Make servants get him up. Important. Tell them important. Must get up."

Out in the driveway Stewart, who had no stories to file, had changed his mind. "Seems to me we had bloody well stay put till they come and get us."

"I've got a call in for Dooman," said Hill. "Let's see what he says."

"OK," said Bellaire. "Anyhow, I'm going to have breakfast first. We won't eat again until night, if then."

There were five solemn plainclothesmen clustered at Hill's door. "Come in, gentlemen," he said, "I've been expecting you."

"We are policemen," one announced. They circled Hill with quiet authority and fanned out to look for Joe Dynan. "Dynan-san?"

"Church," said Hill; "he's gone to Mass."

Finally, Dooman was on the line, and Hill struggled to the phone. When a policeman blocked his way, he shouted to Katsu, hoping that Dooman would hear, "I'll have to ask the police if I can talk with him!" Then he raised his voice further. "War has been declared!!"

"Tell Dooman-san," the plainclothesman ordered the servant, flattening his hand over the receiver, "that Hill-san has left the house."

"I understand perfectly," said Dooman, who knew about the police—yet not about the war. Whistling cheerfully, Dynan returned. Then Bellaire walked in without knocking, and the police had three arrests. Minutes later Benninghoff—immune as a diplomat—was at the door, and told only that Hill was under arrest, while the other two were being held because they were found on the scene of a police investigation. On the pretext of warming his hands at the stove in a corner of the living room, Benninghoff managed to squeeze inside. "War," Hill whispered to him. "Japan's declared war."

When Benninghoff nodded, the police interrupted, suggesting that he go on his way. "Tell the AP and my family what happened," Hill urged.

"All right," said Benninghoff, "but eat a good breakfast. You won't get another meal like this for a long time."

After Benninghoff left, the police took Hill away. The others knew they were next.

Otto Tolischus was awakened by insistent banging on his locked bedroom door. He tugged on a robe. Four plainclothesmen had entered his house, finding no one but a houseboy and the rotund fifty-three-year-old *Times* reporter, a veteran of such break-ins, having worked under Gestapo surveillance. They were from the Metropolitan Police, said one of the dark-suited men. "Put on your coat. The procurator wants to see you."

"The Grew story!" Tolischus thought. The Japanese had got hold of it somehow! He asked whether he could dress and make himself breakfast. "Dress warmly," he was told; "it is very cold outside." His visitors seemed elated about something. Tolischus was certain that it had nothing to do with their finding him in.

"I'll bet you don't know the big news," teased one policeman as they shared precious breakfast coffee, a rare commodity in Japan. But Tolischus was told nothing until they had marched him out the kitchen door to a waiting taxi with a smelly, fuming charcoal-burning attachment that was already beginning to symbolize Japan's oil deprivation. "There is war between Japan and America, Britain, and the Dutch. There has been a battle. Manila, Singapore, and Hong Kong have been bombed." No one mentioned Pearl Harbor.

At the police station his keys were confiscated, and while he waited alone in an unheated room the police searched his home and office. From another room a radio barked what he assumed was war news, but he could make out nothing. Once he thought he recognized the voice of Prime Minister Tojo.*

---

* Other American civilians had roughly the same experience. Thomas Davis of the National City Bank's Tokyo office had his house broken into at five. Charles E. Meyer of Socony-Vacuum Oil was hustled off at five by the usual five plainclothesmen. Richard Tenelly of NBC and Reuters was arrested at the JOAK station as he prepared to make a morning broadcast overseas. He had no news of the war and protested that they had made a mistake. Similar scenes were repeated all over Japan.

•

The dinner party in Hong Kong to which Emily Hahn had gone had ended about midnight. Charles Boxer had left to return to duty; but Emily remained with her hosts to talk. "We listened to a broadcast from Tokyo at four in the morning, but there wasn't anything special in that, and at five o'clock I climbed the hill, holding my long skirt out of the dew and watching the cracked stairs carefully in the dawning light. . . . It was a lovely fresh morning, just turning cool. Hong Kong nights are often stuffy but the dawns are better. It had been raining."

She was breast-feeding Carola—very likely puffing away at a large Corona cigar, as was her wont—when the phone rang at six. "Mickey! The balloon's gone up. It's come. War."

She thought of Carola, of how to behave. "Where?" she asked.

"All over. Pearl Harbor and Malaya and everywhere else."

"How do you know?"

"I can't tell you that." Boxer's voice sounded impatient. "Well, can you manage? I'm going down to headquarters. You had better phone Hilda."

"Yes, I'll do that. You call me back if you have time."

Hilda Selwyn-Clarke had offered to take her in, up on the Peak. Emily left the bedroom to alert her factotum, Ah King, but found him already in the hall, fully dressed, and looking at her for instructions. The news had traveled fast. "I must pack," she said. "Call Ah Choy and tell her. We'll take all the baby's clothes and my winter things. Two suitcases."

Hilda's voice on the telephone was calm and unhurried. "Selwyn's gone downtown already. Very well, my dear, I'll come and pick you up on one of my trips. Could you be ready this afternoon? I'll be going up—and downhill all day."

Putting the phone down, Emily crouched over the sleeping baby, her mind numb. "Being a nursing mother rather dulls your brain."

In the New Territories, Theresa Gaggino's family had a farm near the frontier. A sow had given birth the day before to twenty-three piglets and her father wanted to save them all. "So we got up at four in the morning to feed them. It is very unusual for a Chinese pig to have so many. The sow was named 'Mussolini' and the boar 'Hitler.' A company of Canadian soldiers were nearby. Their job was to blow up the bridge. We were still feeding the piglets when an officer came to tell us that we had to evacuate because the Japanese were massing on the border. My father said he wasn't concerned. The Japanese had been there for a long time now and had not been a problem. In fact, when my father went hunting and shot a bird that would fall on the other side of the border, Japanese soldiers would throw it to him.

"The officer was very insistent that we had to leave and sent a vehicle for us. When Mother told everyone to join us—we had Chinese sharecroppers—he said that only Europeans could go. He said the Chinese would be all right; the Japanese would leave them alone. Mother said that one of the women had just had a baby. Mother would not leave without her. So he relented and let only those two come with us.

"After we left, the Canadians blew up the bridge. When the Japanese came through they killed everyone on the farm."

At 6:50 A.M., with the sun only just rising, the first demolition charges were fired. In forty minutes all rail and road bridges on the frontier, including those spanning the Shum Chun River, were down. Japanese engineers quickly began erecting temporary crossings.

It was clear that the Japanese could do what they wanted with Hong Kong. British forces had no observation planes and little intelligence network across the border. Lieutenant General Takashi Sakai had three divisions available, all with combat experience. They had practiced assaults on strongpoints they knew of in the Territories. At Lo Wu they waited until Lieutenant L. B. Tamworth's engineer party had set off their charges, then, almost before the dust had settled, put a pontoon bridge over the Shum Chun. Major G. E. Grey's Punjabis fell back toward the Gin Drinkers Line, deep to the south.

Sakai was baffled. Advance detachments were finding no opposition as they fanned out south of Lo Wu toward Fanling, and across Laffan's Plain to the villages on the east coast. "Tell them to keep going," he instructed an aide from an improvised trestle table, where he was studying a map. "The English must be there someplace. Where can they go?"

Frank Harrison called Andy Leiper at 6:30. His voice sounded urgent. "Have you heard the wireless news?"

"No, not yet. Has anything happened?"

"Christ, yes. This is *it*. I've just heard a San Francisco broadcast which said that the Japanese have launched a massive surprise bombing attack on the American fleet at Pearl Harbor and that war has been declared. The local radio reports that there are heavy concentrations of Japanese forces moving along the border towards Lo Wu." Andy Leiper began loading his kit bag into his secondhand Austin 10. The telephone rang again. Helen was to report to the War Memorial Hospital as soon as possible.

●

T. G. Crews was Corporal of the Guard at the American embassy in Japanese-occupied Peking, one of a hundred Marines in the detachment that guarded the compound and rode shotgun on trains that carried supplies to American enterprises in North China, including the legation in Tientsin. Guerrilla and bandit bands were active. Leaving the guardhouse across the street from the Chien Men Wall at six in the morning—no patrols walked the top of the wall because it was too cold—he realized that for the two hours of his watch already gone by "something was different. There were usually hundreds of coolies and vegetable carts out on the street. This time it was deserted. Finally a lone rickshaw man came up to my post. He told me that he had seen some Japanese soldiers on top of our wall."

Crews rushed inside, "woke up some Marines and told them to run the Japanese off. They were gone longer than I thought they should have been, so I sent another group to check it out. They, too, didn't come back. Now I pushed the alarm button that summoned help from the main detachment. In a few minutes a truckload of Marines came up and were going up onto the wall when my phone rang." It was the officer of the day. Nothing remotely like what was going on had happened in the four years since Crews had, at seventeen, enlisted and sailed, after boot camp, to China. "Get the Marines off the wall," Crews was ordered. Then he learned that Pearl Harbor had been attacked and the U.S. was at war with Japan.

The Marines "hassling with the Japanese soldiers" were perilously near a shootout. As a pale sun rose over the compound, the Americans came down; the Japanese remained.

●

"Well," said Major Fisher at the Union Building in downtown Singapore, "you all know what it is and we are now getting a communiqué ready."

Cecil Brown took down Fisher's version of events on his portable typewriter so that he could take it directly to the censor for approval. The Japanese had forced a landing in northern Malaya and bombed Singapore. The first landings had been repulsed but a successful landing had been made just below the Thai border, where the enemy was being engaged by British troops. "At this moment," he typed, "numerous aircraft are roaring overhead but I cannot tell whether they are Japanese or British." (The planes were British. The Japanese had left.)

Correspondents picked up, as they departed, Brooke-Popham's fanciful Order of the Day, which had been prudently drawn up the previous May and translated into Malay, Tamil, and Mandarin: "We are ready. We have had plenty of warning and our preparations are made and tested. . . . We are confident. Our defences are strong and our weapons efficient. Whatever our race, and whether we are now in our native land or have come thousands of miles, we have one aim and one only. It is to defend these shores, to destroy such of our enemies as may set foot on our soil. . . . What of the enemy? We see before us a Japan drained for years by the exhausting claims of the wanton onslaught on China. . . . Let us all remember that we here in the Far East form part of the great campaign for the preservation in the world of truth and justice and freedom." At 4:45 A.M. Brown filed his story for CBS with the censor.

From Kota Bharu, his operational headquarters to the north, Flight Lieutenant Richard Allanson was ordered up from Runcie's Airstrip "with the duty of attacking a Jap heavy cruiser single-handed because the ghastly weather that morning had caused it to be impossible for what were then some of our best-trained pilots to remain in formation. It happened to be one of their newest cruisers and very well armed." The cruiser and escorting ship threw up a curtain of fire, and Allanson turned toward the coast for safety, first north into Thailand, then south to the Kota Bharu airbase. The plane was badly shot up but flyable, and when they managed to land, Allanson remarked to his rear gunner, "How pleasant to be on the ground again, Sergeant."

"Oi've never smelt the grass smell so sweet, Sir," said the Cockney gunner. "Oi could smell it w'en we was still at er fahsend feet."

Allanson quipped about the warm reception they had received. "Oh," said the sergeant, "yew missed the best paht of it, Sir. I reckon

yew turned awiy in jest noice toime. The minnit yew turned awiy it
was jest laik Brock's Benefit, it was!"*

.

It was early morning before Colonel Claire Chennault's Flying
Tigers training at Toungoo ("Point A") in Burma heard that they had
lost their volunteer status. Officially they were the American Volunteer
Group, replacing a disbanded group of foreign daredevils and soldiers
of fortune who had flown obsolete aircraft ineffectively against the
Japanese for Chiang Kaishek. Through Lend-Lease, the Chinese acquired dollars; through a presidential executive order signed in April
1941 they were authorized to recruit American officers and enlisted
men for detached service in China. The P-40 fighters shipped over
were labeled "advanced trainers," and while Chennault commanded
the AVG his title was "Adviser to the Bank of China."

During the summer of 1941 about 240 men—105 of them pilots—
signed contracts with William Pawley's "Central Aircraft Manufactur-
ing Company" in southern China, the cover for the enterprise, and
most crossed the Pacific on passports identifying them with civilian
jobs. Once the radioman handed Chennault a dispatch from RAF
headquarters in Rangoon about Pearl Harbor, the need for subterfuges
was over.

Lieutenant Charles R. Bond had only finished painting the squadron insignia on his P-40 two days earlier. The First Pursuit Squadron
(there were three) had decided on Adam chasing Eve as history's first
pursuit, but Chennault had objected to the big red apple as looking
confusingly like a Japanese Rising Sun. On the 6th the apples were
repainted green, and the planes readied to fly, but a monsoon rain had
kept them down on Sunday.

No one was actually an AVG lieutenant. There were no ranks except
assumed ones, and Chennault, who had retired from the Air Corps
more or less at its request as a captain, was a colonel at Toungoo
because he ran the outfit. Harvey Greenlaw, the AVG executive officer,
called himself a lieutenant colonel, and his Mexican-Russian mate,
Olga, called herself his wife. Gregory Boyington had been a Marine
lieutenant who wanted to fly in a war, rather than on boring sub patrol

---

* Brock, a fireworks manufacturer, had been famous for his pyrotechnic displays,
and his name identified particularly spectacular shows.

off the Florida coast. Recruited like the others on the promise of excitement and money, he had sent through, as instructed, his "unannounced resignation," which was attached to an agreement of reinstatement without loss of precedence "if I survived, or if the United States declared war." He had been handed a passport with something remotely resembling his picture in it, identifying him as a "member of the clergy."

A harder-drinking, more womanizing group of clergymen had never existed. That they cohered was due almost entirely to Chennault, whose furrowed, granite face commanded respect more than did his P-40s, of which only sixty of the original hundred remained because they were so hard to handle. One pilot, Boyington joked, already had five flags painted on his plane—American flags—"for he had wrecked five P-40s, which made him a Japanese ace." The scrapped planes were a source of spare parts, the only parts pool available.

Sitting out the rain, Lieutenant R. T. Smith had written to his parents that things were "getting tenser and tenser," with the Japanese reported as having crossed the Thai border. "Of course if Thailand is invaded openly we will probably swing into action from here and never get to China. Makes no difference," he added breezily, "just so we get to doing something!"

Most AVG personnel were still asleep in their grass-covered barracks when Harvey Greenlaw's excited shouting was heard. "Pearl Harbor has been attacked! Pearl Harbor has been blown up! Get up everybody! Hurry! Take off as soon as possible!"

Harvey has flipped, Boyington thought. "Good God, what could we do? It was pitch black. There weren't even any lighting facilities on the field." Soon enough, lanterns were moving about in the waning darkness. Greenlaw was worried about having their planes jumped on, and in panic he ordered pilots up with engines insufficiently warmed. Some lifted off and sputtered down. Others braked just beyond the runway, unable to get airborne and damaging their landing gear in the mud or tipping over and bending propeller blades.

"At this point," Boyington wrote, ". . . the rest of us who hadn't started to take off were instructed to cut our engines, and the planes in the air were called down. They figured it was better to take a chance on the Nips' bombing accuracy . . . than lose our entire air force to the black night." So was "Pappy" Boyington preserved to become one of the leading air aces in the South Pacific, a Japanese prisoner in 1944 after ditching near Rabaul, and an alcoholic bum for a decade after that.

R. T. Smith wrote in his diary about a very different war, almost as if he had been at a different Toungoo. Apparently he was preparing material for another letter to his parents. He had been in the ready-room when "somebody ran in . . . and said that the U.S. was now at war with Japan. We could hardly believe it tho' it was confirmed on the radio. Everybody stood around laughing and kidding about it, altho it was easy to see there was really plenty of tension. Here we are in the middle of the works now." His P-40, number 77, felt "as comfortable as an old pair of shoes." He had put all of forty hours of flying time into it, "and we're ready!"

Chennault was worried, he later confided, more worried than at any other time in his checkered career. He had taken the AVG job knowing that routine advancement had been short-circuited. A cigar-chomping nonconformist stunt flyer who preferred his own strategies to accepted doctrine, all he had to show after four years were a jungle airstrip in Burma and a slightly less primitive Chinese base in Kunming, some adventurous pilots, and hard-to-maneuver P-40s that, his men claimed, climbed like a brick, and needed four hands to fly and prayer to land. "My plane is ready and so am I," one pilot boasted in his diary nevertheless, "—and it is my dearest wish that I get my sights on one of those Jap bastards." Another wrote confidently, "It is unbelievable that the Japs had enough guts to attack Honolulu. . . . Everybody [is] running around like mad wondering what will happen to us. . . . I can't help from thinking the U.S. will easily wipe up the Japs."

But not, Chennault realized, his AVG. The Japanese could easily evade the single British air spotter on the long Burmese border and pounce on his airstrip before a single Flying Tiger left the ground. He would have to defend both ends of the Burma Road, Rangoon and Kunming—650 miles apart—with equipment he could not replace. The RAF could be of little help. He knew what they had in Rangoon—30 obsolete fighter planes and 12 outdated bombers. Chennault was on his own. If he got a general's star, it would be the hard way.

•

There were no lights in the stable at Novo-Vileyka, near Vilnius, where eight thousand Russian prisoners had been dumped to die. The daily food ration was a kilogram of bread among seven people, and a half-liter per PW of a potato soup thickened with husks and straw. Every morning, Yuri Farber, once an electrical engineer in Moscow, remembered, the dead were pulled out of the unheated and windowless barracks. "The corpses were dragged to a pit and sprinkled lightly with chloride of lime, but they were not buried because the next day a new group of corpses would be thrown into the same pit. There were days when the corpses exceeded a hundred and fifty and often, together with the corpses, they would throw in people who were still alive." Since these were *Untermenschen*, that was only a technicality.

Farber had not expected to live into December 6. When called a Jew, he identified himself as Yuri Firsov and pretended not to understand German or Yiddish. His comrades were Ukrainians, with whom he slept, arms wrapped about each other for warmth, although some had typhus and all were infested with lice. On the morning of the 6th, one of them, Pavel Kirpolyansky, was cold and dead. He was dragged off to the lime pit. That night Farber lay between two other Ukrainian prisoners, sharing overcoats. No one had blankets. "We put our arms around each other. I was warm and slept soundly."

•

"Sit down, Grace," said the President. "I'm going before Congress tomorrow. I'd like to dictate my message. It will be short."

Grace Tully took the draft down between puffs of the presidential cigarette. "Yesterday, December 7, 1941," he began, carefully specifying every punctuation mark, "a date which will live in world history, the United States was suddenly and deliberately attacked by naval and air forces of the Empire of Japan. . . ."

The message ran only about five hundred words. She rushed off to type it, and returned it to Roosevelt, who went over it on the telephone with Hull. Then over an abbreviated early supper in the Oval Office with Grace Tully and Harry Hopkins, the President reviewed the pages again.

Reaching for his pen, he began making changes in every sentence, beginning with the first. Crossing out "world history," he penned one word above the line—"infamy."

•

By 11:30 the second wave had begun to touch down. A few planes from the first wave that had lost their bearings homed in with them.

Many more were shot up over Oahu than in the first assault—three dive bombers, five torpedo planes, and one fighter in the first group failed to return; six fighters and fourteen dive bombers in the second. As in the first wave, some planes that managed landing on the heaving carrier decks were too battered to salvage, and were pushed overboard. All pilots reported very heavy fire; the Americans had quickly improvised defenses. More planes were up, and there had been dogfights that cost a few intruders their return trip. Sublieutenant Iyozo Fujita managed to limp back in his Zero with a damaged and sputtering engine, landing precariously on the *Soryu*, yet in debriefing he insisted that whatever the ground fire, the enemy would not be able to put any planes in the air that could endanger the strike force.

One of the last to return was Commander Fuchida. He had remained through the second wave to circle Pearl Harbor and observe results, photographing what he could through the dense smoke. In the process he picked up two planes that had missed their rendezvous and escorted them back. By 12:14 all aircraft that would return had landed, but Nagumo was not ready to leave the area. He hoped to draw more stragglers and wanted to consider a third wave. As Fuchida touched down on the *Akagi*, he saw "refueled and rearmed planes . . . lined up on the busy flight deck in preparation for yet another attack. I was called to the bridge as soon as the plane stopped, and could tell on arriving there that Admiral Nagumo's staff had been engaged in heated discussions about the advisability of launching the next attack."

•

The embassy switchboard was already dead when Ambassador Grew left with Robert Feary, his secretary. They were at Togo's official residence by 7:30. Feary waited at the bottom of the carpeted stairs while Grew went up.

The Foreign Minister was in formal morning dress, his face impenetrable. "He slapped a document on the table, clearly a gesture of finality." Then he read a statement, interpreted by Kasé. First, that the Emperor had commanded his government to convey his views on Indochina. Second, that peace was "the cherished desire of His Majesty" and toward that realization his government would "continue its earnest endeavors." There was a further document, a memorandum in English, which Togo handed to Grew, describing it as the final response

of Admiral Nomura to Secretary Hull. He had seen the Emperor at
3:00 A.M., Togo said, and the paper constituted His Majesty's reply
to President Roosevelt.

Did this mean, Grew asked, realizing the answer, that access to the
Sovereign to whom he was accredited had been refused? Such access,
he insisted, was a usage of international law.

Denying any desire to stand between the Ambassador and the
Throne, but doing so anyway, Togo thanked Grew for his efforts
toward friendship between their nations and led him downstairs, where
the British ambasssador, Sir Robert Craigie, was waiting. They had
time only to exchange glances. Linking arms with his lanky, much taller
guest, Togo led Craigie up the stairs while Kasé showed Grew and
Feary the door.* The police were waiting for them at the embassy
compound. Once they entered, gendarmes padlocked the ornamental
iron gates. No one had used the word *war*.

•

On the inner edge of the Manila Bay mine field, Kemp Tolley's
crew awoke expecting to hoist sails for Indochinese waters. Skipper
Tolley wrote in his log, instead, "At 0615 got underway in accordance
with orders to return to Manila, feeling very glad to be alive. A delay
of several days would have meant the sure loss of the ship [off Indo-
china]. Notified the crew a state of war existed with Japan. Hoisted
foresail, jib staysail, and jib. Tested machine gun battery."

Tolley pushed the *Lanikai* to its all-out speed of six knots. He had
worried unnecessarily about being sent out to observe, or even provoke,
a war.

Walking to the Fort Mills Station Hospital at Middleside on Corregidor, overlooking the Bay, Lieutenant Eunice F. Young met several
other nurses returning from early Mass at the chapel, and discovered
from them that war had begun. They went on together to the hospital,
where they began cutting gauze into bandages. Patients, even very sick
ones, insisted on getting out of bed and reporting for duty. Because
of the threat of air strikes, Lieutenant Young recalled, medical officers
activated contingency plans about moving the hospital. "In years before, sometime in the late 1920s or early 1930s, an emergency hospital

---

* Feary remembered the events in reverse, seeing Craigie leave; but Grew was first
to arrive.

had been set up underground. You walked to it through a tunnel. There were different laterals on each side. One was the hospital. We understood that there was medical equipment there ready for use, so we immediately started checking. We found nothing. There were no beds. There was no electricity hook-up. There was no running water. The electricians and everybody got immediately to work."

In Bacolod, Negros Occidental, where her family were the only Americans, Elizabeth Vaughan was up early and turned on the radio for the 6:15 news. "My world collapsed," she wrote. James Vaughan, an engineer, was away on a business trip. "I went to the telephone to call my husband in Manila to ask him how this would affect us, and to ask him not to wait to return the next day as planned, but [to leave] on the plane today, if possible."

She found all lines closed, except to the military. Four hours later there was a telegram from Jim transferring money and communicating "three words to torment me for days of waiting, 'Other telegram follows.' " Villagers in the Visayas sugarcane country panicked and hoarded anything they could find in the shops; false rumors of Japanese landings blocked the roads. There would be one telephone call from Jim Vaughan, who was soon in the Army in Luzon, and that was all. Elizabeth and her two children never saw him again. He died in a prisoner-of-war camp.

Captain Harold K. Johnson, later a prisoner of war on Bataan and long afterward an Army chief of staff, recalled hearing rumors in Manila the day before Pearl Harbor that an attack had been made on Hawaii. No one gave it much thought because "we were the prime target." The next morning at 6:30, while he was about to eat his breakfast, he received a telephone call: "Colonel Clarke wants you to alert the regiment and move it out of barracks." Captain A. J. Van Oosten assumed that Johnson knew there was a war on. He didn't, and responded skeptically, "Well, I'll tell you. I think with an order like that I probably ought to talk to Colonel Clarke. I wonder if you would put him on the line." What George C. Clarke had not told Van Oosten was that he had only heard the news on his radio, and had no instructions to do anything. "I received no orders from higher headquarters," he told an interviewer later from a hospital. "I never received an official report or directive that there was a war." Still, he didn't want his men in their beds when and if bombs fell.

Johnson listened and then moved quickly. "I could see, all during

Bataan and the prison camp days, those two fried eggs that were never consumed sitting there staring up at me from the breakfast plate."

When, as he did in the relative coolness of every morning, Jose Laurel drove his wife to Los Baños for her thermal bath, the countryside around Manila was still quiet. Wisps of smoke from the rice-cake ovens of roadside *tiendas* curled into the open windows of his car, and Laurel felt hungry, but he was a member of Quezon's Cabinet and knew he had to be at the office shortly. His car, which flew the small triangular green flag of the Civilian Emergency Administration, had a radio, but he had not turned it on.

His two youngest children, Doy* and Dodjie, were already at Mass at the Ateneo chapel, where the Immaculate Conception was being celebrated. As the service ended, a school official announced that the Philippines were at war: students were to go home at once, and not return until classes resumed. The Japanese, they were told, had already bombed several places in the islands. In the gloomy morning, redolent of rain, boys clutching choice belongings waited for family cars and drivers to pick them up.

Already working as Secretary of Justice before his official swearing-in the following week, the elder Laurel at fifty was Chief Justice of the Supreme Court. Politically ambitious, he was relinquishing the honor. (He would be President himself—under the Japanese occupation.) Listening to the war news while driving back to Manila, he understood that he was now a member of Quezon's war Cabinet. He could have been pardoned a qualm. Major General Basilio J. Valdez, chief of the Philippine Army, had his job because he was the President's personal physician. But it was a figurehead post; everyone expected Douglas MacArthur to run the war.

Carlos P. Romulo, soon to be an aide to MacArthur and later a Philippine foreign minister, was editor of the *Manila Herald*. He grumbled at being awakened early by his city editor, "Fatso" Intengan, with a report that the Japanese had bombed Hawaii. "You're crazy," Romulo charged. "Don't print anything as screwy as that!" But to be sure, he telephoned Jorge Vargas, who confirmed the news. Then Romulo telephoned MacArthur, whose private number he had; the general cultivated the press barons. "Carlos, it's here!" said MacArthur.

---

* Young Salvador Laurel, still in short pants at thirteen, would be Corazon Aquino's Vice-President after the ousting of Ferdinand Marcos.

Armando Malay, a newspaperman on the *Tribune* (and a postwar history professor), had no such august contacts and got his confirmation from Manila radio. Further corroboration came from excitable Constabulary gunners, who had begun firing at imaginary aircraft. Malay and his wife carried their baby to the basement and took refuge under the stairs. Then he had second thoughts. Assuming that there would be an extra printed, he wanted to be part of the action. Gulping a hasty breakfast, Malay rushed off to the *Tribune* office. The bus terminals were already crowded with evacuees, yet it was an hour to daylight.

•

When Jack Liddell, Chairman of the Shanghai Council, arrived at the International Settlement's Municipal Building, he found Japanese Consul-General Miura there with uniformed Japanese officers as well as several Britons and Americans with local duties. Ignoring Liddell, Miura took the chair and expressed the hope that normal life in Shanghai would continue. "Japanese forces will not interfere in the International Settlement," he explained, "except for detachments which will be posted at certain places in order to preserve security." The Japanese flag was to be flown and all other national flags removed. Cowed, the municipal officials agreed to remain, unless military interference made their task impossible. Meanwhile, carrying on kept them out of confinement.

One hundred ten miles east of Shanghai, the 15,000-ton *President Harrison*, en route from Manila to Tientsin to evacuate the Marine contingent, was spotted by a patrol plane, which signaled the ship to stop. Instead, the liner picked up speed. Flying on and spotting a friendly vessel, the Japanese plane dropped a message to the ferry *Nagasaki Maru*, forty-two miles away, to follow the *Harrison*. "You are asked to telegraph the fact to our base and keep watch on the ship."

Sighting the ferry as it closed in, and assuming that it was a warship, the *Harrison* turned west toward the mouth of the Yangtze. The *Nagasaki Maru* followed in hot pursuit, an unusual combat encounter between unarmed ships, ending when the liner ran aground on the muddy Yangtze flats. Captain Genzaburo Suge had already radioed their location, and a destroyer crew seized the helpless *Harrison*, the biggest prize of the day.

•

While men on the deck of the *Ford* watched the picket ship *Bulmer* up-anchor from the Manila Bay telephone buoy, three surfaced subs glided by, also heading out. The crews exchanged good-bye waves. At 6:45 a duty launch materialized in the brightening daylight to unload twenty quarts of ice cream; Ken Tillman signed a receipt for it. The delivery made it seem as if nothing had changed—except that men were taking down the *Ford*'s flammable awnings. Doggy Reynolds, Chief Bos'n Mate, watching the ice cream transaction, waited until the transfer was made, then told Tillman, "Guard the shipment like gold. It might be the last anyone on board would see." General Quarters sounded. They were to go into Condition Readiness Two, divided into work teams on four-hour intervals, day and night.

Without opposition and without MacArthur's headquarters even being aware of it, the first Japanese invasion of Philippine soil had already occurred. A day later he was still reporting to Washington that no landings had succeeded. The small force—the 24th Airfield Battalion—had left the Formosan port of Takao early Sunday afternoon. The short voyage to the Batan Islands, off the northern coast of Luzon, was to secure an emergency landing site for aircraft expected to soften up the Philippines for invasion. The two transports were escorted by a single destroyer, four torpedo boats, and so many smaller support vessels that young Florentino Hornedo, on Batan Island, largest in the chain, recalled that islanders thought the line of ships stretched all the way to Formosa.

When the Batanese realized what was happening, their fascination with the sight gave way to panic and many fled into the hills. Meanwhile, in what would become a Philippine pattern, Japanese collaborators emerged—small shopkeepers, vegetable farmers, fishermen, and boat maintenance workers, many who had married Filipino women and whose children used their mothers' local names. Some Japanese turned out to be covert officers, who broke out long-hidden uniforms.

Combat units in the landing force had little to do but take over the airfield near Basco. Construction crews began to improve the primitive landing strip even as the 24th and 50th fighter regiments began operations from it, and the presence of such short-range aircraft over Luzon misled American observers that Japanese carriers were offshore.

•

At Soldiers' and Sailors' Memorial Hall in Pittsburgh, nearly three hours into an enthusiastic America First meeting, Senator Gerald Nye was winding up his attacks on Roosevelt to approving shouts of "Treason!" and "Impeach him!" Suddenly he paused and confessed, "I have before me the worst news that I have encountered in the last twenty years. I don't know exactly how to report it to you; but I will report it to you just as a newspaperman gave it to me." Excited murmurs rippled through the hall.

Nye read Robert Hagy's note about Pearl Harbor, adding, "I can't somehow believe this. I can't come to any conclusions until I know what this is all about." And he went on to charge that when Roosevelt had addressed the nation on radio about the German attack on the destroyer *Greer*, and claimed that it was without provocation, "I tell you the *Greer* shot first. That was the incident the President said was unprovoked—and that's cheating." Roosevelt, he implied, may have cheated again.

America must not let communism "grow in the ruins," Nye exhorted to loud applause. "Keep your chins up!" he closed, sitting down to ringing cheers.

Vaulting to the platform, Hagy handed Nye a third scrap of news—that Roosevelt had called an evening meeting of congressional leaders, very likely to prepare a declaration of war for which the senator's vote, yea or nay, would be expected. Yet another Nye rally in Pittsburgh was coming up, an evening lay sermon at the First Baptist Church, where the pastor was an America First stalwart. Flustered and sweating, Nye mumbled vaguely, "I must, I must try . . . ," insisting as he left Memorial Hall that he would keep his church date, then catch a late train to Washington.

Faced with little choice, R. Douglas Stuart, Jr., who ran the America First headquarters on Jackson Boulevard in Chicago, prepared a statement recognizing the inevitability of a declaration of war and asked "all those who have subscribed to America First principles to give their support to the war effort of this country until the conflict *with Japan* is brought to a successful conclusion." It even pledged "aid to the President as Commander-in-Chief of the armed forces of the United States." Chapters were advised to postpone all scheduled rallies and to cease distribution of noninterventionist literature. Yet the language, complete to the conspicuous italics, carefully left the door open for further opposition to war with Germany.

The pledge to Roosevelt drew some bitter telegrams from diehards, and Stuart prepared a counter-telegram to all members of the national committee of America First, calling a meeting to determine the future, if any, for the organization. European war or not, most regional leaders, even more conservative and intemperate than the national board, would oppose closing down, hoping to use the organization as a weapon against socialism, unions, liberalism, Jews, and other allegedly alien influences.

Although Robert Wood's first bitter words to Lindbergh on the telephone were "Well, he's got us in through the back door," both of them knew that the Boston rally had to be scrapped. For Richard Moore, America First publicity director in Chicago, Lindbergh drafted a statement which effectively ended his activity against intervention. Although Roosevelt had provoked the war, Lindbergh charged, it had to be fought anyway. "We have been stepping closer to war for many months. Now it has come and we must meet it as united Americans regardless of our attitude in the past toward the policy our government has followed. Whether or not that policy has been wise, our country has been attacked. . . . Our own defences and our own military position have already been neglected too long. We must now turn every effort to building the greatest and most efficient army, navy and air force in the world." It admitted no error but failure.

Occupying themselves in the club car while their train churned across the plains of Kansas toward California, Orson Welles and Pare Lorentz wondered if they had already drunk too much when the radio at the bar blared the news about Pearl Harbor. There was no place to go and nothing they could do, Welles remembered. They "stayed there the rest of the day and night drinking and listening to the news with mixed feelings of exhilaration and terror."* By the time that Milton Caniff, traveling in the other direction, and by air, arrived in Washington from Los Angeles, the country was at war. Still, the Chemical

---

* Their film would never be completed. Criticism of the assembly line was suddenly inappropriate. The two actors they had signed in New York would go off to war instead of to Hollywood. One was killed at Iwo Jima. The other, Robert Ryan, survived to become a postwar star.

Warfare man who had contacted him was waiting. "We just sat there at the Fairfax Hotel and finished this thing. They printed it in one night and got it out to the West Coast. We were doing it, step by step, in a cartoon style, easily understood. If you're hit by a fire bomb, this is what to do."

•

It took until 11:27 for General Martin to get four A-20s at devastated Hickam Field off the ground, ordering them "to find the carrier that was south of Barber's Point." All they found after an hour were American ships that had escaped from Pearl Harbor, in the process misidentifying them as Japanese. Aboard the *Portland*, Vice-Admiral Wilson Brown, ordered to "get" an enemy carrier, replied to headquarters that his cruiser had been bombed. "This afternoon?"

"Yes," he radioed. "A plane dropped two bombs, narrowly missing me astern." Very likely it was one of the eager A-20s.

When Captain Brooke Allen managed to get a B-17 in the air from Hickam, he was also ordered south, against his better judgment. Although no one awake at eight o'clock could have missed the incoming direction of the Japanese raiders, north to south, Army and Navy brass stubbornly explored below Oahu for *Kido Butai*. At first their hunch looked good to Allen. He sighted "this beautiful carrier," which fired at him. Since the Japanese had no four-engined bombers, the ship, logically, had to be an enemy vessel. He went into a bomb run and then pulled away, realizing that it was the *Enterprise*, alive with jumpy gunners. He swung about once more, only to find the *Enterprise* again, and decided to go home.

If any proof were needed of the direction from which the enemy had come, it turned up when a map was recovered from the body of a downed Japanese pilot. On it were courses plotted to a point northwest of Oahu, apparently the rendezvous location of carriers and planes. Too late, Martin sent up more aircraft.

By noon, "Brigham" Young had collected the nine surviving SBDs of his *Enterprise* flight—five were downed, one crashed, three too damaged to fly—and sent them up from chaotic Ford Island to cover the seas north and northwest of Oahu to a distance of 175 miles. He had his bearings right, but Nagumo's flattops were beyond range. The planes turned back.

•

Reporters packed the White House pressroom at 5:58 P.M., this time permitted microphones and even newsreel cameras. Klieg lights bathed everyone in perspiration. "I call you in," said Steve Early, "to tell you that both the War and Navy Departments, since the first report [of attacks on the Philippines], have been endeavoring to get in touch with commanding officers in Manila, and have been unable to do so." The President was "disposed to believe . . . that the first report was an erroneous one." But Early had more news that he did not know was equally erroneous. The President had just received a telephone call from Governor Poindexter in Honolulu, who reported "heavy damages and loss of life" in the city and said that "a second wave of planes was just then coming over." Poindexter had been as excitable as anyone on Oahu. Those in the office near Roosevelt heard the governor shriek, "My God! There's another wave of Jap planes over Hawaii right this moment!" The second wave had long come and gone; any activity in the Hawaiian skies consisted of nervous gunners firing at imaginary enemies. The minor damage in Honolulu itself continued to result from erratic and badly fused American AA shells.

Just after noon in Honolulu—5:30 in Washington—the shaken Poindexter had taken a call at his home from General Short. Martial law would be invoked, and it was up to the governor to sign the proclamation. The emergency he had declared had not gone far enough. Poindexter wanted White House approval, he said; he was only a territorial governor, a presidential appointee. But it had taken nearly half an hour to get through to Roosevelt, and throughout the call the harried governor was badgered by the Navy censor, who had demanded at the start, "What are you going to talk about?" The President approved of whatever Poindexter wanted to do, and martial law officially took effect at 3:45 P.M. Hawaii time. Civil government affairs became the responsibility of the Hawaiian Department's judge advocate general, Lieutenant Colonel Thomas H. Green.

At the FBI office, Robert Shivers discovered that no one was guarding the Hawaiian consulates, which still had telephone service. He pressed the Honolulu police into doing something. Until 12:30, no one but an inquiring reporter from the *Star-Bulletin* had looked in on Consul Kita, who professed no knowledge of any attack. He was promised a copy of the first "extra."

The police found Kita in the driveway with his *Star-Bulletin*. Inside the consulate Yoshikawa and an assistant were burning papers. Unaware of events, Honolulu cabbie John Mikami pulled up to take Kita and Vice-Consul Okuda to play golf. Mikami had to announce himself via a policeman, who emerged with a message that Okuda and Kita would be unable to play.

TOKYO	BANGKOK	TOBRUK	PEARL HARBOR
8:00 A.M.	6:00 A.M.	Midnight	12:30 P.M.
December 8	December 8	December 7/8	December 7

HOUR 35

AT 9:30 A.M. on the 8th, Australian army trucks began moving troops from Port Moresby, New Guinea, to Paga Hill, the Fixed Defence site. W. E. Prentice, a Brisbane volunteer, had arrived with his unit only two days earlier on the former holiday vessel *Katoomba*. The only reminder of war while they threaded their way inside the Great Barrier Reef for security was the gray bulk of their escort, the cruiser *Adelaide*. Holiday routine on board ship had prevailed, even to peacetime printed menus for the Dining Saloon. Dinner for the 5th had included "Poached Grouper, Roast Quarter of Lamb and Corned Brisket of Beef." Beer was sixpence a glass. When the *Katoomba* entered the harbor, the atmosphere became even more holiday-like. Young Papuan boys paddled up to the ship and shouted to the artillerymen, "Throw a penny long way!" Surfeited with beer, the troops obliged, and "many small dark boys would dive a long way, their white hands and the white bottoms of their feet showing clearly until the coin was captured."

As Prentice prepared to leave the *Katoomba*, word swept through the ship that Pearl Harbor had been bombed, news confirmed by

American cargo ships huddled in the harbor in the morning mist. Soldiers waiting in the gloom to disembark watched as an amphibian Catalina took off between lines of float-flares. The plane rose and disappeared; then there was "a sudden red flash" and Major Baker, Prentice's C.O., said, "Poor fellows!" Loaded with officers returning to Australia to confer about strategy, the Catalina had not cleared the hills. There were no survivors. War had come to New Guinea. With few modern weapons at home, and none of its seasoned troops, Australia had only distance between it and the Japanese. East Asian commands had been promised by Churchill "three months warning of any serious explosion in the Far East," but that had been empty rhetoric. Curtin could take comfort only in the new battle fleet at Singapore.

Presiding as both Prime Minister and Minister for Defence, Curtin put the Cabinet on record "that the situation should be accepted as involving a state of war against Japan." H. V. Evatt, Minister for External Affairs, reported that the Japanese minister in Canberra had asked permission to cable Tokyo in code, and the request had been denied. "All such communications are to be in plain language." They reviewed the disposition of shipping and labor union disputes delaying the unloading and deploying of war materiel at Darwin, suddenly Australia's front line to the north. The Minister for Labour and the Conciliation Commissioner were ordered "to proceed by air to Darwin immediately." Christmas leave for Services personnel and for workers in munitions industries was ordered canceled, and war production accelerated.

As a Melbourne cyclist was shouting to people on the streets, "The Japs are at us!" and the War Cabinet was meeting in emergency session, John Curtin stepped outside to tell reporters that the events of the morning were "a new war." Going-to-work crowds surged around newspaper offices countrywide, then listened to radios, at work and at home, as the prime minister labeled Japan "an assassin in the night." Looking beyond Malaya and the Indies he called for courage and determination and declared, "Australia is the stake in this contest." Recruiting depots reported their busiest day of the war. In Perth, where the sun had barely risen, hundreds queued up before darkened depots to enlist. The recruiting staff arrived as usual at nine. "I've been meaning to join up for some time," a volunteer told an early-bird reporter, "but the war has come so close that a man must get in it now." His home town, the only major city in Western Australia, was as close to Singapore as to Sydney or Melbourne. The war poster exhorting, "This is Serious!" had taken on a new reality.

•

Balding and bespectacled, mustached and addicted to old-fashioned high collars, Sir Robert Craigie was one of His Majesty's senior ambassadors. A career Foreign Office official, Craigie at fifty-three had been envoy to Japan since 1937, an appointee of Prime Minister Neville Chamberlain, as was obvious from the ambassador's constant exhortations that timely concessions to Japanese pressure were all that would keep war away. In November 1941 war warnings from the stately columned embassy in Tokyo were frequent, and on December 1 he had reported a conversation that his Georgia-born wife, Pleasant (daughter of an American diplomat, Pleasant Stovall), had with the wife of a Japanese Cabinet minister who had confided that "no one on earth can prevent war nowadays." The message went to Singapore as well as to London.

At 7:45 on Monday morning Craigie had received a telephoned request that he call upon the Foreign Minister at eight. Why he assumed that he was to receive a declaration of war yet never turned on his radio or asked any embassy functionary to do so is inexplicable, but he rushed out and was received as usual by Mr. Kasé. Handing Craigie a long memorandum identified as a copy of one just given to Ambassador Grew—the very paper Kurusu and Nomura had delivered to Cordell Hull—Kasé explained that it documented why Japan had just broken off negotiations in Washington.

Scanning it hurriedly for any reference to war or to Britain, Craigie found nothing; and to Togo, who had just ushered Grew out and led Craigie upstairs, the ambassador expressed polite puzzlement. What about the reports "which had been broadcast on the British wireless late the previous evening that Japanese warships and transports were proceeding across the Gulf of Siam?" If true, these carried "the most serious implications."

According to Togo, reports had reached Japan of "large concentrations of British and Indian troops on the frontier of Siam, disposed for purposes of attack, and that Japanese warships had accordingly been ordered to patrol off the coast of Indo-China." Protesting, Craigie recalled that on the 5th he had guaranteed that Britain would not violate Thai territory as long as Japan respected Thai independence.

Japanese forces in the area, he charged, were not acting on their own initiative but were "fully controlled by Tokyo."

Ushering the ambassador out, Togo assured Craigie that he had worked hard to settle differences amicably, and "regretted that things should now have come to such a pass."

None too quickly, Craigie began to suspect "that something more serious was afoot," but it was only when he returned to the Embassy (the whole transaction had taken less than twenty minutes) that he was "met by Pleasant with the news that the Japanese wireless had announced that warlike operations against Britain and the United States had commenced." Both Lady Craigie and Embassy Counsellor Paul Gore-Booth had already begun burning whatever codes and confidential papers remained (some had been previously destroyed), and members of the staff living outside the compound were being telephoned, an operation that ended abruptly when the lines were cut at 8:30. Carrying bedrolls and suitcases, employees were already rushing for the assumed safety of the compound.

Long at his desk, Vere Redman, the press attaché, had arrived as usual just after five to prepare what Craigie described as "the excellent little news sheet which the Embassy issued and circulated daily to counteract the German propaganda and to carry the war into the enemy's camp." Just before telephone lines to the embassy were cut, Mrs. Redman had appealed that she was being held at her flat by gendarmes as hostage for her husband. Sir Robert sent his wife after Mrs. Redman, with C. H. Johnston, his Third Secretary, instructed to remain in the car.

Belying her name, Pleasant Craigie made a scene until the police let her go up to see for herself that Mrs. Redman had come to no harm, but she remained a hostage. With the embassy gates still open, Craigie sent W. E. Houston-Boswall, his counsellor, to the Foreign Ministry to demand her release. Outside the embassy more gendarmes were gathering.

•

Boat day and mail day at the North Borneo (now Sabah) oil port of Sandakan, on the far eastern coast, was Monday. Agnes and Harry Keith were up early to wait for news and supplies from Singapore. Worried about a Japanese invasion, they had stocked a jungle hideout with food, bedding, clothes, even books and the family silver; but as war came closer they had abandoned any idea of escape, realizing that their fate might be worse if caught that way. Leaving Borneo altogether meant abandoning a way of life they liked: "I believed completely in the rightness of my staying," Mrs. Keith wrote; ". . . it was the only thing for *me* to do."

At 6:00 A.M., while they were drinking the first coffee of the morning, they heard about Pearl Harbor—but not about relatively nearby Malaya—on the radio and informed the servants. "Maybe very good, Missee," said their houseman, Ah Yin. "Now America fight." Then he thought further about the Keiths' year-old son, George. "Missee!" he urged. "You take Mistah Groge and go home! Singapore boat go today. If Japs come here, very bad!"

Everyone in the expatriate colony "was writing mail madly" in order to get it out on what might be the last boat. "Also people kept an eye on the sky, and ears cocked for planes. A few women were packing hurriedly; they were getting out."

Eventually "the radio air was full of messages of condolence from Home Offices to besieged garrisons and falling states that were crumbling to bits unaided. 'Good-bye. Be of good cheer. We are sorry we cannot help you. You are doing your duty. God bless you.' " It had not yet come to that, but Agnes Keith "couldn't believe that if the Japanese did take Borneo they would [be able to] hold it more than six months." Then the good world they knew would be restored to them.

·

Befitting the occasion, the Emperor appeared in naval uniform for the Privy Council meeting in the Imperial Palace at eight. All thirty-two members stood, then bowed from the waist. Hirohito walked to his elevated place at the head of one of the two long tables in the chamber, then sat down.

By the Japanese constitution of 1889, treaty-making and war-making were the prerogative of the Emperor and not within the power of the elected Diet. The Emperor also possessed supreme command of the armed forces. In practice he exercised his authority only on the advice of the Cabinet and the Privy Council, neither of which was responsible to the Diet. However godlike, Hirohito reigned; he did not rule.

The Privy Council had the constitutional duty of ratifying all treaties and laws, but the authority was largely empty. Nearly half the Privy Council's members were members of the Cabinet. Most appointees owed their seats to a prime minister's clout, and the armed services in effect had a veto over the prime minister who could not form a Cabinet if no senior officer would serve. (The Army and Navy ministers in the Cabinet had to be a general and an admiral.) By Tojo's time the military had secured such dominance that he was both Army Minister and Prime Minister.

The Emperor, along with the Council president, Yoshimichi Hara, and the elderly vice-president, Admiral Baron Kantaro Suzuki, sat at one table. At the other sat the Prime Minister and thirteen-member Cabinet. Hara, who had been skeptical about war as a route to Japan's economic goals, chaired the meeting.

Tojo counted on the accomplished facts and quick successes to lead to prompt ratification of the war rescript. Hara read the draft aloud as each member followed the text in his copy. As he finished, two members indicated a desire to speak, an unusual circumstance in matters so moot. The Netherlands Indies went unmentioned, went one objection. Tojo responded that they had not yet been attacked. "We hereby declare war on America and England," objected another councillor to the opening of the second paragraph, was "improper for a country like Japan, which puts so much emphasis on politeness and courtesy." "America," he meant, was not a political entity. Several speakers, including Foreign Minister Togo, defended the text. The Emperor, in whose name it was to be promulgated, said nothing.

Hara solved both problems from the chair. "Do we certify," he asked, "that this nation is now legally at war with the United States, the British Empire, and the Kingdom of the Netherlands? And do we approve His Majesty's most gracious transcript as it *now* stands?"

There was a murmur of assent. Hara declared the vote unanimous. Hirohito rose and left the room.

Also at each place were copies of Roosevelt's message to the Emperor, the long Japanese memorandum to Washington breaking off negotiations, and the war rescript. The President's message, this time, was an exact translation, nothing missing. That had not always been the case. On December 2, with the strike force sailing steadily south-southeast, what would be the last Hull counterproposal had been put before the Imperial Conference. Hull's requirements had remained tough—Japanese withdrawal from their conquests—but such qualifying language in his preamble as "This is a basis for negotiation" and "This is a tentative plan"—had been censored out, and the most militant portion of the Japanese position also deleted, to furnish the impression of Japanese flexibility and American intransigence.*

•

In a four-story building on Shanghai Street in Kowloon, Lao Wu, a shipyard laborer, awoke at seven in the back room of his flat and shook his eldest son, Tai Ngau (Big Cow) Wu, a shipyard apprentice, awake. They went into the kitchen to brush their teeth, Lao Wu wondering aloud whether there would be any work with so many ships gone from the harbor. "It's a small thing if we don't have work," said Big Cow, "but it is unthinkable if war really starts." The men he worked with had told him that a Japanese invasion "was just a matter of sooner or later."

Ma Wu, his mother, had overheard, and sighed, "If the Japanese devils really reach Hong Kong, it will be very miserable for us! I only hope that it won't happen!"

In the front room their boarder, Tak-yen Lau, a clerk in a foreign firm, was putting on his necktie. "Don't be afraid," he consoled Mrs. Wu. "How can the Japanese dare to fight with England? England is a powerful country and has a formidable navy. And there's an alliance with America. Many foreigners come to Hong Kong to trade and to invest their money. Just look at the prosperity of Hong Kong! Even the rich are not afraid, so why should we be afraid?"

Listening from the middle room, the lady boarder, Mrs. Li, scoffed at the easy optimism. "Last night when I went to watch a movie, the subtitles suddenly called for the emergency reporting to duty of the Navy, Army and Air Force. What more tension could you want? I was so afraid that I didn't dare watch the film to the finish. I rushed home."

"It's just battle practice," said Lau, "just for show. You have to get used to it. To tell the truth, at a time when it is chaotic everywhere in the world, we can't say that we're not lucky living in stability in Hong Kong!" Then he went into the lavatory and closed the door with a bang.

* In 1951 the diplomat and later prime minister Shigeru Yoshida disclosed the doctoring of the exchanges, intended to leave the impression "that only the American position was being maintained in a one-sided manner."

Big Cow shook his head. "That man," he said, "really dreams his life away."

"Don't bother about people like him," said Wu. "If the Japanese really start a war here, it will be great trouble for us."

Shaking his fist, Big Cow vowed to help repel the Japanese. His shipyard cronies said the Japanese devils had to be resisted.

Mrs. Wu hushed him with the outstretched palm of her hand. "Big Cow, there are Japanese spies everywhere. If they hear you, it will be serious!"

Old Wu led his son off toward the shipyard. They looked for a bus to the Star Ferry docks, to cross to the island. Mrs. Li descended to find her young daughter and son, and escort them to school. Her husband, a sailor, was at sea. Going to the window, Mrs. Wu shouted, "Father of Big Cow, on your way back from work, buy twenty catties of rice if you have the money."

It was about eight when they parted at the junction.

•

More fortunate than Shiro Kozawa and Shingo Kozawa, his two associates at Echigoya and Co., Kurahachi Fukuda was arrested in a police raid on Japanese nationals in Singapore at 6:00 A.M. rather than in the first sweep at 3:15. "All our neighbors," he noted in his diary, were in custody. "We have no time to do anything. . . . All the keys of the firm and domestic ones have been taken with me to the police. During the time in the cab before the final depart[ure] we have fortunately saw our ayah and paid [her] $30 salary for the month of December. . . . We are taken to police station at Beach Road and then to the Immigration Dept. at East Wharf . . . where we all met."*

•

As dawn approached in Bangkok, Premier Phibun's whereabouts were still unknown. Since the Japanese knew where the border incident

---

* Later in the day all 176 Japanese males picked up were shipped to Changi Prison, a bleak, gray cement-block-walled enclosure in eastern Singapore. Nearly two hundred more would be added from Malaya. When the surrender of Singapore came in February, the conquerors used Changi as a detention camp—according to memories of occupants one of the most infamous in Japanese control. By then Fukuda had been shipped to internment in India, where the camp commandant confiscated his diary.

had taken place and had not located the Premier in the vicinity, they assumed that his investigatory trip was a fabrication. Still, Japanese military movements were now like an uncoiling spring that could not be wound back. With no orders for the Bangkok embassy to the plane due to fly over for instructions, officials wondered how to signal neutrality. A racecourse was across the avenue; several Japanese ran across to it and pulled down a cloth banner. As they were spreading it out, the plane roared past and flew south; Thai policemen, seeing the unusual activity, rushed over, snatched the stolen banner, and arrested several onlookers. A Japanese military attaché pursued the Thai police in his car; meanwhile the plane returned and circled several times without perceiving any message.

The chase over, embassy personnel returned indoors to a flurry of bulletins—that Japanese landing near Bangkok harbor had skirmished with Thai police, and that soldiers in the south were resisting the Kra landings. From Tokyo they heard radio broadcasts about the "brilliant attack on Pearl Harbor" and the successful operations to the south. "Our faces flushed," Lieutenant Colonel Iwaichi Fujiwara, an agent at the embassy recalled; "our eyes brimmed with tears, and our bodies were shaken with the exciting news. The national anthem and the military march broadcast at the beginning and the end of the newscast stirred up our feelings even more."

Sleeping poorly, Sir Josiah Crosby was up and out of bed instantly when a caller was announced in the morning darkness. A member of the local British community had heard "from a reliable source" that the Japanese had landed troops in southern Thailand as well as nearer Bangkok, at Bang Poo, a seaside town near the mouth of the Bangkok River. "Whilst it dismayed me," the veteran diplomat recalled in 1945, "I was not astounded by it; . . . the possibility of a Japanese invasion of British territory through Siam had never been absent."

Although he had expected the Japanese, he had resisted the Matador plan. Entreating the authorities in Malaya not to activate it, he raised fears that it would be Japan's excuse to pour through Thailand to save the nation from the British aggressor. He had staved off nothing; the Japanese needed no provocation, and he had hobbled his own side.

Suddenly he thought of the safety of the British population in Bangkok, which he hoped to evacuate into Burma or upper Malaya.

He applied to see the Foreign Minister, but was put off until the afternoon.

•

Timed for 8:30 P.M., the British advance in Libya was mounted by several units, including the 23rd Brigade, the 1st Durham Light Infantry, and the 4th Border Division, augmented by New Zealanders. Two Italian divisions, the Trento and the Pavia, held positions defending Bir el Azazi. Unlike many other Italian units, rated low even by Mussolini, the Pavia Division fought a stubborn rear-guard action, but after midnight the armor of the 32nd Tanks Brigade overcame the Pavias. At a cost of 11 killed and 25 wounded, the Durhams took 150 prisoners, and many guns. The XXX Corps had drawn away the enemy's main force, making possible the Tobruk garrison's ending its own encirclement after 242 days. Although Gen. Claude Auchinleck would declare the siege over as of December 7, Tobruk had not been relieved as much as abandoned by the Germans. While Hitler had drawn airpower from Russia to cover a sea route for resupplying the Afrika Korps, the planes were not yet in place. A new threat to Tobruk was to come.

•

Because of static, Captain H. H. Smith-Hutton, the American military attaché in Tokyo, could not get KGEI in San Francisco on his radio, and over breakfast listened to Shanghai. Tuning in late, he missed the first bulletins. The announcer was advising Americans on the recommendation of the consul general to stay off the streets and to remain calm. Smith-Hutton told his wife, Jane, that something unusual had happened in Shanghai; perhaps the embassy personnel would know more.

It was a two-minute walk to the embassy, which they entered through the garage. Passing the office of the naval attaché, Smith-Hutton saw a crowd around the radio. "Have you heard?" said a colleague. "San Francisco radio says the Japanese have attacked Pearl Harbor."

He confessed that he hadn't heard, and rushed into his own office to call Grew, who found the news hard to believe. He had left the Foreign Minister only fifteen minutes earlier, said Grew; Togo had not mentioned war. Why not check with the Japanese Navy? All they needed to do was turn on local radio, but Smith-Hutton ordered his car and was chauffeured through quiet streets about four blocks to the Navy Department. Asking for Rear Admiral Ryozo Nakamura, aide to the Navy Minister, he was escorted to "the usual waiting room," where Nakamura appeared. Was there any truth to the report? Smith-Hutton asked. If so, when would a declaration of war be issued?

The admiral looked "rather sad," in keeping with his oft-declared friendship for the U.S., and confessed that the report was accurate. He had just learned of it himself. A declaration of war, however, was a Foreign Office matter, and he was sure that the embassy would soon be informed. Personally, he added, he was not happy about it.

"I told him I wasn't either, and I said this might be the last time I would see him. I hoped he would survive the war. He said he hoped the same for me." Customarily they parted in the waiting room, but the admiral escorted Smith-Hutton down the staircase and saw him to his car.

At the Foreign Office, just after Grew had seen Togo, Eugene Dooman was taken in to see the Vice Minister, and asked for confirmation of the NHK broadcast that Japanese planes had bombed Pearl Harbor. "Mr. Dooman," he apologized, "I regret that I am not authorized to say anything."

Since it was still short of nine, opening hour for the embassy, Dooman asked Oyama to drive through Marunouchi, the financial and business district of Tokyo. People were now hurrying as usual to work, emptying out of streetcars and buses and railway stations. The sidewalks were crowded. "The usual babble of talk and laughter," Dooman thought wishfully, "was gone. . . . Having satisfied myself that there was no spontaneous rejoicing . . . , I went to the Embassy and found the gate closed. Policemen on duty . . . told me that I was to return to my house and remain there until I had word that I would be allowed to enter the Embassy."

•

Returning nearly empty-handed from MacArthur, Brereton took a radiophone scrambler call at Nielson Field from his chief in Washington, "Hap" Arnold. Brereton explained his plans, and Arnold filled him in on Pearl Harbor, so that, as Arnold later explained, Brereton would not be caught in the same way and have his "entire air force destroyed."

There were already a flurry of reports of Japanese flights over Luzon, Brereton said. He was sending his planes up.

With daylight, the Philippine Constabulary found that the first things dropped by Japanese aircraft were leaflets. "When we liberate you," one promised, "never again will you be aliens in your own land."

.

Yoko Matsuoka's husband, Takashi, left for work at the Domei Agency at eight o'clock as usual. The American-educated Yoko, recently married at twenty-four, had returned to traditional ways in Japan, serving a breakfast of hot, fermented soybean soup in which white bean curd and bits of scallion floated, a bowl of steaming rice, dark green seaweed, an assortment of pickles, and green tea. The little coal stove tended by her mother—the young couple lived with her parents—faintly warmed the room. The ambience was very different from what she remembered of Swarthmore College.

For a house in which two newsmen resided—her father was an editor of the *Mainichi Shimbun*—it was surprisingly without a radio. Yoko was still cleaning the kitchen table when the telephone rang and she heard the excited voice of her husband, whom she had seen only ten minutes before. He was at the railway station, where he had discovered that Japan was at war. "The news must have broken early this morning. I shall probably have to work until late tonight."

Yoko's seven years in Ohio and Pennsylvania whirled past her eyes. "How incredible!" she thought, as she hung up the telephone. "Why did we start a war we cannot possibly win?"

Her father had not yet left. He changed from breakfast kimono to business suit and hurried to his office, from which he telephoned her. "Our Navy has attacked Singapore, Manila and Hawaii. And we were successful." He sounded relaxed. He had often talked about "the yoke of white imperialism." Her mother "went about her household chores with her usual self-confidence."

American-educated Sumie Seo Mishima, who had returned to Tokyo to marry in 1932, was at breakfast with her husband when, turning the radio dials, he caught the war news. "They've done it!" he shouted excitedly. She "shuddered all over" but could not argue with him. "All that day I was startled by the slightest noise. . . . Somehow it never occurred to me to ask whether Japan would win or lose. I could not associate such sporting terms . . . with the terrible tragedy of a world war."

•

Expecting his leave to be shortened, Private First Class Walter M. Letteer of the 26th Infantry Regiment was not surprised when a Western Union messenger turned up at his door in Rochester, New York. "YOUR FURLOUGH CANCELLED," the yellow form read. "RETURN BY SUNDAY MIDNIGHT. GENERAL ROOSEVELT." Brigadier General Theodore Roosevelt, Jr., was his regimental commander—in Fort Devens, Massachusetts. There was no way he could return in time. Then Letteer looked up. The messenger was still waiting. The telegram had been sent collect, and Letteer owed 53¢ from his soldier's pay of $21 a month.

In Washington, messages poured in to headquarters of the services from men on leave wondering where to go. Some rushed back to their camps to find that their units had already left for parts unknown. At the Navy Department, calls about losses seemed to come in from Admiral Bloch at Pearl Harbor every few minutes. Captain McCrea listened on Admiral Stark's extension, taking down notes and recording each message. Stark had been taking them himself to Frank Knox—an opportunity each visit to carry away fresh instructions. This time he looked at McCrea's grim memorandum and said, "You take this down to the Secretary. I think he's seen enough of me today."

A receptionist let McCrea in. He coughed a few times to attract attention. Knox poked his head out of the little bathroom attached to his office. "Oh," he said; "Captain, it's you."

"Yes, Mr. Secretary."

"This has been quite an afternoon."

"Yes it has."

"You know," Knox confided after his furtive trip to the bathroom, "I'm just mixing myself a drink. Would you join me?"

It was obvious that Knox would need a drink even more after seeing the new message, and McCrea was not going to stand in the way. "Well, Mr. Secretary," he confessed, "I've never taken a drink in the Navy Department [before], but being invited by the Secretary, it's almost a command."

"So with that," McCrea recalled, "the two of us stood there in the little bathroom and drank Mr. Knox's bourbon."

•

Where there was less information, the atmosphere was more heady. At the Majestic, on Elm Street in downtown Dallas, the war news was flashed on the screen during the second daily showing of *Sergeant York*. The applause and cheering were thunderous.

•

As soon as Lieutenant General Korechika Anami learned of the state of war with Britain and the United States, he went to his office at Bukan University in Hankow, taken over as headquarters for his Eleventh Army, and ordered the seizure of all enemy property. Like other major cities of China, Hankow, although deep in the interior, a thousand miles from Shanghai, had its international quarter. A bustling Yangtze port and industrial complex, Hankow could load oceangoing vessels. Japanese cruisers had steamed up the broad Yangtze during the four-and-a-half month siege in 1938 to blast government forces away, and Anami's 75,000 men remained as a garrison for central China. Frustrated that there was no immediate combat role for him, Anami nevertheless dictated a telegram to Emperor Hirohito, whom he had once served as aide-de-camp: "I will do my best and happily die for you."

For the moment his duties were far less glamorous. He ordered the British and American citizens in Hankow assembled. "I want you to be calm," he told the worried group, most of them routed from their beds. (It was only 7:30 A.M.) "I promise that your safety will be guaranteed if you make no trouble. But if you do anything harmful to the Japanese cause, you will be put under strict control."

Then he had the important Chinese businessmen gathered. "I think all of you understand the significance of this war," he announced. "Japan's purpose is still the same as it has been—to establish a co-prosperity sphere throughout Asia. I strongly urge you to put your trust in Japanese military power. And I caution you not to be agitated or tempted by enemy propaganda."

Back at his office he received a report from his Control Section that the confiscation of enemy property was proceeding without incident. There was, however, a problem with the Chinese tobacco vendors, who wanted to close their shops although they had not received any directive to shut down. A delegation of vendors had arrived to see him. They sold mostly British and American cigarettes, enemy brands.

"Do you think that matters to me?" Anami said. "There is no need for you to close your shops. I want you to remain open and go about your business as before." He sighed with relief at having made, at last, an important administrative decision. He smoked imported cigarettes and detested the Japanese variety.

His chief of staff, Major General Isamu Kinoshita, came in with the latest war news—Guam, Wake, Hawaii, Malaya. "How about Hong Kong?" Anami asked. It was a thousand miles south of Hankow, but the closest real action.

Kinoshita reported that the Twenty-third Army was on the move. "I wonder," Anami mused aloud, "what we could do to help down there?" But there was nothing he could do there, or anywhere else. The vastness of China had overwhelmed him. All he could do was protect his personal supply of tobacco, then return home, pick up his powerful bow, and aim arrows at the straw target in his garden.

•

Admirals Kusaka and Nagumo had been fending off requests for a third wave over Pearl Harbor when Mitsuo Fuchida landed. Even a burglar, Nagumo warned, hesitates to go back for more. From the *Soryu*, Rear Admiral Tamon Yamaguchi had reported that both the *Hiryu* and *Soryu* were ready to go again; the skipper of the *Kaga* recommended, at the urging of his pilots, that fuel tanks and other service installations should be bombed. Commander Takahisa Amagai, the flight deck officer of the *Hiryu*, had seen the results of AA fire against the second wave. Less enthusiastic about returning than chancing a surprise attack elsewhere, Amagai suggested, ambitiously, "We're not returning to Tokyo; now we're going to head for San Francisco."

A landing on any of the Hawaiian group had never been part of the plan. Manpower was stretched thin for the other operations, and no one had thought in any case that Hawaii could be won and held. Suddenly it looked easy. Fuchida tallied up what he observed, a litany of sinkings and crippled ships, and one hundred or more planes destroyed on the ground.

Nagumo appeared satisfied. He had delivered a disabling thrust. "We may then conclude," he said, "that anticipated results have been achieved."

"All things considered," Fuchida countered, arguing hard, "we have achieved a great amount of destruction, but it would be unwise to assume that we have destroyed everything. There are still many targets remaining that should be hit. I recommend that another attack be launched." He wanted to deny the Pacific Fleet its support facilities, forcing it back to the mainland. Scratched from a torpedo bomber because of illness, Minoru Genda, Yamamoto's architect of the operation, wanted to attack "again and again." American military capacity in Hawaii had to be crushed. But Genda was known for his aerobatic teams in the Imperial Navy Air Corps—"Genda's Circus." To senior officers—Genda was thirty-seven—he had a daredevil disposition.*

Kusaka observed that the enemy carriers had not been located; they posed a threat that could materialize overhead at any time. Hadn't *Kido Butai* inflicted as much damage as hoped for? Was the little more they could do worth the risk of the fleet? Enemy return fire, Nagumo added, proved "surprisingly prompt even though we took them by surprise; another attack would meet stronger opposition and our losses would certainly be disproportionate to the additional destruction which might be inflicted." Further, he felt wary of remaining so long within the range of big land-based bombers. He knew there were Flying Fortresses on Oahu. (They would prove ineffective against moving ships.)

Kusaka agreed, suggesting an immediate turnabout to the northwest as planned. "The attack is terminated. We are withdrawing."

"Please do," said Nagumo.

The appropriate signal flags were run up the *Akagi*'s yardarm shortly after one o'clock Hawaiian time. *Kido Butai* swung about.

Aboard the *Nagato*, Admiral Yamamoto learned of the decision shortly before nine in the morning by Tokyo reckoning. He had expected it, and his feelings were mixed. That his enthusiasm for the results of the strike was less than complete is clear from the sardonic *waka* he composed. A classical verse form of thirty-one syllables ar-

---

* Genda in the 1950s would be the first chief of staff of Japan's Air Self-Defense Force under the new constitution, then a five-term member of the upper house of the Diet. In 1962 he was awarded the United States Legion of Merit medal for his postwar military leadership role. He died at eighty-four in 1989.

ranged in five lines, he adapted it to his zest for bridge, the most innocent of his gambling compulsions:

> What I have achieved
> Is far from a grand slam,
> Let me in all modesty declare.
> It is more like
> A redoubled bid just made.

That no aircraft carriers were disabled had to have been particularly frustrating to an air-minded admiral who knew how much they represented offensive capacity in modern war. But there was more, as he wrote cautiously to a close friend: "If we had known that air units alone could achieve so much in the Hawaii operation, we wouldn't have used just air units. . . . We didn't know that at the time, and it can't be helped." During the short-term impotence and confusion in Hawaii that had followed the attack, the Japanese might have seized one or more of the indefensible islands, possibly even vulnerable Oahu itself. At the very least, isolated Midway Island might have been taken. Since Yamamoto had rejected invasion ideas as too risky, he had made the future Battle of Midway inevitable.

•

In a subdued mood, at 7:35 A.M., the *Ford*'s section that had been on weekend liberty returned, with news from Manila radio and from the rumor mills of Cavite. A new watch was already waiting to take over: there were still no orders to depart; a lighter was en route with meat and vegetables. But other submarines nestled alongside the oiler *Pecos*, taking on fuel before heading for the open sea.

MANILA	BANGKOK	MALAYA	PEARL HARBOR
HONG KONG	7:00 A.M.	SINGAPORE	1:30 P.M.
PEKING	December 8	6:40 A.M.	December 7
8:00 A.M.		December 8	
December 8			

HOUR 36

THE NEWS CONFERENCE for members of the foreign press not rounded up as "enemy agents" was held at nine in an old wooden structure that housed the Foreign Ministry. The War and Naval ministries had handsome buildings, but foreign affairs had little clout in Tokyo. On his way inside, Robert Guillain, accredited from Vichy France and thus a neutral, met a Japanese newsman on the way out. Wondering whether America had struck first, something Guillain doubted, he asked whether there had been an American declaration of war. "There is just a 'state of war,' " said the reporter.

Guillain looked about for his friends, Bob Bellaire of the United Press, Max Hill of the Associated Press, Otto Tolischus of the *New York Times*, and others. All were missing. Instead there was a sprinkling of neutrals and Axis correspondents, among whom a Foreign Ministry functionary in morning coat was distributing mimeographed copies of the memorandum delivered to Washington, a Japanese version of recent relations with the United States, and a draft of the Imperial Rescript.

"Is this rescript designed for internal consumption," asked Guillain, "or is this really the declaration of war as it was delivered to Washington?" The functionary offered something ambiguous, and Guillain pressed, "At what time was this declaration of war handed to Washington?"

"This time," he remembered, "the only answer I got was a scowl and a look of repressed fury." No declaration had been delivered, even after the fact. Two of the documents in Guillain's hand elaborated upon a break in negotiations, and the third—the Imperial Rescript—was still without the Emperor's seal. With no announcements to wait for, newsmen filed out. There was a lot to read, and radio broadcasts seemed the source of real news.

A Foreign Ministry handout prepared for Japanese media was *An Outline of Information and Propaganda Policies for the War between Japan and the Anglo-American Powers*. From occupation currency to studies of tides and harbor depths across a third of the earth's surface, nothing that could have been anticipated had been left to chance. Japan's cause, the manifesto insisted, was a moral one as opposed to the enemy's "selfish desire for world conquest." The goal was "a new world order" which would enable "all nations and races to assume their proper place in the world," and in which all people could live in peace "in their own sphere." Employment of "their proper place" and "in their own sphere" suggested that the nation of the "Yamato race" with its "shining history"—the mythical Emperor Jimmu had established his court at Yamato 2,601 years earlier—might define its own terms and legitimatize its own "order."

At the War Ministry a domestic press handout cleared the slate for the new phase of conflict. "Imperial rewards" were announced for war dead and "survivals" of the war "on various China fronts" from as far back as April 1940. The release had been held for an occasion when the nation would be preoccupied and the bad news buried on back pages of newspapers. It was the thirty-third time since the Decoration Board had been established that wholesale awards had been announced for the dead, the seventeenth for the living. Of the 2,569 given the Order of the Golden Kite, only 357 survived to receive the award in person, one—Captain Shibao Hayashi—for the fourth time. Few Japanese soldiers expected medals; the practice was to offer decorations—and even then, sparingly—to the near-kin of the dead. For those who would not return there was assurance of deification in the Yasukuni Temple, the national pantheon for warriors who fell for the fatherland.

Before going off to war, many young Japanese who anticipated "rebirth" had boldly brush-stroked, in Chinese ideograms, laconic aphorisms about death and sacrifice. Like "a shattered pearl," Ensign Shigemi Furuno, whose doomed minisub had detached from the *I-18*, wrote,

> I will scatter my bones
> in Pearl Harbor.
> The dawn is bright
> with the joy of our reunion
> at the Yasukuni Temple.

It was two minutes after nine in Tokyo when radio stations JLG4 and JZJ broke into their bulletins with the statement, "This is in the middle of the news but today, specially at this point, I will give the weather forecast: west wind, clear; west wind, clear." Thirty-three minutes later there was a repeat of the announcement. Army and Navy listening posts in the U.S. had been monitoring Japanese radio broadcasts for such words since November 28, when a "Magic" message to the Japanese embassy in Washington, dated November 19, was decoded. "In case of emergency (danger of cutting off our diplomatic relations) and the cutting off of international communications," it went, "the following warning will be added in the middle of the daily Japanese language shortwave news broadcast." It went on to list three secret codes:

1. In case of Japan-U.S. relations in danger:
   HIGASHI NO KAZEAME (EAST WIND RAIN)
2. Japan-U.S.S.R. relations:
   KITANOKAZE KUMORI (NORTH WIND CLOUDY)
3. Japan-British relations:
   NISHI NO KAZE HARE (WEST WIND CLEAR)

The signal would be broadcast "in the middle and at the end as a weather forecast and each sentence will be repeated twice. When this is heard, please destroy all code papers, etc."

Although Colonel Bratton's team in Washington listened hard, no weather broadcast before Pearl Harbor had used the designated language. After the fact, charges were made that some variation of the message constituted the code—not a war warning in any case—although the instructions had been exact and had not been incorporated in any weather forecasts intercepted. On December 5 there had been a message at 7:00 A.M. Tokyo time on JVW3:

TOKYO TODAY NORTH WIND SLIGHTLY STRONGER MAY BECOME CLOUDY
  TONIGHT.
TOMORROW SLIGHTLY CLOUDY AND FINE WEATHER.
KANAGAWA PREFECTURE TODAY NORTH WIND CLOUDY.
FROM AFTERNOON MORE CLOUDS.
CHIBA PREFECTURE TODAY NORTH WIND CLEAR.
MAY BECOME SLIGHTLY CLOUDY. OCEAN SURFACE CALM.

Twenty-three hours and thirty minutes later JWV3 broadcast another possible signal:

TODAY NORTH WIND MORNING CLOUDY AFTERNOON CLEAR BEGIN
CLOUDY EVENING. TOMORROW NORTH WIND AND LATER FROM SOUTH.

The forecast was given three times. If a code, it suggested breaking relations with Russia, which never happened. Yet it was closer to the language of the instructions of November 19 than the forecast of the previous day warning of ruptured relations with Britain. No "winds" warning with an American connection and close to the preconditions was picked up by Bratton's staff. Commander Safford later claimed to have received an "East Wind" decrypt on December 4, broadcast the previous day. No one afterward could trace the dispatch or delivery of the yellow teletype sheet he remembered. The nonexistent text would become notorious as the "winds execute."

•

At eight Charles Boxer telephoned from the Battle Box to find out whether Emily Hahn and their baby were arranged for. She assured him that she was, then asked, doubtfully, "Charles, you'll be all right?"

"Me? Nobody's going to get *me*. . . . I'll be locked up underground, honeybunch. . . . Listen. Hear it? There they are now."

Through her free ear she heard the air-raid sirens, and through the telephone she heard them again an instant later, an effect she remembered as "weird." Then she heard another familiar sound, having been in China for years—bombs exploding. Through it all, Boxer continued talking. "Well, Mickey, I'm sorry about all this."

"Darling, you didn't do it!"

"Anyway, Carola's too young to care; that's a good thing. . . . All the best."

She went out on her stone terrace and looked across the bay, where smoke was rising from the direction of Kai Tak. Her neighbor across the veranda was sucking on his pipe and staring across the bay. They had never spoken before. "Good morning," she said. "Here it is."

"Yes," he said, shaking his head. "Japan's committed suicide."

She went inside and crouched over the baby again. Ah King came in and urged, "Come and eat breakfast." Ah Choy, the wash amah, was folding clothes in the bedroom, and looked up. "You scared, missy?" she asked.

"Nooooo. You're not scared, are you, Ah Choy?"

"Yes," she confessed, and began to cry. Emily forgot again about breakfast and sat over Carola's crib.

Reserve captain Robert Simpson expected to hear from Headquarters on Monday morning, but his first call came just after eight from a Kowloon undergraduate who wanted to know whether the day's exams had been canceled. "They say that the Japanese have started to attack—that the aerodrome has just been bombed."

"I'm sure I'd have heard if that had happened," Simpson said. "So far as I am concerned your examination is still on, and you should get on your way over here and take it."

Then he returned to shaving, and as he wiped his razor he heard the noise of aircraft engines, then the swish and bang of bombs. An AA battery halfway up the hill near the university compound behind him opened fire.

"What's that?" his wife called from the breakfast table downstairs.

"That's war," Simpson said; "they've attacked."

The telephone rang. It was the officer who had called Sunday night. "I'm not offering you a choice this time," he said. "Japanese troops have crossed the frontier at two points. We are at war. Report at once."

Simpson had barely hung up when the phone rang again—orders for his wife and daughter for immediate ANS—Auxiliary Nursing Service—duty, the reason they had been permitted to stay. Effective immediately, the university had become an auxiliary hospital. The three changed quickly into reservist uniforms. His daughter brought the car round and drove him to Army headquarters to report to Brigadier Torquil MacLeod, commanding the Royal Artillery.

In her new blue-and-silver housecoat, Heather Tomlinson was on the veranda outside her house in the compound of Kowloon Hospital, where her husband was on the medical staff. Eda, her baby daughter, was being bounced about in the garden on the shoulders of her amah. Sterling Tomlinson was in the bathtub. As a child on November 11,

1918, Mrs. Tomlinson had watched a very different sort of garden scene—the family washerwoman so excited at hearing that the war had ended in Europe that instead of hanging the clean laundry she threw it on the grass and jumped on it with joy. Suddenly time seemed to go in reverse. "I heard the noise of a lot of planes and looked up and saw them flying in formation towards us. I called to my husband and he said, 'They are probably RAF reinforcements.' I saw them coming [closer] and shouted to him, 'I think they are Japs.' He said, 'Don't be silly'—and then we heard the bombs falling on the airport just down the road. He leaped out of the tub to dress and go to the hospital. I screamed to the amah to come in."

Madame Sun Yatsen had risen early and gone to Kai Tak Airport to meet her sister, Madame H. H. Kung, who was arriving on an early morning flight from Chungking. She had been visiting their sister, Madame Chiang Kaishek, the most ambitious of the formidable Soong sisters. Madame Kung was chancing the hazardous route, in an ancient DC-2, over the Japanese lines. The China National Aviation Corporation planes, with civilian American pilots, operated on erratic schedules to lessen the risk.

The DC-2 touched down; the women embraced. Passengers collected their luggage and began dispersing. Leaving the airport manager's office, Pan American pilot Freddie Ralph, captain of the Sikorsky S-42 flying boat *Hong Kong Clipper*, tied up to a buoy nearby at Kai Tak Dock, was growing more and more anxious about departure. His crew of six had been alerted for an early takeoff because of war warnings; then the flight was indefinitely delayed. At 7:55 the United Press manager in Manila, Dick Wilson, telephoned to his Hong Kong counterpart, George Baxter, from the Peninsula Hotel to report that his return flight was being held, and to ask whether Baxter had heard anything about war in the Pacific.

Had Baxter been listening to his radio he would have known, but British censorship had kept the news from reaching his office. Pan Am in Manila, Wilson said, had radioed that there was trouble somewhere but could not furnish details. As Baxter put the telephone down he heard "the zooming of planes followed by heavy explosions and the rattle of machine-guns. Several of us rushed to the roof from where we could see . . . the Kai Tak airport."

Jan Marsman, a Dutch engineer, had climbed into the bus to Kai Tak when an excited Chinese employee of Pan Am rushed to stop it.

The flight, he shouted, had been delayed. A passenger claimed to know why: war with Japan. Another passenger accused him of being an alarmist. But the bus was diverted to the Peninsula Hotel, where Marsman saw workmen stripping the ballrooms for use as a temporary hospital. Ribbons of gummed paper already crisscrossed the plate-glass windows to guard against the splintering effect from explosions. Carpeting was being rolled up and stacked.

Among the watchers, Marsman noticed T. B. Wilson, agent of the American Steamship Lines, whose megaphoned announcement had ended a ball the night before. They were having coffee together when Marsman observed aircraft circling, then diving, over Kai Tak. "What do you think those planes are?" he asked Wilson, motioning him to the window.

"Oh, hell, just maneuvers, Jan," said Wilson, as columns of smoke billowed from the direction of the airport. "Do they use smoke screens in maneuvers?"

When they saw some of the *Clipper* crew rush, disheveled, into the hotel lobby, they knew that their flight had been more than delayed.

On the HMS *Scout*, in dry dock at Taikoo on Hong Kong Island, Executive Officer Christopher Briggs was called to the quarterdeck phone. It was the staff officer for operations at Naval Headquarters, who said, tersely, "Tell your captain that we are at war with Japan." Briggs ordered the antiaircraft guns readied and steam raised in order to get the ship, whatever its condition, out of dry dock as soon as possible. It was nearly eight before he had a chance to telephone his wife. "We are at war," he told her, calling off their lunch, but asking her to meet him at the gates at noon. "Bring over some clothes when you come."

As she put the telephone down she "heard planes fly towards Kai Tak aerodrome at the end of our road, and my thought was, 'At long last they have sent some planes from Singapore'; then I heard a loud 'wump'—it was the Japanese bombing Kai Tak and the Pan American *Clipper* which was anchored in the bay."

The log of the *Scout* records the air raid as 8:10. On the quarterdeck, Briggs was standing "with the phone to my ear and looking towards Kai-Tak on the Kowloon side when the first enemy planes appeared." There were forty-eight dive bombers and fighters in the flight, releasing bombs as low as sixty feet above the airstrip. "I saw the bombs fall on the airport and the poor *Clipper* got a direct hit and went up in smoke," Briggs wrote. There were six strafing passes over it, to make certain it was destroyed. It burned to the waterline. Reports from eyewitnesses claimed—since Japanese pilots allegedly had defective vision—that Germans had been "definitely observed" in the cockpits. From a considerable distance, and in his pajamas, Sergeant Major E. C. Ford at Fort Davis—a high point on the island—watched with his mates. They had "uncomplimentary remarks about the ability of the Jap Air Force." Private Bob Yates stayed at his gun, on the western edge of Mount Davis. It could only be fired toward the sea.

Five RAF and eight civilian planes were smoking rubble, but no one would learn that from the censored press. "EARLY RAIDS ACHIEVE POOR RESULTS," the *South China Morning Post* would report on Tuesday; and on the next page, as if nothing happened, an advertisement for Pan American boasted, above a picture of the handsome flying boat, "Twice Weekly to Manila in 5 Hours. Weekly to Singapore in 10 Hours."

Even from the lowest hills facing Kowloon it was obvious that the airfield barely now existed. "Master! Have got war!! You lookee see!" shouted servants about to lose their jobs but now awakening employers or calling them to verandas or to windows overlooking the bay. "Well, Missy," was Ah Sze's variant on the theme when he brought breakfast to Phyllis Harrop, an assistant to the police commissioner, "we all fight together now." Divorced from a German businessman who had left the colony, she had retained her spousal passport, soon her most valuable possession. For the moment, her most important piece of paper was her naval pass: she was the only one in the commissioner's office who could get in and out of the dockyard.

Helpless in dry dock, *Scout* had escaped damage. The problem for the Royal Navy, eager to get its ships safely out to sea, was how to release the *Scout*. None of the Chinese workmen had shown up. When the enemy planes disappeared toward Canton, however, one of the European staff arrived and helped the sailors open the valves and flood the dock. The operation began while engineers aboard were raising steam. While the dock slowly filled, a two-hour procedure, the crew made the ship ready and loaded stores and ammunition.

Freddie Ralph had walked out at eight to look over the *Clipper*; a Filipino mess boy went inside. At the first bombs, the crew ran for cover; Ralph dashed to the end of the dock, jumped into the water, and hid in the fetid opening of a large sewer pipe. The mess boy leaped overboard.

Dorothy Jenner had left the Gloucester Hotel on the island and ferried across to catch the *Clipper*. In her handbag was a letter of introduction to General MacArthur from Madame Chiang, a guarantee of an "Andrea" interview. As she was walking out of the airport lounge "the heavens opened. . . . I jumped under a big drainage culvert and almost landed on top of a fellow who was already sheltering there. . . . We introduced ourselves and he turned out to be an Eurasian gentleman called Mr. Pownall, also on his way to Manila." When they could, they got themselves to the Peninsula Hotel, "to await developments."

At the block of flats nearby, once married quarters for service personnel and now an engineers' barracks, NCO Frederick Boughey threw himself, amid flying glass, under a concrete stairwell. Until then he had found the soft life, and the quiet, difficult to get used to after service in France and then in the Blitz. Picking himself up after the planes left, he ignored his minor cuts and ran to the entrance to check on his unit's trucks, "parked nose to tail." He passed a sergeant with a smashed leg, and a dead guard at the gate. Several trucks had taken shrapnel hits and were spouting water from radiators and hoses. Boughey turned round and dashed to the canteen, from which the Chinese manager had fled. Grabbing packets of gum, he unwrapped them and began chewing vigorously. Then he noticed the cigarette rack, already largely looted, and stuffed his pockets. Returning, he saw other soldiers gazing at the streaming trucks; they gaped as he plugged the holes with wads of gum. "It worked like a charm," he remembered. With no orders, he stayed with his truck. (That night, still without instructions, he spread his groundsheet under his truck and bedded down.)

Before joining the hurrying pedestrians on their way to work in Kowloon, Big Cow Wu and his father paused at a tea shop to consider spending ten Hong Kong cents for tea. The shipyard would wait. There were no ships to refit anyway. Suddenly they heard the clatter of airplanes and distant explosions.

"Maybe," said Big Cow doubtfully, "it is only battle practice."

"It does not look like it."

A cloud of smoke rose from the northeast—like a devil stooping in the air, Wu thought.

"That side," cried Big Cow, "is Kai Tak. It *is* fighting!"

Old Man Wu tugged at his son. From their fourth floor they might see what was happening. "Go home and have a look!"

"You go home," said Big Cow. "I have to hurry to the shipyard and talk about this with my friends."

There was confusion in the narrow Kowloon streets, with people on their way to work undecided whether to continue or to rush home. Wu thought of his family in the country, his brother who had been conscripted by the Japanese to carry coolie loads, his mother who had died of hunger, another brother who had, they thought, joined the guerrillas. Perhaps he had better buy some rice right away.

He saw British soldiers in trucks headed north toward the New Territories. Chinese and Indian police were trying to control the street traffic, and Wu thought that people looked frightened. He heard a pedestrian ask, "Mr. Indian Policeman, the Japanese are coming. What will you do?"

"They're a bad lot," said the policeman grimly. Then he shrugged and put out his hands. "I don't know what to do!"

"Fight," suggested the pedestrian.

The policeman shook his head. "The British cannot win," he said. "They do not have the power to fight the Japanese."

The radios in shops were wailing hoarsely, in a babble of stations that left no broadcast intelligible. Queues formed at food counters; Wu joined one at a rice store, fishing in his pockets for money. He had five dollars and a few cents. By the time he got into line there were twenty or thirty people following behind him, discussing what had happened. Only the day before, the purchasers coming out, staggering under bags of rice, would have insisted on delivery. Now they were grateful to be burdened, and received admiring glances from people waiting for a similar opportunity.

Every queue seethed with rumors, each more frightening than the last:

"The Japanese have already reached Shatin, and will soon enter Kowloon city."

"Japanese warships are just outside the harbor, and may land at any time."

"Soon no rice will be sold; rationing will begin and we will be limited to thirty catties a month." (A Hong Kong catty was 1.1 pounds.)

"Soya beans and preserved vegetables must be bought before it is too late."

"It is lucky to be able to get this rice; now for salted fish!"

"Maybe the British have some way out of this!"

"What way will there be? They can only surrender."

"No, the radio broadcast said that they will defend to the last man!"

"Do you believe such words? With what can they defend against the Japanese?"

When Wu's turn came, he bought forty catties of rice—all he could get for his five dollars.

Struggling into Shanghai Street with his load, he saw Mrs. Li returning, her face wet with tears. "Old Man Wu," she appealed, "my husband is somewhere in South America. Who can decide for me? I and my children depend upon you."

Emerging from the block of flats, Mother Wu joined them on the sidewalk. "The worst comes true," she said. "Just as we talk about them, the Japanese come. What shall we do now?"

"It is better to be calm," said Wu, putting down his sacks of rice. "We will help one another and we will pull through."

Lau materialized from the street throng. To prevent inbound floods of refugees, the ferries were not running to the island. His firm, he was sure, had closed. Pale with worry, all he could say was, "The Japanese are indeed coming!"

"Didn't you say," Mrs. Li reminded him, "that the Japanese dared not fight with Britain?"

"Governor Sir Mark Young," Lau assured her, incoherently, "is determined to defend Hong Kong. But unless the Japanese do not come, the British cannot defend this place. If the Japanese are determined to come, it is difficult to say."

"Mr. Lau, the more you say the more I don't understand."

"Who can understand fate now?" Lau sighed. "Disaster is arriving!"

Wearing a grave expression, Big Cow Wu returned from the shipyard and joined the knot of people on the sidewalk. His friends had discussed the situation, he reported. "The Japanese are risking desperately. They attacked the American Pearl Harbor as well as Singapore this morning. The British here will have to surrender. I have heard that the Japanese have entered the New Territories. The British will soon retreat from Kowloon. It will be a time of anarchy, and some bad guys among us are ready to take advantage and do mischief."

"Oh," said Mrs. Wu, "isn't this like meeting the wolf before the tiger arrives?"

Wu himself had grown thoughtful. "We must find more food. We will have to take care of Mrs. Li and her family. The future does not look easy. But the thieves are bound to lose sooner or later!"

•

Even before the Iba Field radar screen first showed incoming blips at eight o'clock, Hap Arnold had called from Washington to warn about dispersal of aircraft. Thirty-six P-40s at Clark Field scrambled to intercept whatever it was; David Gibbs, operations officer of the 19th Bombardment Group and senior officer in Colonel Eubank's absence, ordered all B-17s into the air. Jorge Vargas was at work in Manila issuing directives "by order of President Quezon" when the President telephoned from Baguio. He and his daughter Zenaida were watching with satisfaction seventeen twin-engined bombers just over-head. After all, they had to be American. Then there were explosions. "Jorge," Quezon shouted, "tell General MacArthur that Camp John Hay has been bombed! And call the Council of State for a meeting tomorrow at nine!"

Like Arnold, General Gerow wanted no repetition of Pearl Harbor. At 7:55 Manila time he had telephoned from Washington asking about "any indications of an attack." Davao and Aparri had already been bombed and Batan Island occupied, but MacArthur replied casually only that radar had picked up planes thirty miles from Luzon and that his aircraft would "meet them." He was confident all around, he added: "Our tails are up in the air." While P-40s were winging wildly all over central Luzon, responding to confused reports of enemy sightings, John Hay, less an operational base than a rest-and-recuperation spot, had been hit. No incoming Mitsubishis encountered the lower-flying P-40s.

In the Associated Press office in the *Manila Bulletin* building, Clark Lee and Ray Cronin wondered whether to enlist but concluded that they would be of more use in their own jobs. Yet because of official silence and instant military restrictions there was little to do but listen to the radio and read other newspapers' imaginative extras. Another recourse was to telephone about while they could. They got through to Guam, where the cable office manager told Lee, "Many Japanese planes are attacking us. We have been in and out of our shelter since six o'clock. Our small forces are fighting but the Japanese have landed and are advancing. This can't last long."

The transmission broke off at 8:30 and Lee could not reestablish contact. The Japanese had not yet landed, but Guam was in panic.

From Shanghai, AP newsman Jimmy White cabled, "Japanese seized International Settlement. USS *Wake* captured in Whangpoo. Heavy machine-gun firing audible from *Bund*. British gunboat went down with guns blazing under . . ." The message stopped. At that point the Japanese, Lee guessed, had seized the Globe Wireless office.

A bulletin brought them back to the Philippines. The Japanese were bombing Davao, Mindanao's major city. A PBY had been shot down, and an enemy plane. The ancient aircraft carrier *Langley* was reported attacked.

Thirteen carrier-based bombers and nine fighters in the *Ryujo's* first wave had met no resistance over Davao. The second wave—two bombers and three fighters—encountered the awakened antiaircraft gunners, and Flight Petty Officer Hiroshi Kawanishi crash-landed his disabled plane. Since the Navy forbade a pilot to surrender and become a prisoner of war, *jibaku* had been called for—self-destruction using one's plane as a missile, in a kamikaze death. But there had been nothing worth destroying—the old *Langley* was not in port—and Kawanishi had instinctively tried to save his plane. Now *gyokusai* was required—death rather than dishonor. Kawanishi burned his fighter, then shot himself.

In the streets of Manila and other Philippine cities and towns, crowds emerging from churches or queuing to board streetcars and buses found their lives changed. Few households could afford a radio. News was what was shouted by newsboys at street corners, particularly if in Tagalog. "*Binomba ang* Pearl Harbor!!" cried vendors offering *Mabuhay*. "Pearl Harbor attacked!" yelled the vendors of the *Bulletin* and the *Tribune*. Carmen Guerrero Nakpil, who had been bused with other young women to the ball at the Manila Hotel as partners for young Air Corps officers, had managed only a few hours sleep before Mass at eight at St. Theresa's College. After church, she was sent home. Antonio Quintos, in school at the Ateneo de Manila, was also sent home after Mass. His classmates from the distant Visayas—the central islands of the archipelago—were urged to find the fastest way back. His brother José was on the school football field for a parade when he was told to go home. Apprehensively, he searched for Antonio, and the two left for their father's office—he was a physician in Intramuros. Entering the walled city, José recalled, "In Calle Victoria I saw two American soldiers. They were crying like kids. We were too scared to cry."

Trinidad Subido, a young mother whose husband, Abelardo, had been in the Army since 1939, was living with her mother-in-law. Letters from Abelardo had warned that war was imminent; the family had prepared rice, canned milk, and other essentials for possible evacuation. "Now my mother sewed her jewels into the hem of her skirt. We younger people were annoyed with her but those jewels saved us. She sold them little by little to buy food."

Simeon Medalla, an officer trainee in Intramuros, later a colonel, recalled the small American convoy to the Philippines that no one knew had been rerouted to Brisbane. "MacArthur had promised, people told me, for it was a reassuring idea, that a seven-mile convoy of ships was en route with troops and tanks and guns and planes to turn the situation around.* We waited three-and-a-half years for those ships. Everybody believed that we would win, despite everything, in three or four months. People believed any optimistic statement attributed to MacArthur."

Señora Geronima Pecson, in Zamboanga City on Mindanao, where her husband was a judge, left church and learned of the war. Crowds, she remembered when she was a birdlike nonagenarian and a retired senator, were excited rather than worried. While people sang "The Star-Spangled Banner" in the streets to stress their link with the Americans, she hurried to the local Red Cross office to volunteer her services, later using that association and her husband's position to secure a job in the Malacañang Palace under occupation President Laurel. From

---

* The rumor seems based upon the convoy of *seven* transports escorted by the USS *Pensacola*, loaded with war materiel and troops for MacArthur's command. When it swung south from Honolulu on November 29, it carried nearly 5,000 troops, 52 A-24 bombers, 18 P-40s, 48 75mm guns, 340 motor vehicles, 600 tons of bombs, 9,000 drums of aviation fuel, and 3,500,000 rounds of ammunition. None of it would reach the Philippines.

there, using imaginative bookkeeping, she spirited funds into the mountains to guerrilla bands. "I was a thief!" she crowed proudly at ninety-one. "I was a thief!"

•

Michael Lindsay's political barometer was the presence of American Marines at the embassy in Peking. When they left, he would go. At thirty-two, the tall, lean Oxonian was happily insulated from the teeming city in the lakefront setting of American-run Yenching University. In December 1937 he had sailed from England, via Vancouver and Yokohama, to the jewel of foreign colleges in China. Under the Japanese occupation it had remained independent. Lindsay could travel rather freely, slipping on occasion into Communist-dominated areas, where he had been converted to the cause. In 1940 he had changed jobs, briefly becoming press attaché at the British embassy in Chungking.

One of the attractions drawing him back to Yenching was a pretty young student in Mao's underground. Li Hsiao-li, from a wealthy local family, became his wife in June 1941. Both began sending intelligence about Japanese movements to the Communists in the interior.

With war involving the British and Americans threatening, the Yenching administration wanted to abandon the campus and move to the freer west, but most of the faculty, comfortable in Peking, objected. Lindsay himself lived in the university compound and preferred to stay. Only the two Jewish refugee professors were eager to go.

As usual, on Monday morning before Lindsay left for class, his wife got up before him to consult with the cook and to listen to the Chinese-language news from British radio in Shanghai. When she could tune in nothing on the familiar frequency, Hsiao-li got her husband out of bed to dial the German station in Shanghai. A woman was reading the news in Mandarin. Japan had declared war on Britain and the United States and had attacked Pearl Harbor; Japanese forces in Shanghai had captured British and American naval vessels on the Whangpoo and moved into the International Zone to greetings from friendly citizens; Hong Kong had been attacked.

Lindsay assumed that soldiers surrounded his campus. He thought fast. Several Chinese friends had left pistols with him, and he fantasized about shooting his way out; then his cook discovered that there were no guards at the gates. Hastily, Lindsay and Hsiao-li stuffed radio equipment, concealed by clothing, into suitcases. Appropriating the university president's conveniently parked car—Leighton Stuart was on a visit to Tientsin—they picked up physics professor William Band and his wife, but zoomed out of the back gate without the best man at Lindsay's wedding. Refugee professor Rudolf Loewenthal was innocently teaching an early morning journalism class.

Abandoning the Dodge at Wench'uan just short of a Japanese checkpoint, they "walked off into the countryside, hiring a couple of farmers to carry our luggage concealed in their deep harvest baskets. We headed for the holiday house of a French doctor who had treated wounded Chinese soldiers, but the man [left] in charge, afraid to take us in, passed us on to another foreigner's house further into the hills. . . . Here we were put in touch with a man who was nominally a village head under the Japanese regime but actually worked for the Communists. He hid us in Dragon Spring Temple."

Later, Lindsay heard that the dreaded Kempeitai—the political police—had broken into their house only ten minutes after their flight. They also remembered that they had left behind, in their haste, all of Hsiao-li's jewelry and money, and Lindsay's razor blades, tobacco, and shirt collars, which somehow at the moment seemed more a cause for regret than the abandoned Loewenthal or the president's car.*

•

"Well, it has begun," said Dr. Sun Fo to his counselor and private secretary, Percy Chen. The news of Pearl Harbor had come over the radio in his comfortable study in Chungking, where Dr. Sun—heir of Sun Yatsen—was president of Chiang Kaishek's rubber-stamp legislative Yuan. Chen's Russian-born wife, Mucia, had gone back to Hong Kong to ship their belongings off to Rangoon for forwarding over the Burma Road to Chungking. When rumors began to fly about an attack on Hong Kong, he had wired her a telegram, "IN CASE OF EMERGENCY FLY TO CHUNGKING WITH SUN FO." But the censor in Hong Kong, under orders not to alarm the population, cut out the

---

* Leighton Stuart remained interned in the Tientsin area until 1945. In 1946 he returned as American ambassador to China, at which time the Japanese presented him with a replacement car. Rudolf Loewenthal, who had prudently taken Chinese citizenship, was unharmed. Assisted during the occupation by Roman Catholic priests, he survived to marry a Russian refugee in Peking and after the war got to the U.S.—as did the Lindsays.

words, "IN CASE OF EMERGENCY." And by the time the telegram arrived, Sun had already taken a CNAC plane back to the speck of land in the Yangtze near Chungking that served for an airstrip when the river was low in winter.

"A feeling of panic" overwhelmed Chen. All he could hope was that her Russian nationality might be useful.*

Percy Chen saw his task in the Nationalist capital as trying to keep Dr. Sun "on a liberal path, counteracting the efforts of others . . . who were trying to draw his support for more reactionary policies." He was "also concerned with keeping Chiang Kaishek from making peace with the Japanese and from adventuring against the Communists and breaking the United Front." But the United Front remained a sham. Unified by ideology, the Communists operated with more guile than good intentions. Both sides preferred pretending to fight the Japanese while utilizing stalemate—"protracted war," Mao Zedong called it— to gather strength against the enemy that would be left when exhaustion overtook the occupiers: each other.

Ramshackle Chungking was an accurate symbol of the Chiang government, propped up by semifeudal alliances with regional warlords, and by American dollars that were meant to bolster Chiang against the Japanese but somehow were used more against the Communists when not disappearing altogether into the pockets of Chiang's people.

The "Gissimo" had limited the Communist presence in Chungking to General Chou Enlai—second in the Red hierarchy to Chairman Mao—and a few members of his staff, and forbade foreign reporters to meet with his ostensible partner. Still, newsmen took labyrinthine paths through dark alleys to meet furtively with Chou in his spartan, dimly lighted house and to be asked, "When is the United States coming into this war?"

Despite Chou's desire to see America in the war, that involvement, when it came, seemed more likely to help Chiang than Mao, but the Chinese in general saw the new Japanese adventures in the Pacific as relieving the pressures on the Asian hinterland. The news reached the

---

* The beautiful and resourceful Mucia Chen managed to get on a boat of Chinese refugees to Haiphong, in Indochina, and thence to Kwangchowan, in southern China, claiming to be the wife of a merchant. Chen disappeared into the vastness of China hoping to find her among the exodus from Hong Kong. They met, by chance, in March 1942, on the road from Liuchow to Kwangchowan.

interior in forms often more hopeful than accurate, as Graham Peck, a Yale-educated free-lance artist bicycling through China, discovered. On the way to Chungking he saw "a group of village Kuomintang officials making their way up the long slope from the river, their black-clad figures bristling with the canes, medals, and scarves which were the tokens of their rank and prosperity. They had ignored me during my previous stay, but now they beamed as they hastened to shake my hand. They told me five hundred American planes had bombed Tokyo on December 7 and we were allies. A day or two later, I heard what really happened."

· · ·

At 6:50 A.M. a Dutch patrol plane flew low over the *Marblehead*, signaling "All clear and good luck." The cruiser had cleared the harbor at 6:27 and began steaming south at high speed, rejoined by the destroyer *Parrott*. Two destroyers, the *Barker* and the *Paul Jones*, were detached northward to join Admiral Glassford's cruiser, *Houston*, in Philippine waters. Hart ordered his own patrol planes, largely cumbersome PBY Catalinas, to load bombs and proceed to preassigned stations where they would not be targets. When used for combat rather than reconnaissance they needed fighter escort, which was nonexistent. Recognizing the hazards, one PBY pilot was alleged to have radioed his base, "Have sighted enemy planes. Please notify [my] next of kin."

At 7:00 A.M., not long after Dutch merchant shipping in the vicinity of the Indies was ordered by radio to make for the nearest safe port, the governor general, A. W. L. Tjarda van Starkenborgh Stachouwer, went on the air. "Citizens of the Netherlands Indies!" he began. "In its unexpected attack on American and British territories, while diplomatic negotiations were still in progress, the Japanese Empire has consciously adopted a course of aggression. These attacks . . . have as their objective the establishment of Japanese supremacy in the whole of East and Southeast Asia. The aggression also gravely threatens the Netherlands Indies. The Netherland government accepts the challenge and takes up arms against the Japanese Empire."

To the Dutch the war was no surprise. Major General J. C. Pabst, ambassador in Tokyo, had employed his contacts well, particularly Japanese Communists who had governmental and industrial connections. He had even managed to secure specimens of secret occupation currency printed in Dutch and Malay, and warned Washington and

London. In Japan he awaited word from the Dutch government-in-exile as to what the embassy should now do, but it would be more than four hours—2:30 A.M. London time—before a cable would be sent to him to confirm a state of war. Then, held up by the Japanese, the message would not be delivered until the following day.

In Manado in North Celebes (now Sulawesi), the young garrison doctor, A. J. P. Borstlap, listened to the governor general's message with Annie, his wife, before going off to the military hospital, which served a mixed force of eleven hundred. "Fellow citizens," came Stachouwer's peroration, "men and women of whichever race and faith you are, I call upon you to fulfill a hard and exalted duty to Queen and Kingdom. . . . May God grant that we are worthy for the task before us."

The three hundred Japanese in the area, fishermen and their families and some shopkeepers, had closed their businesses in the first days of December and posted signs that they were on holiday until mid-January. Everyone knew that they had gone to the island of Yap in the Japanese-controlled Carolines, a thousand miles to the northeast, very likely to wait out an invasion of the Indies. "We felt," said Borstlap, "like the noblesse in the Bastille, wondering how long we had to live." The Dutch had no artillery and no air force, and their exposed tip of pinwheel-shaped Celebes, just below Mindanao in the Philippines, was indefensible.

Borstlap clicked off the radio, which had begun to repeat the news about Pearl Harbor. "My wife and I," he recalled, "looked into each other's eyes, silent, knowing 'this is the end; we are doomed.' At last, what we had dreaded so long had come. We understood what lay before us. Breakfast was hardly touched. I changed from my white uniform into green field dress with a Sam Browne belt, put on my helmet and loaded my long-packed backpack, gasmask bag and canteen into the car. Then I took leave of my two daughters who did not understand what was happening but felt the tension of their elders." It was strange, he remembered, how cold and indifferent his leaving his wife, who was seven months' pregnant, seemed—"just a perfunctory kiss like I was going to work."

"Be careful," she said.

"Make the best of it," he responded.

The Japanese would not come to Manado for a month, and he would have one more night with his wife before he was, with two companions, taken prisoner and subjected to a preinterrogation beating. By then, Borstlap knew that the Japanese were decapitating prisoners, and when his group was led, blindfolded, to their execution, he waited "totally unfeeling, for the blow of the sword." He heard the beheading of his comrades, "but over my head a palaver began about my Red Cross armlet . . . and after some time my blindfold was taken off. I was confronted with the gory mess of my two unlucky compatriots and led away." A gaunt wreck, he would survive forty-five months as a prisoner of war in the Kai Gun Camp at Macassar in the Celebes.*

Not long after the Tokyo "winds" broadcast, Colonel (later Brigadier General) Elliott R. Thorpe, the U.S. Army Lend-Lease representative in the Indies, left by car for Pengelegan, a few miles into the hills from the Javanese capital, Bandung. It was the home of the *Chef de Cabinet* of the Dutch general staff; the invitation combined a morning of business, arranged before the war news, with lunch. Lieutenant General Hein Ter Poorten, the military commander in the Indies, would be there also.

Ter Poorten had been bringing him, Thorpe later wrote, intercepts of Japanese transmissions. Several repeated instructions from Tokyo to the Japanese ambassador at Bangkok that military action might take place shortly against Hawaii, the Philippines, Malaya, and Thailand, and that the "go" signal would be a Tokyo broadcast ostensibly furnishing weather information. The code for action against the United States would be "East Wind, Rain."

Thorpe had sent the warning in several texts to Washington. One arrived with the paragraph describing potential locations for attack deleted by the unhelpful Consul General Dr. Walter Foote, who added in a covering note, "Thorpe and [Commander Paul] Slawson [the Naval Attaché] cabled the above to the War Department. I attach little or no importance to it and view it with suspicion." In any case, the text of the Dutch intercept, with the intent Thorpe described, does not exist. It was very likely the known message about breaking relations, imaginatively interpreted.

---

* Annie Borstlap and her daughters Ada and Jolanda, four and two, escaped by boat to Java, but their first flight was aborted. The Catalina was strafed and destroyed as, horrified, they lay flat on their bellies on the jetty waiting to board. Annemarie Borstlap was born during another air raid a few days before the Dutch on Java surrendered. With her sisters and mother she was freed from a Japanese prison camp in September 1945.

Another Thorpe story is less reliable. The next day—December 9 in Java—the chief of the Dutch air force (Major General Van Oyen) reportedly came to Thorpe's office and told him that half of the dozen PBYs being ferried across the Pacific to the Indies had been destroyed at Pearl Harbor. Once the Japanese had departed, "Van Oyen took off for Java with what was left of his planes and made the trip without meeting any hostile aircraft." In Thorpe's interview with Lieutenant Colonel H. H. Griffin in 1983, the number of planes had escalated to fifty, and the casualty count to thirty-six; but there were no Dutch planes in Oahu and none destroyed, and it would have been impossible for the hypothetical planes to get to Java overnight from Hawaii.

•

In room 48 at 7:30 Cecil Brown awoke after snatching a little more sleep. A captain he knew also lived at the Raffles, and had a radio. Brown got him out of bed. Captain Getchell had slept through the bombing. "For Christ's sake!" shouted Brown. "The war is on."

"You're kidding."

"No. Singapore was bombed three hours ago. Could I come over and hear your radio?"

In Getchell's room Brown heard a report from San Francisco that the Japanese had bombed Pearl Harbor.

Back to shave, he received a call about another press conference at eight. On his way to Union Building he picked up a single-sheet extra of the *Singapore Free Press* and learned that the Philippines and Hong Kong had also been attacked. "It is almost unbelievable." The communiqués were "pretty confused." One established that two landings had been effected and that the airfield at Kota Bharu was in jeopardy. The second reported Japanese surface ships "retiring at high speed and the few troops left on the beaches . . . being heavily machine-gunned." Still it was "certain," as he put it discreetly in his dispatch, "that the Japanese achieved a certain amount of surprise."

The censor passed his story, and as he hailed a rickshaw back to the Raffles, O'Dowd Gallagher of the London *Daily Express* observed, "Well, now you Americans are in it."

"Yes, we sure are. I hope to God we don't make the same mistakes that the British have been making."

"Well, you already have. That Pearl Harbor doesn't sound so good."

In the aftermath of the air raid, troops fanned out over Singapore Island to post antiaircraft and other defenses which might intercept the enemy some distance from the city. D. G. Cotton remembered a golf club secretary who prevented the Army from planting gun sites on the course as they "would interfere with play," and rubber plantation managers who had haggled over compensation for felled rubber trees. Now such arguments vanished, and his unit was trucked to a clearing near the Tengah RAF station, on the unpopulous west side of the island. There was one drawback other than the "lusty" yellow rubber ants that dropped off the trees and the "ferocious" red ants underfoot. "We had only one axe."

At Fort Canning, Lieutenant Charles Fisher listened to "a fatuous briefing to the effect that a few Japanese soldiers had landed on a beach in south-eastern Thailand . . . but when last seen, 'the little men' appeared to be running back to their landing craft." At Malayan Broadcasting Mrs. Innes-Kerr found it "a bit disappointing that first morning to hear that the Japs had made landings at Kota Bharu, but we did not suppose they would get very far. . . . Far more worrying was the news that started to come through of the total destruction of the American fleet in Pearl Harbour. It was good that America had been brought in on our side but the news of her initial losses was most dismaying."

•

Thailand's ceremonial regent during the boyhood of King Ananda Mahidol was a royal relative, Prince Aditya. Although December 8 was the Thai national holiday, Constitution Day, his wife, Princess Kobkaew na Ayudhya, remembered his slipping out early that morning to play golf. What was more unusual was that he came back early. "What's the matter?" she asked. "Why such a quick game?"

"They're on the border," Prince Aditya said. Actually the Japanese had been in Thailand since 2:00 A.M. The elite Imperial Guards Division had begun moving overland from the Indochinese frontier to seize the main line of the railway, and the airfields, while one battalion had been landed near Bangkok, in advance of the main force, to overawe the Thai government. The cabinet had already begun an anxious session when, just before seven, Premier Phibun materialized. The invasion was in full swing, and there had been some useless resistance.

Phibun asked whether a cease-fire order was appropriate. Adun, who as Chief of the National Police had a stake in the decision, argued for giving the Japanese what they could take anyway. "It was better to lose our sovereignty to this extent than lose it completely by being taken over as a Japanese colony. Should Japan lose the upper hand . . . and be defeated by England and the United States, these countries should still be sympathetic towards us as a small country which had done its duty in fighting against Japanese aggression." The Thais had resisted Japanese landings in the south as well as British troops advancing up the Yala road in response.

Phibun agreed, and a motion for a cease-fire passed. Rising at 7:45 to inform the waiting Japanese ambassador, Phibun was handed a telegram from Churchill urging the Thais to defend themselves and promising that Britain would come to their aid with all its strength. It was not only too late to affect the decision, but unrealistic in any case; however, most accounts allege a telegram quite the opposite in message—that Churchill had deplored Britain's inability to help the Thais while exhorting them to fight on alone. The postwar fabrication was to excuse the quick capitulation on grounds that Thailand had been deserted. It was even alleged that the message arrived in time for the Cabinet to conclude that it could expect no help from Britain.

The Japanese, Princess Kobkaew remembered, were quickly "all over Bangkok. The thing is, they asked [only] for passage through to Burma, so we agreed, to save our own skins. Once they were here, they didn't leave. The Japanese were very friendly. They really wanted us to be part of their Co-Prosperity Scheme, and they were very nice to us. They paid for what they had taken. . . . In the palace we were above politics. The Japanese didn't do anything bad to us."

Although fighting actually continued at Singora, "a very strong resistance worthy of their honour," according to a premature government bulletin, ended by 7:30 A.M. "The events which had thus occurred," an official announced to the Thai people, "could not be averted. Although Thailand had tried all she could, . . . further struggle would entail the loss of Thai blood without achieving its purpose."

The Thais had strictly taken no sides. "The Thai people," the announcement went on, "are enjoined to keep calm and to endeavour to carry on their work . . . as usual. The Government will try their utmost to alleviate as much as possible the burden of events and the Thai

people are asked to keep the peace and listen to the instructions and
advice of the Government in every way." Those instructions would be
written out by the Japanese military.

•

Correspondent William J. Dunn got out of bed when a cable arrived
from his boss in New York, Paul White of CBS News. It was just past
seven in Rangoon. The message puzzled him. White wanted him to
cable "continuously" without waiting for instructions. Dunn guessed
that he understood. Since he could not make direct radio contact from
Burma, it made no difference when his material arrived. Still, he wondered why CBS wanted an unpredictably large bill run up. At least
from Bangkok, to which he was sailing in two days via Singapore, he
might be able to broadcast via a relay from Tokyo.

Officers of the American Military Mission to China expediting
shipments up the Burma Road from Rangoon were also quartered at
the Strand. Dunn usually met them for breakfast, after which he went
on his daily search for a copy of the local English-language newspaper.
It was about 7:30 when he joined them. "Have you seen the paper?"
one of the group asked casually.

"Of course not," said Dunn. "Anything happen?"

"Nothing much," said Colonel Twitty. E. M. Twitty was commanding officer of the unit, and the others deferentially let him go on.
"The Japs bombed Pearl Harbor."

Dunn had been to Pearl, and remembered his briefing on the impregnable defenses there. He was not taken in, and showed that by
shaking out his folded napkin unconcernedly and taking a long sip of
water. "Anyone hurt?" he asked lightly.

"There must have been," said Twitty. "They sank a flock of ships
and apparently blew the hell out of everything else." Everyone at the
table watched Dunn, and he watched them. Over the toast and coffee
Twitty continued furnishing details, and CBS's star Far Eastern correspondent took none of them seriously. Dunn drained his coffee, took
his leave, and turned down the street to the newspaper kiosk. Only a
few steps from the hotel he saw the American consul striding toward
him, very likely searching out Colonel Twitty. He had a newspaper
clutched in one hand and tragedy etched on his face. "Instantly I
understood Paul White's cable. I reached for the consul's paper, but

the first look at his face had told me the story. My God! Those bastards weren't kidding."

•

Northern Malaya in the west was closer to the Gulf of Siam invasion beaches in the east than the first quiet hours of the war suggested. Alor Star in Kedah State had an RAF base to defend the central sector of the peninsula, yet was only sixty miles from Butterworth, the coastal city across the strait from Penang, on the Burmese side. Kra is a very narrow isthmus. By early morning, bombers "in waves"—to the surprise of the nursing sisters at the Alor Star hospital—were wrecking Alor Star.

Miss P. M. Briggs was one of four nurses at the station—good peacetime duty because the RAF personnel, starved for white women reminding them of home, saw to it that they had a "gay time." But Monday morning the British planes going up after the raiders were old, slow, outgunned, and outnumbered.

There was some antiaircraft fire; Miss Briggs heard the explosion of bombs, and then there was silence. "Suddenly an ambulance arrived. In it was Pongo Scarf, a young RAF officer we knew well. His plane had crash-landed in a field nearby. Pongo was badly wounded. He was given a blood transfusion but his condition was hopeless. His wife Sally was one of our nursing sisters, but during the previous day she had left Alor Star with the rest of the [evacuated] service wives, so poor Pongo died without ever seeing her again."

Miss Briggs was determined that Scarf be "properly buried." She secured a coffin from the local jail and in her compact £132 Morris 8 she and another nurse followed the ambulance to the local cemetery. On the way they encountered a car bearing two Army chaplains, stopped it, and led the clerics to the open grave to say a proper prayer, "so that later when I saw Sally I could tell her that we had done all we could."

The air base at Sungei Pattani was also hit. As 21 Squadron was preparing its Buffalo fighters for action, the operations room reported approaching aircraft. Confusion followed. The station commander, Squadron Leader F. R. C. Fowle, ordered two planes to have their engines warmed up, while Squadron Leader Allshorn detailed two pilots to stand by for instructions. Then Allshorn decided to scramble the entire squadron, but Fowle refused to permit it, despite a telephoned warning of imminent attack. Ten minutes later, five enemy bombers were overhead.

The two standby pilots ran to their planes and took off without further orders just as bombs began falling among the parked Buffaloes. Other pilots, and the ground crew, took cover in a concrete drain while seven planes and the station communications building were hit. Two RAF operators and sixteen Chinese women in a working party were killed. The pilots who had managed to get into the air had only slightly better luck. They could not make proper altitude in their ancient aircraft, and their guns would not operate. They circled, then landed gingerly on the rubble-strewn field.

Seconded from the Sutherland Highlanders, D. K. Broadhurst was working with the Kedah State Police. His being "Army" had kept his family with him, something he was regretting as he watched clouds of smoke rise from the Sungei Pattani air base. "There is no doubt this is war. . . . I rush downstairs."

The children and Marjorie huddled under the staircase for shelter. Servants hurried in and joined them—all but one bewildered and crying boy. Broadhurst tugged on his uniform. Hammond, his driver, was nowhere to be found, and the car was missing. Revolver in hand, Broadhurst requisitioned a passing bus, ordering it to the police station, where he loaded the policemen and drove past puzzled guards into the air base.

In their way were burning oil drums and storage sheds. The heat was fierce. A corpse lay by the side of the road. Oil drums began to burst, scattering the Malay police from the bus.

In a trench nearby, Broadhurst found his terrified policemen and marched them back to the station, from which, later, he could watch Japanese planes return to machine-gun the field. It would be a busy day, with no time later to say good-bye to his family evacuating hastily south.

Adjutant for the Kedah Police was Nicholas Photiades, whose bungalow facing the airfield was screened by trees so that he could hear but not see takeoffs and landings. He was used to the noise and rarely looked up. On Sunday morning his "boy" had awakened him as usual, and a dressing-gowned Photiades sat down on the veranda to his tea and fruit. Planes were going up on practice flights. While he was shaving, he vaguely heard them land.

The sound of planes swooping over the airfield again surprised him. Although they were "making a different noise," he took little interest until a deep boom pulsated across the road. He looked out. Everything seemed normal; planes were still overhead. He went on with his ritual shaving. Then he heard more explosions, also antiaircraft fire. "Something like a piece of bomb" flew over the roof of his bungalow. Flames and smoke arose behind the trees. He continued shaving, feeling that the RAF deserved "full marks" for the realistic air-raid-precautions practice.

Photiades strolled into the bedroom of Kenneth, the civil servant who shared the house. It was unusual for Kenneth to be up so early, but he was sitting on the edge of his bed, drinking tea. "We will have to complain to the RAF and tell them not to make so much noise so early in the morning," Photiades observed.

"Yes, dammit!" said Kenneth. "I'm usually asleep until 8:30 and will have a horribly long day today. I will write very sharply to the Air Ministry."

"I shouldn't think that they will take much notice," Photiades decided. "What about writing to *The Times*? Would that take too long?"

The district commissioner was considering practice mobilization, and Photiades had been struggling with the language of a "calling-up paper." The local state possessed a sultan, in whose name as well as that of King George the document had to be couched. ("You had to combine His Majesty's with His Highness' name and knowing which should come first was tricky.") To perfect his flowery prose he drove to the Volunteers' headquarters to check with someone. In effect he would be calling himself up, as he was a private in the Volunteers. Only Stevens, the transport officer, was there, but they went over the notice together and "streamlined" it.

Getting back in his car, Photiades drove to the police building, which seemed "remarkably quiet." It remained that way until the chief of police arrived, in full uniform and "looking most excited."

"Why aren't you in uniform," Paddy shouted. An Irishman, he was emotional at times.

Photiades offered to change into it "at lunchtime," which excited the chief even more. He brought down his swagger stick on the table with a bang, scattering the precious call-up papers. "Don't you know," he exploded, "that there's a war going on?"

"Yes, of course I do," said Photiades, who could count from 1939 to 1941. "It's been going on now for two years."

"No! Not that one. This is a real one. It's on here now. Didn't you hear the bombing this morning?"

The authenticity of the morning practice suddenly dawned on Photiades. "That explains it if they were real bombs. Who attacked us?"

"The Japanese. They also bombed Pearl Harbour. . . . Don't you listen to the wireless?"

"Thank God!" said Photiades, feeling "an indescribable relief" that the Americans were in the war.

"What are you thanking God for?" asked the chief. But Photiades, dropping the subject, had turned back to his bungalow to put on a private's uniform.

At Kulim Hospital in South Kedah, Henry McGladdery, a junior surgeon, saw the planes fly over en route to Penang and "took them to be ours on some sort of exercise." When Sungei Pattani was bombed, he was ordered there to deal with the casualties. "Off I went, taking my golf clubs with me and expecting to stay in Sungei Pattani for whatever number of months, or perhaps weeks, were needed by our army to drive the Japanese out of Malaya."

•

At General Tomoyuki Yamashita's Saigon headquarters, Lieutenant Colonel Ichyi Sugita, preoccupied until then with plans for moving into Thailand and Malaya, learned belatedly about the attack on Pearl Harbor. The cardinal rule in military doctrine was "know your enemy," and he felt "highly uneasy in my heart about the future destiny of our country." The "military men" who had authorized the operation, he felt, did not know the country or the people. As a general later Sugita would not change his mind.

•

Running the 170-mile Alexandria-Tobruk gauntlet had been a twenty-two-year-old seaman, Kenneth Cunningham, in an Australian destroyer that had sustained hull damage and limped back to "Alex" for refitting. The ship's company was divided and one watch barracked on two luxurious houseboats in the Nile, below Cairo. Completing his week away, Cunningham and his "best cobber," Bluey Collett, arrived at the Alexandria railway station just after 2:00 A.M. "As Blue and I left the dimly lit station in the blacked-out city to make our way back to the ship, I noticed two very excited 'Gyppos.' One of them rushed over to me in high excitement. After decrypting his poor English I assessed that the Japs had bombed the American Navy at Pearl Harbour. . . . The effect on me was electrifying. I shook the Gyppo's hand. (THAT was unusual then.) I punched the air with my right hand in tremendous excitement and yelled to my mate, 'Blue, we've won the war!' We then made our way back to the ship formulating all sorts of scenarios that would achieve an Allied victory."

•

By 7:00 P.M. the White House pressroom was a garbage dump of wastepaper, cigarette stubs, and wiring for cameras, microphones, and lights. The *Christian Science Monitor*'s correspondent, Richard L. Strout—the future TRB of the *New Republic*—had covered the White House since Woodrow Wilson's days, and had never seen anything like it. "The telegraph boys fairly came out of the cracks, the floor was tangled with a black spaghetti of wires, the motion picture lights were on, cameras were busy, men were telephoning, a radio receiver blared (and rattled out static every time somebody dialed a number from the booths). Men with chattering hand motion-picture machines climbed over and under desks . . . and they were followed by others carrying glaring lamps on black cords." To protect their primacy, the wire-services—AP, UP, and INS—had pasted paper on the windows of three telephone booths, usurping them for their own use.

Early and his secretary had emerged three more times, once with news that Guam had been attacked but not much else for early morning editions. Reporters scurried away for quick sandwiches and to check out other leads.

One source of Washington information that would have interested them remained secret for years to come: "Magic." But the machine had been running empty; nothing more had come from Tokyo after the activation message following the infamous paragraph fourteen. Then a new intercept arrived via Station S in Puget Sound, circular 2507 from the Foreign Ministry in Tokyo to diplomatic missions abroad. It was a preliminary report from *Kido Butai*. "The Imperial Naval Air Force," it read in plain text and in English, "has damaged three United States battleships and sunk three in the Battle of Hawaii." And it went on to identify the sunken ships as the *Oklahoma*, the *Arizona* and the *West Virginia*.

When the President's telephone rang again it was, he learned,

"Missy" Le Hand, from Warm Springs, where she was recuperating from a stroke. Marguerite Le Hand had been Roosevelt's secretary, and more, for twenty years, living in a small apartment on the third floor of the White House. Eleanor Roosevelt had long before that ceased intimacies with her husband, in the aftermath of an affair she had discovered he was carrying on; and the pale, blue-eyed Missy, who called Roosevelt "FD," became surrogate spouse while Eleanor remained public wife. Missy had served with charm and devotion and wifelike familiarity, but was high-strung and had kept going with sleeping pills before her breakdown. She had heard the war news in her sanatorium room, and could not bear being left out. Roosevelt told "Hacky"—Louise Hachmeister, at the White House switchboard—not to put the call through.*

•

The Japanese knew all about "the tunnel"—Aliamanu Crater, three miles west of Fort Shafter, from which General Short, now Military Governor, was directing what was left of the defense of Hawaii. The underground command post was his equivalent of Corregidor, a communications center for directing the expected assault on Oahu. Short had troops he could deploy, and he was busy doing it.

In the heat of a Hawaiian midafternoon, even in December, columns of "six-by" trucks loaded with soldiers from Schofield moved along the coast, depositing machine gun companies on the beach. Black smoke from burning ships still rose from Pearl Harbor. Private James Jones had his notebook with him, scrawling inside the cover that it should be sent to his brother in the event of the writer's death. He was developing grandiose ideas about future fame as an author, and as his truck, with machine gun mounted on the roof, wound its way down through fields of sugarcane and pineapple, Jones described his feeling that the war would be a social and cultural watershed the results of which many in his outfit would not survive to see. "I wondered if I would. I had just turned twenty the month before."

F Company was to cover the south shore from Wailupe, east of Honolulu, to Makapuu Point, on the southeast edge of Oahu. The truck pulled off at a designated campsite among the palms, palmettoes,

---

* Le Hand died of a cerebral embolism in 1944. FDR had willed her (as he did Eleanor) half the interest in his estate, but she predeceased him.

and hibiscus. Soldiers unloaded and stretched barbed wire along the sand and dug in machine gun emplacements. If an enemy could be repelled by a few machine guns and their rifles, the 27th Infantry was ready—but for a powerful thirst. There was little fresh water, and they were restricted to one canteen daily per man. Out to sea, so Jones would write to his brother Jeff, the "warm, raggedy roof of clouds" stretched on and on. "It almost seems as if you can look right on into eternity." The desolate beach would be the background for Jones's story "The Way It Is" and his short novel *The Pistol*.

Every movement on the Oahu shoreline was suspicious, every plane in the sky an enemy, every ship on the horizon bent on invasion. At Tripler General Hospital, where Barbara Fowler and her mother had rushed from distant Kahala to volunteer, every alarm complicated patient care. At the first sign of planes near Diamond Head, they had driven up to Wilhelmina Rise to see what was happening. When calls for doctors and nurses had gone out on the radio, they went to Fort Shafter to help out at Tripler, "doing whatever we figured was necessary, not really knowing just what to actually do." Martha Fowler took on the task of keeping wet a severely burned cook from Hickam Field—"so nothing would stick." But each time the sirens sounded "we had to get the least hurt under their beds and pull the curtains across their windows. What a job!"

Taking a break to grab a meal and a little rest, Dr. Moorhead ran into the commandant at Tripler, Colonel Alvin C. Miller. Maybe, said Moorhead, he should return to active duty, since that's where he was. Casually, Miller said that he would see what he could do; later he turned up in Moorhead's operating room and announced, "You're in the Army now!" If Moorhead wanted it, he was now a full colonel. But that would have been an emergency honorific. Moorhead was six months past sixty-seven.

HOUR 37

F OR HIROKO NAKAMOTO in Hiroshima there would be no classes for three days. She had come early on Monday, worrying about passing her sixth-grade examination for secondary school, and a classmate asked, "Do you know we have started a war with America?" Hiroko felt her heart beating very fast. Almost all that the United States had meant to her was encapsulated in a song she had been taught:

> A doll with blue eyes
> Born in America of celluloid
> Arrived in Japan's harbor
> With many tears in her eyes.
> "I don't understand the language.
> What would happen if I got lost?"
> Nice little Japanese girl,
> Please play with her.

America was big and rich, but could it also be bad?

Children were told to return home and follow the news on the radio. Hiroko was eleven, and confused. "Listening, I felt as if my blood were on fire, my body burning. The radio addressed us . . . , saying we must work hard for our country and prepare for the future. We did not know exactly what was meant. But I felt very sober as I went back to finish my last few months in primary school."

Already in her early teens, Junko Matoba had a profound knowledge of the West without ever having been there. Her father, a branch manager for a trading firm, now transferred to its Saigon office, had been in Australia with his family. "My mother and the children came directly back to Kobe without my father. I could not make friends since my education had been occidental. I felt like an outsider in the Japanese environment of militarism and propaganda about the sanctity of the Emperor. Everything seemed artificial. That morning the students were called to assemble to listen to an important announcement on the radio. . . . When [the attack on] Pearl Harbor was announced in such a tone as if Japan had already conquered the whole world, and when the headmistress told us to hail the Emperor with three Banzais, I felt instinctively that Japan was plunging into a lost war. I told the girls around me that, but they did not show any reaction." Nor did her mother, who worried only about reductions in food and clothing rations.

Shusaki Endo's alter ego protagonist, Ozu, in his novel *When I Whistle*, has already known months of dreary privation. Sugar and matches are rationed; university students put in compulsory "volunteer" service every two months at a munitions factory; there are increasingly numerous farewell parties for conscripted friends. One morning in Tokyo, Ozu is shaken from sleep by his mother. He protests, "If it's for school, I'm going to go in the afternoon. Let me sleep some more."

"That's not it! Japan and America are at war!"

Scrambling from his *futon*, he snatches at the newspaper extra: "WAR BREAKS OUT IN PACIFIC BETWEEN JAPAN AND AMERICA."

"Wow!" he shouted. "We did it!"

"What will happen?" his mother asks, wondering about Ozu's student deferment. "Do you think you'll be called up? This is terrible."

"What do you mean?" says Ozu, looking at her troubled face. "Japan will thrash America!"

Bolting his breakfast, Ozu rushes from the house to join whatever excitement he can find. "At Umeda Station a naval marching song was playing over the loudspeakers. After the march a news broadcast caused a great stir among the passengers. At the conclusion of the news, a spontaneous cry of 'Banzai' rose from the crowd."

At the university, student talk is almost entirely about the likely cancellation of draft deferments. In Ozu's philosophy class his professor is excited, his voice rising. "At last the time for a confrontation between the spiritual civilization of Japan and the material civilization of a foreign country has come! The modern age may well be at stake in this war. This morning it occurred to me that the mission of Japan is to deal the death blow to foreign culture . . . in our country!"

The news, Hiroyuki Agawa, twenty and a student at Tokyo Imperial University, agreed, was "terrific. . . . No question of moaning that if there is a war, some of us may die. No lamentations, that was our mood."

Recruited three years earlier by the Foreign Ministry as a university teacher, John Morris, an Englishman, wondered whether he had quasi-diplomatic status and was safe. While Tokyo radio poured out war bulletins, his cook urged, "Go on with your breakfast or you'll be late for work." He decided to check with his neighbor, Reuters correspondent Richard Tenelly, but there were policemen outside Tenelly's house. It was clear that he had been arrested. Morris risked an inquiry and explained his situation. He had to give a lecture at ten.

"We have no orders to arrest you," said a policeman, "so you had better carry on with your work as usual."

Morris took a tram and delivered his lecture. "There was nothing abnormal in the behavior of the students and we carried on as though nothing had happened." But before he could leave the building a university official ordered him to do no further teaching pending instructions from the Department of Education.

To clarify his position, Morris checked with the Foreign Ministry, where someone told him that orders had already been issued that he was not to be arrested; however, it might be best if he kept close to his house for a few days. On his way home he stopped to see his friend Frank Hawley, who worked for the British Council as director of its Library of Information and Culture. But Hawley and his Japanese wife had already been arrested. Hawley's cook advised against trying to visit. When she had brought bedding and food to Sugamo Prison, she had been refused permission to see them.

At his own house, Morris found "about eight policemen. . . .

Everything was in disorder; my books were lying all over the floor; my clothes had been pulled out of the cupboards, the bedding was heaped in the middle of the room. They fired questions at him: "Had I a short-wave transmitter concealed in the house? Had I perhaps a machine-gun, or at any rate a rifle?" They went through his letters, examined his photographs, and confiscated X-ray negatives of his lungs although he denied that they were pictures of secret fortifications. "They also selected for removal some half dozen of my books, all of them with red bindings, since in the minds of the Japanese police, books with red covers are thought to be connected in some way with communism. To these were added a very large pile of [English] newspapers, some a year old. Fortunately, these papers were not consecutive, for, although I did not then know it, it had recently become a penal offense to possess a consecutive file of newspapers." Then, to his surprise, the police left.

A heap of pamphlets on a top shelf escaped notice. The embassy had sent them to resident nationals to be offered to house guests. A Vere Redman production, they touted the British war effort. Prudently, Morris carried the contraband into the lavatory and flushed it away.

The excitement at elite Tokyo No. 1 High School, the vestibule to Tokyo University, kept students from paying much attention to lectures. "One boy in my class," Momo Iida noted, "was particularly impressed because on the train on his way to school, an old army veteran had suddenly stood up in the carriage and started to make a speech to all the passengers in a shaking, emotional voice." The war, he explained, had not merely expanded; it was "something entirely new, a total conflict the like of which we had never experienced before." Now that it had started, there could be "no going back. It was the greatest challenge in Japan's history," and "whatever the cost we had to overcome it." The thought was sobering.

Preparing for college entrance examinations on such a morning was impossible for Mutsuo Saitō. Despite the euphoria around him, in which he shared, he used the morning hours in which he would have been tutored by his crammer to buy "strong rice-straw paper" and a pot of glue, returning home to cover the windows as protection against flying glass. It seemed almost an unpatriotic lack of confidence, but his father approved. Watching from the living room, Kosuke Saitō explained, "What do they think they are doing, going to war with America? Don't they know how rich and powerful it is and how strong

American industry is? Japan can't hope to defeat a country like that."

"Didn't you hear what they said on the radio?" Mutsuo argued. "We've wiped out the American fleet. The whole Pacific is open to us now. Of course we're going to win." While his father thought that "something terrible had started," Mutsuo worried that history would pass him by. Once at the university he could become an officer cadet and then share in Japan's moment of glory. Meanwhile he tacked to his wall a large map of the Pacific to record conquests and victories with miniature rising-sun flags.

At the Christian college in Yokohama where Takaaki Aikawa was teaching, the dean appeared on a platform in the playground after morning gymnastics. "According to the radio," he announced, "war has been declared between Japan and America. I am not sure if this is true or not, but I suppose it is true since it came over the radio."

Aikawa was appalled at the logic and even more appalled, as a Christian, about the war. His school had resisted, as Emperor-worship, the enshrining of Imperial portraits, and until 1937 attempted to teach that Jesus was "the Lord of all," with "no East or West in Him." Militarism had finally won. Many students, sensing no contradiction in loyalties, now bowed as they passed Hirohito's portrait. In the playground Aikawa noticed, in the aftermath of the dean's message, "that the students did not disperse even after the work bell rang. They remained in many small groups. . . . With the excited faces of those who were destined soon to pay the penalties of war with their own precious flesh and blood, they stood around and seemed to us to be discussing the realities of war. I returned to the teachers' room. . . . It was crazy—suicidal!! Why on earth must we fight with them?" He thought of the missionaries who were his American friends and had spent "hard years" building the college. "Now they belonged to the enemy country!"

In Japan to learn her family's language, Iva Toguri had found the red tape of trying to leave exasperating. She failed to complete all the paperwork in time for passage home on the *Tatuta Maru*, although that escape route, on the decoy which quietly turned back to Japan, would have done her little good. "I just did not have enough knowledge of Japanese to understand what was happening the day Japanese radio announced war between Japan and the U.S.," she recalled in 1948. "I could understand the word 'war' but could not believe that war had really broken out. . . . I could only read the English newspaper printed in Tokyo, but I was warned by my uncle and aunt not to be seen reading a paper written in English." She felt trapped, and claimed to have wandered about in a daze.

There were ten thousand stranded Japanese-Americans, some entered in family registers where they lived, as Iva was with her aunt and uncle. Others were registered with the *Kempeitai*. Efforts to conscript "American" young men had begun years earlier, and there had long been economic and psychological pressure to show loyalty to Japan in some manner. Iva would succumb. Broadcasting in English, she became "Tokyo Rose."

Honolulu-born Tosh Kano had gone to Japan in 1933 to study engineering at Nippon University. With jobs hard to locate in the U.S. in the 1930s, he found work in Malaya and the Philippines. Back in Japan in 1940, he was drafted into the army and in 1941 sent to Hiroshima for officer training, then to Tokyo to the Army Engineering Academy. He was sure that war between Britain and Japan was close because his class was studying tactics for attacking Fort Changi in Singapore. On Monday morning, on his way from his boarding house to the *Oi machi* railway station, close to the waterfront, he heard "radio news floating out of a store" that war had come. Between repeats of the war bulletin the announcer warned, "Don't switch off your radio today. We will have much important news."

"Naturally, I stopped walking. My eyes were turned toward the voice on the radio. [I was] eager to catch every word. . . . My fears had come true." In his boarding house at breakfast he had read a morning paper with a headline, "U.S. Shows Stubborn Attitude. Talks Reach Serious Stage." It was all obsolete. He wondered about his parents and his sister in Hawaii, and—although he was overdue now at the Academy—he paused for more news. To calm himself, he lit a cigarette. When the bulletins and band music began repeating, he hurried on to the station.

On the train he saw faces more serious than exultant. Someone claimed, "Even a rat, when cornered by the cat, would turn against the cat. The situation for Japan was like this rat. The ABCD countries have forced Japan into war. If they hadn't set this line around Japan and hadn't blockaded all our trade and economy, Japan would not have started this war."

Another passenger wondered, "Can we win this war? Do you think we can fight bigger and richer countries?" And someone answered, "We fought Russia and won, didn't we?"* A man sitting next to Kano turned to ask, "Heitai-san"—Soldier—"what do you think about this?" Kano turned toward the window and pretended to look out, as if he hadn't heard. "I felt that the man was right about the economic blockade."

When he arrived at the Academy, in the suburb of Matsudo, Kano saw instructions on a blackboard: "No class today; assemble at the Officers' Club." Everyone gathered about the radio listening to martial music and intermittent news, waiting for the reading of the Imperial Rescript. Kano was not afraid of war or of death, but "felt like I had lost all the strength in my body."

•

Orders from Washington came to the embassy in Peking at 9:00 A.M. that the ranking officer was to negotiate a surrender. Incarceration wouldn't last long, T. G. Crews thought, perhaps six months. "We were so much better militarily." Still, it was "not a good feeling." The Marines stacked their rifles in the courtyard fronting their barracks, piled up their ammunition, pulled down the flag, and waited for the Japanese, who did not come for nearly four hours. "I can still hear the hard-heeled shoes of the Japanese soldiers as they clattered in on the cobblestones to take us captive. That morning we had had bacon and eggs for breakfast. Four years later we got another egg, when our POW camp was liberated."

Because Tientsin was close to Manchuria, it had become an alternative White Russian community after Mukden fell to the Japanese in 1931. Eugenia Foyn had met her English husband in Mukden and moved to Tientsin where he was district assistant manager for Caltex. The foreign concession, not so large as Shanghai's, was still a mini-nation. Japanese occupation made life harder, but a foreign passport had offered freedom from most harassment. Since foreigners had to register with the Japanese military, each address and nationality was known, making it easy for soldiers to knock on doors and order each

---

* Japan had overwhelmed the Czar's inept forces after the surprise attack at Port Arthur in 1904, but had been embarrassed by General Zhukov's army along the Mongolian border in 1938–1939, a defeat in an undeclared war covered up by censorship and propaganda.

resident holding what had suddenly become an enemy passport to pack a suitcase and be ready for shipment to an internment camp. For many in Tientsin it was their first news of the war.

Hastily, Francis Foyn began packing his company's ledgers, his stamp collection, and objects of sentimental value. Without telling him, Eugenia dumped all the useless treasures out, filling their few trunks with the practical things that evacuees needed—pots for cooking, jewelry for selling, bedding and blankets for sleeping, household valuables for bartering. When they reached the camp on the Shantung Peninsula, Foyn began unpacking and went into shock. Eugenia shook him and snapped, "You can't keep warm on ledgers." She had been a refugee before, and was a survivor.

Eugenia's sister had kept her Russian passport, and remained a neutral to the Japanese. Some Jewish refugees, long dogged by misfortune, did not have to pile into internment trains either. They held German passports.

•

A heavy overcast seemed to cover all Taiwan as Lieutenant-Commander Koichi Shimada's weather reconnaissance plane returned over Takao harbor at 6:00 A.M. His pilot could not land and had to go north to Taichu (T'ai-chung) until the fog cleared. By the time Shimada was able to report to headquarters at Tainan at 9:00, the attack squadrons had taken off. He worried about a reprisal raid on Taiwan. After all, the Americans must have long known about Pearl Harbor, and had even awakened to his predawn weather mission and jammed his radio signals. "Our defenses were far from complete. The air raid warning system and antiaircraft defenses were totally inadequate. Moreover, we had little of our strength left, since in addition to the attack groups sent against Luzon, we had dispatched planes to provide antisubmarine patrol for the [Luzon] invasion convoys headed for Aparri and Vigan." Until the aircraft returned, when the sun was already lowering, Shimada's fears remained at odds with the local situation. "We were at war with the United States, expecting action at any minute, yet the atmosphere on Taiwan remained peaceful and serene almost to the point of unreality."

•

The sun shone through occasional breaks in the clouds as the *Ryujo's* first-wave aircraft began returning at 9:30 from the Davao raid. Commander Hara on the *Amatsukaze* counted them. One was missing. Weather had been no factor—the day had been calm. Air defense had been nonexistent. The lost plane had developed engine trouble and ditched within sight of the destroyer *Kuroshio*, which picked up its crew.

Pilots reported "an empty bag." There was no carrier in the bay as reported. A seaplane tender, the *Preston*, was strafed but got away. Two seaplanes moored near it were destroyed. "It was," Hara concluded, "a most peculiar operation." He hoped for more interesting action once the second wave was back. Two cruisers and two destroyers—including his own—would not be returning to Palau. Instead, they would round Mindanao and patrol waters off Legaspi Bay in central Luzon, where an invasion force was to go ashore. As they broke away he learned from his radio about Pearl Harbor.

From Nielson Field, more remote from the headquarters hierarchy than the few miles to Intramuros, Brereton bombarded MacArthur's offices with calls asking to go to Taiwan with his B-17s. All morning, even before daybreak, Brereton's airfields had followed up unverified sightings from their own radar screens at Iba Field and from observers seemingly everywhere in Luzon. Some reports were from panicky Filipinos seeing a formation of birds; some may have been from fifth columnists sowing confusion. Flying Fortresses from Clark Field were already in the air to avoid becoming ground targets—all but one, which was having generator trouble. At 9:00 in the Nielson log appears the entry, "In response to query from General Brereton a message [was] received from General Sutherland advising [that] planes [are] not authorized to carry bombs at this time."

Captain Anloff at Fort Stotsenburg had been awakened at a leisurely 7:30 to be told, "Hey! The Japs bombed Pearl Harbor at 2:30 our time. I wonder if you could come over to the office a little early." By the time he arrived, a report was in that three fighter-bombers had attacked a small Army installation at Aparri, on the north Luzon coast, each dropping a well-aimed 500-pound bomb. Yet the Stotsenburg antiaircraft unit, the 200th Coast Artillery, formerly of the New Mexico National Guard, had been told by Manila that there was no evidence that a war was on, and they were to hold their fire unless bombed or fired upon. No one seemed to know that to the north of Luzon, Batan Island had been invaded and occupied since daybreak.

At 9:10 Colonel Harold George of the Interceptor Command reported to headquarters that he had 54 pursuit planes in the air and 36 in reserve, and that none of them had made any "contact with hostile aircraft." Yet more enemy sightings were reported, allegedly twin-engined bombers. Nothing of the danger to the Philippines seemed to disturb MacArthur on the first day of the war; afterward he and his senior staff carried on a public relations campaign to shift the blame elsewhere. In his memoirs, supported by self-serving hagiographies from subordinates, he claimed that Japanese air strikes in the early hours of the eighth had been warded off or had been nonexistent. He was "under the impression," he wrote, "that the Japanese had suffered a setback at Pearl Harbor ["our strongest military position in the Pacific"], and their failure to close in on me [in the Philippines] supported that belief." He knew nothing, by his account, of air strikes on Davao, on Baguio, on Aparri, on Camp John Hay, or of the occupation of the Batan Islands. And although Gerow had telephoned to him from Washington that Pearl Harbor had suffered "considerable damage," and Hart had added the shocking details, MacArthur preferred to rewrite his history. Through Sutherland he had prevented American B-17s from interdicting attack sites on Formosa, but his memoirs generously gave Brereton "complete tactical control of the Far East Air Force."

Had Sutherland been shielding his boss from bad news? Had he been making decisions by reading MacArthur's mind rather than consulting him? Nothing of the sort fits MacArthur's own inglorious know-nothing account. One must return to the image of a stunned, pajama-clad figure, more proconsul than general, sitting on his bed in the predawn darkness and reaching for his Bible rather than rushing to action. A paralysis of will, in part concealed by loyal lieutenants. For many reasons, most of them political, the MacArthur mystique did not unravel with the day.

•

Liu Hung Sak, a reporter for the Hong Kong newspaper *Kwang Ming Po*, awoke in Kowloon to the wail of air-raid sirens and the boom of bombs. Having lived in Chungking he knew the real thing. Dismissing any thought of fleeing for shelter—he had his responsibilities to *Kwang Ming Po*—he raced for the lavatory to wash and hurry on to his job.

An urgent knock on the door of the flat found him still filling his water basin. None of his family dared go to the door, nor would the frightened maid budge. Still in his pajamas, he opened the door to a British policeman with a cocked pistol.

"Are there any Japanese living here?" the policeman asked in English.

"No."

"You must come away with me!"

"Where to?"

"The police station."

"At least I should wash my face and get changed," Sak pleaded, still puzzled. The policeman followed with his gun to the lavatory, and as Sak lifted his razor he was ordered to pack it with his clothes. Recalling past litigation, Sak assumed that he was being confronted with a very untimely slander suit. His paper had weathered many of them.

The policeman accompanied Sak into the bedroom, past the cowering family. Outside, exploding bombs echoed. Then, as Sak was putting on his shoes, the policeman asked for Sak's immigration permit. He scanned it carefully; then he asked, "Is Szechuan in China or Japan?"

Suddenly Sak recalled that the previous tenant, who had left three months earlier, was Japanese. He explained the misunderstanding—that the lists of aliens still included the vanished enemy. Disappointed and waving his gun, the policeman warned, "If I prove that you are not a Chinese, I will use this next time I'm here!" Then he dashed downstairs. From the balcony, the relieved family saw a police car pull away.

It was already nine o'clock. Sak realized that it would be hopeless to get on the ferry to Hong Kong even if it were running. With his neighbor across the hall, Cheungkiang Fan, he went to Kowloon Wharf, where enterprising motor boat pilots and sampan captains were offering rides to passengers willing to pay almost anything to cross. Sak struggled into the crowd waving his dollars, and ten minutes later was at Queen's Pier.

Traffic everywhere in Hong Kong was heavy. Andy Leiper nosed into the Peak Road at Jardine's Corner, amidst a line of military vehicles. Leaving Helen at the hospital, he headed for his bank. He could hear the thump of bombs. The smudges of exploding antiaircraft shells hung in the air, and he could see smoke rising from the Kowloon side. "What I was seeing," he recalled, "was the annihilation of the colony's small air force of antiquated planes. . . . We never saw a British plane in the skies over Hong Kong during the entire course of hostilities."

Each bank had massive queues, and they would get worse, as government orders were to operate from ten to noon only, and to shut down during air raids. Seconds after the doors were opened by the Indian guards and the Chinese policemen herded anxious people inside, Jardine's banking hall was filled to capacity, remaining that way until the sirens howled again.

Although the *Morning Post* would report, loyally, "READY CIVILIAN COOPERATION AIDS MOBILISATION," there was "minor panic in the streets," UP chief George Baxter remembered. Tens of thousands of Chinese rushed to the air-raid shelters "dragging their crying children and what personal effects they could grab. . . . Merchants hurried to board up their windows and bar their doors to prevent the frightened Chinese from swarming into their establishments seeking refuge." The first hours were "pandemonium" with "just as many thousands rushing in one direction as in another regardless of the fact that the air-raid tunnel entrances were all on the lower hillside."

Many in the large Portuguese community (with ties to nearby Macao) were in churches for the Feast of the Immaculate Conception and emerged just as sirens were screaming or bombs booming. Hysteria followed when mothers rushing home to their children were directed instead to take cover in air-raid shelters.

Reporting late on Monday morning, Sergeant David Bosanquet was even later in getting to his antiaircraft battery. There was not enough transport in Hong Kong to convey all units to positions. His gun at Sai Wan had been manned at midnight only after he retrieved his own car and groaned uphill, overloaded with men and equipment, on the same road above Lyemun that he had taken with his girlfriend the night before. He had not slept since Friday. Of little use to anyone in his dazed condition, he dropped into his camp bed, left alone by his commanding officer, Lolly Goldman. Bosanquet came to with the morning sun beating down and Bombardier George Chow shaking him. "You hid yourself pretty well, didn't you?" said Chow. "The CO thought you would like to know that we have been at war for the last two hours and that perhaps you would grace him with your presence."

Bosanquet looked at George Chow's broad grin and assumed a joke. "Come on, get up," Chow insisted. "We're taking over No. 1 gun in ten minutes." When bombs began falling, Bosanquet was suddenly wide awake.

Until mobilization, Captain Simpson, his university students spared their scheduled examination, had never seen the Battle Box. Four levels underground, Brigadier MacLeod greeted him jovially with "What do you think of this set-up?"

Recalling stories of underground earthworks in World War I Flanders, Simpson said, "It seems all set for the Battle of the Somme."

MacLeod laughed. "The sooner our wonderful telephone is knocked out, the better. We may then be allowed up to the outer air, and see for ourselves what's going on."

A staff officer presented Simpson with a steel helmet and a service revolver which had an identity tag dangling from it reading "Mohammed Din." (He would show it to his wife so that if she read of a casualty by that name she could identify him.) His number-two houseboy, who had accompanied them in the car, appealed, "Master, more better you pay me iron hat. Then I go all o'time, look after you." Simpson found another steel helmet for him. "I was on the point of giving him the revolver"—Simpson thought such weapons were dangerous to bear—"but remembered that in Hong Kong it was a very serious criminal offence for any civilian to carry a revolver without a police permit."

.

Relman Morin looked at his watch. It was eight o'clock and still the Japanese had not come for him. He could be the only American in Saigon not yet in custody. Even a pre-breakfast saunter outside his Saigon hotel to buy an extra raised no alarms, and he had brought back a paper he thought "unreal, wholly without substance." Dispatches were credited to Tokyo sources, with a few claimed as *"émissions de France."* It seemed to him a page from *The Great Pacific War*—that Hector Bywater had imagined it all. "Pearl Harbor bombed . . . Manila and Hong Kong attacked . . . a statement from Tokyo that Anglo-American 'encirclement' had forced Japan to draw the sword . . . the Governor-General called upon the French to remain calm, reasserting French neutrality and Japanese respect for it . . . from Batavia, the flash that the Dutch, without hesitation, had plunged into the fighting

. . . the lurid, gloating, childishly excited Japanese accounts of the damage done at Pearl Harbor . . . 'the entire American fleet has been sunk.' "

The lobby was deserted except for a man leaning over the desk talking to a clerk. In the streets the only Japanese was an officer picking his teeth in front of La Pagode, a coffeehouse. In the rue Catinat the proprietor of the Cave Bordelaise was watching his waiters set up chairs and tables on the sidewalk as usual. Morin kept walking, toward a government office. Inside, he asked a *fonctionnaire* about his status.

"You mean because of the war? . . . But you are in a neutral country. You have the same status here that you would have if, for example, you were in Switzerland."

"I understand the British and American consuls have been interned already, and so have the British bank people."

"Not interned," said the official with hairsplitting precision. "Merely detained temporarily in their homes."

Morin retraced his steps to La Pagode, already full of locals drinking their morning coffee. He heard a whisper rustle through the room: "*Américain*." First no one met his eyes; then a patron he knew aggressively invited him to sit down.

"How is it that you are not arrested yet?"

"They seem to have missed me. What have you heard?"

Morin was offered an atrocity story his acquaintance had heard from a local woman. She had seen Sidney Brown, the American consul, dressed in a shapeless, shabby white robe, some coarse and dirty material like a prison kimono, hauled away in the back of an open Japanese truck. "They were exhibiting him like a prize, those dogs. They drove him through all the streets, shaming him. . . . But he was so magnificent. You should have seen him. So grave, so dignified. It was a triumph for him, *mais absolument*."

Good old Sidney, Morin thought with sad pride. But when he saw Brown a week later, the consul was surprised. The Japanese had apologized for having no car available. And they had taken the most direct route to their booking office. "Coarse white robe, hell!" Sidney Brown objected. "That was my best linen suit."

The coffee house vibrated with similarly authentic war news. British planes from Singapore had sortied over Saigon. American cruisers had sunk the Japanese carriers off Hawaii. A seaborne attempt on Hong

Kong was foiled. None of the stories were in the papers, but they left Morin hopeful.

At the hotel he had lunch amid chattering, exuberant people. Although it was Monday, it seemed like a holiday. No one appeared to be going to the office. After a few postprandial brandies it was beginning to look like a thoroughly pleasant war.

Even the internees, thrown together in the large, well-appointed house of the British consul, E. W. Meiklereid, were faring well. The six guests thrust upon him by the Japanese, who guarded the gate leading out to the boulevard, had a well-stocked library, a dining room table on which Ping-Pong balls clattered in off hours, an unconfiscated radio, a staff of servants, and a larder restocked by a houseboy permitted to go shopping with a gendarme. Morin knew none of it. Conspicuously and uneasily, he waited for his arrest.

•

Confused by lack of sleep or by the postponed, withdrawn, and reinstated operational plans, yet well aware that enemy landings since midnight had given him all the authority he needed to activate Matador, Brooke-Popham had failed to use it. Fears that premature violation of the Thai frontier might start a war were moot: the Japanese had simplified that problem. Yet he waited until a reply from London, formally giving him the authority he had requested four days before, arrived at 8:00 A.M. At 8:20 he told General Percival about the message but added, inexplicably, "Do not act." Although the war was real, "Brookham" was expecting a morning air reconnaissance of Singora and Pattani to resolve any last possible doubts.

By the time that whatever he was waiting for happened, and Brooke-Popham sent word to Percival that Matador, or what was left of it, was on, Percival had left for a previously scheduled meeting of the Straits Settlements Legislative Council, to offer a report on the situation. No one at his headquarters undertook to relay the orders north, to General Heath. Lines of authority were too rigid for an underling, however elevated, to chance that. While the Japanese were moving swiftly, puzzled and frustrated British troops remained undeployed except for those drawn into the fighting at the Kota Bharu beachhead.

•

The usual German method for wholesale killings of Jews was the *Aktion*, a roundup by the SS that separated those fit for slave labor from those to be gunned down and dumped in pits. Watching one such nightmare left even Heinrich Himmler feeling faint, after which he exhorted troops not to be haunted by the screams and the blood but to face their racial purification duties with steadfast consciences.

In Polish "Wartheland," mass murders had intensified as the winter made *Aktionen* less feasible in captured Russian territories. Five thousand Jews from nearby villages had been concentrated into Heidenmühle, a farming settlement near Turek, west of Lodz. The Judenrat had been ordered to list all inhabitants as fit or unfit, the latter group to include all Jews over sixty-five or under twelve. It had been obvious that disaster loomed, and the Judenrat turned to the rabbis for guidance. Their recommendation was fasting and prayer while hoping for a miracle, and they ruled that "the law of the land is the law," regardless of its evil. Since defiance only meant more deaths, they had accepted their impotence. Some Jews fled anyway, attempting to lose themselves in the Polish peasantry.

At 2:00 A.M. SS troops surrounded Heidenmühle. Jews who did not emerge willingly were flushed out in house-to-house searches. At bayonet point, by the harsh light of vehicle headlamps and electric torches, inhabitants were herded into one of the villages, marched out to a field, and ordered to line up, men and women separately. Shivering in thin nightclothes, they formed wavering queues, and waited.

•

When Janet and Ed Murrow arrived for dinner at the White House at eight, they expected pandemonium at worst, informality at best. There was both. In the corridors, streams of people scurried. In the family dining room Eleanor Roosevelt herself served scrambled eggs, milk, and a pudding dessert to the Murrows, to her friends Trude and Joe Lash, a few acquaintances who happened by, and to several of the Roosevelt family. From time to time a White House functionary slipped in and handed notes to her, some of which she passed about. Little at Pearl Harbor had escaped damage; the fleet was crippled and the West Coast exposed to attack. Her own mood was polite outrage.

FDR's place at the table was vacant. In the study adjoining his bedroom the President received officials, military and civilian, and had food sent in. Finally, the Murrows got up to leave. No, said Mrs.

Roosevelt. Her husband still wanted to see Ed. Janet went back to their hotel; Murrow sat on a bench in the hallway, chain-smoking and exchanging words, as they passed by, with Henry Stimson, Frank Knox, Cordell Hull, and others who seemed puzzled at the sight of a reporter waiting quietly in the White House inner sanctum.

"There was ample opportunity," Murrow wrote after the war, re-acting to charges of Administration foreknowledge, "to observe at close range the bearing and expression of Mr. Stimson, Colonel Knox, and Secretary Hull. If they were *not* surprised by the news from Pearl Harbor, then that group of elderly men were putting on a performance which would have excited the admiration of any experienced actor. . . . It may be that the degree of the disaster had appalled them and that they had known [it was coming] for some time. . . . But I could not believe it then and I cannot do so now. There was amazement and anger on most of the faces."

Another person to slip out from Mrs. Roosevelt's improvised din-ner was Tom Campbell, a Montana agricultural engineer and farming consultant, who told *New York Times* reporter Bill Lawrence and several other newsmen that he had heard that the Japanese "had sunk all our Pacific battleships at their moorings." The reporters dashed off to tele-phones, but they had been anticipated by Frank Knox. The Navy Secretary, once publisher of the *Chicago Daily News*, had warned news-paper executives to withhold any news that might let the Japanese know "how unbelievably successful their attack had been," as there was concern that "they might follow it up with an amphibious assault against Hawaii, which we would have been powerless to resist."

It was Eric Sevareid's sad-voiced evening broadcast from the White House, CBS commentator Elmer Davis thought, "that really set the wheels turning in American factories. For the first time, he told the grim truth . . . , that damage to the American fleet had been disastrous, that it would be impossible to exaggerate it—that indeed the very core of naval defense in the Pacific had been wiped out." He could give few details, "yet his listeners felt an odd sense of relief . . . that the uncer-tainty was gone, knowing that it was plain now what all of us must do."

Knowing what Americans now had to do was the theme of early editions of Monday morning newspapers across the country, compet-ing with Sunday extras and out by eight in the East. Many editors unlimbered their "Second Coming" type for the front-page headline, the *Philadelphia Record* sprawling "WAR!" hugely across the pink paper of its earliest Monday edition, hawked by newsboys at every intersection where a traffic signal stopped vehicles. The *San Francisco Chronicle* splashed the same exclamation. More circumspect, the *New York Times* spread "JAPAN WARS ON U.S. AND BRITAIN" across its more sedate front page. Even the *Chicago Tribune*, anti-interventionist until the last day, began Colonel Robert R. McCormick's lead editorial on page one under a boxed head, "WE ALL HAVE ONLY ONE TASK." War, he wrote, "has been forced on America by an insane clique of Japanese militarists. . . . It has happened . . . thru no volition of any American. Recriminations are useless. . . . All of us, from this day forth, have only one task. That is to strike with all our might to protect and preserve . . . American freedom."

On the *Tribune*'s masthead McCormick ordered its slogan, "Our country, right or wrong," adapted from Commodore Stephen Decatur's boast in 1815, replaced with "Save our Republic."

The next morning, unwilling to relinquish his suspicion that Roosevelt was somehow conspiratorially behind events, McCormick telegraphed his Washington bureau chief, "The Japanese attack couldn't have taken place if the Hawaiian commanders had been alerted. Why weren't they?"

At 8:20 the first Cabinet officer arrived at the White House. Jesse Jones, the Secretary of Commerce, had first heard about the war from a seat in Griffith Stadium. Others trickled in through a throng of spectators on the back lawn of the White House who had begun singing, hesitantly at first, then with fervor, "God Bless America"—it had already become the informal National Anthem—and "My Country, 'Tis of Thee." Vice-President Henry Wallace followed, then Secretary of Labor Frances Perkins, Secretary of Agriculture Claude Wickard, Secretary of the Treasury Henry Morgenthau, Jr., Postmaster General Frank Walker, Attorney General Francis Biddle, Secretaries Stimson, Hull, and—last to arrive—Knox. The ubiquitous Harry Hopkins took his own minutes.

From behind his desk in the big oval Blue Room on the second floor, around which the Cabinet sat in a semicircle, the President began by remarking that they were at the most grave Cabinet session since Lincoln had met with his Secretaries after the firing upon Fort Sumter in 1861. "You all know what's happened," he said in a low voice. "The attack began at [about] one o'clock [Washington time]. We don't know very much yet."

"Mr. President," Francis Biddle asked, "several of us have just arrived by plane. We don't know anything except a scare headline, Japs Attack Pearl Harbor. Could you tell us?"

The President, recalled Frances Perkins, who had just flown down from New York, asked Frank Knox to "tell the story," which he did, with interpolations from Stimson, Hull, and the President. Interrupting Knox, who offered to fly out to Pearl Harbor the next morning to find out what had happened, and why, Roosevelt urged, "Find out, for God's sake, why the ships were tied up in rows."

Ashen-faced, Knox explained, "That's the way they berth them." To the President, a Navy man who had been Assistant Secretary in 1917–1918, it seemed more like carelessness than orderliness, and Harry Hopkins noted that even the sketchy description of damages and casualties left them "all shocked."

Undersecretary of State Sumner Welles had prepared for Hull a long alternative war message. Ignoring it, Roosevelt read his draft declaration of war. Hull again argued for more detail, with Stimson seconding him. Discussion arose about connecting Germany with the Japanese aggression, but Roosevelt pointed out that there was no evidence of collusion. What he wanted, he explained, was a message that would unite Congress—in Hopkins's description "an understatement and nothing too explosive."

FDR's draft was accepted as presented.

•

Realizing that as *Oklahoma* escapees they would be assigned no duties, Archie Pence and another sailor received permission to take out a motor whaleboat from the *Maryland* to look for survivors in the water and to transport men back and forth from Ford Island to the shipyard. ("Twice we were almost run down by destroyers racing out of the harbor.") Then they used grapnel hooks, in case there were bodies tangled in the wreckage, to clear oily debris from between the *West Virginia* and the *Tennessee*. They gave up late in the afternoon when they ran out of fuel. In the confusion there was no way to pump more.

In the Ford Island dispensary in midafternoon they finally stripped away their oil-soaked gear. Clothes were in short supply. Men extricated from the harbor wore anything available. "It was a common sight," H. J. Bultman recalled, "to see an enlisted man in officer's uniform. By the morning the only thing left in our room on Ford Island was an athletic supporter."

No one told Pence and his buddy where to go or what to do. Having not eaten all day, they wandered about looking for food, but when they reached the Island boathouse they were ordered into a working party loading ammunition onto lighters going out to destroyers and cruisers in the harbor. Sunday breakfast had to wait until darkness.

•

From the opening of the Tokyo Stock Market at nine, there had been a steady decline in prices, suggesting a lack of confidence in the outcome of the war. By ten Finance Minister Okinori Kaya was worried. He knew that Hisatsune Sakomizu had already been at the Stock Exchange Building for hours and had conferred with exchange President Yahaichi Aizawa and with representatives of the brokers' association. Although everyone understood the ministry's interest, traders decided against hasty government purchases, which would appear artificial. Instead, Aizawa offered to stake his own money, and bought a block of shares. Prices immediately went up above the previous day's quotation. Then they fell back as no news of specific war successes followed the announcement of outbreak of hostilities.

Sakomizu and Aizawa were concerned: would others pick up the optimistic note that Aizawa had sounded? They watched the quotation board; the market began to rally. Prices restabilized; then they rose dramatically amid a heavy traffic of messengers and brokers. Sakomizu went down to the floor to investigate. "Haven't you heard?" a messenger explained. "Someone on the floor got a call from a friend in the Navy Ministry. They've attacked Hawaii and destroyed more than half of the U.S. fleet!"

As eleven o'clock approached, newspaper extras began appearing on the floor and prices soared.

WAKE ISLAND	TOKYO	NORTH ATLANTIC	PITTSBURGH
1:00 P.M.	11:00 A.M.	SOUTH ATLANTIC	NEW YORK
December 8	December 8	2:00 A.M.	WASHINGTON
		December 8	9:00 P.M.
			December 7

HOUR 38

T HE FIRST twin-tailed "Betty" bombers approaching Wake Island were hidden by a rain squall almost until they were overhead, their engine noise smothered by the roaring surf. At 11:58 A.M. the Marines of Battery E at Peacock Point saw a wedge of nine unfamiliar aircraft. Then it appeared, according to a civilian workman, as if "the wheels dropped off the airplanes." Bombs—the "wheels"—began falling from 2,000 feet. Eight Grumman Wildcats were on the ground; Major Paul Putnam had been keeping four of his twelve F4Fs on round-the-clock patrol since arriving from the *Enterprise*.

Driving back from the Commandant's office, Pan Am *Clipper* Captain John H. Hamilton and the company's airport manager, John B. Cooke, heard the drone of planes, then felt the repeated shock of exploding bombs. From the front seat, Cooke's Chinese driver, "Tommy," spotted the Japanese bombers, swerved, and braked. "We haven't a Chinaman's chance!" he shouted, opening his door and diving out.

The three men scrambled into an unfinished foundation hole. A bomb hit the coral about twenty feet away, showering them with sand and debris. Yelling that the spot was too hot for him, Hamilton used a lull to run for the cover of a drainage pipe. Cooke and Tommy followed, but when bullets began to kick around them they fled back to their hole, from which they watched a second flight of nine planes make a shambles of Pan Am's hotel, storage sheds, fuel tanks, radio shack, and wood-plank dock.

Ignoring the risks, Marine pilots ran to their aircraft. One hundred-fifty-pound bombs and 20mm incendiary bullets reduced four parked F4Fs to rubble. Fire spread to three more planes; only the last was salvageable. Two pilots died; another would die by daybreak. Twenty other Marines would die; eleven were wounded. Only twenty-one men in the ground crew were unhurt. Nearby, Walter Bayler's communications center was wrecked; tents were burning and gasoline storage tanks and drums, lashed by the trade winds, blazed with searing intensity. At the Pan Am compound, the hotel was afire and ten civilians killed. But the *Clipper*—an unexpected target not in Japanese plans—was hit only by machine-gun fire.

In twelve minutes the raid was over. Not a bomber was downed, and the pilots, low enough for their wide grins to be seen, waggled wings in farewell as they banked in the direction of Kwajalein Atoll to the south. The four Grummans on patrol, inexplicably all to the north, had seen nothing. As they landed, one struck bomb debris on the strip, damaging its propeller and engine. It was 12:10. The Wake air defense was down to four planes.

Examining his flying boat, pockmarked by sixteen machine gun holes, Hamilton estimated that it was marginally airworthy—enough to risk a run for the mainland. By 12:50 the plane was loaded with thirty-seven passengers and twenty-six Pan Am employees, some of whom were not on the morning run, and, to make room for them, stripped of all nonessential weight, including the mail. Wallowing away from the shattered dock and into the channel, the Martin 130 made one attempt at a takeoff, then backtracked for another. On the third try the overloaded craft picked up enough speed to lift off the lagoon. It was 1,185 miles east to Midway.

As the *Clipper* rose, an excited figure was seen running toward the dock. It was J. P. Hevenor, a government employee who had a ticket but had not heard the departure call. He would become a long-term guest of the Japanese.

A letter had arrived with the *Clipper* for Private First Class Verne L. Wallace, but he was manning a lookout post on a coral spit and a friend had picked it up for him. By the time Wallace could open the envelope, the words inside were of little comfort. His girlfriend in Haverford, Pennsylvania, had written, "As long as you have to be away, darling, I'm so very, very happy you are in the Pacific where you won't be in any danger if war comes."

.

At Lautoka, Fiji Islands, the crew of the SS *Mapele*, a Matson Line freighter, had just finished off-loading two thousand tons of cement for a new airport at Nadi and had left with a cargo of sugar for Vancouver via Honolulu and San Francisco. Fiddling with his dials, the radio operator picked up the news of Pearl Harbor and notified the captain, George Mollinson. There were sealed orders for such eventualities. Mollinson read his. The *Mapele* was to sail thirty miles to the west of its usual track—and the ship was to have all surfaces visible from air or sea immediately painted gray.

While the radio shack listened for distress calls (there would be five), the crew began mixing together all the black and white paint on board.

.

By eleven o'clock Ambassador Grew had read a *Yomiuri Shimbun* extra reporting that war had broken out between Japan and the United States and Great Britain. With the Tokyo embassy closed by the police, Grew had much to reconsider, and few of his senior staff about. He was not even aware until afterward that Ichiro Ohta of the Foreign Ministry had called on Eugene Dooman and had to see someone at a lower level instead, Third Secretary Edward Crocker, since Dooman had not been able to reenter.

Extracting a paper from his pocket, Ohta told Crocker, whom he did not know, "I am instructed to hand to you, as representing the Embassy, the following document which I shall read to you." Then he offered in his best school English a message which mentioned nothing about an attack and could only have been conceived in the Wonderland world of diplomatic obfuscation: "I have the honor to inform Your Excellency that there has arisen a state of war between Your Excellency's country and Japan beginning today. I avail myself of this opportunity to renew to Your Excellency the assurances of my highest consideration."

"This is a tragic moment," Crocker replied, adjusting his pince-nez.

"It is," Ohta agreed; "and my duty is most distasteful." Then he proceeded to read a longer document, in English, formally closing the embassy and suspending its functions. No one was to communicate with the outside, and all radio transmitters and shortwave receivers were to be handed over immediately. In the confusion, no one mentioned the radiotelephone, with which embassy personnel were able to communicate across the Pacific for another twelve hours, until it was jammed. And a car radio was forgotten, and used, largely unsuccessfully, to pick up English-language broadcasts. But everyone was locked into the embassy compound, to remain until release to an exchange ship the following June.

Even as Ohta, accompanied by policemen, strode through the embassy issuing instructions, files were being emptied and their contents burned in metal wastebaskets. Anticipating trouble, the naval and military attachés, Commander Henri Smith-Hutton and Colonel Harry Cresswell, had destroyed their codes and files the previous Friday. Now Helen Skouland, the slim blonde in charge of the file room, passed folders and documents to clerks and secretaries who fired them with gasoline from five-gallon tins. In the courtyard, as yet unvisited by Ohta, eyes watered from the smoke and soot, and burning scraps of paper littered the gardens. Charles ("Chip") Bohlen, later an ambassador and State Department bigwig, seized a bucket and sloshed water about.

En route to the embassy in a car with a Japanese-speaking colleague, Bohlen had heard the ringing of the traditional newsboys' bells and asked their chauffeur if it meant anything. He had heard reports of fighting between the British and Japanese fleets, the driver said. "Probably not true; only on Japanese radio." But they bought "one of the flimsy extras, and my companion translated the reports of fighting between the Japanese, and American and British, fleets."

Upon Ohta's official closing of the embassy, Eugene Dooman was permitted to return, with all his personal effects, to be sealed up in the compound. So were other staff members who lived outside. Most were prudent enough to arrive with their mattresses and bedding. The unusable offices became dormitory rooms, while the six most senior officers moved into the embassy residential quarters with the Grews. Japanese servants working in the embassy were called together by the police and given the choice of remaining interned with their employers, or leaving. All of them, even Oyama, chose to stay.*

Deeply depressed, feeling that his ten years in Japan had failed, Grew tried not to show it. He invited his staff into the Residence for a drink, discussing with them bedding arrangements and housekeeping needs, and the uphill fight inevitable to reverse a long series of initial losses. Their link with the outside world would be the Swiss mission. How much, if anything, of international law the Japanese would honor was unknown.

Shortly after eleven, Ambassador Craigie left the columned portico of the British embassy to call on Grew and was surprised not only that no police or soldiers stopped him but that there were no more than the usual number of uniforms in the vicinity. At the American embassy the compound was surrounded by police and curious onlookers. Denied admission, Craigie protested loudly until he was permitted in, just in time to learn that the official Japanese declaration of war had been delivered. Guessing that he would have no chance to talk to Grew again for a long time, if ever, Sir Robert told the ambassador that he had enjoyed working with him during the previous four and a half years, and returned to his waiting car.

At His Majesty's embassy, police now blocked all the entrances, but "the great iron gates were speedily flung open. . . . As my car passed through and I heard the clang of the gates closing behind me, I knew this sound was symbolic of a temporary loss of liberty for all of us."

A few minutes later, Pleasant Craigie observed the Netherlands ambassador, General J. C. Pabst, a veteran of twenty years in Tokyo, urging the police to let him in to see her husband. Refusing, they ordered him back to his car, pushed him in, and slammed the door. It was the last they would see of the gentle Pabst, who died in internment a month later.

---

* Employees locked in for what would be seven months of internment were permitted only one leave—at the New Year. Throughout the claustrophobic weeks, they served dinner always dressed in formal Japanese clothes and with the utmost formality, as if each occasion were an official function. Yet the men knew that their families were subject to contempt for assisting the enemy. Dooman "never could really understand why they remained," but they did. On the day of departure, the head servant said to Dooman, "When you return home and listen to people telling you of the bad things we Japanese have done, please tell your friends about us."

The busy Mr. Ohta was already at the British embassy to repeat the instructions he had just given to the Americans, and to demand the embassy's shortwave transmitter ("They had evidently got us mixed up with the German Embassy!"). Craigie denied having one, and after a fruitless search Ohta's men removed all receiving sets "with a vague promise that they would be returned . . . ; but we never saw them again."

Another foreign diplomat arrived at the gate to confront the gendarmes. Insisting on seeing Lady Craigie, Madame Hansen, wife of the Danish consul general, got her way. She had brought "a number of camp beds" for the embassy staff. Pleasant Craigie was grateful. Even "small telephone lobbies without windows" were being turned into bedrooms. Food and fuel were being pooled—even clothing. Some of the staff had arrived for work without knowing there was a war on, and had only what they wore.

For others, no beds would be needed. The embassy chaplain, the Rev. T. P. Simonds, was arrested in Yokohama and lodged in the city jail. (The Anglican Bishop of South Tokyo, the Rt. Rev. Heaslett, who had lived most of his adult life in Japan, was also jailed.) Before the gates closed, the embassy counselor, Paul Gore-Booth, had retrieved Mrs. Redman, although the authorities were still insisting on arresting her husband. Yoshitane Kiuchi, Chief of the Protocol Department, who, in top hat and tail coat, had returned Mrs. Redman, came back several days later, again in morning coat, but with a gendarme colonel in uniform and a dozen plainclothesmen, to take Redman by force. While protesting that Redman, a diabetic, might die in jail, Craigie was pushed aside and Redman roughed up and removed.*

In a "Final Report" written eighteen months later, Craigie deplored the war with Japan as a disaster for Britain. Anthony Eden sent it to Churchill, who minuted back that the Japanese attack, despite Sir Robert's unfortunate experience, had been "a blessing" for Britain, having brought the U.S. "wholeheartedly and unitedly into this war. . . . Greater good fortune has rarely happened to the British Empire than this event."

•

* Freed when the British were repatriated late in 1942, Vere Redman became Director of the Far Eastern Section of the Ministry of Information in London.

A second air raid over Kowloon occurred at ten o'clock, a half hour after Captain H. L. White, who had been moving his unit from Shamshuipo to Wan Chei Gap, had received orders countermanding the leisurely earlier ones. Now he was directed urgently to the island, with all his ammunition and equipment. His first thought two hours earlier was "new aircraft for the defence of Hong Kong": now he knew better. Bombs fell at the far end of the parade ground and on Jubilee Building, the officers' quarters. The structure shook; plaster flaked off the walls. When everyone unhurt got off the floor, White sent armed parties to round up trucks at gunpoint. ("Chinese drivers would leave their trucks and beat it.") He also dragooned "a gang of coolies" to help with the loading. ("Had to go down to the pier myself a couple of times and pull my revolver on them to keep them from leaving us flat.")

Later he reported "not a single serious casualty all day"; the dead and all the badly wounded had only been Chinese.

On the island, the larger shops opened late, at ten, and then only partially. The Sincere Company, Lane Crawford, Wing On, Tai Sun, and China Emporium opened only their main entrances. Guards materialized at all government buildings, and the courts suspended proceedings. Chinese residents waited outside newspaper offices for posted bulletins as extras were delayed by censorship. The examiners for the Secretary of Chinese Affairs had been late in arriving at work. Someone held the English-language *South China Morning Post* for Monday aloft and complained, "There is no mentioning of the imminence of war in this newspaper!"

By 10:30 Dr. Isaac Newton of Kowloon Hospital had taken in nearly all of the 103 casualties he would see during the day. He had arrived at 8:15 although he had still been in his pajamas at 8:00. When leaving his house in a hurry, Newton had difficulty convincing his houseman, Ah Yuan, that packing a dinner jacket was unnecessary. Collaring sixty coolies for stretcher-bearers, and finding extra beds, was harder work than wholesale surgery. "I felt rather sick inside and did not enjoy my lunch," he wrote in his diary, "but had to push some food in because of the work in front of me."

Doing his daily paperwork, a bespectacled Maryknoll priest, Father Mark Tennien, switched on the radio in the Catholic mission in Japanese-occupied Wuchow, northwest of Hong Kong and Canton. From the windowsill, the radio music was lost in the street noise below—the narrow lane was crowded with peddlers, hawkers, junkmen, Chinese on daily errands, children. Close by he heard the familiar sounds of the bottle-scavenger, his cans and glass clinking in bags swinging from his shoulder pole. Then through them he heard the Hong Kong announcer break through with news flashes about Pearl Harbor, Manila, and even the bombing of Hong Kong. The stunning news had come to him late. He had been used to Japanese bombs in the Yangtze valley since 1938, and had been in China since 1928. Suddenly he and his missioners were no longer neutrals, but wartime enemies.

•

By ten o'clock the Japanese had reopened the Shanghai Bund and ceremonially hoisted the Rising Sun to the mast of the USS *Wake*. In front of the hotels and banking houses on the Bund, a contingent of marines paraded, in celebration and intimidation. Aircraft flew overhead, dropping leaflets in a variety of languages exhorting the population to remain calm and to rely on the benevolence of the occupiers. Sentries were posted at consulates, banks, municipal buildings, cable and telephone offices, and public utilities. By ten o'clock, the Japanese had even found John Powell's secret radio transmitter and seized it, but not before several newsmen had filed stories and Powell had sent one of his own to the London *Daily Herald*.

Powell had returned to the American Club, where he had been living, just in time for a servant to knock on his door and warn that Japanese soldiers were in the lobby and had ordered everyone to leave in two hours. Many had resided at the club for years, expecting to live out their lives there. Few had enough trunks and cases to pack much, and they lost whatever they could not carry away, but all—Powell included—"started packing furiously."

The takeover of Shanghai was rapid and efficient. Captain Otani, who had boarded the *Peterel* with the summons to surrender, had been, as *Mr*. Otani, the Assistant Secretary of the Municipal Council, working under Godfrey Phillips. Without explaining his dual role he telephoned—still as Assistant Secretary—the Chairman of the British Residents' Association, a Mr. Collar, and asked him to the office. Collar hurried to the Municipal Building and found a uniformed Otani, who received him courteously, filled two glasses with sake, and proposed, "I ask you to accept the admiration of the Imperial Japanese Navy for the noble action of *Peterel*."

Then Otani came to the point—although he was serious about the *bushido* displayed by the British sailors. There were four survivors not yet rounded up, he explained; he wanted assistance in finding them. Equal to the occasion, Collar observed that as a civilian he had no authority over military personnel. Otani dropped the matter.

Two British officers unconnected with the *Peterel* had also escaped detention. Major Sidney Hunt and Captain Raymond Dewar-Durie, attached to the consulate, had driven there in civilian clothes on quiet back streets. Dewar-Durie had codebooks and documents in his office and wanted to get at them before the Japanese. As they reached the Bund, where the British consulate was just south of the Garden Bridge, they saw a sentry already at the gate. Parking in the road to the rear of the compound, Dewar-Durie climbed the wall and burglarized his own building, afterward burning the papers from his safe. Abandoning their very recognizable car, they slipped away through narrow alleys.

As foreign civilians, they might have chanced the open country beyond the Settlement perimeter. Yet as military men they could have been shot for wearing mufti; and to reach Free China they would have to hazard hundreds of miles of occupied territory as very conspicuous Caucasians. Locating Nationalist agents they knew, they arranged—for a price—to be smuggled into the hinterland in the trunk of a car. (After weeks on foot and in sampans upriver, they reached Chungking.)

Arch Carey, a Shell Oil employee, went to his office on the Bund and encountered Japanese marines. Since they did not stop him, he went to his department only to find Japanese officers, accompanied by interpreters, swarming about. He would be allowed back later to retrieve personal papers, Carey was told—but nothing else. "These men were not pleasant; they joked about the slogans and war pictures, including photographs of Mr. Churchill which adorned the office walls. At the main entrance to the Shell Building there were elaborate displays of British war posters. . . . These were immediately removed by our new overlords. . . . Out in the streets, barricades had been erected at intersections of all main roads; Japanese marines or soldiers . . . intercepted all foreigners, asking for passes or passports."

The south side of Avenue Edward VII, at the Bund, was the upper boundary of the French Concession, technically Vichy-run. Carey crossed with two colleagues to find a bus, but his companions were turned back. They were not carrying their passports. He promised to send their papers to the Shell Building so that they could leave it.

.

At ten, with Fort McKinley's code room in morning routine, Lieutenant Harold Brown went down to the harbor to exchange mail sacks with the courier boat *Miley*, from Corregidor. Returning to the McKinley vault, he opened his sack and found "a long Jap message setting up an open code to cover certain developments. The open message was to end with the word 'STOP.' I read the message very carefully." Later he recalled three of the phrases. If certain Japanese names were mentioned in a message about the shifting of personnel to other positions it would mean

Japan was at war with Britain, *or*
Japan was at war with the United States, *or*
Japan was at war with Britain and the United States.

Although the cable gave no particulars of dates or times or places, it might have been useful to know about it earlier, but Navy decrypters did not work weekends, and the paper had piled up. Brown took the message to General Sutherland at Fort Santiago.

"Very interesting and timely!" Sutherland observed in a voice thick with sarcasm. He asked whether the code had actually been received, and Brown confirmed that something like it had, although the key names had not been checked. (It was very likely the ubiquitous breaking-relations message.) Why, asked Sutherland, had the decrypting been delayed "to the point of uselessness?"

"I explained," said Brown, "that the message setting up the system had been sent to the Navy to be broken several days ago," but that everyone had been "running behind because of the volume of work." Sutherland listened until Brown had finished, then asked him to take the cable and the explanation to MacArthur's office. After a five-minute wait—record brevity—Brown was ushered in, and made his presentation. "Thank you, Son," said MacArthur, and signaled that the interview was over. "He never moved a muscle or changed his expression during my explanation."

At Fort McKinley, Minnie Breese Stubbs remembered her gas mask. A few weeks earlier the staff had the customary practice session, with each person donning a mask, going through a gas-filled room, and removing the mask an instant before exiting, to learn, with streaming eyes, the effectiveness of the device if an enemy utilized a chemical weapon. Nurse Stubbs was supposed to play golf that morning with Hattie Brantley, as neither went on duty until the afternoon. They had heard about Pearl Harbor and about the bombing of Baguio. Under war conditions, so they thought they were told when their gas masks were issued, "we were supposed to wear them at all times. . . . So we went out to play golf. Put our gas masks and helmets on and then we got to play. We went on with our game."

The surrealist vision of women in gas masks and steel helmets swinging golf clubs on the brilliant green under a torrid tropical sun suggests the air of unreality with which many responded to the outbreak of war. It would be no different in a place like Singapore. Only bombs and bullets and bloodletting could shatter the colonial state of mind.

•

Petroleum engineer R. G. Tyler's telephone rang at 8:30. All Europeans at the Shell oil fields in Lutong, just west of Brunei, North Borneo, were to report to the Rest House. It was the all-purpose meeting place. Ever since he had tuned in Manila Radio as usual at 6:15—one got an early start to the day when living practically on the Equator—he had been expecting the summons. "Quite a jolt," he noted in his diary. He knew that the "half-cocked state of affairs" was about to end, but that it happened via Hawaii was a surprise. By 8:00 he had learned from Singapore Radio that the battle was joined even closer to home. There had been schemes discussed ranging from mild air-raid precautions to complete demolition of the fields. Tyler had gone to his office to wait out the decision.

At the Rest House all hands were issued "Army webbing and knapsack equipment." Everyone was to pack whatever essentials would fit, then stand by for instructions. The miles of pipes and pumps, towers and tanks, Tyler mused, were "the most promising in the world, with potentialities that nobody could estimate . . . , the labour of years." Yet they were indefensible.

•

The HMS *Gossamer* was a Royal Navy minesweeper escorting convoys halfway to Archangel and Murmansk over the North Cape, then escorting return ships back. "Aussie," yelled Able Seaman Page, a Scot, to the only Australian on board, eighteen-year-old Geoff Jellbart, "the Japs have bombed the hell out of Pearl Harbour!"

"Good," said Jellbart. "Now the Yanks have got to come in with us."

In the far warmer South Atlantic, the former liner *America*, now the USS *West Point*, a straggler in the huge convoy from Halifax, Nova Scotia, to destinations unknown, was approaching Cape Town with sufficient British troops to populate a small city. Although the ships and seamen were all American, and technically neutral, the mission was thoroughly belligerent. The soldiers aboard were from a nation at war with Germany, and the ships relieved British vessels shifted to other war duty. Admiral Dönitz could send his U-boats against the Stars and Stripes only at risk of widening the war.

The *West Point*, the *Manhattan*, and the *Mount Vernon*, all renamed from peacetime passenger service, were at the tag end of a cruiser-led convoy code-named "William Sail 12X," which was having trouble staying together in rain squalls and stormy seas. Buffeted by wind and water, the carrier *Ranger* could not launch its patrol planes, and the cruiser *Quincy* was having difficulties retrieving its catapulted sea-plane scouts. H. Norman Honhart, a former gunner's mate recalled to active duty and turned into an officer, had just noted in his diary for December 7 aboard the armed transport *Orizaba*, as clocks moved to the new day, "19th day at sea. A.M. What a night, terrific storm, no rain but high wind. Everything is breaking loose. 23-degree rolls, waves higher than A-deck. . . . [cruiser] *Vincennes* lost a whale boat. Slightly warmer tonight."

Where they were sailing was the subject of daily speculation, and when one of the radiomen aboard the *West Point* rushed into his cabin to wake up his mates with the news from Pearl Harbor he was greeted as if it were more rumor. Ed Moore's response was "Get lost!" But the radioman returned a few minutes later with confirmation.

The news also went to the British wardroom on the upper deck, where there was a radio. When Captain L. W. Gormley, who thought his regiment was en route to Basra, on the Persian Gulf, passed by as duty officer, he noticed "intense excitement." Curious, he went inside and heard for himself, then rushed below to inform his colonel. Crowded below for weeks of monotonous sameness in shallow tiers in what had once been ballrooms, the sleeping troops were, by day, avid consumers of wild speculation about where they were going, and why.

Gormley had "imagined it all," the colonel insisted, sitting up to hear the account of Pearl Harbor. Then, accepting it as fact, he summoned his officers to the wardroom, where they began to arrive in various states of dress and undress. "Gentlemen," he began, "—gentlemen of the British Army. I have a very important announcement to make. This morning you were the goddam British. Now you are gallant allies." First there was puzzled silence. When the import of the quip had sunk in, there were prolonged cheers. Then he ordered that the troops be told, and a tightened alert instituted. There were German submarines everywhere in the Atlantic, and now, perhaps, Japanese ones too.

Aboard the *Orizaba* the order to the American crew was "life jackets 'til we get in."

Among the troops on the *Manhattan* was Ernest Warwick, in the Suffolk Regiment of the 18th Division. He had heard the rumor that his unit was headed around the Cape of Good Hope and through the Suez Canal to help relieve the "Desert Rats" of Tobruk. The 18th had no idea that it had already been redirected by radio to Malaya, where it would arrive totally unprepared for jungle warfare.

It would make no difference. They would dock in Singapore weeks later, running down gangplanks under a hail of bombs from unopposed Japanese aircraft, and go into action just in time to surrender in the streets.

•

Before six hundred of the faithful at the First Baptist Church in Pittsburgh, Senator Nye spoke with defeat in his voice. "I had long hoped that at least the involvement of my country in this terrible foreign slaughter would be left largely to our own determination." But Roosevelt, he charged, had done "his utmost" to provoke Japan. The United States, Nye warned, was unprepared to fight a one-front war, "let alone two." (Isolationists had done all they could to forestall military preparedness, but he made no reference to that.) He warned that the U.S. would wind up on the side of "bloody Joe Stalin," and the suggestion drew laughs. Nye looked up and scolded, "I am not making a humorous speech."

America First was finished, he prophesied. "There isn't much that

America can do [now] but move forward with American lives, American blood and American wealth to the protection of our people." To a waiting reporter he added, leaving the church, "This is just what Great Britain planned for us. We have been maneuvered into this by the President, but the only thing now is to declare war and jump into it with everything we have and bring it to a victorious conclusion."

Reading the *Post-Gazette*, with its bold war headline, a cab driver exploded to Robert Hagy, "That guy [Nye] committed treason this afternoon. If I'd known what was going on out there [at Soldiers' and Sailors' Hall], I would have had a hundred drivers out there and we would really have strung that guy up."

"Now," a man exploded to Hagy in a diner, looking over the front page of his paper while the reporter tucked in a quick supper, "maybe Wheeler and Lindbergh and those other guys will shut their traps."

Considered by most people, including himself, as the leading isolationist, Senator Burton K. Wheeler was taking the next train from Billings, Montana, that moved in the direction of Washington, D.C. At the platform he told surprised reporters that he wanted a declaration of war against Japan. "The only thing now is to do our best to knock hell out of them."

•

In the interstices between gathering news and entertaining guests whom the President could not see, Eleanor Roosevelt somehow found time to communicate with OCD head Fiorello La Guardia. The uncertainty about war was over, but now the exposed West Coast might be attacked. Unproven reports of Japanese planes, surface ships, and submarines off San Francisco were disturbing. She and La Guardia determined to fly west to see about civil preparedness. They would leave on the first plane they could get after Roosevelt's declaration of war address to the Congress the next day.

Also trying to reach the mayor was James Landis, Dean of the Harvard Law School, who doubled as director of the New England OCD district. By then it was well after nine. Landis understood that although La Guardia's grasp of civil defense realities was small, the President had kept him on because people—including FDR—liked him and admired his energy, and he could be surrounded by more expert underlings who would do his work. Still, Landis was dumbfounded by the telephone conversation. After he informed La Guardia of the standby measures ordered, including an alert to all air-raid wardens and auxiliary policemen, the mayor answered, "Very fine, but I think you want to get them to march. Can you get a big parade going in Boston tomorrow?"

"Mayor," Landis explained, "my men don't march. They don't know how to march."

"You ought to get them to march," said the impresario of Manhattan's St. Patrick's Day and Columbus Day parades.

"They know," Landis appealed, "[that] marching isn't going to do anything here. They know exactly what their tasks are." He hung up, and put parades out of mind. Later, when Roosevelt appointed Landis to replace La Guardia, the corps of mayors were "fired . . . all in one night."

From his *Time-Life* offices Henry Luce telephoned his father, the Rev. Henry Luce, in Haverford, Pennsylvania. The elder Luce shared his son's satisfaction. "We will now all see," said the old man, "what we mean to China and China means to us." It would be their last conversation. A few hours later the elder Luce died in his sleep at seventy-three. When Teddy White expressed condolences, Luce observed, "It was wonderful that he lived long enough to see America and China as allies."

•

One of the more belligerent places in the continental United States on Sunday evening was the state of Tennessee. Interviewed at his mountain home by the *Chattanooga Times*, war hero Sergeant Alvin Cullom York recommended that the Japanese be given "a lickin' right away. We should take care of the Japs first and then take on the Germans." In Chattanooga itself, Local 1442 of the United Brotherhood of Carpenters and Joiners met in emergency session and issued an official declaration of war "on the Japanese Government and any other Government that may be allied with her against the United States."

•

Tai Sing Loo's exhausted band of Pearl Harbor volunteers, civilian and military, had worked through lunch hour and beyond. "Every-thinks [sic] were under control," he explained, "and we all secure and roll up the hoses. . . . We were hungry no lunch so I brought each one a Box Ice Cream . . . and we all dismissed about 3:30 p.m."

On Kalakua Avenue in Honolulu, Ed Sheehan joined the knots of people in front of the drugstore, the tavern, whatever had opened, and shared concerns and rumors. Everyone wondered whether the Japanese would return. Wives of men at Pearl moved in and out of the groups listening for people who had been at the harbor and asking questions. "One pretty young woman said her husband was assigned to the *Arizona*. She heard it had been hit. Her lips trembled. What had happened? Was it bad? Were the men all right? I remember telling her I didn't know, then getting away as gracefully as I could."

It was a hot afternoon in Hawaii and there was nothing to do with more corpses than could be refrigerated other than to bury them quickly. At Hickam, Major Vivian Thiebaud was employing a team to identify the dead, many of whom were not wearing dog tags when the attack began. If the body could not be linked to a name, they recorded whatever distinguishing characteristics remained. Four hundred dead from Hickam were buried at Schofield in brief rites that were jointly Protestant, Catholic, and Jewish. By 4:00, the dead were disposed of, the most efficient American operation of the day.

•

Maury Meister's PBY had been in the air nearly twelve hours. At 3:30 A.M. the crew had gassed the plane for nine or ten hours of flight. Now they were praying for enough fuel to reach Ford Island, and a debris-free patch of water on which to splash down. As they banked to come in, Meister saw the water "covered with two to four inches of thick, black, gummy crude oil from the sunken ships and ruptured fuel tanks from disabled ships. . . . A quick glance at the tank farms which stored fuel for surface ships and aviation gasoline . . . showed no visible damage. Fire and smoke rose from Hickam Field. . . . We landed in the oil-surface of the bay and taxied to our ramp where the beach crew was standing by. For some unknown reason when we had left San Diego we had sent [after us] our store of cold weather flight suits, heavy gloves, fur-lined suits. Now we knew why."

The beach crew normally wore bathing trunks to wade into the surf and guide the wheeled pontoons of the PBYs onto dry land. "Now they were wearing flight suits [in the tropical heat] to keep the heavy crude oil off their skin. Put a suit on, bring a plane in, take suit off, place it in trash pile, put on another suit and repeat. . . . We landed about 1530 and were warmly welcomed as we were the last to return and most had thought the worst had happened to us."

Air crews, however weary, were told to stand by once their planes were fueled and ready to go again. "No one seemed to know just what we were to be ready for but be ready. Rumors were everywhere. The Japs had put a landing party ashore; each person could fill in the point of landing. There was a squadron of planes en route from the mainland; they were all shot down with no survivors. . . ."

At undamaged hangars, "some black paint was found and everyone with no specific job was busy painting over the windows. Large strips of canvas were hung over the hangar doors to block out any trickle of light. Canvas cots were set up inside the hangars; armed guards walked the perimeters." There was no fresh water on Ford Island. In sinking, the *California* had severed the pipeline from shore. Only the swimming pools had water, and guards patrolled to protect what was left. Most mess halls were being used for medical treatment, but Meister found one still providing rations. He drew the first food he had seen since three in the morning. "I had just gotten my tray and sat down at a table when General Quarters sounded, and I rushed to my battle station near the hangar. . . . As we looked out toward the open sea we saw two destroyers at full speed just at the entrance to Pearl Harbor, and a patrol plane circling overhead. As the destroyers converged, they started dropping depth charges and . . . what looked like a miniature sub lifted completely out of the water, then exploded in the air."

•

Throughout Luzon all morning, American aircraft—obsolete P-36s and hot-to-handle P-40s—took off, exhausted their fuel, and returned to bases empty-handed. If the Japanese were overhead, they were flying higher than American pilots were wont to go. The B-17s were still aimlessly airborne at ten when General Sutherland telephoned from Calle Victoria. "Chief of Staff informed General Brereton," the Nielson Field log recorded, "that all aircraft would [still] be left in reserve and that the present attitude is strictly defensive. General Brereton stated to General Sutherland that if Clark Field is taken out [of action] we could not operate offensively." Appended is a note, "Bomber command recommends bombs not be loaded at this time due to danger of extensive damage by enemy air action." And a second, erroneous, note: "24 enemy bombers reported in Cagayan Valley proceeding south in direction Manila." Sooner or later a sighting was bound to be accurate. It was seven hours since the news of Pearl Harbor had reached Manila.

Sutherland had barely cradled his phone when he raised it again to issue new instructions in MacArthur's name. A reconnaissance mission to Formosa had been authorized. The catalyst may have been Hap Arnold's radiogram number 749 to MacArthur from Washington: "Reports of Japanese attacks all show that [large] numbers of our planes have been destroyed on the ground [at Pearl Harbor]. Take all possible steps at once to avoid such losses in your area, including dispersion to maximum possible extent . . . and prompt take off on warning note."

At 10:10, Lieutenant Colonel Eubank left for Clark Field. Three Flying Fortresses were to be prepared for photo reconnaissance. The phone at Nielson Field rang again at 10:14. According to the log, "General Brereton received a telephone call from General MacArthur. . . . Bombers will be held in readiness until receipt of reports from reconnaissance missions." But the log added, if reconnaissance reports were not received in time, Formosa would be attacked anyway "in late afternoon. The decision for offensive action was left to General Brereton. All bombers were ordered to arm and be on the alert for immediate orders." The show seemed on the road.

Available B-17s were to be loaded with 100-pound and 300-pound bombs and take off (according to a 10:45 entry) "to attack known airdromes in Southern Formosa at the latest daylight hour today that visibility will permit." Bombers evacuated to Mindanao would return to Clark Field "after dark [to be] prepared for [additional] operations at daybreak." Flying lonely patrol patterns far apart so they would not be in each other's way, the B-17s, finally unleashed, trickled back slowly, one by one.

•

In Burma, Charles Bond found Colonel Chennault's first wartime order posted on the Flying Tiger bulletin board at 9:45 A.M. A twenty-four-hour alert was in effect. All pilots were to carry side arms. (Bond would borrow a .25 automatic, all of four inches long.) In the event of an air raid, personnel were to "repair to the jungle, lying down flat"—an impossible feat, literally, but the colonel's Chinese was sometimes better than his English—"utilizing whatever shelter may be available. . . . Strict watch will be kept for enemy parachute troops at all times."

The first warning sounded on an old brass ship's bell—all they could scrounge from the British—was a false alarm, the first of a half-dozen on the eighth. To assess their strategic situation, Chennault sent up Erik Shilling in a stripped-down reconnaissance aircraft, with two P-40 escorts, to overfly Bangkok and find out what was going on. "Get your pictures and get home," he ordered. "Fly high. No fighting."

They climbed to 26,000 feet in clear weather and sighted Japanese ships by the dozens unloading troops and equipment. Fighter planes were parked wingtip to wingtip. Such forces were likely to move on Malaya and Burma, but there was nothing that the Flying Tigers could do. Nor the RAF.

The Burmese village of Toungoo, on the Sitang River, north of Rangoon and halfway to Mandalay, was only sixty miles from the Thai border. The Japanese had taken Bangkok without firing a shot and were fanning out over Thailand. "The reports are unbelievable," Bond noted in his diary; "we are stunned." They kept their engines warm. "With no radar . . . we have little time to get off. Many of us scan the eastern skies continuously—as if we would have some chance to scramble. . . . We expect to be hit, but I presume they are working on Singapore right now. Who knows?"

Bond had guessed that the AVG might remain at Toungoo rather than move north, although Chennault wanted to protect Chungking. It seemed more important to guard the Burma Road supply lifeline to China than to turn back raids over Chiang's capital. Even a shift to Kunming, in Yunnan Province, seemed out, to the relief of Major W. K. Lin, who was Chinese liaison with the AVG personnel already in Kunming. On the afternoon that Chennault had learned of Pearl Harbor he had received a confidential letter from the unhappy Lin dated December 6 that suggested that nothing had changed since the AVG had replaced the undisciplined Westerners whose high flying for the Nationalists had been accomplished largely in brothels and bars.

Some of the AVG personnel in Kunming, Lin confided, "are always drunk in the hostel, and this is not the worst." One inebriate had seized a cook's meat cleaver and tried to behead a woman who had resisted his attentions, "but fortunately he was prevented." Others drove cars with drunken recklessness, or brought local women to their bedrooms, or smuggled goods from Burma into China to sell at profiteering prices. "This may entail some misunderstanding among the public," the major noted diplomatically, "and at the same time spoils our reputation."

Chennault punished the offenders with harmless reprimands and fines, and a few days later he informed Lin of the "severe action." He asked Lin to continue his "close watch." Then he appealed to Washington for more planes, anything that might carry bombs and interdict the Japanese forces flooding through Thailand toward Malaya and Burma.

To the south in Rangoon, Colonel B. F. Kane, Divisional Engineer for British forces in Burma, had more immediate problems. He had been called to meet with RAF Group Captain John Rutter and Squadron Leader Charles Turl. With them was Chief Engineer for Signals Colin Scott. "The Group Captain introduced his requirements, using to illustrate them a small map of Burma, which I suspect he had torn out of one of our telephone directories. His requirements were simple, though urgent. He wanted three lines to a number of places, this was a minimum: an Op[eration]s line, an Admn. line and one in reserve. From Rangoon to Toungoo, to Lashio, to Taunggyi, to Mandalay, to Myitkine, to Prome, and to Magwa." How long would it take, Rutter inquired, for Posts and Telegraphs to provide these services? That his map had to be what it was suggested the primitive state of preparation, but he had not translated that into the impossibility of his demands.

Colin Scott looked at Kane, and Kane looked in bafflement to Scott. "Our Group Captain had, roughly estimated, asked for 10,000 miles of twin circuit involving the construction of new lines of say 500 miles through dense jungle. Colin paused and took a deep breath before answering: 'Provided we had the materials, which we have not, then at a rough estimate, if we hurry, three years.' "

Rutter would get lines to Mandalay and to the fighter base at Rangoon before the Japanese overran the area he had mapped out.

•

It was not until 10:30 A.M. that Lieutenant Colonel Richard Mallonée, "senior instructor" to the Philippine 21st Field Artillery Regiment, 21st Division, at Bayambang, discovered there was a war on. Filipino units rated low on the communications scale as well as elsewhere. Their 1917 Enfield rifles were long and heavy, unwieldy for the small and short Filipino soldiers, and there was only enough ammunition available for a few minutes' fire. Even so, it required a baffling amount of red tape to get it released from warehouses in Manila.

North Luzon Force had briefed divisions to concentrate within four hours' marching distance of their assigned defense areas and await further instructions. MacArthur's standing orders were for a no-withdrawal all-out defense of the beaches at each potential landing site, although there were neither sufficient trained troops nor materiel— nor dedication—for such a strategy. Although there was chaos among the Filipino officers, Mallonée as foreign adviser had no command authority. Colonel Mateo Capinpin, who ran the division, vacillated between packing up to go and remaining where they were until an invasion seemed imminent.

There was also the question of what potential landing points to defend. Although Mallonée, with twenty years of Philippine experience, had a file of water depths, artillery positions, potential landing areas and fields of fire, Capinpin, ignoring such data, decided "to occupy positions selected during a forty-eight-hour trip over 120 kilometers of front by a major of Constabulary and a reserve captain." A further problem surfaced all over Luzon. There were not enough buses and trucks on Luzon to carry out MacArthur's prewar plans.

Despite the initiation—however disorganized—of the beach defense gamble, even MacArthur from the beginning had grave doubts that it would work. According to Sutherland, MacArthur had confided to him on the day the war began that his troops would have to "remove immediately to Bataan." Yet he told no one else, and gave no instructions to move equipment, supplies, ammunition, or men to what he long realized would be his last-ditch stronghold. To everyone else he would claim for days that the situation had not yet deteriorated sufficiently for the funneling of forces into Bataan. Colonel James V. Collier of the operations staff immediately suggested provisioning Bataan as a "safety measure," but MacArthur turned him down with an "Oh, no!" and was supported by his Intelligence chief, the worshipful Brigadier General Charles A. Willoughby. Not until December 23, with everything on Luzon crumbling about him, and the beaches long since overrun, did MacArthur abandon a scheme already moot. Materiel desperately needed on Bataan was abandoned to looters and to the Japanese.

·

It was 9:30 P.M. in Washington. In the White House, extra chairs were brought into the Blue Room for the ten invited congressmen. Members of the Cabinet relinquished the front semicircle and moved back. Vice-President Wallace and Harry Hopkins remained, as did Grace Tully. Roosevelt knew his guests well; and although he didn't like all of them, there was no sense of strain. The senators were Alben Barkley, Charles McNary, Tom Connally, Warren R. Austin, and Hiram Johnson. The representatives were Sam Rayburn, Joseph Martin, Sol Bloom, Charles Eaton, and Jere Cooper. Johnson and Martin had been die-hard isolationists, but isolationism had expired eight hours earlier, and everyone knew it. Harold Ickes, who had not spoken to cranky Hiram Johnson in two years, now shook hands and offered him his chair.

Pacing outside, uninvited, was rabble-rousing, isolationist "Pappy" O'Daniel, a senator only since liquor interests had purchased enough votes five months earlier to push the evangelical, antidrink governor upstairs and safely out of Austin. To amused reporters, O'Daniel, a flour salesman as recently as 1938, explained that he wanted "to make sure that Texas is represented." The senior senator from Texas, Tom Connally, was already inside; O'Daniel would linger a while, frustrated, then leave.

"As you know," Roosevelt began, "Japan has attacked us." He outlined the gravity of the situation in Hawaii and implied without reading his draft declaration that he would ask them to confirm the state of war. Would they be ready to receive him in joint session at 12:30 the next afternoon?

As they sat in what Stimson described as "dead silence," Roosevelt explained that American defenses, "including the whole west coast of the Americas," had been gravely impaired.

"Nothing about casualties on their side?" asked one congressman.

"It's a little difficult [to know]," said Roosevelt. "We think we got some of their submarines. . . ."

"Well, planes—aircraft?"

"We did get, we think, a number of their planes. We know some Japanese planes were shot down, but there again—I have seen so much of this in the other war. One fellow says he has got fifteen of their planes, and you pick up the telephone and somebody else says five. . . . I should say that by far the greater loss has been sustained by us."

"There is a story coming over the radio that we got one of their airplane carriers."

"Don't believe it. . . . I wish it were true. . . . Of course it is a terrible disappointment to be President in time of war, and the circumstances came most unexpectedly."

The congressmen wondered how Japanese carriers got in so close, and Roosevelt guessed, having little to go on, that the enemy fleet reached a point close enough to move in for the attack after sundown the night before. "Now, let us assume," he said, offering a scenario, "that they launched those planes at a distance of a hundred miles at daylight. That means that they had twelve hours to get to that point in the dark, and running at perhaps 25 knots; that would be 300 miles further away. In other words, at dark, last night, they might very well have been 400 miles away from the island, and therefore out of what might be called a good patrol distance. Patrol out of a given point is 300 miles under normal conditions, but 500 miles is a long way for reconnaissance patrol. . . . At dawn they were 100 miles away from the island—they launched their planes—they steamed this way and that, or reversed their course. The planes dropped their bombs and went back."

Not satisfied that the fleet could be so surprised, Senator Connally, Chairman of the Foreign Relations Committee, asked why American forces in Hawaii were not able to "do anything." Rising from his seat he added, more in despair than in anger, "They were supposed to be on the alert. . . . I am amazed at the attack by Japan, but I am still more astounded at what happened to our Navy. They were all asleep. Where were our patrols?"

Since the President had offered his explanation, Connally turned to Knox. "Didn't you say last month that we could lick the Japs in two weeks? Didn't you say that our Navy was so well prepared and located that the Japanese couldn't hope to hurt us at all? Why did you have all the ships at Pearl Harbor crowded the way you did? And why did you have a long chain across the mouth of the entrance, so that our ships couldn't get out?"

Knox struggled for a reply. His boasting about the readiness of the Navy had come back to haunt him. The Navy, he suggested, had been ready for submarines but not for aircraft.

"Well, they were supposed to be on the alert," Connally insisted.

Getting his comparative times mixed up—Roosevelt was clearly exhausted and more than a bit rattled—he observed that it was "daytime out there while we are all in bed," and a congressman responded, unhappily, "We are in bed too much." Still, the consensus, expressed by an unidentified voice, was, "Well, Mr. President, this nation has got a job ahead of it, and what we have got to do is roll up our sleeves and win this war."

It was getting late. Another congressman asked what would be in the President's declaration-of-war request to the Joint Session.

Evasively, Roosevelt said that he had not yet decided what would be in the message—as, Hopkins noted in his diary afterward, "it would be all over town in five minutes, because it is perfectly footless ever to ask a large group of Congressmen to keep a secret." What the President did not want was any opportunity in the fifteen hours that remained before his address to Congress for diehards to patch together an isolationist alternative.

Since the declaration was the prerogative of the House Foreign Affairs Committee, Roosevelt asked Chairman Sol Bloom before adjourning the meeting about the mechanics of having a motion ready. Bloom had been worrying about it all through the discussion, and "shrank," he confided later, "from exposing the Jews of a future generation to the possible charge that this war had been set in motion by a Jew." The isolationist camp, he knew, was rife with anti-Semitism. (After he left the White House he consulted the House parliamentarian, Lew Deschler, and worked out a way to suspend House rules and have a clerk read the war resolution.)

Offering few crumbs of news to waiting reporters, the congressmen and Cabinet secretaries left the White House subdued and silent. As some of them drove home they noticed that the only place in Washington where all the lights seemed on was the tall, narrow building just to the north of the War Department—the headquarters of Selective Service. Atop some government buildings, antiaircraft guns had begun to appear, some of them, like the weapons used in the Louisiana maneuvers, replicas made of painted wood. Even some authentic guns were useless. Real ammunition was stacked up next to them, but because of shortages—Congress had ruthlessly penny-pinched for years—it was the wrong size.

On the bench in a much-traveled hallway, Ed Murrow still waited for his promised talk with the President. Looking gaunt and ill—"like a deathshead," Murrow thought—Harry Hopkins came by and invited the patient Murrow to wait a bit more comfortably in the bedroom Hopkins occupied at the White House. For a while, Jesse Jones, who had wandered over from the Cabinet meeting for a few private words, joined them. Long Roosevelt's confidant, Hopkins felt crushed by what he realized would be new burdens. Ostensibly Lend-Lease Adminis-trator, he was the President's legs. While they talked, Hopkins put on his striped pajamas and "flung himself on a large four-poster bed. He looked like a tired, broken child, too small for the bed. He murmured to himself, it seemed, 'Oh, God, if I only had more strength.' "

Waiting with other reporters on the White House steps in the cold, Glen Perry watched the grim-faced lawmakers leave, most of them unwilling to say anything. Loftily, however, isolationist Representative Joseph Martin declared on the way out that Congress would be united: "In the hour of danger there is no partisanship." Last to emerge was crusty Harold Ickes. "Mr. Secretary," asked George Dixon of the *New York Daily News*, "would you say the situation is serious?"

"No comment," Ickes growled.

•

As the White House geared up for war, the Navy Department was sending messages to all merchant vessels in Pacific waters that were not sailing under escort. "All merchant shipping en route to Manila are to sail," it instructed, "via the Malacca Straits and south of Celebes to British or Dutch ports instead of north of Balikpapan in Borneo and await further orders. Vessels en route to America to continue their journeys."

In Tokyo, Admiral Wenneker would copy it down and note, "The above is a welcome success for our Radio Monitoring Post which obtained the data for ascertaining the U.S. code and relayed it to Berlin." Known as "Hansa" to the German Navy Signals Service, the code had been broken on November 9. And the Germans had an efficient station in Shanghai.

•

At the Tokyo Kaikan in the Marunouchi district, more than a thousand members of the Central Cooperative Council, a business group formed to support government policies, had been waiting for Prime Minister Tojo. He had been listed to open the conference at

9:30, which had given his Monday morning schedule a normal appearance to further cover the surprise aspect of the dawn, and predawn, attacks. The Cabinet was also to have been present, but Kōtarō Takamura saw no one on the platform; only two large vases of chrysanthemums flanked the rostrum where Chairman Goto was to preside. In the hall, conferees milled about exchanging stories of how they had first heard of the war.

A sculptor and poet, Takamura had, in his twenties, worked in New York for Gutzon Borglum, later the limner of presidential heads on Mt. Rushmore. Now a widower of fifty-eight, he lived in three rooms attached to a studio and wrote single-mindedly in support of nationalist goals. Still an artist, he had come to the meeting with a proposal to improve the aesthetic tone of factories. "The mental health of workers," his manifesto read, "is greatly sustained by the wholesome perception of beauty." He wanted paintings, sculpture, murals, and "everyday necessities" in factories—even "the beauty of machines"— to represent, as "an exaltation of national spirit," the best in Japanese design. Now, he thought, "the situation has suddenly changed, and the proposal I submitted seems inappropriate and already belongs to the past."

On the train he had heard only that war had begun in Hawaii at three in the morning, Tokyo time—Takamura had left too early for newspaper extras, and had not turned on his radio. All that Goto had announced from the platform was that they were facing "a very serious historical moment." The Prime Minister had been called to the Imperial Palace and could not open their meeting until one o'clock. "All members," Goto added ("in a slow and heavy voice," Takamura remembered), "are requested to wait quietly."

There was buzzing in the hall that an Imperial proclamation would soon be read. Takamura paced nervously about the waiting rooms, looking out the windows into the warm winter sunlight flooding Marunouchi, where people and traffic rushed along as if nothing had changed. At 11:30 he hurried back into the conference hall. Lunch and tea would be served at noon, but people were standing expectantly, heads bowed, eyes cast down at the floor, waiting for the proclamation to be broadcast. "My body became tense, my vision became blurred." He felt "pinned" to his place on the floor.

At 11:40, in the presence of Marquis Kido, the Emperor affixed his seal to the war rescript, but not in the form it had been ratified by the Privy Council. He could not undo the war, but he could couch his feelings within careful limits. He had Kido insert a line that made the Emperor's position clear. After a sentence on friendship between nations as "the guiding principle of Our Empire's foreign policy," Hirohito added, "It has been truly unavoidable and far from Our wishes that Our Empire has now been brought to cross swords with America and Britain." Then at the close, objecting to the use of war for purposes of "raising and enhancing the glory of the Imperial Way within and outside our homeland," he had the line amended to "preserving thereby the glory of our Empire."

He could only justify war for purposes of national preservation,* he explained to Kido, confessing that it was heartrending to declare war on countries he admired, and to become an enemy of the British royal family, which had been so kind to him when he was a young prince traveling abroad. Kido offered no reply. Curiously, he added in his diary, "I was very grateful to see the Emperor being so confident and dauntless on the day of the great war on which the fate of the nation depends."

Kido's office notified the Prime Minister that he could now make his war broadcast to the people.

---

* The concept that the war was initiated as an act of national preservation—as an unavoidable act of self-defense—has persisted into Japanese schoolbooks and semi-official language. Decades after the war, *Japan Echo*, for example, a publication backed in part by Foreign Ministry funds, declared, "Japan, simply to assure its own survival, was given little choice but to wage war with the United States. . . . Washington took actions calculated to provoke a fight with Japan."

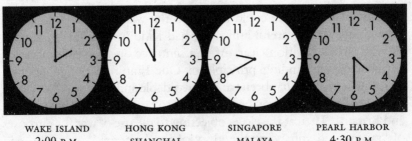

WAKE ISLAND	HONG KONG	SINGAPORE	PEARL HARBOR
2:00 P.M.	SHANGHAI	MALAYA	4:30 P.M.
December 8	MANILA	9:40 A.M.	December 7
	11:00 A.M.	December 8	
	December 8		

HOUR 39

ITHOUT RADAR—and there was no chance Wake would have it in time—the atoll was doomed. The enemy would return unheard above the roaring surf. Some stranded civilian workers, their jobs aborted, offered to enlist in the Marines; others fled into the boulder-strewn bush, among the flightless peewee birds, sand rats, and scrub. The still-unscathed one-story temporary structure erected as an infirmary for the contractor's laborers became the island aid station, manned by a civilian doctor, Lawton S. Shank.

As the wreckage everywhere cooled it was picked over for salvageable tools and parts, and the runway cleared. To frustrate an airborne landing, the strip was mined. To block a seaborne invasion, a Navy lighter loaded with dynamite and concrete was anchored in the main channel. To make room for more wounded, the dead were hauled from the Navy hospital in a cold drizzle and, pending burial, put into an empty refrigerator shed. It was unlikely to be needed for further food shipments. Wake's future seemed certain: further wounded and dead, and no chance of resupply or rescue.

From Truk, the major Japanese base in the Marshalls, a force commanded by Rear Admiral Kajioka from the light cruiser *Yubari* had already embarked. Marines filled two converted old destroyers; garrison troops followed in transports; two light cruisers, six destroyers, and two submarines were sent ahead. Before any arrived, Wake was to be softened by further raids.*

.

The first real impact in Japan of war with the U.S. was the order, published in the supplement to the December 8 *Official Gazette*, eliminating Mickey Mouse and Popeye the Sailor from Japanese cinema screens. Bowing to the new Foreign Transactions Control regulations on trading with the enemy, the Shochiku and Toho managements, the two major exhibitors in Tokyo showing British and American films, immediately withdrew the popular favorites. In Yokohama the Asahi News Theatre seemed not to notice, keeping in its bill "American Football," a Popeye cartoon, and "Song of a Lake," a Disney short featuring Mickey Mouse. (The authorities would have to step in.)

The foreign film gap was filled with safe French and German films, René Clair's *A nous la liberté*, the Berlin musical *Ein lied geht um die welt*, *Heimat*, and *Der Kosak und die Nachtigall*.

.

A spokesman from MacArthur's headquarters telephoned the Associated Press just before eleven to report that the general had issued a message of "serenity and confidence" to the Philippine people. Also, the aide announced, there would be a press conference at Fort Santiago.

Clark Lee went to represent the AP, driving into Intramuros through one of the archways in the thick stone walls. The overgrown moat, covered with neatly cut grass, was used by officers for golf. The building on the left was the Sisters of Charity nunnery; at the end of the passageway was a garage in which Lee saw MacArthur's brilliantly polished black Cadillac with the red license plate on which were the three silver stars of a lieutenant general. Behind it was a bomb shelter for Army staff, with underground offices and a switchboard.

In a small whitewashed room at the right of the garage the newsmen met Major LeGrande A. Diller, who explained that the meeting was only to issue press credentials. There was no news yet. He did not

* A report in the American press that Major Devereux radioed to Hawaii defiantly, on behalf of his trapped force of 522 Marines and 1,200 construction workers, "Send us more Japs," became a wartime legend. When released from a Japanese prisoner-of-war camp in 1945, Devereux denied it.

know when MacArthur would see them. They were to come back at four. Reporters knew that there was plenty of news; they had access to telephones and telegrams and had heard air-raid sirens swelling and wailing all morning, and shots fired, although they realized that jumpy Constabulary men—raw recruits—fired their Enfields and Springfields with little provocation. "There was not much fear," Lee felt, "because everybody thought the Jap planes would come over Manila and our boys would knock them out and it would be pretty as hell to watch. We said to each other: 'The minute that first bomb fell on Pearl Harbor the United States got moving. From all over the United States those big bombers are flying to San Francisco. They'll hop to Hawaii and then on down to Australia and up here. They'll be here within a week. The aircraft carriers will ferry pursuit planes from Hawaii.' "

MacArthur would issue his first press release before the day was out, and it would be clear that Major Diller had little to do with its composition. From December 8, 1941, until March 11, 1942, the day the general left the Philippines, 109 of the 142 communiqués issued by his office identified only one person by name: Douglas MacArthur. Even units doing the actual fighting often went unnamed, and not because military secrets were involved—the Japanese knew their enemy. As far as No. 1 Calle Victoria was concerned, all troops under the American flag were "MacArthur's men," and the communiqués were dated "GENERAL MACARTHUR'S HEADQUARTERS." It was a triumph of ego, and for many months to come the only triumph.

Shortly after eleven o'clock, Lieutenant Colonel George C. Clarke and Lieutenant Harold Johnson, Clarke's operations officer for the 57th Infantry Regiment, Philippine Scouts, returned from a meeting in Manila of local commanders. The word was that USAFFE was convinced that the Japanese would make their first landings with paratroops, and that paratroop defense positions were to be prepared, especially at airfields. Each of the battalions of the 57th was ordered to the perimeter of Nielson Field, siting weapons, digging foxholes, stringing wire. An observation post was established on the high ground near the radio tower used by Pan American Airways. With commercial air flights a casualty of the first hours of war, headquarters units of the Far Eastern Air Force, already using part of the operations building of the Pan Am Terminal, began spreading out.

·

Although Liu Hung Sak had reached his newspaper office in Hong Kong by ten, he changed his mind about reporting for work right away. Extracting dollars from his bank and buying whatever food he could carry home seemed higher priorities than a sacrificial professionalism. He waited in long queues, ducking into an air-raid shelter each time the sirens screamed. Frustrated, he chose early lunch at the misnamed Dairy Farm, a restaurant on the mezzanine floor of a large and apparently safe concrete building; then he returned to the bank queue, drawing $500 and $100 notes. He carried his catties of rice— about ten days' supply, he guessed—to the *Kwang Ming Po* building.

·

In Chungking, Pao-huang Tang, Kuomintang desk officer just promoted to military attaché in London, and eager to leave, returned home from his office almost as soon as he had arrived there. He handed Rosalie a newspaper. It was full of war news, but primacy of place was given to Pearl Harbor. The problem created by the new situation was whether the fighting would be stepped up and their departure made difficult or even impossible. Since December 1, when Colonel Tang had brought his Eurasian wife the news about his assignment, they had planned to leave via Hong Kong, Honolulu, and the United States. Now Hong Kong and Honolulu were under attack.

Twenty-three, and the daughter of a Flemish mother, Rosalie had studied in London and Brussels, and then at Yenching. She was a teacher and writer—she gave English lessons to the Russian military mission—but under wartime conditions she had become a midwife at an overcrowded infirmary in less than celestial Little Heavenly Bamboo Street. The new occupation seemed an irony, since she was unable to bear children of her own. Although Tang's masculine pride required a boy, for a thousand Chinese dollars (inflation would soon make that insufficient to buy a cup of rice) she had, only a few months before, bought a baby girl she named Yungmei. Girls were cheap. From their single rented room in an old house in the bomb-ruined center of the city, perched on a cliff, they could hear newsboys in the grimy fogbound streets below shouting about extras, and people surging out of their houses and flats to buy the papers.

Tang was elated; he reported that the Military Council was jubilant, and Chiang Kaishek so happy that he sang an old opera air. Kuomintang officials were going about congratulating each other over the

American catastrophe in Hawaii as if a great victory had been won. It was what they had been hoping for—America linked to China's destiny. "And . . . the telling criticisms of Chinese chaos, inefficiency, and defeat," Rosalie wrote later, "could now be shrugged off with a triumphant 'And what about you?' "

For Chungking, Rosalie Tang* remembered, it was a schizophrenic day. Compounding the joy over Pearl Harbor was glee over what they preferred to believe were continuing German victories in Russia. A Red Army defeat would weaken Stalin's surrogates in Yenan. Chiang had long ordered his officers to read *Mein Kampf* as well as his own speeches.

•

Prime Minister Tojo timed the reading of the Imperial Rescript, and his own war message, both broadcast nationwide, for the lunch break. The ubiquitous outdoor loudspeakers would catch people not indoors at home or at work. All radio shops had outdoor loudspeakers, although little to sell inside but a small Bakelite receiver which transmitted domestic broadcasts. Few Japanese had what was called a "super"—a device to enhance reception and pick up foreign stations. Their sale and use were forbidden. It had been more than an hour since street newspaper sellers with extras had been shouting, at each bus or tram emptying of passengers. "*Senso! Senso!*—War! War!" Noonday crowds clutched at news of sensational, almost unbelievable, victories even before rushing to the tofu vendors and noodle sellers on their heavily laden bicycles or under their precariously balanced trays.

The peripatetic vendor of snacks was a welcome sight in Japanese cities. He represented food obtainable without the *gaishoku ken*—the ration card distributed through the neighborhood associations. At home after work the main dish would be a cup of rice, a helping of soybeans or millet, and, Chikara Inoue remembered, "some very coarse item for a side dish. It was all lacking in flavor and one felt hungry afterwards."

A bright sun had warmed the chilly morning, bringing out masses of the curious who wanted to be in the middle of something important, perhaps the signal day of their lives. There was more satisfaction,

* A novelist, later, as Han Suyin (*A Many Splendored Thing*); her husband would be killed in October 1947, fighting the Communists in Manchuria.

mingled with a sense of anxiety, than the euphoria described the next day in the Japanese press, although it was a fact that enlistments soared. Proud parents, often with town and village bands thumping up enthusiasm, accompanied young men to recruitment offices, and where the community was too small for one, to the railway station and the nearest point from which to join the armed forces.

That war was justified was questioned by few. Pushes into China had long burdened the Japanese with food shortages and rationing, and a standard of living that diminished daily. Many lived in paper-windowed wooden shanties and wore clothes manufactured from synthetic fabrics that looked shabby even when new, and often fell apart when washed. It was the encirclement of Japan that seemed responsible, and aping the arrogant, racist West had only brought grief. Now the colonial powers would be beaten at their own game with their own weapons. The Japanese had adopted modern military hardware as they had acquired business suits and concrete office buildings.

As NHK pumped out radio reports of startling successes in unfamiliar places—Guam, Kota Bharu, Pearl Harbor, Bangkok, Mindanao, Singapore—crowds multiplied about street amplifiers. Walking among the clerks and typists and shopgirls and businessmen in the Ginza district of Tokyo as the news spread, Robert Guillain heard "no shouts, no cheers, for one never applauded in this country; but across every face was spread a look of smug pride. . . . 'It was as easy as that,' all those masks said. 'That's how we are! One day at war, and Japan has already beaten America!' There was no . . . hysteria of any kind. It was as though everything that had happened seemed to them almost natural."

At precisely noon an NHK announcer began reading the Imperial Rescript. (No ordinary citizen had ever heard the Shōwa Emperor's formal, high-pitched voice.) A respectful silence fell everywhere within hearing radius. People bowed in the direction of the Palace. When the voice faded, many listeners prostrated themselves in submission; some wept. After a pause, an announcer introduced General Tojo, speaking from a JOAK microphone in the film-screening room of his official residence.

Japan was at war, he began. "In spite of all that our Empire has done, ardently desiring the preservation of the peace of East Asia, our efforts have ended in failure. . . . The United States refused to make the least concession; instead, joining in league with Britain, the Netherlands, and Chungking, it demanded unilateral concessions on our part, such as unconditional and wholesale evacuation of our military and naval forces from China, nonrecognition of the Nanking Government, and the annulment of the tripartite pact between Japan, Germany, and Italy." (He made no mention of Indochina.) The nation's very existence was threatened.

"On reading the Imperial Rescript," he went on—the document his own aides had written—"I am filled with awe and trepidation. Powerless as I am, I am resolved to dedicate myself, body and soul, to my country. . . . And I believe that every one of you, my countrymen, will not care for your life but gladly share in the honor to make yourself His Majesty's humble shield." He anticipated a long war, but it was "a heaven-sent opportunity to test the mettle of us Japanese of the Shōwa Era." He pledged himself and his countrymen, he concluded, to "the grand imperial enterprise."

Keeping war fervor at a high pitch, NHK followed Tojo with a recording of "Umi Yukaba," ("Across the Sea"), adapted from the ancient and revered *Manyoshu*. Loudspeakers that had been broadcasting since early morning blared the solemn hymn:

> Across the sea, corpses soggy in the water;
> Across the mountains, corpses heaped upon the field.
> I shall die only for the Emperor,
> I shall never look back.

In Nagasaki, Sumiteru Tamaguchi's history teacher had brought a portable radio to class to listen to the news bulletins. In schoolrooms all over Japan Tojo's voice rang out with accusations that the West wanted to dominate the world and had to be crushed. Sumiteru joined in the enthusiasm because it was imprudent to do anything else. A Buddhist and a pacifist, he resented his bellicose teacher and the smug new song immediately a hit with children up and down the home islands:

> Siren, siren, air raid, air raid,
> What is that to us?
> Enemy planes are only mosquitoes or dragonflies.

After the stirring anthem about dying for the Emperor, class was dismissed for the day. Sumiteru walked out alone, wondering why he should have to fight anyone.

After pausing for a press photo, Tojo hurried out. The Central Cooperative Council could not open its meeting until he had formally convened it. And as the conferees at the Tokyo Kaikan listened to the radio addresses and waited, Kōtarō Takamura, like the others, felt "purified and transparent, . . . as if suddenly awakened in a new world." A fissure had opened in time, with yesterday "long gone" and the present "exalted and given a new meaning." In an "excited voice," a Council functionary raised emotions further by reading a bulletin describing "the victorious results" at Pearl Harbor. "There arose great spontaneous applause," and, overcome, Takamura "dropped tears on the floor. I felt a tragic thrill. . . . Moreover, when I felt for our Majesty's rejoiced heart at these good tidings, I was not able to suppress my overflowing tears."

Just before noon, Navy Ministry staff members assembled in the Ministry's Conference Hall One to hear the Minister, Vice-Admiral Shigetaro Shimada, read the Imperial Rescript. It already appeared clear from early reports that the Americans had suffered catastrophic losses, and that Japan had forced a radical revision in traditional strategy, shifting the anticipated *Kantai Kessen*, the "Great All-Out Battle," from the homeland waters, as the U.S. planned, to the enemy's lair. Yet Commander Atsushi Oi heard the admiral's voice seem to break as he came to the Emperor's statement that war had been "far from Our wishes." He appeared to be "weeping in his heart" that the situation had come to this, and Oi was "moved to tears." Years later he read Shimada's memoirs and found that the admiral had been one of the war hawks.

•

Father Gordon was up, he thought, before the others at Notre Dame Academy in Midsayap. Looking out his window in the darkness, he saw a fire across the road in the yard of the girls' dormitory. It was only five o'clock but the boys were cooking breakfast. "Fr. [Frank] McSorley said the Mass and gave a fine sermon on our Blessed Mother. I had forgotten to tell the flagbearers and color guards just what they were to do. (I guess I didn't know what they should do anyway.) . . . Breakfast was then served. After about thirty minutes the bugle sounded and all fell in for the drill. . . . All the boys lined up and . . . escorted the [girl] Sponsors in long flowing evening gowns with a kind of shoulder pad effect of starched pineapple cloth to the Reviewing Stand."

As the morning lengthened, crowds gathered for the drill competition. "They can't help it once they hear the sound of music." Teenagers turned left-face while others went right-face, some shouldering arms left-shoulder while others shifted to right shoulder. Captain Guballa patiently proceeded from platoon to platoon. The smallest boy in the school won a special prize for the Manual of Arms drill.

In the high, hot sun parents snapped pictures and children complained of thirst. "I had ordered 450 popsicles to be sent out from Cobato the first thing in the morning," Father Gordon noted. At eleven the ices arrived, and while they were being distributed he took Captain Guballa and his assistant Mr. Abrogan, a former Constabulary lieutenant, up to the *convento* porch out of the sun. "Fr. McSorley was talking with them while I tried to get some ice for a cold glass of beer. (I never saw anyone put ice in beer till I came over here.) We tuned in the radio. 'Pearl Harbor bombed!' (How ignorant, I didn't know where it was.) But then 'Davao bombed!' It seemed impossible. Why, Davao is only about 150 miles from Midsayap! . . . We kept getting different broadcasts but really, nothing too definite. The Captain had taken one mouthful out of his glass—he was pacing the room, he couldn't believe it. 'Davao, Davao,' he kept saying. And out in the school playground everyone was running around playing and joking."

Guballa ran to his Philippine Scouts barracks, "not knowing what to do; they had received no orders. In fact they couldn't receive any orders—they have no wireless set, not even an ordinary radio." He ordered two Japanese who lived close by arrested.

·

By 9:30 R. G. Tyler learned that the "*final* emergency scheme" for the North Borneo oil fields was to be activated. Senior staff accompanied by squads of British soldiers were ordered out with guncotton charges to blow the heads off the flaming gas wells. With a roar the liberated gas went thundering hundreds of feet in the air. Men watched in awe, then went back to their tasks on the ground, the pandemonium muffling the bursts of explosives and the hiss of acytelene torches employed to destroy plant machinery, blow tanks, and fire storage sheds. One of the world's major sources of petroleum and gas was being rendered inoperable so that the enemy would have to start from scratch, even to re-drilling.

The main pumping station, Tyler recorded wryly, "was a particularly magnificent sight—viewed as a spectacle only." Blazing oil overflowed the firewalls; pulsating clouds of gas flamed into the sky; sheets of burning oil drifted downstream in the Baram River near Miri; a pall of black smoke hung over the great field, darkening a sky already heavy with gathering thunderclouds. The Japanese could not have done a better job of destruction with a thousand planes. And the British had been forced by events still remote and unclear to attempt it themselves.

•

At the Singora Beachhead, with General Yamashita himself now ashore, resistance ceased at ten. After a morning of scattered fighting, Thai troops had learned that Bangkok had surrendered.

The Japanese 5th Division began spilling inland toward Thai airstrips. Even as Mitsubishis began landing, a few angry Thais, falling back, sent shells onto the rain-sodden runways, sending up puffs of mud and spray. At the shoreline, motorized landing craft, upturned by the waves, floated, Tsuji thought, "like puffed-up globe-fish."

From the police station, now Japanese headquarters, Major Osone, still in plain clothes, wandered about looking contrite. Tsuji reassured him that had he "handled the situation correctly," the Thais might have informed the British, who then might have moved north sooner. Since the Thais could not report what they didn't know, the local surprise was complete. And casualties were low. A roll call after the cease-fire counted nine dead and seventeen seriously wounded.

Yamashita climbed a low hill near the lighthouse and looked out to sea. Transports were lowering boats with supplies and troops. There was no sign of the British. He sat down and ate some cold rice from a square tin and read four radio messages brought out to him by an aide. From Tokyo came confirmation that Hawaii, Hong Kong, and the Philippines had also been attacked. From Bangkok he heard that the Imperial Guards had landed and were moving south to join him. From Pattani there was a radio message that the landing there had been unopposed. From the 18th Division commander at Kota Bharu he learned that stiff resistance was continuing and that one transport had been sunk. Retrieving his rice tin, he seized his chopsticks and lifted out what was left.

Looking up, Tsuji saw one of their own planes dip low to drop a message: "Large enemy mechanized force this day . . . passed through Changlun moving north." Since the British had no tanks, Tsuji assumed that the pilot meant motor transport and Bren gun carriers. To head off an attack on their beachhead, Tsuji ordered a regiment to forestall the British, a unit led by another lieutenant colonel, Shizuo Saeki, "a strong old man" but "a poor hand at making his way in the world. The more able of his classmates had [already] become lieutenant generals."

By mid-morning, Ambassador Tsubogami was in effective control of Thailand. Phibun and Direk had left the Cabinet to negotiate with him over the country's future and had found their flexibility limited to the selection of one of four Japanese options. Bowing to each other, Phibun and the ambassador parted on the premier's promise to take the alternatives back to the Cabinet. Their war was over.

Returning to his ministers, Phibun explained his predicament, and asked Direk to read aloud the first alternative—that Japan and Thailand would sign an offensive and defensive alliance. Prince Wichit Wichitwathakan read the other three. Thailand could join the Tripartite Pact with Germany, Italy, and Japan, becoming a full Axis ally. Or Thailand could cooperate informally with Japanese military operations. Or Thailand could formally agree to permit Japan to undertake the defense of Thai borders. Each option anticipated passage of Japanese forces, their logistical assistance, and cessation of resistance. In return, the Japanese offered postwar retrocession of some territories long lost to Burma and Malaya.

The third option appeared least risky. Phibun and a majority with him supported guaranteeing Japan "all convenience" and the deletion of the lost lands provision as suggesting the wrong reasons for cooperation. But Phibun let one of his most pro-Japanese ministers, Pananon Vanit, speak for him, breaking in only long enough to voice resentment over the timing of the invasion because it had come too quickly to prepare the nation. He wanted the Japanese to pass through quickly and move out of the country, Phibun said, for Thailand did not have the resources to maintain them. Vanit added his annoyance that the Japanese had moved into central Thailand. It was a further embarrassment to the leadership.

Later in the day Consul General Asada, who had learned every word of the Cabinet discussion, dismissed it all as role-playing for history. Vanit himself would turn up at the Japanese embassy, shake Asada's hand, and exclaim in high spirits that everything was going fine. Yet the Cabinet had seemed sullen when, with its capitulation document ready to be typed and signed, Foreign Minister Direk left to secure the Japanese signatures.

Ostensibly the Thais had given in to brute force. Although only a few companies of Japanese troops had arrived by water to intimidate Bangkok directly, the government was persuaded by what it knew of Japanese capabilities to sign what Tomokazu Hori, press spokesman for the occupiers, called a "thorough understanding." It would be thorough enough to oversee every aspect of life in the country. Whatever their nationality, the publicity release went on, individuals, "so long as they do not take actions injurious to the Japanese," were safe, and "should joyously carry on their respective occupations, with peace of mind."

•

At 9:30 A.M. Australian Lieutenant Colonel Frederick G. Gallaghan, at the Kota Bharu air base, received a message that Brigadier B. W. Key, with the 8th Indian Brigade, had retaken Number 15 pillbox and was pressing forward to Number 14, and then that Number 12 had been retaken, with troops moving toward Number 13. The information was erroneous: the "Dogras" had failed to achieve their defensive objectives in the muddy shoreland, divided by creeks and rivers, slippery with reeds, and difficult to traverse. The Japanese were about 1,500 yards from the airfield; it was beginning to suffer bombings and machine-gunnings by planes from Thai bases captured intact.

Sitting around their remaining aircraft as they were being patched and serviced in the morning rain, the Australian crews of RAAF Squadron 1, Kota Bharu, weighed what they knew of the situation. Suddenly, with no warning—they had no radar—Peter Gibbes saw "dozens of fighter aircraft. We assumed them to be RAAF Wirraways as we *knew* the Japs had no aircraft carriers in the invasion fleet and no airstrips anywhere near. We stood up and waved, only to be mercilessly strafed for the following ten minutes. Several personnel were killed and many Hudsons set on fire and badly damaged, including the one I had flown

that night. At once we realised that things were far more serious than
we had imagined from the info we had been fed."

.

While Lieutenant Goodpaster's engineer unit was working under
lights in the old Quarantine Station to get a stockade ready for the
Canal Zone's 250 Japanese internees, new orders arrived. "We were
told we [had] better build for the Germans as well, and this would
increase the total [capacity] to something like 750 or 1,000. And then
. . . we were told to include the Italians and that we had better plan
on enough to include the Central Europeans. . . . So we were building
a cantonment for 1,800 people who were picked up . . . within a matter
of a couple of hours. They were snatched out from wherever they were.
The round-up completely broke the [spy] rings we knew existed there."

Until the stockade could be finished sufficiently to house everyone,
the internees—including many from nations with which the U.S. was
not yet formally at war—were thrown into the Panamanian Carcel
Modello ("model jail, a great misnomer").

As a beginning, Goodpaster was throwing up industrial fencing.
Then he intended to have the prisoners build their own tent-frames,
dig their own latrines, erect their own kitchens. Meanwhile his engineers began their war by digging sewer lines in the semidarkness. "As
the people were flocking in we put up our guard towers and barbed
wire. . . . In the meantime, things were getting thoroughly wild in
some parts of the Canal Zone. Where people got over-excited, guards
started shooting at each other . . . and at least one or two post commanders evacuated all their people. . . . At Howard Field they took
them all out into the jungle off the base. . . . We heard all kinds of
rumors, and the Panamanian papers [by Monday morning] were saying
that Japanese carriers had been sighted off the coast, and so on."

"Everyone was emotionally charged that night," Robert Fox remembered. "We heard . . . rumors that the Japanese were coming up
the Chagres River [on the Pacific side] and would be attacking the
canal. . . . In retrospect we felt they blew it there, for we simply were
not ready for them. . . . A novice guard, remembering that he was to
call 'Halt!' three times before firing, actually did call 'Halt! Halt! Halt!'
in rapid succession, then emptied his rounds into the front of an approaching vehicle. Fortunately, no one was hurt although he totally
disabled the vehicle. . . . Of course . . . we were all wearing 1917-

version tin helmets, canvas leggings, and holsters and gunbelts with full clips of ammunition, something most of us had never done before."

•

Rotating her remaining combat patrol craft, *Enterprise* put up a fresh six-plane group, F4Fs this time, and a half-hour later sighted four cruisers and twelve destroyers commanded by Rear Admiral Milo F. Draemel. With orders to join Halsey, TF 8 had sortied hurriedly from Pearl Harbor in the aftermath of the attack, and Draemel's aborted golf game. The Navy gunners were nervous and took potshots at the planes, which recognized friendly ships and prudently kept their distance.

Soon one of Halsey's SBD pilots on patrol reported seeing a Japanese carrier and cruiser sixty miles south of Oahu and imagined that he was being attacked by enemy fighters. No one thought of the impossibility of the sighting. The ships may have been the shadows of clouds on the sea; the planes were Air Corps A-20 light bombers also searching in the wrong place for a Japanese force long gone. From the *Enterprise*, a hundred miles away, knowing only the misinformation he was radioed, Halsey ordered up what he called "the only weapons I had left," eighteen TBD Devastator torpedo bombers. With them went six SBD Dauntless escorts fitted with smoke generators to shield the approach of the torpedo planes, and for protection six F4F Wildcat fighters.

In the gathering dusk, the patrol found nothing and began returning, but, concerned about their attempting to land at sea in near-dark, Halsey ordered the fast F4Fs, led by Lieutenant Francis ("Fritz") Hebel, to fly north to Oahu. Then the torpedo group, low in fuel and laden with 2,000-pound aerial torpedoes, homed in on the carrier. Despite the possibility of lurking subs, Halsey had to order the ship's lights turned on. Few of his pilots were trained in night landings, and they were coming in fully armed.

The recovery process was hairy. One Devastator nearly lived up to its name when it thumped down hard and dislodged a torpedo. The blue-overalled flight-deck crew chased down the skittering "fish" and secured it. Although the Japanese had not found a flattop to torpedo, the United States Navy had almost done it for them.

It was 8:30 before the last plane landed. Halsey was in a rage over the "confusing and conflicting reports that had poured in on us all day. . . . It is bad enough to be blindfolded, but it is worse to be led around the compass." His force was "perilously low" on fuel. The *Enterprise* was safe at 50 percent of capacity, but Halsey's cruisers were down to 30 percent and his destroyers at 20 percent would soon be in trouble. They pressed on in the darkness.

•

Over Luzon, the sixty minutes from 11:00 A.M. through noon were a confusion of alleged sightings usually reported as "enemy planes, number unknown." A bulletin was even issued at 11:10 that Clark Field "had not been bombed." Just after eleven Garry Anloff at Fort Stotsenburg took a phone call from the postmaster at Aparri, reporting "that over a hundred twin-engined aircraft had just gone over his post office. I talked to P-40 pilots stationed at Iba. They had telephone orders not to go up. And they were sitting on the ground, engines warming." At 11:55 Sutherland telephoned Brereton "at the direction of General MacArthur" to ask for an update on plans for bombing Formosa, and Brereton reported that the Del Monte (Mindanao) B-17s would be moved that afternoon to San Marcelino, a pasture-like emergency field just west of Clark, and would shift to Clark when the first flight took off.

As Sutherland and Brereton talked, the Japanese bombers targeting Clark Field, already airborne for two hours, were less than an hour away. Overflying the Batan Islands and crossing Luzon at Aparri, they saw no opposing planes in the air. To Saburo Sakai in one of the lead escorting Zeros, Luzon materialized as a deep green against the dark blue of the ocean. His group cut west over the South China Sea, in order to close in on Clark Field from over the water and offer less opportunity to be spotted by radar or by observers. They expected a spirited defense. The news of Pearl Harbor had certainly reached every level of MacArthur's command.

To the south at Iba, a radar plotter left his post at 11:30 for lunch. He was puzzled as to why they weren't "up on the Mountain" with their equipment as he expected when assigned there, but his lieutenant explained that the Air Corps wanted the radar vans close by. Worried that they were an attractive target, the radarmen had tried to dig a foxhole near their vans, but in the sandy soil on the edge of the South China Sea it caved in. Refusing to be denied, they scrounged fifty-five-gallon oil drums and filled them with sand, setting them up in a large circle.

Morning plottings had screened large numbers of aircraft. Toward noon they had picked up "bigger planes" about one hundred miles to the north, on a track toward Iba and Clark—and possibly Manila. New at the job, the radar unit had acquired a lot of recent experience— more than a week of apparent "dry runs" of planes flying so high that P-40s sent up couldn't find them. The big incoming group—perhaps a hundred planes—was noted on the plotting board "and the information was passed on to our radio tent where it was sent to higher officials, I'm not sure to whom." That part wasn't the plotter's job.

•

The mail arrived on time at Government House, Singapore. Sir Shenton Thomas opened a letter with the return address of the Japanese consulate general. Signed by Suermasa Okamoto, the consul general, it was dated the 7th and thanked Thomas for his invitation. "It is exceedingly kind of Your Excellency to ask me to have lunch with you tomorrow, 8th December, at 1:00 p.m. I feel I am highly honoured and I shall be delighted to accept your kind invitation." But Okamoto would take tiffin in wartime custody at Changi.

TOKYO	SHANGHAI	WASHINGTON	PEARL HARBOR
1:00 P.M.	HONG KONG	NEW YORK	5:30 P.M.
December 8	MANILA	11:00 P.M.	December 7
	12:00 noon	December 7	
	December 8		

HOUR 40

Tᴏᴋʏᴏ ɴᴇᴡsᴘᴀᴘᴇʀs were rushing out with superpatriotic responses to the war. Reproducing the Emperor's statement, *Hochi* editorialized, "The entire people are overwhelmed with a sense of awe at the granting of the Imperial Rescript, and we can hardly suppress the explosion of our feelings. What is destined to come has at last come. The Japanese people have long waited for this day. . . . Let us scourge Britain and America, the enemies of peace."

Asahi Shimbun blamed "America's policy of applying fantastic principles to the situation in East Asia. The Americans spoke as though their appointed task was to police the world." Much like *Asahi, Chugai Shogyo* assailed the economic and military "encirclement" of Japan by the West, and America's attempting to force "imaginary and selfish principles" upon the nation in order to obtain "absolute control of the Orient." The war was for the "emancipation of East Asia." Japan has long persevered, but the time had come to "purge . . . British and American influence from the Pacific, the South Seas and East Asia."

The idea of war with America overwhelmed the individual imagination. "My nature was utterly changed," novelist Osamu Dazai wrote. "There was a feeling of being utterly transparent, as if shot through by a strong ray of light, or the breath of the Holy Spirit—a feeling as if a single cold petal had melted inside my breast." Yet despite his ecstatic epiphany, Dazai was "itching to beat the bestial, insensitive Americans to a pulp."

Similar "turbulent emotions" welled up in the young novelist Sei Ito. "I felt a curious inner tranquillity, . . . the feeling of relief bubbling up inside me. There was the joy of being given a direction clearly, a lightness of the whole being." And Yoshoro Nagayo wrote, "I never thought I should live to see such a wonderful day, such a thrilling day, such an auspicious day! Heavy clouds were hanging over our heads; then, with the promulgation of the Imperial Rescript . . . the clouds scattered, the fog disappeared." Suekichi Aono remembered "how my heart pounded with the news of [first] victory. What a great plan there must have been, what a grand design! In no time, England and America have been cut down to size. A people which has an Imperial Army so absolutely worthy of faith and trust as ours is indeed a lucky people."

Shoichiro Kamei argued, "Peace is far more to be feared than war. . . . War, rather than the peace of slaves!" Novelist Yōko Ōta, whose *Land of Cherry Blossoms* had just been made into a hit film in which the hero vows to "rejuvenate senile China with the blood of young Japanese men," remained "glued to newspapers and the radio, cried, and felt fully alive," as if she were "a fresh new flame." Most Japanese, Yoshio Nakano observed, were "over the moon." When he heard Hirohito's rescript read, Daigaku Horiguchi wrote, he realized that only a Japanese could appreciate the privilege granted:

> The joy of fighting for the Emperor
> And dying for him in battle
> Is something a foreigner cannot understand,
> A joy that only we can experience.

Economist Tadao Yanaihara, then forty-eight, felt strangely humble. "So they've declared war on Britain and the U.S. at last. The time has come to gaze with resolution upon history, to love one's country, to maintain a view of humanity and its destiny. Whatever transpires, our hearts are at peace, because they are with God. Have we not studied religion for such a time as this?"

Not all intellectuals were so reconciled to events. Hearing the claims of sunken American warships at Pearl Harbor, political scientist Kiheiji

Onozuka, a more reflective seventy, told his diary, "The good ship Japan has just been sunk." *Asahi Shimbun* journalist Soichi Kinoshita, only thirty-eight but well aware of what censorship kept from publication, thought, "What mad violence!" Then, he recalled, "Another feeling ran down my spine: 'We'll be beaten.' "

At his home in Hakone, almost in the shadow of Mount Fuji, former Prime Minister Prince Fumimaro Konoye heard of the war on his radio. When his initial shock turned to rage—he saw safety in limiting Japanese adventuring to East Asia—he took the next train to Tokyo and made no secret of his anger. To make certain his views were known—they could not have appeared in the censored press—he went for lunch to the Kazoku Kaikan, the Peers' Club. While everyone around him was reveling in the first successes, Morisada Hosokawa remembered, Konoye became despondent. Rising from his seat he walked toward the hallway, turning back to say, "It is a terrible thing what has happened. I know that a tragic defeat awaits us at the end. I can feel it. Our luck will not last more than two or three months at best."*

•

At the dockyard gates in Hong Kong Alice Briggs handed her husband a basket of clothes to be put aboard the *Scout*. They talked briefly while Briggs worried about preparations on the destroyer: he was responsible for everything but the engine room. All his wife knew was that it was safer for the ship at sea than in dry dock. When they parted, she knew little more; nor did Briggs, until his captain had returned to the ship, took Briggs aside, and asked, "Will you promise not to tell your wife what I have to say?" Then he relayed his orders to sail after dark with the four-stacker *Thanet* to Singapore by way of Manila. Briggs could write a guarded letter to Alice, for delivery via the operations officer at the base. Going to his cabin, Briggs began, "By the time you get this we will have sailed and it may be quite a time before we meet again."†

At 12:15 ZBW (Radio Hong Kong) broadcast Sunday prayers. At 12:30 a program of dance music began, continuing until the radio

---

* He would commit suicide in 1945, just after the end of the war.

† It was. Taken prisoner, Alice Briggs would not be reunited with her husband and daughter for four years.

went dead to prevent the Japanese, engaged in another air raid over the island, from using its signals for navigation.

•

Just before noon, two Japanese sailors shouldering rifles appeared at John Powell's room in Shanghai's American Club to evict him. "Both were drunk, and their arms were full of bottles of beer looted from the club bar. They made themselves at home and proceeded to consume the beer, at the same time ordering me to hasten my departure." Powell took to the Metropole Hotel only what he could carry, abandoning "practically all of my clothing and numerous pieces of carved ivory, and art treasures, including some rare Mongolian and Tibetan rugs, pieces of brocade and jewelry I had picked up in my newspaper travels . . . and had treasured for many years." He had ample warning that the Japanese were coming, and had even sent his family away; the loss of his hoard was predictable. So it was with most foreigners in the Settlement, who had lived as if their residence were fixed by immutable law.

Some—particularly absentee landlords—had little choice. Sir Victor Sassoon* had found no one to whom to sell his hotels, offices, and apartment buildings, long in jeopardy. They were confiscated during the morning. So were the Shanghai branches of the National City Bank of New York, the Chase Bank, the Hong Kong and Shanghai Bank, and the Chartered Bank of Australia and India. J. A. MacKay, manager of the City Bank, was marched off to internment after two Japanese officers, once employed in the New York office of the Yokohama Specie Bank and familiar with American practice, took charge. Planning had been thorough.

For Powell, who had only a few dollars in his pocket when the Japanese arrived, his lapses in preparation meant spending what remained of the day in a queue at the City Bank office, where he kept his personal and business accounts. "I discovered that a considerable portion of the foreign and Chinese communities apparently had a similar idea, for a line had formed which not only extended around the block, but overlapped. The line was made up not only of Americans,

---

* Sassoon, who had left for India, sailed from Bombay in February 1942 around the Cape of Good Hope to England. On board the *Tjiluwah* he was overheard by "Han Suyin" to say, "We'll be back in Shanghai next year."

but of large numbers of other foreign residents, particularly Russians, Scandinavians, Portuguese, Jewish refugees and Chinese, all of whom thought that an American bank offered better protection than the banks of other nationalities."

It took him about five hours to reach the doors through which depositors were admitted in small groups. When his turn came he was ushered into the office of the three American executives of the bank, who stood "with their hands in their pockets looking on more or less helplessly while two Japanese sat at the desk with the bank's books open before them. One of the American officers whispered to me that the Japanese had been trained in New York . . . and 'understood.' " Powell could withdraw nothing in dollars, and was only permitted to have Nationalist Chinese currency, which he knew would rapidly depreciate and would soon be replaced by worthless paper issued by the puppet Nanking administration. The single Japanese failure of foresight had been to arrive without newly printed currency for Shanghai, as they had arranged for other areas intended for occupation. But Powell would not need money for long. After twelve days of limbo his *China Weekly Review* offices, sealed on the 8th, were seized. Everything was removed, even the clock on the wall, and he was taken off to prison.

Laura Margolis discovered to her surprise that Captain Inuzuka "had installed himself in the penthouse of our hotel which had belonged to Sir Victor Sassoon." A Joint Distribution Committee bank credit of $30,000 had to last the month and over eight thousand refugees were totally dependent on welfare funds for their food. The banks were predictably inhospitable about JDC credit. "There was only one thing to do and that was to go up and see him and show him the telegram." She had become friendly with Inuzuka's live-in "secretary," later his wife. "Mrs. Inuzuka opened the door for me. . . . The refugees were in a panic. Mr. Siegel stayed with them in the lobby of the hotel, to quiet them. He was very open and honest. . . . This was a deputation of all the refugees from Hongkew, maybe fifteen down there. They had elected their own committee to come and see us and say 'Now what? What is going to happen to us?' I just put the cards on the table."

In the sumptuous Sassoon penthouse, high above Shanghai, Inuzuka pondered the fate of his Jewish charges. They could be his problem, or that of Laura Margolies. "If you allow us to borrow money against this," she offered, "we can operate, for how long we can't guarantee. This is the only asset we have. You're an occupying power now. Occupying powers don't like riots. Hungry people riot. You and I and our countries can be fighting out there"—and she pointed away, to the world beyond Shanghai—"but I think it would be to your benefit to let me use the credit I have. I can't use it as an enemy national unless you give me an OK."

The argument worked. But before Inuzuka agreed, "I had to go through the tea ceremony—like a movie. He finally said yes, but on one condition."

"You give me a list of the people from whom you borrow the money," he insisted, ruling out the banks, "and it cannot be enemies of Japan."

Below in the lobby she explained that until loans were arranged, the JDC could feed eight thousand people four days or four thousand people for eight days. And she had to find funds from neutrals—borrowing, paradoxically, from people the Japanese could assume "were betting on the Allies winning the war." Russians in the Settlement were neutral. So were French, Swiss, Portuguese.

Margolis and Siegel were in business. The refugee community settled down to a spartan survival.

·

At noon Melville Jacoby cabled Time-Life from Manila that the press corps had "lost wireless contact with the U.S."—a phenomenon that suggested a shift from voluntary censorship to official blockade of news. War panic, he reported, had taken hold in Manila, with "runs on banks, grocery stores, gas stations." (Vargas quickly ordered withdrawals limited to two hundred pesos weekly.) Taxis and buses and trucks had been taken over, paralyzing public transport; some of the requisitioned trucks brought 20,000 sandbags to protect Quezon's Malacañang Palace. Philippine Scouts were riding about in buses freshly painted orange, rounding up Japanese nationals and hauling them to internment camps. Four thousand were picked up in Manila. In Iloilo, city police rounded up 153 enemy aliens, mostly shop owners, and too many for the local jail. The authorities took over the Japanese school. In a holiday mood, thousands jammed the streets to watch, the most jubilant of them the Chinese townspeople, who waved Nationalist flags.

All inter-island vessels were commandeered by the Navy, while international shipping scurried back into Manila Bay for safety—including the British *Taiping*, bound for Australia, and the Vichy French *Maréchal Joffre*, on which there were sixteen Japanese whom officials wanted to take into custody. Six somehow evaded police at the pier. The hapless *San Jose*, awaiting clearance to lift anchor for Hong Kong with the Canadian contingent's vehicles, was ordered to off-load its equipment. There was no chance now of going farther north.

To prevent enemy planes from homing in on radio signals, all commercial radio broadcasting was banned between 5:30 P.M. and 6:30 A.M. The publishing or broadcasting of weather information became illegal. Ex post facto, all schools were ordered closed at 7:00 A.M. (By the time the regulation was issued, all of them were empty.)

Manila Bay was quiet. Four more submarines were leaving the bay. The work of stripping down the *Ford* and its harbor companion, the *Pope*, continued. Burnable items had to go, including personal letters or pictures that might give information to the enemy. Winter clothing useless in their operations area was removed on a lighter. Gray paint dulled the shine on brass fittings and gun barrels. When that ran out, the crew used boiler compound from the fireroom. Rumors that the destroyer would be used to evacuate women and children seemed verified when a sailor covering the shine on a torpedo mount noticed a partly open crate that had been lifted aboard and shouted, "Hey! *We are getting women aboard*. Look at all the Kotex!" "Doc" Zlotelow, the Chief Pharmacist's Mate, scoffed, "Damn it, shut up! These were the only bandage material I could get." While gibes flew about wounds being dressed with the unmentionable articles, Zlotelow took them below.

•

General Maltby would later deplore the failure of Lieutenant Tamworth's sappers and Major Grey's Punjabis to provide Hong Kong "the measure of delaying action anticipated." Tamworth did manage sixteen demolitions; Grey's outnumbered and underequipped troops did all they could do while the Japanese flooded around them. At Taipo Market, halfway down the eastern coast of the peninsula at Tolo Harbor, the forward party of a Japanese battalion, pouring through the deserted village at noon, found a bridge intact and began rushing across, only to be caught on the exploding span. Suddenly more cautious, the main body of troops paused, giving the British the chance to destroy fuel pumps and tanks. Few such opportunities arose, but in the Taipo area, at least, the headlong advance slowed.

Another of Grey's units was a platoon of Afridi soldiers from northern India, led by the tall, bearded Jemadar Sherin. Protecting a bridge demolition crew, the platoon watched a Japanese detachment cross a rocky field with what appeared to be a dozen village women marched before them as a defensive shield. Trembling and sobbing, the women were being pressed forward by soldiers with bayonets. Sherin called Grey on his field phone.

"Do your job," said Grey. "Halt the enemy . . . , blow up the bridge, and fall back to Gin Drinkers."

Sherin ordered his Afridis to fire, consoling himself that the Japanese on similar occasions in China had raped hostage women, then killed them. He'd be sparing them that. When the detachment, with its captives, came within 150 yards, Sherin's men opened up. There were no survivors.

•

As soon as two Buffaloes were patched up to fly, Flight Lieutenant J. R. Kinninmont and Sergeant N. R. Chapman, the Sungei Pattani squadron clerk, took them up. Over Thailand, about two miles below Singora, they were discovered by twelve Japanese Type-96 fighters. The sky, Kinninmont remembered, "seemed full of red circles." Their Buffaloes were no match for the Japanese and getting away did not prove easy:

> I pulled up to meet one as he dived down. . . . I was in such a hurry to shoot something that I didn't use my gun sight. I simply sprayed bullets in his general direction. Somebody was on my tail and tracers were whipping past my wings. . . . Chapman was turning and shooting with four Japs. I decided to get out. I yelled to Chapman (over the radio telephone) 'Return to base. Return to base.' and went into a vertical dive. As I went down I glimpsed the sergeant diving straight for the ground with three Japs on his tail, shooting; then I lost sight of him. At three thousand feet I had a quick shot at a four-engined Kawanisi Jap flying-boat and missed.

Three fighters went after Kinninmont. When he dived, one followed. A tight turn to the left was too late: he felt bullets splatter into the Buffalo. Opening the throttle, he felt the first real fear in my life. . . . It struck me in a flash. This Jap was out to kill me. I broke into a cold sweat and it ran down into my eyes. A noise throbbed in my head and I suddenly felt loose and weak. My feet kept jumping on the pedals. My mouth was stone dry and I couldn't swallow. My mouth was open and I was panting as though I'd just finished a hundred yard dash and I felt cold. Then I was jibbering. . . . 'Watch those trees. ———, that was close. He'll get you next burst. You'll flame into the trees. No, he can't get you. ———, he mustn't get you. You're too smart. He'll get you next time. Watch him, watch his guns. Watch those trees. ———, it's cold.' My feet were still jumping on the pedals. I couldn't control them. Then I saw his attacks were missing me. I was watching his guns. Each time they smoked I slammed into a tight turn. And then my whole body tightened and I could think. I flew low and straight, only turning in when he attacked. The Jap couldn't hit me again. We raced down a valley to the Thai border and the Jap quit.

Kinninmont had celebrated his twenty-first birthday three weeks before. He survived the episode, and the war. Chapman, an Australian like Kinninmont, was five years older. He lasted only five more weeks.

Just as they returned and parked their planes next to three others standing by, fifteen enemy bombers approached without warning from about 6,000 feet. No warning system existed; their communications had gone up in the morning raid. This time—it was 10:45 A.M.—the rest of their aviation fuel went up in flames, about 200,000 gallons. It was just as well. Only four serviceable Buffaloes remained; all the station buildings were destroyed, and a false poison gas alarm added to the chaos. Once the crews had eaten whatever bread and bully beef they could find for lunch, Squadron Leader F. R. C. Fowle ordered the remnants of the squadron to withdraw to Butterworth, forty miles west. Before he could evacuate, however, he was ordered to attempt another reconnaissance of Singora. Although headquarters in what was left of North Malaya was desperate to find out how the Japanese had made out on the Thai coast, their successes were obvious. They were flying from Thai airfields, and had achieved mastery of the Malayan skies.

At the Kota Bharu air base, incoming aircraft were warned to land somewhere else to the south. Two planes from Tom Lamb's 36 Squadron, up from Seletar, had failed to pick up his radio message to reassemble at Kuantan, halfway down the peninsula, and flew low over the Kota Bharu runway. Wrecks blocked a normal approach, and as they descended even lower, Flight Officer Callick and Flight Sergeant Lyall saw their own troops frantically waving them off. Callick ran out of fuel just as he touched down at Kuantan. The plane swerved violently, wrecking the undercarriage. It was no consolation that the plane was obsolete anyway.

From what was left of the Sungei Pattani airstrip, the intrepid Kinninmont took off again in his scarred Buffalo, this time chased about over Singora by five Zeros. Again he got away, reporting forty ships in Singora harbor, enemy flying boats on the lake at Singora, and vehicles heading down the highway toward Alor Star. Although the war in Malaya was less than twelve hours old and the enemy had been resisted bravely and fiercely, Malaya was already doomed. All the British had left with which to defend the country was its vastness.

Control of the air over northern Malaya, largely defended by colonial Indian troops, gave the Japanese the opportunity to drop leaflets suggesting that the Indians were being given the burden of defending a land not their own while British soldiers far away in Singapore were being spirited away to safer climes. The Japanese propagandist was a master of English cliché. "TERRIBLE RIOT IN SINGAPORE. SECRET EVACUATION OF BRITISH TROOPS," the leaflet headlined. "A terrible riot has broken out in Singapore! British and Australian troops are being secretly evacuated from Singapore! Malayan and Indian Soldiers! Pack up your troubles in your old kit bag and co-operate with the Nippon Army. British and Australian Soldiers! Return to your homes at once by hook or by crook. You may never get another chance to see your beloved ones in England or Australia!"

•

At sea off San Miguel Bay on their second day out, Clare and Leon Grove, with two friends who were also executives of Alatco, a bus and trucking company in southern Luzon, were enjoying expatriate life on their yacht, *Taringtang*. They had anchored at a beach to cook a breakfast of bacon, eggs, toast, and coffee; afterward they had fished until one of the party caught lunch—a pompano. Jimmy James had to be urged to break the holiday spell and dial Don Bell's 12:45 broadcast from Manila, and—so Clare Grove noted in her log—"we missed the first few minutes." What followed was "staggering"—Japan had attacked "American soil," and not the Philippines, but Hawaii. "We heard something about Baguio and Davao, but could not be sure just how they were connected with this attack. A battleship had been bombed by the Japanese and a Japanese aircraft carrier had been sunk by the Americans."

Don Bell advised staying tuned for further developments. They did, while hoisting all sails and keeping the *Taringtang*'s motor running. Hurriedly, they headed back to home port, Pasacao, on the southern neck of the island well below Manila. "Apparently war was in the air!" Mrs. Grove wrote innocently.

It took some time to recall all the B-17s in the Luzon skies to Clark Field for the Formosa mission. The Fortresses had wasted tons of fuel and needed their tanks topped; gasoline trucks moved out to service them as they queued up in neat rows. Pursuit planes also began peeling back from patrols; lunch hour was approaching. Despite the many sightings reported, and raids on other fields and bases, no concern was evident about dispersal of aircraft. It was more convenient to service planes wingtip to wingtip.

Reports of enemy planes telephoned in by ground observers continued to arrive from as far north as Aparri. Few were taken seriously. The Japanese had no long-range bombers like the B-17; their carriers, it seemed, were far away at Pearl Harbor. Although there had been minor raids elsewhere before breakfast, false alarms were more frequent. Weary and frustrated B-17 pilots wanted to have lunch, check out their missions on maps they knew were inadequate, and get airborne toward a real target.

At Nielson Field, Colonel Harold George of Interceptor Command was in his plotting room when sightings of high-flying enemy planes flooded in. He felt certain that the target was Clark Field. The Air Warning Center at Neilson, set up before Iba's radar was operative, received reports from designated watchers throughout Luzon—postmasters, mayors, and other minor public officials—and plotted them on a sixty-foot-long table cut into the shape of the long, crooked Philippine archipelago. As the reports came in by telephone, telegram, and teletype and arrived from the Message Center by runner, an officer read them aloud to the plotters, who, using cue sticks, pushed miniature planes into place. Before noon, with a clot of toy planes bearing down on central Luzon, George's aircraft warning officer, Colonel Alexander H. Campbell, teletyped another warning to Clark. From Iba, radar-generated information alerted Clark; and Campbell himself telephoned. Static fuzzed some radio signals; the teletype went unread, possibly because the operator at Clark had gone to lunch. An unidentified lieutenant did pick up the telephone to assure Campbell that he would relay the warning "at the earliest opportunity." He may have then gone to lunch too, having only responded to a message half-heard and misunderstood.

As Campbell plotted the Japanese closer to Iba and to Clark, he urged George "to do something about it." George insisted on waiting until the planes reached a predetermined distance. Then George's aide, Major John T. Sprague, typed out a message and showed it to Campbell, who asked what "kickapoo" meant.

"Go get 'em," said Sprague, confidently, taking it into the Message Center. The Japanese were then about fifteen minutes from target. Four squadrons of fighters were ordered up. Since multiple alerts had already gone to Clark, no new one was transmitted.

Five minutes later a plane ferrying additional cameras from Nielson arrived at Clark. The three-plane reconnaissance to Formosa had been further delayed because only one B-17 was fitted with photographic equipment.

Iba's grass strip was hit first, by 53 twin-engined Mitsubishis escorted by 50 Zeros. Sixteen P-40s of the 3rd Pursuit Squadron, short on gas after a futile patrol over the South China Sea—they were flying too low—were either on the ground for refueling or in the process of landing.

As a radar plotter at Iba returned from lunch he saw "soldiers running for cover" and looked up. Although he had reported a large group of incoming aircraft, he failed to make the connection and observed to a sergeant, "Look at those nice planes."

"The only trouble is that they're Japs!" the sergeant shouted, running hard.

The radarman ran for his circle of sand-filled barrels, diving in as the attackers began a strafing run. "Somebody fell asleep," he thought as he saw planes being hit on the ground and pilots trying to get some of them airborne "shot down before full flight." From behind the barrels he watched as his radar vans and radio tent were shattered, "and a bomb hit the place where our caved-in foxhole was." His lieutenant, the only one with a rifle, stood up in the melee to fire at the dive bombers. Crouching, the private heard a single machine gun chattering and watched several officers fire their .45 pistols in futile anger.

"I believe one or so P-40s was left," he wrote later. "It cannot be blamed on the Aircraft Warning Company."

At about 12:45 the tight formation of 27 high-flying twin-engined bombers flashed into view at Clark from the west, and Iba, followed by a second wave of 26 (one had dropped out at the start because of engine trouble). A ground crewman looked up and said admiringly, "Look what the Navy's showing us!" And indeed they were Navy planes—of the Japanese 11th Air Fleet. Bombs glinted in the midday sunlight, and, to the high wail of sirens, men streamed from the mess halls.

Having finished lunch, Lieutenant W. Dupont Strong, a B-17 pilot, was walking to his barracks when he heard "a low moaning sound." He looked up and saw "a whole crowd of airplanes" approaching from the northwest. He ran for a slit trench. "By the time I hit the trench, the bombs had begun to hit the ground." Other pilots, one of them Captain Alison Ind, "rushed out in a futile attempt to take the big machines off. . . . One after another, these vitally needed, expensive, irreplaceable bombers collapsed in bullet-riddled heaps or sagged to the ravenous flames that were consuming them."

Aircraft were caught taking off, landing, or on the ground for refueling. Ordinary alertness might have compensated for the inadequacy of radar. (The Iba installation was the only working radar in the Philippines.) More value placed on the B-17s might have kept them from useless air time, but ground-pounding senior officers still considered bombers as inefficient artillery, less useful than a good 150mm howitzer battery, which could deliver more iron and explosives closer to a target (except that it had no wings to get to distant targets). And pursuit planes were fine for close-formation flying to thrill spectators at air shows, but good for little else.

Private First Class Victor Mapes, a ground crewman for the B-17s, saw the Fortresses coming in "to re-gas. They lined them up on the runway and the crews cut out for chow. I was listening in the barracks to a very loquacious radio commentator named Don Bell, when all of a sudden he said that Clark Field was being bombed." (There had been erroneous earlier reports of an eleven o'clock bombing.) "As far as I knew, and I was there, nothing was happening, but just to make sure, some of us went outside to the back of the barracks." Coming over the foothills were the Japanese. Shouting "Attack!" the men scrambled for a revetment, pulling on their gas masks as they ran. While trying

not to suffocate in the useless gas masks—orders were to wear them—
they crawled into a concrete latrine to hide from the low-flying Zeros
with their machine guns. "I saw a guy throw his shoe at a plane, another
his .45. . . . It seemed like it went on forever."

Another refuge was a tank. Sergeant Forrest Knox and a buddy
leaped in, quickly closing the turret. "What do we do now?" asked
Knox's buddy.

"I don't think we can do anything."

"We can't stay here."

"Sure we can."

Knox decided to have a look. He pushed back the hatch and confirmed that the raiders were Japanese. "They've got a big flaming ass-
hole on the fuselage," he yelled inside. The two began training the
tank's gun at the swooping Zeros. "I was firing so much," Knox recalled, "that the empty ammo cases kept building up on the deck.
. . . I don't think I hit anything. They never bothered to explain how
far you had to lead an aircraft in order to hit it. . . . When it should
have been duck soup because they were so close, I was missing them
by fifty feet."

Private First Class Robert Brown of the 17th Pursuit Squadron
was at Clark Field when the first V formation of bombers droned over.
"When the big guys got through, the fighters started raking us, pulling
up right over the top of me. Scared and amazed? I couldn't believe
someone was attacking the United States. Absolutely unreal! All these
Zeros so close I could see the big red dots on their wings. Hell, who
could believe this? Us? And here's our planes all sitting on the ground."

Only one of eight antiaircraft guns at Clark put up any fire, but its
shells burst uselessly low. In his barracks, Anton Bilek saw his sergeant
rush in shouting, "It's the real thing. Here they come!" Bilek had joined
the Army two years earlier to learn a trade and had gone to sheet-
metal school for aircraft repair. He would have a lot of work on his
hands, but as the sirens screamed he grabbed his helmet, gas mask,
and World War I-vintage Springfield rifle and dashed for a machine
gun pit. "So that's what it sounds like," he said to a buddy about his
first taste of war. With weapons too ineffective to fire, they watched
while the Japanese "didn't miss anything. . . . We look around and see
all this devastation, airplanes burning, hangars burning, gas trucks
burning. Men yelling and screaming. Wounded and dead all over the
place." Flash fires in the long cogon grass, Lieutenant Edgar D. Whit-

comb, a B-17 navigator, recalled, were "roaring and crackling like an evil beast." All that remained of his plane were four charred engines.

The 200th Coast Artillery's 3-inch antiaircraft shells were helpless against the Japanese. The newest ammunition had been manufactured in 1932; most fuses were corroded, and only one of every six shells even exploded. Saburo Sakai in his Zero was puzzled. His squadron was almost unmolested although the bad morning weather had cost them valuable hours after Pearl Harbor. "Instead of encountering a swarm of enemy fighters diving at us in attack, we looked down and saw some sixty enemy bombers and fighters neatly parked. . . . They squatted there like sitting ducks. . . . Finally, after several minutes of circling over the field, I discovered five American fighters at a height of about 15,000 feet, some 7,000 feet below our own altitude. At once we jettisoned the external fuel tanks, and all pilots armed their guns. . . . The enemy planes, however, refused to attack, and maintained their low altitude . . . flying around at 15,000 feet, while we circled above them."

The first wave, escorted by Zeros, began their runs from 22,000 feet, carpeting the runways with flames. A few bombs fell short, hitting the crowded Officers' Mess. Japanese bombardiers had studied the layout of Clark Field from reconnaissance photos and knew exactly where each Flying Fortress was parked under peacetime conditions. And they were still there. Saburo Sakai took pictures. "Our accuracy," he recalled, "was phenomenal—it was, in fact, the most accurate bombing I witnessed by our own planes throughout the war. The entire air base seemed to be rising into the air with the explosions. Pieces of airplanes, hangars and other ground installations scattered wildly. Great fires erupted and smoke boiled upward." Lieutenant Colonel Eubank insisted that Bomber Command had not known of the approaching force. "The formation was almost directly overhead at the time the air-raid warning siren was sounded and the bombs began exploding a few seconds thereafter." There were claims that telephone lines to Clark had been sabotaged and that teletyped warning messages had not been received. But every cautionary rule of warfare had been ignored since daybreak. Offensive aircraft had been wasted in futile patrols; aircraft meant for pursuit were flown timidly and ineffectively; aircraft ordered by Washington to be dispersed were lined up for convenience and destroyed on the ground. With ten hours to prepare since learning of

Pearl Harbor, the Philippines Command by misusing its B-17s had permitted a second Pearl Harbor to happen.*

Desperate attempts were made by pilots of some P-40s to get up, and as the Zeros escorted the two waves of bombers away, there was a brief chance in the chaos. Then the Zeros returned at low level to strafe the field and finish the job, destroying ten planes before Lieutenant Joseph H. Moore of the 20th Pursuit Squadron succeeded in leading three other P-40s into the air. One, piloted by Lieutenant Randall B. Keator, allegedly shot down a Zero, while Moore claimed two.

Sakai denied it. Ten minutes after the bombers exited to the north, his flight of Zeros had returned, circling down to 13,000 feet to view the flaming shambles, diving at steep angles to cannonade the few undamaged B-17s, then climbing steeply out of range. "Five fighters jumped us. They were P-40s, the first American planes I had ever encountered." (Actually there were only four.) "Four of the planes arched up and over into the thick columns of smoke boiling up over the field, and were gone." The fifth, Sakai reported, spiraled to the left, and he fired into it from two hundred yards, blowing the canopy off the plane. "The fighter seemed to stagger in the air, then fell off and dove into the ground."

Quezon was still in Baguio when Jorge Vargas telephoned to report that Clark Field had been bombed and its B-17s destroyed. Excitedly, Quezon asked why American planes had not been able to head them off.

"I do not know, Mr. President," said Vargas. "Probably they were also destroyed."

Reviewing pilot claims later from the airfield at Tainan, the Japanese logged thirteen planes destroyed in the air over Clark Field, thirty-five on the ground, including nearly all the Flying Fortresses in Luzon—half the B-17 force. They had lost no bombers and only five

---

* Since history often repeats itself because people ignore its lessons, the Japanese would have their own Clark Field later in the war. In New Guinea on August 17, 1943, two months after the Americans landed in force south of Lae, B-25s and P-38s wiped out more than a hundred planes of the Japanese 7th Air Army lined up in neat rows on airstrips at Wewak. "At the time," Major General T. Tanikawa (a colonel in Malaya in 1941) confessed, ". . . our defenses were not alert. It was a decisive Allied victory."

Zeros—one to an antiaircraft gun. Four crashed "during the flight home"—perhaps due to P-40 fire. None, Sakai insisted, had gone down in a dogfight; but Americans sought the small solace of believing that they had bested a few of the enemy. Heroes were needed, and sometimes created, as with Captain Colin Kelly's claim soon after to have sunk the battleship *Haruna* in level bombing from his high-flying B-17. The aged *Haruna*, one of the oldest capital ships in the Japanese navy, survived into 1945; in December 1941 it was nowhere near Luzon. Although the bombardier, Sergeant Meyer Levin, thought he had hit something, he may have only bombed the shadow of a small cloud. The crew bailed out safely from the crippled plane—all but Kelly, who (so his copilot, Donald Robins, thought he observed) was hit by debris falling along with them, probably a vertical stabilizer. As unaware of the facts as anyone else on the American side, Franklin Roosevelt awarded Colin Kelly a posthumous Medal of Honor. The nation was grateful even for the wraiths of victory.

Primitive Del Carmen Field was a tent city on land that had formerly grown sugarcane, with a mile-long grass strip for its obsolete planes, and 238 officers and men. Most had arrived less than three weeks before on the troopship *Coolidge* and were in the process of readying an air base for an expected shipment of P-40s. In the brush around the tents were piled hundreds of 500-pound bombs, which had puzzled Sergeant Thomas E. Gage, as they could not possibly be used by P-40s. "This is going to be a bomber base," he was told, "and we are supposed to be the air cover for it." All the gasoline was stored in fifty-five-gallon drums, fortunately on the other side of the field from the bombs. There was one tank truck. The "depot" was a large metal building that formerly processed sugarcane.

Since their P-40s had not yet arrived, they depended upon Seversky P-35As, planes ordered by Sweden in 1939. With the Philippines short in aircraft, 48 of the fighters were diverted to the Pacific, tools for servicing them calibrated, Stockholm-style, in metric. Out of date for use against the Zero, they were a maintenance mystery, besides, to their ground crews.

With communications as rudimentary as everything else, aircrews heard about the war only on the noon news, when E. J. ("Shorty") Batson ran from the cook shack to the orderly room to shout, "Hey! We just heard on the Manila radio that Pearl Harbor has been bombed!" Not waiting for a response, he raced off. Sergeant Gage heard a rumbling "like thunder" and looked out of the orderly room tent in the direction of the booming, toward Clark Field. The sky appeared "covered with what I thought were hundreds of little black dots." His first surmise, which left him shaken, was that they were enemy planes. Then, as they turned into puffs, he realized that he was seeing antiaircraft fire. "Well, I hot-footed it . . . and told Lieutenant [Edward] Jennings that Clark Field was being bombed. Giving me a fishy stare, he wanted to know if my report was official. And I said, 'Hell, no, Lieutenant. Look out the back of the tent and you can see for yourself.'"

Pilots rushed to their P-35s; crews remained with the planes until the engines fired. "No orders came. We sat there and sweated in the sun. . . . After a while, some got out under the wings [in the shade]. We never received any orders. . . . I think Lieutenant Merritt finally told a few of them to go up and see what was happening. . . . One of our planes with Lieutenant Stuart Robb in it ran into a Zero and got his canopy shot off and his engine shot out. He came down dead stick and landed and had glass cuts on his hands and face. And one of the other lieutenants said that those guys up there are playing for keeps. He had some holes in his plane. Another said he wasn't going to go back up in this piece of junk."

Gage remembered hearing the usual slurs about the military incompetence of the Japanese. "Our navy would wipe them off the ocean in one week. They were too small and couldn't see, couldn't shoot, couldn't fly. And their equipment was shoddy because they copy things and didn't copy them right. One of their Zeros dropped a belly fuel tank on our field and after the fun was over . . . I looked at that belly tank and it was a beautiful piece of mechanism—perfectly made and high quality—and I said to myself that somebody is full of bull!"

Adjacent to Clark Field was old Fort Stotsenburg, home of the 26th Cavalry, Philippine Scouts, largely officered by Americans. Rack after rack of bombs shattered the installation, which from Mitsubishi altitude looked like part of Clark. Decoding messages in the signals office on the second floor was Major Raymond Herrick, who seized his steel helmet and hit the floor when strafing Zeros poured .50-caliber bullets into his building. Meanwhile teletype messages kept printing, and from his prone position Herrick seized one. Just then a bullet ricocheted off the wall and hit Herrick on the back of his helmet, knocking him unconscious.

When he came to, he felt a large lump rising on his head. He noticed a message still in his hand. Still on his stomach, he decoded it: "A state of war exists between the United States and the Imperial Japanese Government."

Artillery captain Alva R. Fitch, later a general, was based at Stotsenburg, the command post of Major General Jonathan Wainwright. On Saturday, Fitch had been on the Manila docks, supervising the off-loading of 75mm self-propelled guns, and back at Stotsenburg had spent Sunday, well into the night, hurriedly training personnel on how to use them. "We figured the war was that close." But the next morning, although officers had been awakened at 5:45 with the news of Pearl Harbor, there were "no orders" from Manila. He roused his battery anyway, loaded all vehicles, and prepared to leave for action somewhere, but "no orders came so we dug personnel trenches in the Battery area for protection against enemy aircraft." At 11:30 he had gone to Officers' Call. "There was very little information and no orders." Coming away, Colonel Louis Daugherty told Major William Thomas that the war news was probably phony and that it was all just "an alert."

Whether it was command paralysis of will, or catastrophically poor communications, few units received orders to do anything different than they had been doing before. A private in an antitank company of the 31st Infantry, Leon Beck, remembered how each Friday their schedule for the week would be posted on the company bulletin board. "On Monday our training schedule showed that after reveille and breakfast we were going to have instruction in extended-order arm-and-hand signals in the field. And on the morning of December 8, that's exactly what we did. Since we had no orders canceling this exercise we went into the field just as if nothing had happened."

Alva Fitch had not known it, but Wainwright had been given some vague employment for his men, and the few motions they were going through, largely standing in place, carried out the mission. Shortly before nine that morning, MacArthur's headquarters—which usually meant Richard Sutherland—telephoned Wainwright that Baguio, ninety-five miles to his north, had been bombed. He was "to take every precaution against a possible Jap paratroop landing at Clark Field." Obsessed by fears of fifth-column activity and paratroop drops, MacArthur dismissed Japanese aircraft handling and marksmanship. He was sure that his B-17s were only vulnerable through sabotage and from the ground.

Wainwright had no infantry at Stotsenburg, but he did post an artillery unit to the east, to rake the open parade ground—seemingly a natural paratroop landing site—with shrapnel if necessary. Then he went to his house to pack his personal belongings, in anticipation of further action. Preparing to return to headquarters just after 12:30, he walked out onto his porch in time to hear the roar of aircraft echoing against the foothills of the Zambales Mountains, which loomed north and west toward the sea.

At 12:48, officers lunching at Stotsenburg also heard approaching planes, and rushed outside. They counted fifty-three bombers, "very high." They speculated, Fitch recalled, "for a very few seconds, and then took to the ditch." When Clark Field "erupted in a column of smoke and dust," he ran toward the barracks, "where I found the Battery engaged in antiaircraft operations with Springfield rifles, with far more danger to themselves than to the airplanes. . . . I am still surprised that none of them were killed by their own barrage."

With still no orders in hand when the attack was over, Fitch moved his men and guns up the China Sea Trail and bivouacked in the jungle. Soon they found "a large part of the officers and men" from Clark in the area, having taken to the hills in a disorganized rout. "They were thoroughly demoralized. Many of them stayed in the hills for two or three weeks, coming out to forage at night."

Arriving overhead in a P-40 from Nichols Field just after the raid, Lieutenant Samuel Grashio was appalled. "It was astounding. Where the airfield should have been was an area boiling with smoke, dust, and flames." Unable to land, he marked time, returned, and discovered chaos. "Command, leadership, discipline, even simple order, had vanished utterly. Officers, enlisted men and civilians had scattered headlong in all directions."

"We couldn't find anyone from our unit," Private First Class Mapes remembered, "so we wandered away. We saw a man in his '38 Ford lying there, shot. Looked like he was trying to get off the base. Then there was a dead pilot in the cockpit of a B-17. We could barely see him because of the fires that were still burning. When we got to the edge of the jungle there was firing and yelling. Everyone was trigger happy. It was dangerous to be moving. We spent the night at the edge of the jungle behind two logs."

"The very air of Stotsenburg rattled with concussion," Wainwright recalled. In the din, the general's houseboy, Felemon San Pedro, ran out, "his eyes like big black marbles. . . . He had put on my steel helmet."

"Mother of God, General, what shall I do?"

"Go get me a bottle of beer," the hard-drinking Wainwright yelled back. The beer seemed to help both of them. Wainwright drained it, handed Felemon the empty bottle, and hurried toward his headquarters building, passing an antiaircraft battery on the edge of the parade grounds. Its black bursts followed the bombers ineffectively. While looking up, he heard "the moist impact of metal against flesh and bone." Turning, he saw a gunner falling, his face "a bloody blob. A bomb splinter had streaked all the way over from Clark Field, whose edge was twelve hundred yards from us." Wainwright ordered the battery commander—Alva Fitch—to get the young soldier to a doctor, but the gunner came to, wiped a hand across his bloody face, and insisted unsuccessfully, "Stay by my gun . . ."

From Sadieville, Kentucky, Robert Brooks was the son of poor black sharecroppers. "He lied about his race," Sergeant Maurice E. ("Jack") Wilson of the 192nd Tank Battalion remembered. "We was all white. . . . And he lied to get in a white outfit. He was yellow . . . , had kinda kinky hair. I called him Nig all the time, and didn't know he was a nigger." Brooks was dead on arrival at the Stotsenburg hospital.

Wainwright wrote out his first order for a Silver Star. And thinking still of the young soldier and his useless equipment, the general added in his memoirs, "We were in a war for which we were no more prepared than a child is to fight a cruel and seasoned professional pugilist." Later the parade ground at Fort Knox, Kentucky, was named for Brooks, who fell at the edge of a Philippine parade ground.

Doing what he could to organize the removal of the dead and wounded from Clark, Wainwright evacuated 193 casualties with Fort Stotsenburg's ambulances and trucks. "Ninety-three . . . were killed at Clark. Seven more died in our hospital." One of his officers assigned to the 24th Field Artillery, Philippine Scouts, Captain Jerome Mc-Davitt, remembered being ordered, when the Japanese had gone, "to sneak out the dead bodies and place them in the morgue. That after-noon four other American officers and myself, along with our Phil-ippine Scouts, put many [more] men into the morgue." According to Garry Anloff, "There was a garbage can outside the surgery section at the Stots hospital with arms and legs sticking out of it; we had one hell of a clean-up job."

Anloff was at Clark in the aftermath when Eubank "called one of the overage colonels manning the telephone at MacArthur's headquarters and said, 'I want to report that you no longer have to worry about your Bomber Command. We don't have one. The Japanese have just destroyed Clark Field.'"

One B-17 had been late in returning to Clark. Piloted by Lieutenant John Carpenter, it landed amid the rubble, the only survivor of its squadron. (It was to have been the lead camera plane for the Formosa raid.) Another had flown in from Mindanao and was surprised, but got away. On Saturday and Sunday, B-17 crews at Del Monte Field had spent the daylight hours pitching tents—"unlaughable labor," Lieutenant Ed Jacquet put it. Monday morning Lieutenant Earl Tash and Lieutenant Doug Kellar took their B-17 back to Clark Field for engine repairs. The Flying Fortress crews at Del Monte had no idea they were at war. Tash and Kellar had arrived over Clark Field as what appeared to be a large dust cloud rose from the runways. They decided to circle nearby Mount Arayat until the dust settled. On a new try at a landing, they encountered aircraft over the field. Still, they lowered their flaps and wheels and were on a final approach when three planes above them pounced and began firing. Quickly, Tash raised flaps and wheels, gunned the B-17 upward, and ordered Bibbin to fire away.

They fled back to Mindanao with a radioed appeal to have an ambulance meet the plane. The bomber "seemed to wobble all over the sky and make awful big circles to get onto the field. When it stopped rolling," Jacquet remembered, "there was the 'meat wagon' [waiting] and someone saw something drip out of the bottom of the ship: blood! Upon closer inspection [we saw] both ailerons hanging down when only one should be down. Here and there sunlight could be seen through the side of the ship—bullet holes. Then Sergeant Bibbin, the radio[man and] gunner, was taken out with almost all his right shoulder blown off."

Clark Field continued to burn. In each of fifteen B-17 positions little more remained than a charred mass of blackened earth and metal with four projections that were the hulks of engines. "Grass fires," Jacquet recalled, having arrived the next day, "had leveled all the tall

grass around the field. . . . A gas trailer pulled by a ten-wheeler truck
. . . had [loaded] every size of wheel and tire you could think of. They
were the few tires that could be salvaged out of the trucks that had
been on the field."

Although it was a day after the raid, Jacquet was still encountering
the unremoved dead. "What froze me in my tracks was a man lying
there. He seemed in a running attitude with a comic magazine in one
hand, but he was lying on his face. . . . His clothes had been blown
off and he was sort of roasted." There were skeletons of other burned
out planes—bullet-riddled hulks, some with bodies of pilots who had
tried to get airborne. In the wreckage of the mess, corpses sprawled
with unswallowed food oozing from limp mouths. "There were prone
Americans lying all around, lots of them. They all seemed to be trying
to run away from the center of the field when they were caught—men
I had known and worked with. . . . With a heavy heart I kept on across
the field . . . but never stopping until I got to a small bomb hole in
the sand that still had the bottom half of the bomb in it. I couldn't
resist and looked in. Then I stopped and scooped out rivets—many
different sizes—and small iron castings all crammed inside the beau-
tifully machined bomb casing." And he wondered whether they had
come from the floor sweepings of American machine shops and factories, sold only months before as scrap to the Japanese. "They made
wonderful shrapnel for anti-personnel bombs."

Lieutenant John Posten of the 17th Pursuit Squadron recalled the
dead "still lying where they fell. There was a whole B-17 crew lying
dead next to their burning ship. . . . The 20th [Pursuit Squadron] got
only three ships off the ground; the rest were riddled before they could
get the motors started. . . . Three of them tried to take off as the
bombing was going on, but were killed. . . . A friend of mine reported
seeing a pilot trying to fight his way out. . . ." Crewmen on the field
were shot before they could take cover, and others who took cover in
a gasoline shed were blown up with the shed. . . . That night we all
went back into the hills to sleep. We didn't do very much sleeping,
though."

In the Manila suburb of San Juan, Carmen Guerrero Nakpil heard
the news about Clark Field and realized that it was very bad, perhaps
worse than reported. "Some of the boys I danced with might be dead."

•

It was nearly eleven when Treasury Secretary Morgenthau returned from the White House to brief his senior assistants. Everyone available had been working into the night to get the paperwork going which would put the American economy on a war footing. "It is just unexplainable," he confided, "much worse than anyone realizes. . . . Knox feels something terrible. . . . Stimson kept mumbling that all the planes were in one place. . . . They have the whole fleet in one place, . . . this little Pearl Harbor base. They will never be able to explain it."

From the hour it happened, the failure of alertness and the failure of Intelligence would be endlessly debated, while the Clark Field debacle, covered up by rhetoric and attenuated by distance, largely disappeared into the shadows. Although vagaries of weather alone kept the Clark Field attack from occurring almost simultaneously with Pearl Harbor, conspiracy theories concocted by former isolationists and by military apologists—ignoring Clark Field—would continue to allege that FDR wanted, and even encouraged, the Pearl Harbor disaster in order to engage in a war which only rage at a surprise strike would have made acceptable. Yet that Machiavellian scenario would *not* have required a catastrophe: a raid repelled at great loss to the enemy would have done just as well. Afterward, complaints from commanders in Hawaii arose that they had not been warned unambiguously that war was imminent, or that Pearl Harbor was a likely target, this despite a decade of war games and maneuvers predicated upon a carrier-raid on Oahu.

On the last day of March 1941, the commanders of the Naval Base Defense Air Force and the Army's Hawaiian Air Force had issued an estimate of the situation that read almost as if the Japanese would borrow from it. "The most likely and dangerous form of attack on Oahu," it predicted, "would be an air attack . . . launched from one or more carriers which would probably approach inside of 300 miles. . . . Any single submarine attack might indicate the presence of a considerable undiscovered surface force probably composed of fast ships accompanied by a carrier."

The very next day, April 1, 1941, the Chief of Naval Operations in Washington had independently sent a message to the commandants of all naval districts, including Hawaii, that "past experience shows that the Axis powers often begin activities . . . on Saturdays and Sundays or national holidays of the countries concerned." Each headquarters, Admiral Stark advised, should "take steps on such days to see that proper watches and precautions are in effect." Hawaiian commanders had ignored that and much else. Their own cautionary words of months past would now haunt them.

•

At 11:30 A.M. General Percival finally recognized that Matador was stillborn. Defense forces were ordered to take up positions astride the Thai frontier. With Bren gun carriers, some troops were to cross the border on the Singora road and forestall any Japanese advance from the north. "Our Punjabi soldiers," Desmond Brennan recalled, "impatiently lined up at the frontiers," but nothing happened "to disturb the idyllic tranquillity of our mountain resort." His servant "fussed over me and my clothes and I suggested to all and sundry that the Japs had realized the frightful beating we were about to give them and had all gone home." But the highlands of Kedah State were to the west of the peninsula, and the enemy had not yet arrived. Only two days later would Brennan's B Company of twenty-five ambulances have its first casualties. One Indian soldier had a bullet penetrate his helmet and give him "a new part in his hair and the outer table of his skull before making a large exit hole in this so-called head protector. The second gentleman had both testicles neatly severed by a splendid marksman. I realized at once that the helmet was of little use as a head protector and seriously considered using it as a jockstrap."

Brennan's code orders for moving north had been food for thought. Two weeks earlier they had gone to Ipoh on receiving the code instruction "armour," a clever choice since there wasn't a tank in Malaya. Then they moved to battle stations on the receipt of the ironic code word "awake."

•

It was after midnight when Ed Murrow was summoned to Roosevelt's study. The President was sitting at his desk over beer and sandwiches and invited Murrow to share from the White House tray. Roosevelt was wearing a shapeless gray jacket the color, Murrow thought, of his tired face, but he was "so calm and so steady." Murrow wanted to talk about Pearl Harbor, but Roosevelt first wanted to know about London, about how the British were bearing up, about people he knew there. He told Murrow that he had talked with Churchill, and quoted the Prime Minister's response, "We're all in the same boat now."

"Did this surprise you?" Roosevelt asked Murrow about Pearl Harbor.

"Yes, Mr. President."

"Maybe you think it didn't surprise us!"

As the talk turned to the surprise attack, and Roosevelt began ticking off the appalling losses in ships sunk at their moorings, aircraft wrecked on their runways, soldiers and sailors dead and missing, he raised his voice in anguish at the lapses in alertness. Pounding his fist on the table as he referred to the planes destroyed he added, "On the ground, by God, on the ground!" As the talk turned to the Philippines, another visitor entered. Colonel William Donovan, just in from New York, was engaged in setting up a new Intelligence organization, separate from the often-feuding armed services, and soon to be the OSS. With Donovan they mused about how the attack would affect American opinion. Both visitors agreed that the country would vigorously support a declaration of war.

Had it all been, Roosevelt wondered, a joint Axis plan? What about the simultaneous attacks on Malaya and Hong Kong? (He knew nothing yet of the Philippines.) Donovan had no evidence of it, and guessed that Hitler was as surprised as they were.

After thirty-five minutes, Murrow emerged, wondering what to do with his scoop. He was not told that anything was off the record, but he knew much more than official releases conveyed. He walked to the White House Press Office in the West Wing. Eric Sevareid was working late, and knew where his CBS colleague had been. Reporters looked at Murrow expectantly. "It's pretty bad," he said; then he turned and exited into Lafayette Square.

From Buenos Aires, the new focus of Japanese and German activity in the Americas, the correspondent for the *Yomiuri Shimbun* would furnish Tokyo readers with a very different picture than Westerners received of how the fact of war was brought home to Washington. President Roosevelt, *Yomiuri*'s man in Argentina reported, "acted like Napoleon when [he] set foot on St. Helena." Just before Japanese "sky fighters" swept down upon Hawaii, Roosevelt and Hull had been outlining "the next step to be taken in order to make the Japanese nerve crack and . . . give in without fail to their demands." When the news of the strike on Pearl Harbor was conveyed to them, "the President was unable to comprehend the full gravity of the news. He acted like one who had been stricken by palsy, his face pale with the immensity of the crisis he had invited."

At the State Department, continued the dispatch, attributed imaginatively to the United Press, undersecretaries Sumner Welles and Adolph Berle "were dumbfounded. Their vocal cords failed to move and they had a lost look as if the earth had left them hanging in midair." Citizens in New York and Washington were "speechless." In Washington the emergency Cabinet meeting called for by an astonished Roosevelt was "called off." When reporters first saw him, "the hand in which he held a cigarette holder was continually shaking and in a trembling voice he told . . . of the losses and casualties sustained by the American forces. There was no longer that million-dollar smile of his." Outside the White House, heavily armed guards allegedly went on duty everywhere. "Pennsylvania Avenue and three other streets were fenced and persons other than those who had official business were prohibited from walking on the streets."

•

Having already declared a complete nightly blackout, the Army in Hawaii ordered all private cars off the highways unless authorized by the police. Then, at 6:04 P.M., the police radio announced, "From now on, nobody allowed out of their homes [during blackout hours.]" Instructions followed closing all saloons and prohibiting the sale of liquor; shutting down all schools indefinitely; rationing gasoline; suspending all food sales until an inventory of food stocks could be made; establishing a strict censorship; and suspending all civil courts and instituting provost courts in their place.

Hawaii could not live on pineapples and sugar, its chief crops. An inventory would show a thirty-seven-day supply of most staples, but also imminent shortages of potatoes, rice, and onions. How to import food when Hawaiian waters were crawling with enemy subs became an immediate problem. How to evacuate civilian dependents and stranded tourists was another dilemma for the new military government. Fighting a war suddenly became more than merely defending the islands.

•

Finishing his address at the Tokyo Kaikan, the Prime Minister was followed by several lesser speechmakers, whom no one seemed to hear. "The powerful and succinct words of Tojo," Kōtarō Takamura wrote, "penetrated the minds of the conferees." A motion of support for the war was acclaimed by voice vote, and everyone—nearly two thousand, Takamura estimated—"marched out in four lines toward the Palace, bearing banners . . . condemning America and England." At the Palace grounds they found other groups similarly gathered, each with a declaration to declaim. Everyone sang the national anthem and joined in cries of "*Banzai!*"

Tojo also had a more ritual appearance to make, one required of politicians in grave times. With Navy Minister Shimada he went off to the Meiji Shrine, sacred to the memory of the Emperor's grandfather, and then to the Yasukuni Shrine, repository of the souls of Japan's war dead since the opening of the nation to the West in 1853. Clapping a gong to summon the spirits of the gods that dwelt in each temple, they reported the new war and invoked the gods' blessings for its successful conclusion. Crowds gathered around them, and voices were heard, the press reported, "praying for the early capitulation of the British and American forces."

It would not take long for a popular song to exploit the shrine in glorifying death:

> Your mother weeps with joy;
> It is too great an honor for us
> That you are worshiped as a god
> at the Yasukuni Shrine.

·

At the Walker mansion on Nuuanu Avenue in Honolulu, where fifty guests, including Admiral Kimmel, had been invited for a festive twenty-first anniversary celebration, no one called in regrets and no one came. Not even the caterers or the band.

MELBOURNE	VLADIVOSTOK	TOBRUK	LOS ANGELES
3:00 P.M.	MANILA	BERLIN	SAN FRANCISCO
December 8	HONG KONG	VILNA	PORTLAND
	1:00 P.M.	6:00 A.M.	9:00 P.M.
	December 8	December 8	December 7

HOUR 41

IN MELBOURNE the War Cabinet adjourned after recalling Parliament to Canberra and putting emergency measures into effect across Australia. Prime Minister Curtin began preparing a radio address to the nation. "We are at war with Japan," he began, and he went on to itemize the unprovoked attacks that had imperiled Australia's "vital interests." "I point out," he told Australians, "that the hands of the democracies are clean."

It was the first real war the Pacific had experienced, Curtin said, offering a geography lesson that included attacks "as far apart as Honolulu, Nauru, Ocean Island, Guam, Singapore and British Malaya." He might have extended his list, but instead, curiously, Curtin closed with the words of the feisty yet unwarlike Algernon Swinburne, whose lyrics were notorious when Curtin was a schoolboy. War, said Swinburne, son of an admiral whom he had caused constant embarrassment, brought out the best in people:

> Come forth, be born and live,
> Thou that has help to give. . . .

Another surprising outcome of an unprecedented day, Australians heard a staid statesman quoting on a national radio transmission a once-vilified Victorian poet whose sex-obsessed verses had made respectable citizens squeamish.

•

In Kuibyshev, American Lieutenant Colonel Townsend Griffiss, representing the United States Army's Air Corps Ferry Command, applied to Russian officials, given the changed situation, for permission to deliver planes via Alaska and Vladivostok in Siberia. Suspicious that American desire for the route had "relation to questions of strategy as well as . . . to aircraft deliveries," the Russians refused. They were, Griffiss reported, "reluctant to take action which might precipitate hostilities with the Japanese." His mission "unpromising," he would be ordered back to London.

The only Americans in Vladivostok with official status were the consulate staff. Monday afternoon's diplomatic problem was a by-product of a Lend-Lease shipment which had arrived just before the Japanese opened hostilities in the Pacific. The Soviet freighter *Mayakovsky* had loaded a cargo of American manufactures at Vancouver, British Columbia, including locomotives and railway freight cars. After three days at sea, an unemployed Detroit laborer, Edward Henry Speier, thirty-four, emerged, hungry, from the cab of a supposedly sealed electric locomotive. He was put "in a warm room" aboard ship and jailed on arrival in Vladivostok.

Vice-Consul Donald Nichols accompanied Consul General Ward and Diplomatic Agent Ankudinov to the Militsiya, where at 1:05 P.M. they were permitted an interview with Speier. Ward asked the stowaway his name. "Is this a court?" Speier asked.

"No, you are talking to the American Consul General and Vice-Consul."

Speier spilled out his life history. He left the U.S., he said, to avoid "being made a soldier," and because he was "not given a chance to work in the United States." It was his sixth attempt since December 1940 to get to Russia. He had been living in the locomotive cab on a siding in Richmond, California, since July 30, 1941. When it had not been loaded on a freighter and he had run out of money for food, he left and washed dishes in a local restaurant, returning to the cab to sleep. He had remained in the locomotive when it was shipped north to Canada on a rail flatcar. "Speier suffered from the heat while in California," Vice-Consul Nichols reported to Washington, "but as the locomotive moved northwards he almost froze, and once . . . the locomotive fell off the flatcar and he had to remain in it while it was being reloaded. During the course of his experience he was considerably shaken up and bruised. . . . He had no desire to go anywhere in the world other than Vladivostok, where he expected to obtain employment."

Speier spoke no Russian, claimed to be a Communist, and was willing to bear arms for Russia but not in defense of a "capitalist state." He was, he contended, one of "Uncle Sam's disinherited sons, kicked around and not given a chance to work," even thrown in jail often because he "tried to eat" and had no money to pay his restaurant bills. Now "Uncle Sam wants to pat me on the back and make a soldier of me, but I am not so dumb. . . . If I am to have a bayonet in my belly I want it to be for a good reason. . . . In every country there are good and bad people, but whereas in the United States the bad people are running the Government, in the Soviet Union the bad people are all in jail."

Speier would need some passport, whether he chose to go or stay, Nichols observed. Insisting that he only wanted to be left alone, Speier agreed to sign a passport application if the oath of allegiance were stricken. He was uneducated, Ward thought, and possibly unbalanced, and "well versed in the ordinary Communist dialectics and clichés. . . . He is a very uncouth person and seasons his conversation liberally with profanity and obscenities."

The Russians offered to send him back if the U.S. wanted Speier for draft evasion. Washington preferred that the Soviets keep him.

•

For L. E. Tutt of 414 Battery, 104th Regiment, the relief of To-bruk, after 242 days, came without fanfare and flags. "Our first sight of troops from the outside was not an encouraging one. At dawn we saw a huge convoy of vehicles and ambulances threading their way through our position and on towards the town. Not a victorious army but the detritus of a division which lost almost everything. They were not relieving us; rather they were taking shelter behind our wire. There were empty water carts, Bren [gun] carriers with just a driver, in short the tail of units which have lost, or become separated from, the fighting heads. They were the remnants of some of the forces which had so bravely set out to meet with us."

For the Italians on the other side, relief had not come fast enough, as the 1st Durham Light Infantry had made contact with the Pavia Division overnight, inflicted an undetermined number of casualties in the darkness, and taken 130 prisoners. Gambarra had countermanded Rommel's withdrawal orders, setting up what would be a prolonged row over how the retreat should be conducted. The Italians saw their honor at stake. Libya was their colonial showcase; Rommel saw it only as a space between Tunis and Cairo.

The morning issue of *Tobruk Truth* emphasized the big events elsewhere, headlining, "War Flares Up in the Pacific & Japan Attacks American and British Bases." Imaginative reports about Japanese losses were printed, including the reported sinking of a carrier off Pearl Harbor, and the downing of dozens of aircraft. Mustard gas bombs, it reported dramatically—and equally erroneously—had been dropped on Singapore.

Sergeant Sherman Clay, twenty-three, an American volunteer on detached service from the U.S. Army, heard the news from a British noncom. "I guess you Yanks," he said, "can no longer justify staying out of this bloody war."

"Bitingly cold this morning," Edward Porter noted at his antiaircraft battery. Scanning his *Tobruk Truth* he concluded, "Now the whole world is at war. . . . Our little affair here now seems a sideshow."

No longer trapped in Tobruk, L. E. Tutt's 414 Battery would be shipped directly to Burma, through Suez, to fight the Japanese.

•

Unaware that Muñoz Grandes's Blue Division had withdrawn beyond Volkhov, Russian aircraft continued to bomb the empty positions for hours, never noticing two stragglers, an airplane spotter and an infantryman who had overslept. They walked unmolested along the Otenskii-Shevelevo road to the west until they caught up to their units. There was no attack on the Spanish bridgehead, which would only be evacuated at noon the next day.

•

At daylight in the unheated PW camp at Novo-Vileyka in Lithuania, the whistle sounded for work parties. Yuri Farber began to shake Andrey, who slept to one side of him, beneath a shared overcoat. "He did not respond; he was dead. I tried to wake my second neighbor,

Mikhaylichenko. He was dead, too. I had slept the night between two dead men."*

·

There was little activity at the ferry landing on Terminal Island, across the inlet from San Pedro, California. Behind it lights still shone on the oil derricks of the Signal Hill oil field, and in the backdrop of Long Beach buildings. In the chicken-wire detention pen at the landing were three hundred Japanese plucked from their cars and boats. Soldiers patrolled the streets in pairs. Japanese children were still coming by, peering into the chicken-wire to seek out a missing parent. The main street of Fish Harbor, usually gay on a Sunday evening, was nearly dark, with only one Japanese restaurant open. Inside, the bald, elderly Japanese proprietor screamed to anyone who would listen that he had been in the U.S. since 1906.

A one-armed ex-sailor competed for attention, boasting about the port's defenses while worrying about his fishing schooner, and how he would get out in the morning. "How do they expect us to make a living? I'd sneak my boat out but they've got enough dynamite in that harbor to blow the whole Jap navy to bits. Hell, I wouldn't try to get a canoe through that."

In the light evening rain in Los Angeles, an itinerant guitarist named Woody Guthrie wandered from bar to bar along the Main Street skid row with a folk-singing partner he identified as the Cisco Kid. The pair sang for coins and free drinks, but encountered only the usual down-and-outers and none of the cash customers. Singing in the Ace High Bar, Guthrie passed his hat, finding few donors until some sailors turned up. Servicemen seemed happy about the war. "We can whip them in no time," said one. Another craved "a close crack at them Jap bastards." Patriotically, the bartender was not accepting payment for beer, and a sailor raised his gift suds and announced that the news was all right. "I . . . got a good uniform on. Got a free glass of beer. Got some real honest music. Got a great big war to fight. I'm satisfied. I'm ready. So here's to beatin' the Japs."

Girls in the booths volunteered themselves, unsurprisingly, to dance, and a overage civilian enthusiast announced, "By God, we gotta

---

* Farber survived. Moved to the death camp at Ponary, from which few emerged, he tunneled out and escaped to the Russian lines in April 1943.

treat our soldiers and sailors like earls and dukes from here on out."

For the sailors milling about, Guthrie began to sing a song he had been improvising about how the Japanese were certain to lose the war they had so unwisely begun. But just as his audience was getting into it, the smashing of a plate-glass window brought the war next door. Looking out, they could see that the Imperial Bar—run by a Japanese couple—was under siege. Exhorted to strike a blow for Pearl Harbor, the denizens of neighboring pool halls and flophouses had flooded into the street.

"We came to git 'em an' dam' me we're gonna git 'em," a leader of the rabble vowed. "Japs is Japs. We're at war with them yeller-belly Japs!"

"An' we come to git our share of 'em," another patriot agreed.

"Get 'em! Jail 'em! Kill 'em!" chanted the mob, Guthrie remembered.

The Cisco Kid, Guthrie, the sailors, the other patrons from the Ace High, and even the bartender slipped out of the bar to watch. Behind the broken window, the Japanese proprietor and his wife stood terrified. Guitar in hand, Guthrie, his partner, the sailors, and a woman carrying a jug of cheap red wine moved gingerly over the shards of glass on the sidewalk to a position between the throng and the Japanese. As a few in the mob moved belligerently toward Guthrie's group, he strummed his guitar and in his flat Oklahoma twang began to sing:

> We will fight together;
> We shall not be moved
> We will fight together;
> We shall not be moved
> Just like a tree
> That's planted by the water,
> We shall not be moved.

As the wistful melody cut through and the words became recognizable, the mob quieted. In the drizzle some began to sing along with Woody, and it seemed natural to link arms and sway rhythmically. Grumbling, some loiterers began to slink away, a departure hastened by the arrival of police cars. Summoned to handle a riot, the L.A. police department saw instead a bedraggled band singing an old union song in the rain in front of a broken window behind which stood two very puzzled Japanese.

At the Pendleton Army Air Base in Oregon, Private First Class Ross A. Sheldon was "lounging around the barracks" when a buddy returned with a report that the Japanese had bombed Hawaii. No one believed it. Then two others came in with news that civilians in nearby Pendleton were buying soldiers drinks. "That clinches it," said a private. "Now I know we're at war." In Portland, to the west, Tomihiro Chiye had gone with his mother to a church social. When they returned, they found their door open and the house ransacked. Neighbors told them that the FBI had come and taken Tomihiro's father to the Multnomah County jail. A law degree, American citizenship, lumber mills, hop-yards, hotels, and real estate investments had meant nothing.

Resplendent in his rented tuxedo, Peter Ota's father, who had come from Okinawa in 1904, was at a wedding in Los Angeles. When the reception ended, the FBI agents were waiting. A dozen wedding guests occupied cells in the county jail in their tuxedos, and for several days their families had no idea what had happened to them. When Ota's wife and children next saw him, he was wearing a denim jacket with a large number on his back.

In the early hours of darkness in the San Francisco area, air-raid sirens—actually fire alarms, since the city had no air-raid warning system—sounded three times. Radios went off the air each time, but the lights of the city blazed as usual. The Pacific Gas and Electric Company finally sent men downtown to extinguish the streetlights one by one. Searchlights along the bay crisscrossed the night sky, failing to pick up the nonexistent enemy planes.

General John DeWitt told newsmen that Japanese aircraft had been overhead: "I don't think there's any doubt the planes came from a carrier." His office contended that thirty enemy planes had flown over from the south, passing over the Mare Island Naval Base, then splitting up over San Francisco into two groups. Army pursuit planes had tracked the northbound flight but lost it; the southern group had escaped. Reacting to widespread skepticism, DeWitt complained, "There are more damned fools in this locality than I have ever seen. Death and destruction are likely to come to this city any moment. These planes were over . . . for a definite period. They were enemy planes. I mean Japanese planes. They were tracked out to sea. Why bombs were not dropped, I do not know. It might have been better if some bombs had been dropped to awaken this city."

The city seemed awake enough. Dennis Keegan, a University of

San Francisco senior, crossed the Golden Gate Bridge with a friend in a battered Chevy and was stopped for inspection by a National Guardsman. Ignorant of the air-raid alarms, he drove on downtown.

> Market Street was bedlam. The United Artists Theatre had a huge marquee with those dancing lights, going on and off. People were throwing everything they could to put those lights out, screaming Blackout! Blackout! The theater people had not been told to turn them off. . . .
> No cars could move. The streets were full of people, blocking the tracks, the trolley line. People were throwing rocks, anything they could find. A streetcar came along, one of those old-fashioned, funny San Francisco streetcars. It had a big round light. A man ran up with a baseball bat and smashed the light. But the city was lustrous, all the office building lights were on. I said to my friend, "Let's get the hell out of here before they smash our headlights."

At his rooming house he flipped on the lights and the landlady screamed, "Dennis, turn the light out! The Japs are comin'! The Japs are comin'! The Golden Gate Bridge has been bombed!" She and her daughter were clutching one another in terror.

"Mrs. Kelleher," said Keegan, "I just drove over there a few minutes ago. There's nothing wrong with the bridge." But they remained so paralyzed with fright that he turned out the lights.

In Seattle, DeWitt's alert also led to mob behavior to enforce the emergency blackout. By eleven all lights were out but for a blue neon sign at a busy intersection. Led by the nineteen-year-old wife of a sailor on a destroyer, the throng heaved anything portable—rocks, bottles, shoes—at the sign, then at darkened storefronts. While policemen watched, looting began, spreading to a six-block area. "We've got to show them they can't leave their lights burning," explained the Amazon. "This is war. They don't realize one light in the city might betray us. That's *my* patriotism."

•

On Oahu, there was no panic. The Japanese were so substantial an element of the population that they were hardly noticeable. Still, many prudently kept off the streets, although not Ted Tsukiyama, a Nisei. Hearing a radio announcer instruct all members of university ROTC units to report immediately, he jumped into his uniform and rushed to the Manoa campus. "There were reports that Japanese paratroops had landed on St. Louis Heights. Our orders were to deploy and meet the enemy and delay their advance into the city. . . . As we thought of the sneak attack a wave of fury and anger swept over us. . . . It was going to be them or us. But fortunately, the enemy never showed."

Hideo Naito, an alien, then a cook at the Royal Hawaiian Hotel, was given a Red Cross arm band by a hotel official (who duly identified such awardees to the Red Cross office). As Naito walked home from Waikiki to Liliha and guards stopped him, he shouted, "Red Cross Emergency Aid!" Then each guard in turn would shout to the next, "Red Cross Emergency Aid!" And Hideo Naito returned safely from cooking hamburgers for hotel guests.

Yasutarō Sōga took down a telephone message for his wife. She was to report to her Red Cross unit to help make surgical dressings. But there was a change in the rules. "No other language than English was to be used in the surgical dressing room."*

On the radio Ed Sheehan heard that a complete blackout had been ordered. Any cars authorized to travel at night had to have headlights painted blue at a police station. When he and Jimmy Jones—who had a car—decided to report back to Pearl, they first drove via the police station to be painted, then headed down Dillingham Boulevard in the dusk. Few cars were on the streets; most were stopped by police or soldiers demanding identification.

Also checking with the police was the San Jose State College football team. The players had arrived on December 4, even before the Willamette University game with Hawaii. (Football was a more leisurely college sport in 1941.) Lolling at the Moana Hotel over breakfast, they had heard firing in the distance. Running outside to Kalakua Avenue, they found cars speeding west toward Pearl Harbor, drivers shouting that there was a war on. There seemed nothing that the team could do except listen to the radio, but as evening came they reported to the police and volunteered themselves. Offered shotguns, which few of them had ever fired, they were assigned to guard duty.

At the Pearl Harbor main gate, Marines in smudged and disheveled uniforms examined, with blue-tinted flashlights, the badges of Sheehan

* By the close of the day 482 persons were in wartime custody in Oahu: 370 Japanese, 98 Germans, and 14 Italians. Eventually, further suspicion prevailed and 980 Japanese in Hawaii were declared security risks and sent to internment camps on the mainland. Not a single Japanese resident would be convicted of espionage or sabotage.

and Jones. They could see figures moving about on the blacked-out ships and docks. Even in the machine shop, supervisory personnel were waving blued flashlights, and men shuffled about uneasily in small groups. The blackout was to be absolute. Striking a match to light a cigarette might lead to being shot.

An unseen Samaritan brought in a large urn of strong coffee which workmen gulped down. Some tried to sleep stretched out on the floors or on tool chests. Most made empty conversation, exchanging old and new rumors. They swapped casualty stories. Some had gone out to the capsized *Oklahoma*. Frantic knocking signals had been heard from sailors surviving in air pockets. Rescuers had tried to cut through the hull plates with acetylene torches. Then, worried about igniting gases, they switched to chipping—slowly cutting through the thick steel plates with air-driven tools. At about eight, several exhausted chippers returned to the shop to confer with their bosses. It was terrible, they said, to listen to the agonized tapping of the trapped men. "There are men dying in there," one said, "who still don't know what the hell happened." Hundreds had been entombed below; most were assumed dead.

Volunteers slid about the slimy bottom of the upturned ship listening for traces of tapping and returning knocks of recognition while marking the locations. Because the keel was hollow the sounds were often echoes from elsewhere. Men had to climb into the upside-down darkness to grope for a true source, and cut again. The first two sailors located were asphyxiated because the acetylene flame consumed their fading oxygen. Now the pneumatic equipment let the trapped air escape faster than man-sized holes could be cut, and besides, caused the water to rise and men to drown. Yard hands were numbed and frustrated.

After some coffee the chippers went back.

•

In the captain's quarters on the *Prince of Wales* at 12:30 P.M., Admiral Sir Tom Phillips convened a strategy session of his top brass—his chief of staff (Rear Admiral A. F. E. Palliser), the captain of the Fleet (Captain L. H. Bell), the skippers of the *Prince of Wales* (Captain J. C. Leach) and the *Repulse* (Captain W. G. Tennant), and their staff officers. His information, said Phillips, was that the Japanese were landing at Singora and Kota Bharu and were being covered by big warships—perhaps a battleship of the *Kongo* class, plus heavy and light cruisers and twenty destroyers. If the Navy could get in close, the invasion fleet might be scattered and there was a good chance of "smashing the Japanese forces" that were only a mile or two inland at most. A success would give the British in Malaya months more to ready defenses. Fighter support overhead was uncertain at best, but his ships were useless in port. The two big vessels needed depths of at least thirty-six feet and twenty-seven feet in which to operate: they were built to be oceangoing, and they might secure the region if they could achieve surprise.*

Without aircraft cover they could use the concealment of bad weather—it was usually bad in the South China Sea in December—or (forgetting the thirty-six-foot draft) slip among the innumerable islands off the Malay coast, avoiding, of course, possible mine fields. Phillips would steam due north up the Gulf of Siam, away from land-based enemy planes, then make a run due west to the beachheads and catch the enemy by surprise. Before the Japanese could retaliate, the big—but fast—ships would retire at top speed for Singapore.

Admiral Sir Andrew Cunningham, commander in the Mediterranean, had written privately of Sir Tom's appointment when he heard of it, "What on earth is Phillips going to the Far East Squadron for? He hardly knows one end of a ship from another!" He had spent most of his career as a desk officer, but his senior officers on the *Prince of Wales* agreed that the big capital ships had not been sent to Singapore to remain inactive, and that the risks were acceptable. That Churchill's government had broadcast to the world the presence of the *Prince of Wales*—although not the *Repulse*—and that the Japanese might be taking steps to shadow and interdict it was ignored in the enthusiasm for the operation.

The meeting over, Phillips ordered immediate preparation for departure. They would slip out at dusk. He would conduct the strike himself.

•

Surfacing near an entrance buoy at the mouth of Pearl Harbor, Commander Nabuki Nakaoka of the *I-68* saw what seemed to be a large new explosion coming from the direction of Ford Island. Al-

---

* High-flying Japanese planes had photographed them in the harbor earlier that day, according to Captain Kameo Sonokawa of the Genzan Air Group.

though the blast was very likely one of the many delayed explosions on ships still afire, he assumed that a midget sub had penetrated and found a new target. Thirty minutes later, still on the surface in the darkness, the *I-68*'s radio picked up a radio signal from Ensign Masaharu Yokoyama and Petty Officer Tei Uyeda: "I have succeeded." The submarine mother ship *Katori*, with the strike force and listening hard for all sub messages, picked up the same signal. Since all midget subs had orders not to radio from the harbor—if they got in at all— both ships assumed that Yokoyama had made a major strike—perhaps a capital ship—and had slipped out of Pearl Harbor. Both the *I-68* and *I-69* hovered in the vicinity hoping to retrieve the heroes, but messages from the sub would cease at 1:11, and no one could identify the claimed success.

To make symbols of the sacrificial submariners, the Imperial General Staff would posthumously promote all missing crewmen two ranks, and Yokoyama was awarded credit for sinking the *Arizona*. Since a repair ship was moored outboard of the *Arizona* it was impossible for a sub's torpedo to have hit the battleship. The carrier pilots who actually did were irate.

Discovered by an American destroyer during its vigil, the *I-68* dived down to the seabed and was rocked by depth charges. When there was quiet again, Nakaoka tried to rise, but found he was caught in the harbor submarine net. Rocking the sub back and forth, Nakaoka managed to free it, but he had sprung some leaks and had to surface. Fortunately the night was dark, and he could limp back to the *Katori*.

MALAYA	MOSCOW	BERLIN	PEARL HARBOR
SINGAPORE	ADDIS ABABA	CHELMNO	NIIHAU
12:40 P.M.	9:00 A.M.	LODZ	7:30 P.M.
December 8	December 8	7:00 A.M.	December 7
		December 8	

HOUR 42

AT NOON the correspondents at the Raffles bar were concocting schemes to get to the front in a hurry. There would be little but press handouts to report from Singapore. While at lunch with several newsmen an hour later, Cecil Brown was summoned by a Malay clerk to the telephone. He left his ice cream unfinished.

"Do you want to go on a four-day assignment?" It was Services Public Relations. "I can't tell you what it is, or where you are going, but I must have an immediate yes or no and you must leave at once. At once."

"All right," Brown decided. "I'll take it."

He went back to his ice cream and told Tom Fairholl and O'Dowd Gallagher. "I hate to leave Singapore," he said, perhaps to make them feel better about being passed over, "when this story is just beginning."

"I agree with you," said Gallagher. "I wouldn't go."

As Brown was adding that there was no one to cover for CBS if he left, Gallagher was called to the telephone. He returned more red-faced than usual, panting, "Cec, it's the *Prince of Wales*. We've got to pull out right away. . . . They're asking one American and one Britisher to go."

By the time they had thrown changes of clothes in bags, grabbed cameras, and dashed into the Raffles lobby, a Navy escort was waiting. Brown set his belongings down, seized a telegraph blank at the front desk, and addressed it to CBS: "OUT TOWNING FOUR DAYS SWELL STORY. BROWN."

"Have a good time," said the lieutenant.

•

As the *Ford* awaited orders off Cavite, each lighter that took away awning canvas or brought supplies had its own new rumors to pass along to the ship's working parties, some of them true. A Pan American flying boat had landed in the harbor—whether from east or west no one knew. The Air Corps had been wiped out to the north on Luzon, and with practically no antiaircraft protection in Manila harbor, ships would be easy targets at Cavite. Pearl Harbor was a debacle, despite radio reports of only a few sinkings. Fireman John Sherrill was sunk in gloom. "My twin brother is on the *Arizona*, and I just know he's dead or seriously wounded—I feel it."*

One piece of scuttlebutt was that both *Ford* and *Pope* were to convey some auxiliary vessels south. They would actually clear the bay after midnight to do that, only to be ordered back thirty hours south of Corregidor.

•

After a night to mull over what had gone wrong, Fedor von Bock set down his thoughts about the disintegrating situation. At a conference of his senior commanders on September 29, he had stressed that Moscow had to be taken by November 7—before the onset of the early Russian winter. He had promised Hitler as much. But the weeks after the great summer victories, when Hitler spread out his forces north and south to seize Leningrad and the Caucasus, were wasted opportunities. Now all three objectives were ungained.

At first von Bock could not put charges of overreaching against Hitler on paper. Instead, he wrote of the autumn rains and mud which bogged down his advance, and "the breakdown of the entire supply system." Russian railway trackage was a different width than that to the west, which meant that German engineers had to re-lay Russian

* Warren Joseph Sherrill did go down with the *Arizona*.

tracks—thousands of miles of them—or transfer troops, equipment, and supplies at the Polish border to Russian rolling stock, where it existed. And Russian roads were poor at best, nonexistent at worst, resulting in massive vehicle breakdowns. Fuel, ammunition, and replacements were slow in coming.

Realizing that his Army Group Center had captured more than a million Soviet soldiers and killed hundreds of thousands more, while two other armies, north and south, were doing the same, von Bock marveled at Russia's "ability to recuperate after suffering losses that would have toppled other nations." And he deplored the widespread "disruption and destruction of our supply lines," which kept "dire necessities" from reaching the front. Partisan activity to his rear had developed after German advances that were too rapid to assimilate the occupied lands. An informal army he had not subdued existed behind him while he faced a resurgent enemy before him.

Twenty-four more enemy divisions were in front of his army group, he added, than three weeks earlier. His troops were depleted and exhausted. Besides, the Russians—subhumans in Hitler's propaganda—had manufactured better tanks, and more of them, and had replaced "their lost artillery" with "their very effective rocket launcher."

Closing, he summoned up the courage to blame Hitler at least by indirection. Von Bock had demanded, unsuccessfully, "the authority to strike down the enemy when he was wobbling. We could have finished the enemy last summer. . . . Last August, the road to Moscow was open: we could have entered the Bolshevik capital in triumph and in summery weather. The high military leadership of the Fatherland made a terrible mistake. . . . Now we are all paying for that mistake."

He had barely finished when he learned of Pearl Harbor and the heavy American losses. "This will certainly widen the war," von Bock worried. "The Americans now have a legal basis for assisting the English and Russians, which they have been doing all along. How different would things be if the Japanese had attacked the Russians."

It did not get into the High Command minutes that one of Sunday's discussions at Wolfschanze had been to formulate a decree to satisfy Hitler that civilian resistance in occupied territories had to be crushed by means more cruel than torture or physical death. Hitler wanted a form of psychological warfare he described as *Nacht und Nebel*—night and fog. Individuals "endangering German security" were to be disposed of in a discreet manner, to "disappear" into the night and fog so that friends and relatives would never know their fate. Adding the new horror to death disconcerted even the loyal professionals whose discipline was killing. Field Marshal Keitel volunteered the most strenuous objections. All the more reason, Hitler seemed to feel, to have the decree issued in Keitel's name.

In his memoirs Keitel claimed that he inserted code words into the text to imply that there had been opposition to the edict, that the High Command had been overruled, and that it was the product of Hitler alone. Keitel had pondered overnight, produced a draft to the Führer's satisfaction, and sent it to Himmler for promulgation from Berlin. "After lengthy consideration," it read, "it is the will of the Führer that more severe measures be taken against those who are guilty of offenses against the Reich or against the occupation forces. The Führer is of the opinion that in such cases . . . an effective and lasting deterrent can be achieved only by the death penalty or by taking measures which will leave the family and the population uncertain as to the fate of the offender. . . . The attached directive for the prosecution of offenders corresponds with the Führer's conception."

The *Nacht und Nebel* decree—he claimed—left Keitel queasy, but he signed it and shipped it off. It would become popular later in other countries borrowing their ideology from the Nazis, especially post-Perón Argentina.

•

With other reporters assigned to Kuibyshev, Henry Cassidy of the Associated Press was permitted to explore the snow-covered highways west of Moscow after the Germans had fallen back. The fired and frozen villages, empty of inhabitants, were each a "chamber of horrors." Although snow and ice had clothed bodies and broken vehicles "in a merciful cleanliness," Cassidy was still appalled by the sweep of the devastation. Russia was a huge country, and the distances as well as the destruction were vast.

> The first village, Bakhlanova, still smoldered in the charred ruins, out of which rose only four of its original collection of fifty houses. There the Germans had time to apply their torches before retreating. The next village, Petrovskoye, was intact. . . . From that point the road wound like a narrow tunnel through frosted pine forests, littered by all that remained of the once-proud German sixth and seventh tank divisions. For twenty-five miles stretched this graveyard of the panzers, marked by masses of charred

vehicles, piles of frozen bodies, and a jumble of personal effects. . . . Hundreds of bodies of the troops who once had manned those machines could be seen sprawled grotesquely in the snow. Hundreds more lay buried beneath the drifts or beneath white birch crosses.

All over Germany, posters with line drawings and a rhymed text appealing for woolen clothing, blankets, and rags to tide the troops over the Russian cold were being turned into tatters by the winter weather.

·

As the morning sun rose over the mountains on the edge of Addis Ababa, George Weller of the *Chicago Tribune*, bored with covering the final dregs of the war to eject Mussolini's troops from Ethiopia, looked out of his window on the courtyard of the shabby Hotel Imperial. Italian civilians had not been bothered. One of them, a maid in an oversized black sweater, bustled about in the December chill. Up and about outside was the British major in charge of local motor transport. "Lovely morning," he said, seeing Weller.

"Beautiful," said Weller.

"Are they going to let you interview Tiger Tim?"

"Yes, this afternoon," said Weller, understanding the reference to the frail Imperial Lion of Judah, one of the many ornate titles of Emperor Haile Selassie, now restored to his tatty throne.

"Have you swotted up a lot of questions to ask him?"

"That's what I'm doing."

The dialogue gradually faded; the major looped his swagger stick over his right wrist and headed in the direction of a muddy Italian Army truck to see who was in it. Then he paused and returned; looking up at the window he observed to Weller, "This morning's radio gave me a jolt. I suppose you expected it all along."

"Sorry," said Weller, "too busy to listen. What did you hear?"

"I mean about Japan."

"Did the Washington talks break down again?"

"I mean about the bombing."

"What bombing?"

"The bombing of Pearl Harbor."

"The bombing of *what*?"

With his mind elsewhere, Weller conducted a desultory interview with the Emperor, a black beard lost in an Ethiopian general's uniform.

Then Weller telegraphed to Chicago in baseball language for permission to move "from the African right field to deep center: [East] Asia."

•

It was the birthday of the Virgin, and Polish churches were filling up with worshipers. Near the River Ner (Narew), in an abandoned mill in the Ladorudz Forest at the edge of Chelmno, which the Germans had renamed Kulmhof, what became known as the "Final Solution" (*Endlosung*) of the Jewish Problem in Europe, begun on the evening of the seventh, continued in the first light of the next morning. Eighty of the Kolo Jews ("merchandise" in Nazi documents) were loaded into the first of the three large refitted trucks through the double rear doors at "nine per square yard" and hauled in the direction of a clearing in the woods. The van moved at a slow, deliberate speed over the narrow asphalted road, to furnish time for the deadly, odorless carbon monoxide to fill the sealed cargo area. The emptied "Saurer vehicle" returned from the forest eight or nine times, until all seven hundred of the Kolo contingent had been "resettled."

For four more days, deportees would be trucked from Kolo, until the camp was vacant and ready for more captives. Each day the Nazi officer in charge would warn the drivers, Michael Podklebnik recalled, to "drive carefully and slowly," for early in the operation a van failed to make a curve, and skidded onto its side. According to a forest warden named Senjak, "The rear of the van opened, and the Jews fell out on the road. They were still alive. Seeing those Jews crawling, a Gestapo man took out his revolver and shot them. He finished them all off. Then they brought Jews who were working in the woods. They righted the van and put the bodies back inside."

Podklebnik was kept alive to dig pits in the woods for the bodies, including, he found on January 12, his own wife, seven-year-old son, and five-year-old daughter. "I lay near my wife and two children and wanted [the Germans] to shoot me. One SS man told me, 'You still have enough strength, you can work,' and he pushed me away. That night . . . I wanted to hang myself but my friends would not let me. They said as long as my eyes were open, there was some hope."*

---

* Humor was a rare commodity, but in the Warsaw ghetto Chaim Kaplan wrote in his diary that Jews were waiting for the day of the defeat of the Germans with such anticipation "that they wouldn't even commit suicide for fear of missing it."

Gravediggers were trucked to the woods daily. A few days later Podklebnik saw his opportunity and jumped out. "By the time they turned round and started shooting, I was already in the forest." He had no idea that he was also evading the gas chambers that would replace the inefficient vans in 1942.

Behind the barbed wire of the larger ghettoes of Poland—Warsaw, Lodz, Bialystok, Lublin—there was hunger, but one could survive. A busy public life continued, formal and informal, even the beginnings of underground resistance. Smugglers, peddlers, beggars, speculators plied their occupations; there were even newspapers for sale although Nazi law forbade Jews from reading German papers. And between the lines Chaika Grossman, in the Bialystok ghetto, read "that Moscow had not fallen and that the Soviet Union was holding out. If the German paper wrote that 'O.K.W. reports that we have taken Staraya Rossa (or some other place) in a counter-attack,' the Jews knew that the Russians had attacked and that the Germans had to counter-attack. That was a good sign."

In the Lodz ghetto the news of Pearl Harbor spread quickly. For two months, Hans Landa had been in the city the Germans had re-named Litzmannstadt, deported with his parents from Prague. "The news of the Japanese attack and the U.S. joining the war," he remem-bered, years later, from Caracas, Venezuela, "were immediately known in the camp. German newspapers from the outside were regularly smuggled into the ghetto." Hope rose "that Germany would lose the war in the long run, but the possibility of survival was small. The most important thing was to get some food for our stomachs, and fighting the lice and the freezing cold."

In Polish Lwow (now in the Soviet Ukraine as L'vov), few of the declining population of Jews speculated much about German reverses in Russia or what difference America might make in their expectations. Life did not seem likely to last long enough for a turnabout in the war to mean much. A sector of slum north of the Lwow-Tarnopol railway line had been decreed as a ghetto. Jews not living in it had to vacate their homes without compensation and move by December 14; non-Jews had to leave the area. After the fourteenth, Jews found outside the ghetto would be shot; non-Jews caught helping them faced the death penalty. Although the city was a chaos of wagons and carts and bundle-burdened men and women, impatience with the pace of relo-cation only spurred on *kapo* brutality. Amidst it all, the *Judenrat*—local self-government at the point of a pistol—had to supply hundreds of laborers daily to build a forced-labor camp at Kurowice, with a sign already in place at the entrance, as would be at each extermination camp, "ARBEIT MACHT FREI": work makes one free.

Work at the camp was at least twelve hours a day, performed in the cold and rain and snow by thinly clad, poorly fed inhabitants who slept on the floors of windowless and unheated buildings, suffering, without medicines, typhus and dysentery and vermin. In the Lwow ghetto, it was unsafe for an able-bodied man to be seen on the street: the *Judeneinsatz* searched day and night for replacements for slave laborers already worked to death.

It was a little better for Polish Jews who had fled into Russia. Sarah K.—her surname changed—no longer had to wear a yellow armband with the Star of David, but her husband had been forced into the "hungry, feeble, lice-infested" émigré army of Polish general Wladislaw Anders, to fight the Germans. She would never see him again. In early December she was in Atabassar, a drab town in northern Kazakhstan. "There was no coal nor other heating material available, so the [one] room in which we lived was not heated and the walls were covered with ice. We slept on the floor, covering ourselves with our overcoats and the remnants of a blanket. . . . Due to malnutrition and lack of vitamins, my brother developed night blindness. He moved very slowly, touching the walls of the buildings."

Not only Jews were in Polish death camps. Stefania Lotocka had been arrested in Lukow in March and charged with Communist sympathies. In Ravensbrück she had slept in frost since October. "In our thin porous dresses made from nettle fibres we had to stand at rollcall for hours at a time. Our constant hunger made us feel even colder. . . . The so-called 'bread' had only a four percent content of wheat, the balance being a mixture of ground-up acorns and sawdust. . . . We were on the edge of starvation. Icicles hung from the ceiling of our barrack, and during the night a hoar frost formed on our blankets." Still, life had improved. They had just been assigned to workbenches to plait straw into boot covers for German troops suffering the Russian snows.

"Exhausted and hopeless after our work on the sandpiles, we felt that this new indoor work in a warm barrack was the fulfillment of a dream. My group worked from four p.m. to midnight. . . . We stood for eight hours without respite, suffering not only from the foul air [of the straw dust] but also from the shrieks and jibes of other workers who were not of our political group. They were, in fact, German prostitutes."

•

For twenty-one-year-old Douglas Collins of the RAF, Fort Komaron, a moldering pile in Hungary, was no improvement over Stalag VIIIB in eastern Silesia. Captured just short of Dunkirk in 1940, he had been recaptured after another escape and imprisoned where he had been picked up. Almost immediately he had begun scheming with other internees to escape into Poland or Romania—some place where he might get waterborne to freedom. Perhaps some surreptitious help from the American Embassy in Budapest . . .

"A new diversion" occurred soon after Monday dawn, when two Australians captured in Greece and escaped from a camp in Austria were marched in. Fresh faces, with fresh news and stories. They were "bloody glad" to be out of Austria, one confided. "We had the lousiest jobs in the world. How'd you like to spend your time burying Russians? . . . They're dying by the thousands." And Jake Jacobs and "Kiwi" Phease described the locked boxcars arriving from the Eastern Front with staggering skeletons and cannibalized corpses, "packed masses of stinking humanity" clubbed down when they rose from the "death cars."

One of the crucial German mistakes in Russia continued to be the abuse of prisoners. In the early months, low in food, weapons, and morale, trapped Russians had given themselves up, literally, in armies. Since Stalin's government had not signed the Geneva Convention on Prisoners of War, Hitler saw no reason for anything but the most barbaric conditions for an allegedly subhuman enemy whose survival was not to be encouraged anyhow. In the winter cold they starved and froze, and stank less. But once the facts reached the front through captured Germans, surrender ceased to be an alternative. As General Guderian put it, ruefully, when Russians fought to the death in the snow and frost, "We started to mistreat them too soon."

Stalin's treatment of German prisoners was little better—tit for tat. A Polish officer saw Germans, stripped of warm tunics and boots, being shipped to Siberia in open freight cars in subfreezing cold. By standards of the Soviet *gulag*, little believed in then in the West, the handling of prisoners as hardly better than refuse was not unusual.

One survivor remembered being shunted east in a cattle truck and drawing his guard's attention to developing frostbite in a foot. "What of it?" the guard asked.

"I could develop gangrene and lose my foot."

"Don't worry, we have plenty of feet in the *gulag*."

"Our own experience in Germany," Collins realized, such horrors new to him, "paled to nothing."

They traded adventure tales. Jacobs and Phease had been in Tobruk and Benghazi before being thrown into the debacle in Greece. "A big foul-up. We had the wops on the run in North Africa and Christ alone knows why they had to pull us out and send us over to join the big retreat." It had been different in Libya. "You should have seen those Eyeties. Couldn't give themselves up fast enough."

Interrupting the exchanges of the newcomers with an unusual forgetfulness in discipline, the Hungarian commandant "rushed up waving a newspaper, an incredulous look on his face."

"The Japanese have sunk half the American fleet in Hawaii."

Chronic disbelievers, the prisoners nevertheless accepted the grim news. "And the new cataclysm reached out to touch *us*, too, for the U.S. and Britain now declared war on Hungary, Romania, and Bulgaria. . . . The conflict had become larger and our chances of escape smaller."

•

In Athens, where the Greek resistance was still spiriting across the Mediterranean British soldiers stranded after the failed April intervention, Jean Demos concealed another page of her furtive diary in the tin box buried in a corner of her garden.

8 December 1941

The Germans have made a new law. "Anyone who hides one of the Allies will be shot."

They shot Panayiotis Charidis for having provided some Englishmen with food. And they arrested Fotini Argyropoulou for having concealed the Australian, John Richardson.

The field of action narrows. But we have still many allies scattered about, hidden here and there. They get away as quickly as possible. The departures to Egypt continue and are more frequent.

Alexandra Poubourra worked splendidly. She herself went with our friends to the little port where the caique picked them up. But now they have arrested both Alexandra and her brother. In prison they are torturing them to make them reveal the names of the people they were working with. Merciless beating, burning with hot rods and lighted cigarettes. But not a single name escapes them.

•

There were few places on Niihau where one could keep a prisoner of war. Hawila Kaleohano was not even sure there was a war, only that his Japanese visitor was hostile, unwelcome, and suspicious. Since Kaleohano's sister's house nearby was larger, his brother-in-law agreed to put the pilot up for the night. A small party of the curious at Joseph Keale's looked over Nishikaichi, who only wanted everyone to go away so that he could retrieve and repair his Zero, or destroy it. The Hawaiians sang to someone's guitar, fed their guest sweet potatoes and roast pork, even urged him to strum the guitar, which he plucked like a *samisen*. Mostly he looked out at the water for a sign of the sub that was supposed to be part of the rescue plan.

No lights showed from Kauai. It seemed very strange; the Hawaiians were certain that their visitor had something to do with it. Confronting him with the phenomenon, he confessed with hand motions to attacking Oahu. It was clear to Harada that the islanders understood, and that it was prudent to interpret honestly. They decided that the pilot had to be escorted in the morning to the weekly boat at Kii, fifteen miles to the north, to be taken to Kauai. Nishikaichi said nothing, but he had no intentions of going meekly.

•

Having sailed southward all day looking for the Japanese strike force in exactly the wrong direction, the *Lexington* group was now looking for a missing scout plane—one of its own. Although the misdirected search for *Kido Butai* frustrated the brass aboard as well as onshore, it was one of the happier outcomes of a very bad Sunday. Even together, the *Lexington* and *Enterprise* task forces would have been overwhelmed by the six-carrier fleet of Admiral Nagumo. The American flattops survived to fight another day. If there had been trouble on the horizon, they would have blundered into it—but *Kido Butai* was now steaming away, and Japanese subs, despite a plethora of opportunities, remained ineffective.

During daylight, the *Lexington* and her escorts kept crews busy stripping flammable peacetime gear and heaving it overboard. As darkness came, all ships were informed by the *Enterprise* that the lost plane had not been heard from. The destroyer *Lamson* was detached to look for the pilot. "We were also directed," Warren F. Dalton, a seaman on the *Lamson* recalled, "to turn on our 36-inch searchlight every half hour and rotate it around the horizon in the hope that the downed pilot would see it. All night long, while supposedly searching for the Japanese, we were alone, illuminating the sky and ourselves."

MANILA	MOSCOW	BRUSSELS	PEARL HARBOR
HONG KONG	LENINGRAD	HEIDENMÜHLE	8:30 P.M.
3:00 P.M.	10:00 A.M.	8:00 A.M.	December 7
December 8	December 8	December 8	

HOUR 43

SUDDENLY, after ten years with the *New York Times*, Junnosuke Ofusa was out of a job. As Otto Tolischus's assistant, he felt sure that he would find the police in the office, as they had questioned him at least twice a week in better times. Ofusa inquired about his boss anyway when he saw gendarmes in the building, and found that Tolischus was in the Akasaka police station. Trying to telephone the American embassy to report the arrest, Ofusa was threatened with arrest himself. Besides, he was told, the line had been cut. He wouldn't get through.

At 4:00 P.M. the policemen returned to Akasaka from the *Times* office, having searched it thoroughly to seek grounds for an espionage charge. A plainclothesman permitted Tolischus to accept from home a bag with his warmest underwear—bought for such a contingency— but Tolischus also learned that he was detained under paragraph 8 of the National Defense Act. "You sent political, diplomatic, and economic information to foreign agents harmful to Japan. That means penal servitude up to ten years."

Relieved not to be charged with spying, Tolischus contended that he had done nothing incompatible with his work as foreign correspondent and that he had worked with the knowledge, and often the cooperation, of the Japanese government, submitting everything he cabled to the censor. Whatever passed the censor absolved the writer.

Refusing to sign a statement alleged to represent his interrogation, he began writing one of his own. The police pounded the table with their fists until Tolischus, intimidated, signed their version. "I know I am a prisoner of war," he objected, "but I protest against being treated like a criminal."

As a concession, since he had eaten nothing all day, Tolischus was permitted to have his cook bring him dinner. Meanwhile, the police counted out before him 1,700 yen found in his house, then put most of it in their pockets, claiming that they would turn the money over to Ofusa. Tolischus was permitted to keep 250 yen—about $72.50 with the yen worth twenty-nine cents. A taxi was summoned to take him to another jail in the blacked-out city. "I am very sorry there is war between Japan and America," the plainclothesman confided after a long silence in the darkness.

"You can't be any sorrier than I am," said Tolischus. Then, realizing that they were turning into a driveway, he asked, "Where are you taking me?"

"To Tokyo Detention Prison," said the policeman. There Tolischus found correspondent colleagues and other Americans rounded up as he was, a few in faded blue convict kimonos. Some had not even known about the war.

Max Hill was there. At the Shibuya police station, he had been charged with sending stories "detrimental to Japan's diplomacy." Hill denied filing anything the censors had not approved. Two policemen led him out to the street where another charcoal-burning taxi was waiting. There were few police vehicles: gendarmes rode the buses and streetcars, or walked.

In detention, Hill relinquished his clothes for a prison robe and rice-straw *zori* sandals. All his possessions, including watch and pen, were taken. A onetime Domei colleague observing the proceedings offered advice. "Hill-san," he said, "you must tell the American people the war can never end until they realize that Pearl Harbor was a counterattack and not an attack."

Hill shook his head. "That day will never come," he said. They shook hands. Hill bowed. The Domei man bowed. Then Hill went back among the correspondents for whatever was the duration. Once a number was sewn on his prison coat, he received "a battered and dented bowl of paper-thin aluminum and wooden chopsticks. Hill was now *happyaku-rokuju-nana-ban*, number 867.

•

Canadian soldiers in Hong Kong had spent much of Monday morning commandeering vehicles. At three o'clock Captain Harold Pierce of the Royal Canadian Signals reported to the Battle Box that eighty-five trucks and twenty-five cars had been rounded up—anything that could transport soldiers around the island. Pierce even acquired ten one-ton trucks used to carry "night soil" from the flushless latrines at Shamshuipo. Chinese saboteurs working for the Japanese quickly slipped into the improvised motor pool and ripped out distributor heads, slashed tires, and removed ignition wires. Forty vehicles could not be put back into operating condition.

The Army motor pool was at the Happy Valley Race Course. Since no provision had been made for accommodating or feeding the drivers, some went home, taking their ignition keys with them. Although it was a case of muddle rather than malice, treachery would be common, with drivers regularly disappearing with their loads of supplies, or arranging to wreck their vehicles in ditches. There was no scarcity of rice, but stocks were seldom where they could be used. Nine months' supply of food for the island had been stored, but it quickly ceased arriving at the right places, in part because more vehicles were seized than the military needed, resulting in a breakdown of civilian transport. Water was a more serious problem: most of it was piped from the New Territories. Engineers began the hopeless task of boring for potential sources below the rock that was Hong Kong.

On Kowloon 350 trucks and drivers were collected and registered at the Traffic Office. Some were employed to load rice onto thirty lighters to be towed across to the island. Police launches eventually towed a few, but most would be left at wharfside to be gutted by incendiary shells and bombs or retrieved by the Japanese.

Anticipating bomb damage and looting, the managements of English clubs began dispersing their liquor stores. Members not already on military duty rushed from homes and offices to load cases of the precious elixir into cars queuing at street entrances. Soldiers en route to postings in the hills would call out, "How about a bottle, mate?" Usually the appeal succeeded.

Circulating in Hong Kong was the rumor that "German staff officers" were leading the Japanese advance into the New Territories, for the Japanese were "little more than monkeys" who could not have sliced through British defenses without Western help. There were no German officers on the ground any more than there were German pilots in the air.

.

At the Shell oil fields in North Borneo, the flash and roar of burning gas and oil was meeting its match in the fork and crackle of lightning and the heavy rumble of thunder. Sheets of rain drenched the flaming wells and torched machinery. Flaring through the downpour, the blazing gas was almost the only light at midday. Electric power had gone, as had telephone and radio communication with the Lutong Refinery, which field workers assumed was also set ablaze. Spasmodic explosions shook the area, man and nature competing in a wild Götterdämmerung.

Where the storm had doused fires, R. G. Tyler and other Shell engineers rushed about in waterlogged clothes, in what had become a shallow lake, to re-torch whatever survived. Meanwhile, Tyler noted in his diary when the surreal day was over, "we were working in complete ignorance of what may be taking place elsewhere." All they knew is that they would shortly be taking flight, abandoning the native work force to the dubious mercies of the enemy.

.

In New Delhi, Thomas Murray Wilson, American representative to British India (with the rank of Minister), noted "a record number of callers and telephone calls." Worried Americans abroad were seeking advice about what to do now that they were citizens of a belligerent nation. "The news of the Japanese war action," he observed wryly on a notepad, "came after all as a complete surprise. I think it is marvelous that we Americans can be so completely surprised when something happens that we have been looking for for a long time." One caller, a journalist named Chaman Lall who was planning a series of talks on All India Radio, wanted Wilson to prepare one to which Lall had given the preliminary title "A Hundred Million Loving People"—presumably Americans. "That was quite enough for me," Wilson wrote, "because there is very little love in my soul these days."

.

In a wan sun, Freiherr von Heyl, fur-hatted in the cold, left his bunker to inspect "yesterday's battlefield." He found thirty dead Russians. "One still twitched, but he was hopelessly wounded." Von Heyl left him writhing in the snow. In his diary he mentioned none of his own casualties. Perhaps they had been carried off earlier. North of the village of Mokschino a newly arrived self-propelled heavy gun was put into position—just in time, as the Russians struck hard over the frozen lake to the north. Russian pressure not applied to one segment of the Moscow front was shifted to another.

•

At 8:00 A.M. three SS officers arrived at Heidenmühle to give appropriate orders for the *Aktion*. Germanized Poland had to be further Germanized. It was only a small thing as *Aktionen* went. A week before, tens of thousands had been murdered in Riga, and more Latvian Jews were scheduled for an *Aktion* in a few days. The head of the Jewish police was instructed to read the names of the "unfit" from the official list. He began the roll call. No one responded. The unfit had been fit enough to flee.

The silence hung heavy as the roll call continued past nine. Finally an officer ordered the line of men to file past, and another directed them to the right or left. About eleven hundred Jews sent left were marked for death.

Through bribery and other forms of intercession the *Judenrat* managed to gain reprieves for four hundred. The others were shipped to Chelmno.

•

In Brussels, Anne Sommerhausen picked up her Nazi-censored morning paper and found each headline more disturbing than the last. "Pearl Harbor!" she wrote in her diary. "The shock is so overwhelming that we cannot even feel relief at the thought that soon, probably within a few days, America will be on England's side." Reading the same headline, a German soldier observed to her with hazardous frankness, "Now Germany is *kaputt*."

A second story was of local concern. The *Oberfeldkommandatur* had closed all movies, theaters, and other public amusements indefinitely "because an unknown person seriously wounded a German army officer with a dagger last night. Dozens of hostages are being taken into custody, and there will be reprisals if the criminal is not arrested by December 16 at noon." At least she knew that Mark, her husband, a lawyer and former member of Parliament, would not be among them; he was safely in a prisoner-of-war camp. Belying his gold-rimmed glasses and soft-spokenness, he had joined the Army at sixteen when the Germans invaded in 1914, and in 1940 had volunteered again. Her three sons were, happily, too young.

The third headline, least predictable, was the longest. "MARRIAGE OF HIS MAJESTY LEOPOLD III ANNOUNCED BY CARDINAL VAN ROEY IN A PASTORAL LETTER READ IN ALL CHURCHES ON SUNDAY." A Protestant, Anne Sommerhausen had not heard the news. The long-widowered king, who had surrendered his army when German panzers raced across Belgium and left his situation hopeless, was under house arrest in the royal Château of Laeken, where the ceremony had taken place secretly on September 11. Leopold had given Mary-Liliane Baels, the beautiful governess of his children, the title of Princess of Rethy rather than Queen, and had put any possible offspring out of the line of succession.*

"I stood dumbfounded. . . . The King has been shut up in his château since the capitulation, and no word to the people has come from him since June 1940. I have felt pity for him. But now, now? My husband, too, is a prisoner. And 60,000 other Belgian men are. All are separated from their wives and their children. And the King, who seemed to want to share their hardships, marries!"

Through the day she reasoned herself into "a more charitable" attitude. "If I could, by exceptional German clemency, see Mark, be with him while he is a prisoner, wouldn't I join him?" She wondered about the fate of her petition to have Mark released and returned to work. A few prisoners had trickled back, mostly Catholic and Flemish rather than Walloon and Protestant, she thought, "because Walloons are known to be more hostile to Germany."

•

With word of the wider war, some British go-it-alone strategies underwent rapid change. In Scotland, the 3rd Grenadiers, preparing

---

* There would be three children from the marriage. Leopold, then forty, would never regain his throne. His brother Charles became regent until Baudouin, the King's son by Queen Astrid, came of age in 1951.

for an invasion of Pantellaria, a tiny island near Malta, moved off from a camp in Dumfriesshire, just west of Greenock. Landing at dawn on the Isle of Bute, they waded ashore up to their waists in ice-cold water only to learn that the scheme had been abandoned. Pantellaria would remain Italian until 1943.

In Northern Ireland, the 5th Division was ordered to step up its schedule for invading Vichy French Madagascar. Fears had arisen that the Japanese might use the big island as they had Indochina, effectively closing off the Indian Ocean. Two untrained brigades with no amphibious experience were to supplement the strike force, but the mission was to be limited to capture of the deep-water harbor of Diego Suarez.

Instead of quickening the pace of the operation, the modifications would slow it down. When the attack took place on May 7, 1942, the Japanese, busy many thousands of miles away, offered only the failed interdiction of a minisub of the Pearl Harbor type. Before the mother sub could retrieve the beached crew, British commandos seized them.

In England, Princess Louise's Kensington Regiment was completing Home Guard exercise "Scorch." The 1st Battalion, as the Enemy, had captured Colchester and fanned out as far as Chelmsford and Cambridge before being wiped out by decree of the service umpires and returned to their billets. The fun over, working parties went back to giving assistance to labor-short local farmers.

·

At the head of his six escort fighters, Lieutenant Fritz Hebel spotted before him in the blackness an island dotted with fires. Assuming that it was Kauai, where cane fields were often burned, he turned east and led his Wildcats over Molokai before he realized that what he was seeing were ships and installations on Oahu still ablaze more than twelve hours after the attack. He directed the F4Fs across the channel west to Makapuu Point on Oahu, where he followed the fire-illuminated coastline south and west over Diamond Head and Waikiki toward Pearl Harbor. Since thick smoke partially obscured the runway lights on Ford Island, Hebel led his planes toward Hickam Field to the north; then he saw the lights at Luke Field again.

Honolulu downtown was a confusion in the semidarkness. Blackout and curfew orders were only spottily observed. Many people had not heard of them. Cars jammed the streets as curious citizens poked around looking for war damage and even for shrapnel souvenirs. Other cars threaded up lookout points over Pearl Harbor, their occupants attracted by the clouds of smoke and eager to assess the unreported losses. Ford Island and undamaged ships in the oil-slick harbor were alive with jittery gunners, apprehensive that the Japanese might return, possibly even with parachute troops.

Hebel radioed the Ford Island tower for landing instructions. He was instructed to turn on his navigation lights and come in; meanwhile Fourteenth Naval District headquarters notified nearby ships and Army antiaircraft units, "Hold your fire. Friendly planes coming in to land." "All the runway lights were lighted," Maury Meister recalled, "and we could see several planes coming in a loose formation." They were to approach, Harry Rorman thought, from 180 degrees south, but instead they came in rather more from the west. It may have made a difference.

In the control tower, "Brigham" Young, who had flown in earlier from the *Enterprise*, was put on the tower radio so that the pilots would deal with a familiar voice. Ordered to use their lights, to assure anyone below that the planes were friendly, the fighters closed in on Ford Island. Hebel descended to five hundred feet and turned on his red and green running lights. Automatically, he banked to the right to circle the island counterclockwise as if he were executing a carrier landing, and swept low over battered Battleship Row. It was nearly nine, Honolulu time.

As Hebel's lead plane peeled off and began to land, from Dry Dock One, apprehensive AA gunners on the *Pennsylvania* opened fire. When the fighters aborted landings and zoomed up, the evasive action convinced other jumpy gunners to join in. On the *Maryland*, rumors had spread that the *Enterprise* had been sunk at sea. The landing lights of the approaching aircraft, then, had to be a trick. The Japanese had come back after all!

From the cruiser *Honolulu* Seaman Boggs had watched the planes come in from Diamond Head. Unready earlier, the ship now had .30-caliber guns mounted bow and stern. The signal from Ford Island was that these were friendly aircraft, and the crew could see landing lights, but in everyone's mind, Boggs thought, was the worry that "they may be Japs coming in for another sneak attack." When the planes broke formation—it was not apparent from the *Honolulu* that they had been fired on—"there was about a five-second hesitation and then everything in the harbor opened up." Hand guns, rifles, machine guns—anything within reach was turned on the Navy's own F4Fs. As spent AA shells began raining on the wrecked runways, adjacent Hickam Field reported being bombed.

"My God, what's happened?" Hebel radioed in shock. Through heavy fire he tried to slide in at Wheeler Field. His stricken plane stalled and crashed in a field near Aiea, cartwheeling through the cane stubble. (Dragged out of the burning wreckage, Hebel died the next day.) Ensign Eric Allen had no chance to gain altitude; hit over Ford Island, his Grumman Wildcat burst into flames. He bailed out, and as he drifted down, he was shot in the chest.

Aboard the battered *California* for salvage operations—bombs had penetrated its fourteen-inch steel decks—Lieutenant Louis E. Kelley watched the forward AA guns on the *Maryland* open up on three planes, one of them—Allen's—dropping immediately astern of the *California*. Seeing aircraft burning and falling, all that Clair Boggs could think was "We got you, you little yellow sons of bitches."

Picked up unconscious and covered with oil, Radioman First Class Howard O. Pollan lay in a mobile hospital overlooking Aiea Landing. He had been given no food—but "a pair of hospital pajamas at least ten sizes too large." (Only the next day did he get himself cleaned off.) Looking out he could see the sky red with gunfire and was sure they were being attacked again. But what was disturbing him more was a nightmare memory of the morning that he could not resolve. Years later the picture cleared. What he had seen in a flooded compartment of the torpedoed *West Virginia* "was a man being swirled around the room by the water gushing in through the side."

Landing hard, Allen struggled, despite a collapsed lung, through the oil-slicked and debris-choked water toward the *California*. He was picked up by sailors from the minesweeper *Vireo*. Until they cleaned the gummy black grease from his body they did not know that Allen had been struck by a bullet. Or that he was an American. (He died at two in the morning.)

In the darkness of the machine-shop interior at Pearl, workmen had been spinning yarns to pass the time. Sammy Morgan, a Scot who had seen trench service in the 1914 war, was reminiscing about killing a Boche "with me shovel" when a humming sound overhead was followed by what seemed to be the blast of every gun in the harbor. "Tens of thousands of tracers streaked skyward from every direction," Ed Sheehan remembered. ". . . An explosion followed, almost over our heads, and the roof trembled with the concussion. A plane had been hit. We saw it flaming down toward Ford Island."

The men fell to the floor as the building shook and rattled. For the first time all day Sheehan felt sufficient terror to begin to say his Hail Marys. Only old Sammy Morgan remained upright, outlined in the flickering of fire which illuminated the window.

Flying the third plane, crippled and twisting out of control, Ensign Herbert Menges may have been dead by the time his Wildcat spun over Ford Island and crashed into Palm Lodge, a tavern in Pearl City. A fireball rose, then flamed out. It was 9:01 P.M.

Flicking out his lights to evade gunfire, Ensign David Flynn pulled up and headed back to sea to find the *Enterprise*; it was his twenty-seventh birthday and he was hoping for the gift of his life. Ten miles out he realized that he was running out of fuel; as the Wildcat choked into a stall he glided over Barber's Point and headed for the Marine field at Ewa; then, fired on, he took to his parachute as the plane burst into flames. Soldiers passing as Flynn reached the ground took him to crowded Tripler Army Hospital.

Cranking up his wheels, Ensign Jimmy Daniels flew southwest, over Barber's Point, until he heard the Ford tower trying to reestablish contact with the *Enterprise* flight. Returning, he barely cleared the foretop of the beached *Nevada*, opposite Hospital Point, drawing fire from the battleship as he flew on. As he taxied in, .50-caliber machine gun bullets sprayed around him, but the firing stopped before his pockmarked Wildcat did. Preceding him, Ensign Gayle Hermann landed without lights, his F4F absorbing eighteen bullets. Counting the holes the next morning he congratulated himself on surviving. In May he would be lost in the Battle of the Coral Sea.

Escaping the flak, Ensigns Bucky Walters and Ben Troemel, in two SBDs from Scouting Six, gunned over the Pali peaks toward Kaneohe. Low on gas, they descended without warning. Walters's Dauntless headed toward a parked truck on the runway; working his brake and rudder frantically, he evaded it, also missing a wrecked car and a mobile crane. Troemel had a further obstacle—his partner's plane. Skidding in a crooked path, he also cleared a concrete mixer.

Elated at landing without a scratch, the pilots jumped out to find an irate station commander. He had blocked the field to make a Japanese landing impossible. In the darkness, the SBDs had managed to come in anyway.

However ineffectual the runway obstacles proved, American gunnery on Oahu had been deadly against defenseless Americans. A spent machine gun bullet had even penetrated the port side of the *Argonne* and killed a seaman who had been rescued from the *Utah*. Another *Utah* survivor was wounded. A sailor from the *Nevada* was hit on Ten-Ten Dock.

From his surfaced submarine, Commander Yasuji Watanabe of the *I-69*, just off southern Oahu, recorded seeing "a flame like a ship exploding in Pearl Harbor. After this very heavy antiaircraft followed." It was 9:01; the explosion was very likely that of Menges's plane. It had been a costly sixteen minutes.

It almost proved expensive for the *I-69* as well. While Watanabe was surfaced, recharging his batteries, the destroyers *Blue, Ramsey*, and *Breeze* found the sub, which had to make an emergency dive. He plunged to two hundred feet, below the level at which he knew Americans set their depth charges, and took his chances, as his normal submerged depth was one hundred feet. He was putting his craft under dangerous pressure. Slightly damaged, the *I-69* set out for Kwajalein in the Marshall Islands as soon as it was safe to resurface and signal the strike force.

The fate of the *Enterprise* and its planes became even worse in the retelling abroad, at a time when the bad news was censored in the U.S. From Buenos Aires a Japanese correspondent reported hearing via Panama that the *Enterprise*, sinking after a Japanese bombing attack on the carrier, flew its remaining seventy planes off for safety, but confused American gunners on Oahu "mistook the planes from the doomed vessel for Japanese and shot down an estimated 40 of them."

•

It was two o'clock Malay time when Lieutenant Colonel H. D. Moorhead's advance party of Indians reached the padlocked gate on the Thai side of the Pattani road. Neither Thais nor Japanese were there. Someone smashed the lock. Weary after nearly three days of waiting, often in the rain, for marching orders, the vanguard of the 11th Indians found frontier positions on their own side brimming with water, loops of barbed wire still unstrung, and land mines not only not dug in but never unpacked.

Hardly had Moorhead's men crossed the border when a small force of Thai constabulary, perhaps three hundred, opened a barrage of small-arms fire from behind roadblocks at what seemed every bend in the road. Vanishing rearward into the jungle, the Thais continued harassing fire. By dusk the Punjabis had penetrated only three miles north, losing any chance to reach the critical Ledge position before the Japanese did.

•

In Singapore the Duff Coopers, who had commanded the dinner-party circuit the week before, disappeared from public view. Diana had dengue fever, a delayed souvenir of coming East via a port in Australia, Darwin. Without his promised ministerial powers, Cooper cabled Churchill, his position as a "tourist" was "difficult." By the time the authority to form a War Council that no one else wanted had arrived, he was lobbying for evacuation of Europeans southward, and a withdrawal to defend only Johore and Singapore. Although Cooper was imposed upon him, Shenton Thomas warned London anyway that favoring the white minority would demoralize the population. When the Colonial Office got around to ruling that evacuations were to be made without racial discrimination, few vessels remained to hazard further voyages out.*

•

As the Foreign Office in Berlin opened for business Monday morning, priority went to chargé d'affaires Hans Thomsen's radiogram from Washington, fired off in what was the middle of the night in Germany but only 8:36 P.M. in the U.S. He was responding to events that had surprised him, and everyone else, in the capital, and he had completed his first soundings too late to catch anyone of consequence in the Wilhelmstrasse. The news of Pearl Harbor, he reported, "struck the American government and public like a flash of lightning" ("*Blitzschlag*"). The entire American war plan to defeat Germany, revealed by the *Chicago Tribune*, would have to be "abruptly thrown overboard. . . . The bombastic forecasts that a war with Japan would be a walkover ["*Spaziergang*"] have been immediately silenced." Senator Walter George—the first authority that Thomsen could quote—had already

---

* Duff Cooper announced his departure on January 9, a month before Singapore surrendered. In his diary for the date Sir Shenton excoriated his antagonist as "arrogant, obstinate, vain; how he could have crept into [Cabinet] Office is beyond me."

suggested with new pessimism that Japan would take "a two- or three-year war."

· · ·

At 3:39 P.M. Philippines time, two hours and two minutes after the last Japanese plane had peeled away from Clark Field to the north, a shaken Lewis Brereton telephoned Richard Sutherland to tally the bad news and to report that he was on his way to the secluded MacArthur. Sutherland made no attempt to stall. Eleven minutes later, Brereton and MacArthur were in conference at No. 1 Calle Victoria, in rooms only that Monday afternoon equipped for total blackout.

At San Fernando, on the northeastern limits of Lingayen Gulf, over which the enemy squadrons had come and gone, leaflets fluttered down explaining to Filipinos, "Way to permanent peace causing this conflict between Japan and U.S. [is] Roosevelt attempting to curb our independence. We all know that unless the U.S. has not oppressed Japan, this war has not been started. Our mission is to end this war as far as possible, and in order to achieve this end we should cooperate fully." Japanese English was not as precise as Japanese bombsights.

· · ·

On the heaving deck of one of a long skein of transports in the South China Sea, Lieutenant General Homma, under orders to subdue the Philippines in fifty days, spent the gray late afternoon hours writing on a pad. Under radio silence himself, he could pick up signals from Takao and Tokyo. Watching Homma, Hidemi Kon, a novelist turned war correspondent, realized that the general was easing the strain of waiting by composing verse. Kon observed a group of soldiers deferentially approaching. Bowing obediently, one asked the general if he would please write verses for them to sing in the coming battle. Homma smiled, and turned a fresh page. Within minutes he peeled off lines for them celebrating the decimation of American air power that would be making their landing little more than an exercise:

> Great birds over the sea,
> Great eagles over the land,
> Ranging their silver wings
> Fly toward the southern sky. . . .
> Clark Field they destroy at a single blow.

Where is the Sky Fortress?
Where is the shadow of the P-40?
What a splendid action in the enemy sky!

Bowing once more, the soldier thanked the general for the song;
his small group drifted away.

•

At Nielson Field a runner from the Air Warning Center, Private
Preston Hubbard, reported for duty at 2:00 P.M.—just as several
P-40s returned with bloodied pilots and holes in fuselages and wings
"as big as my fist." Hubbard was "impressed." Whether they were hit
by the Japanese or by friendly fire was unclear. The Japanese had seen
few P-40s in the air, and while the Americans had flown low enough
to be hit by their own AA fire, enemy bombers overflew defensive
bursts. With justifiable foreboding, Brereton rushed from MacArthur's
office by air to Clark Field. The extent of the catastrophe was clear.
Eubank admitted that 17 B-17s had been destroyed or rendered inoperable. Fighter losses at Clark alone totaled 45, with others damaged
and unflyable. Runways were cratered and littered with debris. Ground
installations were in ruins. He had no idea of the human toll. Air
strength had been halved, although cannibalization of parts later rescued a few P-40s and one Fortress. Evasively, MacArthur reported his
losses to Washington by counting what he had left rather than what
he had lost. The "only objective of importance" attacked by the Japanese, he reported, omitting Iba, had been Clark Field. "Damage
[there] heavy and casualties reported at about twenty-three dead and
two hundred wounded.* Our air losses were heavy. . . . Now have
available seventeen heavy bombers, fifty to fifty-five P-40s and fifteen
P-35s. No losses of other types. I am launching a heavy bombardment
counter-attack tomorrow on enemy airdromes in southern Formosa."
In reality MacArthur had lost 55 of his 72 P-40s, and 30 P-35s,
which were no match for the Zero anyway. Outnumbered as his air
force would have been at the start, it had now been eliminated as a
factor in Philippines defense. In message 1135 to Arnold, MacArthur

* The figures were raised to 55, but even then did not reflect eyewitness accounts,
including that of General Wainwright, for Iba and Clark. Sergeant H. G. Tyson of the
3rd Pursuit Squadron at Iba reported 45 dead of 160 in his unit, and 16 of 18 fighters
lost although two were patched up and flew again.

alleged, very likely to explain the accuracy of enemy bombardiers, that the Mitsubishis were "at least partially manned by white pilots." Colonel Constant Irwin of MacArthur's Intelligence staff repeated the excuse in an interview in August 1942: "The job was so well done that there is reason to suspect the pilots of these planes were Germans."

The same rationalization for failure emerged from Singapore, where Dickson Brown reported to Lord Beaverbrook's *Daily Express* about mythical planes that were never brought down, "German airmen are being used in large numbers in attacks on Malaya. . . . Many of the shot-down planes had German crews who were either killed or captured. They are said to have carried out their attacks with great skill and daring." It was racist nonsense. Although Japanese aircraft had proved not to be made of rice paper and string, the men flying them were too proficient not to be white.

The opportunity for a preemptive strike had evaporated, and the wherewithal for any other move was gone. The next day MacArthur had to raise his casualty figures and concede to Washington that the "damage at Clark Field" made impossible the proposed attack on Formosa. (In later years he denied ever discussing with Brereton an attack on Formosan airfields.) His failure to act when he could have done so had closed off his capability to execute any of the missions he had assigned to himself under Rainbow 5. But General Arnold in Washington blamed Brereton, asking him sharply via transoceanic telephone "how in the hell" an experienced airman had let himself be caught with his planes down. Weakly, Brereton explained that he had tried every way he could "to get authority to attack Formosa" but that he had been "relegated to a 'strictly defensive attitude' by higher authority."

There was plenty of guilt to go around. From Australia in 1942 and for years afterward, MacArthur and his aides, from Sutherland to Courtney Whitney, threw up smokescreens defending USAFFE headquarters. They charged that on three occasions in the five days preceding the outbreak of war, Brereton had been ordered to move all B-17s to the presumed safety of Mindanao but had disobeyed orders. Only half—two of four squadrons—had been transferred by December 7. Brereton claimed that Del Monte Field was too primitive and crowded to handle all his Fortresses, and that more were expected from the U.S. and would have to be based in Mindanao as well. (USAFFE knew that another flight of B-17s had left for the Philippines from California on the evening of the 6th.) Brereton also wanted to retain the opportunity to strike at the Formosan bases and ports from which an invasion force would come, whether or not his squadrons were overwhelmed in the attempt. It was what his heavy bombers had been designed to do. Perhaps the real dereliction had been the failure, during the months when MacArthur had been anticipating the promised 165 heavy bombers and 240 fighters, to prepare airfields from which they could operate. Much could have been done with local labor and materials; little if anything was actually accomplished.

No one, nevertheless, had dispersed aircraft, nor flown air cover for parked planes. And Army communications were so inefficient that flimsy allegations of spying and sabotage were raised in defense. One fiction was that a Filipino who operated a bar near Clark Field had a powerful shortwave transmitter and used it to inform the Japanese that the B-17s were back and on the ground. After the raid he was allegedly discovered still at the dials of his transmitter, and a "grim sergeant . . . went into the place with a tommy gun" and dispatched him. An absurd claim, from Lieutenant Joseph H. Moore, commander of the 20th Pursuit Squadron, was that he discovered a mirror tied to a tree above his quarters at Clark Field after the raid and that reflections from the mirror guided the Japanese to the field. Having overflown Clark more than once, the Japanese had photographed the area so accurately that they could have furnished MacArthur with maps. Although there were sympathizers and even reserve Japanese officers waiting in humble occupations for their compatriots to come, the rumored army of fifth columnists and saboteurs was exaggerated.

Brereton felt that he had been unfairly singled out for censure. Long before the attack, MacArthur had received a radiogram from Arnold ordering him to "take all possible steps at once to avoid [further] such losses in your area." Appealing for MacArthur's help "in setting the facts straight" to Washington, Brereton got instead a blistering order to "go back and fight the war." Then, whitewashing himself in magnanimity, MacArthur explained in an imaginative cable to Arnold, "Every possible precaution within the limited means and time available was taken by the Far East Air Force. Their losses were due entirely to the overwhelming superiority of enemy force. They have been hopelessly outnumbered from the start but no unit could have done better. Their gallantry has been conspicuous. . . . No item of loss can be properly attributed to neglect or lack of care. They fought from fields not yet developed and under improvised conditions of every sort which placed them under the severest handicap as regards to an enemy fully prepared in every way. You may take pride in their conduct."

"Hap" Arnold's indirect rebuke to MacArthur was as much admonishing as would occur, although George Marshall would confess to a correspondent in Washington two weeks later, realizing (as he could not have intimated) that Manila had the "Magic" code-breaking capacity denied to Pearl Harbor, "It's all clear to me now except one thing. I just don't know how MacArthur happened to let his planes get caught on the ground."

There were more problems than Marshall knew about. Although Iba, Clark, and Nichols fields were relatively modern by American standards, only Iba had radar—and its equipment was destroyed in the Monday raid. (Radar was being installed at Clark at the time of the attack.) And MacArthur had dug deep logistical and strategic holes for himself, in which he was now trapped. Roosevelt knew even less, and in his first wartime news conference, the next day, he parried a reporter's question about Clark Field by claiming lack of information and shifting to another query. Even after the war a 1946 congressional joint committee investigating Pearl Harbor dismissed Philippine matters as outside its scope.

After the war, then Lieutenant General Claire Chennault wondered why commanders in Manila had not been subjected to an inquiry. "If I had been caught with my planes on the ground . . . I could never again have looked my fellow officers squarely in the eye. The lightness with which this cardinal military sin was excused by the American high command . . . has always seemed to me one of the shocking defects of the war." Francis B. Sayre, Philippine High Commissioner but no admirer of MacArthur, said later, "We supposed that an official investigation would follow. But the war was on then, and [our] minds were immersed in the immediate problems of resistance."

A "combat history" of the war in the Philippines, prepared under the orders of Lieutenant General W. D. Styer in Manila and directed by Colonel W. E. Buchly, a self-described "regular army cavalryman and long time pre-war veteran of the Philippines," explained the Clark catastrophe as a "sneak attack." The self-serving account is an invention. According to this 1946 version of events, the Japanese "employed a clever ruse to arrange that many of the Clark Field planes would be on the ground. Decoy planes from Formosa flew close enough to alert the Clark Field air raid warning net, thus drawing American fighter planes into the air . . . and causing bombers to be sent aloft so that the field would be clear." Buchly alleged that the "decoy" aircraft then "fled to Formosa after keeping the American planes in the air long enough to force them to return to Clark Field for refueling. While the crews ate their lunch, the Japanese struck."

Similar "Jap trickery," the Army cover-up continued, "failed" at Iba Field, where pilots took to the air in time to down thirteen enemy aircraft while losing only four P-40s. The heroics were as imaginative as the statistics. The unreliability of *Triumph in the Philippines* is capped by a line characterizing MacArthur's forces on December 8 as "woefully small but . . . well dispersed, tactically disposed, and ready for action."

Whatever MacArthur's indecisiveness at the beginning, the Philippines were written off in American global strategy even before the first shot was fired. For that reason, perhaps, his rewards for defeat were greater than most captains received for victory. On December 17, a week before the evacuation of Manila, he was given his fourth star as general, and a few months later the nation's highest award for courage under fire, the Medal of Honor.

In line with the close reciprocity Filipinos have always drawn between gifts and gratitude, President Quezon had a more Philippine bauble to confer. MacArthur and Quezon understood each other. As Field Marshal of Quezon's army, MacArthur had been effusively loyal to his patron. Quezon was only the first of the Philippine presidents to consider the national treasury his own, and his role that of living father of his country. In both capacities, from Corregidor, he issued as his first executive order of 1942, on January 3, a transfer of $640,000 in American currency from Philippine funds to MacArthur, Sutherland, Deputy Chief of Staff Richard J. Marshall, Jr., and MacArthur's aide, Sidney L. Huff. The already wealthy MacArthur was to receive half a million; Sutherland was enriched by a paltry $75,000; Marshall and Huff received $45,000 and $20,000 respectively. Only Sutherland kept any personal record of the transaction. Although long-standing law forbade the military from accepting emoluments from persons, firms, or governments being served, MacArthur, back in American uniform, may have felt justified by a 1935 regulation that permitted military advisers to the Commonwealth to accept Philippine compensation.*

From Corregidor, MacArthur would contact the President's deputy, Jorge Vargas, to claim the $35,000 expense allowance due him as chief of the national army and uncollected all year. Despite the chaos, he wanted it, he told Vargas, in blue-chip stock. "Jorge," he inquired from Corregidor on December 28, "I have already received my salary for December but I have not yet taken the 70,000 Pesos contingency fund that is due me."

"What do you want me to do, General?" asked the harried Vargas, who had been left behind to deal with the Japanese, then closing in on Manila.

"Can you buy me $35,000 worth of Lepanto stocks?"

"We will try, General, we will try," Vargas assured him, and after many calls—Wall Street was closed—reached the American manager of the Philippine National Bank's New York office.

"After the war," Vargas revealed, "MacArthur became a millionaire on account of that last-minute purchase."

Roosevelt knew about both sleazy transactions but did not prevent them or use them later against MacArthur. While alive he was too politically dangerous to punish, and if dead, he would have become a saint whose martyrdom would have further energized Roosevelt's adversaries. MacArthur was ordered out of danger and off to Australia to lead the Allies back.

Clark Field had not been a second Pearl Harbor. The attack had not come just after dawn, by surprise, on a sleepy Sunday. The Japanese had attacked, nearly unopposed, long after MacArthur and his staff had heard about Hawaii, and at midday Monday, following warning after warning about enemy overflights and air raids, and even after the first Philippine territory—the Batan Islands—had been overrun. Instead of American losses largely being obsolete battleships, or newer ones almost as useless in a modern war of mobility, the Philippines

---

* MacArthur also extracted a promise from the ailing Quezon to reappoint him as Field Marshal of the Philippines after the war, with the same pay and allowances as he had received until returning to the U.S. Army. To Quezon it may have appeared as confidence in a future not easily perceived from the gloom of Malinta Tunnel below Corregidor. On June 19, 1942, having been extricated from the Philippines, Quezon visited Dwight Eisenhower and offered him (Ike wrote in his diary) "an honorarium for services rendered . . . as MacArthur's chief of staff in Manila." Eisenhower politely rejected any "material reward" as "inadvisable" and "impossible."

had lost its air cover and whatever ability there was to retaliate. Pearl Harbor had been an unexpected target, a daring gamble. Clark Field and Cavite were inevitable targets. Not only had a war warning been received in Manila ten days earlier, the war had actually begun.

The bungling pointed ultimately to the general in the penthouse eyrie at the Manila Hotel and his circle of sycophants. ("You don't have a staff, General," George Marshall would tell him in 1943. "You have a court.") Yet it seemed better in Washington to co-opt the former isolationist Right by permitting its stalwarts to march behind Mac-Arthur's banner than to alienate the internal opposition by replacing him. War hero in 1918, Hoover's Army chief of staff and strongman who had put down the pathetic Bonus March of war veterans, Roosevelt's Army chief until the President could get rid of him, Douglas MacArthur was an icon.

Faceless military technocrats who had lapsed in vigilance, Kimmel and Short were expendable; MacArthur, the very image of a hero since the Argonne, resolute with clenched chin and cap overflowing with excess gold braid, was the essential symbol of the fighting spirit he had not evidenced. America was suddenly in urgent need of heroes, and, as Dwight Eisenhower would observe in his diary, in MacArthur the public "built itself a hero out of its own imagination. . . . I still think he might have made a better showing at the beaches and passes, and certainly he should have saved his planes on December 8, but he's still the hero."

Few generals have profited so spectacularly from their own failures. Or from the luck of being nine thousand difficult miles from head-quarters at home. For MacArthur there would be no postwar post-mortems; instead he would be proconsul of Japan.

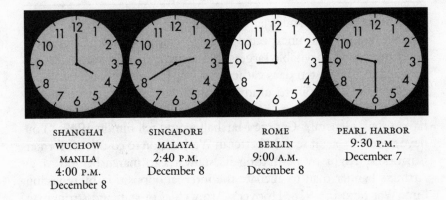

SHANGHAI
WUCHOW
MANILA
4:00 P.M.
December 8

SINGAPORE
MALAYA
2:40 P.M.
December 8

ROME
BERLIN
9:00 A.M.
December 8

PEARL HARBOR
9:30 P.M.
December 7

HOUR 44

AT FOUR IN THE AFTERNOON, the 21st Philippine Division, to which Lieutenant Colonel Richard Mallonée was frustratingly attached, was set to move to Bugallon on Lingayen Gulf. All the division had seen of war was the downing of a lone P-40, pounced on by several Zeros. They watched as the pilot bailed out, his plane in flames. Soon after, a local boy trotted in on a pony to report that the American needed help. Mallonée sent four litter bearers and a doctor, and the party returned with the dying pilot.

As some trucks and buses loaded with infantry began leaving the camp, a division staff officer stopped to explain to Mallonée that they had no transportation for the artillery. "He advised us to sit tight and await orders." Soon they received a message from a Manila trucking company that five vehicles were en route, with nineteen more to follow. But there were still no buses for the remaining personnel. Then suddenly buses materialized, piecemeal. "We did not know how many there would actually be. . . . As each bus moved into place, all men in its vicinity swarmed over it and fought each other for seats, then had to be forced out to load equipment. . . . [Lieutenant] Hendry, the mildest-mannered and most even-tempered of the American officers, had to use a flailing piece of bamboo."

Orange, the basic Pacific war plan of the United States, had envisioned a delaying action confined to the Manila Bay area, specifically the Bataan Peninsula and the island of Corregidor. When chief of staff, MacArthur had participated in developing Orange, which defended Luzon only against Admiral Dewey. Although the strategy hadn't worked for the Spanish in 1898, it did have the merit of concentrating limited resources. MacArthur, however, had begun visualizing the islands as his personal fiefdom, no part of which was expendable. Rainbow 5, his beaches strategy, was reluctantly agreed to by Washington as a preliminary to Orange.

Named for his "Rainbow Division" command in 1918—everything had to reflect his persona—and intended for the independent republic of 1946, if ever workable, Rainbow 5 was a paper tiger in 1941. The plan was to have mobile Filipino troops and fast motor boats defend the entire thousand-mile-long archipelago of seven thousand islands. But his Filipino troops were mostly five-and-a-half-month draftees with little modern equipment. The PT boats to break up landing attempts hardly numbered a handful. MacArthur, in seclusion, could not make up his mind which of the contrary plans to implement. While he publicly maintained an optimistic facade, his defenses were falling apart.

Scattering supplies and men about Luzon, let alone other islands, was a logistical catastrophe in the making. Mallonée's horror at the confusion in the movement of one division to one beach was repeated everywhere in northern Luzon. Harold K. Johnson and Bradford G. Chynoweth, two future generals, but soon, thanks to Rainbow 5, to be PWs, experienced similar frustrations. They deplored the dispersal of foodstuffs and equipment to the beaches—to be abandoned to the enemy—at the expense of Bataan, where troops, Johnson included, had to go on half-rations as early as January 7, 1942. "Unbelievable ineptitude" was Chynoweth's assessment.

Little materiel could have been stored on Bataan. There were no roads on which to haul supplies, and no facilities in which to store them. MacArthur's preparations, according to Captain Anloff, "were zero. There were no roads on Bataan although roads existed on paper. One road went down only to Limay, and stopped. . . . Just before the war I took the map to the G-3 in Manila and asked for an update. He said this road from Limay to Bagac, across the peninsula to the ocean, does not exist; it is only a carabao [water buffalo] trail. Other roads also quit, just stopped. We were two months into the war and already holed up on Bataan before the Engineers had a road across. We had to store ammunition under canvas. When they finally sent ammo to Bataan the Army rented barges and brought it as far as Little Baguio Hill. All the other ammo on Luzon fell into the hands of the Japanese."

Some supplies never went anywhere. While MacArthur's staff busied itself deciding where it was to go, "mountains of food burned on the dock," Chynoweth wrote, "—and then Bataan starved. In my own little sector we had no shortage of rifles, but no ammunition for them. Our ammunition was stored in Manila and they wouldn't send it when I begged." "Wait until your warehouses are built," he was told. For protection against strafing by enemy aircraft, which he expected at any time, Chynoweth ordered his troops to dig foxholes. Because of the shallow water table on the islands of the Visayas, any hole more than one foot deep struck mud or ooze. Twelve inches, he decided, was better than nothing.

When thirty-five Mitsubishis bombed Iloilo he remembered the concerns of the captain of the *Houston*. But the *Houston*, once Admiral Hart's flagship, had left with the *Boise* for Balikpapan in Borneo.

Clark Lee returned to Intramuros for the promised USAFFE briefing. Major Diller looked serious. He recited a list of air attacks repelled in northern Luzon and reported imaginatively that fighters had turned back an attack on Clark Field at eleven. "However, at about one this afternoon Clark Field was badly bombed. Many planes were destroyed and it appears that casualties were heavy."

Reporters asked for more details. "I don't have any," he said. "There is only one telephone line to Clark Field and that has been cut."

Finding that difficult to believe, Lee turned to Melville Jacoby. "Haven't those people ever heard of the radio or the automobile? Can't they send up there and find out what happened?" Headquarters knew the truth, but it was too grim to make public. Then a frightened Manila physician arrived at the *Manila Bulletin* building with a tale for Lee about what he had experienced when driving past Clark Field. He had thought he had seen a "practice" until the smoke and flames, and the fleeing survivors, appeared.

A skirmish with the new censorship took place. Lee lost.

•

From the moment he heard the news of war, Mark Tennien knew he was in danger and that his own presence in Wuchow was no longer of use. But he had not known his next move. Paralysis had set in, interrupted only by the arrival of a radiogram late in the day. Somehow slipping past the Japanese censors and monitors in the Wuchow telegraph office, perhaps because it had been taken down by a Chinese loyalist, it had been copied out and delivered rapidly to the mission: "PROCEED CHUNGKING IMMEDIATELY. ESTABLISH DISTRIBUTION OFFICE MISSIONS. CLEAR EVERYTHING THROUGH CHUNGKING." Nothing could have been more naive than to send such a message into Japanese-controlled territory.

As he packed his most precious possessions gathered over thirteen years, he thought of what he was abandoning, material and spiritual. What he had given his best years to was disappearing in a day. And he remembered that fourteen Maryknoll volunteers had just arrived in Hong Kong on the Clipper that weekend. Not only might they never get to China; they might never get out of Hong Kong.

His bags stuffed, Father Mark lugged them onto his motorbike and threaded his way to the riverfront, hoping to evade, in the crush of the crowds, the Japanese military, and to hire a junk to go up the Yangtze toward Chungking. After some hairbreadth escapes, he would make it in a month, by water, rail, and road.

•

Late in the afternoon, a heavy overcast blanketed Hong Kong. Happily for CNAC it also closed in on Kowloon, and Kai Tak, where cleanup crews had cleared the runways of debris. All RAF antiques had been victims on the ground, as were eight CNAC transports. But the joint Chinese-Pan Am airline still had five planes that had survived in hangars, and in keeping with unorthodox China National Aviation Corporation operations, the survivors had been wheeled out once the Japanese were gone, and camouflaged with bamboo, straw, and mud among nearby Chinese huts. When enemy planes returned during the day, the CNAC transports seemed part of the adjacent village.

People with flight priorities—arranged by American authorities in Hong Kong or by the Chungking government—were brought to the field and assigned to seats on the DC-2s. American dollars magically escalated one's chances of exit, although those chances seemed fragile as the overloaded planes barely cleared the rooftops and vanished. "Free" territory was two hundred miles inland. "There was nothing else I could do," said a pilot, "but sweat a little." In the gloom, Japanese guns barked blindly at the roar of CNAC engines over the China coastline.

•

With Jack Liddell presiding, a full-dress meeting of the Shanghai Municipal Council convened at 4:30 P.M. Although the Japanese claimed not to be interfering with foreign-owned public utilities, they had already seized the buses of the British Shanghai Omnibus Company. Still, the council's understanding was that the occupiers wanted the Settlement infrastructure maintained. Emergency committees were set up to control food supplies, coal, transport, and other necessities.

Even as the council deliberated, life had changed very perceptibly for the worse. "Dangerous" enemy nationals were being hauled to the Bridge House, a small apartment hotel north of Soochow Creek, for water-assisted "interrogation" by the *kempeitai*. Other suspect foreign residents were marched across the bridges to internment camps in Hongkew. Some Americans were escorted to the Metropole Hotel downtown to begin lives of dreary semiconfinement. Unarrested nationals not immediately destitute could go to the cinemas and restaurants or to the nearly useless banks. They could read the "reformed" British and American newspapers operated nominally by their managements but supervised by Japanese Army officers. In the compound of the Anglican cathedral, a general store materialized where residents sold their remaining belongings to each other to raise cash for food.

Queues were everywhere—for food, money, lodging, and registration of foreigners, for whom there was the added frustration that the English of the interrogators was so poor. The expert linguists went to the banks and utilities. Delays were long. The afternoon was turning wet and cold. "The Japanese appeared to enjoy our discomfort," Arch Carey recalled, "and took motion pictures of us waiting on the pavements . . . doubtless for propaganda use in programs for Asians to humiliate us, but most people turned their backs on the photographers. We all kept up a cheerful front, although inwardly we were disgusted. Chinese onlookers gathered to see the unusual sight of white men, women and children standing in line on sidewalks with Chinese police and some Japanese armed guards keeping order." In the streets, the once-docile Chinese began treating their former masters with studied insolence.

Returning to the Shell Building, Carey managed to retrieve some private papers. With the connivance of Chinese maintenance workers still loyal to former employers who might yet be back, he had important documents taken to the rooftop incinerator, "working overtime that day." Carey also searched for toilets down which to flush other sensitive papers. There were no guards in the lavatories. "Finally, on our way out . . . , all of us were searched by armed Japanese marines, and this was the last visit to the offices for most of us for some time. However, three of us were instructed to be present [the] next day to hand over the building to the Japanese. . . . I represented the Property Department." When the time came, the building was confiscated with all the trappings of legality. The Japanese officials who took it over bowed the British out in the traditional style as if the transaction were thoroughly proper and peaceful.

In the children's ward on the top floor of Hôpital Sainte Marie in the French Concession, Jim Ballard thought about his mother and father and hoped that they would soon come to reclaim him. "In the corridor below the landing Jim could hear the French missionary sisters arguing with the Japanese military police. . . . Despite the hard mattress, the whitewashed walls with their unpleasant icons above each bed— the crucified infant Jesus surrounded by Chinese disciples—and the ominous chemical smell . . . , Jim found it difficult to believe that the war had at last begun. Walls of strangeness separated everything. . . ."

What remained real was the mudflat on the Whangpoo to which his father (at least in the lens of fiction) had helped drag wounded sailors from the *Peterel*, and where they had sat for six hours beside a dead petty officer. He remembered seeing Stephen Polkinghorn and another officer taken away, and the expressionless eyes of curious Chinese huddled above them on the quay. Jim wanted to sneak home to Amherst Road. Jordan Avenue, running to the west of the hospital— even the more distant Avenue Foch—would take him there.

•

Beginning his ceremonial business day in Rome, figurehead King Victor Emmanuel expressed to Count Ciano perfunctory satisfaction over the Japanese success at Pearl Harbor. America's military capacity was very great, Ciano replied cautiously. "In the long run," the worried king admitted, "you may be right." And he dropped the subject. "Mussolini," Ciano noted, "was happy. For a long time now he has been in favor of clarifying the position between America and the Axis." *Maresciallo* Cavallaro was certain that the strategic balance had instantly improved. Ships and planes employed in Southeast Asia could not be used in North Africa. "England's war potential in the Mediterranean," he would write hopefully to General Bastico in Libya, "is destined to be reduced, while ours is increasing with the [German] contribution of superior air power." He saw less likelihood, too, for a British move against Vichy colonies in Africa. "It's a matter now for us," he urged Bastico, "to make sure that there is a linking between this moment and the [future] one in which the situation will prove to be decidedly modified, even reversed, in our favor."

•

Concerned about Margot Rosenthal, Ruth Andreas-Friedrich stopped at Mrs. Rosenthal's apartment block on the way to the office. She was already hiding hunted Jews in her cellar, procuring food for them with forged ration tickets. Her job at the vast, once-Jewish, Ullstein publishing house in Berlin gave her access to clandestine, professional-looking printing. She pushed the bell for the *Pfortner* and asked about Margot.

"The one on the second floor? The Jewess, you mean? They came and took her away. Day before yesterday. Oh, along about six."

•

From Washington, the German chargé at the Embassy, Hans Thomsen, had radioed Berlin that war with Japan was certain to relax belligerent American activities in the Atlantic—that "it would be logical [for the U.S.] to avoid everything which might lead to a two-front war," and that "full participation of America in [the] war is not to be expected before July 1943. Military measures against Japan are of defensive character." All of America's energy, he predicted, would be transferred to its *"own* rearmament, [with] a corresponding shrinking of Lend-Lease help and a shifting of all activity to the Pacific."

Thomsen's suggestion that America would want to avoid a two-front war was the very reason that Hitler wanted it. When would the U.S. be weaker and more beleaguered? He instructed Karl Dönitz to send U-boats against American-flag vessels even though no declaration of war had yet been made. "The U.S.," he explained to Ribbentrop, "is already shooting against our ships. They have been a forceful factor and through their actions have already created a situation of war."

He ordered Ribbentrop to begin the expulsion of American diplomats in Germany. Having, Hitler thought, much more reason to be elated than had Mussolini, whose opinions counted for nothing, he confided afterwards to his headquarters personnel that "the date chosen" by the Japanese had been "of exceptional value to us. . . . It was at the moment when the surprises of the Russian winter were weighing most heavily on the morale of our people and when everybody in Germany was oppressed by the certainty that sooner or later the United States would come into the conflict. Japanese intervention therefore was, from our point of view, most opportune."

•

Just after midnight in California, troops of the 17th Infantry Regiment, 7th Division, left Fort Ord in a convoy of trucks, ordered northward to protect the Pacific coastline from invasion. They were to look for "land forms that had been pre-selected on plans," Private (later Lieutenant Colonel) Sumner Hudson, Jr., remembered. At each location they were to site machine guns and to place men fifty yards apart. Earlier on Sunday Hudson had camped at the base of Ocean Boulevard in Carmel on a high sand dune overlooking the ocean. He and his buddies held weekend passes good until six on Monday morning, but as evening came they had misgivings about another December night in a pup tent on the beach. Now they were headed up the coast and over the Golden Gate to camp, somewhere, on a colder beach.

•

Just after 4:00 P.M., in a lowering sun, the bombers of the Eleventh Air Fleet returning from Luzon came into sight over Taiwan. At Takao, Lieutenant Commander Shimada greeted them, learning as they landed that the speedier fighter planes were coming in slightly later because they had remained over the targets to strafe ground objectives after the bombers had dropped their loads. As the first "Betty" came to a stop and the crew clambered out onto the runway, Shimada heard fragments of one airman's surprised reactions: "Are we really at war? . . . We met no opposition. . . . What is the matter with the enemy?"

When more crews landed, "it became apparent that . . . there had been some slight reaction from antiaircraft guns but no interception by enemy fighters.* Even more astonishing was . . . that our fliers had found the enemy's planes lined up on the target fields as in peacetime. . . . We were bewildered, too, because it seemed almost as if the enemy did not know that war had started. Could it be that no warnings from Pearl Harbor had yet gotten through to the Philippines?"

Because of the fog delay, Nichols Field had been dropped in favor of the closer Iba, but Nichols was reinstated as the next day's primary target. Preparations were under way even as the planes kept returning from Luzon. By sundown it was clear that seven Zeros and one bomber had been lost to weather, mechanical failure, or enemy action—a small price. The bag of destroyed American aircraft, mostly on the ground, was 102.

•

At 8:30 A.M. the Eden-Maisky party embarked from Invergordon, in rough seas, for Scapa Flow, where they were due at five to board the *Kent*. In Maisky's presence, Eden had first telephoned Churchill to confirm that the trip was still on. Eden was feeling "chilled and sick," and after a sleepless Sunday night had breakfasted on a half-bottle of soda water. A naval surgeon had diagnosed gastric flu, but Churchill was unmoved. A later conversation from Scapa Flow left plans unchanged even when Churchill let it be known that with King George's assent he was on his way to the U.S. to confer with Roosevelt. "That's all right," Churchill told Cadogan: "that'll work very well: I shall have Anthony where I want him!" Cadogan visualized "three-cornered [telephone] conversations."

Telling "what he knew of the Japanese attack on Pearl Harbour," Churchill was "quite naturally in a high state of excitement," Eden remembered. "I could not conceal my relief and did not have to try to. I felt that whatever happened now, it was merely a question of time. Before, we had believed in the end but never seen the means; now both were clear."

On the telephone Churchill "began laying plans. . . . The emphasis of the war had shifted; what now mattered was the intentions of our two great allies. We must each go to one of them." They agreed to

* An exaggeration. A few P-40s and P-35s had managed to get airborne.

send every telegram to each other twice, to double chances of safe arrival; then Churchill added, "Wait a minute, someone else wants to speak with you."

It was Ambassador Winant, who was still at Chequers. "It was good to hear the relief in his voice."

Running a fever, Eden was bundled into bed aboard the *Somali* and never noticed the rocking of the vessel in the black, churning water.

•

Rumor-fed panic made the early hours of darkness on Oahu frightening ones. Everywhere, especially on Ford Island, there was fear of enemy-poisoned drinking water. Watch logs of stations and bases all over the island reported parachutists landing at locations as far apart as Barber's Point and Kahuku. Some carefully described the invaders as garbed in "blue coveralls, red emblems." All day long and into the night, snipers were reported on secondary roads, and at ten came a bulletin that Japanese were on the beaches below Hickam Field, landing from gliders, and that Pearl Harbor was "receiving naval bombardment."

Lieutenant W. R. Hunnicutt, whose destroyer, the *Bagley*, had chased briefly after the Japanese strike force only to identify Halsey's *Enterprise* group, found that after dark there were few lights along the Oahu coastline. "Whenever a light blinked on there soon followed the crack of a .30 rifle from one of the Marine patrols and the light was extinguished."

At about ten, a launch tied up close to the stern of the *Honolulu*. In the blackout, a young sailor on the cruiser wanted to shoot, but Seaman Clair E. Boggs was certain that the men on the dock were American. He challenged them, warning that if they did not identify themselves, he would fire. When the first warning elicited mumblings neither sailor could identify, Boggs issued another challenge. "Go ahead and shoot" is what he thought he heard, but knowing no password for the day and recognizing Yankee in the voice, he passed up a shot. "A Jap," he concluded, "would be more polite about it."

The next morning he saw the sailors return to their launch and asked them why they had cavalierly called his bluff. They were really scared, one said, and had shouted up at the *Honolulu*, "USS *Chew*."

After-the-fact vigilance was extreme. Ships offshore fired at anything moving, imagining submarines everywhere; troops onshore imagined Japanese invaders returning, and fired back. Two units at Schofield barracks became engaged in a fire fight across a gully, ending when a G.I., nicked by a ricocheting bullet, launched into expletives that were recognizably un-Japanese. One skirmish on a beachfront strip was fictionalized by Private James Jones, a participant, in *From Here to Eternity*.

Apparent intruders were fired at in the darkness and identified afterward. A sentry who challenged a suspiciously moving form nearby three times and received no response bagged his mule. A certainly apocryphal Japanese milkman reportedly crashed his truck into parked planes on Hickam Field, destroying nearly a squadron of them before he was allegedly shot.

Another rumor claimed that Japanese farm workers had cut huge arrows in the cane fields pointing to Pearl Harbor. Acres of cane moved suspiciously in the trade winds, especially at night, and Sergeant Gene Camp, with the 251st Coast Artillery at Camp Malakole, a unit which had reinforced the Marines guarding the West Loch of Pearl Harbor, remembered the results. "More than one stalk of sugar cane was cut down by rifle fire repelling imaginary intruders." A report reached the *Pennsylvania* that the Japanese had landed in California at Long Beach and were marching on Los Angeles. The Panama Canal was reported bombed, bottling in the Atlantic Fleet. On the *Maryland*, one of the least damaged ships, crewmen heard that the *Pennsylvania* had captured two Japanese carriers and was towing them back to Pearl Harbor—a remarkable feat for a vessel in dry dock.

At the shipfitter's shop in the dry-dock area at Pearl Harbor, Ed Sheehan heard that the United States had surrendered Hawaii to Japan. "This last rumor we refused to believe."

Crowded with dirty, hungry, injured sailors from wrecked ships and strafed shore installations, Ford Island was a chaos in the darkness. A refugee from the shattered *West Virginia*, tied up alongside the *Tennessee*, James E. Alley had climbed through the muck and up the hawser of the *Tennessee* but could not get aboard. He had to lower himself back into the black oil and swim to the island. There was no fresh water except in the guarded swimming pool, and salt water was ineffective in sloshing off the oil. A gunner's mate offered Alley a rifle but no ammunition, and he could find no food in the mess hall. The day had been a blur. He and others from the "Wee Vee" went to sleep in their slimy clothes on the mess hall tables.

Through the day and into the night a flood of improbable yet thoroughly detailed misinformation had been received on ship and shore radios and telephones. A pitched battle between Marines and enemy paratroops on Ewa Plain had never happened. Enemy submarines were reported *in* Pearl Harbor, and indeed for a time there was at least one minisub there, possibly two. Strange vessels were reported everywhere, all of them proving to be American. Darkness brought a new sighting, a Marine officer reporting an enemy dirigible two degrees to the right of the moon and three degrees below it. The next morning, Marines would fire thousands of three-inch AA shells at Venus, the planet looking to suspicious eyes like sunlight reflecting off the wings of an unidentified aircraft.

•

For an afternoon audience at the Foreign Office, Willys R. Peck, the American Minister to Thailand, left his legation at three. Vice-Consul Estes accompanied him in one of the few Chevrolets in Bangkok. No gendarmes interfered, although incidents would multiply quickly thereafter, from the pulling down of the American flag and the raising of the Rising Sun to Peck's having a Japanese bayonet poked at his ribs. For the moment, the diplomatic district of the city was sultry and quiet.

Told what they already knew, the Americans were assured that the Thais had only permitted Japanese attacks on the British. But, since the Japanese had their separate quarrel with the U.S., Peck should warn his nationals to behave themselves. He did what he could to arrange sanctuary in the Legation, preparing an invitation to be sent to Americans by Thai couriers offering the theoretical security of the diplomatic compound. "American citizens . . . should bring with them mattresses and bedding for their family, their available stocks of food, a charcoal stove, and several large cooking utensils. Personal effects should be limited to one suitcase per person."

Fifty-three Americans and seven Filipinos arrived before Japanese soldiers roughly handled and turned away latecomers. Although the Thais would resist being forced into a declaration of war on the U.S. until January 25, 1942, the regime had already become a puppet government. Stubbornly, Seni Pramoj in Washington stuffed the declaration in a drawer and refused to deliver it; nevertheless, Americans in Thailand remained prisoners until exchanged.

•

The Malay cabbie dropped Brown and Gallagher off at the dock at the Naval Base where the imposing expanse of the *Prince of Wales* loomed. It was 2:30 P.M. The gangplank was down, and they carried their own belongings aboard. "Very happy to have you with us," said Captain J. C. Leach, the skipper. They shook hands heartily all around.

"This was the real thing!" Brown decided. The pride of the Royal Navy, the *Wales* had carried Churchill across the Atlantic. Churchill had hoped that the presence of big capital ships would deter Japanese aggression, or at least inhibit naval operations in Malay waters. Further—as the newsmen did not know—John Curtin, the new Labour prime minister of Australia, like his predecessor Robert Menzies, had been reluctant, when the homeland seemed threatened, to keep his troops so far away, in Egypt and Libya. Churchill had cabled him that the decision to send the *Prince of Wales* and the *Repulse* "should convince you of our wish to act toward your government in true comradeship and loyalty."

To Brown, who knew nothing of the missing carrier *Indomitable*, the *Prince of Wales*, with its tremendous guns, looked capable of handling anything. He was in luck. "We must hurry," Captain Leach urged after the welcoming formalities. "We have the launch all ready for you." And the correspondents discovered that they were assigned to the *Repulse*, which was to accompany the bigger and newer ship. They began to protest. "I'm terribly sorry," said Leach, "but we're just jammed up. I have 1,760 men on board and we just don't have an inch of room. You will be very comfortable on the *Repulse*. . . . We're all going on the same mission. You talk it over."

While the launch waited, Gallagher and Brown huddled over a joint decision. The *Repulse*, they realized, was a military secret. The Japanese were only supposed to know of the presence in Singapore of the *Prince of Wales*. Gallagher and Brown could not even use a *Repulse* byline and, said Brown, "*Wales* is the big name," the "glamor ship." It had been one of the ships that had stalked and sank the *Bismarck* in the North Atlantic, and still bore the scars of that encounter.

Gallagher agreed. "From a story point of view the whole thing is a washout, but there's no time for any other correspondent to be sent out . . . to go on with this story."

With misgivings unabated, they climbed into the launch. From the top of the gangway Leach called down to them to have a good time. "Thank you, sir," Brown called back. "Take care of yourself."

HOUR 45

I PACKED for the baby and myself, and the amah and Carola and I went off to stay with the Selwyn-Clarkes," Emily Hahn remembered at eighty-three. "It was not an easy day . . . wondering what to do and where to go. Everybody was in the same boat." And everybody who was anybody in Hong Kong seemed to be holed up in Hilda Selwyn-Clarke's spacious house on the Peak. "We had a Chinese doctor and his wife and son, and Constance Lam, a girl who adored the doctor and who was now acting as housekeeper . . . , and Miriam, a Chinese nurse who was Mary [Selwyn-Clarke]'s governess, and the Valentines. Douglas Valentine was Selwyn's assistant, and Nina, his wife . . . — and a lot of other odd bits and pieces, doctors and such. . . . Oh, we were crowded, and the wonder is that we didn't all blow up, but we didn't. We behaved almost admirably. . . . I don't deny that I avoided the baby. I made sure that . . . I turned up for her feedings when it was time, but for the rest I stayed out of her way. It just hurt too much, looking at her."

Meanwhile, they waited for more enemy planes and more bombs "on the tipmost top of the proud Peak," and "for planes to come up from Singapore and drive away those impertinent little pests." None of Hilda's anxious houseguests knew that the planes in Singapore—inadequate as they had been—would never come. In Stanley Prison, Francis Braun knew even less. The Chinese guards told "enemy aliens" nothing. "However there were plenty of signs of unusual activities. The wailing of sirens sounded everywhere and the occasional boom of the guns of Stanley Fort with their shells flying overhead became quite nerve-racking. . . . During one of the salvoes, a young priest quite forgot the dignity of the cassock he was wearing. He came charging across the connecting span wringing his hands in despair and appealing, 'Oh, my God, save my life! Oh, my God, save my life!!' "

To Heather Tomlinson the hours that followed were "chaos. I took some food and coffee to Sterling in the operating room; there were hundreds of Chinese bleeding from wounds. Sterling came out covered with blood. I went home and wondered what to do." Then her husband returned and told her that she had to move quickly, across the bay to the island. He had to open a first-aid station there—and besides, the Japanese could not be contained in the New Territories above them. They packed three suitcases. The baby's amah had to be left behind.

•

The *Taringtang* docked at twilight at Pasacao, where the Groves learned that a blackout was in force. Unable to use automobile headlamps, they raced the setting sun and arrived in Iriga to find "the folks" finishing "the usual game of tennis." There was no sign of war, but they learned about Pearl Harbor, Hong Kong, even about "Baguio, Davao, [and, erroneously,] Nichols Field." In the blackout, they sat about the dinner table with their two children and Leon Groves's two partners, hardly able to eat—"first because of the dimness of light and second because we could think or talk of nothing but what was to happen now, and when? . . . We shall sleep with anything but a secure feeling. We feel that the chances of an invasion of the Philippines are remote, but what type of action will be taken by Japan?"

Life would alter quickly. After internment by the Japanese, and their escape, the family, aided by guerrillas, survived three years of jungle life.

"At the end of the afternoon," High Commissioner Sayre recalled, "I conferred with General MacArthur in his office. He was pacing the floor, and I could see from his face how grave the situation must be. He read to me the radio [message] telling of the tragic losses at Pearl

Harbor. Whereas our entire military strategy had been based on holding Corregidor and some territory on the Bataan peninsula . . . and
waiting for the American main fleet to fight its way west to our rescue,
we now learned that there was no American fleet." MacArthur told
Sayre of the Clark Field catastrophe, "and it was hard to believe that
we were not in some horrible nightmare from which we would
awaken." The general, Sayre remembered, had conferred with him and
with a very concerned Admiral Hart ten days earlier, after the war
warning from Washington. MacArthur had paced back and forth, puffing his black Manila cigar and "assuring" them that "the existing alignment and movement of Japanese troops convinced him that there
would be no Japanese attack before the spring."

Francis Sayre had "saved enough" out of his annual office appropriation for sand, bags, tools, and emergency supplies for a basement
shelter in the High Commissioner's residence. He bought "quantities
of food and supplies and numerous large garbage cans which were
placed along the corridors for storing water." If there were a siege, he
would be ready.*

•

"Hai sentito?" was the question that echoed from passerby to passerby as Branko Bokun walked through Rome to his friend Ivo's office.
"Have you heard?" Bokun had no idea what the excitement was all
about, but Ivo seemed to know everything that was happening. A
polyglot Yugoslav from Dalmatia, now annexed to Italy, he was working in the censorship office reading suspect mail in Russian, Serbo-
Croatian, Spanish, French, and English. Bokun, on a false passport as
a Rome University student from Hungary, had met Ivo, who loved
to boast about his work, in the block of flats in which they lived. A
young clerk for the Serbian Red Cross in Belgrade, Bokun had been
recruited as an informant by the former Intelligence chief in Yugoslavia.
Since the April invasion and conversion of Serbia into a German "pro-
tectorate," he concealed himself as director of the Red Cross office.

"Heard what?" Bokun finally asked Ivo, who motioned to him to
wait. He was talking with higher-ups. "The Japanese were right,"

---

* Before the fall of Bataan, he and MacArthur were evacuated by submarine. The
grand commissioner's residence in Manila, with all its stocks, had long been abandoned
to the Japanese.

Bokun could make out from across the room. "They had no choice but to attack Pearl Harbor."

The other visitor pointed out that Italy would be in more trouble with America now in the war, and Bokun understood that the Italians had no stomach for the war in any case. Only a few days earlier the Vatican newspaper, *Osservatore Romano*, had sold out in a few hours because it had published pictures of Italian prisoners of war, mostly from North Africa, in English camps playing football, enjoying the good life. Mussolini, so local gossip went, protested that the action had been treasonable. "Seeing these photographs, the Italian soldiers will run to the English waving even their white underwear, to surrender!" British Intelligence, he was sure, had subverted the Pope's editors.

"The Japs were provoked by the Americans," said the elderly man with a shaved head like Mussolini's—an informer for the *Duce*, Ivo later explained. "The decrepit Roosevelt, under the influence of the American Jews and Communists that surround him, forced America to enter the war." Since the invasion of Russia, the *Duce* double went on, Roosevelt had been trying to find a means, and "the easiest way to deceive the naive Americans was to provoke an incident with Japan." He pointed out at length that American cardinals and archbishops had been speaking out openly against intervention, which would assist godless Communism.

"Is that all true?" Bokun asked Ivo when they were finally alone.

"I'm afraid it is. . . . Stalin has his men in important positions in Washington, and they would do anything to save Communism."

Had Bokun been able to understand English, and listened to Ezra Pound on Italian radio, he would have heard Ivo's views reinforced.

•

"Where is there still a neutral piece of land?" State Secretary von Weiszäcker asked himself. Most states in Latin America were "American followers" and would join the war, depriving Germany of listening posts and sites for covert operations. Japan, he judged, was clearly the aggressor—the navy "had steered the policy and forced the conflict. . . . The military impact should be very great in order to justify this." In any case, he felt that as a result of the Japanese attack, Germany had in effect been at war with the U.S. since six on Sunday evening. "Now our legal relationship with the U.S.A. will also be clarified quickly." He had yet to talk to colleagues about the extension of the war, and when he did he would be extra-cautious. "The war, as Japan conducts it, arouses enthusiasm here. The U.S. involvement dampens it in turn." He confided to his diary that a Pacific diversion "eases the burden after all and may later even open new perspectives." The language was diplomatic circumlocution. Pearl Harbor might, to von Weiszäcker, furnish a way out of the war.

However pro-Axis, and despite its contribution of troops to the Russian front, Spain remained a neutral. Less cautious than his brother-in-law, General Franco, Serrano Suñer, the Foreign Minister, instructed his underlings to demonstrate their gratitude to Emperor Hirohito by visiting the Japanese legation in Madrid and leaving their calling cards.

•

With European Central time imposed on Paris by the Germans,* the late-autumn night now lasted until nine in the morning. "It was terrible, terrible," Simone De Beauvoir remembered, "to wake up in the blackness that went on so long each day because they changed the time. . . . We lived on Berlin time, so we never really knew what time it was, only that it was black all the time, black." Curfew at six left few French citizens any daylight hours not spent at work. In their morning newspapers, read in half-darkness, most Parisians learned that their world had changed. Some knew earlier: it was unsafe to tune in the BBC before midnight, but after that, hidden radios clicked on in basements and attics all over France.

The news seemed bleak. America was in the war only because it had suffered a catastrophe. Gerhard Heller, a Francophile who oversaw the conformity of French writing with Nazi ideology, read "*l'Amérique va entrer en guerre*" as a "*mauvais signe*" of a longer German winter, "*l'aggravation de la situation pour Allemagne.*" For writers whom Heller censored, privation was gradually extinguishing hope for anything more than that the meat-and-potato rations would not diminish further, and that coal would last the winter. For Heller and his compatriot

* Ironically, what began as Occupation imposition in 1940 became national policy after the war. Paris and Berlin are on Central European time, the synchronization now a symbol of European unity.

in Paris, Ernst Jünger, *l'aggravation* meant no immediate loss in the quality of life: for Nazis there was plenty of champagne. But Heller now could see the war lost.

•

In "Unoccupied France," eighty-five-year-old Marshal Pétain mused to the American ambassador, Admiral Leahy, "Never before has the whole world been at war; . . . I don't know what will come of it." Marshall M. Vance, the U.S. Consul in Lyon, communicated a very different reaction to Washington—that American entrance into the war had been "quietly but extremely encouraging to French morale." It had not been all that quiet. Despite fears of Nazi or Vichy surveillance, visitors came to the consulate entrance to offer Vance good wishes and to admire the American flags flown from the main office and from the British Interests Section across the river. Until the morning of the eighth, the Stars and Stripes had been flown only on holidays.

Diplomatic offices were also information-gathering units—in some cases, disinformation-gathering, as with the reports from Vichy France and Switzerland, from American businessmen with German connections, of new plans for the invasion of England. Much as the Nazis wanted to subdue Britain before the U.S. could make a difference in Europe, an invasion was, in fact, off. The Germans had their hands full in Russia; England would have to be strangled by submarines. Nevertheless, Paul Squire, the American Consul in Geneva, reported from "a very good source" that the Germans were "preparing an all-out attack on England for January and have underground airplane shelters in Northern France where they hold in readiness large numbers of a new type of six-motor planes, each carrying a 20-ton tank." The strategy, Squire added, was "to land as large a force as possible in England, to dig in without necessarily attempting to conquer the entire island, and then to announce to the world that they have mastered the whole of Europe and suggest to the British that the time has come to talk business."

In order that their elite units could be diverted to subduing England, he continued, "The Germans have prepared, for some weeks back, strong positions behind their present lines in Russia, so as to take care of any enemy initiative on that side."

None of it was true, but the idea anticipated German V-1 and

V-2 revetments along the Channel and North Sea coast in 1944 and 1945, the last-ditch attempt to make England unwilling to continue the war.

•

By late afternoon the Kota Bharu airstrip was untenable. The Australians at the field had almost nothing serviceable left after enduring more bombing and strafing. Several batteries of "Dogra" artillery had been ordered to the Sabak and Kuala Krai beachheads fronting Kota Bharu, but mud, rain, and swollen streams impeded their movement. No longer concerned about British air strikes, the Japanese landed more troops and nudged forward across the gluey, slippery flats and through dank jungle.

At about 4:00 P.M., with stray bullets now pinging into the area from the fighting near the airfield perimeter, a rumor reached the squadron that the enemy had broken through. It was a legitimate fear: the beaches were only two miles to the east. In the early darkness, panic gripped the ground personnel. Torching the remaining buildings, they took off in the few flyable planes, each crammed with evacuees. Abandoning fuel and explosives that should have been destroyed, they left the airstrip usable as well by not returning to crater it after taking off: they had no room aboard for bombs. (The Japanese had carefully employed only 150-pound bombs in order to leave the runways repairable.) Peter Gibbes recalled the bullets from the beachhead landing about the field, and his being "packed tightly into the fuselage of a Hudson for the flight to Kuantan some 160 miles south."

One shot-up Vildebeeste, an antique surviving from 36 Squadron, needed only a tire to be able to get airborne. Flight Lieutenant G. S. Richardson improvised by stuffing divots of coarse grass through the bullet hole, then clearing the "KB" airstrip. Flying south, Richard Allanson signaled that they should drop down at Runcie's Airstrip. He wanted to retrieve their kit bags. They touched down on the grass runway and regained their possessions—all but Allanson, whose baggage had been stolen. Somehow, Richardson made it up again with his grass-stuffed tire, but near Kuantan his engine stalled because oil had leaked away through an undiscovered bullet hole. He managed to put the plane down with a dead prop. His luck was holding. (It would run out later, at Endau, to the south.)

By 6:15 the Kota Bharu airfield belonged to the Japanese. Yet, said

Gibbes, one of the last to leave, "We all felt (and were constantly told) that Singapore would hold and was impregnable." Some alleged later that the airfield and town had been abandoned prematurely, but a telephone message from Major General A. E. Barstow, commanding the 9th Indians, had advised Brigadier Key that although holding Kota Bharu was now left to his discretion, he was not to "risk annihilation." With the Japanese already infiltrating through his exposed positions and encirclement looming, Key began planning a withdrawal.

Before long, Allanson was back at his home base on Singapore island, Seletar—a prelude to prisoner-of-war status. Listed as "missing in action, believed killed," he kept himself alive as a captive "by making efficient traps to catch rats and mice. . . . I always carried a walking stick to assist with my impaired ability to walk, with which I also managed every now and then to kill the odd snake or lizard. All of which offered a reasonable amount of protein."

·

There was little of a material nature that could be done to buttress the defenses of Malaya, but Buckingham Palace came to the aid of Sir Shenton Thomas with a telegram of indirect encouragement from King George VI:

IMPORTANT GOVERNOR SINGAPORE PERSONAL
I have it in command from the King to convey to you the following message from His Majesty. Begins. The storm of Japan's wanton attack has broken in the East and Malaya bears the first assaults of the enemy. At this fateful moment I assure you of my high confidence in your leadership. I am at one with you, and their Highnesses the Rulers and the peoples of Malaya, in the trial which you are sustaining. I know that the Empire's reliance on your fearless determination to crush this onslaught will be fully justified, and with God's help the devoted service of every man and woman in Malaya shall contribute to our victory.
Ends.　Private Secretary.

Sir Shenton filed it.

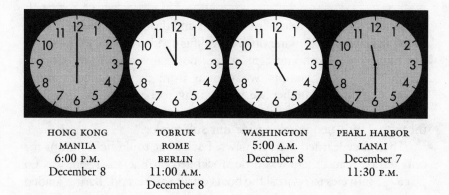

HONG KONG	TOBRUK	WASHINGTON	PEARL HARBOR
MANILA	ROME	5:00 A.M.	LANAI
6:00 P.M.	BERLIN	December 8	December 7
December 8	11:00 A.M.		11:30 P.M.
	December 8		

HOUR 46

U NDER cover of early darkness the aircraft tender *Langley*—a pioneer carrier designed for 1920s planes—slipped its moorings at Cavite and vanished southward, without lights, to join Admiral Glassford's cruisers at Iloilo in Panay. Except for submarines, almost no fighting ships remained in Manila Bay. Not realizing the pitiful ineffectiveness of American torpedoes, Admiral Hart counted heavily on his twenty-four active subs—three others were being overhauled—and kept their three tenders at hand. His naval air arm consisted of 28 PBY Catalinas and five utility planes. Six gunboats and six motor torpedo boats completed his fighting force in the Luzon area. In effect the Navy was naked and helpless, even as a rear guard to cover withdrawals.

At dusk three PT-boats commanded by Lieutenant Robert B. Kelly cast off for Mariveles on the short cruise from Cavite, detouring to drop passengers at Corregidor. From the "Rock" to Mariveles they had to feel their way through the mine fields. With warning lights turned off, "it was something else," Kelly recalled in 1942. The Army on Bataan "heard the roar of our motors and thought it was Jap planes. Searchlights began winking on . . . , feeling up into the sky for planes— our motors were echoing against the mountains on Bataan, so they couldn't tell where the noise was coming from. . . . For a few minutes it was a question whether we were going to be blown to hell by a mine or by one of our own shore batteries. But finally we snaked through, [and] tied up alongside our sub tender."

Then they learned the bad news. Each boat could hold rations for only ten days and there was little stockpiled on Bataan. There was no place at Mariveles to conceal the boats during an air raid. Barges loaded with gasoline drums had been towed out into the Bay and anchored there, as no one had wanted wharves set afire by burning gasoline. PT boats would have to refuel at sea with 100-octane gasoline by hand and through a funnel. There were a lot of things, crews discovered, that no one had thought of.

•

Frustrated at not going up against the Japanese over Singapore, Flight Sergeant Lockwood went off duty at Seletar Air Base at six, stopping on his way out to ask his adjutant, Flight Lieutenant Young, for a few hours off to get married. "It's a hell of a day to pick for a wedding," said Young, but he offered four hours' leave in mid-afternoon.

At the Tanglin Garrison Church a chaplain pronounced the vows. As best man, Lockwood's Squadron Leader, Joe Farmer, furnished the ring. "We had a glass of wine and a piece of cake at Joe Farmer's house in Outram Road, and I then took my new wife to Seletar and put her in Married Quarters."

Thirty minutes after his leave was up, Lockwood—a navigator and bombardier—was flying, "picking up torpedoes and bombs, dropping some on the Japs [at Kota Bharu] and ferrying some to Gong Kedah and Kuantan. . . . That was my honeymoon."

Flying from captured strips at Singora and Pattani, General Sugawara's 3rd Air Group struck repeatedly at airfields in northern Malaya. With almost no AA protection, British pilots crouched helplessly in slit trenches while their planes were wrecked on the ground. Enemy pilots—Brooke-Popham had dismissed them as "not air-minded"— were skilled and experienced. With sundown fast approaching, only fifty British aircraft—most of them obsolete Buffalos or useless Wir-raways—were still operational, less than half of Pulford's strength in Malaya the day before.

To MacArthur in Manila, Brooke-Popham radioed for help, appealing for long-range bombers to attack Japanese airfields in Indochina. Sir Robert did not know that half of the Philippines bomber force lay in ruins on the runways of Clark Field.

•

Instead of salvaging supplies and ammunition, the Spanish Legion used its remaining trucks to withdraw the wounded from the Leningrad front. Troops stuffed themselves before leaving with whatever would be left, including chocolates and cognac. Learning of it, von Chappuis rebuked Muñoz. The general brushed off the reproaches. He had disengaged without losing a man, and had issued his own command, he explained, about holding the new line. "Nailed to the ground. Not one step backward."

When General Ernst Busch called von Chappuis from his 16th Army headquarters at Dno, southwest of Lake Il'man (out of which the Volkhov flowed) von Chappuis complained that the 250th (Spanish) Division was "a hole in the line." He needed, he said, more troops. Busch sympathized, but had none. The behavior of the Blue Division was known to the High Command, he said, but it could not be replaced just yet.

On the instructions of Busch, von Chappuis summoned Muñoz Grandes. "Can your division hold?" he asked.

Muñoz evaded a flat yes or no. Morale, he insisted, was good, but he had suffered heavy losses and was down to less than a third of effective strength. "Even in spite of the cold, the wish is there, but the battalions are so weak . . . that it is doubtful if they can hold."

"Then I shall recommend that you be pulled out for rest and resupply behind the front."

The suggestion smacked of dishonor. "We will recuperate in the line," Muñoz insisted. "My soldiers will fight to the death."

Reporting to Busch, von Chappuis recommended that the Blue Division be withdrawn. Muñoz Grandes "no longer had the necessary energy and initiative for successful leadership." The commanding general for the Leningrad operation, Wilhelm Ritter von Leeb, knew that most divisions were in as desperate a plight as was the battered Blue. Muñoz remained.

•

To get back to the Libyan front, Alan Moorehead and another reporter had taken the "appalling" train as far as Mersa Matruh in western Egypt. During the night Moorehead heard about Pearl Harbor. The off-again on-again desert war had left newsmen distrustful of press claims in Cairo of "Rommel Surrounded," or "Rommel in Rout," or now, "Germans Desperately Trying to Escape British Net." The train had derailed; they spent "a freezing night" on a siding, then managed to complete the trip in a hospital plane off to pick up more wounded. As they rode along the coast road from the airstrip they realized that the shape of the battle had altered once more—at least until the Germans dug in and restocked. What they saw suggested rout. It was the price Rommel paid to slip his army away to fight another day.

At Gambut, east of Tobruk, they came upon an abandoned German tank base, with tents complete to concrete floors and electric lights, canvas baths and still-ticking alarm clocks, and Bakelite Afrika Korps-issue containers reminiscent of good hotels—"filled with buttons and cotton and thread, endless bottles of mouthwash, eye lotion, body powder, toothpaste, liquid soap, water purifiers, headache powders, ointments, hair oils and shampoos, even a chocolate that was supposed to 'pep you up' according to the label. (I tried some, nothing happened.)" There were "neat little cooking stoves with telescoping pots and pans" in a well-stocked field kitchen, and "thousands of pairs of woollen gloves and underclothing, stockings, sweaters, shirts, tunics and caps. . . . It was a profusion the people of Germany have not seen for years and although much of the stuff was ersatz it was warm and well made." Moorehead plucked some things without realizing that what he saw presaged a long war. The Wehrmacht had all of Europe as supplier.

The chief prize was the tank workshop, bedded in concrete and equipped under canvas with precision instruments and spare parts. Thirty tanks still waited for repair. A few smoldered, but the Germans had run out of time to render all of them useless. It was clear from the high tide—the camp abutted the coast—that soldiers had run to the sea to throw maps and papers away. The Mediterranean had thrown them back. Some letters and paper debris remained in the tents, including the Afrika Korps desert paper *The Oasis*, a sophisticated production compared to the *Tobruk Truth*. It included an incomplete serial story, "The Heroes of Hellfire Pass," news of successes in Russia, and exhortations that it would be a humiliating thing if Germans on other fronts were let down by the Afrika Korps. "For some reason the writers insisted that the fall of Leningrad had taken place. (Rommel . . . had officially circulated the news that Moscow had fallen.)"

The "scarred white village" of Tobruk was no showplace. "The sand was full of shrapnel and broken bits of metal. . . . You could distinguish the men of Tobruk from the other[, relieving,] soldiers. Their clothing, their skin, and especially their faces were stained the same colour as the earth. They moved slowly and precisely with an absolute economy of effort. . . . They seemed to fit perfectly into the landscape." Well fed and fitted out with the latest German luxuries, Moorehead savored the victory more than did the silent veterans of the siege. That the Germans would be back, almost to the outskirts of Cairo, seemed impossible.

•

Leaving the Albergo d'Italia for the railway station to catch the noon Rome-Rapallo train, Ezra Pound was in a quandary. He was returning, as he explained with shaky confidence a few weeks later, "to seek wisdom from the ancients. I wanted to figure things out. I had a perfectly good alibi, if I wanted to play things safe. I was and am officially occupied with a new [Italian] translation of the Ta S'eu of Confucius. . . . That is, I have WORK thaaar for some years. . . . There was to face this, the SITUATION. That is to say the United States had been for months ILLEGALLY at war, through what I considered to be the criminal acts of a President whose mental condition was NOT, as far as I could see, all that could or should be desired. . . . It was obviously a mere question of hours . . . [before] the United States of America would be legally at war with the Axis."

Pound had already contacted Rome Radio, arranging time off from propagandizing ("a month clear") to settle his strategies. He had also visited a hectic American embassy, returning "indignant and discouraged," his daughter claimed. "They would not allow him on the last

Clipper out of Rome. It was reserved for American diplomats and press.
. . . If he and his family wanted to leave Europe it would have to be
by slow boat. Months on a route full of mines and torpedoes."

"Is that the way they want to get rid of me?" he exploded to Mary
Pound. Panic had precipitated his inquiry. There was no chance amid
the clamor that he would secure any priority for his family, or even
money for tickets; and he knew he was unwelcome. His "recoming to
U/S/" was out.

•

Morning newspapers in Germany gratefully moved news from Russia and Libya off the front pages. Overnight, Joseph Goebbels's Propaganda Ministry had geared up for praise of the Japanese moves in the
Pacific as a "justifiable defense measure against President Roosevelt's
machinations to enlarge the war." According to DNB, the official
German news agency, Roosevelt's designs to envelop the Far East in
war had at last been realized. "While persisting at length in dollar-
diplomacy warfare together with the Jews against the newly resurrected
Germany, President Roosevelt has deliberately pursued the policy of
spreading the war to other countries and other continents."

Germans read of "newly released" documents (prepared by Goebbels) revealing that it was Roosevelt who "instigated" Poland against
Germany in 1939, pushed France and Britain into war against Germany, and who "scrapped his oath" to keep American boys out of
overseas wars by "giving shooting orders" to the Atlantic Fleet. "Dollar
Imperialism has scored a great victory over the intelligence of the vast
majority of the American people."

According to the *Volkischer Beobachter*, organ of the Nazi Party,
Roosevelt had already "prolonged the European war," resulting in the
downfall of innocent nations such as Yugoslavia and Greece, and spread
it further "by aiding the Soviet Union."

•

Realizing that he was likely to be picked up at any time, Mazuo
Kato had gone home to his apartment. Two FBI agents were already
waiting in the lobby to warn him that he was to inform the Bureau
any time he left the building. He assured them that he was going
nowhere—which proved to be a reasonable assumption, as his landlord

had lost no time in changing the lock on Kato's door. He managed to get a new one and, relieved to be alone again, telephoned his colleague Clark Kawakami, who told Kato that just after he had left the embassy, everyone inside was interned. Guessing that another opportunity for such indulgence might be long in coming, he took a hot bath, then went to bed. It was still dark at 5:00 A.M. when the expected rap at the door came. Two young FBI men instructed him politely to dress and go with them.

He asked for permission to shave and brush his teeth. They followed him into the tiny bathroom to make sure that he had no plans to slash his wrists or cut his throat. One asked if he had any weapons and accepted his word that he had none. Kato wondered whether he should pack his belongings, and was told that was unnecessary—a thought that disturbed him greatly when he sat in the rear of an unmarked sedan and wondered whether he was being taken for the kind of American-style gangland "ride" so graphically depicted in George Raft movies. He kept his fingers on the door handle, in case he might need to fling himself into the street.

On K Street near 15th the car stopped, and in an FBI office Kato answered a few identification questions and was brought a roll and coffee. It was the beginning of internment.

·

Although most casualties had been brought in by eleven in the morning, nearly twelve hours later all the hospitals on Oahu still had emergency surgery to perform. Surgical teams worked through the night and into the 8th. At Schofield Barracks, Leonard Heaton would wield his scalpel for twenty-four hours, pausing only long enough to perform some of the administrative duties abandoned to him by the vanished Colonel Canning.

For Dr. John Moorhead and his improvised civilian staff at Tripler General, *clean* had replaced *sterile*. All sterile packs had long been exhausted. Autoclaves could not keep up with demand. Instruments and gloves were boiled. Blood was running short despite queues of volunteers willing to give it. Many wounded, remembered medic John T. Snyder, who had begun the day driving an ambulance, were so badly injured "that limbs were just hanging or so shattered that there was no hope of saving their extremities. In a room off one of the surgical suites there were several large cans that were filled with arms and legs, placed there for disposal. Some of the arms still had wrist watches on the wrists and rings on the fingers."

The hospital was blacked out when Sergeant (later Major) John Walen, just off guard duty, walked in to look for his wife and infant son. He "clunked his helmet and flashlight by my bed," Phyllis Walen wrote. "He grabbed me and held me tight."

•

At the Singapore Naval Base, Gallagher and Brown went aboard the *Repulse* at 5:15 P.M. Almost at once the big ship began gliding out into waters lit by a brilliant red sunset. A very young Royal Marines lieutenant assigned to them had a scrawny black kitten, and in the exhausting heat they dangled a string for it to paw. The scene suggested a boring voyage, and Brown asked the lieutenant, "What the hell are we going to do for four days?" It didn't seem long enough to do anything significant.

"Oh," he said, "we may have something. We might even have movies. We had a picture last night aboard." Brown asked what it was, and the lieutenant said, "*Arise My Love*, with Claudette Colbert."

With the sunset lengthening the shadows of the palms on the Johore shore, the *Prince of Wales* drew up alongside. As it passed, escorted by several destroyers, the crews of each ship stood at attention. From the bridge of the *Repulse*, Captain William Tennant waved his white hat. Two men on the bridge of the *Wales* waved back—Captain Leach and Admiral Tom Phillips.

In the wardroom below was a notice tacked to the bulletin board, under the signature of Captain Tennant. "We are off to look for trouble. I expect we shall find it. We may run up against submarines, destroyers, aircraft or [other] surface ships. We are going to carry out a sweep to northward to see what we can pick up and what we can roar up. We must all be on our toes. For the two months past the ship has felt that she has been deprived of her fair share of hitting the enemy. . . . There is every possibility that things are going to change completely."

O'Dowd Gallagher copied the entire message in the curious powder-based fluid given to him on board. Hurrying to the naval base he had forgotten his ink bottle, and was offered an Admiralty concoction guaranteed not to run even if his paper became wet.

From his office window at the base, O. W. Phillips, Chief Engineer (later a rear admiral) for the station, had watched the ships leave, and "a deep sense of foreboding" came over him. After the noon strategy session Sir Tom had looked in to say that he was taking the fleet to sea, and requested Phillips (no kin) to work closely with the chief of staff, Rear Admiral Arthur Palliser, to "keep the pot a'boiling." Now O. W. Phillips, a veteran of battleship service in the Great War, could only think of Coronel—the November 1, 1914, battle in which the fleet of Admiral Sir Christopher Cradock, sailing from the Atlantic into the Pacific to hunt down Admiral Graf von Spee's squadron heading southeastward from the Carolines, was met and mauled. Cradock lost his two biggest ships—and his life.

Phillips turned to his secretary, Commissioned Engineer Albert Wall, and asked, "Wall, do you know any Latin tags?"

"A few, Sir," said Wall; "which one are you thinking of?"

Quos Deus vult perdere, primus dementat," said Phillips. "Those whom the Gods wish to destroy, they first make mad. I think Tom Phillips is going up the east coast of Malaya."

He felt that he had to unburden himself to someone else about it before it was too late, and walked down to Palliser's office. Palliser had been his naval college classmate at Dartmouth.

"I advised him to go," said Palliser.

"That's just too bad," Phillips said, unable to contain himself.

"Do you want to spread grief and amazement?" Palliser reproached.

As the capital ships passed Changi Signal Station at the eastern end of the island, Sir Tom Phillips was handed a radiogram over the signature of Air Vice Marshal Pulford: "REGRET FIGHTER PROTECTION IMPOSSIBLE."

"Well," Phillips shrugged, "we must get on with it."

•

At the Naval Ministry in Tokyo, Admiral Wenneker discovered that the Japanese knew that the *Prince of Wales* had left Singapore, "probably to disrupt landing at Singora," almost as soon as the big ship had lifted its gangplank. Congratulating Captain Nakamura on behalf of the German embassy, Wenneker learned nothing of what the Japanese planned to do about the *Prince of Wales*, but Captain Maeda was assigned to brief him daily on operations, and Wenneker discovered the Navy's disappointment that no aircraft carriers had been in port at Pearl Harbor. Nevertheless, said Nakamura, solemnly, "As from today, Japan has entered the greatest epoch in the whole of its history."

Returning to the embassy, Wenneker found a cable for him from the Admiralty in Berlin. A raider, "Ship 45," had returned safely, preceded by two prizes seized at sea. "Ship 16," while supplying a submarine, had fallen victim to the *Devonshire*. And "Ship 41," which had sunk the *Sydney*, had "perished itself."

•

South of Taipo Market was a footpath along the harbor that led to Taipo-Ku, a route along which Major Grey's Punjabis, defending Hong Kong, had fallen back. Placing his men along the high ground overlooking the water, he waited for the enemy. The narrow road funneled the Japanese into marching formation, and they proceeded into machine gun and rifle fire. Then Grey's men disappeared to re-form farther south. At 6:00 P.M. the exhausted Japanese approached a causeway, with sea on both sides. They had walked thirty miles since dawn and had been up all night as well. With mule trains bringing up the rear, they began crossing. Again Grey's men swept the road with gunfire. Bolting mules and overturned wagons added to the confusion, and to the suggestion that it was a primitive Balkan war rather than the era of the airplane and tank. But the Japanese kept coming. At 6:30 the Punjabis blew up the railway tunnel south of Taipo and fell farther back to the mythical safety of the Gin Drinkers Line.

Times reporter Colin MacDonald, "Our Special Correspondent" to London newspaper readers, groped his way through the up-and-down streets of blacked-out Hong Kong. In the blue-lit dimness of the commodore's office in the naval dockyard he met a Mr. Wint of the British embassy in Chungking. MacDonald had flown out to file dispatches, evading Chinese censorship; Wint was on diplomatic business. Now both were trying to leave by whatever circuitous route. "You have a good chance," said the commodore, shaking their hands. His chances were a good deal less.

Encountering MacDonald in the Peninsula Hotel, refuge for frustrated air passengers, Dorothy Jenner discovered that he had found a way to exit Hong Kong. There were tons of good stories to file from the colony, but she wanted out. Everything seemed hopeless, and she had already experienced a week of its desperate prewar gaiety since flying in with him from Chungking. She remembered the "few tunnels" just being dug for air-raid shelters. "The nice man who took me on the tour blathered on about, 'We'll have the toilets here and the rice storage somewhere there.' He hadn't a clue really. By comparison with the tunnels honeycombing the hills round Chungking it was all so amateurish. I hadn't the heart to tell him that they were at least six months too late. . . . He was rather like an over-earnest boy scout and he approached the war as he would a weekend camp."

She begged MacDonald to take her with him. Although Dorothy Jenner's wiles were legendary, honed by decades of employing her buxom charms on susceptible males from Rudolph Valentino to British millionaires and minor Continental royalty, "he [MacDonald] was horrified at the suggestion and informed me brusquely that no British naval vessel had ever put to sea with a woman aboard. The fact that these were exceptional times and called for exceptional measures didn't seem to cut any ice with him at all. . . . I thought the best thing I could do was get back over to the Hong Kong side. The Japanese had already walked into the New Territories and I didn't want to be the first European to greet them."

MacDonald and Wint boarded the *Scout* in gathering darkness. The destroyer lifted anchor at 6:30, following the *Thanet* down the harbor and through the mine field into heavy seas. Beyond the Kowloon hills the sky was lit by flashes of distant guns. Tense and watchful, the crew imagined the outlines of a Japanese cruiser, but they were under orders to take no offensive action and to arrive intact. "Many vague shapes were seen flitting by in the darkness," MacDonald reported later to the *Times* from an unidentified place that was Tarkan, Borneo, "most of them Chinese junks which we dodged at high speed."

•

In the Oahu darkness, Bess Tittle and her three-month-old son, David, were being evacuated from the Schofield Barracks area, where they had been crowded with other service wives and children for alleged safety. Dinner had been the enlisted men's fried chicken. As they gathered for the bus convoy to somewhere, clutching suitcases and aluminum sterilizers loaded with cans of milk and baby bottles, a jeep pulled up. It was her husband, Norman, commander of a radar company only since the day before. He had been at Fort Shafter through the raid and into the night.

"What luck to find you so quickly," he said. "I'm on my way to the tunnel."

After a parting kiss Captain Tittle left for Aliamanu Crater, General Short's not-so-secret emergency command post.

The line of evacuee vehicles crept slowly toward the Wheeler Field gate, where buses halted, then began backing and turning awkwardly to avoid bomb debris. The buses moved forward in the slow lane. Army vehicles with blue headlights whirred past on the shoulder of the road and in the other lane. "Look!" someone cried. "A moonbow!" The women craned their necks to look at the phenomenon—in Hawaii, at least, a sign of good luck. Below, stretched out before them, was the panorama of Pearl Harbor, where the tilting superstructures of partly sunken ships were backlit by burning oil. It seemed to Mrs. Tittle a scene out of Dante. The horror of it kept them speechless: "We simply did not believe what we saw."

Near midnight, they stopped at what appeared in the dark to be a school. "In the eerie light of masked flashlights, we surveyed the scene. The floors were covered with mattresses occupied by women and children. A cacophony of low, anxious voices, children's wails, and soothing authoritative directives met our ears."

"There is plenty of room upstairs," a woman in a Red Cross uniform announced. No one seemed interested in the invitation. They were there to keep out of danger, and "an upper story," Bess Tittle thought, "was not the best place to be during an air raid."

It was also near midnight when Ensign Sakamaki awoke. When he had first come to in his drifting minisub, it was already as dark above as it was below. Both crewmen wept with exhaustion and frustration. He was still in sight of Diamond Head, which was silhouetted in the moonlight. He could not navigate accurately, but he tried to set a course for the small island of Lanai, where he might be able to rendezvous with a mother sub and scuttle his unmanageable boat. When he turned on the power the sub vibrated violently without actually moving. White smoke curled up from the damaged batteries.

Nothing worked right. The sub drifted onto another reef. The two men lifted the hatch, set the fuse to blow up the boat, and jumped into the powerful waves. The sub failed to sink; Sakamaki failed to drown. At 7:07 A.M. on the beach near Kaneohe Air Station, an Army sergeant would pick up Sakamaki, the first Japanese prisoner of war.

TOKYO	HONG KONG	MOSCOW	MIDWAY ISLAND
8:00 P.M.	MANILA	LENINGRAD	12:00 midnight
December 8	7:00 P.M.	2:00 P.M.	December 7/8
	December 8	December 8	

HOUR 47

T OWARD EVENING, as the air grew chill, crowds that had thronged the Meiji and Yakusuni shrines in Tokyo after Tojo and Shimada had visited* began to drift away. A few voices could still be heard praying for the prompt capitulation of the enemy. Dusk had made the war real, for the government had decreed that streetlights would no longer operate at night. No one expected air raids—the home islands were far from the war—but for purposes of air defense and fire control, as well as to conserve power, lights inside houses were also to be dimmed. According to the Home Vice-Minister, such orders had to be "faithfully followed" although "the whole nation can remain undisturbed with firm faith in the Government."

As the first blackout came to Tokyo, the Navy Ministry released a communiqué about what newspapers were beginning to call the Battle of Hawaii. The American fleet had lost at least two battleships sunk and four heavily damaged; four heavy cruisers were "badly crippled"

---

* Late in the 1980s Prime Minister Yasuhiro Nakasone became the first postwar political leader to visit the Yakusuni Shrine in his official capacity, this after Hideki Tojo and the thirteen others condemned by the victors as "Class A War Criminals" had been secretly enrolled at the shrine as "martyrs."

and many smaller ships sunk or damaged. Further, an aircraft carrier was believed to have been sunk in Hawaiian waters and was identified as the *Enterprise*. The sunken capital ships were reported as the *Oklahoma* and *West Virginia*.

The estimates were partial and erroneous. Although a sub had targeted the *Enterprise*, Halsey's ship had evaded the torpedoes. In Pearl Harbor the damage was far greater than the first Japanese boasts. In one day the U.S. Navy alone had lost 2,008 men—more than in all of World War I.

Recalling the prophetic *The Great Pacific War*, retired Major General Yahei Oba, hearing the news on his radio, began an article for the next day's *Nichi Nichi* suggesting that the 1926 novel had not been sufficiently daring. "No naval expert ever dreamed that the Japanese fleet would venture to this American outpost. Even Hector Bywater predicted that the Japanese, with their present capital ships, would be incapable of dispatching their valuable men-of-war to Pearl Harbor. Bombs over Honolulu . . . sufficiently proved that nothing is impossible for the Japanese. . . . Even the German Luftwaffe did not hazard such an epochal gamble. Indeed, this was an unexpected and bold adventure defying any other sort of boldness."

Having marched back from the Palace grounds to the Tokyo Kaikan, their bellicose banners still raised, the businessmen of the Co-operative Council heard more speeches, then bowed heads for a closing ceremony. Kōtarō Takamura went home by subway train. Feeling contemplative, he walked up the slope of nearby Komagome Heights in the darkness. At eight o'clock the sky was already bright with stars, "close and glaring. One, which looked like Jupiter, outshone the others and appeared to oscillate vaguely as if floating in ether." Returning home, where he lived alone, he put his day into a poem, from "ancestors' voices" and his trembling at listening to the rescript, to his willingness to sacrifice himself for the Emperor and "that night . . . when Jupiter shone large." Perhaps Mars would have been more appropriate, but Takamura remained honest to his material.

•

By early evening in Hong Kong, the world had totally changed. Shops had closed one after another, or sold things behind half-closed doors. The prices of everything edible, especially rice, had escalated. Two Chinese newspaper extras had appeared, and Kianghai Yau, who managed the Yik Kee soft-drink shop in Shaukeiwan, watched his clientele depart earlier than usual, buying extra packs of cigarettes before abandoning their chess boards. A young man who had taken over the tiny business from his father, who had recently died, Yau was afraid. "We closed the store," he remembered, "by fitting thick planks together to block the doorway, leaving the central door half open." From the back room, where employees took their meals, they could see patrons enter. Yau sat down with Uncle Nam, an uncle only because of his age, who was cook and general handyman as well as "honest cashier."

"There was a loud noise outside. I and Uncle Nam went to the door to have a look, and saw a gang of men gathering outside. They divided themselves into smaller groups and began knocking at the doors of each shop. These were gangsters making use of the crisis to blackmail shops for protection fees." After strongarming payment, they wrote boldly in chalk on the doors "XX XX House"—their code for "protected shop." No one was eager to pay, "but there was no way out under such circumstances. Strangely, the policemen disappeared while this happened."

"Just wait until they come here," said Uncle Nam. "I won't let them get away so easily."

"Uncle Nam, let it be," said Yau. "Don't irritate them. We can only bargain."

"Uncle Nam," pleaded the shop assistant, Ah Ching, "better good far off than evil at hand! Although you may know how to fight, they have a lot of people . . . ."

Before Ching could finish, five men up to no good marched into the shop. Nam confronted one, "a man of about thirty with a big nose."

"Ah Sen," scowled Uncle Nam, "even you are involved in this business?"

The man with the large nose appeared embarrassed, and looked away toward his companions. One of the others, "with thick brow and large eyes," caught the signal. He patted Nam's shoulder briskly and said, loudly and unconvincingly, "Sorry we disturbed you! My brothers were thirsty, and we wanted to have a drink." He looked in the direction of the bottles of soft drinks in their wooden boxes.

While Nam stared at them, Yau rushed to the bottles and offered lemonade and root beer. The men tilted back their heads and poured the liquid down. Then, leaving ahead of the others, the big-nosed thug joined the gang in the street. The shop crew watched silently. When the others drained what obviously were drinks on the house, they left together. The thick-browed ruffian of the group stopped to chalk letters on the door proclaiming that Yik Kee Shop was protected. Inside, Uncle Nam explained that he once coached martial arts in Shamshuipo, and had taught Ah Sen. "This fellow often got himself into trouble. . . . Once on the road I saved him. He would have died long ago. . . ."

It was dusk, when the night markets usually became crowded, but the streets were emptying. Yau felt restless. He ought to go home to his mother and the younger children, he said. Uncle Nam warned against it. The roads were unsafe. Then the street lamp at the tram stop flashed and went out, and another air-raid warning wailed. In the gloom, Nam turned on a light that was shielded by layers of black cloth. He and Ah Ching set out a chessboard, and began to play under the dim glow.

It was nearly dark when Liu Hung Sak left the *Kwang Ming Po* newspaper office to try to get a boat from Hong Kong back to Kowloon. First he took a crowded bus to Happy Valley, well out of his way, staggering under his load of rice. He had a friend there who secured news no one else seemed to have. En route, Sak ran into his neighbor Cheungkiang Fan, then another friend, Hansen Chen. They decided to have dinner together in the Wise Man Café in the basement of the Hong Kong Telephone Building. "Since morning, the small cafés had either closed down or inflated their prices. The larger restaurants like Wise Man would not blackmail their regular clients. The building was also safe from air raids. . . . Few lights were on. Business was very bad. There was a sad and gloomy air about. . . . We were the only customers in civilian clothes."

Over rice bowls they chatted about the war, Chen remarking that he saw "no need to go away." Sak blamed his own surprise on the "groundless propaganda" by which the British encouraged local optimism.

They emerged into Hong Kong's first "real blackout." The streets "were quiet like a city of the dead." Sak felt his way along, still carrying his sacks of rice and depending on his hearing and sense of direction. ("I seemed to be the only human being in the street.") Turning into Wellington Street he collided with a hurrying stranger who cried "Oh!"

but kept going. Sak felt a painful bump begin to swell above his eyes, and struggled back to his blacked-out newspaper office for treatment before trying to find out whether the Star Ferry was still running.

•

With the coming of darkness in the Philippines, defensive preparations around the perimeter of Nielson Field ceased. The regimental commander of the 57th Infantry, Colonel George C. Clarke, was the only man in his mostly Filipino unit who had any combat experience—in the trenches of France in 1918. Emotional and imaginative, Lieutenant John Olson thought, Clarke was "prone to exaggerate the risks and to see danger in every shadow." Every safeguard that could be taken against sabotage or against parachute troop landings had to be taken. (Not a single paratrooper landed in Luzon, although it was an *idée fixe* with Calle Victoria.)

Lights were forbidden unless completely screened. Smoking was prohibited after dark. Everyone was to sleep fully dressed, although gasmasks and helmets did not have to be worn if they were placed beside the sleeper to be instantly available. Four-hour watches were instituted, and soldiers with foxholes already dug were required to sleep in them. Listening and watching posts were established, and each man on such duty was equipped with a whistle to warn of enemy paratroops. If the men were not keyed up by the onset of war, Clarke's precautions ensured a jumpy state of excitement as everyone prepared for a long night of alarms, from the Guadelupe Gate to the Pasay Road and the Pasig River.

•

At dinner with other Chinese officials in Chungking, preceded by much celebratory drink, Pao-huang Tang and his wife, Rosalie, saw nothing but "a circle of beaming faces." Referring to the failed American attempt to negotiate with Nomura and Kurusu, one desk soldier crowed, "America will no longer be able to play a double game." The Chinese, Rosalie Tang remembered, laughed at the gullible Americans. "For it was a Sunday, the week-end, when the 'fat boys,' as the Americans were nicknamed by the Japanese, had been caught. 'They were too busy drinking and whoring,' cried a very drunk Chinese brigadier, raising his glass to toast the future. Now America would *have* to support Chiang, and that meant U.S. dollars in the pockets of the officials, in the pockets of army commanders, and guns to Hu Tsungnan, for the coming war against [the Communists in] Yenan." For that, they understood, Chiang Kaishek would have to put aside his predilection for the Axis powers, and declare war on Germany—and even Japan.*

•

As daylight was failing, a Punjabi force from the 6th Brigade of the 11th Indians, riding Bren carriers, halted to set up defensive positions. They were ten miles across the Thai border, on the road north from Kitra, above Alor Star, toward Singora. The Punjabis had no idea that moving south on the same road were advance units of Lieutenant Colonel Shizuo Saeki's regiment from the Japanese 5th Division. When his advance tank and troop carriers blundered into the Punjabis and were sprayed by antitank crews, three tanks were disabled, but infantrymen behind them leaped from their trucks and, numerically superior, outflanked the Indians.

Under severe mortar fire, the British withdrew, the Punjabis destroying bridges as they retreated. It was the end of what was left of Matador. In darkness, no air cover for the Punjabis was possible. By day or night, there was no longer any effective air support anywhere in Malaya.

•

Siberian troops had been identified among the dozens of fresh divisions before Moscow. They were well booted and clothed. "I would never have believed," Guderian was writing home, "that a really brilliant military position could be so bloodied up in two months." From General Hoepner's 4th Army on the southern wing to von Kluge's 9th Army to the north, Russian forces moved, to Guderian's amazement, "with unprecedented speed and in great numbers." He hoped to defend his new "short line" with "what is left of my forces. The Russians are pursuing us closely and we must expect misfortunes to occur. Our casualties, particularly from sickness and frostbite, have been bad. . . . The loss of vehicles and guns owing to frost has been far greater than was feared. We are making what use we can of sleds. . . . I am not

---

* There was surreptitious cooperation between the Kuomintang and the Japanese, Chiang hoarding his energies for the inevitable confrontation with Mao Zedong. But Chiang purchased his American largesse with reluctant declarations of war on Germany and Japan on December 9.

thinking of myself," he closed guardedly, "but rather about our Germany, and that is why I am frightened."

Guderian ordered more of his tanks blown up where they lay frozen in the mud, to deny them to the Russians.

"We may now think of changing over to the final winter positions," Halder wrote from Rastenburg. At the same time, Guderian was deploring, "If a decision had been taken at the proper time to break off and settle down for the winter in a habitable line suitable for the defence, we should have been in no danger." Halder's bland comment foreshadowed Hitler's Directive 39, announcing that the "severe winter weather which has come up surprisingly early in the East, and the consequent difficulties in bringing up supplies, compel us to abandon immediately all major offensive operations and go over to the defensive."

"The decision was just in time," Keitel thought after the war, "to avert the worst consequences. . . . Hitler was at last brought to realize that we could not check [the Russians], and gave reluctant permission for a short withdrawal. . . . We had been badly misled about the quantity of reinforcements that the Russians could produce. They had hidden their resources all too well." That the withdrawal had to be staged, rather than headlong, was a decision by Hitler that "correctly realized," Keitel concluded, "that to withdraw even by only a few miles, was synonymous with writing off all our heavy armaments, in which case the troops themselves could be considered lost. . . . Without heavy armament they were absolutely defenceless, quite apart from the fact that artillery, anti-tank guns and vehicles were irreplaceable." If the army were to withdraw without weapons, it would "suffer the same fate as Napoleon had in 1812."

For the Wehrmacht and its proud professionals, the events culminating on the 7th had been close to catastrophic; for Hitler, the circumstances had made possible his absolute control of his generals. Brauchitsch's resignation, offered on the 7th, had not been accepted, but it would be on the 21st. Henceforth, Hitler would be his own commander-in-chief. He would order an end to a situation where generals raced each other to the telephone link to Wolfschanze to complain about the other's withdrawal jeopardizing their flanks. The war was too brutal and too big to be left to proud professionals. By Christmas, nearly forty senior commanders, with ranks as high as field marshal, would be relieved and sent home. Hitler would keep track of every detail; and Junker dominance of the Army was officially as well as effectively over.

•

Although at Hitler's headquarters General Walter Warlimont saw "an ecstasy of rejoicing" as the news of Pearl Harbor spread, it was shared by few generals. Most were more concerned with the withdrawals grudgingly authorized by Directive 39 than with a distant expansion of the war. Army Group Central, von Bock reported by telephone to Halder, "is not anywhere in a position to check a concentrated attack." Halder noted "Grave concern about Kluge's right wing and Guderian's left wing. . . . Decision to withdraw involves loss of enormous quantities of material. . . . Unless we can form reserves, we face the danger of a serious defeat." In Libya, he added, not realizing that Rommel had not waited for orders, "Rommel must call a halt and fall back."

"Due to the onset of Russian winter," the High Command announced without further explanation, "operations in the East are being curtailed. On most parts of the East Front only local engagements are taking place." In the center, Halder confided to his diary, "The Yakhroma front has fallen back without trouble, and so has freed small reserves for liquidation of the situation at Klin, which is now in progress. On the whole, the desired shortening of the front has been accomplished." The confession was full of loaded words, each of which spelled withdrawal. East of Kalinin, he noted, "we have nothing back of the line."

Immediately after his staff conference, where he had offered no thoughts about the new war, Hitler and a large entourage, including Keitel and Jodl, entrained for Berlin. Since the Führer had left no "official instructions" behind, Walter Warlimont was puzzled. Nothing had been said about "the entry of our Far Eastern ally," or that the Japanese successes put no new pressure on Russia, where it was urgently needed, yet drew in the United States. And if Hitler were saving such utterances for a public statement in Berlin, he was already preceded there by the head of the Press Section of the Foreign Ministry, who, with Hitler barely aboard his special train, had called in foreign newsmen to declare that President Roosevelt, "the instrument of negation and evil," had embarked upon a policy of indirectly meddling in the European war and keeping Japan out of the war until he was ready to attack Japan. Now, Dr. Paul Schmidt judged, "the Shylock in the White House" had received the proper response, the very one American mothers had worried would happen and against which cool-headed anti-interventionist congressmen had warned. "The world," said Schmidt, "has been called to arms."

A happy Ambassador Oshima was preparing for a one o'clock appointment with Ribbentrop to clarify Germany's position, diplomatic language for pressing Germany to make good its offer to join the war against the U.S. Ribbentrop knew exactly why Oshima was coming and had already spoken with Hitler by telephone. He had no doubt that the Führer would be declaring war; it was only a matter of timing. Hitler had already ordered Dönitz's U-boats to sink American ships without warning, and he was returning to Berlin for a ceremonial war message.

Since Japan had done the attacking, Ribbentrop had pointed out to Hitler, the letter of the Axis accord did not require Germany to join against the U.S. On the other end of the line, Hitler was silent for a long moment. "If we don't stand on the side of Japan," he said, finally, "the Pact is politically dead. But that is not the main reason. . . . The United States is already shooting against our ships. They have [already] been a forceful factor in this war and through their actions have already created a situation of war [against us.]" Besides, Hitler knew, the American "Victory Plan" had confessed to such military weakness as to be unable to take on Germany until July 1943. Why wait for that?

•

Claude Letulle waited as long as he dared before retrieving the air-dropped leaflet he had secreted under a rock. French prisoners of war at the camp in Poland called Rawa—a stockade servicing an open-pit coal mine at Rawa Mazowiecka, east of Lodz—had been watchful since a warning had appeared on the wall of Barracks 34. Scrawled in French by a despised collaborator they hoped someday to kill, and signed with the name of the SS *Oberstrumführer* of the camp, it threatened, "ANY PRISONER CAUGHT PICKING UP OR HOLDING AN ENEMY LEAFLET WILL BE SHOT."

"We were excited," Letulle remembered. "Something was happening. We had to get one of those papers. They had to be coming from Russia because it was close by and had planes that could easily reach us. We wondered whether the Americans were joining the war. . . ."

Any time the Germans were nervous it meant good news for us, and I began to gain confidence that someone could subdue them."

The day before, a Russian plane had approached "so low that it almost touched the trees," and SS guards began shooting to keep prisoners still as thousands of leaflets fluttered down, "a good many within reach, but we couldn't move while soldiers and their dogs watched." Gaining an unexpected Sabbath rest while the leaflets were gathered up, the prisoners watched to see if any were overlooked. Letulle spotted one, which he hid under a rock when they resumed work.

Although they had learned to sleep in the unheated barracks where the walls, covered with bedbugs, seemed in motion, after marching back through the entrance to the camp for the night under the "ARBEIT MACHT FREI" piety the Nazis erected above the barbed wire, sleep, this time, was difficult. They had been stripped and searched for contraband as they returned their tools, but nothing had been found. Now, waiting past the morning hours for the light to weaken—the days were short—Letulle helped a man move the rock to recover the leaflet while, by prearranged signal, another laborer screamed in feigned pain.

As guards rushed to the shamming prisoner, Letulle moved away to empty his wheelbarrow, in the process stuffing the paper into his shirt. Since they had been searched before, and the area combed, he risked returning to barracks with the leaflet, printed in French and Polish:

> PRISONERS, DO NOT ABANDON HOPE. THE GERMANS ARE NOT AS GREAT AS THEY THOUGHT. THEY HAVE NOT SUCCEEDED IN TAKING MOSCOW AND THEY WILL NEVER DOMINATE RUSSIA. WITHIN A FEW MONTHS WE WILL OVERTHROW GERMANY AND FREE YOU. THEN WE WILL TURN YOUR EXECUTIONERS OVER TO YOU FOR JUDGMENT.

In the darkness later, Letulle cautiously passed the leaflet around the silent barracks. "Afterwards I tore it up and we each swallowed a piece."

•

On a routine patrol—the war news had changed nothing in their sector—Squadron Leader Janusz led his 315 Polish Squadron, in Spitfires, over the English Channel. When he saw two Messerschmidt

109Fs about to attack from the direction of the high morning sun, he turned toward them. They disappeared beyond the French coast, but they had already done some damage. A Spitfire could be seen in the water. The pilot, who had bailed out, was climbing into his dinghy. "We patrolled over the pilot for a short time," Janusz reported, "and then set course for England. I then saw two Me's attacking the sqdn from behind and above and I turned to engage. The Me saw me and turning away went into a dive." Janusz followed, got within two hundred yards, and fired a cannon burst. Then he closed again and loosed a second burst. "After that I saw black smoke from the cockpit and gave him a third burst as he was going down steeply into the sea from about 1,500 feet."

Although Janusz had to break away because of another German in view from the port side, he saw the splash of water and returned contentedly to base. Another pilot, he found, had bagged a Focke-Wulf 190, and Flight Lieutenant Czcykowski reported a second Me 109 going "straight into the sea." But Flying Officer Grosnoski, in the dinghy, had disappeared. Pilots were often machine-gunned as they floated helplessly, just as Janusz had made sure that the Nazi airman he had cannoned even as the fighter was going down would never climb out.

•

Felix Morley's telephone rang well before sunrise. He assumed some business had arisen affecting Quaker and pacifist Haverford College, of which he had just become president. The unhappy caller was his old newspaperman friend Kyoshi K. Kawakami, whom he had known since 1925 and who represented in Washington the *Hochi Shimbun* of Tokyo. The scholarly, courtly Kawakami, who had an American wife and American-born children, had been arrested the night before and hustled into internment at the Gloucester Point immigration station in New Jersey, across the Delaware from Philadelphia. Morley was his closest contact. "Could I visit him and provide the only two comforts the old journalist really wanted—a head of lettuce and a copy of *Les Misérables?*"

Three years later, Joe Jordan, one of the students Morley had taken to meet Kawakami in order "to see the war in perspective," reminded him of the visit in a letter from Okinawa, where Jordan had just landed with the Marines. By then Jordan had seen a different war than Morley knew, and would be killed in action there on Japan's doorstep.

•

When twangy-voiced, bespectacled Harry Truman got back to Washington, it was 5:30 A.M., and still dark. At 6:00, when he opened his front door, he found his wife Bess "up getting breakfast." It had been a struggle getting back. On a political trip to Missouri, he was at the Pennant Hotel in Columbia, he told his cousin Ethel, when "the boy who drove me down . . . called me from Cross Timbers . . . and told me the Japs had bombed Honolulu." By the time that Bess had telephoned about a joint session of Congress the next day, Truman was exploring ways to fly back. "I had no car and no dinner," he wrote to Ethel later, but he explained his predicament to the manager of the small airport across the street from the hotel, who offered to fly Truman to St. Louis. It took 40 minutes for the first 130 miles. Then he attempted whatever connections there were to Washington. Failing hops to Chicago and Memphis, he managed to get the 11:00 P.M. flight to Pittsburgh when someone was bumped to seat a United States senator.

In the sturdy TWA DC-3 he sat up through the night and further stops, listening to the news on the plane's radio. Arriving at 3:30 A.M., Truman waited in the dreary Pittsburgh terminal for the Washington connection. Marking time also were Senator Dennis Chavez of New Mexico, Senator James J. Davis of Pennsylvania, "and Curley Brooks, the great Republican isolationist from Chicago." Newly elected, "fat, curly haired" C. Wayland Brooks, so Truman told Ethel, was an American Legion stalwart, "has a synthetic blond wife, and is a most important *Chicago Tribune* senator. He looked as if he'd swallowed a hot stove, and that's the way all those anti-preparedness boys looked the next day. It wasn't because they'd been up all night getting there either."

Crawling into bed, Truman told Bess to wake him at ten for the Declaration of War session at the Capitol.

At the White House after a few hours' sleep, the President was awakened "before the sun" to confront the avalanche of messages and decisions that had to be made. Breakfast was black coffee. His war message had to be reviewed in the light of the new day. Directives had to be issued. Dozens of staff had to be seen, from General Marshall to Arthur Prettyman, Roosevelt's valet. The President may have looked forward least to Prettyman's visit at eleven, when Roosevelt had to be prepared for his address to Congress. He would have to stand, and to offer the illusion of walking into the House chamber on the arms of aides. A President disabled by physical infirmity could not be seen that way when the nation was mobilizing for war. Appearance was reality.

He would be, he knew, rolled back from the Oval Office to the family quarters on the second floor. There, Arthur Prettyman would help him onto his bed, lift his legs, and lay the polio-limp limbs out straight. Off would come the trousers and shoes. On would go twenty or more pounds of stainless steel leg braces, with shoes fixed at the bottoms, and straps and pads for the lifeless knees, and thigh bands with buckles. (The bottoms of the braces were black, blending into the shoes and socks.) Then striped morning trousers were slipped over, and the President pulled into a sitting position so that he could be eased back into his wheelchair, and his cutaway coat put over his shoulders. For standing, and the suggestion of walking, the knee braces would be locked; he would be lifted erect by Colonel Edmund W. Starling, head of the White House Secret Service, and eldest son James Roosevelt, a Marine captain. Propped on one side by a cane, the other shoulder supported by James, he would enter the House Rotunda, the audience standing as soon as the doorkeeper announced, "Mr. Speaker [of the House], the President of the United States." Then would come the address asking for a declaration of war against Japan, America's response to what he would call, memorably, a day of "infamy."

Reminding Churchill not to jump the gun, the President prepared a cable to be sent via the American embassy, "I think it best on account of psychology here that Britain's declaration of war be withheld until after my speech at 12:30 Washington time. . . . Any time after that would be wholly satisfactory. Delighted to know of message to De Valera." Overnight via Winant had come the text of an appeal to the Irish prime minister, attempting to turn the half-American (but fanatically anti-English) Eamon de Valera from a neutrality beneficial to the Germans. "Now is your chance. Now or never! A nation once again! I am very ready to meet you at any time." But the old revolutionary would be unmoved.

In a message-drafting mood, the Prime Minister prepared another, to the Japanese ambassador in London, declaring that a state of war existed between Great Britain and Japan. He signed it, "I have the honour to be with high consideration, Sir, your obedient servant,

Winston S. Churchill." Later he explained the diplomatic close by saying that if you are going to kill a man, you might as well be polite to him. It had not yet become clear to anyone except, perhaps, Churchill, that whatever reverses were to come for his side, the Axis partners, on their first day as joint combatants, had lost the war.

THE
DAY
AFTER

December 8

"If seven maids with seven mops
  Swept it for half a year.
Do you suppose," the Walrus said,
  "That they could get it clear?"
"I doubt it," said the Carpenter,
  And shed a bitter tear.

—LEWIS CARROLL,
  Through the Looking-Glass (1871)

A GROTESQUE PARODY of the servants sweeping up after a rowdy party, the immediate aftermath of December 7 suggests a long day. It appears to begin on the 8th with the formality of a simple declaration of war. It closes on the 11th with another, hysterical, one.

No one knew how many seamen were dead or missing at Pearl Harbor. Trucks with amplifiers crawled around the ruined docks, instructing crews from abandoned ships like the *Arizona* and *Oklahoma* to muster at designated places to be recorded and counted. Men in hospitals, scattered on informal duty on other vessels, asleep where they could find shelter, or entombed in sunken ships, remained temporarily or permanently missing.

At dawn on the 8th, launches from the hospital ship *Solace* began scanning the oil-slicked water for human remains. At Aiea Landing, corpsmen began the grisly task of matching flesh to names. A medic on the *Solace*, James F. Anderson, was out "on the awful job of going out alongside the battleships and picking up the remains of the bodies that had floated to the surface." Crews tried "to salvage any part of a human body that could be identified," usually through fingerprints or dental work. "It was a gruesome job but we had to do it—the detail was assigned to us. The parts were brought to the [naval] morgue, where we would clean them of oil and try to identify them." The Marine sergeant overseeing a doctor and his detail watched the squad recoil from the horrific duty and quietly said, "Men, this is war, and the doc here is your officer. You do as he says. If you don't, you can be shot."

The Army was attempting its own identifications, preparing a list of 211 descriptions at Hickam Field alone. Among them, Lieutenant David Denver Gray noted "Case #4. Charred remains. No identifications. No personal belongings." And "Case #188. Badly mangled and decomposed remains. Identification impossible." Unnumbered and last was "Japanese aviator—identity unknown."

At Hickam a B-17, with its landing gear collapsed and its engines broken from its big wings, sprawled across a landing strip; another, flung about by a bomb, raised its tail section gauntly outside Hangar 5. The hulk of a Flying Fortress was a hundred yards away. At Wheeler Field, where 151 Air Corps planes, including 75 new P-40s, had been parked wing to wing, bulldozers pushed the wreckage into large piles for disposal. Ground crews filled in the craters in runways. At Bellows, as at other airfields on Oahu, the same clearing task was under way, often complicated by the search for charred bodies.

To the northwest, *Kido Butai* steamed away without encountering a single American ship or plane. Admiral Nagumo kept to a withdrawal speed of 25 knots until turning to the west 550 miles above Midway. Then, to conserve fuel, he reduced speed to 15 knots. Eventually he would detach two of his six carriers, and two destroyers, to cover the capture of Wake Island. Nagumo had worried about meeting an American carrier force, and counted himself lucky. The fortunate ones were the Americans. Outnumbered and outgunned, with only two active carriers between the American mainland and the Philippines, the U.S. Navy could not have afforded to lose much more. Frustration about not finding the enemy left the Navy in further gloom, but that lack of contact spared the ships that, in June, would win the Battle of Midway.

In Pearl Harbor, the search for the living continued. Chippers working away at the upturned hull of the *Oklahoma*, where faint tappings could still be heard, rescued 32 men. (Bulkhead markings later revealed that some of the 415 men who remained entombed survived until Christmas Eve, seventeen days after.) Smoke still funneled up from the crumpled *Arizona*. The salvage effort went on even as the base geared up for the war that had so taken it by surprise. A minisub was pulled from the bottom; a Zero was dragged out of the water onto the Ford Island seaplane ramp, and Seaman James Archer picked through the pilot's flight suit for identification. Where not covered by his leather helmet, his face was already gone, eaten away by crabs.

The official count at Pearl Harbor encompassed losses far beyond what Admiral Yamamoto expected to inflict, but the outcome was at odds with the facts. His Navy colleague, Admiral Onishi, had warned that a "Hawaii operation" would "put America's back up too badly" for easy compromise. Eighteen ships, eight of them battleships, were either sunk or crippled. Over 300 aircraft were destroyed or badly damaged on the ground. Yet 15 of the ships would be raised, repaired, and returned to fight; more than half of the 347 lost aircraft were obsolete. 2,403 Americans were killed; 1,178 were wounded. The dead would be avenged. "Remember Pearl Harbor!" became a motto, a battle hymn. America's back was up.

Late in the afternoon of the 8th, Hawaii time—already well into the 9th in Tokyo—Halsey's combined task force began entering Pearl Harbor, more at risk from American gunners and patrol craft than from the receding enemy. The destruction appalled him, and he loyally blamed the enemy for attacking rather than his own side for its somnolence. "Before we're through with 'em," he vowed, "the Japanese language will be spoken only in hell."

Aboard the *Salt Lake City*, Communications Officer Church A. Chappell noted in his war diary the return of the *Enterprise* and its escorts late on the afternoon of the 8th. What followed was an evening filled with fear and false reports. "Machine gun fire all around ship and station. Red rockets fired. Beware of drifting mines, one-man subs which come to surface and throw hand grenades . . . , spies swimming in harbor . . . , landings at Fort Weaver." Even the harbor pilot bringing them in was "full of doleful rumors."

Captain Ellis M. Zacharias spoke to the cruiser's crew by intercom to voice regret that they had to see what Pearl Harbor looked like. It had "served to give you all an entirely wrong impression." Whatever the damage, he explained, "the effect of what took place there is going to be greatly beneficial to us for many reasons. . . . There is nothing that could have consolidated public opinion and expedited our future plans of operations . . . as quickly as this did." Further, he noted, the real weapons of future war, aircraft carriers, were unscathed. "Our job right now is to protect this carrier. . . . We must not relax."

From the *Enterprise*, Halsey warned of excessive eagerness. "We are wasting too many depth charges on neutral fish." But just before dawn on the 10th an SBD from the carrier, piloted by Lieutenant Edward L. Anderson, spotted the *I-170* and dive-bombed it. Crippled, the sub remained surfaced, and a target for Lieutenant Clarence E. Dickinson's SBD, which sank it. Later in the day the *Enterprise* evaded a torpedo, and, on two successive days, the *Salt Lake City* engaged surfaced submarines with gunfire. Tag ends of *Kido Butai*, the subs left behind to hit the vessels emerging from Pearl Harbor were the least successful part of the operation.

On the morning after Pearl Harbor an urgent plea to replace destroyed aircraft was reviewed in Washington. It was one of Marshall's easiest decisions. With aid to the Philippines effectively blocked, he shipped heavy bombers instead to Hawaii. To bolster the crippled Pacific fleet, the Navy transferred three battleships and an aircraft carrier from sub patrol in the Atlantic. With 12 B-17s and 25 PBYs, an organized daily search of Hawaiian waters to a distance of 700 nautical miles in all directions began. The remaining B-17s were held on thirty minutes' warning as a strike force. The barn door was now securely locked.

By Tuesday the Willamette University football team, unable to go home to Salem, Oregon, was put on guard duty, two hours on and four off—a regimen not conducive to sleep. The women in the Willamette party found themselves volunteered as nurses' aides. It was a lark, unlike any football trip before or since, and some regretted going home.

In some places it was a quick war. Guam was indefensible, but correspondent Vincent Sheean claimed in Washington that the Navy had used its limited funds for the defense of the island to build two golf courses. Even if true, Guam would have been overrun in a few hours. At 5:45 A.M. on the 10th, west of the Date Line, with the invasion twenty-five minutes along, Governor McMillin ordered a cease-fire, sounded on three blasts of an automobile horn. The Stars and Stripes, after forty-two years, was lowered from Government House.

On the tiny Hawaiian island of Niihau, an even smaller war took

longer. The downed pilot, Shigenori Nishikaichi, had convinced
Yoshio Harada, a Japanese resident of Niihau, to join forces with him.
With machine guns pulled from the wrecked Zero, the two had turned
on the usually phlegmatic villagers. "How can you do this to us?"
demanded big Ben Kanahele, a huge Niihauan, when his wife, Ella,
was taken hostage.

"I'm afraid," explained Harada. "I don't know what will happen if
I go against the pilot."

Shot in the chest when he lunged at Nishikaichi, Kanahele seized
the pilot anyway. Grunting in pain, he lifted Nishikaichi and threw
him against a stone wall. His skull shattered. To make certain he was
dead, Kanahele drew his hunting knife and slashed Nishikaichi's throat.
Horrified, Harada broke free from Ella and pressed a shotgun against
Kanahele's stomach. Ella clutched Harada's arm and the bullet missed.
Pushing her away, Harada fired again, blowing away his own belly.

When an Army rescue team arrived the next day, the Sunday after
Pearl Harbor, they found the bodies of Nishikaichi and Harada lying
by the bloodied stone wall, stinking in the Hawaiian heat. In his home
prefecture, a monument was erected to Nishikaichi, and his exploits
were fictionalized in films and cheap novels, where he absorbed thousands of bullets while beating off waves of enemy soldiers.

•

Never had a President been so protected as was Franklin Roosevelt
when en route from the White House to the Capitol just before noon
on the 8th. In one of a motorcade of ten black limousines, he sat in
his dark naval cape next to Marine Captain Jimmy Roosevelt. Secret
Service men displaying automatic riot guns perched on running boards
on both sides of the car. On either side was an identical limousine
with three men on each running board and four inside with shotguns.
Marines checked the credentials of every invited guest and reporter,
even the elderly Edith Bolling Wilson, who had watched her husband
ask for a declaration of war in the same chamber in 1917.

Introduced at 12:30 P.M. by Speaker of the House Sam Rayburn,
Roosevelt put on his glasses, adjusted his loose-leaf notebook, and
began his businesslike six-minute speech. It was not an occasion for
ringing Churchillian phrases. He wanted a quick vote for war and
sweeping sums to prosecute it. Afterward no one would remember any
phrase except the "date which will live in infamy."

Representative Jeanette Rankin, who had been in the House even before women's suffrage and had voted against the war in 1917, arose once more to announce her *nay*. "Sit down, sister," said John M. Dingell. Even enemies of the President tried to persuade her to change her vote and make the resolution unanimous. They had to settle for 338 to 1.

In the Senate the count was 82 to 0. Gerald Nye himself voted for war. Some isolationists could not return in time to cast ballots, but none would have voted *nay*. Some would call for prosecuting those culpable at Pearl Harbor, but the culprits intended were the politicians and military bureaucrats in Washington, not the bunglers in the field.

Roosevelt's war message had been deliberately short on details about Pearl Harbor. The enormity of the losses might have created a despondency about the war exactly fitting Yamamoto's hopes. Even cranks like Colonel McCormick of the *Chicago Tribune* withheld the grim statistics. At a dinner for "Wild Bill" Donovan, Arthur Krock of the *New York Times* took a telephone call and returned to the table too shocked to hold his tongue. "My God!" he announced. "Ninety percent of our fleet was knocked out at Pearl Harbor!"

"Arthur has good sources," said Donovan.

It was difficult to keep anything secret in Washington. America First also had the facts, leaked by Senator Nye and others on the 9th after Secretary Knox and Admiral Stark had confidentially revealed them in a closed meeting of the Naval Affairs Committee. Ruth Sarles of the Washington office of America First reported to Robert K. Wood that one senator remarked as he left the secret session, "We would be lucky if we kept Hawaii." Eight battleships had been sunk or crippled, she reported; "half our effectives are wiped out." The government, she guessed, "will sit on the lid as long as possible." In one of the earliest conspiracy allegations, isolationist Senator Guy Gillette claimed to her that he had seen documents that established American advance knowledge of "the plan of attack." Most modern bombing planes and "all but seven percent of our ammunition," she was also told, had been shipped to hated England, leaving the U.S. with only the resources for three weeks' fighting. Still, there was no way to frighten or goad America First stalwarts into keeping the faith. Their cause was lost and the movement would self-destruct. Ruth Sarles would need another job.

•

Not only had new Russian ambassador Maxim Litvinov arrived in Hawaii on the last *Clipper* to get through; he managed an overnight transcontinental flight from San Francisco in time to watch the war begin in Washington. Leaving the old Pullman mansion on 16th Street—the Soviet Embassy—he turned up in the chaos of Monday in Thomas Saltz's haberdashery in the grubby gray denim suit in which he had flown from Moscow, looking as if he had slept in it at least since Singapore. Saltz turned Litvinov into a reasonable equivalent of an ambassador. Calling at the White House on the afternoon of the 8th in his vested new respectability to present his credentials, he was greeted by a surprised Roosevelt with "You get that suit in Moscow?" But Litvinov wanted to talk about whether the "providential" happening that had brought the U.S. into the war would prevent delivery of vital war materiel to Russia.

They exchanged ideas for forty-five minutes; then the President, who had managed only five hours' sleep, had himself wheeled to his bedroom and seized an hour's nap.

Across the United States, for little reason but vague fear, Japanese were being taken into custody. Except in the West, most were treated with courtesy. In New York, Governor Herbert Lehman's first executive order after learning that the nation was at war was to order the state police to protect Japanese nationals. In Washington, D.C., some irate citizens chopped down enemy cherry trees, and in New Jersey a Japanese schoolboy was refused passage on a bus.

•

Public euphoria pervaded Japan. The Government Information Bureau announced that the conflict would be known as the Great East Asia War (*Daitōa Sensō*), and that the "obnoxious" term *Far East*, derived from the British conception that England was the center of the world, "would not be used any more." As Kōtarō Takamura put it in the *Yomiuri*, Japan's enemies

> . . . raise their heads in arrogance
> While we are constructing the Great East Asia family.

Citizens on public duty were urged to wear a kind of uniform. For women, although slacks were considered too Western, it was to be *mompe*, unstylish baggy pants. Civilian men were to wear *kokuminfuku*, the austerity national uniform, a khaki shirt and trousers with puttees wrapped around the calves, and an army cap without insignia. These were to be worn, at a minimum, on the 8th of every month, to commemorate the victory at Pearl Harbor. On the 10th, a rally in Tokyo sponsored by the daily newspapers had as its theme "Crushing the U.S. and Britain," and the *Nichi Nichi* afterward editorialized, "There has never been a more constructive war than this. Every bullet fired from Japanese guns carries with it the destruction of the old order and helps to bring a new and better one."

Communiqués overflowed with Homeric epithets that in another culture might have engendered skepticism about the facts; but the facts were largely real, a litany of victories. The fleet was the "invincible navy," and fliers were "wild eagles." A downed Japanese plane was "self-destroyed," as if each pilot had, in pre-kamikaze fashion, become a flying bomb. The dead were "hero-gods." Horrors perpetrated, if not celebrated, were glossed over simply, as in history textbooks in contemporary Japan, with, "War makes people cruel. So we cannot say one nation is more cruel than another."*

At ten o'clock on the morning of the 9th, Emperor Hirohito arrived at the Imperial Sanctuary on the Palace grounds, his slender form lost in an ancient Court robe. He carried a scepter in his right hand. Behind him the sacred trees in the ceremonial garden were hung with strips of yellow and white cloth, from some of which small mirrors dangled and glittered. (A mirror in Shinto belief symbolizes one's forebears; seeing one's self is seeing one's ancestors.) In the pavilion adjoining the Sanctuary were seated Prince Takamatsu and Prince Mikasa, brothers of the Emperor. Behind them were Prime Minister Tojo and his Cabinet; Dr. Hara, President of the Privy Council; and six former prime ministers, including Prince Konoye.

As His Majesty was seated, facing the others, a Court Ritualist rang a bell; when its reverberations died away, another aide presented the Emperor with a small branch from one of the sacred trees. Rising, Hirohito entered the inner shrine and informed the spirits of the sacred souls of the departed, especially those of his father, Emperor Taisho, and his grandfather, Emperor Meiji, of the declaration of war against the United States and Britain. Then he remained for a moment in prayer—to ask, so Tokyo newspapers reported, for the divine blessing

---

* From a five-page lesson on "War" in a 1988 text for senior high schools.

of the Emperor Jimmu, founder of the Empire, in realizing the ideal which had inspired Japan since its origins.

As Hirohito bowed his way out, his Empress entered to repeat the prayer. Next to worship was Count Yoshisada Seiganji, representing the Household of the Empress Dowager, mother of Hirohito. Then, in turn, homage was rendered by the other dignitaries in the Pavilion, and the Sanctuary emptied. The ancestral spirits had been well and fully informed, and their divine protection requested in ample measure.

As the ceremony ended, tens of thousands thronged the plaza of the Imperial Palace to pray for the welfare of their Imperial Majesties and for victory. In Hibiya Park the government had arranged a massive "Smash America and Britain" rally for the noon hour. Rousing choruses of patriotic songs echoed off nearby office buildings. As lunch hour ended, the park emptied.

In the Imperial Palace itself, the Emperor had discovered from American radio that the Pearl Harbor attack had begun more than an hour *before* the Foreign Ministry's note to Washington was delivered. The message itself was no declaration of war, and to Britain the Japanese had presented nothing whatever, but Hirohito told Foreign Minister Togo that he was angry that his wishes about timing were not followed. Tojo accepted the responsibility. It seemed a small matter.

•

Although General Sir Hastings Ismay was Secretary of the Committee of Imperial Defence, he did not learn that the Japanese were attacking Hong Kong, Thailand, and Malaya until the early hours of December 8 in London. Ismay did not spend his Sundays near a radio or a telephone. By Monday evening he had convened a conference to consider Britain's precarious position in East Asia. No one expected to send Hong Kong anything but fine phrases about the good fight, but how were the *Repulse* and *Prince of Wales* to be used to save Singapore? Churchill suggested two alternatives, Ismay remembered. "Either they should vanish into the ocean wastes and exercise a vague menace like 'rogue elephants'; or they should go south and join the remnants of the United States Fleet. The discussion continued far into the night without any decision, and it was agreed to have another look at the problem the next day." No one in Whitehall knew that the ships were already in the South China Sea.

At midnight December 9, twenty-four hours into the war for Malaya, Admiral Phillips on the *Prince of Wales* received a message that the Japanese were landing an invasion force at Kuantan, halfway down the Malayan coast. Sir Tom had been prudently steaming for home, his ships having been spotted by Japanese reconnaissance. Turning around, he would surprise them. In darkness he could move into position to shell the intruders and wreck their beachhead.

At daylight a destroyer went ahead and found nothing. Phillips prepared to continue south to Singapore. Overhead a plane was sighted but not identified; by 10:50 A.M. radar picked up a cloud of aircraft. Seventeen minutes later the *Repulse* and the *Prince of Wales* were under attack from dive bombers and torpedo planes.

Cecil Brown had despaired of seeing any action, but kept his diary going in hopes of doing a "color" story. Phillips had more than that in mind when he left Singapore. He had sent a message to the *Repulse* and the four accompanying destroyers that there might be transports, even cruisers, to sink. "We are sure to get some useful practice with high-angle armament, but whatever we meet I want to finish quickly and so get well clear to the eastward before the Japanese can mass too formidable a scale of air attack against us."

By 11:17 both big ships had been hit and set afire, set upon, Gallagher wrote, "like a pack of dogs on a wounded buck." At 11:51 Captain Tennant of the *Repulse* radioed the *Wales* through the smoke and fire, "Have you sustained any damage?"

Phillips's answer came back: "We are out of control. Steering gear is gone." Also gone was all ability to defend the ship, as his guns were powered by electricity, and torpedoes had wrecked the system. "Left to right, up and down," AA gunner Frederick Hodgson remembered years later, "were useless."

"Bloody good bombing for those blokes," muttered a gunner on the *Repulse*. "Cecil, you are never going to get out of this," Brown remembered saying aloud to himself before he unbuckled his soft new Singapore-made shoes and jumped into the oil-slick below. "My mind cannot absorb what my eyes see. It is impossible to believe that these two beautiful, powerful, invulnerable ships are going down. But they are."

"Captain," a junior officer pleaded with Tennant, who seemed ready to go down with the *Repulse*, "you must come with us. You've done all you could for this ship. More than most men could."

When Tennant did not budge, his men forced him up on the deck. The ship was almost on her beam ends, near a final plunge. They pushed Tennant over the side and jumped after him into what seemed more thick diesel oil than seawater. Arthur Bartholomew watched the ship go down "stern first, her props still turning." Then the *Repulse* was "just bubbles under the smoke."

Unwounded, the destroyers picked up the survivors, with Japanese planes apparently leaving the smaller ships alone for the rescue work. Bartholomew was plucked by the *Electra*; Frederick Hodgson of the *Wales* floundered toward the *Express*. "Her life saving nets were hung over port and starboard sides . . . and everyone was grasping them to climb aboard." On deck he was given artificial respiration to push the oil from his stomach.

Overhead, once the Japanese had left, British planes appeared, too slow and too few to have done any good earlier. The pilot of the first fighter to reach the spot was Flight Lieutenant Tim Vigors in a Brewster Buffalo, no better than the Australian-made Wirraway, which in its American version was a Harvard trainer. There was little better or more modern in Malaya. (Australia itself, denuded of soldiers and equipment by Churchill to battle for North Africa, boasted *one* unarmed Hurricane fighter, grudgingly sent from Britain for training.)

Flying over the rescue ships, Vigors remembered Dunkirk, where he had seen a similar ordeal—"many men in dire danger waving, cheering, and joking as if they were holiday-makers at Brighton waving at low-flying aircraft. . . . I take my hat off to them."

Interrogating survivors, O. W. Phillips asked, "What did you think when you found you were going up the east coast of Malaya?"

"We thought," one said, "the management had gone mad!"

Early on Wednesday the 10th, while Churchill was working on official papers in bed at 10 Downing Street, as was his morning routine, his telephone rang. Admiral Sir Dudley Pound, the Navy chief, had trouble controlling his grief. Churchill heard "a cough and gulp," then silence. "Prime Minister," he finally began, "I have to report to you that the *Prince of Wales* and the *Repulse* have both been sunk by the Japanese—we think by aircraft. Tom Phillips is drowned."

"Are you sure it is true?"

"There is no doubt at all."

"Poor Tom Phillips," said Churchill to himself, putting the phone down. Never in war, he confessed, had he "received a more direct shock."

Ismay and General Sir Leslie Hollis had slept in their offices. On their way to bed, Ismay had confessed to Hollis that he had dreamed the night before that the *Prince of Wales* had been sunk; and he had awakened in a cold sweat. At dawn the next morning—it was early afternoon in Malaya—a gray-faced Hollis knocked on Ismay's door. "Your dream about the *Prince of Wales* was true," he said; "and the *Repulse* as well."

The catastrophe could not be concealed, and as Mollie Panter-Downes described the shock and gloom in London, "It was as if some enormously powerful watchdog which had been going to keep the burglars away from the house had been shot while exercising in the front yard." Yet, Cecil Brown observed, once he filed his story and cleaned himself up, "Raffles Hotel still has dancing every night, but there are not as many dancers." At dawn the next morning, in a gesture reminiscent of the war of 1914–1918, Lieutenant Haruki Iki, whose nine-plane squadron had dealt some of the devastation, returned to drop flowers over the watery graves of the *Repulse* and the *Prince of Wales*.

In Japanese Victory vocabulary, Singapore would become *Shonan*, or Light of the South. It was expected to fall quickly. While Malaya itself became a puppet state, Singapore would be a crown colony ruled from Tokyo. Moving south, General Yamashita's troops seemed almost unimpeded. Strafing and bombing had softened up the enemy, now retiring quickly out of fear of being cut off from below.

•

It took Japanese troops little more than a day to sweep through Kowloon to the Gin Drinkers Line. While the Scots, Punjabis, and Rajputs reeled back, English and Canadian defenders fled from air raids which knocked out their shore and AA batteries. Sent largely to improve morale in Hong Kong, the Canadians were too busy to be uplifted by a cable from the Minister of Defense in Ottawa that "in the days that lie ahead [they would] worthily uphold the best traditions of Canadian arms." Brigadier Lawson replied, "All ranks much appreciate your message."

General Maltby's Order of the Day to his Middlesexers and other troops observed that it was "obvious to us all that the test for which we have been placed here will come in the near future." He expected every man "to stick it out unflinchingly," and become "an example of high-hearted courage to all the rest of the Empire."

A sentry with the Volunteers, Ralph Ingram watched the last take-offs from Kai Tak. The blasted runway had been hurriedly prepared for two DC-2s that materialized out of the night sky and were guided down by deftly handled searchlights. CNAC's Pan Am pilots had been enticed one more time—they made sixteen trips after the first raid on Kai Tak—to extract wealthy Chinese businessmen and government officials who waited with suitcases crammed with valuables. Three of the eight well-paid CNAC pilots went without sleep for more than fifty hours; all made it out, along with the crew of the destroyed *Clipper*. As the planes dipped down, then took off again with strained urgency, terrified refugees fleeing Kowloon cowered in fear of falling bombs. For VIPs like Chinese Finance Minister H. H. Kung and Madame Sun Yatsen there would be no languishing as prisoners of war. Pan Am Traffic Manager Charles L. Schafer, who had worked on camouflaging the planes, elected to wait. He wanted to help load and dispatch one more DC-2, on which he would leave. A Japanese bomb destroyed it, and his last chance to escape.

As Kowloon went, so went the island's water supply. Overlooking the crucial Jubilee Reservoir in the western section of the Gin Drinkers Line was the Shing Mun Redoubt, a complex of pillboxes and underground tunnels and the key to the Line. It was overrun by 1:00 A.M. on the 10th, and by midday on the 11th, orders were to evacuate what remained of Kowloon in a postdarkness mini-Dunkirk.

Courage, sometimes of an unorthodox variety, was the only commodity that remained in abundance on Hong Kong. Before she fled the Peninsula Hotel on the Kowloon side, easygoing Dorothy Gordon Jenner took a Canadian captain to her bed. "These were strange times," she explained. Neither were concerned for the moment about his wife and children in Winnipeg. She gave him "the kiss of my life" as he left, to be killed that night on the island at Magazine Gap. Then she buttonholed the commissioner of police for a job, and soon was working as well as sleeping in the "Battle Box," in Phyllis Harrop's makeshift office. Both made it through Stanley Prison.

"Glumly" nursing her baby through the bombardments, Emily Hahn was unencouraged by a message about gallant Hong Kong from King George VI, but was inspired to survive by "Red Hilda" Selwyn-Clarke, who punctuated every explosion with "Oh, my God!" and insisted confidently about little Carola, "You'll never keep her alive. Never." Mother and daughter would survive prison camp, as would Carola's father, Major Charles Boxer.

Andy Leiper returned to the Chartered Bank of India branch on Queen's Road on the 10th to find his taciturn Chinese head cashier unwilling to work amid the bombings, but quite willing to have his crew run the Cash Department from the bank's safer and newer building in the Des Voeux Road. "I no fear die," he confided. "Soldiers no can run when Japanese come. Why *we* run? I think more better we stay. All shroffs think so." Until the surrender of the colony on Christmas Day they continued paying out Hong Kong dollars, however worthless they had become.

Except, perhaps, for MacArthur's highly personal communiqués from the Philippines, the Hong Kong press was the most imaginatively upbeat news source in East Asia. On the day that the Gin Drinkers Line was breached, and Kowloon ordered evacuated, the *South China Morning Post* bannered, "FUTILE RAIDS GIVE COLONY TIMELY PRACTICE." Smaller headlines announced, "Vain Bomber Attacks on Warships," "Accurate Artillery Fire Checks Enemy Land Forces," and "Another Quiet Night." A smaller headline read, "No Panic in Alarm." More realistically, an adjacent column reported a government regulation: "Rice Shops Must Open." Hong Kong residents received their most accurate information by grapevine, and through that medium they knew from the start that the war was lost, and that they would soon have new masters.

•

In Indochina, where masters had been effectively, if not officially, exchanged for months, Relman Morin was not picked up by the Japanese until the morning of the 9th. His second cup of coffee still unfinished, he was reading, in a Saigon morning paper, that American bombers from the Philippines had raided Tokyo. A bulletin from the Japanese military in Hanoi denied it, adding that it would be "impossible for anybody, any time, to bomb Tokyo. *C'est une chose impossible.*"

Morin was still smiling with delight at the possibility when there was a rap on the door of his hotel room. Five Japanese came in. "Our two countries are at war," explained a gendarme, "and we have come to protect you."

"From what?" Morin asked.

For two days he was under house arrest, guarded by two soldiers so innocent of Western ways that they had never seen a typewriter or a bathroom shower. Eventually an officer visited, prior to taking Morin into internment at the British consul's large house, and explained that the entire American fleet had been sunk. Morin doubted it. "Well, in that case we'll simply build another fleet. It might take five or ten years, but we can go on building ships indefinitely."

"If America doesn't surrender and we don't surrender," the officer asked, with some surprise, "then how will the war end?"

"Somebody will have to be invaded," said Morin.

•

In the Philippines, where the Army's air umbrella had been turned inside out on the first day of the war, the Navy's turn came on the third. By Hawaiian standards it was a paltry affair, with no capital ships to go down, but Cavite's subs and destroyers, and an occasional cruiser, made up one of the formidable forces in East Asia. On the sub tender *Otus*—a freighter until commandeered in March—Seaman Paul B. Noel expected any Japanese raid to be routed by powerful AA fire. When the twin-engined bombers appeared on the 10th, flying in formation, east to west, at 20,000 feet, they had looked puny and harmless. The yard AA guns went into action, including the four on the *Otus*. "They were a delight to watch," Noel remembered, "as the guns hammered out wicked volleys. Tracers guided them right for the targets, except that they soon wavered, arched into half of a loop far beneath the Japanese planes, and fell harmlessly into the sea." The Navy's antiaircraft guns, no better than the Army's, fired shells fused for explosion at 10,000 feet, quite sufficient for the last war.

Fires burned throughout the yard as ammunition stores detonated and fuel tanks ruptured. A shiny new fire engine proved to have an inoperable pump; frayed old fire hoses gave way under pressure, leading to stories that they had been sliced through by enemy agents. Anything inoperable because of carelessness, incompetence, unpreparedness, or obsolescence was attributed to Fifth Column tampering. Ordered to get under way, the *Otus* was halted by a fouled anchor. It had to be cut away with a blowtorch.

Red and yellow flames, topped by pillars of black smoke, could be seen as far away as Manila, making damage reports difficult to fudge.

Lieutenant George T. Ferguson, just back from doctoring on the Yangtze Patrol, described the scene as "One Bloody Mess," with many of the casualties from friendly fire. "Bombs hissed down and empty AA fragments dropped all around. . . . Casualties poured in so damn fast [that] we filled Canacao Hospital in [a] couple of hours." Ferguson found a trench to hide in but only after shrapnel had pierced his knee.

Once the fires were out, the yard reeked with burned and decaying flesh. Ferguson had to lead a detail to dispose of the unidentifiable dead. Some bodies were cremated. His squad dumped most unrecognizable remains into bomb craters and covered them with earth and rubble. Ferguson estimated that he disposed of about two hundred casualties. In prison camp later with some of the survivors, he sometimes wished he had been one of the dead.

Higher-ups fared little better. Admiral Rockwell took cover in an open ditch. In the blazing rubble he lost everything but the sweat-soaked clothes on his back. "We spent that night in an open school yard nearby and for the next two weeks [we] were like so many rabbits—running from one hole to another dodging bombs that fell almost every day." How the surviving ships of the Asiatic Fleet could be used effectively became an immediate problem. With the loss of the British capital ships off Malaya, Singapore had instantly become a ghost base. On December 11 Washington ordered Admiral Hart to renege on his promises and send his Singapore-bound destroyers to Darwin, Australia. Any further vessels he extricated from the Philippines, now written off as lost, were to go south as well.

The British in Malaya characterized the reversal as a failure of good faith; but even the ships left to help the Dutch were as good as gone. The fictional Lieutenant Maki in the 1933 Japanese novel had sunk the cruiser *Houston*; in reality it would survive to be sunk once more, this time off the Indies.

The 11th, by official report, had been a day of victories for American forces in the Philippines, who needed one. Air raids had wiped out almost all combat-ready aircraft. A few P-40s still flew; the remnant of the B-17 force was in hiding in Mindanao. Everyone realized that the logical landing site on Luzon for the Japanese was Lingayen Gulf, northwest of Manila, and it seemed no surprise when Major LeGrande Diller released for MacArthur a statement that a major landing there had been thwarted. Most of the invasion vessels had been sunk and the beaches littered with Japanese corpses.

Life photographer Carl Mydans, seeking pictures, found the beaches quiet. A few Filipino troops were visible. There had been no battle. An unidentified and possibly mythical boat in the lower Gulf had touched off a barrage from coast defenses. The boat had disappeared. Based on Diller's story, American newsmen in Manila worked up material for banner headlines; Mydans merely returned to Diller's office in Intramuros and challenged him, "I've just been to Lingayen and there's no battle there."

"It says so here," Diller insisted, pointing to his communiqué.

When the Japanese landed on the undefended upper shore of Lingayen Gulf, they moved toward Manila almost unopposed.

•

On the evening of the 9th President Roosevelt spoke to the nation by radio. His confident voice and the "fireside chat" format were the ideal medium for admission of serious setbacks and warning of further attacks, even "along our coast lines. It should be clear now," he cautioned, "that our ocean-girt hemisphere is not immune." Safety could not be measured "in terms of miles on any map." Still, he predicted that American might would regenerate; the war would be taken to the enemy. What he did not say was that his planners worried about a number of possible Axis moves, from an invasion of Alaska or Hawaii to bombing raids on the Panama Canal or the West Coast. The Japanese might seize the Galapagos Islands off the coast of Ecuador, or—with the Germans—foment revolutions in Latin America, even Mexico. In the east, Greenland and Iceland might be blockaded or captured, and Atlantic coast oil refineries shelled by surfaced submarines. The failure in Oahu had underlined the need for more and better aircraft warning systems, and the sub threat to coastal shipping was real. It looked like a long war.

Until the release of the Victory Plan and the attack on Pearl Harbor, Hitler had preferred to deal with America *after* he had subdued Europe. He had prevented Admiral Dönitz's submarines from attacking the slow American tankers and freighters silhouetted against the bright Atlantic shoreline. Even permitting American Lend-Lease had been a more modest price to pay than full war mobilization. But, since the War Department document—overly optimistic, it turned out—estimated that the U.S. would be sufficiently mobilized by 1943 to land in force on the Continent and defeat Germany, it seemed in Hitler's interest to go to war sooner, with a weaker America.

•

Calling on Foreign Minister Ribbentrop in Berlin on the 8th, Ambassador Oshima was assured that Germany and Italy would declare war on the U.S. Hitler's generals would have been happier had Japan made a move against Russia, but the Führer was willing to take what he could get. He did not consult his anointed second-in-command, Göring, who privately felt that the entry of America into the war would ensure "that one day the enemy's numerical superiority would be colossal."

Hitler arrived in Berlin by train from Rastenburg at 11:00 A.M. on the 9th. A message from Hans Thomsen, his chargé in Washington, confirmed that Roosevelt had revealed no plans to ask for a declaration of war against Germany—that the President might find it difficult to persuade Congress to vote for a two-front war. Dönitz, however, had already been authorized to let his subs fire on American ships without warning, a signal that the Führer's own declaration was coming. Hitler had not returned from Wolfschanze for nothing.

Later on the 9th the Washington embassy was instructed to burn its secret files and codes, and Hitler began drafting a speech to the rubber-stamp Reichstag. The Foreign Office had prepared for him a list of "that lout" Roosevelt's violations of neutrality, of which the most recent, and the most flagrant, was the Victory Plan targeted at Germany.

From the Propaganda Ministry, Dr. Goebbels worried about home opinion, and how it would react to war with the United States. It would be crucial to denigrate American films, American jazz, and other familiar transatlantic products, to emphasize that America had "virtually no culture of her own." Further, Japanese victories were already, by contrast, worsening the public's "already poor opinion of the Italians." In warning about "excessive euphoria" over quick Japanese successes he may have been hinting, too, at another possible comparison—the bogging down of the Germans themselves in Russia. His department chiefs knew how to read between the directives.

•

The fall of the Tikhvin salient on December 9 returned to the Russians a path across frozen Lake Ladoga out of the reach of German artillery fire. Colder weather had been thickening the ice, making possible heavier loads on the "Road of Life." Even at minimal rations, Leningrad needed a thousand tons of food trucked in daily, not counting fuel and ammunition. Fuel for essential civilian needs—factories remained unheated, and few homes warmed to tolerable levels more than a single room in which everyone lived and slept—was computed at 35.31 cubic feet of wood per 8 square meters (about 9 square yards of living space). A black market log sold for 200 rubles, about two weeks of a workman's wages. On December 9 any surplus household wood was ordered confiscated and distributed to the needy. Electric power remained so weak that ninety more streetcars were removed from service. All barber shops, laundries, and public baths were shut down because water could not be heated, and Leningraders at home ceased shaving and bathing. Even bakery production, however essential, was erratic because of frozen water lines and fuel shortages. The city was not out of danger, although the perils were now shared by the Wehrmacht.

On the Moscow front the fighting raged on while Guderian's forces retreated southwestward from Tula. In some places Zhukov's armies regained fifty-mile swaths of territory, enough that Stalin was able (on the 13th) to confirm the rollback of the Germans from Moscow. But as some Russian forces doing the counterattacking were often, as Halder noted in his war diary at Wolfschanze, "hastily gathered" and without combat experience, German "tactical patchwork," as he described it, kept withdrawals from becoming routs.

Lacking confidence in his generals, Hitler would order the retreats stopped, although it would take him until the following week, when he returned from his Reichstag speech, reviewed the situation, and discovered that the crumbling had continued. "You'd better make yourself comfortable where you are," General Hans von Greiffenberg telephoned to Lieutenant General Günther Blumentritt, Chief of Staff of the Fourth Army. "A new order has arrived from Hitler. Fourth Army is not to retreat a single yard."

In Libya the retreating Rommel, who would not backtrack very far, waited behind Gazala for reinforcements, then withdrew further, even from Benghazi. But he would return, with air support and equipment unusable then in frozen Russia. And he realized that he had the Führer's confidence: Rommel could not have helped but know that in

Hitler's speech to the Reichstag on the 11th he had been singled out
for praise. A bright spot in the war picture had been needed, since the
Führer's confidence in his Russian command had reached bottom.

While the "criminal" Roosevelt "chats from the fireside," Hitler
told the Reichstag, "our soldiers are fighting in snow and ice." Germany
had maintained peace with the U.S. despite "unbearable provocations,"
for Roosevelt had wanted war to escape from the consequences of his
failures at home. Backed by "the millionaires and the Jews," he was
forced to "provoke" the attack on his own country, and had finally
succeeded. "It fills the German *Volk*, and I believe, all decent people
throughout the world, with profound satisfaction that the Japanese
government, after years of negotiating with this swindler, has finally
had enough of being subjected to scorn and indignities." Roosevelt
should finally understand—"I say this because of his limited intellect—
that we know that his aim is to destroy one state after another. As for
the German nation, it needs charity neither from Mr. Roosevelt nor
from Mr. Churchill. . . . It only wants its rights! It will secure this for
itself even if thousands of Churchills and Roosevelts conspire against
it."

Hitler's war message was not a mere obligation to Tokyo. The U.S.
appeared badly hurt, and unprepared for world war. Yet forcing Roosevelt's hand was a service to Washington and a gift beyond price to
London. Without it, the President could not have had a willing Congress behind him: Hitler was not beating the U.S. to the punch, and
he knew it. Unlike Göring, he expected a divided America, lacking in
will to prosecute a two-ocean war.

As Hitler went on to announce that American diplomats would
have "their passports returned to them," usually an act signifying war,
the marionettes of the Reichstag rose from their seats in what Otto
Brautigam described as "tumultuous homage" (*sturmischen Huldigung*)
for the "*grossten Führer und Staatsmann*." The staged bedlam drowned
out Hitler's actual declaration. Only afterward did radio listeners in
Germany have the fact confirmed to them that their country was officially at war with the United States.

Telephoning Walter Warlimont at Wolfschanze, Alfred Jodl asked,
"You have heard that the Führer a moment ago has declared war on
America?"

"Yes," said Warlimont, "and we couldn't be more astonished."
Hitler had not confided in his staff, who had hoped that Japan would

keep the United States busy. Now Jodl instructed him on Hitler's orders to examine "where the United States is likely to employ the bulk of her forces initially, the Far East or Europe."

"Agreed," said Warlimont; "this examination is obviously necessary, but so far we have never even considered a war against the United States and so have no data on which to base this examination. We can hardly undertake this job just like that."

"See what you can do," Jodl insisted. "When we get back tomorrow we will talk about this in more detail." Privately, Göring spoke of German suicide (*Selbstmord*).

A paragon of efficiency, Warlimont would lay a lengthy and astute reappraisal on Hitler's desk. The "Roosevelt plan," he concluded, "operates on a level where the possibility of its being fulfilled in practice in the future is doubtful." Yet "from our point of view, [it] is not to be overlooked. Consequently, in the discussions about German strategy, which has essentially achieved its war aims already, views about the defensive have come to the fore." Warlimont's bureaucratic code was clear enough. Germany would now struggle to keep its conquests. Only the overwhelming of enemy shipping to Europe and Africa could "stem the collapse of all the enemy's offensive planning and force him to give up the struggle." However couched, it was not the assessment that Hitler wanted.

Roosevelt's second war message to Congress seemed only a postscript to the vote against Japan. It passed both houses unanimously. (Miss Rankin voted *present*.) War with Germany (and Italy) appeared to be entered into almost casually.

"The stars in their courses are fighting for us," Churchill's private secretary John Martin observed in his diary Thursday evening. Despite the catastrophe off Malaya and the debacles in Hawaii and Luzon, there were grounds for hope. "The P.M. was soon full of bounce again," another Churchill aide, John Peck, wrote to a colleague in Washington, "because the news from Russia and Libya more than balances our misfortunes." He might have added "from Washington." The balance of inevitable power had been altered in a day. However wider the war, it would be won.

CURTAIN CALL

Doomsday

Alas for the Day! . . . A fire devoureth before them
. . . and behind them a desolate wilderness. . . .
Wonders in the heavens and in the earth, blood
and fire, and pillars of smoke. The sun shall be
turned into darkness, and the moon into blood.

—Joel: 1, xv; 2, iii, xxx

I T WAS the afternoon of August 5, 1945. To a group of six hundred Army officers assigned to the Hiroshima garrison, Professor Yoshitaka Mimura of Hiroshima Bunri University, a theoretical physicist, was explaining the scientific possibilities of new weapons which might reverse the tides of war. Japan had little Navy or Air Force left. Within months, a massive invasion of the home islands seemed likely. "Could you tell us, sir," a young lieutenant colonel asked, "what an atomic bomb is? Is there any possibility that the bomb will be developed by the end of this war?"

Mimura chalked a rough sketch on the blackboard to illustrate the chemical reactions required. Scientists at Tokyo University, he explained, have "theoretically penetrated" the secrets of nuclear fission. If they could apply their theories practically, an atomic bomb "could be even smaller than a piece of caramel candy, but, if exploded five hundred meters above a populated city, it could possibly destroy 200,000 lives."

"When can we have that bomb?"

"Well, it is difficult to say," Mimura answered, knowing nothing of any Japanese enterprise to apply fission theory to bomb-making. "But I can tell you this much: not before the end of this war."

When Paul Tibbets, flying back to Savannah after maneuvers in North Carolina, had heard the news of Pearl Harbor on his radio, the B-29 Superfortress had been only a concept on the drawing board. "Little Boy," at 9,000 pounds the sole bomb-bay cargo in his B-29 Superfortress on the morning of August 6, 1945, had only been the concept of a committee of scientists on a Saturday morning in Washington the day before Pearl Harbor.

Like Colonel Tibbets, Major General Curtis LeMay had first heard the Pearl Harbor news on his radio when returning from a training exercise. Running the B-29 show meant picking the plane and the people for the Hiroshima flight. "I want the best crew you've got to drop this first one," LeMay told Tibbets. "And that doesn't necessarily mean you." But Tibbets had picked himself, and waited five hours into the *Enola Gay*'s lumbering course from Tinian, a once-Japanese neighbor of retaken Guam, to explain to his crew why their mission consisted of only two planes rather than the cloud of aircraft that normally pounded the beleaguered cities of Japan. Their one-bomb raid would pack thousands of times the punch of Pearl Harbor. "We are carrying the world's first atomic bomb."

The "first special bomb," as identified in a directive from the War Department to the 509 Composite Group, 20th Air Force, was to be delivered "as soon as weather will permit visual bombing after about 3 August 1945 on one of the [following] targets: Hiroshima, Kokura, Niigata and Nagasaki. To carry military and civilian scientific personnel . . . to observe and record the effects of the explosion . . . , additional aircraft will accompany the airplane carrying the bomb. . . . Additional bombs will be delivered on the above targets as soon as made ready by the project staff."

Only one more was ready. It was en route to Tinian, and no further instructions were needed to drop it.

Airmen knew that they were lugging a big experimental payload, 28 inches in diameter, 120 inches long, but they had never before heard the word *atomic*. In *The Great Artiste*, an accompanying B-29 that carried no explosives other than defensive hardware, some of the crew needed no explanation. They were scientists monitoring the equipment that would photograph and measure the effects of the explosion.

At eight-fifteen and seventeen seconds in the morning, Japan time, the bomb-bay doors of the *Enola Gay* opened. From *The Great Artiste* an instrument package drifted down from a parachute. Forty-three seconds later, with the *Enola Gay* at 31,600 feet in a 155-degree diving turn to the right racing away from the impact point, "Little Boy" erupted 1,890 feet over Hiroshima like a thousand rising suns.

The plane lurched upward on lightening its load; it shuddered again in the shock wave, then trembled in the echo effect. "I think this is the end of the war," Tibbets observed to Bob Lewis, his copilot. "Bingo!" the *Enola Gay* radioed to Tinian.

Monitoring the instruments in *The Great Artiste* was Luis Alvarez, later a Nobel Prize winner in physics. On December 7, 1941, he had been working at the M.I.T. Radiation Laboratory on radar. Now he saw a bright flash illuminate the crew compartment, "the light from the explosion reflecting off the clouds in front of us. . . . I looked in vain for the city that had been our target. . . . My friend and teacher Ernest Lawrence had expended great energy . . . building the machines that separated the U-235 for the Little Boy bomb. I thought the bombardier . . . had dumped Ernest's precious bomb out into the empty countryside." The target had ceased to exist.

•

For Honolulu-born Tosh Kano, the war had begun when he was drafted out of engineering school in Tokyo to fight in China. A third of his unit had died, but he had returned for officers' training and was in Tokyo, on his way to the Army Engineering Academy, when he saw the first bulletins posted about Pearl Harbor. Released in March 1945 because of ill health, he was back in Hiroshima, where he had a wife, a daughter, and an infant son. Walking to the barracks of the local Fire Protection Brigade, where he now worked, he was quick to warn a group of giggling girls on their way to high school that an air-raid alarm sounded at twenty-five minutes after midnight (American weather planes had been active) was still in effect. "We are very sorry," they chorused. "*Gomen-nasai.*" Looking up as he heard the hum of a plane, he saw a high-flying, silvery B-29 release "something shining with a parachute." It appeared to be a leaflet drop: he had not seen "Little Boy" fall from another plane. "Be careful, girls," Kano admonished. Late now for duty, he hurried through an underpass toward the barracks.

Hiroko Nakamoto had heard the news of Pearl Harbor at school in Hiroshima, connecting America only with the song she had learned about a celluloid doll. In sixth grade then, she was now, under war conditions, a working girl, hurrying, at 8:15, to a factory job. Alerts through the night had kept her awake; she was groggy from lack of sleep. From beneath half-closed lids she saw a blinding light—"as if someone had taken a flashbulb picture a few inches from my eyes. There was no pain. Only a stinging sensation, as if I had been slapped hard in the face. I tried to open my eyes. But I could not. Then I lost consciousness."

Tosh Kano "felt" the bright flash as he emerged from the underpass; then a pressure wave pushed through the tunnel which had shielded him. He was jolted forward—"just like a strong wind coming out of a narrow passage"—and blown into a drainage ditch. His cap, glasses, and briefcase scattered. Instinctively he lay low and covered his face with his hands. Then he raised his head to look around, and saw a whirlwind of debris. A "ball of pinkish fire" sizzled through the underpass, and again he flattened himself into the ditch. As it passed he smelled a strong, gassy odor. He could see nothing through the black cloud that crawled along the ground. In the darkness he heard people crying in pain, calling for help.

Novelist Yōko Ōta, whose wartime works like *Daughter of Battle* pulsated with patriotic enthusiasm, was asleep under her mosquito netting. The air-raid alert had been lifted at seven, and she had returned groggily to bed in the northeast suburb of Hakushima Kuken-cho. On the day of Pearl Harbor she had felt like "a fresh new flame"; now she thought she was dreaming of being "enveloped by a blue flash, like lightning at the bottom of the sea. . . . With an indescribable sound, almost like a roll of thunder, like a huge boulder tumbling down a mountain, the roof of the house came crashing down. When I came to, I was standing there, dazed, in a cloud of dust. . . . Yet there was no flame, no smoke. And I was alive. . . . I looked about me dazedly, half expecting to see my dead body stretched out."

All her furniture and belongings, from the twelve pieces of luggage packed for the countryside to the three thousand books in the library, were gone; there was only a small mound of broken roof tiles. "Of the mosquito net and even of the bed, there was not the slightest trace. . . . Outside, as far as the eye could see—which was much farther than usual—there stretched ruined house after ruined house." Her sister, Nakagawa, materialized, white dress covered with blood and face swollen like a pumpkin. Yōko looked at her own kimono. It was drenched in blood from shoulder to waist.

They stumbled to the cemetery just past the board fence beyond the garden. The fence was gone, as were the shrines. A lone *torii* stood gauntly, and blood-soaked survivors sat expressionless on gravestones. Thin wisps of smoke began to issue from the flattened buildings. Yōko's mother handed her Nakagawa's baby. It was still asleep.

Closer to the blast center, Hiroko Nakamoto lay inside a shattered house; she had no idea how she had got there. Dazed and in shock, she began stumbling down a ruined street. The air was heavy "with a sickening odor." She saw bodies everywhere. A stalled streetcar was filled with dead people. She passed a miraculously unscathed woman. "She looked at me, then turned away with a gasp of horror. I wondered why. I felt as if one side of my face was detached, and did not belong to me. I was afraid to touch it with my hand."

People who could walk through the nightmare were moving toward the river—"burned people with clothes in shreds or no clothes at all, men and women covered with blood, crying children." The wooden bridge she crossed every day to her factory was afire. Hiroko stopped. For the first time she looked at her body. It was a mass of burns from the ankle up. "I realized that the left side of my face must be burned, too. . . . Not pink, but yellow. The flesh was hanging loose. I went down to the water's edge and tried to put the skin back with salt water from the river, as I saw others doing."

A White Russian émigré who had joined the British army as a medic, Constantine Petrovsky had gone into action on the night of the first raid on Singapore, in the first hours of the Pacific war. When the garrison had surrendered, he began nightmarish months of prison camps in Malaya, Thailand, the Philippines, and finally Japan. His lot of sick and starved prisoners worked twelve-hour shifts in a coal mine near Hiroshima. Petrovsky and an American PW doctor cared for the sick without medicines. No appeals for supplies had worked. "Look, we don't have now, Captain," he was told. "It's Americans bombing us all the time."

With no newspapers, no radio, no news other than overheard conversation among guards, they understood nevertheless that the war had turned around. Seeing the first B-29s confirmed it. "Americans were coming to Japan day and night. . . . When the planes attacked, they put down red flag, alert, and on loudspeaker [warn] that American are coming, and everybody is to go out to the shelter. We saw this red flag and [heard an] alarm. But only high up was zzzzzzzzzzzzzhhhh going—[one] plane. . . . I went out where I was looking after the sick room, looked at the sky and suddenly phew! Like earthquake." A column of smoke arose "like a mushroom, spreading out, black. . . . I said, 'My God! They shot one plane, one bomb, they got oil tanks.' "

He saw the Japanese officers shuddering. One exclaimed, "That's a lucky shot." But later a Japanese doctor came in and announced that he was leaving—that the war was, in effect, over. He was needed in the city. "Americans no good," he said.

"Why?" Petrovsky asked.

"They dropped bomb. Hiroshima finished. Everybody dead."

"Can't be one bomb," said Petrovsky.

"Oh, yes, we don't know. But that happened."

A different kind of prisoner of war, "Jim" Ballard had been interned with his family near Shanghai. The raids and the devastation of the summer of '45 had left his camp in chaos, and they had been marched from detention in Lunghua to the grassy center of an abandoned football stadium. Jim guessed "that they were being walked to death around the countryside." A Japanese soldier patrolling the cinder track stared down at Jim and was about to kick him with a ragged boot. "But a flash of light filled the stadium, flaring over the stands in the south-west corner of the football field, as if an immense American bomb had exploded somewhere to the north-east of Shanghai. The sentry hesitated, looking over his shoulder as the light behind him grew more intense. It faded within a few seconds, but its pale sheen covered everything within the stadium."

Jim and the Japanese soldier waited for the rumble of sound that followed bomb-flashes, "but an unbroken silence lay over the stadium and the surrounding land, as if the sun had blinked."*

A teacher at a Christian school in Yokohama when the war began, Takaaki Aikawa was working reluctantly at Nippon Hikoki, an airplane factory. The radio news at noon had mentioned "considerable damage"

---

* Given the distance across the China Sea, only unusual atmospheric conditions could have made the novelized account in *Empire of the Sun* possible—a reflection off a high cloud layer. Some of the adult captives, Ballard recalls, claimed to have seen the flashes, probably from the Nagasaki bomb, overwhelming the fires from conventional bombing on the China coast.

at Hiroshima "by a small group of enemy planes." It took two days, however, before newspapers were permitted to print anything about the atomic bomb. "Most unforgettable" to Aikawa was a photograph of the streetcar which Hiroko Nakamoto had encountered, frozen by the blast. "As it stopped, it suddenly changed into a car of the dead, skeletons still hanging on the straps just as they had hung on them as living persons a few moments before." Another picture became famous as the "Thinking Man." Sitting on the stone steps of a bank, waiting for it to open, a man had been obliterated. "The flash printed his shadow on the stone wall of the bank, a shadow in the posture of the *Thinker* of Rodin. And there it has remained."

Like all Japanese cities, Hiroshima had been home to a host of household Buddhas, impassive and friendly, large and small. Like the city's flesh-and-blood inhabitants, Buddhas by the tens of thousands—wood, stone, ceramic, bronze—were incinerated, imploded, glassified, pulverized, blistered, liquefied, fused. At Pearl Harbor a thousand men had died instantly on the exploding *Arizona*. Four years later the technology of war had reached a decisive new level of efficiency.

Momo Iida remembered as a schoolboy on the first day of the war hearing an old soldier on a train declaring that the war would be like none before. When the news of the bomb came, Iida recalled the prophecy, and also his father's explanation—the elder Iida was an inventor and manufacturer of small household appliances—that with nuclear power "a bomb the size of a matchbox could burn up the whole of the world." Now Japanese radio warned that more attacks "of this new type of bomb" might occur, and citizens were urged "to wear white clothes as a protective measure." The wearer of white might, perhaps, not become a shadow.

On the night after the bomb, kamikaze pilots training at Kumigaya Air Base to fly to their deaths heard the whine of an air-raid siren. They ran to shelters carrying white sheets over their heads. The kamikaze hopefuls did not want to lose their opportunities for heroic suicide. Among them was Mutsuo Saitō, who had run about on the morning of Pearl Harbor protecting his house with pasted-up rice paper, which had approximately the same value against incendiary raids as white sheets against an atomic bomb.

Repatriated from his Washington embassy post to Japan with his American wife, Gwen, and their daughter, Mariko, Hidenari Terasaki lived the last year of the war, ill with heart trouble, in the food-desperate countryside. From public exhortations, Gwen expected that Japan "would fight until the entire country was destroyed, the Japanese people broken and almost extinct." Then Mariko returned from the village post office with a letter for her father from a newspaperman friend. It was their first news of Hiroshima. "As yet," he wrote, "we know of no defense against this new and terribly destructive weapon." Terasaki remembered that years before in Shanghai a "European Buddhist monk"—probably Trebitsch Lincoln—had told them one evening "that he foresaw a bomb so powerful that it could wipe out an entire city— a bomb that would change the course of history. . . . At the time we thought the monk was mad, but on this August day in 1945 we remembered his predictions and were afraid."

Soon afterward, Terasaki was back in Tokyo as English interpreter for the Emperor, who claimed that his Pearl Harbor role had been little more than pawn. "Indeed, the oil embargo cornered Japan," Hirohito explained. "If at that time I suppressed opinions in favor of war, public opinion would have certainly surged [against me], with people asking why Japan should surrender so easily when we had a highly efficient army and navy. . . . It would have led to a coup d'etat." He would have been killed by the militarists. "That would have been fine," he shrugged, "but Japan could have perished."

Now that a single enemy plane could do the work of a cloud of them, Japan seemed close to perishing. The "great hordes" of B-29s conducting daylight raids "looked beautiful" to "Pappy" Boyington from his prison camp, from which he was marched daily to dig tunnels deep below the surface of Honshu. A Flying Tiger in Burma on the first day of the war, and a fighter ace in the South Pacific later, he could not imagine from his combat experience "what kinds of bombs were going to be dropped to necessitate a tunnel two hundred feet underground." Then a Japanese guard "tried to tell me about the atomic bomb. He could speak no English . . . and I couldn't fathom at first that it was only one bomb he was talking about." Only after the surrender had been signed, and Boyington was on his way home, did he learn of the reality of the bomb.

In a prison camp at Hakodate, near Sapporo, at the southern tip of Hokkaido, onetime *Peterel* telegraphist Jack Honywill was working the coal mines. Life was stark and he remembered with gratitude the meal he had been given en route from an even worse camp, a bowl of rice and pickled grasshoppers, first described as prawns. On fire-watch he was approached by one of the sentries who spoke a little English. "Hiroshima," he said. "One bomb. Finish." Honywill thought that the guard must have awakened from a nightmare, but then all work stopped.*

Shot down after sinking the battleship *Haruna* in Kure harbor, erroneously reported sunk by the crew of Colin Kelly's B-17 off Luzon in the first days of the war, B-24 pilot Tom Cartwright and the surviving crewmen of the *Lonesome Lady* had been taken to nearby Hiroshima for interrogation. An unsophisticated junior-college freshman when his Sunday movie in Amarillo was interrupted, he had since learned a lot about war. Now his interrogators wanted to know what he knew. Cartwright and his comrades had been instructed before their mission to answer freely rather than suffer brutality. What did it matter if the enemy learned of the disasters that lay ahead if they kept on fighting?

On August 2 he was taken to Tokyo for further questioning. His crew remained behind in Hiroshima Castle. A few days later he was grilled again.

What was the "new kind of bomb" that could end the war? Cartwright didn't know, and wasn't told why he was being asked. But to loosen his tongue, a huge soldier, brandishing a samurai sword, was motioned in, and Cartwright was blindfolded and marched out with him. "This is your last chance to keep your head," the interrogator warned.

Despite his terror, Cartwright convinced both captors that he knew nothing. Led back to his cell, he was unaware that his crewmen had been killed by the blast of the first atomic bomb. Later the Japanese identified twenty Americans among the Hiroshima dead, including some apparently executed elsewhere in the city, and concealed in the nuclear toll. Eight alleged casualties had been murdered in medical experiments at Kyushu University.

One American had survived the holocaust, but not for long. After

---

* More than half the *Peterel*'s complement survived PW camp, and a few were still alive when in 1977 a new *Peterel* was commissioned, complete to the misspelled name. One survivor, A. E. Mariner, exultantly went aboard, and Earl Mountbatten wrote to him that the Queen put up her binoculars and observed, "There is Jim Mariner. I can see him putting both arms up over his head." The original *Peterel*'s skipper, Stephen Polkinghorn, a tenacious ninety-nine, read about the event in a war veterans' home in New Zealand.

the raid a young soldier wearing only shorts was tied to a pole near Hiroshima Castle. He was found stoned to death by chunks of broken concrete—retaliation, perhaps, for the bomb.

•

Squadron Leader Tom Lamb had flown a torpedo bomber into the Malayan chaos. Feeble after years of malnutrition and exposure, he was at a prison camp at Palembang, Sumatra, when Flight Sergeant "Mel" Melville brought the news "in great excitement." Their radio, concealed in the screw-leg of a stool, had picked up a bulletin that a bomb had "blown half of Japan into the bloody sea." It seemed true. Guards began bowing and the food improved.

At a camp on Java the news reached the POW population after another secret radio, built into a wooden shoe, picked up a broadcast from Delhi. The Dutch and British prisoners, captives in one of the richest rice-producing areas in the world, were so near starvation that the report seemed merely the product of hunger and hallucination. The "listening officer"—a New Zealander—had missed the opening of the broadcast, but he was able, Colonel Laurens van der Post, who had been in Singapore at the beginning, remembered, to relate "that something tremendous had happened. He wasn't quite certain precisely what it was, but in the course of the morning of the day which was now ended, something more like an act of God than of man had been inflicted on Japan at a place called Hiroshima. Exactly how and what had been done he couldn't explain. All he knew was that it was something new and terrible in human experience, more terrible even than earthquakes, tidal waves or volcanic eruptions."

Van der Post wondered whether they had picked up some dramatized radio fiction like Orson Welles's *War of the Worlds*, which once had caused a panic in America. When the New Zealander again twisted his contraband coils and picked up Perth and San Francisco, the awesome event was confirmed. They returned to their ragged blankets on the stone floor with certainty that the unexplained, but man-made, cataclysm would end the war. All they had to do was survive a little longer, not an easy thing given the Japanese contempt for prisoners of war and their likely refusal to similarly degrade themselves.

Once a junior senator who had to hurry back from Missouri to vote on the war resolution in 1941, Harry Truman in August 1945 was President, and en route home by sea from a conference near Berlin with Stalin. Prudently, Truman had prepared a statement before he had left Washington, which an assistant read to reporters at the White House. Hiroshima had been leveled by "an atomic bomb," it began, a device which was "a harnessing of the basic power of the universe. The force from which the sun draws its power has been loosed against those who brought war to the Far East." On board the cruiser *Augusta* the President told sailors on being handed the radio message about Hiroshima, "This is the greatest thing in history." A single bomb had made it certain that the war would end, and very soon. But Truman also understood that the bomb had opened a new and unpredictable chapter in world affairs.

Japanese Home Service first broadcast a bulletin that "a small number of B-29s" had penetrated into Hiroshima and "reduced to ashes . . . a considerable number of homes." The unidentified explosives, it reported, were attached to parachutes, and their effectiveness "should not be regarded as slight." It would be necessary to "formulate strong steel-like measures to cope with this type of bomb."

•

Living in Hanamaki, far to the north of Tokyo, since his studio had been incinerated by the fire-raids, Kōtarō Takamura

> . . . heard that broadcast.
> Sitting upright, I was trembling.
> Japan was finally stripped bare. . . .

The news came to Marquis Kido in devastated Tokyo through military chiefs who spoke of a "new type of bomb" which they had been assured could not be made during the likely span of the war. Kido reported to the Emperor, who confessed to being "overwhelmed with grief" at the catastrophe. Although he realized that the Army hierarchy might resist, Hirohito said, the dread new circumstances required that Japan "bow to the inevitable." However unconstitutional it was for him to place his Imperial self in the decision process, he requested an emergency session of the Cabinet. "I thought," Hirohito told Hidenari Terasaki, "that the Japanese race would be destroyed if the war continued."

The Cabinet debated the unthinkable, with only Foreign Minister Togo, a survivor from the first day, outspokenly for ending the lost war before more Hiroshimas occurred across Japan. It would take a few more anguished days, and another bomb—and Russia's hurrying into the war—before Tojo's replacement as Prime Minister, the elderly Baron Kantaro Suzuki, would give the Emperor the legalistic cloak for the moral authority already exercised privately. Suzuki formally asked for the Throne's "wishes," and Hirohito was given the opportunity, he claimed later, "for the first time to exercise my own free will." The Army wanted one more great battle, this time on the home islands, to salvage Japan's honor at whatever cost. When the Americans began the expected invasion of the home islands, the first thrust was likely to occur against Kyushu. Just south of Honshu, it was the second major island in the group. Whether guesswork or good intelligence, the fix was accurate. The storming of Kyushu, codenamed "Olympic," was already scheduled for November 1.

"When I thought about what that would be like," Lieutenant Sam Hynes, a young marine pilot based on Okinawa remembered, "I felt doomed, with a Japanese fatalism." He knew the cost of taking Okinawa, on Japan's doorstep. "I imagined the desperate defense of the homeland, the suicide attacks, the fierce concentrations of AA fire. The whole population would fight against us. In my imagination farmers attacked with pitchforks, crying 'Banzai!' and geisha girls held grenades between their inscrutable thighs; every object was a booby-trap, and all the roads were mined. We would all be killed, I thought, by fanatics who had already lost their war."

The Japanese in August 1945 would not have foreseen this as fantasy. Many expected the Emperor to announce what was anticipated as "the Honorable Death of a Hundred Million," and legendary director Akiro Kurosawa, then a young filmmaker cranking out propaganda for the military, thought it would happen. "Those people . . . probably would have done what they were told, and died. And probably I would have done likewise. The Japanese see self-assertion as immoral and self-sacrifice as the sensible course to take in life. We were accustomed to this teaching and never thought to question it."

Firebrand young officers in the Imperial Guards preferred a coup, and continued hopeless fighting, to dishonor, and tried to seize the Palace and radio NHK to prevent the Emperor's broadcast appeal to lay down all arms. In one of the many ironies of that frantic period, the radio anchorman on duty at NHK who found technical reasons to keep the fanatical Major Kenji Hatanaka from subverting Hirohito's address to the nation was Morio Tateno, who had first announced from NHK the attack on Pearl Harbor and the beginning of the war.

There was added irony in another frantic—and failed—post-Bomb conspiracy, the plot to kidnap a child of royal blood and bring him up secretly as post-occupation successor to the Emperor, who some expected to be dethroned, or to choose abdication. Navy Ministry funds were to be covertly used, and the scheme was entrusted to Captain Minoru Genda, once aide to Admiral Yamamoto and the planner of Pearl Harbor. A child was plucked, but the scheme came apart. (Genda even managed to find a place for himself in the postwar Japanese establishment.)

The planning center for Japanese Navy home defense had been Kure, on the southeast coast of Hiroshima Bay, and for ground forces the Second Army Group headquarters in Hiroshima itself, both in southernmost Honshu. Field Marshal Sugiyama, the Army chief, had commanded the efficient Second Air Fleet in Malaya at the start of the war. Now Hiroshima was flattened; Army sources were mute and unreachable; firestorms fanned across what was once a city.

From Kure, where the searing flash and the soaring mushroom cloud had been visible, urgent appeals had gone to Tokyo. Wires had also gone to Nara, near Osaka and halfway between Tokyo and Hiroshima, to locate Captain Mitsuo Fuchida. Leader of the first wave of carrier planes over Pearl Harbor, rescued later from a ditched plane during the Battle of Midway, Fuchida was a survivor. As Air Operations Officer for the Navy, he had been at a conference at Hiroshima on the defense of Kyushu; it had ended just the day before. Leaving his assistant, Lieutenant Toshio Hashizume, at their hotel in Hiroshima, the Yamato (since obliterated by the bomb), he had flown to Nara to troubleshoot a problem at the new underground naval headquarters being built remote from Tokyo. The headquarters would lack a navy. The fuel-starved home fleet was down to one battleship, four small carriers, four cruisers, and twenty-eight destroyers. Many were damaged and barely operable.

Could the essential Fuchida return urgently to Hiroshima to explore the whereabouts of a second, apparently unexploded, bomb? Witnesses had seen a second B-29 drop something by parachute. If Fuchida could find it, the secret of the awesome explosive might be solved. He flew back, circling over the smoking rubble that had been

Hiroshima. Near the river, at what seemed the blast center, the charred skeleton of a domed building somehow stood. Little else remained; the fires were going out. There was nothing left to burn.

With Captain Yasukado Yasui, Fuchida flew about the nearby hills until darkness, spotting nothing resembling a crumpled parachute. At dawn the pair began again, searching likely sites in a truck from Kure. Up a mountain road, five miles north of Hiroshima, they saw what appeared to be white silk billowing in the wind. Stopping, they climbed out and cautiously followed the parachute cords down to a metal cylinder, three feet long and about a foot wide. It did not look like a bomb, but it was clearly what observers had described. Tugging at a metal ring, they dislodged the contents—instruments connected by wires, including a thermometer and a radio transmitter. They had found Luis Alvarez's scientific package, which had measured and reported the performance of the bomb. To Yasui, Fuchida explained the likely purpose of the contents, adding, "Whatever made us think we could beat America?"

Gingerly, they pushed the wires and instruments back into the cylinder, loaded it into their truck, and left the hills from which they could still see the horror of Hiroshima.

Sources and Strategies

Some incidents in this global narrative, fuzzy in date or time, have been fixed through the internal logic of events or through the evidence of details. "Early morning," "dawn," or the onset of darkness can mean one thing in one latitude or longitude, another somewhere else. A worldwide account must also recognize the simultaneity of time, which can mean night in one band of longitude, day in another—and even different dates and days of the week. Events are described in approximately simultaneous time worldwide, but not "our" time. Chronology is more simplified now than it was in 1941, when Bangkok and Singapore were twenty minutes apart, and Java was a further ten minutes off Malayan time, and Hawaii was two and a half hours earlier than California time.

Accounts of participants, set down just after an event or nearly five decades later, can be equally faulty in detail, but for different reasons, and some individuals involved in the events of that crucial December have given accounts incompatible with earlier testimony. Official histories and contemporary communiqués can be dubious in omission or commission—often deliberately so. This narrative attempts to reconcile accounts as well as times where possible, to select the most probable descriptions of events where variations are irreconcilable. Memory plays tricks on remembrancers. History and legend often fuse, or replace each other. What should have been becomes instead what happened, or never happened in the way described in citations. Stories in contemporary newspapers, press handouts, or later histories are not necessarily "true" because they appeared in print. War is messy, inefficient, unpredictable, and confused. Perhaps that is the only certainty.

To cite all the *published* sources utilized—books, newspapers, articles, memoirs, official documents—would require another volume almost as long as this one. Since that is impractical, I have identified in notes for each chapter only those oral, manuscript, and documentary materials unique to this narrative. A few exceptions to the rule are limited-access publications not likely to be found in most research libraries. There is a vast literature on Pearl Harbor itself as well as on the vast arena of war beyond Hawaii.

All manuscript material and oral history material in my possession of an American nature, including letters and tapes from participants which could not be used in the book, have been presented to the U.S. Army Military History Institute, Carlisle, Pennsylvania. Documentary material relating to Britain and the Commonwealth nations has been given to the Imperial War Museum in London. These may be consulted at the discretion of each institution. A reader who requires the location or identification of a particular published source not clear from the context may consult me, enclosing a stamped, self-addressed envelope.

As I have noted, some published accounts are simply not accurate, yet are accepted as fact because they look authoritative in print. Spectators have remembered the wrong football teams playing each other on December 7; the New York Philharmonic broadcast has been assigned the wrong music, soloist, and conductor; congressmen have recalled sitting at conferences in the White House with colleagues who were distant from Washington. People—including military men—have recorded hearing the war news hours before the attack on Pearl Harbor happened, and have identified ships and planes simply not in the vicinity of the action described—even planes which did not exist. Dozens of Dutch PBYs are destroyed at Pearl Harbor; sailors there are entombed on the wrong battleship; FDR finds his "day of infamy" phrase as an instant epiphany; and Fuchida flies into the inferno of Hiroshima a few minutes after the Bomb is dropped. I have attempted to exorcise some of these historical ghosts, mostly silently.

Times of events have been made consistent with reality in accounts where memory has erred. In some cases, participants misstated the time by hours—even days. In some cases the culprit is the International Date Line.

East Asian nomenclature is largely that of the period, in names of both people and places. Even the historical figure now known by the unintentionally ironic name he gave to his reign at its beginning, the Emperor Shōwa ("Bright Peace"), remains Emperor Hirohito. (Mao Zedong is an exception because his surname is unchanged.) The present Chongqing remains Chungking, and the Yangzi River is still Yangtze. Elsewhere, where useful, a contemporary spelling is added in parenthesis. Most Asian names are given Western style, again with exceptions where familiarity renders any other practice awkward and intrusive. Chiang Kaishek's name, for example, appears last-name-first. Japanese and Thai names are given Western-style where a name would be unrecognizable to the lay reader otherwise (i.e., Tojo Hideki is, here, Hideki Tojo). The index lists all family names in the usual sequence.

In the following notes, the United States Army Military History Institute is abbreviated to USAMHI. The Imperial War Museum is IWM; the Hoover Institution on War, Revolution and Peace at Stanford, California, is HI; the Australian War Memorial [Library] in Canberra is AWM. The National Archives, Washington, is NA-W; the Archives branch in Suitville, Maryland, in NA-S. SW is the author.

THE DAY BEFORE: December 6, 1941

Data on the prewar American military mission to London is from Gen. Charles L. Bolte's papers and oral history, USAMHI. The Japanese novel *Future War between Japan and the United States* was translated by War Department staff; a transcript is at USAMHI. A translation of the Marquis Kido diary by Yuri Takahashi was furnished to SW by Junko Matoba. Copies of Gen. H. H. Arnold's radiotelephone messages to MacArthur, Short, and Brereton are in the Morton papers at USAMHI.

HOUR 1

Pvt. Hisaeda Akiyoshi's Guam diary is at AWM. Capt. Garry Anloff's memories throughout from his letters to SW and taped interviews. Lt. Freiherr von Heyl's diary extracts throughout are from his privately printed war diary, *Wie Ich den Krieg erlebte*, which he gave to SW. Translations are by Beata Engel Doyle. Edited and translated by John W. M. Chapman, volume 4 of the war diary of Admiral Ulrich Wenneker is published in a bound typescript-reproduction as *The Price of Admiralty* (Ripe, Sussex:

Saltire Press, 1989). The volume covers the period September 10, 1941–January 31, 1942.

Hour 2

Previously unpublished Leningrad diary accounts are from the journal of Lidiia Osipova at HI, as translated by Adriana and Richard Martin. Translations from the diary of Marshal Ugo Cavallaro are by Beno Weiss. A run of the *Tobruk Truth* was consulted at AWM. Douglas MacArthur's restored penthouse suite, with some of his own memorabilia in it, is in use again at the Manila Hotel, without a corridor of bedrooms now put to other uses. It had been burned by retreating Japanese troops early in 1945. When not in use as a VIP suite it can be seen on application.

Hour 3

Admiral Hart's message to the *Gold Star* is in Daniel J. Mullin's *Another Six Hundred*, a privately printed diary-narrative of Destroyer Division 59 (hereafter Mullin). Recollections of Gen. Bradford Chynoweth are from his unpublished memoir in USAMHI. Captain Arthur G. Robinson's memoir-log, "The U.S.S. *Marblehead*. The story of a Gallant Ship," is at HI. General Sir Lewis Heath's papers are at IWM.

Hour 4

Anthony Heckstall-Smith's memoir is at AWM. Copies of Ambassador Winant's cables are at the Australian Defence Forces Academy, Canberra. Dr. Julien M. Goodman wrote to SW about Fort McKinley.

Hour 5

Lieutenant Charles Fisher's memoir is at IWM.

Hour 6

The U.S. military attaché's report from Kuibyshev is in NA-S.

Hour 7

Flying Officer Richard Allanson's memories of Malaya are from letters to SW. America First papers are at HI. General Ira Eaker's oral history is at USAMHI.

Hour 8

Evatt-Casey cables throughout are at the Australian Defence Forces Academy, Canberra.

Hour 9

Von Weiszäcker diary extracts are translated by Beata Doyle.

HOUR 10

Details of Kathleen Harriman birthday dinner at Chequers are taken in part from a letter from Kathleen Harriman Mortimer to SW.

HOUR 11

Grace Tully's corrected typescript is at the FDR Library, Hyde Park, New York.

HOUR 12

The source (Kleinfeld and Tambs—*Hitler's Spanish Legion*) for the Blue Division barracks bombing near Leningrad literally places the unexploded but ticking bomb in the impaled body of a soldier, suggesting a melodramatically inaccurate recollection.

HOUR 13

Seaman Robert Ogg investigation papers, including his denials of melodramatic extrapolations made from his testimony, are at NA-W.

HOUR 14

Former Ambassador Seni Pramoj wrote to SW about the suppressed Thai declaration of war on the U.S.

HOUR 15

Major C. R. Templer's Hong Kong diary is at IWM. Lieutenant Charles Utter described his Canal Zone memories in letters to SW.

HOUR 16

Details of Shamshuipo and Stonecutter's Island are based upon SW's visits to both sites in April 1988.

HOUR 17

The Singapore memories of Donald Pearson, Mrs. Innes-Kerr, D. G. Cotton and John Mutimer are from unpublished accounts in IWM.

HOUR 18

Alice Briggs's account of Hong Kong is from her privately printed memoir; Christopher Briggs added his own version in letters to SW. John Tonkin's POW reminiscence, written in 1971, is in IWM. That Task Force 12 picked up sonar signals from the trailing *I-74* was reported to me on 8 November 1990 by a Navy captain now retired who had been a junior officer then on the *Lexington*.

HOUR 19

Alfred Littlefield Smith's account is based on his interview published in *U.S. Navy Medicine*, Jan-Feb 1986 and a letter to SW from Jan Kenneth Herman, Historian, Naval Medical Command.

HOUR 20

Accounts of the *Peterel* and its sinking are in the IWM.

HOUR 21

Ed Sheehan's accounts of Pearl Harbor Sunday are based upon his Honolulu-published memoir, *Days of '41* (1976), and his letter to SW.

HOUR 22

Arthur Gomez told SW in Hong Kong about the Mickey Mann incident in the New Territories. Robert K. M. Simpson's unpublished memoir is in the University of Hong Kong Library. Kurahachi Fukuda's diary is at the IWM. Vera Inber's diary description of a child's swaddled corpse on a sled is validated by a photograph reproduced in this book. General Ian Campbell's prisoner-of-war diary is at the IWM. A transcript of Ryuichi Yokoyama's account of *Kido Butai*, taken from Tokyo Radio, is at NA-W.

HOUR 23

Emily Hahn's memories of Hong Kong are from her memoirs, notably *China to Me*, and from a letter to SW. These are supplemented by a letter from Charles Boxer to SW. Ruby Motley's memoir of Manila is at the USAMHI; Howard W. Brown's Philippine papers are at NA-W. Monica Joyce in North Sydney did the detective work on Dorothy Jenner's age.

HOUR 24

Karl von Wiegand's papers are at HI. Francis Braun's account of Hong Kong appeared in his Hong Kong-published *The Banknote that Never Was* (n.d.). Claire Chennault's papers are at HI.

HOUR 25

Eugene Dooman's memoir is at HI. Ernst Jünger's diary is translated by Beata Doyle. Herbert R. Lottman in a letter to SW identifies Céline, who in the published diary is thinly concealed as "Merline."

Hour 26

Michael Branch's memoir is at IWM. The Libyan diary by an unknown Milanese soldier is at AWM.

Hour 27

Laura Margolis Jarblum's memories of Shanghai are from letters to SW and a taped interview. Father E. C. Gordon's diary is published in part in Lina Araneta Santiago's *Four Decades for Our Lady* (Manila, September 25, 1979). Peter Gibbes wrote about his RAF experience in Malaya to SW; E. C. Ford wrote about Hong Kong to SW.

Hour 28

Dr. Desmond Brennan wrote to SW about Malaya. Charles Simon's memories of Penang are in a letter to SW. W. R. Halliday's experiences of Singapore are in a letter to SW. For Mullin see Hour 3. H. L. White's Hong Kong diary is at IWM. Army movements and conversations at the War Department are from "U.S. Army Investigations into the Handling of Certain Communications Prior to the Attack on Pearl Harbor," SRH-115, 1944–45," declassified from Top Secret, NA-W. Exact times of communications are from a memorandum for Gen. W. Bedell Smith, June 8, 1942, by J. R. Deane, Secretary, General Staff, USAMHI.

Hour 29

Mollie Reilly's memoir of Singapore is at IWM. Walter C. Phillips's typed Philippines memoir is at USAMHI.

Hour 30

The Pearl Harbor memories of Alfred Perucci, Doyle A. Bell, Harry Rorman, Maury Meister, Archie Pence, and B. C. Besser are from letters to SW. William Gentry and Cecil Vandiver responded to questionnaires from USAMHI. The H. Alexander Walker episode was told to SW by Walker's son Harry in Honolulu in November 1988. Robert Richards's B-17 at Bellows Field is described from photos in the National Air and Space Museum and Stanley Thomas's account in the Bristol (Connecticut) Museum Newsletter, January 1984. Scouting Six details not previously in print are from the Navy Investigative Report at the Arizona Memorial Museum, Pearl Harbor, furnished by Daniel Martinez. Harry W. O. Kinnard's and John R. Deane's oral histories are at USAMHI.

Hour 31

SW checked the "Bethlehem Steel, 1898" mortars at Corregidor himself. War Department "radios" to the Philippines from Gerow, Arnold, Marshall, and others are in the Morton papers at USAMHI. Harry Hopkins's memos are in the Hopkins Papers, Georgetown University Library. Leonard Heaton's medical narrative, including John

J. Moorhead material, is from his oral history at USAMHI. Ivan D. Yeaton, William C. Braly, and John Wright deposited oral histories at USAMHI. Data from Philip Gibbs, Phyllis Walen, David T. Coiner, Paul Becker, and A. J. Winser are from letters to SW; Ronald Moton's memories are from taped interviews and letters. All *Ford* material is from Mullin. Texts from American radio broadcasts of John Daly, George Fielding Eliot, and others are from contemporary recordings. Quotes from Webley Edwards's Honolulu broadcasts are from C. C. Waite to SW, and Ed Sheehan. T. C. Carter's Singapore memories are at IWM.

Hour 32

Jorge Vargas material is from the Vargas Papers, University of the Philippines, Quezon City. J. G. Ballard wrote to SW about his novel and its relation to reality. Arthur Collins and Andrew Goodpaster furnished oral histories to USAMHI. Lindbergh/ America First documents, including Ruth Sarles's papers, are at HI. W. R. Halliday, Robert Fox, George M. Trostle, William Gregg, Lucile R. Addington, Bob Thomson, Tom Cartwright, Donald Greene, Ray Wax, John P. Smith, Oree C. Weller, and Robert Kidd wrote to SW. The Stilwell papers are at HI. Theodore Parker, Jack Rogers, Jack Marshall, Fred Warrick, R. H. Patterson, and Henry Miley contributed oral histories or questionnaire responses to USAMHI. George Kondo was interviewed by SW. Both Gen. John W. Hewitt and John Morris in an oral history and in a questionnaire response at USAMHI report the Polo Grounds summons to Colonel Donovan. The Cabinet War Rooms at Whitehall, with the large relief map of Malaya still on the wall, are open to tourists.

Hour 33

Ian Watt, C. H. Lockwood, David Marshall, and Atsushi Oi wrote to SW. Charlie Gan, Guan Chuan Tan, and Constantine Petrovsky contributed oral histories to the Singapore Oral History Department. Edwin Thumboo and Lee Kijo Lin were interviewed by SW in Singapore. John Boulter's and John Mutimer's memories are from IWM papers. Dietrich Zapf wrote to SW about Hildburghausen. John Horton's description of Hart's Manila office is from his "Waiting for Pearl Harbor," *Washington Post*, December 7, 1986.

The Brereton-MacArthur evidence about responsibility for the Clark Field disaster suggests shared blame, since Brereton or his surrogates could have ordered air cover for Clark during lunch hour and both before and after. MacArthur's large share begins, in real evidence of refusal to use his B-17s, with the Nielson Field summary of activities for December 8, in which an early entry is "07.15 General Brereton visited No. 1 Victoria and requested permission of General MacArthur to take offensive action. He was informed that for the time being our role was defensive, but to stand by for orders."

The earlier hour of the MacArthur rebuff in the diary fixes Nielson time as that of Brereton's return and reporting to his staff. However, the loose sheets of the diary—all carbon copies—for the dates December 8–13 identify the year as 1942 with corrections in ink to 1941 for 8–10 and no correction for 11–13. The year again appears as 1941 beginning with the 14th, at which point the paper becomes different, but the next two dates are mistakenly 1942. After that, the year is typed accurately; the slips in date suggest a typist reverting to the new year in the early weeks of 1942.

Hour 34

Edward Settles and Edward H. Howard wrote to SW about Guam. Eugene Dooman's papers are at HI. Theresa Gaggino wrote to SW about Hong Kong and T. G. Crews about Peking. Bradford Smith quoted R. T. Smith's diary in a letter to SW. The corrected typescript of FDR's "Infamy" address to Congress is in the FDR Library at Hyde Park. Eunice Young's memoir of the Philippines is at USAMHI, as is Harold K. Johnson's oral history. George C. Clarke was interviewed by Lewis Morton; see the Morton papers at USAMHI. José Laurel's privately printed memoir is at the Laurel Foundation, Manila; SW was given a copy by Laurel's son, "Doy." SW interviewed Florentino Hornedo about the Batan Islands and Armando Malay about Manila.

Hour 35

W. E. Prentice wrote to SW about New Guinea. Lao Wu's memoir (Hong Kong University Library) was translated by Kay Li. Kurahachi Fukuda's Singapore diary is at IWM. Willys R. Peck's and H. H. Smith-Hutton's papers are at HI. Australian War Cabinet proceedings are at the Defence Forces Academy, Canberra. The text of Private First Class Letteer's telegram from Brigadier General Roosevelt is at USAMHI.

Hour 36

Heather Tomlinson wrote to SW about Hong Kong. Bob Yates was interviewed by SW in London. Carmen Guerrero Nakpil, Antonio Quintos, José Quintos, Trinidad Subido, Simeon Medalla, and Geronima Pecson were interviewed by SW in Manila. Michael Lindsay supplemented his memoir in letters to SW. A. J. Borstlap wrote to SW about the invasion of Celebes. Elliott Thorpe's oral history about Java and Pearl Harbor is at USAMHI and at odds with his published memoir. Information about the Thai royal family on the first and only day of their war is from conversation with Harry Rolnick in Hong Kong and a follow-up fax from him. Memoirs of P. M. Briggs (Mrs. Briggs Thom), F. R. C. Fowle, D. K. Broadhurst, and Nicholas Photiades are at IWM. Ichyi Sugita wrote to SW about Malaya, Kenneth Cunningham about Egypt, Barbara Fowler Ball about the Philippines, Frederick Boughey about Hong Kong.

Hour 37

H. J. Bultman wrote to SW about Ford Island. Tosh Kano's diary is at the IWM. Hiroko Nakamoto's celluloid doll song—only mentioned by her—was found for SW and translated (separately) by Mieko De Angelo and Naomi Matsuoka. Liu Hung Sak's Hong Kong memoir (Hong Kong University Library) was translated by Kay Li. Eugenia Foyn's daughter, Molly Soltay, told Rodelle Weintraub in Hong Kong about her family's experience in Tientsin.

HOUR 38

The Hong Kong memories and diaries of H. L. White, Isaac Newton, and Sidney Hunt are at IWM, as is R. G. Tyler's Borneo diary and B. F. Kane's Burma memoir. Minnie Breese Stubbs responded to a USAMHI questionnaire. Kōtarō Takamura's memoir of December 8 in Tokyo appeared in the *Chuokoron* for January 1942, furnished by Norio Irie, and was translated by Tsutomu Takahashi. Geoff Jellbart, H. Norman Honhart, and Ernest Warwick wrote to SW about the Atlantic convoy experience. Major Lin's appeals to Chennault are in the Chennault papers, HI.

HOUR 39

The Iba radar plotter was a private who wrote to SW but asked to have his name withheld. All other original sources in the Clark Field section were referred to earlier. Chikara Inoue wrote to SW (translated by Edith Sarra) about ration cards and radio "supers." Frederick E. Gallaghan's diary is in the AWM.

HOUR 40

Tom Lamb wrote to SW about Malaya. Clare Grove's Luzon log is at HI. Edward Jaquet wrote to SW about Clark Field and the B-17 debacle, supplementing his memoir in the Winter 1985 *Daedalus Flyer*, the organ of American pilot-officers. Also writing to SW about the Philippines, largely about Clark Field, were Victor Mapes, Forrest Knox, Robert Brown, Anton Bilek, Edgar D. Field, Thomas E. Gage and William Thomas. Alva Fitch's oral history is at USAMHI.

HOUR 41

The Pendleton Army Air Base story is extracted from a letter to SW from Ross A. Sheldon. Ellis Markham and Oree Weller wrote to SW about the trapped sailors in the *Oklahoma*. Lieutenant Colonel Griffiss and Vice-Consul Nichols filed reports now in NA-S. Sherman Clay wrote to SW about Libya. L. E. Tutt's and E. G. Porter's diaries are at IWM.

HOUR 42

Nacht und Nebel documentation is in the IWM. Hans Landa wrote to SW about the death camps from his experience as a survivor. Douglas Collins's memoir is in the IWM. Warren F. Dalton wrote to SW about the destroyer *Lamson*.

HOUR 43

Thomas Murray Wilson's papers are in the Georgetown University Library. Joseph Moore and Constant Irwin were interviewed by Louis Morton (Louis Morton Papers, USAMHI). Nicholas Photiades' memoir of Malaya is at IWM.

Hour 44

Sumner Hudson wrote about preparations in California in a letter to SW. James Alley, Clair E. Boggs, W. R. Hunnicutt, Howard O. Pollan, and Louis E. Kelley wrote about Pearl Harbor to SW. Seni Pramoj wrote to SW about Thailand.

Hour 45

Reports of Consuls Marshall M. Vance and Paul Squire are in NA-S. G. S. Richardson wrote to SW about Malaya.

Hour 46

C. H. Lockwood, John T. Snyder, and Bess Tittle wrote to SW. O. W. Phillips's Singapore memoir is at IWM.

Hour 47

Kianghai Yau's Hong Kong incident (Hong Kong University Library) is translated by Kay Li. John Olson's Philippines recollection was a response to a USAMHI questionnaire. Squadron Leader Janusz's flight report is at IWM.

THE DAY AFTER: December 8

James F. Anderson and James R. Archer wrote to SW about Pearl Harbor. The Army list of unidentified Oahu dead is at USAMHI. Church A. Chappell's papers are at HI; they include a copy of Ellis A. Zacharias's address to the crew of the *Salt Lake City*. Frederick Hodgson and Arthur Bartholomew furnished oral histories to the Singapore Oral History Dept. Ralph Ingram's Hong Kong memoir is at IWM. Paul B. Noel wrote about the Philippines to SW. George T. Ferguson's diary is extracted in *U.S. Navy Medicine*.

CURTAIN CALL: The Day of the Bomb

The command to drop the bomb was from General Thomas T. Handy, deputy to Gen. George C. Marshall, to General Carl Spaatz, Commanding General, Strategic Air Force, dated from Washington on 25 July 1945, and marked "CONFIDENTIAL." It was declassified on 18 June 1948. The possibilities of seeing the distant flash of an A-bomb explosion in southern Japan from the China coast were explained to SW by meteorologist Charles L. Hosler and nuclear scientist Forrest J. Remick. The descriptions of the metamorphosed Buddhas at Hiroshima are based upon SW's experience of them. Earl Mountbatten's letter to Jack Honywill is in the IWM *Peterel* papers. Tosh Kano's diary is at the IWM. Tom Cartwright and Tom Lamb wrote to SW; Constantine Petrovsky contributed to the Singapore Oral History archives. The identification of

Trebitsch Lincoln is SW's own inference from the evidence in the Terasaki account. Hidenari Terasaki's pages of notes of his conversations with the Emperor were rediscovered after his death by his half-American daughter, Mariko Terasaki Miller, and published many years later in the Japanese monthly *Bengei Shunju* (November 16, 1990).

ACKNOWLEDGMENTS

I am indebted to the people and institutions identified below for their memories, their good offices, and their access to materials relevant to this study. Interviews, oral history materials, letters, and documents used significantly are cited in the source notes. Some individuals and institutions for whose help I am grateful are cited in the picture credits and source notes rather than below.

•

Carolina Afan, David Aiken, Masayuki Akiyama, Henry Albinski, W. H. Allison, James R. Archer, Bernard Asbell, Nick Bailey, Deirdre Bair, Barbara Fowler Ball, H. G. Barlow, George Barton, William G. Berberet, David T. Best, Lothair Blum, W. Michael Blumenthal, Geoffrey Bolton, A. G. Brauer, Frank A. Broad, Ralph E. Brown, Phillip Bruce, R. J. Bultman, Jr., Eugene C. Camp, James D. Campbell, III, Liwa Chiu, Harry P. Clark, Christopher Clausen, David T. Coiner, Kenneth R. Creese, Emilio A. Cruz, Thomas M. Culbertson, Elena Danielson, John Denehy, John Dorsey, Beata Doyle, William Duiker, Andrea M. Edang, Pam Elbinger, Raymond D. Emory, Jenny Emrys-Roberts, George Enteen, A. L. Fangman, John W. Finn, Alice Fleischer, Herman C. S. Fong, Paul A. Fraser, S. Friedlander, Jan

Geilenkirchen, Wayne T. Gise, Steven Greenfield, William Gregg, Frank Grilho, Thomas Hale, Alan Hanley-Browne, Eileen Hanley-Browne, Thomas Hardwick, John P. Haynes, Jan Herman, Lester James Hildreth, Jr., Charles L. Hosler, Norio Irie, Ernest J. Irvin, Laura Margolis Jarblum, Keith Jay, Lou de Jong, Francisco Sionil José, Monica Joyce, Jürgen Kamm, Laura Kauffmann, Ben Keeton, David Keogh, Billy F. Kerslake, Philip Klein, Heinz Kosok, Thomas J. Lamb, Jackie Lane, Sotero Laurel, Jake W. Layton, Jr., Robert Lee, Dorothy Levy, Kay Li, Herbert R. Lottman, W. R. Lucius, David Lusk, Armando J. Malay, Charles Mann, Ellis Markham, William Martin, Daniel Martinez, Junko Matoba, Herbert Mattlage, John McCarthy, Michael McKernan, Simeon Medalla, Maury Meister, George H. Mers, James Milholland, Jr., William J. Miller, Maria Louisa C. Moral, Ruth Niel, Vicki Norton, Ruth Nuzum, Steve J. Pechac, Archie B. Pence, Consuelo Salazar Perez, Lila Thomas Peterson, Roger Pineau, Emily Gain Piper, Ralph Pixton, Howard O. Pollan, Serafin D. Quaison, Shirley Rader, Jack T. Randall, Susan Reighard, Forrest J. Remick, H. K. Reynolds, Harry Rolnick, Eileen Root, Robert A. Ryan, Lina Araneta Salazar, Antonio M. Santos, Edith Sarra, Nicholas B. Scheetz, William Schmalstieg, Ernst Schurer, Mina Schwalb, Ed Sheehan, Ross A. Sheldon, Charles E. Shelton, William A. Sheppard, S. T. Simmons, George Simson, Elisabeth Sinn, Bradford Smith, Hugh Smith, Tom Smyth, Molly Soltay, Richard J. Sommers, Jervis Sparks, Sandra Steltz, Gillian Stevens, Gerhard Strasser, Victor C. Stratton, Ernst Strauss, Lorenzo M. Tañada, Hiromi Tanaka, Gilbert Thompson, Edwin Thumboo, Peter Thwaites, Paul Tognetti, Dorothy Traiger, John Turner, Henry E. Wagner, Jr., C. C. Waite, Phyllis M. Walen, Charles W. Watson, Van Watts, David Weintraub, Mark Weintraub, Rodelle Weintraub, Beno Weiss, Oree C. Weller, Bruce Weigl, A. J. Winser, Philip Winsor, Muriel Winterscheid, Lady Wright, Vincent Yang, Bob Yates, Philip Young.

•

Arizona Memorial & Museum, Pearl Harbor; Atomic Bomb Memorial Museum, Hiroshima; Australian War Memorial, Canberra; British Library, London; Dai Ichi Insurance Company, Tokyo; Eisenhower Library, Abilene; The Johns Hopkins University; Franklin D. Roosevelt Memorial Library, Hyde Park; Georgetown University Library; History Library, Australian Defence Forces Institute, Canberra; Hong Kong Public Record Office; Hong Kong Radio 3; Hoover Institution, Stanford; Imperial War Museum, London; International House Library, Tokyo; Kyoto University; Laurel Foundation, Manila; National Aeronautics and Space Museum, Washington; National Archives, Singapore; National Archives (U.S.); National Library of the Philippines, Manila; National Museum of Science & Industry, London; National University of Singapore; Naval Institute, Annapolis; Nihon University, Mishima; Pan Am Library, New York; Pattee Library, The Pennsylvania State University; Pearl Harbor Survivors Association; U.S. Army Military History Institute, Carlisle, PA; University of Hong Kong History Workshop; University of Hong Kong Library; University of the Philippines, Quezon City; University of Wuppertal Library; Vargas Foundation, Quezon City.

INDEX

Ackerson, Frank A., 238
Addington, Glenn, 313–14
Addington, Lucile R., 313–14, 674
Aditya, Prince, 435
Adun, Detcharat, 172–73, 205–06, 436
Aebersold, Paul, 284
Agawa, Hiroyuki, 447
Aikawa, Takaaki, 449, 658–59
Aizawa, Yahaichi, 464
Akers, Anthony B., 321
Akin, Spencer B., 256
Akiyoshi, Hisaeda, 23, 669
Aldridge, James, 278
Alfieri, Dino, 81–82
Allanson, Richard J., 72–73, 381–82, 599–600, 670
Allen, Brooke E., 250–51, 394
Allen, Eric, 558
Allen, Woody, 302
Alley, James E., 590, 677
Allshorn, Sq. Ldr., 438–39
Alvarez, Luis, 655, 666

Amagai, Takahisa, 215, 411
America First Committee, 8, 9, 95, 308, 310–12, 392–93, 477–478, 634, 670, 674
Anami, Korechika, 410–11
Anders, Wladislaw, 555
Anderson, Edward L., 632
Anderson, James F., 629–30, 677
Anderson, Lale, 80
Andreas-Friedrich, Ruth, 61–62, 586
Andrews, Maxine, 302–03
Anloff, Garry, 24–25, 43, 345–46, 453–54, 506, 528–29, 581–582, 669
Aono, Suekichi, 509
Arazym, Martha, 149
Archer, James, 631, 677
Argyropoulou, Fotini, 557
Arnold, H. H., 13, 70, 100–01, 303, 407, 425, 573–76, 669, 673
Asada, Wannito, 172, 502–03
Astor, Vincent, 99
Auchinleck, Claude, 38, 152, 406

Austin, Warren R., 486
Aweau, Sam, 232
Aydelotte, Frank, 52
Ayudhya, Princess Kobkaew na, 435–436

Baels, Mary-Liliane, 565
Bahr, Walter, 267
Bair, John, 309
Baker, Maj., 398
Ball, Lawrence, 264–65
Ballantine, Joseph W., 262
Ballard, J. G., 293, 585, 658, 674
Band, William, 429
Banta, Jack, 305
Barkley, Alben, 486
Barstow, A. E., 600
Barthelmes, Karl, 231
Bartholomew, Arthur, 639, 677
Bastico, Ettore, 217–18, 586
Bateson, Harold, 194
Batson, E. J. ("Shorty"), 524–25
Baugh, Sammy, 306
Baukhage, H. R., 79, 354
Baxter, George, 419, 456
Bayler, Walter, 288, 330, 466
Beatty, Frank E., 268
Becht, *Forstmeister*, 209
Beck, Leon, 526
Becker, Paul, 271, 674
Belin, Ferdinand Lammot, 55, 100, 113
Bell, Don, 517–18, 520
Bell, Doyle A., 233, 324, 673
Bell, L. H., 545
Bellaire, Bob, 375–76, 414
Bellinger, Patrick N. L., 238
Benninghoff, Merrell, 188–89, 210, 375–77
Bennion, Mervyn, 244
Benton, William, 95
Bergdoll, Charles, 249
Bergholtz, Olga, 161
Berle, Adolph, 135–36, 363, 534
Besser, B. C., 244, 673

Bicknell, George W., 109–11, 123, 237, 245
Biddle, Francis, 34, 239, 462–63
Bilek, Anton, 521, 676
Billotte, Philippe, 357
Black, Hugo, 246
Blake, Gordon, 249
Blanco, Juan Eugenio, 92–93
Bloch, Claude C., 220, 300–01, 409
Bloom, Sol, 486, 488
Blumenthal, W. Michael, 293
Blumentritt, Günther von, 647
Bock, Fedor von, 25–27, 68, 160, 184–85, 549–50
Boettiger, Anna Roosevelt, 269
Boettiger, John, 269
Boggs, Clair E., 567–68, 589, 677
Bohlen, Charles ("Chip"), 468
Bokun, Branko, 595–96
Boldin, I. V., 69
Bolte, Charles L., 669
Bond, Charles R., 482–83
Bonesteel, Chesley, 326–27
Borstlap, A. J. P., 432–33, 675
Borstlap, Ada, 432–33
Borstlap, Annemarie, 432–33
Borstlap, Annie, 432–33
Borstlap, Jolanda, 432–33
Bosanquet, David, 156–57, 456–57
Bostrom, Frank, 249
Bothne, Adolph M., 244
Boughey, Frederick, 422, 675
Boulter, John, 359–60, 674
Bowen, Kelly, 275–76
Bowker, Jack, 143
Boxer, Charles, 165, 332, 378, 417, 642, 672
Boyington, Gregory, 382–84, 660
Bradley, Omar, 314
Brady, Francis M., 345
Braly, William C., 257, 674
Branch, Michael, 40, 185, 673
Brantley, Hattie, 475
Bratton, Rufus, 109, 124–25, 185–186, 196, 211–12, 213–14, 239, 416

Brauchitsch, Werner von, 28–29, 159, 619
Braun, Francis, 171–72, 594, 672
Brautigam, Otto, 648
Brennan, Desmond, 203–04, 532, 673
Brereton, Lewis H., 180–82, 240, 256, 344–46, 407–08, 453–54, 481–82, 506, 572–576, 669, 674–75
Brewster, Kingman, Jr., 308
Briggs, Alice, 135, 510, 671
Briggs, Christopher, 134–35, 420–421, 510, 671
Briggs, Lyman J., 52
Briggs, P. M., 438, 675
Briggs, Patricia, 135
Broadhurst, D. K., 439, 675
Broadhurst, Marjorie, 439
Brooke, Alan, 61, 152, 336
Brooke-Popham, Robert, 10–11, 47–48, 64–65, 104–05, 106, 162, 196–97, 222, 281, 334, 381, 459, 602–03
Brooks, C. Wayland ("Curley"), 624
Brooks, Robert, 528
Brown, Bob, 257
Brown, Cecil, 64–65, 358, 381, 434, 548–49, 592, 608, 638–40
Brown, Clifton, 196
Brown, Dickson, 574
Brown, Harold, 474
Brown, Howard W., 166, 672
Brown, Robert, 521, 676
Brown, Sidney, 458
Brown, Wilson, 322, 394
Bryan, Obby, 372
Bryant, H. L., 58–59
Buchly, W. E., 576–77
Buddha, 4
Bulkeley, John D., 321–22
Bultman, H. J., 464, 675
Bundy, Charles W., 213
Buracker, William H., 66–67
Busch, Ernst, 603
Bush, Vannevar, 51–52, 62

Byas, Hugh, 279
Bywater, Hector, 9, 457, 614

Cadogan, Alexander, 61, 86–87, 179, 588
Caldwell, Charles, 256
Callan, Tommy, 305
Callick, Flt. Officer, 517
Camp, Gene, 590
Campbell, Alexander H., 518–19
Campbell, Ian, 161, 672
Campbell, Tom, 461
Caniff, Milton, 123–24, 393–94
Canning, Austin J., 265, 607
Capinpin, Mateo, 485
Carey, Arch, 143, 193, 472–74, 584–85
Carmichael, Richard, 248
Carpenter, John, 346, 529
Carter, T. C., 352, 674
Cartright, Tom, 315, 661, 674, 677
Case, Otto A., 73–74
Casey, Hugh, 256
Casey, Richard G., 79, 84, 670
Cassidy, Henry, 551–52
Cavallaro, Ugo, 40, 177–78, 586, 670
Cave, Wing Cmdr., 352
Chaffin, Harold, 248
Chamberlain, Neville, 399
Channon, Henry ("Chips"), 338
Chapman, C. C., 289
Chapman, N. R., 515–16
Chappell, Church A., 631, 677
Chappuis, Friedrich-Wilhelm von, 30–31, 92, 206, 603
Charidis, Panayiotis, 557
Chavez, Dennis, 624
Chen, Hansen, 616
Chen, Mucia, 429–30
Chen, Percy, 429–30
Chennault, Claire, 382–84, 482–84, 576, 672, 676
Chiang Kaishek, 8, 50, 98–99, 429–430, 495–96

Chiang Kaishek, Madame, 164, 333, 419, 422
Ching, Henry, 333
Chiye, Tomihiro, 542
Chou Enlai, 430
Chow, George, 456–57
Chuman, Frank, 317
Churchill, Clementine, 338
Churchill (Harriman), Pamela, 86–87, 338
Churchill, Randolph, 86
Churchill, Winston, 5–6, 14, 61, 68, 80, 82, 86–87, 90–91, 107, 121–22, 144, 151–53, 174, 259, 283, 301, 336, 338–41, 356, 366, 398, 436, 470, 532–33, 571, 588–89, 592, 625–26, 637–40, 648–49
Chynoweth, Bradford, 42–43, 581–582, 670
Ciano, Galeazzo, 299–300, 349, 585–86
Clark, Mark Wayne, 312
Clarke, George C., 388, 494, 617, 675
Clay, Sherman, 539, 676
Clayton, Will, 246
Clement, William T., 255–56
Close, Upton, 355
Cobbett, J. C., 158
Coiner, David T., 270–71, 674
Collar, Mr., 472
Collett, Bluey, 441
Collier, James V., 485
Collins, Arthur S., 304–05, 674
Collins, Douglas, 556–57, 676
Compton, Arthur Holly, 52, 62, 309
Compton, James, 365
Conant, James Bryant, 52, 62
Connally, Tom, 246, 486–87
Cooke, John B., 465–66
Cooper, Alfred Duff, 107, 571
Cooper, Diana Duff, 107, 571
Cooper, Gary, 24, 67
Cooper, J. E., 275
Cooper, Jere, 486

Corbin, Clifford L., 246
Cotton, D. G., 130, 435, 671
Cradock, Christopher, 609
Craigie, Pleasant, 399–400, 469–70
Craigie, Sir Robert, 340, 387, 399–400, 469–70
Cranborne, Lord, 133
Creighton, John M., 83
Cresswell, Harry, 468
Crews, T. G., 380, 451, 675
Crocker, Edward Savage, 467–68
Cronin, Ray, 289, 425
Crosby, Josiah, 106, 145, 173, 196–197, 405–06
Crüwell, Ludwig, 38, 56–57, 146, 217
Cumming, Seaman, 143
Cunningham, Alan, 38
Cunningham, Andrew, 546
Cunningham, Kenneth, 441–42, 675
Cunningham, Winfield Scott, 288
Curtin, John, 229, 274, 398, 536, 592
Curtis, Lionel, 177
Curts, Maurice E., 245
Czcykowski, Flt. Lt., 623

Dalton, Warren F., 559, 676
Daly, John, 277, 337, 674
Daniels, Jimmy, 569
Darlan, Jean Louis, 299–300
Daugherty, Louis, 526
Davidson, Howard C., 250
Davis, Elmer, 461
Davis, James J., 624
Davis, R. H. S., 46
Davis, Thomas, 377
Dazai, Osamu, 508–09
De Beauvoir, Simone, 597
De Gaulle, Charles, 357
DeLany, Walter, 84
De Valera, Eamon, 625
DeWitt, John, 318–19, 542–43
Deacon, E. T., 253
Deane, John R., 238–39, 673
Dedijer, Vladimir, 167

Demos, Jean, 557
Deschler, Lew, 488
Destouches, Ferdinand Louis
     ("Céline"), 178–79, 672
Devereux, James, 287–88, 493
Dewar-Durie, Raymond, 473
Dewey, George, 581
Dickinson, Clarence E., 253, 632
Diller, LeGrande A., 493–94, 582,
     644–45
Dillon, John H., 238
Dingell, John M., 634
Direk, Chaiyanam, 106, 172–73,
     502–03
Dixon, George, 489
Djilas, Milovan, 167, 206–07
Dönitz, Karl, 96, 476, 586–87, 621,
     645
Donovan, William ("Wild Bill"), 306,
     308, 533, 634, 674
Dooman, Eugene, 175–76, 188,
     374–77, 407, 467–69, 672,
     675
Douglas, William O., 50
Dow, Leonard J., 248
Dowie, Donald, 162, 334
Downes, Donald, 307–08
Downs, Ken, 352
Draemel, Milo, 269–70, 323, 505
Drake, Waldo, 69–70
Drummond-Hay, Grace, 170–71, 367
Dunbar, Stoker, 292
Dunn, James, 55
Dunn, William J., 227–28, 437–38
Du Plessis, Bubbles, 347
Dykstra, Clarence, 309
Dynan, Joe, 375–76

Eaker, Ira, 70–71, 303, 670
Earle, John B., 220
Early, Stephen T., 34, 247, 268–69,
     324, 395
Eaton, Charles, 486
Eden, Anthony, 61, 86, 90–91, 161–
     162, 179–80, 356, 470, 588–
     589

Edgers, Dorothy, 58–59, 77–78
Edwards, Webley, 263, 274, 674
Egusa, Takashige, 273, 281–82
Ehrenburg, Ilya, 297
Eichmann, Adolf, 209
Einstein, Albert, 52–53
Eisenhower, Dwight David, 42, 304,
     312, 363, 578, 579
Eliasberg, Karl, 161
Eliot, George Fielding, 277, 337, 674
Elizabeth II, 661
Elliott, George E., 202–03, 221–22,
     230
Endo, Shusaki, 446–47
Ennis, Edward, 239
Enola Gay, 654–55
Ertegün, Mehmet Münir, 246
Esparza, Jose Antonio, 30–31
Eubank, Eugene L., 345–46, 482,
     522, 529, 573
Evatt, H. V., 79, 398

Fabian, Rudie, 257
Fairholl, Tom, 548
Fan Cheungkiang, 455, 616
Farber, Yuri (also Firsov, Yuri), 384–
     385, 539–40
Farmer, Joe, 602
Farnum, William C., 251
Farthing, William E., 231–32, 243
Feary, Robert, 386–87
Fellers, Bonner, 176–77
Fenollosa, Ernest, 259
Ferguson, George T., 644, 677
Fermi, Enrico, 62
Ferrer, Mariano, 92–93
Fielder, Kendall, 111, 123
Finn, John W., 233
Fish, Hamilton, 301–02
Fisher, C. R., 358, 380–81
Fisher, Charles A., 63–64, 435, 670
Fitch, Alva R., 526, 528, 676
Flynn, David, 569
Foote, Walter, 433
Ford, E. C., 195, 421, 673
Forgy, Howell, 267

Forty-Seven Ronin, The, 15
Fougier, Rino, 40
Fowle, F. R. C., 438–39, 516, 675
Fowler, Barbara, 444, 675
Fowler, Martha, 444
Fox, G. Robert, 304–5, 504–5, 674
Foyn, Eugenia, 451–52, 675
Foyn, Francis, 451–52
Franco, Francisco, 31, 597
Franken, Lt., 350
French, Edward F., 213–14, 219
French, Sir Wilfred, 99
Friedheim, Eric, 306
Fritchey, Clayton, 279
From Here to Eternity, 271–73, 590
Fuchida, Mitsuo, 146, 214–15, 229,
    232, 233–34, 236–37, 386,
    411–12, 665–66
Fuchikami, Tadao, 229
Fugi, Shigeru, 255
Fujita, Iyozo, 273, 386
Fujiwara, Iwaichi, 405
Fukuda, Kurahachi, 158, 404, 672,
    675
Fukudome, Shigeru, 12
Fukunaga, Kyosuke, 9–10
Fuqua, Samuel, 329
Furuno, Shigemi, 416

Gage, Thomas E., 524–25, 676
Gaggino, Theresa, 378–79, 675
Gallaghan, Frederick G., 503, 676
Gallagher, O'Dowd, 434, 548, 592,
    608, 638
Galland, Adolf, 299, 349
Gambarra, Gastone, 39, 539
Gan, Charlie, 360, 674
Gander, Evelyn, 292
Garland, "Judy," 204
Gellepis, Tony, 267
Genda, Minoru, 140–41, 146, 238,
    412, 665
Gentry, William, 241, 673
George VI, 315–16, 440, 600, 641
George, Anthony, 192

George, Harold H., 240–41, 454,
    518–19
George, Walter, 571–72
Gerow, Leonard, 186, 213–14, 219,
    256, 425, 454, 673
Gervasi, Frank, 173
Gibbes, Peter J., 197–98, 258, 503–
    504, 599–600, 673
Gibbs, David, 425
Gilchrist, Andrew, 106
Giles, "Monkey," 332
Gillette, Guy, 634
Glassford, William, 170–71, 367,
    431, 601
Glinka, Mikhail Ivanovitch, 149
Glover, Jimmy, 104–05
Goebbels, Joseph, 8, 80, 151–52,
    606, 646
Goetz, Ray, 333
Goheen, Robert, 365
Goldman, Lolly, 456
Gomez, Arthur, 157, 672
Gonzales, Manuel, 252–53
Goodman, Julien, 59, 670
Goodpaster, Andrew J., 304–5, 504,
    674
Gordon, Edward Charles, 195–96,
    499–500, 673
Gordon, John B., 310
Gore-Booth, Paul, 400, 470
Göring, Hermann, 8, 167–68, 209,
    299–300, 328, 648–49
Gormley, L. W., 476–77
Grace, B. A., 355
Grannis, Lawrence C., 218–19
Grasett, A. E., 121
Grashio, Samuel, 527
Gray, David Denver, 250, 630
Gray, Stewart, 333
Great Artiste, The, 654–55
Great Pacific War, The, 9, 457, 614
Green, Thomas H., 395
Greene, Donald, 315–16, 674
Greenlaw, Harvey, 382–83
Greenlaw, Olga, 382
Gregg, William, 313, 674

Greiffenberg, Hans von, 647
Grew, Joseph, 9, 89, 98, 116–18,
    134, 175–76, 188–89, 210–
    211, 374–77, 386–87, 406–7,
    467–69
Grey, G. E., 379, 514–15, 610
Griffin, H. H., 434
Griffiss, Townsend, 537, 676
Grosnoski, Flying Officer, 623
Grossman, Chaika, 554
Grove, Clare, 517–18, 594, 676
Grove, Leon, 517–18, 594
Grumbar, Harry, 331–32, 353
Guballa, Macario, 195, 500
Guderian, Heinz, 25–28, 69, 159,
    556, 618–19, 647
Guenther, Dr., 350
Guillain, Robert, 414–15
Guthrie, Woody, 539–40

Haape, Heinrich, 149–51
Hachmeister, Louise, 443
Hagy, Robert, 310–12, 392, 478
Hahn, Emily, 164–65, 378, 417–18,
    593–94, 641–42, 672
Halder, Franz, 28–29, 35, 55–56,
    67–68, 159–60, 298, 619–20
Halifax, Viscount, 82–84, 280, 283
Halliday, W. R., 205, 355, 673, 674
Halsey, William F., 66–67, 247–48,
    286, 322–23, 505–06, 631–32
Hamilton, John H., 329–30, 465–66
Hamlin, Mrs. Charles S. ("Bertie"),
    99, 268
Hanabusa, Hiroshi, 199
Hansen, Madame, 471
Hara, Tameichi, 342, 453
Hara, Yoshimichi, 15, 402
Harada, Irene, 369
Harada, Yoshio, 369, 558, 633
Hardaway, Robert, 265
Hardwick, Tom, 73
Harkness, Richard, 63
Harriman, Averell, 86–87, 338–40
Harriman, Kathleen, 86–87, 671
Harris, Cmdr., 139

Harrison, Frank, 155–56, 379–80
Harrop, Phyllis, 421, 641
Harsch, Joseph C., 69–70, 270
Hart, Thomas C., 41–42, 43–47,
    83–84, 134, 139, 181, 255–
    257, 280, 321, 324, 343–44,
    454, 595, 601, 644, 670, 674
Hasami, Capt., 126–27
Hashimoto, Cmdr., 334
Hashizume, Toshio, 665
Hatanaka, Kenji, 664
Hatanaka, Masaharu, 297
Haviland, J. W. III, 371–73
Hawley, Frank, 447
Hayashi, Shibao, 415
Hayne, "Jack Dusty," 291
Hayter, William, 283–84
Hearn, Thomas, 319
Heaslett, The Rev., 470
Heath, Sir Lewis, 48, 670
Heaton, Leonard D., 264–65, 607,
    673–74
Heatter, Gabriel, 354
Hebel, Francis ("Fritz"), 505, 566–
    568
Heckstall-Smith, Anthony, 56, 670
Heller, Gerhard, 597
Hendry, Lt., 580–81
Hermann, Gayle, 569
Herrick, Raymond, 525–26
Hevenor, J. P., 466
Hewel, Walther, 297–99
Heydrich, Reinhard, 209
Heyl, Ludwig C., Freiherr von, 26–
    27, 184, 564, 669
Hill, Max, 116, 118, 374–77, 414,
    561–62
Himmler, Heinrich, 209, 460
Hirohito, Emperor (Showa, Em-
    peror), 11–12, 15, 32, 50, 55,
    63, 82–84, 89, 98, 113, 133–
    134, 174, 175, 186, 225,
    234–35, 341–42, 401–03,
    490–91, 497–99, 597, 636–
    637, 660, 663–65
Hiroo, Akira, 199

Hiss, Alger, 83
Hitler, Adolf, 6, 8, 27–29, 31, 35, 55–56, 67–68, 159–60, 167–168, 284, 297–99, 301, 406, 549–51, 556, 586–87, 619–621, 646–49
Hodgson, Frederick, 638–39, 677
Hoepner, Eric, 26, 618
Hollis, Leslie, 640
Holman, A. B., 292
Homma, Masaharu, 182, 572–73
Hong Kong Clipper, 419–22
Honhart, H. Norman, 476, 676
Honywill, Jack, 143, 291–92, 660–661, 677
Hoover, Herbert, 260
Hoover, J. Edgar, 239, 354
Hopkins, Harry, 63, 87, 99–100, 108, 245–46, 256, 262, 300–302, 338, 339, 385, 462–63, 486–89, 673
Hopping, Halstead, 252
Höppner, Rolf-Heinz, 209
Hoppough, Clay, 109
Hori, Tomokazu, 503
Horiguchi, Daigaku, 509
Hornbeck, Stanley, 98
Hornedo, Florentino, 391, 675
Horton, John, 343–44, 674
Hoshino, Naoki, 138–39, 341–42
Hosmer, Ellsworth A., 102
Hosokawa, Morisada, 510
Houston-Boswall, W. E., 400
Howard, Edward Neal, 371–72, 675
Hu Shih, 221, 245–46
Hubbard, Preston, 573
Hudson, Sumner Jr., 587, 677
Huff, Sidney L., 577
Hull, Cordell, 33, 50, 54–55, 63, 83–84, 89, 94, 98, 108–09, 162, 171, 180, 183, 201–02, 213, 220–21, 247, 262, 300–02, 365–66, 385, 402, 461–63, 533–34
Hunnicutt, W. R., 589, 677

Hunt, Sidney, 473, 676
Hutchinson, William K., 306
Huxley, Aldous, 333
Huxley, Maria, 333
Hynes, Sam, 664

Ibusuki, Masanobu, 248–49
Ickes, Harold, 246, 364, 486, 489
Iida, Fusata, 273, 659
Iida, Momo, 448, 659
Iki, Haruki, 640
Inada, Shuichi, 341
Inagaki, Kiyoshi, 199, 226
Inber, Vera, 160–61, 672
Ind, Alison, 345, 520
Ingram, Ralph, 641, 677
Innes-Kerr, Mrs. E., 129–30, 435, 671
Innes-Kerr, "Tam," 130
Inoue, Chikara, 496, 676
Intengan, "Fatso," 389
Inuzuka, Koreshige, 193–94, 512–13
Irwin, Constant, 574, 676
Irwin, Pete, 326
Ismay, Hastings ("Pug"), 104, 121, 338, 637–40
Isoda, Saburo, 263
Itaya, Shigeru, 232–33, 331
Ito, Sei, 509
Iwase, Naoji, 199

Jacobs, Jake, 556–57
Jacoby, Melville, 513, 582
Jacquet, Ed, 529–30, 676
Janusz, Sqdr. Ldr., 622–23, 677
Jellbart Geoff, 476, 676
Jenner, Dorothy Gordon ("Andrea"), 165, 422, 610–11, 641, 672
Jennings, Edward, 525
Jodl, Alfred, 27, 159, 298, 620, 648–649
Johnson, Harold K., 388–89, 494, 581, 675
Johnson, Hiram, 486
Johnson, Lyndon B., 50, 247

Johnston, C. H., 400
Jones, James, 271–73, 443–44, 590
Jones, Jeff, 444
Jones, Jesse, 462, 486, 489
Jones, Jimmy, 544
Jordan, Joe, 623–24
Jünger, Ernst, 178–79, 349, 598, 672

Kageneck, Graf von, 150–51
Kaiser, Mrs. Henry, 318
Kajioka, Rear Adm., 492
Kaleohano, Hawila (Howard), 369, 558
Kaleohano, Mabel, 369
Kaltenborn, H. V., 354, 364
Kamei, Shoichiro, 509
Kaminsky, Harold, 220, 225
Kanahele, Ben, 633
Kanahele, Ella, 633
Kanaoka, Empei, 255
Kane, B. F., 484, 676
Kano, Tosh, 450–51, 655–56, 675, 677
Kaplan, Chaim, 553
Kardelj, Edward, 206–07
Kasé, Toshikazu, 189, 374, 386–87, 399
Kato, Mazuo, 78–79, 112–13, 129, 212, 365
Kato, Tatsuo, 126, 145, 276–77, 606–07
Katsuno, Consul, 258
Kawakami, Clark, 112–13, 607
Kawakami, Kyoshi K., 623
Kawanishi, Hiroshi, 426
Kaya, Okinori, 216–17, 464
Keale, Joseph, 558
Keator, Randall B., 523
Keegan, Dennis, 542–43
Keep America Out of War Committee, 8
Keitel, Wilhelm, 159, 298, 551, 619–620
Keith, Agnes, 400–01
Keith, Harry, 400–01

Keith, John O., 108
Kellar, Doug, 529
Kelley, Louis E., 568, 677
Kelley, Ruth, 118
Kellogg, Paul, 87
Kelly, Colin, 524, 661
Kelly, Robert B., 322, 601–02
Kennan, George, 347–48
Kennedy, John Fitzgerald, 306
Kennedy, Malcolm, 57
Kesselring, Albert, 159
Key, B. W., 503, 600
Kidd, Isaac Campbell, 244
Kidd, Robert, 321, 674
Kido, Koichi (Marquis Kido), 11, 138–39, 190, 211, 225, 324, 374, 490–91, 663, 669, 672
Kimmel, Husband E., 20, 69–70, 74–75, 84–85, 102, 187–88, 212, 220, 226, 230–31, 234–235, 236, 243, 245, 252, 310, 322–23, 535, 579
King, Edward B., Jr., 24
King, Ernest J., 6
Kinnard, Harry, 245, 673
Kinninmont, J. R., 515–17
Kinoshita, Isamu, 411
Kinoshita, Soichi, 510
Kirpolyansky, Pavel, 385
Kita, Nagao, 22, 59, 88, 90, 183, 395–96
Kitts, Willard A., III, 236
Kiuchi, Yoshitane, 470
Kluge, Guenther von, 26–27, 618, 620
Knox, Forrest, 521, 676
Knox, Frank, 34–35, 108–09, 186–187, 201–02, 213, 238–40, 246–47, 268, 300–02, 364, 409–10, 461–63, 487–88, 634
Kobayshi, Yuichi, 259, 276–77
Kon, Hidemi, 572
Kondo, George, 316–17, 674
Konoye, Fumimaro, 11, 510

Koyama, Toshio, 342

Kozawa, Shingo, 404

Kozawa, Shiro, 404

Kramer, Alwin D., 58–59, 60, 77–
78, 108, 183, 186

Kramer, Mary, 108

Krick, Harold D., 126

Krock, Arthur, 634

Kühn, Otto, 22

Kung, H. H., 641

Kung, Madame H. H., 164, 419

Kurosawa, Akiro, 644

Kurusu, Saburo, 33–34, 54–55, 79,
100, 110, 113, 162, 171, 180,
201–02, 221, 262, 276, 300,
325, 365

Kusaka, Ryunosuke, 140, 229, 233–
234, 238, 330, 411–12

Kuzmin, Matvei, 149

Kuzmin, Vasili, 149

Lademan, J. W., 41

La Guardia, Fiorello, 87, 269, 478–
479

Lall, Chaman, 563

Lam, Constance, 593

Lamb, Tom, 516, 662, 676, 677

Landa, Hans, 554, 676

Landau, Leo, 157

Landis, James, 478–79

Landon, Truman H., 101, 231–32,
248–49

Lane, Glenn, 264

Lange, Herbert, 208

Lash, Joseph, 460

Lash, Trude, 460

Lau, Takyen, 403, 424–25

Laurel, Dodjie, 389

Laurel, Salvador "Doy," 389

Lawrence, Bill, 461

Lawrence, Ernest O., 52–53, 284–
285, 655

Lawson, John K., 155, 640–41

Layton, Edwin T., 74–75, 102, 231,
236

Layton, Sir Geoffrey, 163, 340

Le Hand, Marguerite ("Missy"), 442–
443

Leach, J. C., 545, 592, 608

Leahy, William, 351, 598

Leary, H. Fairfax, 244

LeBlanc, Arthur, 99

Lee, Clark, 289–90, 296, 425–26,
493–94, 582

Leeb, Wilhelm Ritter von, 159–60,
603–4

Lehman, Herbert, 635

Leiper, G. A. ("Andy"), 155–56,
158, 379–80, 455–56, 642

Leiper, Helen, 158, 380, 455–56

LeMay, Curtis, 307, 654

Leopold III, 565

Letteer, Walter M., 409, 675

Letulle, Claude, 621–22

Levin, Meyer, 524

Lewis, Bob, 655

Li Hsiao-li, 428–29

Liat Chuachin, 361

Liddell, Alvar, 339

Liddell, Jack, 390, 584

"Lili Marlene," 80

Lily, Col., 362

Lin Lee Kijo, 361, 674

Lin, W. K., 483–84

Lin Yutang, 278

Lincoln, Trebitsch, 660, 678

Lindbergh, Anne (Mrs. Charles), 310

Lindbergh, Charles A., 8–9, 95, 308,
309–10, 311, 327–28, 338,
393, 478, 674

Lindsay, Michael, 428–29, 675

Litvinov, Maxim, 187, 635

Lockard, Joseph L., 202–3, 221–22

Lockwood, C. H., 357–58, 602, 674,
677

Lockwood, John, 162, 334

Lockwood, Pat, 357–58

Loesser, Frank, 267

Loewenthal, Rudolf, 429

Long, Breckinridge, 99, 246, 363

Loo Taising, 285–86, 479–80
Loos, Anita, 333
Lopez, Placida, 24
Lorentz, Pare, 94–95, 393
Lorenz, Heinz, 297
Lotocka, Stefania, 555–56
Luce, Clare Boothe, 278
Luce, Rev. Henry, 479
Luce, Henry, 277–78, 479
Lyall, Flt. Sgt., 517
Lynch, Wilf, 120

MacArthur, Douglas, 6–7, 42–43,
    44–45, 181–82, 256–57,
    275, 325–26, 343, 344–46,
    389, 407, 425, 453–54, 474,
    482, 485, 493–94, 506, 526,
    572–79, 581, 594–95, 603,
    669, 670, 674–75
MacArthur, Jean, 257
MacDonald, Colin, 165, 610–11
MacGregor, Iain, 128, 332
MacKay, J. A., 511
Mackensen, Hans Georg von, 300
MacLeish, Archibald, 328
MacLeod, Torquil, 418
MacNeice, Louis, 338
MacVane, John, 337
Mahidol, King Ananda, 435
Maisky, Ivan, 179–80, 356, 588
Makabe, Shinzo, 317
Makabe, Wilson, 317
Malay, Armando, 390, 675
Mallonée, Richard, 484–85, 580–81
Maltby, Christopher M., 115–16,
    121, 128, 155, 514
Mamerow, John, 345
Manders, Pug, 307
Mann, Gerald, 247
Mann, Mickey, 157, 672
Mao Zedong, 50, 430, 618
Mapes, Victor, 520–21, 527, 676
Margolis, Laura, 194, 292–93, 512–
    513, 673
Mariner, A. E. ("Jim"), 291, 661

Marshall, David, 360, 674
Marshall, George C., 62, 82, 100–01,
    125, 180, 186, 196, 212,
    213–14, 229, 300–02, 312,
    314, 318, 326, 363, 576, 579,
    624, 632, 673, 677
Marshall, George Preston, 306
Marshall, Jack A., 314, 674
Marshall, Mrs. George C., 125
Marshall, Richard J., Jr., 256, 577
Marsman, Jan, 419–20
Martin, Frederick, 109, 249–52, 394
Martin, Harold M., 232, 324
Martin, John, 339–40, 649
Martin, Joseph, 486, 489
Martinez, Miguel Rodrigo, 92
Masaoka, Mike, 318
Matoba, Junko, 446
Matsudaira, Minister, 211
Matsumura, Heita, 237–38
Matsunaga, Sadaichi, 331
Matsuoka, Takashi, 408
Matsuoka, Yoko, 408
Matsuoka, Yōsuke, 193
Maugham, Robin, 38–39
Mayer, Ferdinand ("Fred"), 33, 54–
    55, 100
McCarthy, J. R., 253
McClelland, J. W., 280–81
McCloy, John J., 239–40, 363
McCollum, Arthur, 183, 186
McCormick, Robert R., 7, 73, 278,
    462, 634
McCrea, John, 300, 409–10
McDavitt, Jerome, 528
McGladdery, Henry, 441
McIntyre, Marvin, 50
McIntyre, Ross T., 34
McLaughlin, Irene Castle, 310–11
McLeod, D. K., 227–28, 457
McMahon, William J., 275
McMillin, George Johnstone, 41, 370,
    632
McMorris, Charles H., 84, 231
McNary, Charles, 486

McSorley, Frank, 499–500
Medalla, Simeon, 427, 675
Meiklereid, E. W., 459
Meister, Maury, 241–43, 282, 480–481, 567, 673
Melville, Dave, 256
Melville, "Mel," 662
Menges, Herbert, 569
Menzies, Robert, 592
Merdinger, Charles J., 136, 245
Merline (*see* Destouches)
Merritt, Lt., 525
Meyer, Charles E., 377
Michela, Mike, 297
Miedl, Alois, 167
Mihailovic, Draza, 166
Mikami, John, 396
Miles, C. V., 158
Miles, Sherman, 124, 186, 210–11, 213–14, 140
Miley, Henry A., 315, 674
Miley, Peggy, 315
Miller, Alvin C., 444
Miller, Doris, 264
Miller, Jim Dick, 329
Miller, Roger, 253
Mimura, Yoshitaka, 653
Mishima, Sumie Seo, 408–9
Mitsubishi Estate Group, 279
Miura, Consul-Gen., 390
Miyo, Tatsukichi, 233
Mölders, Werner, 349
Mollinson, George, 467
Mollinson, James A., 231, 250
Moltke, Helmuth von, 177
Montgomery, Robert, 59
Mooney, James D., 308
Moore, Ed, 476
Moore, George F., 257
Moore, Joseph H., 523, 575, 676
Moore, Richard, 393
Moorehead, Alan, 604–05
Moorhead, H. D., 570–71
Moorhead, John J., 264, 44, 674
Moreell, Ben, 364
Morgan, Sammy, 568–69

Morgenthau, Henry, Jr., 11, 462, 531
Mori, Juzo, 331
Mori, Mrs. Motokazu, 109–11
Morin, Relman ("Pat"), 23–24, 139, 295–96, 457–59, 642–43
Morley, Felix, 623–24
Morris, Frank, 306
Morris, John, 447–48
Morris, Leland, 348
Motley, Ruby F., 166, 672
Moton, Ronald, 272, 674
Moulton, H. Douglas, 214
Mountbatten, Earl, 661, 677
Mullin, J. Daniel, 209–10, 275, 670
Muñoz Grandes, Agustin, 30–31, 92, 148, 206, 539
Murata, Shigeharu, 146–47
Murphy, Robert, 351
Murphy, Vincent R., 230, 236
Murray, Allan, 24
Murray, George D., 66
Murrow, Edward R., 327–28, 337, 460–61, 488–89, 532–33
Murrow, Janet, 328, 460–61
Muselier, Émile, 357
Mussolini, Benito ("Il Duce"), 40, 177–78, 299–300, 586, 587, 596
Mutimer, John, 130–31, 361–62, 671, 674
Mydans, Carl, 645

Nagai, Tsuyoshi, 235
Nagano, Osami, 11, 14–15
Nagayo, Yoshoro, 509
Nagumo, Chuichi, 137, 203, 238, 330, 386, 394, 411–12, 558
Naito, Hideo, 544
Nakamoto, Hiroko, 445–46, 655–657, 659, 675
Nakamura, Ryozo, 407, 609–10
Nakano, Yoshio, 509
Nakaoka, Nabuki, 546–47
Nakasone, Yasuhiro, 613
Nakijima, Timostsu, 238

Nakpil, Carmen Guerrero, 426, 530, 675
Nasu, Yoshio, 223, 335
Nelson, Donald, 246, 364
Neuhoff, Maj., 150
Neumann-Silkow, Walther, 56, 217
Newman, Joseph, 320
Newton, Isaac, 471, 676
Newton, John H., 136, 322
Nichol, Bromfield B., 214, 252
Nichols, Donald, 537–38
Nicolson, Harold, 338
Nieto, Manuel, 343
Nimitz, Chester, 51
Nishikaichi, Shigenori, 368–69, 558, 633
Nishiura, Susumu, 138
Noah, 3
Noel, Paul B., 643, 677
Nomura, Kichisaburo, 33–34, 54–55, 162, 180, 201–2, 213, 220–221, 262–63, 276, 300, 325, 365
Noyes, Leigh, 20, 238
Nye, Gerald P., 308, 310–12, 392, 477–78, 634

Oba, Yahei, 614
O'Brien, Pat, 306
O'Daniel, W. Lee ("Pappy"), 247, 486
O'Neill, Bill, 333
Ofusa, Junnosuke, 560–61
Ogata, Lt., 113
Ogg, Robert D., 101–03, 671
O'Hara, John, 296
Ohta, Ichiro, 467–70
Oi, Atsushi, 366–67, 499, 674
Oishi, Tamotsu, 141
Oka, Yutaka, 318
Okada, Keisuke, 216
Okamoto, Suermasa, 507
Okamura, Katsuzo, 78–79, 112, 180, 201, 213, 247, 365
Okazaki, Katsuo, 117
Okuda, Vice-Consul, 396

Olson, John, 617, 677
Onishi, Takijiro, 12, 631
Ono, Kanijiro, 140
Onozuka, Kiheiji, 509–10
Oppenheimer, Frank, 284
Oppenheimer, J. Robert, 284
Oppenheimer, Kitty, 284
Oshima, Hiroshi, 6, 102, 298, 349, 621, 646
Osipova, Lidiia, 37, 669–70
Osone, Yoshihiko, 258, 501
Ota, Nakagawa, 656–57
Ota, Peter, 542
Ōta, Yōko, 509, 656–57
Otani, Inaho, 290–91, 472–73
Ott, Eugen, 20–21
Oualid, William, 169
Outerbridge, William W., 188, 219, 220, 225
Ozawa, Jisaburo, 46, 113–14, 145

Pabst, J. C., 431–32, 469
Packard, Reynolds, 261
Page, George ("Giorgio") Nelson, 259
Palliser, A. F. E., 525, 609
Panter-Downes, Mollie, 640
Parker, Edward N., 275
Parker, Theodore W., 326–27, 674
Passy, Col. (André de Wavrin), 357
Patriarca, F. A., 252
Patterson, Cissie, 278, 354
Patterson, Joe, 278–79
Patterson, R. H., 314, 674
Patterson, Robert P., 124
Pawley, William, 382
Payne, Robert, 359
Pearson, Donald B., 129–30, 671
Peart, Florence, 337
Peck, Graham, 431
Peck, John, 649
Peck, Willys R., 591, 675
Pecson, Geronima, 427–28, 675
Pence, Archie, 243–44, 463–64, 673
Pennefather-Evans, John, 203

Percival, Arthur, 47–48, 105, 196, 222, 223, 459, 532
Perkins, Frances, 7, 462
Perry, Glen C. H., 355, 489
Perucci, Alfred D., 233, 673
Pétain, Henri Phillipe, 168, 299–300, 598
Petrovsky, Constantine Constantino-vich, 362, 657–58, 674, 677
Phease, "Kiwi," 556–57
Phibun Songkhram, Luang, 115, 144, 172–73, 205–06, 404–05, 435–36, 502–03
Philippines Clipper, 287–88, 329–30
Phillips, Godfrey, 472
Phillips, O. W., 608–09, 639, 677
Phillips, Tom, 44–45, 83, 134, 196–197, 280–81, 352, 545–46, 608–09, 638–39
Phillips, Walter C., 220, 673
Photiades, Nicholas, 439–41, 675, 676
Pierce, Harold, 562
Piercy, Arthur, 157
Places (Selected)
  Burma, 6, 20, 227–28, 382–84, 437–38, 482–84
  Canal Zone, 9–10, 118–19, 192, 219, 303–05, 504–05, 590
  China, 8, 9, 11, 98–99, 142–43, 170, 192–94, 278–79, 290–293, 380, 390, 403–04, 410–411, 428–31, 451–52, 472–474, 495–96, 511–13, 583, 584–85, 617–18, 658
  Formosa (Taiwan), 74, 181, 190, 191, 293–95, 344, 452–53, 482, 587–88
  Guam, 9, 19, 23, 41, 370–73, 632
  Hawaii
    Aliamanu Crater, 443, 612
    Bellows Field, 232
    Ewa Marine Base, 90, 232–33, 253, 282, 569
    Ford Island, 90, 111, 126, 214,
      239, 241, 248, 252–53, 270, 394, 481, 566–78, 631
    Haleiwa Field, 251, 273–74
    Hickam Field, 90, 109, 229, 231–32, 248–52, 287, 326, 394, 479–80, 630
    Honolulu, 395–96, 480, 534–535, 543–44
    John Rodgers Field, 21
    Kaneohe Naval Air Station, 229, 232–33, 273, 324, 569
    Kauai, 287
    Lahaina Roads, 203, 229
    Niihau, 368–69, 558, 632–33
    Opana (radar site), 202–03, 221–222, 229–30
    Pearl City, 21, 569
    Pearl Harbor, 9, 12, 19–22, 59, 67, 69–70, 74–75, 84–85, 88, 90, 101–03, 110–11, 125, 137, 140–41, 146–47, 153–154, 188, 198–200, 203, 215, 218–20, 225–26, 229–39, 241–56, 261–86, 290–311, 316–17, 321–24, 329–331, 337–44, 364–65, 367–368, 385–86, 409, 411–17, 434, 454, 461–64, 479–81, 487–88, 505–06, 544–45, 546–47, 566–70, 589–91, 612, 613–14, 629–32, 659, 665
    Schofield Barracks, 123, 265–66, 270–73, 443, 607–08, 611
    Shafter, Fort, 19, 111, 203, 219, 245
    Tripler General Hospital, 265–266, 444, 569, 607–08
    Wheeler Field, 70, 229, 245, 265, 271, 274, 568
  Hungary, 556–57
  Iceland, 95–97, 326–27
  Indochina, 4, 23–24, 30, 44, 60, 118, 129, 139, 186, 295–96, 441, 457–59, 642–43

Japan, 4, 9, 11–13, 14–15, 21–22,
    32–33, 89–90, 116–18, 126–
    127, 134, 138–39, 162, 175–
    176, 188–90, 210–211, 216–
    217, 225, 233–35, 254–55,
    341–42, 366–67, 373–77,
    386–87, 399–403, 406–09,
    414–17, 445–51, 464, 467–
    470, 489–91, 493, 496–99,
    508–10, 535, 560–62, 609–
    610, 613–14, 635–37, 653–
    666
Libya, 4, 14, 29, 37–40, 56–57,
    80, 93, 99, 117, 146, 177–78,
    185, 217–18, 228, 299–300,
    406, 441–42, 538–39, 557,
    604–05, 647–48
Malaya, 6, 20, 60–61, 152–53,
    347
    Alor Star, 438
    George Town, 205
    Ipoh, 204, 532
    Kota Bharu, 30, 46, 72, 114,
        145, 162, 186, 198, 211,
        222–25, 258, 280–81, 334–
        336, 501, 503, 516–17, 599–
        600, 602
    Kra Isthmus, 58, 61, 87, 94,
        129, 162–63, 201, 222–23
    Kuala Lumpur, 47, 197–98
    Penang, 204–05
    Singapore, 10–11, 30, 46–48,
        63–65, 72, 82, 84, 94, 104–
        106, 113, 129–32, 134, 144–
        145, 158, 162–63, 196–97,
        202, 205, 222–24, 280–81,
        331–32, 352–53, 355–62,
        380–82, 404, 434–35, 459,
        507, 545–46, 548–49, 571,
        592, 600, 602–03, 608–09,
        637–40, 657
    Sungei Pattani, 204, 438–41,
        515–17
Midway Island, 23, 32, 136–37,
    322

Netherlands Indies, 6, 7, 43, 58,
    60, 202, 324–25, 431–34,
    489, 662
Philippines, 6, 7, 9
    Bataan, 485, 581–82, 602
    Batan Islands, 391, 425, 454,
        506
    Cavite Naval Base, 44–46, 139,
        144, 209–10, 257–58, 275–
        276, 321–22, 387, 391, 413,
        549, 579, 601, 643–45
    Clark Field, 24, 182, 191, 294,
        343, 344–46, 425, 453, 481–
        482, 506–07, 518–31, 572–
        579, 582, 588, 595, 603
    Corregidor, 257, 387–88, 474,
        578, 581, 601
    Del Carmen Field, 524–25
    Del Monte Field, 182, 344, 529,
        574
    John Hay, Camp, 425, 454
    Iba Field, 182, 191, 240–41,
        425, 506–7, 518–20, 573,
        576, 588
    Luzon (see individual locations)
    Manila, 24–25, 42–45, 143–44,
        170–71, 289–90, 343–46,
        388–90, 425–28, 513–14,
        517–18, 582, 617, 644–45
    Manila Hotel, 45, 180–81, 255,
        289, 367, 426
    McKinley, Fort, 59, 156, 474–
        475
    Mindanao, 41, 195–96, 342–
        343, 344, 426–28, 453, 499–
        500
    Negros, 42–43, 582
    Nichols Field, 24, 294, 527, 576,
        588, 617
    Nielson Field, 345, 407–08, 453,
        481–82, 494, 518
    Panay (Iloilo), 42, 601
    Santiago, Fort (Intramuros), 166,
        257, 325–26, 343, 344, 474,
        493–94, 572, 594–95

Philippines (*cont.*)
    Sternberg Hospital, 166
    Stotsenburg, Fort, 24, 241, 326,
        453, 506, 525–29
    Poland, 207–09, 460, 553–57,
        564, 621–22
    Russia
        Klin, 149
        Kuibyshev, 296–97, 356, 537
        Ladoga, Lake ("Ice Road"), 35–
          36, 646
        Leningrad, 27, 29, 30–31, 35–
          37, 56, 92–93, 148–49, 160–
          161, 296, 539, 603–04, 647
        Moscow, 25–27, 35, 58, 68,
          76–77, 117, 122–23, 132–33,
          149–51, 160, 184–85, 296,
          549–52, 618–20, 647
        Orel, 159
        Tikhvin, 29, 36, 56, 159–60,
          206, 646
        Tula, 26, 69
    Thailand, 20, 23, 44, 47, 58, 79,
        82, 106–07, 114–15, 118,
        129, 145, 152, 172–73, 197,
        205–206, 211, 258–59, 280–
        281, 336, 404–06, 435–37,
        459, 501–03, 515–16, 569–
        570, 591, 618
    Wake Island, 3, 23, 32, 66, 287–
        288, 329–30, 465–67, 492–
        493
    Wolfschanze, 27–28, 31, 55–56,
        67, 159, 297–99, 550–51,
        620, 648–49
    Yugoslavia, 79–80, 166–67,
        206–07, 595
Podklebnik, Michael, 208, 553–54
Poindexter, Joseph E., 368, 395
Polier, Justine, 87–88
Polkinghorn, Stephen, 290–92, 585
Pollan, Howard O., 568, 677
Popoff, Ivan, 176
Portal, Sir Charles, 152
Porter, Edward, 539, 676
Posey, Elizabeth, 309

Posten, John, 530
Potter, Phil, 354
Poubourra, Alexandra, 557–58
Pound, Ezra, 259–61, 596, 605–06
Pound, Mary, 260, 606
Pound, Sir Dudley, 61, 152, 639
Povich, Shirley, 306
Powell, John B., 193, 472, 511–12
Pownall, Henry, 301, 422
Pramoj, M. R. Seni, 107, 591, 671,
    677
Prokofiev, Serge, 338
Prentice, W. E., 397–98, 675
Prettyman, Arthur, 624–25
Prüller, Wilhelm, 132–33
Pugh, John R., 326
Pulford, C. W. H., 222, 281, 352,
    603, 609
Purnell, William ("Speck"), 181, 256
Putnam, Paul Albert, 66, 330, 465–
    466
Pye, William, 74–75

Quezon, Manuel, 117, 181, 290, 343,
    425, 513, 523, 577–78
Quezon, Zenaida, 425
Quintos, Antonio, 426–27, 675
Quintos, José, 427, 675

Raeder, Erich, 6
Rafsky, Harry, 248
Ralph, Freddie, 419, 421–22
Ralston, J. L., 122
Ramsey, Logan, 230
Ramshaw, J. C., 46, 334
Rankin, Jeanette, 634, 649
Ravenstein, Johann von, 217
Rayburn, Sam, 247, 486, 633
Redman, Vere, 400, 448, 471
Reilly, Molly, 224, 360, 673
Reintgen, Karl-Heinz, 79–80
Rennie, John, 369
Reynolds, "Doggy," 391
Reynolds, Quentin, 351–52
Ribbentrop, Joachim von, 20, 298,
    349, 587, 621, 646

Riccardi, Arturo, 40
Richards, Robert, 249, 673
Richardson, G. S., 599, 677
Richardson, James O., 226
Richardson, John, 557
Richthofen, Lothar Freiherr von, 159
Ridruejo, Dionisio, 92
Ringelblum, Emanuel, 208–09
Rintelen, Hans von, 177
Robb, Stuart, 525
Roberts, Chalmers M., 354
Robins, Donald, 524
Robinson, Arthur G., 43, 324–25, 670
Rockwell, F. W., 321–22, 644
Rodeivitch, Maya, 165
Rodrigo Martinez, Miguel, 148
Rodzinski, Artur, 187, 308–09
Rogers, Jack A., 674
Rokossovsky, Konstantin, 77
Rommel, Erwin, 38–39, 56, 99, 146, 177, 217–18, 539, 604–05, 620, 647
Romulo, Carlos P., 389
Rooks, A. H., 42
Roosevelt, Eleanor, 87–88, 246, 268–69, 328, 443, 460–61, 478–79
Roosevelt, Franklin, 5–9, 11, 13–14, 34, 43–44, 50–52, 55, 58, 63, 79, 82–84, 87, 89, 96, 98, 99–100, 108, 113, 116, 124–126, 133–34, 152, 171, 174, 175, 186, 189, 201–02, 221, 234–35, 243, 245–47, 259, 261, 262, 268–69, 274, 277, 278, 283, 284, 299, 300–02, 310, 325, 328, 339–40, 351, 357, 373, 385, 392–93, 395, 442–43, 461–63, 479, 486–489, 524, 531–34, 572, 576, 578, 596, 606, 620–21, 624–625, 633–35, 645–46, 648–649
Roosevelt, Franklin, Jr., 269
Roosevelt, James, 99, 625, 635
Roosevelt, Theodore, Jr., 409, 675
Rorman, Harry, 236, 673
Rose, Count de, 351
Rosenthal, Margot, 61–62, 586
Royce, Rosita, 94
Rubinstein, Artur, 308–09
Rumelt, Ruth Jane, 325
Runcie, "Mad," 72–73
Rusk, Dean, 364–65
Rutter, John, 484
Rybakov, Vasili, 149

Sachs, Alexander, 52
Saeki, Shizuo, 618
Safford, Lawrence F., 10–11, 58–59, 108, 238
Saitō, Kosuke, 448–49
Saito, Masahisa, 294
Saitō, Mutsuo, 448–49, 659
Sak, Liu Hung, 454–55, 495, 616–617, 675
Sakai, Saburo, 293–94, 506, 522–24
Sakai, Takashi, 116, 379
Sakamaki, Kazuo, 199–200, 226, 282–83, 612
Sakomizu, Hisatsune, 216, 464
Salisbury, Harrison, 307
Saltz, Thomas, 635
Samejima, Tomoshige, 367
San Pedro, Felemon, 527–28
Sarles, Ruth, 634, 674
Sasso, Maurizio, 172
Sassoon, Victor, 511–12
Sata, Naohiro, 330–31
Sato, Jisaburo, 367
Sawyers, Frank, 338–39
Sayre, Francis, 181, 576, 594–95
Scanland, F. W., 282
Scarf, Pongo, 438
Scarf, Sally, 438
Schafer, Charles L., 641
Schick, William R., 249
Schmidt, Paul, 620–21
Schmidt, Rudolf, 159
Schmundt, Rudolf, 80
Schratz, Paul R., 95–97, 327

Schultz, Lester, 108
Scott, Colin, 484
Seaborg, Glenn, 62
Selassie, Haile, 552–53
Selwyn-Clarke, Hilda ("Red Hilda"),
    165, 378, 593–94, 641–42
Selwyn-Clarke, Mary, 593
Selwyn-Clarke, Selwyn, 165, 593
Sergeant York, 24, 67, 410
Settles, Edward Wayne, 370–73,
    675
Sevareid, Eric, 354, 461, 533
Shall America and Japan Fight?, 231
Shank, Lawton S., 492
Sharkay, Al, 263
Shaw, Bernard, 129
Sheean, Vincent, 632
Sheehan, Ed, 153–54, 263–64, 266–
    267, 278, 285–86, 480, 544–
    545, 568–69, 590, 672, 674
Sheldon, Ross A., 542, 676
Sherin, Jemadar, 515
Sherman, Frederick C., 137
Sherr, Joe R., 166
Sherrill, John, 549
Sherrill, Warren Joseph, 549
Shiba, Commander, 21
Shimada, Koichi, 190–91, 452–53,
    587–88
Shimada, Shigetaro, 235, 373–74,
    499, 535, 613
Shimazaki, Shigekazu, 273
Shinjo, Kenkichi, 212, 276, 277
Shinozaki, Mamoru, 362
Shintani, Ishimatsu, 369
Ships
    Adelaide, 397
    Akagi, 88, 140, 146, 215, 219,
        234, 238, 248, 386, 412
    Amatsukaze, 342, 453
    America (*West Point*), 476
    Argonne, 153, 570
    Antares, 218–19
    Arizona, 153, 236–37, 244, 256,
        281–82, 329, 442, 480, 547,
        549, 629, 631, 659

Astoria, 322
Augusta, 663
Avocet, 154
Awagisan Maru, 334
Awatea, 120
Ayatosan Maru, 223, 334
Bagley, 589
Barker, 431
Bismarck, 592
Black Hawk, 43
Blue, 244, 570
Boise, 582
Breeze, 570
Bulmer, 391
California, 154, 244, 266, 282, 568
Cassin, 153, 285–86
Chew, 589
Chicago, 136, 322
Chikuma, 202–3, 229
Chokai, 145
Chosa Maru, 30
Coast Farmer, 323
Condor, 188, 198–99
Crossbill, 188, 198
Cynthia Olsen, 320
Detroit, 153, 270
Devonshire, 610
Don José, 123
Downes, 153, 285–86
Dunlap, 214
Electra, 639
Enterprise, 66–67, 140, 203, 214,
    247–48, 252–53, 286, 322,
    330, 394, 465, 505–06, 558–
    559, 567–70, 589, 614, 631–
    632, 673
Express, 639
Ford, John D., 275–76, 391, 413,
    514, 549
Gold Star, 41
Gossamer, 475–76
Greer, 392
Haruna, 524, 661
Helena, 154, 235, 254, 266
Hiryu, 215, 237, 411
Hobart, 228

Ships (*cont.*)
Honolulu, 22, 567, 589
Hornet, 140
Houston, 10, 431, 582, 644
Idaho, 327
Idzumo, 143
Indianapolis, 322
Indomitable, 5
Isabel, 44, 143–44
Jaegersfontein, 267
Kaga, 233–34, 330
Katoomba, 397
Katori, 547
Kearny, 8
Keosanqua, 198
Kent, 588
Kido Butai, 32–33, 88, 101–03,
    114, 137, 140–41, 190–91,
    199, 202–03, 214–15, 229–
    231, 233–34, 270, 322, 341,
    394, 411–13, 442, 558, 630,
    632
Kormoran, 228–29
Kuroshio, 453
Lamson, 559, 676
Langley, 426, 601
Lanikai, 44, 144, 275
Lexington, 22, 136–37, 203, 322–
    323, 558–59, 671
Louisville, 280
Lurline, 69, 319–20
Luzon, 139, 321
Manhattan, 476–77
Marblehead, 43, 324–25, 431, 670
Marechal Joffre, 514
Maryland, 237, 244, 463, 567–68,
    590
Mapele, 467
Matsonia, 320–21
Mayakovsky, 537
Miley, 474
Minneapolis, 322–23
Monaghan, 220
Montgomery, 270
Mount Vernon, 476
Nagasaki Maru, 390

Nagato, 32, 234, 254, 412
Neosho, 154
Nevada, 22, 136, 244–45, 270,
    281–82, 329, 331, 569, 570
New Orleans, 267
New York, 313
Oahu, 44
Oasis, 605
Oglala, 235
Oklahoma, 22, 244–46, 254, 266,
    281, 282, 442, 463, 545, 614,
    629, 630
Orizaba, 476–77
Otus, 643
Parrott, 275, 431
Paul Jones, 431
Pecos, 413
Penguin, 370–73
Pennsylvania, 153, 235, 254, 283,
    285–86, 567, 590
Pensacola, 323, 427
Peterel, 142–43, 290–92, 472–73,
    585, 660–61, 672, 677
Phoenix, 244
Pope, 514, 549
Porter, 324
Portland, 322–24, 394
President Coolidge, 42, 279–80, 524
President Harrison, 390
President Johnson, 315
President Taft, 10
Preston, 453
Prince of Wales, 5, 45–46, 47, 65,
    107, 163, 281, 359, 545–46,
    548, 592, 608–09, 637–40
Quincy, 476
Ramsey, 570
Ranger, 476
Repulse, 5, 45–46, 47, 65, 107,
    163, 281, 359, 545–46, 592,
    608–09, 637–40
Reuben James, 8
Ryujo, 211, 342, 426, 453
Sakura Maru, 334
Salt Lake City, 631–32, 677
San José, 514

Scott, 280
Scout, 420–21, 611
Sendai, 334
Shaw, 154, 253, 285
Shirogane Maru, 194
Solace, 264, 329, 629
Somali, 589
Soryu, 235, 237, 273, 368, 386, 411
Sotoyomo, 154
Sturgeon, 257
Swan, 270
Sydney, 228–29, 610
Taiping, 514
Taringtang, 517–18, 594
Tatsumiya Maru, 29–30, 78–79
Tatuta Maru, 112, 180, 192, 449
Tennessee, 153, 266, 270, 463, 590
Thanet, 510, 611
Thomas Jefferson, 318
Tirpitz, 57
Tjiluwah, 511
Tone, 202–03, 229
Toyo Maru, 13
Uranami, 46, 145, 162
Uritsky, 33
Utah, 140, 282, 570
Vega, 267
Venice Maru, 23
Vestal, 244
Vincennes, 476
Vireo, 568
Wake, 142–43, 329, 472
Wakefield, 347
Ward, 188, 198, 219, 225, 230, 236
West Point, 476
West Virginia, 244, 254, 264, 266, 329, 442, 463, 568, 590, 614
Wichita, 95–96, 327
Yorktown, 140
Yu Sang, 156–57
Yuhari, 492
Shirao, Tateki, 89–90
Shivers, Robert, 109–10, 239, 395

Short, Walter C., 13, 102, 111, 123, 202–03, 212, 229, 230, 245, 252, 270, 301, 368, 395, 443, 579, 669
Shostakovitch, Dmitri, 296
Siddartha, Prince (*see* Buddha)
Siegel, Manuel, 292, 512–13
Silver Shirts, 8
Simon, Charles, 204–5, 673
Simonds, T. P., 470
Simonov, Konstantin, 68–69
Simpson, Robert K. M., 157–58, 418, 457, 672
Simson, Ivan, 105–06
Sipes, Charlie, 311
Skouland, Helen, 468
Slagle, Bill, 275
Slawson, Paul, 433
Slessor, Kenneth, 228
Smedberg, William, 94
Smith, Alfred Littlefield, 139, 321, 672
Smith, Harold, 34, 58
Smith, John P., 319, 674
Smith, Merriman, 354–55
Smith, N. E., 321
Smith, R. T., 383–84, 675
Smith, Walter Bedell, 312
Smith, William, 84
Smith-Hutton, Henri, 406–07, 675
Smith-Hutton, Jane, 406
Smuts, Jan, 347
Snyder, John T., 607–08, 677
Sōga, Yasutarō, 544
Sommerhausen, Anne, 564–65
Sommerhausen, Mark, 565
Sonokawa, Kameo, 546
Sorge, Richard, 35
Spaatz, Carl, 303, 677
Spaatz, Ruth, 303
Spee, Graf von, 609
Speier, Edward Henry, 537–38
Sprague, John T., 519
Squire, Paul, 598, 677
Stachouwer, A. W. L. Tjarda van Starkenborgh, 431

Stalin, Joseph, 29, 35, 50, 67–68, 76–77, 356, 556, 596
Stark, Harold F. ("Betty"), 82, 94, 108, 125–26, 183, 186, 212, 238, 268, 300–02, 531–32, 634
Starling, Edmund W., 625
Stead, Gordon W., 336
Steinhardt, Laurance, 278
Stevenson, Adlai E., 364
Stevenson, Ellen Borden, 364
Stewart, Max, 375–76
Stilwell, Joseph W., 319, 674
Stilwell, Mrs. Joseph W., 319
Stimson, Henry L., 7, 34, 108–09, 201–02, 213, 246, 261–62, 300–02, 363, 461, 486, 531
Stolze, Lt., 151
Strashun, Ilya Davidovich, 160–61
Strong, W. Dupont, 520
Strout, Richard L., 442
Stuart, Leighton, 429
Stuart, Robert Douglas, Jr., 73, 95, 392–93
Stubbs, Minnie Breese, 474–75, 676
Sturges, Preston, 333
Styer, W. D., 576–77
Styron, William, 302
Subido, Abelardo, 427
Subido, Trinidad, 427, 675
Sugawara, Gen., 602
Suge, Genzaburo, 390
Sugita, Ichyi, 441, 675
Sugiyama, General, 665
Sullivan, Mark, 94, 278
Sulzberger, C. L., 296–97
Sümmermann, Max, 217
Sun Fo, 429–30
Sun Yatsen, 164
Sun Yatsen, Madame, 419, 461
Suñer, Serrano, 597
Sutherland, Richard K., 182, 256, 344–45, 453–54, 474, 481–482, 506, 572, 574, 577
Suyin, Han (see Tang, Rosalie)
Suzuki, Kantaro, 402, 664

Suzuki, Teiichi, 117
Swain, Charles D., 286
Sweeney, Warren, 308
Swenson, Raymond T., 248–49
Szilard, Leo, 62

Taft, Robert, 5
Takamura, Kōtarō, 489–90, 499, 535, 614, 635, 663, 676
Takata, Ichitaro, 112–13
Takemura, Bunsho, 118
Takeshita, Masahiko, 341
Tamaguchi, Sumiteru, 498
Tamura, Hiroshi, 114–15, 172–73
Tamworth, L. B., 379, 514–15
Tang Pao-huang, 495–96, 617–18
Tang, Rosalie (also Han Suyin), 495–496, 511, 617–18
Tang Yungmei, 495
Tanikawa, T., 362, 523
Tanner, William, 219
Tash, Earl, 529
Tateno, Morio, 366, 665
Taylor, Ken, 251, 273–74
Taylor, Maxwell D., 312
Tedder, Sir Arthur, 177
Templer, Cecil Robert, 115, 671
Tenelly, Richard, 377, 447
Tennant, W. G., 545, 608, 638–39
Tennien, Mark, 471–72, 583
Ter Poorten, Hein, 433
Terasaki, Gwen, 213, 659–60
Terasaki, Hidenari, 78, 107, 213, 308, 659–60, 663, 678
Terasaki, Mariko (Miller), 213, 659, 678
Theobald, Robert A., 310
Thiebaud, Vivian, 480
Thomas, Elbert D., 318
Thomas, Daisy, 163
Thomas, Francis J., 281–82
Thomas, Lowell, 354
Thomas, Sir Shenton, 84, 205, 223–225, 281, 352, 360, 507, 571, 600
Thomas, William, 526, 676

Thompson, C. R. ("Tommy"), 305, 338–39
Thomsen, Hans, 96, 571–72, 586, 646
Thomson, Bob, 334, 674
Thomson, George P., 52
Thorpe, Elliott R., 433–34, 675
Thumboo, Edwin, 361, 674
Tibbets, Paul W. Jr., 302, 654–55
Tillman, Ken, 275, 321, 391
"Tito," Joseph Broz, 166–67, 206–07
Tittle, Bess, 611–12, 677
Tittle, David, 611
Tittle, Norman, 611–12
Tobruk (see Libya)
Tobruk Truth, 37–38, 185, 539, 605, 670
Togo, Heichachiro, 13, 88
Togo, Shigenori, 15, 40, 60, 175–76, 189–90, 210–11, 225, 234–235, 386–87, 402, 406–07, 637, 663
Toguri, Iva ("Tokyo Rose"), 449–50
Tojo, Hideki, 11–12, 138, 210–11, 255, 373–74, 402, 489–91, 496–99, 535, 613, 636–37, 664
Toland, John, 101
Tolischus, Otto, 117, 134, 377, 414, 560–62
Tolley, Kemp, 44, 144, 275, 387
Tomlinson, Heather, 408–09, 594, 675
Tomlinson, Sterling, 408–09, 594
Tomoda, Mr., 175
Tomura, Morio, 89
Tonkin, John, 135, 671
Train, Harold, 75
Triumph in the Philippines, 576–77
Troemel, Ben, 569
Trostle, George M., 312–13, 674
Trout, Robert, 377
Truman, Bess, 624
Truman, Harry, 624, 662–63
Tsubogami, Teiji, 172–73, 502
Tsuji, Masanobu, 48–49, 129, 223, 258–59, 334–35, 362, 501–502
Tsukiyama, Ted, 543–44
Tully, Grace, 60, 63, 89, 385, 486, 671
Turl, Charles, 484
Turner, Richmond Kelly, 35, 238
Tutt, L. E., 538–39, 676
Twitty, E. M., 437
Tyler, Kermit A., 221–22
Tyler, R. G., 475, 500–01, 563, 676
Tyson, H. G., 573

Ugaki, Matome, 47, 255
Urey, Harold, 52
Urrutia, Enrique Jr., 311
Usher, Stoker, 291
Ussher, James, 3
Utter, Charles W., 118–19, 303–04, 671
Uyeda, Tei, 547
Uyeno, Shirow, 317–18

Valdez, Basilio, 389
Valentine, Douglas, 593
Valentine, Nina, 593
Vallat, Xavier, 168–69
Van der Post, Laurens, 662
Van Oosten, A. J., 388
Van Oyen, Maj. Gen., 434
Van Valkenburgh, Franklin, 244
Vance, Marshall M., 598, 677
Vanderfield, R. D., 355
Vandiver, Cecil, 241, 673
Vanit, Pananon, 115, 502–03
Vargas, Jorge, 290, 343, 346, 425, 513, 523, 578, 674
Vaughan, Elizabeth, 388
Vaughan, James, 388
Victor Emmanuel III, 585–86
Vigors, T. A., 355–56, 639
Vogt, John H. L., 67, 252–53

Wadsworth, George, 260
Wainwright, Jonathan, 326, 526–29, 573

Wakatsuki, Jeanne, 316
Wakatsuki, Mr., 316
Wakatsuki, Mrs., 316
Walen, John, 608
Walen, Phyllis, 255–56, 608, 674
Walker, Frank, 462
Walker, H. Alexander, 243, 535, 673
Walker, Una, 243
Wall, Albert, 609
Wallace, Henry, 486
Wallace, Verne L., 466–67
Wallis, Cedric, 155
Walters, Bucky, 569
War of the Worlds, 276
Ward, Consul Gen., 537–38
Warlimont, Walter, 298, 620, 648–649
Warrick, Fred, 314, 674
Warwick, Ernest, 477, 676
Watanabe, Yasuji, 254–55, 570
Watson, Edwin M. ("Pa"), 50, 247
Watt, Alan, 284
Watt, Ian, 347, 674
Watt, "Tassie," 204
Wax, Ray, 319, 674
Wedemeyer, Albert, 7
Weichs, Maximilian Freiherr von, 26
Weiszäcker, Ernst von, 81–82, 176, 596–97
Welch, George, 251, 273–74
Wellborn, Charles, 94
Weller, George, 552–53
Weller, Oree C., 329, 674, 676
Welles, Orson, 94–95, 276, 393, 662
Welles, Sumner, 463, 534
Welsh, Mary (Hemingway), 338
Wenneker, Paul W., 21, 126–27, 489, 609–10, 669–70
Weygand, Maxime, 351
Wheeler, Burton K., 308, 478
Wheeler, Mrs. Burton, 308
White, Paul, 437
When I Whistle, 446–47
Whitcomb, Edgar D., 521–22
White, H. L., 471, 673, 676
White, Jimmy, 426

White, Theodore H., 277–78, 479
Whitney, Courtney, 574
Wichitwathakan, Prince Wichit, 502
Wickard, Claude, 462
Wiegand, Karl von, 170–71, 367, 672
Wilkins, Fred, 277
Wilkinson, Theodore S. ("Ping"), 124, 183
Williams, Douglas, 351–52
Williamson, R. W., 275
Willoughby, Charles A., 485
Wilson, Dick, 419
Wilson, Edith Bolling, 633
Wilson, Henry S., 287–88
Wilson, Maurice E. ("Jack"), 528
Wilson, Orme, 246
Wilson, T. B., 420
Wilson, Thomas Murray, 563, 676
Winant, John Gilbert, 82–83, 86–87, 90–91, 161–62, 174, 338–40, 589, 625, 670
Winn, Molly, 125
Winser, A. J., 287, 674
Wise, Stephen S., 88
Wood, Robert E., 73, 393, 634
Woodrough, Fred D., Jr., 59
Wright, John M., 257, 674
Wu Lao ("Old Man"), 403–04, 422–425, 675
Wu, "Ma," 403–04, 422–25
Wu Taingau ("Big Cow"), 403–04, 422–25

Yamaguchi, Tamon, 411
Yamamoto, Akira, 234
Yamamoto, Isoroku, 10, 13, 32, 74, 88, 234, 254–55, 412–13, 631, 634, 665
Yamashita, Tomoyuki, 46, 48–49, 114, 259, 362, 441, 501, 640
Yanaihara, Tadao, 509
Yasui, Yasukado, 666
Yates, Bob, 155, 421, 675
Yau Kianghai, 614–16, 677
Yeaton, Ivan D., 280, 674

Yokota, Minoru, 320
Yokoyama, Masaharu, 547
Yokoyama, Ryuichi, 162, 672
York, Alvin Cullom (see also Sergeant
    York), 479
Yoshida, Shigeru, 403
Yoshikawa, Takeo ("Tadashi Mori-
    mura"), 21–22, 88, 90,
    140
Young, Eunice F., 387, 675

Young, Howard L. ("Brigham"), 214,
    252, 394, 567
Young, James R., 279
Young, Mark, 424

Zacharias, Ellis M., 631–32, 677
Zapf, Dietrich, 350, 674
Zhukov, Georgi, 35, 69, 76–77,
    122–23, 647
Zlotelow, "Doc," 514